G000230385

THE FUNDAMENTAL TECHNIQUES OF CLASSIC PASTRY ARTS

THE FRENCH CULINARY INSTITUTE

Published in 2009 by Stewart, Tabori & Chang
An imprint of ABRAMS

Text copyright © 2009 by The French Culinary Institute
Photographs copyright © 2009 by Matthew Septimus

All rights reserved. No portion of this book may be reproduced, stored in a retrieval system, or transmitted in any form or by any means, mechanical, electronic, photocopying, recording, or otherwise, without written permission from the publisher.

Library of Congress Cataloging-in-Publication Data:

Choate, Judith.
The fundamental techniques of classic pastry arts / The French Culinary
Institute with Judith Choate. p. cm.
Includes bibliographical references.
ISBN 978-1-58479-803-3
1. Pastry. 2. Cookery, French. I. French Culinary Institute (New York,
N.Y.) II. Title.

TX773 .C5258
641.8'65—dc22

2009006902

Editor: Luisa Weiss
Designer: Debra Drodvillo/Notion Studio
Photo Art Director: Julie Hoffer
Production Manager: Tina Cameron

The text of this book was composed in Granjon and Trade Gothic.

Printed and bound in China
10 9 8 7 6 5 4 3 2

THE ART OF BOOKS SINCE 1949

115 West 18th Street
New York, NY 10011
www.abramsbooks.com

THE FUNDAMENTAL TECHNIQUES OF CLASSIC PASTRY ARTS

THE FRENCH CULINARY INSTITUTE

Judith Choate *with*

The Pastry Chefs of The French Culinary Institute

Photographs by Matthew Septimus

Stewart, Tabori & Chang *New York*

Contents

Sessions

Foreword

Pastry chefs are a breed unto themselves, different from culinary chefs or bread bakers. How? Well, think about it. Pastry covers many disciplines: cake baking, dough working, candy making, chocolate tempering, complex cake construction, and sugar pulling, just to name a few. All these tasks take incredible precision. Once you mix a cake and place it in the oven, there is no chance of adding a little more sugar while it is baking. Thus, a great pastry chef must have a fastidious nature. At The International Culinary Center and The French Culinary Institute, we find that there are many career changers drawn to our pastry course from other precise fields . . . for example, medical personnel, accountants, architects, and a startling number of dentists!

Walk into a pastry kitchen, and it is much quieter than a culinary kitchen. You can see the concentration and intensity on the faces of the cooks. The utensils they use are exacting: thermometers, scales, and sculpting knives. Missing is the cacophony of clanging pots hitting the stovetop or the shouting of orders or the visual excitement of a flare-up of flames on a grill.

As fun as it might sound to spend your days working with chocolate and sugar, studying to become a pâtissier should not be likened to an adult version of the game of Candyland. The profession demands that the pastry chef be disciplined and intelligent, have physical stamina, understand proportions, and possess artistic sensibility. Perhaps above all, technique is the most important of the fundamentals. That is the driver of The FCI course, and in this text, we share with you all the basic techniques that an aspiring pastry chef must master. The course's architect was none other than Jacques Torres. Chef Torres, known to many as Mr. Chocolate, is one of the few anointed master chefs of pastry alive today. In France a master pâtissier is chosen after a grueling competition. The title won is M.O.F. (Meilleur Oeuvrier de France—literally, Master Craftsman of France). Chef Torres, at the time he won the title, was only twenty-six—the youngest ever to have achieved this vaunted honor. In addition to winning all types of awards and being the pastry chef of the acclaimed restaurant Le Cirque in New York City, Chef Torres brought a humility to writing our course. He did not want only to reflect his unique style, so he consulted all the top pastry chefs in the city. That approach bestowed on The FCI a course that is relevant, thorough, and exciting. The recipes are reflective of what is being produced in the top pastry kitchens today—and include the classic dishes that are fundamental, timeless, and demand the knowledge of professional techniques.

The true wealth of this book is that it distills ten years of trial and error in teaching students. We have a seasoned and brilliant pastry faculty at The FCI who have taught and refined this curriculum over the years. Their consolidated wisdom is captured in these pages. Work through this book and you will not only acquire the fundamental professional techniques, but you will also have the benefit of hundreds of years of professional expertise.

Let me close by inviting you to visit us at The French Culinary Institute in New York City and see this curriculum in action, not to mention marvel at some of the most delicious cakes and sweets known to mankind!

Dorothy Cann Hamilton

7

Introduction

"My approach is to perfect a strong foundation of pastry and baking basics. Once these are mastered, there is no limit as to what you can create."

Chef Jacques Torres

When Dorothy Hamilton asked me to lead the pastry course at The French Culinary Institute, I was amazed to learn that I would have no budget constraints as I built the pastry kitchens and staff. For my entire professional life, the driving force in the kitchen was, for the most part, economics; I was taught to make the best of what was available to me. But at FCI, my only requirement was to built the best kitchens and staff possible, so that we might give students the maximum opportunity to learn. What a pleasure that was, and what a pleasure it has been to participate in the training of new generations of creative pastry chefs.

In the few years since I began my career in the United States, the profession of pastry chef has changed and grown dramatically. No longer is there the time for a young cook to go from job to job, learning the specialty of the house at each stop. Because of exploding demand, obtaining skills and techniques must be accelerated in an educational setting like The French Culinary Institute, where doors are opened for a successful future in the pastry kitchen. I like to say that we teach a young chef to use the head, while experience teaches how to use the hands.

Pastry work is extremely demanding, both mentally and physically. While we can teach the techniques of the craft, there are several attributes that a cook must possess in order to succeed.

1. Because so much of our work is repetitive, the number-one requirement is discipline. Repetition in the pastry kitchen creates the result; a task can be mastered only be being practiced over and over again. Musicians have an adage that translates well to pastry chefs: Amateurs play a

piece until they get it right, while professionals play it until they can't get it wrong. Discipline gives the pastry chef the willingness to practice until it is impossible to fail.

2. Dedication to the craft builds a sense of structure and responsibility for all aspects of the pastry kitchen. This concern extends not just to the end product, but to fellow workers and customers as well.

3. Desire for knowledge about the art of pastry making will ensure that learning never stops. After more than twenty-five years as a pastry chef, I am still excited to discover anything new that applies to my work. An untried ingredient, a unique skill, state-of the-art equipment, advanced technology—all these contribute to improving my craft.

4. Consistency is its own reward. There is much pleasure to be gained when each cake, cookie, or roll looks exactly as you expect, day after day.

Contemporary pastry chefs are required to learn fast, evolve quickly, experiment with science and technology, and still present a beautifully executed dessert that will please the palate. Mastery of the craft is built on a solid base of classic techniques, and I know that FCI offers the framework that makes this possible. I welcome the opportunity to introduce you to our course in the pages of this comprehensive book. Enjoy learning, experiment, be creative—and, if you can, come visit our classrooms to appreciate fully our dedication to living the sweet life.

Jacques Torres, Dean of Pastry Arts,
The French Culinary Institute

Session 1

Introduction to the Professional Pastry Kitchen: Basic Principles and Terms

Theory

Understanding the Structure of the Professional Kitchen

When moving from the home kitchen into the professional kitchen, it is necessary to rethink the habits of a lifetime. Cooking cannot make the leap from chore to art without many principles, rules, and terms becoming second nature. Before the basic cooking skills are taught, the fledgling cook must acquire a complete understanding of the classic culinary terms, the rules guiding personal and work-space hygiene, and the standards of food preparation. When contemplating cooking or pastry making as a profession, it is important to realize from the outset that a professional cook's life is a disciplined one guided by a set of unwavering standards. If you follow these standards and guidelines, the rewards will be greater efficiency and ease of preparation, as well as more enjoyment performing the tasks at hand.

Instruction to work in the professional pastry kitchen must not only teach the cook to follow a recipe with precision but also to execute that recipe with speed and organization in a commercial atmosphere. Unlike general cooking, where a cook can usually adjust a recipe to personal taste, it is not so easy to reconfigure a pastry recipe. Because it is as much a science as an art, working with pastry requires that ingredients always be measured accurately so that they will conform to a calibrated formula. The pastry chef must first understand the interaction of ingredients—how they react to temperature, fusion, blending, and storing. Only then can the chef test the limits of the imagination, creating exciting dishes with a stamp of originality.

Chef's Regulation Dress Uniform

Starting at the top with a *toque*, or chef's hat (a tall, often disposable, paper, pleated, or plain hat), down to the highly polished black leather shoes to protect from spills, the chef's dress code is standard worldwide. The complete, traditional uniform is a double-breasted white jacket, a neckerchief tied neatly around the neck to absorb perspiration, a white apron tied at the front with a thick, absorbent towel (to grasp hot pans and dishes) tucked into the ties, and black-and-white houndstooth cotton or cotton-poly blend pants. Since kitchen chores will make the uniform increasingly soiled as the day progresses, the head chef or chef-owner will always have a fresh jacket to wear when appearing in the dining room or other public spaces. With the more relaxed climate of recent years, some chefs who work in their own kitchens may be found in brightly colored pants and extravagantly embroidered jackets, as well as clogs or other utilitarian shoes. In an even more relaxed atmosphere, chefs' uniforms are also being worn by home cooks, probably as much for their convenience as for the feeling of professionalism that they impart. No matter how styles have changed, the entire *brigade* in a large hotel kitchen anywhere in the world still wears the standard-issue uniform.

Dean's Tip

"A carpenter's rule is, Measure twice, cut once. A pastry chef's rule is, Scale twice, make once."

Dean Jacques Torres

Organizational Structure

The professional kitchen is a highly organized and structured operation, in which each associate has a specific function with clearly defined responsibilities. Known as a *brigade*, this system of organization was instituted in the vast kitchens of London's famed Savoy Hotel in the late-nineteenth century by the esteemed French chef Auguste Escoffier. It is assumed that the large number of kitchen personnel demanded that a new system of order be established to direct the flow of communication and to ensure the coordination of the multitudinous tasks required in this busy setting.

The *brigade* includes a team of cooks and their *commis* (assistants), who are apportioned into different stations, or *parties*. The entire *brigade* is headed by the **Executive** or **Head Chef** whose job is to orchestrate the overall food production and ensure the efficiency of each station. The Head Chef is assisted by the **Sous-Chef**, who works with individual station leaders called **chefs de parties**. Each *chef de partie* is assisted by a *commis* or apprentice-assistant. The size and scope of the *brigade* will vary according to the size of the kitchen and the requirements of the establishment. There will be many more specific stations and specialized tasks in a large hotel kitchen than in a small restaurant or catering kitchen that may require just one person to cover many stations.

In a large hotel kitchen, a *brigade* would consist of:

Executive or Head Chef: An administrator whose responsibilities include all kitchen-related operations, including menu planning, costing, and scheduling. This person is also responsible for maintaining communication with department heads throughout the hotel system.

Working Chef, or **Chef de Cuisine:** An active cook who works in the kitchen during preparation periods and during service. Also responsible for ordering and other designated administrative duties. Reports to the Executive Chef. In a very large hotel, the Executive Chef may have many more administrative duties than a *Chef de Cuisine*. In smaller establishments, the **Chef de Cuisine** may also be the Executive Chef.

Banquet Chef: In charge of all banquets and parties, with the same responsibilities as a *Chef de Cuisine*. Reports to the Executive Chef.

Pastry Chef, or **Chef Pâtissier:** Responsible for the preparation and plating of all desserts and pastries. Reports to the Executive Chef. In a very large kitchen, there may also be a **Sous-Chef Pâtissier**.

Sous-Chef: Second in command under the *Chef de Cuisine*. Responsibilities include supervising all cooks in the *brigade*. In a large establishment, there will be a day *Sous-Chef* and an evening *Sous-Chef*, as well as a late-night *Sous-Chef* if room service is offered. Duties include overseeing the preparation and service of food and control of all stations and kitchen operations in the *Chef de Cuisine*'s absence.

Floor Chef, or **Chef de Partie:** In charge of a specific station with an assistant, or **commis**, during preparation and service. Each *Chef de Partie* is assisted by a single (**premier**) *commis*, or even by several *commis*. In Europe, the *commis* is assisted by **apprentices**.

Specific stations might be:

Poissonnier: Responsible for the cleaning and preparation of all fish, along with their sauces and garnishes.

Saucier: Responsible for the preparation of all stocks and sauces, as well as all meat and poultry. In a very large kitchen, there may also be a **Rôtisseur**, who would be responsible for roasted, grilled, and fried meats. In a small kitchen, the *saucier* and *poissonnier* may be the same person.

Garde-Manger: Responsible for the preparation of all cold articles (hors d'oeuvre, *pâtés*, *galantines*) and sauces. This position is extremely important in a large hotel kitchen that is responsible for large catered events, cocktail parties, and room service. In such cases, this station may have up to twenty-five people working in it.

Entremetier: Responsible for all vegetable and egg dishes, as well as soups and side dishes.

Potager: Responsible for all soups. This position is usually found only in a very large hotel where gallons and gallons of soups are made daily.

Dean's Tip

"Organization, cleanliness, and planning are 50 percent of a successful recipe."
Dean Jacques Torres

Technique
Setting Up the Standard Workstation (*Poste de Travail*)

The professional kitchen workstation is a universal setup that never changes. It can even carry over to the home kitchen, as working in this systematic fashion sets good organizational skills. The work area consists of an immaculate cutting board placed on a damp cloth or paper towel to prevent slipping. If the cook is right-handed, knives, spatulas, and other necessary equipment are placed to the right of the board. For those who are left-handed, materials are placed to the left. Bowls to hold ready-to-prepare fruits or vegetables, dry goods, or other products are placed at the top of the board.

When peeling fruits or vegetables, place the unpeeled items in a container positioned on the left and transfer them, as finished, into a bowl on the right. Catch the peelings in a bowl placed in the center of the cutting board for easy cleanup. Keep the entire area clean and organized at all times.

It is on the workstation that a cook will prepare the necessary **mise en place** ("put in place") for a particular dish. This French term defines the organization of all the properly cut or otherwise prepared ingredients that will be required to put the dish together up to the point of its final cooking. The appropriate amount of each ingredient is measured out and placed in its own container or bowl. Equipment is also put in place, so that the cook may proceed easily with the actual preparation. Putting together the complete *mise en place* ensures that the cook may prepare a recipe without interruption.

Principles for a Healthy Environment

Before any work can begin in a professional or culinary school kitchen, standards of cleanliness must be set and held. Excellent health and external cleanliness are prerequisites for the maintenance of a hygienic, disease-free environment. Not only is personal sanitation required, all materials and equipment, as well as the workspace itself, must also be antiseptic. To the novice, these rules may seem unnecessary or extreme; **however, any variance from these principles can result in extremely serious, even disastrous, results to the health of others**. Adherence to the following principles will help ensure that this does not occur.

- General daily hygiene must be practiced; bathing, shaving, and tooth brushing are mandatory.

- Hair must be clean, well-groomed, and covered with an immaculate hat. If long, it should be restrained.

- Nails should be trimmed, clean, and polish-free.

- All jewelry should be removed before entering the kitchen to avoid mishap through loss or entanglement with utensils or machinery.

- Perfumes, colognes, and aftershave lotions are not permitted.

- Hands must be washed upon entering the kitchen and after touching raw ingredients, telephones, money, soiled linens, meat, chicken, fish, eggs in or out of the shell, fresh produce, and soiled equipment or utensils, as well as after using chemicals or cleaners; picking up anything from the floor; performing personal actions such as using the lavatory, coughing, sneezing, smoking, eating, or drinking; or at any time necessary when working to ensure that the hands are always immaculate.

- Proper hand-washing techniques include generously soaping; vigorously rubbing for at least 20 seconds to cover the backs of the hands, wrists, between the fingers, and under the nails; and rinsing under warm (38°C/100°F) running water. Dry with a paper towel and use the towel to turn off the water and open any doors necessary to exit the washroom.

- Do not enter the kitchen if you have a skin or respiratory infection, intestinal problem, or rash of unknown origin, as these may cause the spread of disease.

- If working in a school or professional environment, clean uniforms should be regularly issued and impeccably maintained. In a home kitchen, clothes should be clean and covered with a clean apron or smock. Street clothes should never be worn.

- Wear inexpensive and easily disposable rubber gloves when working with products that spoil easily or are known to readily transmit bacteria. These might include chicken, shellfish, sauces, eggs, stocks, meats, cream, and ice cream.

- Never use a kitchen towel, wipe cloth, or side towel for personal reasons.

- Never taste anything with your fingers. Use a fresh, clean spoon for each tasting.

- Never smoke, drink alcoholic beverages, or use controlled substances in any kitchen.

- Cover your face with an easily disposable paper towel or tissue when you sneeze or cough and discard it immediately. If you have to use a cloth, place it in a resealable plastic bag and remove it from the kitchen immediately. Wash your hands immediately. If the cough or sneeze seems to be an indication of the onset of an upper respiratory infection, ask to be excused from kitchen duties.

- Never sit on worktables or preparation areas.

- In the event of an accidental cut or burn, make immediate use of a first-aid kit or, if necessary, call for emergency assistance.

Theory
Principles of Sanitation

Preventing food-borne illness is the moral obligation of the food professional and is essential to the success of any food-related business. State and local boards of health set rigid standards for food service establishments, offer mandatory safety courses for food professionals, and routinely inspect food establishments to ensure that their standards are upheld; however, it ultimately remains the responsibility of the establishment to impose the most rigorous practices in the working environment. In the home kitchen, it is the responsibility of the main cook to create impeccably clean conditions.

There are numerous principles that must be observed in the purchase, storage, preparation, and service of food to prevent contamination from the three most common contaminant sources—biological, chemical, and physical.

Biological Contamination

Bacterial contamination is the cause of most food-borne illnesses. It is interesting to note that some bacteria are beneficial (such as those needed to produce cheeses and cultured milk products, beer, and wine), and it is presently thought that most bacteria are benign. But those that are harmful can be deadly.

Bacteria are tiny, one-celled microscopic organisms that are present everywhere and on everyone. They multiply by splitting in two, and under ideal circumstances, a single bacteria cell can multiply into 281 billion cells in three days.

Undesirable bacteria can cause spoilage in food that can usually be identified by the presence of odor, a sticky or slimy surface, discoloration, or mold. Bacteria that are also disease agents are known as pathogens. Pathogens may not be detectable through odor, taste, or appearance, and this makes them particularly noxious. They are the greatest concern in all kitchens. To lessen the risk of contamination, all food must be purchased from reliable sources and then protected from bacterial infection by the practice of good hygiene, along with sanitary handling and proper storage.

Conditions conducive to bacterial growth include:

Food: Almost all foods, except those that are dry or preserved with sugar or salt, can be hosts for bacterial growth. High-protein foods such as meat, poultry, fish, game, eggs, or dairy products are active supporters of speedy bacterial expansion.

Foods that particularly support the rapid growth of bacteria are known as **potentially hazardous foods**, or PHFs. These include animal products such as raw or undercooked meat, poultry, fish, shellfish, or dairy products, and fully or partially cooked vegetables, raw seeds, or sprouts. A partial list of PHF items includes undercooked bacon, cooked beans, cut cheeses, fresh shelled eggs, shelled hard-cooked eggs or hard-cooked eggs cooled in liquid, unrefrigerated fresh garlic in oil, cooked pastas, meats, cheeses, pastry cream or cream-filled pastries, sour cream, soy protein and soy products, as well as any sauces containing PHF ingredients.

Acidity or alkalinity: Acidity and alkalinity are measured by a pH factor that spans from 1 (strongly acidic) to 14 (strongly alkaline), with pure water measuring 7 (neutral) on the pH scale. Almost all bacteria thrive in a neutral or midlevel pH environment.

Time: All bacteria need time to adjust to their host environment before beginning to grow. For cooks, this allows a brief period to leave food at room temperature as preparation is commencing.

Temperature: Bacteria grow best in temperatures ranging from 4°C (40°F) to 60°C (140°F). This range is referred to as the **food danger zone**.

Oxygen: Most bacteria are aerobic, which means that they need oxygen to grow. However, some of the deadliest bacteria, such as those that cause botulism, are anaerobic, or able to grow without access to air.

Moisture: All bacteria require liquid to absorb nourishment; therefore, moist, damp foods such as cream-based salads make the perfect host.

There are two categories of diseases caused by pathogens: intoxications and infections.

Intoxications are the result of poisons or toxins produced in food as a result of bacterial growth rather than from the bacteria themselves. Infections are caused by bacteria or other organisms that attack the human body.

Bacteria have no means of locomotion; they must be carried from one place to another by means of hands, coughs, sneezes, other foods, unsanitary equipment or utensils, or environmental factors such as air, water, insects, and rodents. Only sterilization will eliminate bacteria, so it is extremely important to understand the simple rules governing bacteria's growth and travel to help prevent bacterial contamination in the kitchen.

Rule 1 **Keep bacteria from spreading.** Do not touch anything that may contain disease-producing bacteria. Protect food from airborne bacteria by keeping it covered at all times.

Rule 2 **Prevent bacterial growth.** Keep all food at temperatures that are out of the food danger zone.

Rule 3 **Kill bacteria.** Heat food to a temperature of 75°C (165°F) or above for 30 seconds through any heat source. Equipment used as a cooking vessel should be washed with hot water and detergent, then rinsed or sanitized.

Chemical Contamination

Chemical poisoning is the result of defective, improperly maintained, or incorrectly used equipment. Such poisons might include antimony from chipped gray enamelware, lead found in containers or soldering material, cadmium found in plating elements. All these toxins can cause illness in humans. Other chemical contamination can result from commercial cleaning compounds, silver polish, and insecticides.

To prevent chemical contamination,

° all food must be stored separately from cleaning or other chemically based materials;

° all containers must be properly labeled and washed or otherwise cleaned; and

° all equipment must be thoroughly rinsed in extremely hot water.

Physical Contamination

Physical contamination is the result of the adulteration of food by a foreign object such as broken glass, hair, metal shavings, paint chips, insects, stones, and so forth. If you stringently follow safety guidelines, physical contamination should not occur. However, if it does, all foods affected should be discarded immediately.

Infectious Disease Chart

Disease: **Botulism (*Clostridium botulinum*)**
Category: **Intoxication**
Source: Contaminated soil on vegetables or other food
Food usually involved: Home-canned, low-acid vegetables; commercially packed tuna, smoked fish, or mushrooms; garlic packed in oil
Prevention: Use only commercially processed products that are properly dated and packed; never use anything packed in a damaged or bulging package or can.

Disease: **Staphylococcus (*Staphylococcus aureus*)**
Category: **Intoxication**
Source: Food handling: urine contamination by food handlers, open wounds and sores
Food usually involved: Custards, dairy-filled bakery products, hollandaise sauce, ham, poultry, protein-based salads, potato salads, other high-protein foods
Prevention: Maintenance of excellent hygiene and work habits. Keep kitchen workers away from all food when carrying any infection or disease.

Disease: **E. coli (*Escherichia coli*)**

Category: **Intoxication or infection**

Source: Intestinal tract of humans, some animals (especially cattle); contaminated water; fecal contamination/feces

Food usually involved: Raw or undercooked red meat, unpasteurized dairy products, fish from contaminated waters, some prepared food such as mashed potatoes and cream-based desserts

Prevention: Thoroughly cook all food, especially red meat; avoid cross-contamination with appropriate storage and handling; practice good hygiene.

Disease: **Salmonella (*Salmonella enteritides*)**

Category: **Infection**

Source: Contaminated poultry, poultry products, meat, eggs; fecal contamination by food handlers

Food usually involved: Poultry, meat, poultry stuffings, inadequately cooked or untreated egg products, gravies, raw food, shellfish from polluted waters

Prevention: Practice good personal hygiene. Properly store and handle all food. Control insect and rodent infestation. Properly wash hands and sanitize equipment and all surfaces after handling raw poultry and/or raw eggs. Use only certified shellfish.

Disease: ***Clostridium perfringens***

Category: **Infection**

Source: Soil; fresh meat; human carriers

Food usually involved: Meat and poultry, reheated or unrefrigerated gravies and sauces

Prevention: Cold foods kept at 4°C (40°F) or below. Hot foods kept at 60°C (140°F) or above.

Disease: **Strep (*Streptococcus*)**

Category: **Infection**

Source: Coughs and sneezes; infected food handler

Food usually involved: Any foodstuff contaminated by an infected handler and served without further cooking

Prevention: Quarantine infected kitchen workers to prevent them from handling food.

Disease: **Infectious hepatitis (A, B, C, D, and E viruses)**

Category: **Infection**

Source: Shellfish from polluted waters eaten raw; contaminated water used for drinking or washing either body or foodstuffs; fecal contamination by food handlers; sharing of contaminated materials such as toothbrushes; intravenous drug use; sexual contact or through skin breaks

Food usually involved: Raw shellfish, any food handled by an infected person

Prevention: Practice good hygiene. Maintain good personal health habits. Use only certified shellfish.

Disease: **Trichinosis (*Trichinella spiralis*) and tapeworm (*Taenia solium*)**

Category: **Infection**

Source: Infected pork or beef or their by-products

Food usually involved: Pork products, especially those that have been improperly or insufficiently cooked

Prevention: Cook all ground and injected pork products to an internal temperature of at least 68°C (155°F) or higher for 15 seconds. Cook all pork chops or roasts to 63°C (145°F) for 15 seconds and 4 minutes, respectively. The meat may also be frozen for a minimum of 8 days to prevent the development of trichinosis and taeniasis.

Theory

Introduction to Safe Food Handling and Food Storage Temperature

Temperature control is critical to safe food handling. Bacteria grow best in warm temperatures, that is, those between 4°C (40°F) and 60°C (140°F). In this temperature range, disease and germs flourish, and most bacteria, including those that spoil meat and vegetables and cause milk to go sour, grow best. Pathogenic bacteria find their nourishment in the 21°C (70°F) to 52°C (125°F) range. Since the normal temperature of the human body is around 98.6°F, one can see how germs, if unchecked, can readily multiply once ingested. Temperatures of 60°C (140°F) or over will kill most non-spore-forming bacteria and all pathogenic organisms. Although freezing temperatures (0°C/32°F) will not kill bacteria, they will hamper or slow down growth so food can be preserved through freezing and—for shorter times—refrigeration.

A food thermometer should always be used to determine the exact temperature of foods. Never use the hands-on method to make this determination.

Partially processed or leftover food must be refrigerated at 5°C (40°F) or below. Refrigerated food should be removed from the refrigerator just prior to serving or reheating. To reheat, food should be heated rapidly to serving temperature so that the internal temperature quickly reaches 74°C (165°F) and is held at that temperature for at least 15 seconds. **Never** reheat food in a steam table, as it does not provide adequate heat to rapidly bring the refrigerated food to the appropriate temperature.

Storage

All food should be dated and labeled before storage and stored in a manner that prevents contamination from exterior sources and inhibits the growth of any bacteria already in the product. Once stored, all foodstuffs should be rotated according to **FIFO**—the first-in, first-out system. Following are the basic guidelines for safe storage.

Dry Storage

° Dry food storage refers to those foods that do not support bacterial growth because they are dry or dried. This includes flour, sugar, salt, cereal, rice and other grains, oil and shortening, and canned and bottled goods.

° All dry containers should be closed tightly to protect from insect or rodent infestation, as well as to prevent contamination from dust or other airborne materials.

° Dry food should be stored in a cool, dry place and raised off the floor, away from the wall, and not under a sewage line.

Freezer Storage

° All food items to be frozen must be tightly wrapped in plastic film followed by aluminum foil, packaged freezer bags, or sealed in Cryovac packaging to prevent freezer burn.

° All stored items should be labeled and dated.

° Frozen food must be kept completely frozen at -18°C (0°F) or lower until ready for use.

° All freezers must be equipped with an outside thermometer so that the freezer temperature can be read without opening the door or entering the holding box.

◦ Frozen food must be stored to assure cold air circulation on all sides. This means that food should not be stored directly on the freezer floor.

◦ Frozen food must be thawed under refrigeration or under cool, running water. Never thaw foods at room temperature because, at some point, the temperature of the thawing product will reach the food danger zone.

Refrigerated Storage

◦ Other than those foods listed for dry storage, all perishable foods that are not frozen should be refrigerated to protect them from contamination.

◦ Refrigeration may be done with the use of a walk-in refrigerator, reach-in refrigerator, refrigerated show case, refrigerated counter, or refrigerated table.

◦ All refrigerators must be equipped with a calibrated thermometer.

◦ Interior walls and shelves of the refrigerator should be kept immaculately clean.

◦ All refrigerated foods should be properly labeled and wrapped or stored in a suitable container to avoid contamination.

◦ Within the refrigerator, always store raw and cooked foods in separate sealed containers.

◦ Do not allow any unsanitary surface (such as the outside of a container) to touch any refrigerated food or food product.

◦ Hot food to be refrigerated must be chilled as quickly as possible over ice or in a cold water bath before placing in the refrigerator to avoid compromising the refrigerator temperature. For instance, a gallon of hot liquid placed in a refrigerator may take up to ten hours to go below 5°C (40°F) and, while cooling, will raise the refrigerator temperature considerably.

◦ Most perishable foods keep best at a lower refrigerator temperature.

◦ Air must be able to circulate around all sides of refrigerated items; therefore, do not overcrowd a refrigerator. Keep all food off the floor of a walk-in refrigerator unit.

◦ Always keep the refrigerator door closed except when placing food into or removing food from the interior.

Holding Food for Later Use

◦ Bring food to holding temperatures as quickly as possible.

◦ Food should be cooked and processed as close to the time of service as possible.

◦ Prudent menu planning prevents excessive leftovers. Leftovers are not to be mixed with fresh food during storage.

◦ Chilled food should be kept at 5°C (40°F) or below at all times.

◦ When holding cold food, such as gelatins or custards, over ice or in a refrigerated table for service, do not mound food above the level of the container, as this food would not be kept sufficiently chilled.

◦ Food that is going to be served hot soon after cooking should not be allowed to drop below an internal temperature of 60°C (140°F).

◦ Hot, perishable foods should not be kept below 60°C (140°F).

◦ If food is not to be served immediately, it may be kept at a temperature in excess of 60°C (140°F) by the use of warming cabinets, steam tables, or other devices suitable for this purpose. However, this should not be done for more than a couple of hours.

Equipment and Utensils Required for a Functional Kitchen

A well-stocked professional kitchen is built around a formal arrangement of restaurant ranges, stock kettles, refrigeration, ice makers, dishwashers, workstations, and cleanup areas. The attendant cookware, knives, and other preparation materials can expect to see long and hard use and should be made of exceptionally strong elements that wear well. Any well-supplied home kitchen will have much of the same equipment, with less emphasis on quantity but the same insistence on quality. Top-quality equipment and utensils purchased for the kitchen will offer many years of valuable use.

Materials

The following materials are those that are typically used for professional cookware. These same elements are also found in most commercially available home cookware.

Professional cookware materials

Copper (a) is the most even heat conductor. It is often used for saucepans, sauté pans, sugar-boiling pots, and casseroles. Lined copper pans should be lined with nickel, tin, or stainless steel (except for the unlined sugar-boiling pots used in candy making, where the lining will cause the copper pot to heat and cool too quickly) and will be extremely heavy. Unlined copper pots should never be used to prepare acidic substances (those having high content of vinegar, wine, citrus juice, tomato juice, or sour milk, among other acids. The meeting of chemical compounds causes a toxic reaction that can lead to serious illness. Never cool cooked foods in an unlined copper pot, as it will affect the color and taste and can cause them to become toxic.

Aluminum (b) is also an excellent heat conductor used for saucepans, sauté pans, and casseroles. Aluminum cookware is often coated with a layer of stainless steel or nickel to prevent a negative reaction (a metallic taste and color change) when used with acidic substances. Never cool cooked foods in an unlined aluminum pot, as it will affect the color and taste and can cause them to become toxic.

Cast iron (c) is an extremely strong, heavy metal usually used for Dutch ovens, griddles, baking pans, frying pans, and skillets. Relatively inexpensive, it is long-lasting and conducts and retains heat extremely well. It is available either uncoated or enameled (coated with a thin layer of borosilicate glass powder fused to the cast iron to prevent corrosion). Before use, uncoated cast iron must be seasoned by generously coating the inner surface with an unflavored cooking oil (such as peanut, canola, or rapeseed) and placing the pan in a preheated 121°C (250°F) oven for two hours. This keeps the metal from absorbing flavors and prevents food from sticking. Once seasoned, the pan should be gently cleaned and wiped dry before storing.

Black steel (d) is inexpensive, conducts heat quickly, and does not warp under high temperatures; it is used to make frying pans and omelette and crêpe pans. Black-steel pans are often not washed, as this causes rust. Instead, the pan is wiped clean, rubbed with salt to remove any remaining particles, and seasoned with a light coating of oil after each use to retain its nonstick capabilities.

Stainless steel (e) is an excellent nonreactive metal but an extremely poor heat conductor. It will not rust and does not require seasoning. To be useful in a pro-

Dean's Tip

"Taking care of your equipment is one of the most important aspects of being a successful chef."

Dean Jacques Torres

fessional kitchen, stainless-steel pots and pans must be quite thick, with an outer or internal layer of copper or aluminum to help conduct heat.

Enamelware (f) is inexpensive, with a decorative layer of enamel over thin steel. It is a poor heat conductor and food tends to stick to the bottom, scorching and burning. It is impractical for the professional kitchen.

Nonstick (g) cookware is often referred to by its various trade names such as Teflon or T-Fal. Nonstick pans are useful because they require minimal fat for baking or browning, baked goods do not stick to the bottom or edge, and they are easy to keep clean. However, with heavy use, the coating wears off quickly, rendering the pan useless. Never heat a nonstick pan to a high temperature without any added fat, as the coating will be damaged and become toxic. Always use a wooden spoon or utensils made for cooking with nonstick pans.

Pots and Pans

As you work in the kitchen, always use the appropriate name for each pot and pan. It is extremely important that the correct names be learned, as often the chef or another cook will call out for a piece of equipment that must be delivered as quickly as possible. If the name is not at the tip of the tongue, time will be wasted while the desired piece of equipment is searched for. The assortment of pots and pans in a professional pastry kitchen is referred to as the *batterie de cuisine* and will contain some or all of the following items:

Angel-food cake pan: A two-part tube pan with slightly flared sides. It is used to bake light, airy angel-food cakes. The center tube is attached to the removable bottom, which makes the cake easier to remove from the pan.

Bain-marie **or water bath:** A technique in which a bowl (or other container) holding food is placed in a larger bowl of hot or warm water so that the food is encased with gentle heat. A *bain-marie* may be used either on top of a stove or in an oven, or to keep food warm.

Assorted flan rings, cookie cutters, and cake rings

Loaf and tartlet pans, *barquettes*, and *brioche à tête* molds

Black-steel pans: Heavy-gauge steel baking pans whose thickness and dark color promote more even baking and browning. They are most commonly available in American-sized sheet pans, French sheet pans (slightly smaller than American), and round disks called *tourtiers* that are used for baking tarts.

Brioche à tête **mold:** A round, fluted pan with flaring sides available in various sizes. It is used to bake brioche breads.

Bundt pan: A cake pan that had arched, often fluted or decorated sides, and a center tube. It is generally about 3½ inches tall and 10 inches in diameter and is used to make bundt or other dense cakes.

Cake pans: Most commonly round, from 2 to 5 inches deep and ranging from 2 to 30 inches in diameter, cake pans can be aluminum or steel. Specialty shapes are also available in metal and glass. **Springform** cake pans have detachable sides.

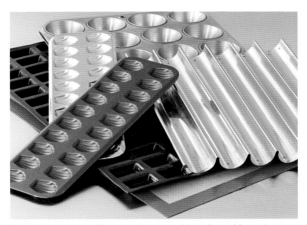

Madeleine pans, muffin tins, silicone molds, tuile molds, and a silicone liner

Charlotte mold: A metal, pail-shaped mold with heart-shaped handles and distinct flaring sides. It is used to make either hot or cold *charlotte* desserts.

Double boiler: A two-part pan in which the top part fits, about halfway down, snugly into the bottom part. The top half holds ingredients to be melted or heated while the bottom holds simmering water to conduct heat to the top. This system is used to warm or gently cook heat-sensitive items such as chocolate, light sauces, or custards.

Hotel pan: A rectangular stainless-steel pan with a lip designed to rest in a steam table or rack. It comes in various sizes, most typically a full hotel pan (12¾ by 20¾ by 2, 4, or 6 inches deep) and a half hotel pan. Also available at a third and fourth of the basic size. Solid-bottomed pans are used to cook, ice, store, or serve foods, and perforated ones are used to drain foods.

Kugelhopf mold: A deep, round mold with a center tube and fluted sides used to make the classic sweet bread most often associated with Austria but also claimed by Alsace and Germany.

Langues de chat pan: A rectangular steel pan with shallow indentations used to make the classic French cookie. It can also be used to make ladyfingers or other small pastries.

Loaf pans: Rectangular pans used as forms for breads or loaf cakes. A **pain de mie** pan or a **Pullman** pan is a long mold used to make loaves of bread that yield square slices.

Madeleine pan: A rectangular pan with shallow, shell-shaped indentations used to make the classic small French *petits fours* known as *madeleines*. They are available in a variety of sizes, with indentations from 1½ to 4 inches long.

Muffin pans: Multi-welled pans used for making individual muffins or small cakes. Available in a number of sizes, including mini-muffin pans.

Poêle: A low, slanted-side pan used for cooking omelettes, crêpes, potatoes, or other items. An American equivalent might be a skillet. At The French Culinary Institute, nonstick *poêles* are used for omelette making.

Ramekins: Individual baking dishes, usually made of ceramic material, used for baking custards such as *pots de crème*, *crème caramel*, and *crème brûlée*. Ramekins are usually decorative enough to be used at the table.

Rondeau: A large, round pan with handles, usually no more than 5 to 6 inches deep, generally used for braising and stewing. It should be of heavy construction and can range in capacity from 12 to 20 quarts.

Russe: A saucepan with a single, long handle that is used for making sauces.

Sauteuse: A round, shallow pan with a single, long handle and sloping sides that is used to sauté.

Sautoir or plat à sauter: A large, round, shallow pan with a single, long handle and straight sides that is used to sauté or to make sauces. It should be of heavy construction to prevent warping at high temperatures.

Sheet pan: A rectangular aluminum or stainless-steel pan with very shallow sides that comes in various sizes, most typically a half-sheet pan (46 by 66 centimeters/18 by 26 inches) and a half-sheet pan (46 by 33 centimeters/18 by 13 inches). For a home oven, a recipe that requires a full-sheet pan can be baked in two **jelly roll pans**, which are normally 44 by 29 by 2.5 centimeters (17¼ by 11½ by 1 inch).

Silicone molds or baking pans: Flexible molds or pans made from silicone rubber that are nonstick and resistant to heat and cold as well as fat. They evenly hold heat or cold, which creates uniformly baked or set products. Their flexibility allows the finished product to be removed easily.

Knife types

Square boys: Also known as steam-table pans, these are almost square pans that are usually 6⅞ by 6¼ by 2½, 4, or 6 inches deep. Most often used to store items in the refrigerator or on the cooking line. Other sizes are also available.

Tart pans: Shallow molds used for sweet or savory tarts. Available in a wide variety of sizes (from 1 inch to 14 inches in diameter). The two most common are **flan rings** and those that are fluted with removable bottoms. Flan rings are metal rings approximately 1.3 centimeters (½ inch) high that are put on a parchment-lined sheet pan. Removable-bottom pans are two-part molds. They consist of a flat disc (the bottom) and a ring with a lip to support the bottom.

Tartlet pans: Similar to tart pans but smaller, these are usually round (although other shapes are available) and vary in size from 1 inch to 5 inches in diameter. They can be made from tinned steel, stainless steel, Teflon-coated steel, and silicone rubber and may have straight, sloped, or fluted sides. **Barquettes**, or **boats**, are small, oval-shaped tartlet pans.

Tube pan: A round, usually deep cake pan with a hollow tube in the center. The tube allows dense cakes, such as pound cakes, to cook evenly with heat generated from both the center and the exterior of the pan.

Knives

Knives are usually the personal property of each chef, and an individual's knife kit is guarded with great care. At the outset of a professional culinary career, a prudent investment in fine knives will be a lifelong one. Many kitchens also have an array of knives on hand for general use, but they are often not of the highest quality. Most knives are made either of high-carbon or forged stainless steel and, in fact, have often been referred to as simply that, a steel. This metal is generally resistant to rust and corrosion and does not stain easily. The knife handle can be made of wood, plastic, metal, or natural substances such as horn or shell. In fine knives, the base of the blade (called the tang) runs the length of the handle and is held in place by a number of rivets, creating a strong, well-balanced utensil. There are now very good knives

of a one-piece construction (Global and Furi brand knives). Currently, blades are being made from an extremely hard, durable material called ceramic zirconia that, reputedly, does not rust, corrode, interact with food, or lose its edge. There are many styles of knives needed to properly cut and shape food. Each has a specific use that is often defined by its name.

There are a few rules that govern knives and their use:

Carbon steel: An alloy of carbon and iron, its advantage is that it will hold a fine edge. Its disadvantage is that it requires a high degree of maintenance, as it corrodes very quickly and cannot be used in humid, salt-air climates or with highly acidic food.

Stainless steel: A combination of iron and chromium or nickel that is a very popular medium for chef's knives. It is resistant to abrasion and corrosion, but it is also difficult to sharpen and does not maintain a fine edge.

High-carbon, no-stain steel: Contains many different materials, such as chromium, molybdenum, and vanadium. Most knives made for professional use are made of such compositions. Blades made from this material are less resistant to abrasion than pure stainless steel knives and are much easier to sharpen. They are also resistant to corrosion.

Every professional knife kit contains all of the following knives, along with auxiliary cutting and shaping utensils:

Chef's (or French) knife (a): The most versatile of all knives, this is used for chopping, slicing, dicing, and filleting. The blade can range from 6 to 14 inches in length.

Utility knife (b): Another versatile knife, used for coring vegetables and fruits and slicing tomatoes and other fruits and vegetables.

Boning knife (c): Used to bone various meats and poultry. This knife has a 6- to 7-inch curved blade, which may be firm or flexible.

Fillet knife (d): The most important feature of a fillet knife is a very sharp, flexible blade that is essential to complete the exacting process.

Slicing knife (e): Used for slicing large cuts of meat or fish such as roasts, ham, or smoked salmon. There are a number of types of slicing knives, with blades ranging from 12 to 16 inches. Some may be round-tipped, while others may have pointed tips. Pointed-tipped knives may also be used to make exact cuts such as those required when cutting large cakes.

Paring knife (f): A small-bladed knife used for peeling fruit and vegetables and turning vegetables.

Serrated knife (g): A bevel-edged blade that is used for slicing breads, rolls, and other soft items.

Steel (h): A hardened, finely ridged rod with a handle and guard and a round or slightly flat profile that is used to keep a knife edge aligned.

Sharpening stone (i): A natural stone, carborundum stone, or diamond-studded block that is available in a wide range of grits (degrees of coarseness) and is used to sharpen knives. The grit abrades the blade's edge, creating a very sharp cutting edge. A coating of water or mineral oil keeps the grit free of particles while being used.

Miscellaneous Tools of the Professional Kitchen

All kitchens, whether professional or home, are equipped with an assortment of tools that go beyond the essentials. As with pots and pans and knives, when used carefully, the highest-quality tools will last the longest.

Some of the small tools that might be found in a professional kitchen are:

Bench brush: A soft-bristled brush similar to a whisk broom that is used to brush excess flour off dough and workbenches.

Box grater: A square metal box with different size holes on each side used to grate cheese, chocolate, fruits, and vegetables. It can, in a pinch, be used to zest citrus fruits.

Cake comb: A small stainless-steel triangle, each side of which has serrated teeth of a different size. It is used to create decorative lines or swirls in the icing of a cake.

Cake rings: Steel rings that are used as forms for baking and shaping. They are usually made of stainless steel and range in size from 5 to 76 centimeters (2 to 30 inches) in diameter and 4 to 15 centimeters (1½ to 6 inches) in depth.

Candy thermometer: A thermometer calibrated in either Celsius or Fahrenheit used when cooking sugar to various stages.

Channel knife or *canneleur*: A small knife used to channel citrus fruit and various vegetables into decorative patterns for garnishes.

Chef's fork: A longer-handled, longer-tined fork that keeps the chef's hand slightly away from the heat when turning items during cooking.

Chinois: A conical strainer with a handle. There are two types: a ***chinois etamine*** (also known as a bouillon strainer) is constructed with fine metal mesh and used for fine straining. A **perforated *chinois*** is used when fine straining is not required. Both are often referred to as "china caps" because of their conical hat shape. However, for clarity in the kitchen, it is common to refer to the *chinois etamine* as a *chinois* and the perforated *chinois* as a "china cap."

Cornet: A paper cone, usually formed from a triangle of parchment paper, used to pipe icings, chocolate, or batters or to place writing or fine-lined decorative work on finished cakes or confections.

Cutters: Available in a variety of shapes and sizes, cutters (or cookie cutters) are used to cut out dough, tempered chocolate, and other items. Those not made in a specific shape such as a heart or flower, generally come in sets of round, graduated sizes that are either plain or fluted around the edge.

Cutting board: Made of hardwood such as maple or plastic such as polypropylene, cutting boards provide a safe surface on which to cut foods and protect the knife edge from damage. Cutting boards should periodically be soaked in a disinfecting solution of bleach and water. A worn board should be discarded, as small food particles may become trapped in the uneven surface and thereby contaminate foods being cut on it.

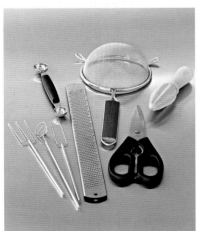

Miscellaneous pastry tools

Dipping fork: A long-handled, three-pronged fork used to dip solid ingredients into chocolate for coating.

***Entremet* rings:** Similar to cake rings, these are stainless-steel or plastic rings that are used to form individual desserts.

Five-wheel cutter: Also known as a **bicycle**, this utensil is used to cut four equal-size strips of dough. The wheels may be adjusted to vary the size of the strips.

Food mill: A metal basketlike utensil with interchangeable disks and a hand-turned crank used to separate solids from seeds, skin, and tough fibers.

Kitchen scissors: Sturdy shears used to cut butcher's twine or kitchen papers or for trimming fish and poultry.

Laser thermometer: Either a traditional or digital thermometer that has a laser component. The thermometer is held over the surface of the material to be measured and the laser (infrared beam) reads the surface temperature. The mixture should be stirred lightly as the temperature is being taken. It is a very helpful tool for measuring the temperature of tempered chocolate.

Lattice cutter: A metal rolling tool that cuts pastry into a perforated, lattice design.

Marble work surface: Because it remains cool, marble is recommended for use when rolling out pastry or working with chocolate or other heat-sensitive products.

Measuring cups: Available in a wide variety of sizes and materials, measuring cups can be made of metal, plastic, or glass.

Measuring spoons: Available in metal and plastic, measuring spoons are, in the pastry kitchen, only used to measure very small amounts that would not read on a scale. They usually come in sets that range from 1.2 to 15 milliliters (¼ teaspoon to 1 tablespoon).

Needle-nosed pliers or tweezers: Very useful for removing fine bones from fish or for removing tiny, unwanted particles from a finished dish.

Offset spatula: A solid metal spatula with a blade that is bent near the handle, allowing the spatula to fit easily under and lift up ingredients. Offset spatulas come in a variety of shapes and sizes.

Parchment paper: A thin paper that has been treated with chemicals to make it nonstick. It is available in rolls and sheets.

***Parisienne* scoop:** Also known as a **melon baller**, this scoop is used to cut fruit or vegetables into small ball shapes.

Pastry bags: Available in a variety of sizes and materials, each with a defined purpose. Traditional styles are

Digital and balance scales

Assorted thermometers

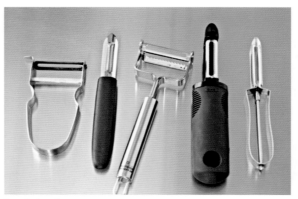
Assorted peelers

Strainers, chinois, a tamis, and a food mill

Five-wheel cutter, lattice cutter, and roller docker

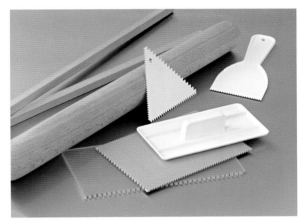

Rolling pin, cake dowels, and assorted cake combs

Assorted pastry decorating tips

made of canvas or linen, but contemporary commercial bags are made from a fabric that has been impregnated with plastic or rubber for ease of cleanup. Disposable, thin, plastic bags are a convenient alternative. Pastry bags are used in combination with pastry decorating tips to pipe batters or icings as well as to speed up portioning of food items.

Pastry brush: A small paintbrush used to brush on egg wash (see page 62) or *nappage* (see page 56), and to soak cakes with liqueurs and glazes. A separate brush should always be used for egg washes to avoid cross-contamination.

Pastry decorating tips: Small metal or plastic V-shaped pieces of varying sizes that fit into the end of a pastry bag to produce a specific design, size, or shape. The most widely used are plain and star tips. Cake decorators use many different shapes to pipe borders, designs, and flowers. A plastic coupler is also available for use when it is necessary to change tips often, as in cake decorating.

Pastry weights: Small reusable metal disks placed in a lined uncooked pastry shell that will prevent the unfilled pastry from rising up and bubbling during baking. If unavailable, the metal weights may be replaced with dried beans or rice.

Pastry spatula: A long, thin spatula that can have an offset handle. Used to assist in cake decorating and for spreading batters or icings.

Pizza wheel: A sharp metal disk with a handle or encased in a plastic cover that is used to neatly cut baked pizza. It is also a useful tool for cutting raw doughs into pieces.

Propane torch: A small, handheld torch ignited by propane that is most frequently used to glaze crème brûlée.

Ricer: A basket- or cone-shaped utensil with small holes and a plunger that is used to force solid foods into small grains resembling rice. Also known as a **potato ricer**.

Roller docker: A small, handheld tool with small spikes or knobs used to perforate or "dock" doughs to prevent air bubbles from deforming the pastry during baking. Available in either metal or plastic.

Rolling pin: A wooden, metal, marble, or glass cylinder used for rolling out doughs. A **French pin**, which has no handles, is the most common in the professional pastry kitchen. For rolling large or heavy doughs, a pin with ball-bearing handles is desirable.

Rolling rack: Also known as a **speed rack** or **bun pan rack**, a rolling rack is a cart with slots on the side to hold sheet pans in place. It always has wheels so that it can be rolled around the kitchen with ease.

Scales: Scales are essential in pastry making. Three types are commonly used in a pastry kitchen: dial portion scales, digital portion scales, and balance scales. Many chefs now prefer digital models. A variety of scales are available in a variety of maximum weights and types that can give an accurate measurement of all ingredients. All scales are marked to tell the user the scale's sensitivity (i.e., 2 kg x 5 g means a maximum of 2 kilograms and in divisions of 5 grams). Digital scales are very easy to use, as they have a tare button, which allows the user to weigh an item, tare it (take the measurement back to zero), and prepare to weigh another item. A balance scale requires the user to put the item to be weighed on one side of the balance and weights on the other. When both sides float freely, the desired weight has been achieved.

Scrapers: There are a number of styles of scraping utensils. For example, a metal **bench scraper** (also called a **bench knife**) is used to clean off a work surface and divide doughs, and a plastic **bowl scraper** is used to thoroughly remove doughs from mixing bowls, as well as to fold ingredients together.

Silicone baking liners: Reusable, nonstick silicone mats—sold most often by the brand name Silpat— that can be used in place of parchment paper in baking. They are made of woven fiberglass that has been injected with food-grade silicone and provide an excellent surface onto which nothing will stick. They come in sizes that will fit either half-sheet pans or full-sheet pans.

Each liner lasts about 2,000 bakings. They should be washed with soap and water both before and after using. After using, they should be cooled flat before storing. They should not be cut, used as a cutting board, or washed with abrasive materials, all of which will render them unusable.

Skimmer: A long-handled, perforated flat spoon used to place items into or remove them from liquids, such as taking fruit from a poaching liquid or putting items into a deep fryer.

Spatulas: Large, wide metal spatulas are used for flipping and moving foods on hot surfaces. Some have offset handles. There is also a variety of spatulas made of softer rubber or composite materials for scraping bowls, folding ingredients, or spreading.

High-heat silicone spatulas are used for stirring hot foods such as custards. Wooden spatulas are also used, particularly for making omelettes in coated nonstick pans, stirring roasting bones for stock, deglazing pans, making *roux*, and stirring *pâte à choux* and *crème anglaise*.

Spider: A long-handled device with a shallow, almost-bowl-shaped disk at the end made of mesh or perforated wire.

Spoons: A wide variety of sizes and shapes of metal and wooden kitchen spoons are available with whole, slotted, or perforated bowls. Used for the same purposes as a skimmer

Stem thermometer: This common kitchen thermometer is provided to all students upon entering FCI. It measures degrees through a metal stem just past the dimple, which is located about 2 inches from the tip. The dimple must be placed in the middle of the food item to record an accurate temperature reading. To calibrate a stem thermometer, place it in heavily iced water for 3 minutes, stirring occasionally. Carefully adjust the nut under the reading dial if necessary. At this point, the thermometer should read 0°C (32°F). This type of thermometer should not be used for oven readings, as it will melt.

Tamis: A worsted cloth strainer often made from wool, used to do fine straining of liquids or dry ingredients. Also known as a **tammycloth** or **drum sifter**. Also available in fine metal mesh.

Tongs: Tongs do not puncture foods as forks do, so they are an essential and versatile tool in every kitchen. They are helpful in turning, lifting, and plating food. They are particularly useful when moving food items to be eaten raw or without further cooking so that contamination from hands or other contaminants can be avoided.

Trussing needle: A long needle used for trussing or sewing stuffed items together.

Turntables: A flat, turnable disk on which a cake (or other item) can be placed and rotated to facilitate icing and decorating.

Vegetable peeler: A small fixed or pivoting blade with a handle, used to peel vegetables and fruit. A wide variety of types are available.

Whisks (wire whips): Thin, flexible wire whips are used to blend mixtures that are not too dense. **Balloon whisks** are made of heavy-gauge wire and have large, somewhat spherical centers; they are used to incorporate air into foods such as egg whites. **Piano whisks** are straight.

Wire racks: Also known as **cooling** or **dipping racks**, these are metal mesh racks of varying sizes used for cooling or glazing. Placing a hot item on a wire rack speeds cooling by allowing air to circulate around the entire item. When used with glazing, the mesh allows the glaze to drip off the item rather than pool around the base of it.

Zester: A small hand tool similar to a channel knife except that it cuts pieces much thinner. It is generally used to cut decorative strings of citrus peel.

Zesting plane: Also known by the brand name **Microplane**, this plane was devised from a tool originally designed for woodworking. It is used to quickly and cleanly remove the zest from citrus fruits. The small zest it cuts is used to flavor rather than decorate food.

Small Appliances

Some of the smaller appliances and equipment found in a professional kitchen are:

Assorted small appliances

Ber mixer: An electric or battery-driven immersion blender, often handheld, that can be placed directly into a mixture for blending.

Electric blender: A machine that purées, emulsifies, and crushes, composed of a solid bottom housing the motor and a blender jar (often two different sizes) with a lid that fits over it. Never fill a blender jar to capacity, as the force of action will raise the lid with cold items, and a combination of force and steam will raise the lid when blending hot items. Even when filled the recommended two-thirds full, the lid, covered with a clean kitchen towel, should be held in place with both hands to prevent splattering or burning.

Electric food chopper or Buffalo chopper: A heavily built machine with a rotating bowl that passes under a hood where vertical blades chop the food. If all the parts are not properly aligned, the machine will not work.

Electric food processor: A machine, often Cuisinart or Robot Coupe brand, with a heavy motor encased in a plastic or metal housing with a detachable bowl and cover and various blades with specific functions. The food processor can chop, blend, mix, purée, knead, grate, slice, and julienne. The machine processes its best when the bowl is filled to half its capacity, and it will work only when all the pieces are properly aligned.

Mandoline: Traditionally, a hand slicer made of a flat metal frame supported by folding legs that has a number of different-sized, extremely sharp blades used to cut vegetables or fruit into a variety of sizes, shapes, and thicknesses. Even if you feel that you are expert at its use, it is good practice to always use the protective guard when slicing with a mandoline. There is now an inexpensive Japanese-style mandoline available with a simplified design that is used for the same purpose.

Standing electric mixer, or table mixer: This is probably the most used piece of equipment in a pastry kitchen. An electric, variable-speed, stand mixer that comes in a variety of sizes with a number of attachments, it is used to mix, beat, blend, and knead batters and doughs. The stand is movable. The stainless steel bowl is inserted into the stand and locked into place before the desired attachment is installed. The two most commonly used attachments are the **paddle** and the **whisk**. The paddle is a flat, fan-shaped piece of

27

metal used for stiffer items such as firm batters or doughs. The whisk is made of balloon-shaped thin wires that are quite fragile and easily broken when used on mixtures that are too firm. It is recommended for incorporating air into light mixtures such as heavy cream and egg whites.

Steam-jacketed kettle (electric or gas): Used for making large quantities of stocks, soups, sauces, or pastas,

these kettles are usually freestanding; some can be tilted, and some may be fitted with spigots. The lid is usually attached, and they range in capacity from 2 quarts to over 100 gallons. The food is heated by steam that circulates through the kettle wall and provides even heat.

Tilting shallow kettle (electric or gas): A large stainless-steel unit with a hinged lid, used for making large quantities of sautés and braises.

Large Appliances

Both the professional kitchen and the home kitchen require equipment for heating, refrigerating, and freezing food. Some of these appliances are:

Stoves, Ranges, and Ovens

There are many different types of stoves, ranges, and ovens. Some have multiple uses, while others have a defined purpose.

Burners may be placed in a range top with an oven (or ovens) either below or above, or they may be placed alone into a stovetop that is fitted into a specific place.

The burner types available are:

Open burner (gas): Direct, adjustable heat.

Flat top (gas or electric): A thick, steel plate over the heat source offers even, indirect heat. However, a flat-top burner requires smooth-bottomed cookware and time to adjust to changes in temperature settings.

Ring-top (gas): Concentric rings and plates that can be removed to expose the burner so that indirect heat can be converted to direct heat. Usually these burners have a higher BTU (British thermal unit, a universal measurement for energy) than a regular open burner. Ring-top burners are particularly well suited to stir-frying.

Some of the available ovens and other cooking or heating sources are:

Conventional oven (gas or electric): The indirect heat source is located on the bottom, underneath, or in the oven floor. An adjustable shelf is set at the desired level for proper cooking.

Deck oven (gas or electric): A type of conventional oven that comes with single or multiple levels. The food is set directly on the oven floor. Allow a minimum of 20 minutes to preheat to temperature.

Open burner

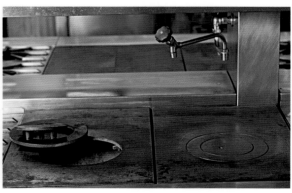

Flat top burner

Convection oven (gas or electric): In a convection oven, a fan blows hot air through the oven, allowing food to brown more efficiently than in a conventional oven. Most often used for pastry and other baked goods for its even heat. Allow a minimum of 15 minutes to preheat to temperature. If a recipe is written with a temperature designated for a conventional oven, the temperature in a convection oven should be *lowered* by 10 percent.

Combi-oven: Temperature, moisture content, and airflow can be controlled with this type of oven. Its design includes features from a conventional oven, a convection oven, and a steamer. Used for both cooking and holding food, it is ideal for use with catering and banquets.

Salamander (gas or electric): An open boxlike apparatus that usually sits above a range top with the heat source located in its roof. It has adjustable racks to control cooking speed and is generally used for intense browning or glazing.

Grill (gas, electric, wood, or charcoal): The heating source is either built in (gas or electric) or added (wood or charcoal) and is located below a heavy-duty cooking rack. In many models, the rack can be moved to allow for instant heat adjustment. Preheating usually takes about 20 minutes.

Deck oven

Convection oven

Grill

Salamander

29

Refrigeration and Freezing Equipment

In addition to heating equipment, all kitchens require some type of refrigeration and freezing devices. Some of those available are:

Walk-in refrigeration: A large, box-shaped unit with a door large enough to allow a person to walk in without

Reach-in refrigerator

Under-counter refrigerator drawers

bending, walk-in refrigeration may be for cold storage or freezing. Generally it is outfitted with storage shelves. A compressor, often located outside the box, cools it.

Reach-in refrigeration: A single- or multiple-unit commercial refrigerator that is simply a larger version of a home refrigerator. Reach-ins come in various sizes and are equipped with adjustable shelving. Small freezers may also be reach-ins.

Under-counter refrigerator or refrigerated drawers: A small appliance used primarily around the work areas of professional kitchens to keep food cold until time of cooking or service.

Freezers: Most professional kitchens do not use freezers, with the exception of small ones used to hold frozen desserts in the pastry kitchen.

Miscellaneous Large Equipment

Hobart mixers: Large, nonportable electric mixers that come in a variety of sizes ranging from 20 quarts to more than 100 quarts. They are similar to the smaller table mixers, but are substantially larger, with stronger motors. The major difference between the two is that Hobarts have gears and only three possible speeds. In order to change gears, the mixer must be brought to a complete stop before moving to another speed. They have a number of safety devices to prevent injury. The wire screen on the front of the bowl must be in place or the mixer will not run. The bowl must be fully raised as well. There is also a timer on the machine that, when set, will operate the machine for a defined period of time. It is always best to start and end mixing on a large Hobart at the slowest speed.

Sheeter: Used in commercial bakeshops where large amounts of dough are rolled, this mechanical roller is composed of two stainless-steel rollers that can be adjusted to vary the gap between them. To the left and right of the rollers are conveyor belts that are reversible in direction. The dough is passed back and forth through the rollers, with the gap being lessened each time until the desired thickness is reached. Sheeters are most useful when making large batches of laminated doughs such as *pâte feuilletée*, croissant, and Danish pastry doughs.

Theory

Principles of First Aid

Burns, abrasions, and cuts are part and parcel of work in the kitchen. These occupational hazards must be dealt with promptly and knowledgeably to ensure that additional damage is not done to the victim or to the workplace.

Follow these simple kitchen safety rules and many, many accidents will be avoided:

Burns, abrasions, and cuts are part and parcel of work in the kitchen. These occupational hazards must be dealt with promptly and knowledgeably to ensure that additional damage is not done to the victim or to the workplace.

° A well-maintained fire extinguisher should be within arm's reach at all times.

° Immediately clean spills from floors and work spaces. If a mop or other cleanup tool is not within reach, spread salt over floor spills to absorb moisture and prevent falls.

° Always use the guards and other safety devices provided for small equipment.

° Never attempt to remove food from a machine that is in motion, and always unplug electrical appliances before unloading, disassembling, or cleaning.

° Do not touch or handle electrical equipment, switches, or outlets with wet hands or if standing in water.

° Make certain that pilot lights are always lit and relight when necessary. Make sure that the kitchen is well ventilated.

° Do not attempt to lift very heavy objects without assistance, and when obliged to lift heavy pots, bend your knees and lift up.

Burns

Burns are often the most serious kitchen accidents, so it is extremely important to know how to treat them.

Burns are classified in three categories:

First-degree burn: A burn caused by quick contact with a moderately hot surface or liquid, resulting in inflammation and reddening of the skin. Painful but not serious.

Cover the burn with a Band-Aid but **do not put any burn cream on the area**.

Second-degree burn: Most often associated with scalding, this is a very painful burn that forms a blister on a localized area. Do not pop or attempt to open the blister. Cover the burn with antiseptic or antibacterial cream and sterile gauze.

Third-degree burn: An extremely serious burn that destroys all layers of the skin. The damaged skin appears white but may well be charred. In the kitchen, these burns are most often the result of contact with hot (200°C/400°F) cooking oil or fat. Keep the victim warm to prevent shock. **Immediately call emergency medical assistance or, if necessary, transport the victim to the nearest medical facility.** Do not undress the victim unless the clothes are saturated with a liquid that is still burning. Do not touch the burn or attempt to treat it yourself. In an educational or professional setting, make certain that all necessary medical insurance and liability forms are complete and that all insurance and liability information is made available to the victim.

There are a number of steps to take that will greatly diminish the possibility of kitchen burns. Learn them early and you will save yourself and others from injury.

○ Always warn your coworkers when you are moving hot pots, pans, and utensils, or when they are stationary but remain hot. It is particularly important to alert dishwashers and other cleanup personnel who handle soiled cookware and utensils. At home, these warnings should be directed to others present, especially young children and the elderly.

○ Always use a side towel to handle hot cookware and utensils.

○ Keep pot handles on the stove turned in from the front and away from open flames. Remember that heat travels and consider that all areas of a pot are potentially hot.

○ Do not overfill pans.

○ Do not attempt to lift or move large containers of hot liquid or food without assistance.

○ To prevent steam burns when removing the lid from a pot, always lift the lid up from the back, directing the steam away from your face.

○ To prevent oil or fat burns when frying, place the food into the pan from the front to the back, allowing the farthest edge to fall into the fat away from your hand.

○ Remember that **oil and water do not mix** and never attempt to put out a grease fire with water. If a small grease fire occurs, use salt or baking soda to extinguish it or cover it with a large lid to deprive the fire of oxygen.

○ Keep containers of liquid away from the deep-fat fryer.

○ To prevent hot grease splatters, dry all food well before placing it in hot fat.

Cuts

The seriousness of a cut is determined by its depth and place of occurrence. Obviously, a paper cut on the finger is treated quite differently from a knife slice that severs a vein or artery. When possible, cuts should be held under cold running water for at least one minute to cleanse the area. Then, using a clean towel, pressure should be applied to stop the flow of blood. If possible, elevate the cut area above the victim's heart to slow the flow. If the cut does not stop bleeding after a few minutes, is very deep, or bleeds profusely, it may require medical attention and stitches. Immediately call emergency medical assistance or transport the victim to the nearest medical facility while maintaining pressure to the cut area. Manageable hand cuts or those that have stopped bleeding should be covered with an antibiotic ointment, a clean bandage, and a rubber finger cover. This is to protect the cut from infection as well as to prevent the spread of bacteria from the wound to any food being prepared, as uncovered wounds are a ready source of food contamination.

Kitchen cuts can be avoided if a few basic precautions are taken.

○ Learn good knife skills. Hold your knife properly, keeping the fingertips of the hand opposite your knife curled down when slicing and dicing.

○ Carry a knife properly at all times—at your side, point down, with the sharp edge to the back.

○ Warn coworkers when moving about the kitchen with an unsheathed knife.

○ Avoid cutting with the knife point moving toward you.

○ Pay keen attention when using a knife. Do not talk.

○ Keep all knives sharp. The cook has less control of a dull knife as it takes more pressure to cut and is more likely to slip.

- Keep cutting boards stationary by placing a damp kitchen towel or a layer of damp paper towel underneath.

- Clean all knives carefully immediately after use, always keeping the sharp edge away from you.

- Never place a knife in a sink of water or under dishes; this presents a safety hazard.

- Never try to catch a falling knife. Jump backward to keep your feet out of range.

- Never try to catch a falling roll of plastic film or aluminum foil, as the cutting edge is extremely sharp and dangerous.

- Be extremely careful when using a mandoline, as the blades are razor sharp. It is a good idea to always use the hand guard.

Theory
The Basic Rules for Peeling and Cutting Fruit

The basic rules of peeling and cutting fruit have evolved with practical considerations. Smooth peeling and uniform cutting ensure even cooking and enhanced presentation. Once learned, these rules are never forgotten and, without exception, offer a basic element that will move a dish from the everyday to the sublime. In the beginning of the learning process, it is extremely important to practice these techniques over and over again.

The Peeling Process (*Épluchage*)

Related terms are ***éplucher***, ***écosser***, or ***éffiler***. The peeling process encompasses all of these activities.

Épluchage, literally defined, means cleaning, peeling, and unwrapping—or dissection.

Éplucher means to peel by removing the skin or outer layer of a fruit.

Écosser means to shell or hull, as with peas.

Éffiler means to pull off stringy side filaments, as with string beans. Memorize the proper name for each process and use it at all times.

- The term *émonder* means to remove the skin of a fruit, like a tomato. Remove the core, score the opposite end in a crisscross, and dip in boiling water for a few seconds. Dip in ice water to chill; then push off the loose skin.

Proper peeling techniques are as follows:

- All items to be peeled should be thoroughly clean and free of impurities before being placed on the cutting board.

- When peeling vegetables, the workstation should be set up as described on page 12.

- Peeling motions should be regular, consistent, and precise, removing as little of the flesh as possible. Most items can be peeled using a paring knife with a 3- to 4-inch blade or a functional vegetable peeler of which there are now many types available.

- Peeling should proceed in an orderly and clean manner with the remains discarded as soon as the work is complete.

grande ronde

petite ronde

pare

tranche

jardinière

julienne

macédoine

paysanne

brunoise

Methods of Cutting Vegetables and Fruit (*Taillage*)

Although traditionally these are the proper cutting methods designated for vegetables, their use applies also to fruit in the pastry kitchen. Proper cutting results in vegetables and fruit of uniform size and shape and ensures that the items will cook evenly. It is particularly important to follow the guidelines for proper cutting because it allows more than one person to prepare items for a specific recipe. Appropriate cutting also is used to enhance the aesthetic of the finished presentation. These methods should be practiced over and over until the appropriate cut can be made almost

with closed eyes. Just as the old joke says that the way to Carnegie Hall is through practice, practice, practice, so it is also that practice is the only way to master proper cutting techniques and sizes.

Again, it is extremely important to memorize the proper cut, as it is the only reference you will have to preparation of a properly peeled and cut item. It is a good idea to practice these cuts outside the classroom using basic vegetables or fruit such as potatoes, carrots, and celery (which, once cut, can be tossed in a pot with a bit of water and stock, seasoned, and cooked to make a simple, healthy soup) or apples and pears (which, once cut, can be tossed in a pot with a bit of water, sugar, and spices, and cooked to make a simple fruit sauce). When practicing on other items, either put them together for a soup, practice cooking methods, or make a raw or cooked salad, either tossed or composed.

The traditional nomenclature for cutting procedures is as follows:

Émincer: To thinly slice.

Ciseler: To finely dice onions and shallots by cutting down through the entire vegetable, both lengthwise and crosswise. This striation of cuts produces a fine, tiny dice that keeps the juices from being forced out, which is what happens with standard chopping.

Tronçonner: To cut into 4- to 7-centimeter (1- to 2-inch) segments.

Parer: To trim round slices of washed, peeled vegetables cut in *tronçons* to obtain flat surfaces on every side so that even pieces can be uniformly cut.

Traditional *taillage* is as follows:

Pared items are first cut into slices that are called **tranches**, then into sticks or dice. Each cut size has a specific name.

Jardinière: Thin sticks, 5 millimeters (³⁄₁₆ inch) square and 4 to 5 centimeters (1- to 2 inches) long.

Julienne: Very thin sticks, 1 to 2 millimeters (¹⁄₁₂ to ¹⁄₁₆ inch) square and 5 to 7 centimeters (2 to 2½ inches) long.

Macédoine: Small cubes, 5 millimeters (³⁄₁₆ inch) square.

Brunoise: Minute cubes, 1 to 2 millimeters (¹⁄₃₂ to ¹⁄₁₆ inch) square.

Paysanne: This cut is tile-shaped or triangular, usually cut from *jardinière* sliced 1 to 2 millimeters (¹⁄₃₂ to ¹⁄₁₆ inch) thick, or it may also be cut without preshaping the item. Vegetables cut into *paysanne* are most often used for soups called **potages taillés**.

Chiffonade: This method of cutting produces thin strips or ribbons of herbs or leafy vegetables.

To cut into *chiffonade*:

1. Wash and thoroughly dry the leaves.

2. Lay the leaves in a flat stack of three or four.

3. Roll the stacked leaves into a cigar shape.

Dean's Tip

"It is impossible to make a good product with poor ingredients. Always buy and use the best possible ingredients to achieve the best possible results."

Dean Jacques Torres

4. Cut the leaf roll, crosswise, to form very thin strips or ribbons.

Émonder is the French term used to refer to removing skins from peaches, apricots, and tomatoes by submerging them in boiling water.

Peler et épépiner (peeling and coring) are the terms used to describe working with pears and apples. To core pears and apples, cut the fruit in half lengthwise. Using a *parisienne* scoop (see page 24), cut out the stem, the seeds, and finally the flower end. To core the whole fruit, work from the bottom of the fruit and core through the center, using a corer or melon baller. To cut apples or pears for tarts, peel, halve, and core. Using a chef's knife, make thin (no more than ⅛-inch) slices, cutting across the core area.

Mangoes are first peeled and then two cuts are made on either side of the long flat pit in the center of the fruit. The two large pieces that come off can then be sliced as desired. For cubes, it is easier to make the two cuts without peeling the fruit and then, using the tip of a paring knife, cut the flesh into cubes of a desired size, taking care not to break into the peel. Turn the section up and out by pushing on the peel, and cut the cubes away from the peel.

Stone fruits may or may not be peeled. Soft fruits, such as peaches, are generally peeled by the process called *émonder* (see page 33). They are opened by using a paring knife to cut through to the pit following the crease that runs around the length of the fruit. Once the two halves have been made, they should be slowly twisted in opposite directions to separate them. They are then cut as desired, usually in thin slices, lengthwise.

Lemons can be decorated with ridges using a channel knife or *canneleur*. After fluting (cutting into ridges) the whole lemon, cut it crosswise into slices or half slices. Lemons (or any other citrus fruit) can also be cut into baskets or cut in half with a paring knife in such a way as to leave a zigzag edge known as **dent de loup**, or wolf's tooth. Lemons cut in this manner are often used as decorative garnish. **Peler à vif** means to remove the peel of citrus fruit, particularly lemon.

Citrus suprêmes (see photos) are made by cutting off the bottom of the fruit so that it can be held upright. With a chef's knife, all of the peel and the pith are removed in straight, even downward strokes; then the fruit is removed by cutting between each membrane to create a solid segment that has no peel, pith, or membrane attached.

Session 2

Ingredients Commonly Used in Pastry Making

Theory

Flours

Flour is produced when grasses, seeds, nuts, or vegetables are finely ground. The ground matter is generally processed through some type of sieve to generate a fine, sometimes almost powdery substance. The use of the term, flour, is always based on the presence of starches or complex carbohydrates. Whether creating something sweet or savory, flour is one of the primary structural elements used in baking, so it is a key ingredient for bakers and pastry chefs.

Beyond being a basic building block for pastries, cookies, cakes, and breads, flour has other important qualities. It provides nutrients, creates texture, lends the desired appearance, generates flavor, and serves as an agent for the incorporation of liquid through binding and absorption.

When attempting to understand how the proteins in a flour act, it is helpful to think of them as strands of wool. In their original state, they are loose and have neither elasticity nor strength. When water is added to actual wool and then pressed or worked, the mixture will turn into felt, a strong, dense fabric. To bring this analogy back to flour, imagine that the strands are two proteins called **glutenin** and **gliadin**. Just as with wool, these proteins absorb large amounts of water and, when mixed or kneaded, begin to combine and gain strength. The resulting mix is called **gluten**. As the flour and water are worked further, the proteins begin to cross connect and to form large sheets. The structure becomes elastic and strong, which enables it to trap gases and air that will leaven (increase the volume and lighten the texture) the product, resulting in the gas bubbles that create the familiar spongelike texture of breads and cakes.

When flour is milled, it is tested and classified according to its ratio of gluten-forming proteins to starch. The protein content of a specific flour will affect the strength of the dough. With wheat flour, the protein content will be determined by the type of wheat used and where and when it was grown, as well as the part of the wheat kernel used.

The amount of water or other liquid in a recipe will also affect the formation of gluten, with large amounts of water increasing the gluten factor. Temperature also speeds the development of gluten; a warm environment will cause it to build up more quickly than a cool one. Fats play an important role as well because they coat the glutenin and gliadin strands, preventing them from bonding with one another or the liquid. Recipes using large amounts of fat will generally be softer and more tender because the fat "shortens" the dough—that is, it shortens the gluten strands.

Wheat Flours

Wheat is one of the world's largest cereal grass crops, second only to rice. Its popularity as a flour is based on its ability to develop gluten when mixed with water or other liquids. This development provides the elasticity which, when worked, will result in the gas bubbles that create the familiar, spongelike texture of breads and cakes.

Wheat berries, the whole kernels of wheat, are composed of three distinct parts: bran, germ, and endosperm. The bran is the hard, protective cover. The germ is the embryo from which a new plant grows. The endosperm is the food source for the germ. Whole-wheat flour is created when all three parts are ground together. White wheat flours are created solely from the endosperm. Both the bran and germ are rich in vitamins and are used as additives or as animal feed.

Wheat flours are milled and refined for different uses and treated to improve their properties and food value. The protein content of flour is the element that will generally determine its use. Flour with a large percentage of protein is termed "hard" and that with a lesser amount is "soft." In the United States, wheat flours are divided into categories based on their protein density. Starting from the hardest and moving to the softest, they include bread flour, all-purpose flour, and cake or pastry flour.

Milling is a long, multistep process. Once delivered to the flour mill, wheat is cleaned and tested and may then be blended with other varieties of wheat to create the desired flour type. The wheat is then tempered with the addition of water for 10 to 20 hours. Afterward, it is rolled or crushed, sifted, and purified, a process that may be repeated up to twelve times. Purification simply involves forcing air through the flour to push the larger pieces to the top for easy separation.

After milling, flour must go through a number of other steps before it is ready for commercial use. To strengthen and elasticize the gluten and to whiten the flour, it must be oxidized or matured. This is either done naturally, by exposing the flour to air for two to three months, or chemically, by adding potassium bromate, which quickly "ages" the flour with no effect on the color. This latter process is used only in the United States. Some flours are also bleached with chlorine dioxide.

Once mature, the flour is enriched with the addition of certain nutrients that have been lost during the milling process. Vitamins B_1, B_2, D, niacin, iron, calcium, thiamin, riboflavin, and folic acid are added. Mold inhibitors may be also be added, and the miller may add malted wheat or barley flour for better fermentation.

Types of Wheat Flour

All-purpose flour: A medium-protein blend of various grades of flours that can be used for almost any type of baking. Created primarily for use in the home kitchen—professional bakers will generally use a specific flour (bread, cake, pastry) to better control the protein content of the product. All-purpose flours tend to have wide variation from mill to mill. Most recipes calling for all-purpose flour should generally be mixed as little as possible, as gluten development is usually not desired. Also available is "self-rising" all-purpose flour, to which baking powder and salt have been added.

Whole-wheat flour: The whole grain is used to produce a flour that is substantially higher in nutrients, fiber, and fat than white flours.

Bread flour: A strong white flour with a high-protein content that makes it especially suited for yeast-risen doughs. Bread flour, primarily used to create yeasted breads and yeast-dough based pastries such as croissants (*viennoiseries*), tends to be slightly granular with a yellowish color. It can be used in combination with lower-protein flours in recipes such as puff pastry (*pâte feuilletée*) or cream puff dough (*pâte à choux*), both of which rely on the gluten structure in the dough to trap steam and enable the dough to remain flaky.

Gluten flour: Used to increase the protein content of weaker flours. It may also be added to some bread recipes that require high gluten development. The addition of gluten flour to a bread dough will shorten the kneading time, require the addition of more liquid, and create a tighter crumb in the finished product.

Cake Flour: A very low-protein flour used to create cakes, quick breads, cookies, and certain pastry doughs. It is often blended with higher-protein flours to achieve the required strength for a specific dough. Cake flour is very white and, when squeezed in the palm of your hand, will remain in a clump when you open your fingers. Doughs or batters using cake flour should be mixed very gently to restrict gluten development. In fact, in some cake recipes the flour is delicately folded into the batter to avoid this development. Tart doughs are generally gently mixed or finished by hand to inhibit gluten enhancement.

Pastry flour: A medium-low-protein flour, falling between all-purpose and cake flours, that is well suited to the creation of many pastries, tart doughs, and cookies. Like cake flour, pastry flour is often used in quick breads in which low gluten development is desirable to maintain a fine crumb in the finished product.

Graham flour: A whole-wheat flour in which the endosperm is very finely ground and the bran and germ are coarse. It is an American flour invented by Dr. Sylvester Graham, who also created the graham cracker.

Semolina: Milled from high-gluten, high-protein durum wheat, semolina flour is used primarily for making pasta and noodles. The flour granules are so hard that they will cut the gluten strands as the gluten develops. Semolina flour is occasionally called for in bread making, pizza dough, ethnic cakes, and some cookies. It is also used to make many flatbreads.

Instant flour: Exceedingly fine granular flour that is used, primarily, in the home kitchen as a thickener for sauces and gravies. It is processed so that it can quickly absorb liquids without clumping. It has a very low-protein content and is used by some pastry chefs

to make quick puff pastry (*pâte feuilletée rapide*). It is also excellent for making flour-based pastry cream (*crème pâtissière*) as it quickly absorbs the liquid and tends not to form lumps, which frequently occur when using other starch thickeners.

Some Other Flours

Although we are most familiar with wheat flours, flour can be made from many, many different starchy foods. Legumes such as soy beans, acorns, nuts, ancient grains such as teff and amaranth, as well as potatoes and other tubers are but a few ingredients used to make flours around the world. The following are some of those used in the American kitchen:

Buckwheat flour: Seeds of an herb, native to Russia, that are ground into a strongly flavored flour used to make pancakes and some breads in the United States, as well as the traditional Russian *blinis* that accompany caviar. It is also used in Japan to make soba noodles.

Chestnut flour: Flour created by finely grinding dried chestnuts that is used in various parts of the Mediterranean to make polenta and desserts.

Chickpea flour: Flour made from dried chickpeas (also known as garbanzo beans) that is primarily used in East Indian and Italian cooking.

Cornmeal and corn flour: Cornmeal—dried corn kernels ground into fine, medium, and coarse textures—is used for breads, griddle cakes, a few desserts, and breading. Bleached with lye, cornmeal is called *masa harina* and is used to make traditional Mexican dishes such as tortillas and tamales. Corn flour is finely ground cornmeal that is used in baking and for breading. In the United Kingdom, corn flour is the term used for the ingredient called cornstarch in the United States.

Nut flours: Almost any nut can be ground into flour, but it is the oilier ones, such as almonds, macadamias, and hazelnuts, that are most often used, alone or in combination with wheat flour, to produce cakes and pastries. Many nut-based flours are used to make traditional cakes throughout Central Europe.

Potato flour: Also known as potato starch, this flour is ground from cooked, dried potatoes. It is gluten-free and consists mostly of starch with a little protein. It is used to create a moist crumb in baked goods and as a thickener.

Rice flour: Extra-fine, almost powdery flour ground from white rice that is used for some baked goods and edible papers. It consists mainly of starch. Also available is whole-grain brown rice flour and glutinous rice flour. The latter is used mainly in Japanese cooking as a thickener or to create desserts.

Rye flour: A low-gluten flour ground from rye, a cereal grass. It is always mixed with a high-protein flour when used to make breads and pastries. Available in light, medium, and dark as well as pumpernickel flours.

Leavening Ingredients

Leavening in pastry depends on the action of air, water, or carbon dioxide, each of which expands substantially when heated. This expansion can be produced mechanically, chemically, or organically—or through a combination of means.

Mechanical Leavening

Mechanical leavening occurs when air is physically incorporated into a mixture to make it puffy or when the steam in a mixture expands under heated conditions. (When the liquid in a mix turns to steam, it can expand to eleven hundred times its original volume.) Two familiar examples of mechanical leavening are creamed butter cakes and egg foams such as meringues. When butter and sugar are mixed together for a creamed butter cake, the sugar cuts into the butter and causes it to trap air. When egg foams are beaten, the protein in the eggs causes the air to be trapped.

Pâte à choux and *pâte feuilletée* are two examples of doughs that rely more on steam than air for leavening. In a *pâte feuilletée*, layers of butter alternate with layers of dough. During baking, the liquid in the butter and in the dough change into steam, which causes the dough to rise to about ten times its prebaked size.

Chemical Leavening

Chemical agents, usually baking soda or baking powder, cause a chemical reaction in a dough that produces gases during baking and cause it to rise. Used to make cakes, cookies, quick breads, muffins, biscuits, and crackers, these chemical agents both produce carbon dioxide in reaction with added acids, liquids, and heat. The resulting products are very light, airy, and tightly grained. When using chemical leaveners, great care must be taken not to overdevelop the gluten in a mix, as overworking will not only affect the ability of the dough to rise, but will also toughen the baked product. Uneven or flat tops and tunnels are two examples of undesirable gluten development in quick breads or muffins.

Baking soda, also known as sodium bicarbonate, is a naturally occurring substance found in all living matter. It is extracted from an ore, *trona*, or manufactured.

When mixed with an acid, it releases carbon dioxide and leaves a small amount of salt. This reaction is immediate, and therefore the batter cannot be left to sit for any period of time or the texture will be radically affected. Some of the acids used with baking soda are buttermilk, citrus juices, sour milk or cream, yogurt, molasses, chocolate, honey, or cream of tartar. If baking soda is not mixed with enough acid to allow it to fully break down, an unpleasant, almost soapy taste will result in the end product.

There are three types of **baking powder**: single acting (also called fast acting), slow acting, and double acting. Single acting is made from an acid that quickly dissolves and produces gases when placed in cold water. Slow acting does not react until heat is applied. Double acting has both elements, so that some leavening (about one-third) occurs during mixing and the remainder during baking. The latter allows a mixed dough or batter to be stored for several days with no loss of leavening power.

Organic Leavening

Organic leavening works by using the fermentation process launched when yeast is used to produce carbon dioxide that makes a product rise. Yeast requires food, moisture, oxygen, and a warm temperature to do its work, and dough provides the best of all possible environments for it. When mixed into a dough, yeast devours sugars and damaged starches and converts them into alcohol and carbon dioxide. This takes some time to occur. The dough must also have a very well-developed gluten structure to trap the gases inside and have enough elasticity to grow and stretch once placed in the oven. The fermentation process helps produce the distinctive flavor and aroma of so many yeasted products.

The speed of fermentation is affected by temperature, food, water, and time. Generally, yeast lives and continues to ferment at temperatures ranging from 4°C (40°F) to 54°C (130°F) but is at its most active at about 24°C (75°F). Yeast will slowly begin to die when the temperature is above 59°C (138°F) or goes below the freezing point. A wet dough will rise more quickly than a dry dough as well. All other factors will affect the amount of time required for the yeast to ferment properly.

There are many types of yeast, but the most common type used for food preparation is the species *Saccharomyces cerevisiae*. It is commercially available as baker's and brewer's yeast.

Baker's yeast: There are three types of baker's yeast: dry yeast, compressed fresh yeast, and starters created from captured wild yeast spores.

○ **Active dry yeast** is composed of tiny, dehydrated granules containing organisms that are alive but

dormant because of lack of moisture. When mixed with warm (40°C/105°F to 46°C/115°F) liquid, they become active. It is available as regular or quick-rise, with the latter taking about half as long to do its leavening work. They can, however, be used interchangeably with an adjustment to the specific rising time. Either type should be stored in a cool, dry place and can be refrigerated or frozen. However, the yeast should be brought to room temperature before using.

○ **Compressed fresh yeast** must be refrigerated and used within a week or so of purchase. If frozen, it must be defrosted at room temperature and used immediately. Doughs made from thawed frozen yeast have a shorter shelf life, usually no more than two days. Although the general recommendation for substituting fresh for dry (or vice versa) is two parts fresh yeast for one part dry, it is always best to check the manufacturer's package directions. To test whether fresh yeast is still vigorous, dissolve it in warm water with a pinch of sugar and set it aside in a warm spot for 10 minutes. If the mixture begins to foam and swell, the yeast can still do its leavening job.

○ **Starters** (also called **levains**) are simply cultivated, captured wild yeast spores. To create a starter, flour and water are mixed together and left to rest for a substantial period of time. Yeast spores from the environment collect on the mixture and begin to multiply. The starter is fed and watered regularly to cultivate the yeast and prevent the spores from dying. Once a large amount of starter has been created, a measured amount can be mixed into a dough to provide leavening while the remainder continues to be fed and watered for future use. Some starters are very, very old and have been handed down from generation to generation. It is this naturally fermented mix that produces breads with a very distinct, but desirable sour taste and aroma.

Compressed fresh yeast

Sugar

Sugar, also known as sucrose, is the water-soluble substance obtained by processing sugarcane, sugar beets, and sorghum. It also is the greater part of maple sap. Although the most commonly used sugar comes from cane and beets, it is also available in other forms such as dextrose (corn or grape sugar), fructose (levulose), maltose (malt sugar), and lactose (milk sugar). Not only does sugar add sweetness, it can also preserve foods, caramelize the surface of cooked or baked foods, delay coagulation in egg-based mixtures, and add stability to, strengthen, and tenderize doughs and other mixes. To the commercial baker, one of its most important benefits is that it retains moisture, which prolongs a product's shelf life. It is indispensable in the pastry kitchen! Although sugar is available in many forms, we will mainly focus on "regular" sugar. That is, the type of sugar most commonly used in the home kitchen. It should be noted that there are also many types of granulated sugar, but most of them are available for use only in the commercial processing of foods and baked goods or by professional bakers. These sugars differ in crystal size, with each type of crystal providing unique functional characteristics.

White Sugar

White sugar is sucrose that has been highly refined through a purifying process using phosphoric acid or any number of filtration strategies and then decolorized to leave pure white crystals, or granules. The types of white, granulated sugar are as follows:

"Regular" sugar, extra-fine sugar, fine sugar: "Regular" sugar is the granulated sugar found on the supermarket shelf and in almost every kitchen's sugar bowl. It is the most common sugar for everyday use and is called for in most home-baking recipes. In commercial food processing or baking, this same granulated sugar is called fine or extra-fine sugar. It is ideal for bulk handling because the fine crystals are not susceptible to caking.

Fruit sugar: Fruit sugar, a commercial sugar used in dry mixes such as gelatin desserts and pudding and drink mixes, is slightly finer than "regular" sugar. It has a more uniform crystal size, which prevents separation and does not allow the smaller crystals to settle to the bottom of the package, an important issue in packaged mixes. It is not available for home use.

Bakers Special: Finer than fruit sugar, Bakers Special was developed for use in the commercial baking industry. It is commonly used for sugaring commercially made doughnuts and cookies as well as in commercially produced cakes to produce a fine crumb texture. It is not available for home use.

Superfine, ultrafine, or bar sugar: The finest granulated sugar, quick-dissolving superfine sugar is ideal for fine-textured cakes and meringues, as well as for sweetening fruits and iced drinks. In the United Kingdom, a sugar quite similar to superfine sugar is known as caster (or castor) sugar, named after the type of shaker in which it is often served.

Confectioners' or powdered sugar (also often called 10X): This is simply granulated sugar that has been ground into a powder, sifted, and lightened with about 3 percent cornstarch to prevent caking. It is available in different grades, each ground to differing degrees of fineness. That labeled 12X (also known as fondant or icing sugar) is the finest, 10X (generically called powdered sugar) is less fine, and 4X is even coarser. The type generally available in supermarkets for home use is 10X. The other two are used in commercial applications. Confectioners' sugar is often sifted before being used in icings and confectionery and to sweeten heavy cream that will be whipped. It is called icing sugar in the United Kingdom and *sucre glace* in France.

Coarse sugar or crystal sugar: Larger than the crystals of "regular" sugar, coarse sugar is usually processed from the purest sugar liquor. It is highly resistant to color change or inversion (the natural breakdown of sucrose to fructose and glucose) at high temperatures. These characteristics make it a desirable sweetener for fondants, confectionery, and liquors. It is also used to decorate cookies and other baked goods.

Glazing sugar: Extremely fine confectioners' sugar (most often 12X) that has maltodextrin added for stabilization and absorption of moisture. Used to create a high gloss on glazed products that will last over an extended period of time.

Sanding sugar: Used primarily in commercial baking and confectionery to decorate baked goods. The large crystals reflect light beautifully and create a sparkling appearance.

Cube sugar: "Regular" sugar that has been moistened, pressed into molds, and cut into a specific shape, generally a cube.

Brown Sugar

Brown sugar is granulated white sugar that has been combined with molasses to achieve a rich, dark flavor and light texture. It is most commonly marketed as light or dark, with the light being the most delicately flavored. Normally quite soft with delicate grains, brown sugar is now also available in a dry, granular form, as well as a liquid. Its rich flavor adds depth to baked goods, sauces, and other mixes.

Brown sugar (light or dark): Because it contains more moisture than granulated "regular" sugar, brown sugar tends to clump and harden when exposed to air. Dark brown sugar has more color and a stronger molasses flavor than the lighter varieties. The rich flavor of dark brown sugar lends itself to use in gingerbread, mincemeat, plum puddings, strongly flavored sauces, and other deeply flavored foods. Lighter types are generally used in baking and in making butterscotch, condiments, and glazes.

Muscovado or Barbados sugar: A British specialty, this is an unrefined sugar with a strong flavor that comes from the sugar cane juice from which it is made. Also known as moist sugar, its coarse crystals are stickier in texture than American brown sugars. Although it

has a strong molasses flavor, this does not result from the addition of molasses. It is, rather, a natural result of the production process.

Free-flowing brown sugars: These finely powdered specialty sugars are produced by a special process that renders them dry. They don't lump and can be poured like "regular" sugars.

Turbinado sugar: A less refined type of granulated sugar that contains a small amount of molasses in the individual crystal as well as on its surface. It is coarser than "regular" sugar, light brown, and has a gentle molasses flavor.

Demerara sugar: This specialty raw cane sugar is very popular in the United Kingdom. Native to the Demerara region of Guyana, has large, slightly sticky golden crystals. It is most commonly used to sweeten drinks or cereals.

Liquid Sugar

Liquid sugar is simply granulated sucrose dissolved in water. There are quite a few types of liquid sugar, most developed before contemporary methods of sugar processing made transporting and handling granulated sugars practical. Liquid sugars are generally dark-colored, and although they can be used in place of dissolved granulated sugar, the color inhibits their use in many products.

Invert sugar: Invert sugar, an equal mixture of fructose and glucose, is produced in the chemical breakdown of sucrose. A bit of acid is added to sugar syrup, and the mixture is then heated to create the inversion. It is substantially sweeter than granulated sugar and is commercially available only in liquid form. It produces smooth, finely textured bakery goods, drinks, candies, and syrups. One type, a mixture of invert and dissolved granulated sugar, was developed exclusively for use by the carbonated beverage industry. Total invert sugar is, as its name implies, completely made up of invert sugar and is used to retard sugar crystallization and retain moisture in commercially made food products. In the pastry kitchen, invert sugar is generally called Trimoline or invert syrup. It is available at bak-

granulated

glucose

light brown

Demerara

honey

invert

molasses

dark brown

confectioner's

pearl

dark corn syrup

45

ery and cake-making supply stores. If it is unavailable, replace it with an equal amount of light corn syrup.

Corn syrup: Also known as glucose syrup, corn syrup is created by treating cornstarch with enzymes to turn it into a simple syrup. To varying degrees, the manufacturing process breaks the starches down into glucose molecules. Low-conversion corn syrups are extremely thick and only slightly sweet. When used in baking, these syrups help retain moisture, create tenderness, and retard burning and caramelization. All-purpose corn syrup, also called medium-conversion syrup, is the most commonly available, in both light and dark forms. The dark has caramel flavor and color added; because its flavor is more distinct, it is generally used only in heavily spiced cakes or cookies. Corn syrup is often used to prevent crystallization of other sugars in a cooked product.

High-fructose corn syrup (HFCS): This is a mixture of pure corn syrup and a corn syrup that has undergone enzymatic processing to enhance its fructose content. The end result is a very sweet syrup that is often used as a sugar replacement in commercial food processing. Its use is now controversial, as many nutritionists feel that it has contributed to the worldwide increase in obesity. HFCS55, used primarily in bottled colas and other soft drinks, is approximately 55 percent fructose and 45 glucose, while HFCS42, used mostly in commercial bakery products and other processed foods, is 42 percent fructose and 58 percent glucose.

Molasses: Also known as sorghum syrup, molasses is the strong-flavored, concentrated liquid that remains after sugar has been extracted during the refining process. It may come from either sugar cane or sugar beets, but that from sugar beets is not used in a kitchen setting. Sulfured molasses is made from green sugar cane with sulfur dioxide added as a preservative, while unsulfured molasses comes from the mature plant, requires no preservative, and has a less potent flavor. Molasses contains a substantial amount of sucrose and other sugars, as well as acids and various elements that add to its viscosity, taste, and color. Dark molasses is less sweet and stronger in flavor

than light. Blackstrap molasses, used as a food supplement because of its high vitamin and mineral contents, may be found in health-food stores; it is not generally used in baking. Molasses helps finished baked goods retain moisture, which in turn lengthens shelf life. In the pastry kitchen, it is most often used to sweeten heavily spiced cakes and cookies.

Honey: Honey is a natural sweetener that is simply the nectar gathered from flowers by bees. It is available in its comb as well as extracted from the comb. The latter is the most commonly available and is the only one used in baking or candy making. The natural flavor of honey is dependent on the flavor of the flower from which it has been collected, although the darker the honey the more intense its flavor. Orange-blossom and clover honeys are the two most popular, but there are many more varieties collected from every part of the world. In baking, honey is used to add moisture and a tender but chewy texture to cakes and cookies.

Sugar in Action

Although sugar has been an important commodity worldwide for centuries, the chemical and biochemical properties of it have only been explored over the past 150 years. Up to this point, cooks could only guess why sweetened, preserved fruits, jams, and jellies did not spoil, or why cakes were moist and light of crumb when sugar and fat were creamed together. Since sugar is such an integral part of pastry recipes, it is extremely important for today's pastry chefs to know the whys and wherefores of sugar's role in food preparation. These will be explored in great detail in the following pages.

The following list is a brief introduction to sugar's functions beyond those of sweetener and flavor enhancer.

1. Sugar incorporates air into fat in the creaming process of a batter or dough;

2. acts as a tenderizer by absorbing liquid and arresting the development of flour gluten, as well as checking starch gelatinization;

3. nourishes yeast to speed its growth in a mix;

4. collaborates with protein and starch molecules during cooking and baking;

5. provides caramelization to the surface of cooked or baked goods, producing a golden color and inviting aroma;

6. stabilizes beaten egg foams by aiding in the whipping action;

7. postpones the coagulation of egg proteins in puddings and custards;

8. moderates the gelling process with fruit preserves and jellies;

9. assists in the prevention of spoilage in preserved fruit products;

10. boosts the tenderness and color of preserved fruits;

11. helps prevent surface discoloration in frozen fresh fruits;

12. amplifies the smooth texture of ice creams;

13. assists many varieties of candy during changing degrees of recrystallization; and

14. develops invert sugar to control recrystallizaton.

Sugar in the Bakery

A look through any cookbook will tell you that almost every baked good requires some type of sweetener. Although a myriad of sweeteners can be and are used, most recipes call for sugar because of its ability to enhance the product's flavor, color, and texture, to add tenderness and evenness of grain, to help retain moisture and extend its period of freshness. With those products requiring yeast, sugar will also assist in fermentation. All these issues are critical to preparing high-quality baked goods, so it is extremely important to fully understand the role of sugar in doughs, batters, and sweet mixes, as well as how it interacts with other ingredients in a recipe. Sugar is, in fact, one of the baker's most versatile ingredients.

Working together, sugar, solid fat (such as vegetable shortening or butter), eggs, liquids, and leavening agents (those products that increase the volume and lighten the texture of baked goods) are the basic functional ingredients for almost all baked goods. It is this mix that forms the final structure of a product. The sensory and systemic characteristics of any baked product will be determined by the amount, essence, and interaction of these ingredients.

The Basic Functional Roles of Sugar in Baked Products

Gluten development: Flour proteins are hydrated during the mixing of batters and doughs, thereby forming gluten strands. Gases produced during leavening are trapped by the thousands of small, balloonlike pockets in the gluten. Highly elastic, the gluten strands allow the mixture to stretch as the expansion of gases occurs. If too much gluten develops, the mixture will become tough and fixed. Sugar performs an extremely important role as a tenderizing agent during the mixing process.

During mixing, sugar competes with the gluten-forming proteins for the liquid in the mix,

which stops the proteins from fully hydrating and slows their development. When the correct amount of sugar is used in proportion to the other ingredients, the gluten will be kept at its maximum elasticity, which, in turn, keeps the gases formed in the leavening process within the interior grid of the dough so the mixture can rise and expand. The final baked product will have a fine texture and a tender crumb, as well as expanded volume and height.

Leavening: Sugar provides an instant, usable source of nourishment to yeast. Under the correct temperature and moisture conditions, the yeast cells break down the sugar, releasing carbon dioxide gas at a speedier rate than would occur if only the carbohydrates in flour were available.

Creaming: Mixing sugar and solid fat together distributes the sugar crystals throughout the fat molecules. In the process, very small air cells are created because air trapped on the sugar's irregular crystal surface gets pulled into the mixture. During baking, the tiny air cells expand and grow as they are filled with carbon dioxide and other gases from whatever leavening agents have been added to the mix, resulting in a light airiness in the baked product.

Egg foams: Sugar coalesces with egg proteins to stabilize the whipped foam mixture in all foam-type cakes such as angel food or sponge. The addition of sugar makes egg foam substantially more elastic so that the air cells can expand and grab the leavening agent's gases.

Egg protein coagulation: Egg proteins form bonds with each other as the temperature rises during baking. When a cake has little or no shortening, the sugar molecules scatter through the egg proteins and slow down their coagulation during baking. In addition, sugar molecules raise the temperature at which egg proteins form bonds by surrounding them and interfering with their ability to create bond formations. The cake "sets" or forms the desired solid, screenlike texture once the egg proteins coagulate.

Gelatinization: The heat of baking causes the flour starches to absorb liquid and swell. As more and more liquid is absorbed by the starch, the cake batter changes from a soft, fluid mix to a solid, set shape, creating the lightly textured layers desired by the baker. This process is called gelatinization. Sugar slows gelatinization by racing with the starch to absorb the liquid. This delay allows the sugar to tenderize the finished cake. The result is that the temperature at which the cake will "set" or solidify is raised, allowing the perfect amount of gas to be produced by the leavening agents so that the desired fine, uniformly textured cake with a soft, delicate crumb is achieved.

It is unclear if the same effect that occurs with cakes happens when making breads; however, it is assumed that sugar does influence gelatinization in breads with a high sugar content, resulting in a tender texture and fine crumb.

Caramelization: Melted granulated sugar oxidizes, turns amber-colored, and exudes an inviting aroma and flavor when it reaches about 175°C (347°F). A nice crust forms and acts as a barrier, allowing the baked product to retain moisture. This rather nebulous creation resulting from the breakdown of sugar is known as caramel, and it can be achieved on the stovetop, in the oven, or on the grill.

Maillard reaction: Maillard reactions—similar to but different from caramelization—occur among sugar and the amino acids, proteins, and peptides and are generally induced by heat. Sugar chemically reacts with proteins in the heat of the oven to contribute a golden brown exterior to baked products. The greater the sugar content of a mix, the deeper the end brown color. In addition, the crisp exterior that results helps the baked product retain its moisture for a longer period of time. These reactions also contribute to the wonderful, inviting aromas that emanate from baking breads, cakes, and cookies.

Surface cracking: Because of the low liquid content and the relatively high concentration of sugar in many cookies, sugar crystallizes on their exterior and produces a desirable crisp surface. When sugar crystallizes, it emits heat that causes the water it absorbed during mixing and baking to evaporate. Simultaneously, the gases in the leavening agents inflate, creating the crackled effect on the dry surface of the cookie as it cools.

The following section explains which of these functions apply to specific types of baked product.

Shortened cakes: Sugar furthers the incorporation of air into the fat in all shortened cakes. It aids in the production of volume during mixing and baking and helps create a fine crumb texture. It also absorbs liquid and promotes the complete hydration of the gluten strands during mixing, which helps ensure a soft, tender cake. This tenderization extends throughout baking as sugar continues to absorb liquid and delays gelatinization.

Unshortened cakes: Cakes that contain no fat but are made with a large amount of whole eggs or egg whites, such as angel food and sponge, are called unshortened. In these cakes, most of the cellular structure comes from egg protein and from the air beaten into them. When whipping the eggs, sugar is added to stabilize the beaten egg foam. Often some of the sugar is combined with the flour before the dry ingredients are folded into the airy eggs to separate the flour's starch particles and keep them from clumping when folded into the egg foam. Sugar also raises the temperature at which egg proteins set, delaying coagulation just long enough to allow the optimum amount of air to be captured into the mix. This process creates a cake that is exceedingly light and tender, with superb volume.

Pound cake: Although prepared with some type of fat, pound cakes (known in France as *quatre-quarts*) are generally leavened with nothing but the air provided by a large quantity of beaten eggs. Creaming the sugar and fat together also contributes to a fluffy batter by creating more tiny air pockets to expand as the cake bakes. The addition of sugar absorbs liquid and facilitates the complete hydration of the gluten strands during mixing, which helps ensure a soft, tender cake. Tenderization extends throughout baking as sugar continues to absorb liquid and delays gelatinization. Sugar content also produces a very fine crumb texture and the desired volume along with a golden exterior.

Cookies: In most cases, cookies are chemically leavened with baking powder or baking soda and have more sugar and fat and less liquid than cakes. During creaming, sugar serves to introduce air into the cookie dough or batter. In general, about half the sugar content of a cookie dough will remain undissolved at the end of the mixing period. As the cookie bakes, the high temperature will melt the fat and cause the dough to become more fluid. The undissolved sugar begins to liquefy as well, and the sugar solution increases in volume, causing the dough to spread. In addition, sugar helps create a golden exterior and wonderful sweet flavor as it caramelizes. In some cookies, such as gingersnaps, sugar assists in the development of a crackled surface.

Yeast breads: Sugar increases the speed at which yeast produces the carbon dioxide necessary to leaven the dough. During mixing, sugar also absorbs a very high proportion of liquid, which delays the formation of gluten. This delay makes the dough's elasticity ideal for snaring gases that form the desired dough structure. Maillard reactions also contribute to the creation of a slightly crisp, golden crust and the appetite-stimulating aroma of baking bread. In addition, flour proteins as well as some of the yeast fermentation by-products react with sugar to assist in creating the desired color and flavor of a yeast bread.

Quick breads: Prepared without yeast but with some type of leavening agent, relatively small amounts of fat, and little or no sugar, quick breads require special care to provide the desired tender crumb. Because of the lack of sugar, the overdevelopment of gluten is a continual risk. Consequently, the flour and liquid have to be combined gently, often stirred by hand just enough to moisten the dry ingredients. With muffins, a common quick bread, overmixing will produce large air tunnels and tough cell walls, resulting in a coarse, uneven grain and chewy texture in the baked product. When a larger amount of sugar is used, this is no longer an issue.

Sugar in Cooking

Sugar is a key ingredient in the preparation of custards, puddings, sauces, pie and tart fillings, and meringues. In most of them, sugar not only sweetens, but it performs essential chemical and physical duties. Even in dishes that do not register on the palate as sweet, sugar contributes valuable taste and flavor tips.

Custards: Unlike baked products, which are primarily flour-protein constructions, custards are egg-protein constructions. If, when cooking, the heat causes the egg white to solidify too rapidly, the liquid ingredients in the mix will be squeezed out in droplets. The condition is known as syneresis, or "weeping." The sugar in a custard mix breaks up those clumps of protein molecules to allow them to move through the liquid. This, in turn, raises the temperature at which the custard will set and allows the egg proteins to coagulate slowly and merge with the other ingredients, giving a smooth, stable consistency to the cooked custard.

Puddings, sauces, and pie fillings: The body and smoothness of dessert sauces, lemon, butterscotch, and other pie fillings, as well as chocolate puddings depend on sugar's ability to disperse among the starch particles of the thickening agent used. When a dry starch, such as flour or cornstarch, is directly added to a hot liquid, the exterior particles tend to cook first, encapsulating the raw starch particles inside. Unappealing and unpalatable lumps are created, and the mixture does not properly thicken. If one part starch is mixed with two parts sugar before being added to a hot liquid, the starch particles will disperse throughout and cook at an even rate, resulting in a smooth texture. When lesser amounts of sugar are called for, a small amount of cold liquid should always be blended with the sugar to further disperse the particles before adding it to a hot mixture. Sugar should also be added to raw cocoa powder (which is about one-third starch) before combining it with hot liquid.

Meringues: Because of the rotating action of the mechanical beaters or a handheld whisk when egg whites are beaten, the egg protein partially coagulates and holds air bubbles. Although on the one hand sugar retards foaming and decreases the volume and lightness of an egg foam, it also helps stabilize the foam. An additional stabilizer such as cream of tartar or salt creates an even more adhesive protein film to hold the air bubbles. This results in a more stable foam that is stiffer and higher than it would be without these additions.

The nature of a meringue is determined by the amount of sugar added per egg white. For example, when making a meringue tart or pie shell to hold fruit, ice cream, or other soft, sweet mixtures, 57

grams (2 ounces) sugar are added for each egg white, or twice as much sugar by weight as egg white. This creates a very stiff meringue, which is then baked in a very slow oven and subjected to a long period of drying. The end result should be a dry, firm, crisp meringue shell, with no browning.

When making a meringue topping for a pudding or pie, just 28 grams (1 ounce) sugar are required per egg white, or equal weights of sugar and egg white. This creates a softer meringue, with a slightly crisp crust and golden-brown color that can be baked at higher temperatures than one that is heavily sweetened and can therefore caramelize more, creating the appealing color.

If no sugar is added to a meringue topping, the air bubbles in the beaten foam will not hold. When baked, the end result will be flat, colorless, and gummy.

Nonsweet foods: Sugar can be a significant flavoring agent when added to a variety of nonsweet foods, ranging from sour fruits to cooked meats such as pot roast, salad dressings, and mixed salads like coleslaw. In addition, baked beans, tomatoes, and some vegetables such as corn, peas, and carrots may benefit from the addition of sugar. Sugar can minimize starchy flavors (as those in corn and beans) while it highlights the more desirable, inherent ambrosial flavors.

Sugar will also blend in and diminish intense salty, acidic, or sour elements, making the finished dish more pleasing to the palate. Some dishes, combining both sweet and sour flavors, owe their palatability and tang to the balance of sugar with vinegar, citrus juices, or other acidic ingredients. Sugar mellows the acidity in tomato-based dishes, complements the saltiness of cured meats in glazes (such as those with a pineapple or sherry base), and reduces the acidity of piquant ingredients such as vinegar or citrus juices in salad dressings and some vinaigrettes. The sweetness of piquant sauces such as mint jelly, applesauce, or cranberry sauces or jellies often used with meats serves to complement the rich, fattiness of the protein. If the meat to be used in a stew or pot roast is lightly sprinkled with sugar before browning, the sugar will add to the caramelization resulting in a browner, more flavorful end.

Candies: As the primary ingredient in candies, sugar displays a range of physical and chemical properties. A wide variety of candies can be produced when sugar concentration, type and degree of heat, and agitation of other ingredients are controlled. Although there are now many sugar substitutes available, none is a suitable replacement for sugar in candy making, as they do not exhibit the unique sweetening, bulking, and manufacturing properties of sugar.

Basic candy-making method: When making candy, sugar is mixed with water (usually at two parts sugar to one part water by weight) at room temperature to the point at which no more sugar will dissolve, creating a saturated solution. This solution is placed over heat and stirred continuously until most of the sugar has dissolved, creating a supersaturated solution. The solution is heated to the boiling point and beyond, forcing more and more liquid to evaporate and allowing the solution to become even more concentrated.

The final sugar concentration dictates the consistency of the candy. One of the keys to successful candy making is regulating the specific concentration of the syrup by using a candy thermometer and by testing a small sample in cold water. The stages and temperatures of hardness for each type of candy are shown in Table 1 (see page 53).

Obtaining the correct concentration of the sugar crystals in the solution can be tricky. Because sugar molecules are prone to recrystallizing as the concentrated supersaturated solution becomes increasingly concentrated, these solutions are notoriously unstable. Care must be taken not to introduce foreign particles or agitate the solution during heating—as both of these can cause premature recrystallization.

Crystalline and noncrystalline candies: Crystalline candy can be subdivided into two categories: 1) those with perceptible crystals, such as rock candy, and 2) those in which the crystals are too slight to be detected on the palate, such as fondant and fudge.

Crystalline candies: The most basic crystalline candy,

rock candy, is created by immersing a string into a supersaturated sugar solution, heating the solution to the hard-ball stage (121°C to 129°C/250°F to 265°F), and then allowing it to cool. As long as the mass remains immersed in the solution without stirring or the addition of other interfering agents, the sugar molecules clump around the string, and the crystals will grow in size. Only chemically pure sucrose will recrystallize in this fashion.

The creamed form of crystallized candy is produced by creating small, imperceptible sugar crystals. The supersaturated sugar solution is heated to a specific concentration (see Table 1, page 53) determined by using a candy thermometer or cold water sample test. The mixture is then cooled and beaten to produce very small homogeneous crystals and create a "cream."

The creaming process is dependent on interfering fat-and-protein-containing agents such as milk, butter, egg, heavy cream, chocolate, or cold gelatin, which prevent the sugar molecules from clumping into larger crystals by coating the sucrose molecules and preventing them from sticking together.

Invert sugar, the result of the breakdown of sucrose into fructose and glucose, is another interfering agent that helps prevent recrystallization. This happens in candy making when the supersaturated solution is heated and invert sugar is created. The amount of water in the solution, along with the length and degree of heat used, will control how much of the sucrose will be inverted. The process can be accelerated with the addition of an acidic ingredient, such as fruit, cream of tartar, molasses, brown sugar, honey, or chocolate. An appreciable proportion of invert sugar is required to prevent graininess and to keep the finished candy moist.

Noncrystalline candies: These amorphous candies are much simpler to produce than crystalline candies. For these candies, recrystallization is avoided by adding interfering agents to the sugar solution or by cooking it to a high enough temperature to halt recrystallization. With candy brittles, butterscotches, caramels, or taffies, invert sugar, molasses, corn

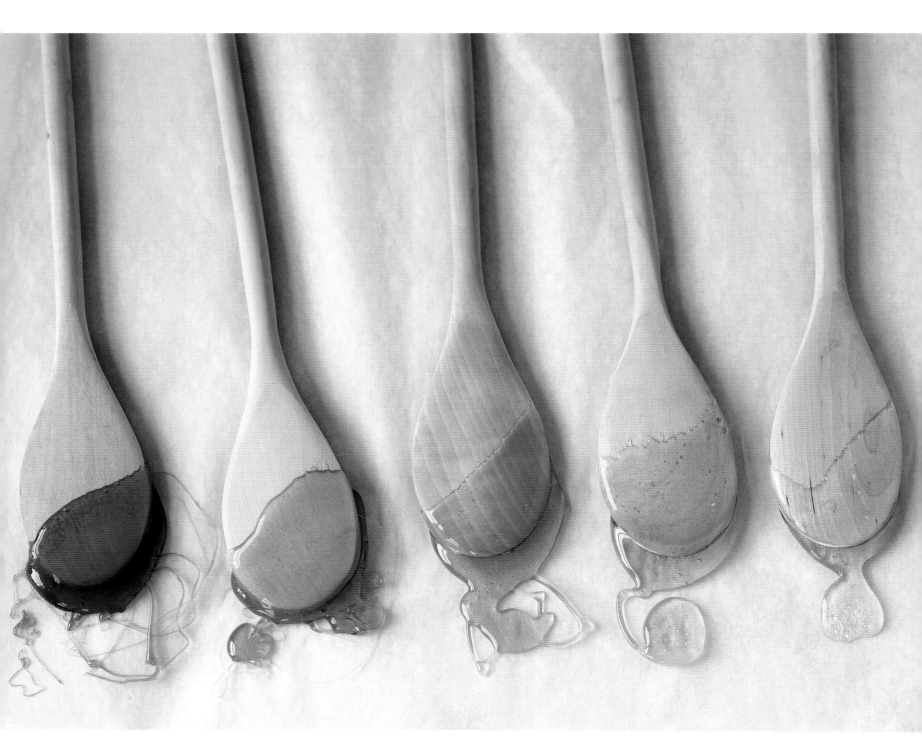

Stages of Sugar Syrup in Candy Making

Boiling Point Temperature (°F)	Candy	Cold Water Test	
230–234°F	Syrups	Thread:	Pulls into a thread, but will not form a ball
235–240°F	Fudge, Fondant	Soft ball:	Forms a soft ball that will not flatten when removed from water
244–248°F	Caramel	Firm ball:	Forms a firm ball that will not flatten when removed from water
250–266°F	Nougat, divinity, rock	Hard ball:	Forms a hard ball that will not flatten when removed from water but is still plastic
270–290°F	Taffy, butterscotch	Soft crack:	Separates into threads that are not brittle
300–310°F	Brittle	Hard crack:	Separates into threads that are hard and brittle
320°F		Clear liquid:	Liquefies and turns light amber in color
338°F		Brown liquid:	The liquefied sugar turns brown in color

Note: To do a cold-water test, use a teaspoon to portion a few drops of the concentrated syrup into a small amount of ice water. Use fingers to form a thread or ball.

syrup, or an acidic ingredient is added to prevent the formation of crystals. The mixture is cooked to a higher temperature than for crystalline candies, reducing the water to 2 percent (or less), which, in turn, prevents recrystallization.

Some noncrystalline candy can be produced using dry heat. For instance, peanut brittle is created by melting dry sugar, which, because water is not present during the cooling period, does not recrystallize and instead forms a glassy, solid mass.

Icings: Sugar's role in the creation of pleasing icings and frostings is quite similar to the part it plays in the preparation of candies. Not only does it assist in the flavor enhancement, structure, and bulk of the finished product, but it also serves as a moisture barrier, keeping the cake or confection fresher for a longer period of time.

Sugar in Frozen Deserts

Frozen desserts such as ice cream, ice milk, frozen custard, and sherbets require sugar to ensure a creamy texture and pleasing mouthfeel. Sugar is preferable to all alternative sweeteners in frozen desserts because of its functional characteristics. When, for example, high-fructose corn syrup—a popular commercial sweetener—is substituted, the freezing point is lowered by about two times and an icy texture results.

Freezing point: The ability of the dissolved sugar in the liquid mixture to attract and hold water reduces the water available for crystallization during the freezing process. The ice crystals that then form are smaller because there is less "free" water. When the water in the liquid mixture begins to freeze, the sugar in the solution that remains unfrozen becomes more concentrated. This further lowers the freezing point of the unfrozen mixture. Exposing the solution to a temperature much lower than the its freezing point will ensure quick, consistent cooling, creating a frozen product with tiny ice crystals that produce the desirable smooth, creamy texture. (Large crystals would be gritty and sandlike.)

Flavors and mouthfeel: Colder temperatures often numb the taste buds, but the sweetness of sugar enhances flavors and lessens the need for additional flavor intensifiers. It also increases the viscosity of frozen desserts and imparts an unctuous, creamy mouthfeel. HFCS or other corn-derived sweeteners will produce an undesirable syrupy taste and mask or alter the base or complementary flavor of the frozen item. If fruit has been added to the mixture to be frozen, sugar will also balance its acidity.

A sugar content of about 16 percent by weight is recommended for ice cream. To create the desired flavor and mouthfeel, additional sugar is required when a high-butterfat ingredient such as heavy cream is replaced with lower-fat milk or fruit purées, as when making ice milk or sherbet.

Sugar and the Preservation of Fruits

There is historical evidence that apples were sliced and dried in neolithic Britain, indicating that methods of preservation existed centuries ago. Drying seems to be the earliest, but records show that by the second century B.C., Italians were preserving fruits in honey, and three centuries later the great Roman culinarian, Apicius, wrote of preserving grapes in boiled water, mulberries in wine boiled down to a syrup, and quinces in wine and honey.

Methods of preserving quince had been developed by the first century, and early Greek physicians valued it for its medicinal qualities—as an aid to digestion and a cure for stomach ailments. The ripest, sweetest quinces could be preserved in their raw state, packed tightly together and submerged in honey. However, if the fruit was not very ripe, it would not soften in the honey, so people began cooking it in a mixture of wine and honey prior to preservation. Since quince is a high-pectin fruit, if the fruit was left to cool in the cooking liquid, a thick, fairly solid jellied conserve was achieved. The mix was frequently seasoned with exotic spices, including pepper. The cooked fruit could be lifted from the gel and used on its own or the conserve served as a sweetmeat at the end of a meal. Our word *marmalade* comes from the ancient Greek for "honey apple," which was often applied to quince. In fact, the Portuguese word for a sweet, solid quince paste (which dates to the fifteenth century) is *marmelada*.

The conserves and marmalades of medieval Europe were semisolid and, as in the ancient world, were used primarily as a sweetmeat or an aid to digestion. However, other fruits in addition to quinces were used, and for the first time, sugar was used to sweeten and preserve fruit.

Although sugar, along with spices, had made its way through the Roman Empire, its use was almost exclusively medicinal. It was not until the late Middle Ages that sugar was used in the preservation of fruits throughout Europe. There are early recipes from the Middle East in which sugar was used as an ingredient in some sweetmeats and conserves—the word *jam* is assumed to derive from the Arabic, meaning, as it does in English, "close packed" or "all together." It is thought that these early Middle Eastern recipes are the root stock for the famous marmalades of Portugal and their subsequent spread through Europe. Today's jams, jellies, and other sweet spreads are descendants of these primitive examples. The softer, more liquid preserved mixes that we know today came about after Nicolas Appert (1749–1841), a French *confiseur*, discovered processing methods using sealed jars in the nineteenth century.

Sugar performs a number of tasks when used as a method of preservation. When a high concentration of a sweetener, such as cane sugar, honey, molasses, or maple syrup, is combined with fresh fruit, the sugar dehydrates the fruit. The natural moisture of the fruit is saturated by the sweetener and the development of microorganisms is inhibited. Sugar has the added bonus of preventing the breakdown of the structure of the fruit. As the sweetener works itself into the fruit's structure, it helps the fruit maintain its original texture. In addition, sugar also aids in the gelling process and in the preservation of flavor, color, and texture.

The wide range of mixtures known as preserves includes jams, jellies, marmalades, conserves, fruit butters, and fruit cheeses, as well as simple fruit preserves. Scientifically, all preserves are known as **gels**. No matter the name, they are all based on the ancient methods of fruit preservation.

The description of each one is as follows:

Preserves: Whole or large pieces of fresh fruit cooked very slowly in a sugar syrup. Slow cooking, rather than boiling, is used to prevent disintegration of the fruit. The result is a soft, slightly gelled mix.

Jams: A mixture of chopped, crushed, or ground fruit cooked with sugar to make a thick but soft spread.

Jellies: Clear spreads made from fruit or vegetable juices cooked with the addition of pectin and sugar that will hold a firm shape.

Marmalades: A mixture of coarsely chopped or shredded fruit and fruit peels cooked with sugar and, sometimes, pectin. Throughout the English-speaking world, *marmalade* generally refers to a spread made from citrus fruits and peels.

Conserves: Generally used interchangeably with the word *preserves*. In contemporary commercial terms, a conserve is usually a luxury product. In America, it is often a coarsely ground fruit mixture combining some citrus fruit with other fresh or dried fruits, such as raisins, and nuts. It is often found on the Thanksgiving table in a cranberry-orange-walnut mix.

Fruit butters and fruit cheeses: Both of these are reductions of fruit purées mixed with sugar that require long, slow cooking to achieve a smooth texture. Fruit butters are spreadable, butterlike, and homogenous, while fruit cheeses are firm products that can be unmolded and sliced. Fruit cheeses are generally served as accompaniments to cold meats or poultry or with a cheese course.

Fruit pastes: Puréed or strained fruit, sugar, and either natural or added pectin mixtures that are very thick and firm. Once set, the paste is cut into decorative shapes and dredged in either confectioners' or granulated sugar. These are often served as part of a **petits fours** or **mignardises** selection. The most famous fruit pastes are the traditional **pâtes de fruits** of France.

Jam Making

The standards of identity (otherwise known as recipes) for the commercial manufacture of preserves established by the Food and Drug Administration specify a ratio of one part fruit to one part sugar, a formula upheld in most cookbooks as well.

For preserves to gel and reach the desired consistency, the sugar must be added because it attracts and holds water. This process leaves less water available to which **pectin** can form bonds. Pectin, a natural gelling component of many fruits (citrus, apples, and some berries are particularly rich sources of it), will gel only in the presence of sugar and acid (usually lemon, another citrus juice, or citric acid) in certain proportions. Optimum acidity is a pH (the measure of acidity or alkalinity) between 3.0 and 3.5. The pectin molecules link to each other, forming a network to trap the fruit pulp and sugar. The acid advances the process by reducing the small electrical charge carried by pectin molecules in water, which tends to make the molecules repel each other. Once released, the chainlike pectin molecules can bind the sugar solution and fruit pulp together.

The ripeness and type of fruit used for preserving will cause the amount of natural pectin to vary. For instance, apples, grapes, and cranberries are more pectin-rich than cherries and strawberries. If a fruit is unripe or naturally low in pectin, commercially produced pectin may be added to produce the desired level of gelling. When using commercially produced pectin, the amount of sugar called for may differ from the traditional one part fruit to one part sugar.

If they are properly prepared and bottled, preserves will be bacteria-free and clear of any yeast cells until they are opened and exposed to air. Once the package is opened, sugar hinders the development of microorganisms by its ability to attract water. This process is accomplished through osmosis (the process whereby water will flow from a weaker solution into a more concentrated one when separated by a semipermeable membrane such as a fruit's outer surface). When cooking jellies and jams, water is drawn from these microorganisms toward the sugar syrup (which must have a concentration of at least 65 percent) and the microorganisms become dehydrated and unable to multiply. Consequently, spoilage is halted. In addition, since sugar attracts and holds water more readily than any other components of jellies, jams, and preserves, it prevents the fruit from absorbing water and keeps the natural color from fading through dilution.

Commercial products: In addition to sugar, industrial preserves may contain a number of alternative sweeteners, for both economic and marketing purposes. A great many commercial preserves include high fructose corn syrup (HFCS), as its sweetening ability is comparable to that of sugar. The one critical disadvantage of HFCS is that it is liquid and, as such, may contain up to 29 percent water. This extra moisture may be evaporated in the last stages of production and cause the expansive fruit flavors to be diminished in the finished product.

Concentrated fruit juices may also be used as a sweetener. Since these are similar in composition to sugar syrups, products sweetened with them have the same caloric content as those that are sugar sweetened.

Jellies and Jams in the Pastry Kitchen

Jellies and jams are frequently used in the pastry kitchen: Jams serve as fillings for cakes, cookies, and sweet pastries. Jellies are used for glazes, *charlottes*, and *mousses*. Raspberry and apricot jams and, infrequently, sour cherry and black currant jams as well as finely cut citrus marmalades are the most important jams for pastry making. The recommended jams and jellies for use in cake making are those that are high-quality, firm-textured, and redolent of the base-fruit flavor. Inexpensive mixes will result in an unpleasant, sweet-sour taste, runny texture, and unusable end product. If a commercial product is loose, it can be thickened by cooking it over low heat until the desired consistency is reached.

Other gelled products frequently used in the professional pastry kitchen are:

Nappages: Also known as glazes, these jellylike products are usually prepared using apricots or a combination of apricots and apples. The cooked, sweetened fruit is strained to achieve a quite thick, clear glaze. Sometimes pectin is added as the fruit cooks to ensure the desired consistency. When used as a finishing glaze rather than a coating, a *nappage* is melted over low heat and, frequently, diluted with water to thin to a spreading consistency.

Ovenproof jams or jellies: These mixtures are formulated to take high heat in the professional pastry kitchen. They contain a special type of pectin along with citrates, which allows them to be heated to 190°C (375°F) for as long as 10 minutes while retaining their pliability and consistency when used as an element in a cookie or other pastry.

Canned Fruit

When fruit is canned, it must be placed in a sugar syrup that has greater sugar concentration than the fruit itself. This sugar syrup diffuses into the fruit and boosts the inherent flavor. As the fruit is cooked in a syrup, the cell walls become more permeable, which creates a tenderer texture, and the retention of sugar ensures that the fruit remains plump and inviting. If a whole fruit has a tough skin and is canned with the skin on—as with Kieffer pears and kumquats—the fruit must be precooked or the skin must be pricked all over to enable the absorption of the sugar syrup.

Frozen Fruit

If a fruit is to be frozen, it must have either a dry sugar pack or be frozen in a sugar syrup to retain its fresh flavor and color. With a dry sugar pack, the fruit is carefully mixed with a designated amount of sugar to evenly coat each piece. The choice of either method is dependent on the eventual use of the frozen fruit.

Although some items, such as blueberries, raspberries, cranberries, and rhubarb, may be dry-packed without sugar, they will benefit from either a dry or syrup sugar pack. When frozen fruit comes into contact with the air, enzymatic browning (discoloration due to oxidation) results, and sugar greatly lessens the chance of this. In some instances, particularly when freezing nectarines, peaches, and apricots, ascorbic acid is added to a syrup pack to further prevent discoloration. By retarding fermentation, the presence of sugar will also lessen flavor changes. When frozen fruit is thawed, the sugar content helps retain the natural texture, fresh-fruit aroma and flavor, and the normal size of the fruit.

Fruits Glacés or Fruit Confits (Candied Friuts)

Fruits glacés are fruits, either whole or in pieces, that have been preserved through cooking in a sugar syrup and then glazed in the same syrup. Occasionally, they are coated in granulated sugar after glazing. Fruits most frequently preserved in this manner are cherries, pineapple slices or pieces, mango, apricots, citrus peel, citron (a large, lumpy, semitropical citrus grown for its thick skin), and angelica (celerylike herb that, when candied, is used as pastry décor or as an ingredient in fruitcakes). Specialty confectioners now preserve many exotic fruits and even vegetables in this fashion. Poor-quality glazed fruits are not recommended, as they often are oversaturated with sugar and taste of artificial preservatives. On the other hand, premium glazed fruits, usually imported from France or Switzerland (and occasionally Australia) are considered delicacies. Fruits preserved through candying can be used alone as confections or as part of a *petits fours* presentation, as cake or pastry decorations and dessert garnishes, or added to baked goods for flavor, texture, and color.

The process used to glaze fruits is a simple one, though lengthy. The fruit is slowly cooked in sugar syrup until most of the water in the fruit has been replaced by sugar and the fruit is translucent, almost glasslike in appearance. Over a period of days, the syrup is drained daily, and its sugar concentration is increased by the addition of sugar for each subsequent cooking. The texture and shape of the fruit is retained by this long process and gradual addition of sugar. Once the translucency has been achieved, the fruit is dried and finished as desired.

Candied citrus peel is prepared by first blanching the peel several times to remove the oily bitterness of the zest and the dry astringency of the pith. The cooking syrup is usually made from equal parts sugar and water; corn syrup, glucose, or honey may be added to prevent crystallization. The same long, slow cooking process described above is employed to achieve translucency. The result should be a firm, tender peel with a slight hint of zestiness. In addition to being glazed or coated in granulated sugar, candied citrus peels are often dipped in dark chocolate (either completely or one half) and served as a confection. Candied citrus peel is also often used in cakes, particularly breakfast cakes or traditional fruitcakes.

All candied fruits can also be preserved in their cooking syrup instead of being dried. Although the syrup will often crystallize, it can be liquefied by bringing it to a boil over a low heat. Technically, these fruits remain somewhat perishable, especially those that have no artificial preservatives added. They will keep, tightly covered and refrigerated, for 2 to 3 months, or frozen for up to 6 months.

Marrons Glacés

Among the most famous of all French confections are **marrons glacés**, or glazed chestnuts, which are used primarily as *petits fours*. They are simply chestnuts that have been peeled and candied using the same process as that used for fresh fruit. They are either stored in the cooking syrup or glazed.

Dried Fruits

Drying fruit causes a substantial amount of the water content to evaporate, leaving an intense concentration of sugar and profound fruit flavor. In addition, this concentration and evaporation allow a long shelf life. Almost any fruit can be dried, although the most commonly available are plums (prunes), grapes (raisins), currants (Zante grapes), apricots, figs, and dates. Recently, producers have brought dried cherries, cranberries, blueberries, and strawberries to the commercial marketplace. Much of the American dried fruit business is centered in California. As with many other products, those produced by small farms generally will ensure the highest quality and most intense flavor.

Fruit is dried by a number of methods. Figs and grapes are dried on the tree or vine; pears, apples, and stone fruits are generally dried on trays in the sun; plums (prunes) are dried using artificial heat. To preserve color, cut fruit is often exposed to sulfur dioxide to prevent discoloration. Plums, when drying as prunes, are usually dipped in a sulfur bath. Potassium sorbate is frequently used to prevent mold forming on plums and figs. The high sugar content of dates and raisins is generally enough to preserve the fruit once concentrated through the drying process;

however, golden raisins (actually just the familiar Thompson seedless grape) are bleached with sulfur dioxide to hold their pale color. Untreated dried fruits generally have an unappealing brown color and a drier texture than treated fruits, but they are much in demand to those concerned with health issues.

Once dried, all fruits should be stored, airtight, in a cool, dry environment. Refrigerated, dried fruits should last at least a year and freezing will add even more storage time. In addition, freezing will frequently tenderize the fruit when thawed.

Puréed Fruits

Although many fruit purées are commercially available, at The French Culinary Institute we often make them using ripe fresh fruit that we have on hand. Purées can be made using either fresh or cooked fruit or berries. Fresh fruit should be washed, stemmed, cored, and, if necessary, peeled—or, in the case of berries, washed and patted dry. If making fresh fruit purée, the fruit should be cut into small pieces and then processed to a smooth purée in a blender or food processor. If cooking, the fruit should be cut into small pieces and placed in a heavy-bottomed saucepan with just enough water to keep the fruit from sticking. The pan should be covered and placed over medium-low heat. As soon as the liquid begins to simmer, cook the fruit, watching carefully, just until it is soft but has not burned or stuck to the bottom of the pan. Additional water can be added, but the more water added, the less concentrated the fruit flavor. The cooked fruit is then processed to a smooth purée in a blender or food processor. For the smoothest consistency, the purée should then be pushed through a fine-mesh sieve. If the fruit has a tendency to oxidize, as do apples and pears, lemon juice can be added to the puréed fruit to halt oxidation. Fruit purées can be stored, covered and frozen, for up to 3 months.

Understanding the Egg

Eggs stand alone as the most versatile and nutritious food given to mankind. One large egg contributes approximately 6.5 grams of protein (or about 13 percent of the average adult's minimum daily requirement), as well as substantial amounts of iron, choline, thiamine, phosphorus, and the vitamins A, D, and E. The yolk contains most of the fat, cholesterol, vitamins, and half the protein, while the white, also known as the albumen, is composed almost entirely of water and proteins called albumins. It also contains niacin, riboflavin, and minerals. The most common eggs used today are those of chickens, although turkey, goose, duck, and quail eggs are also sold.

An egg is composed of a brown or white outer shell and seven interior elements. The shell color does not affect the thickness of the shell nor the quality, flavor, nutritive value, or cooking characteristics of the egg but is determined by the breed of chicken that produced it. The outer shell consists primarily of calcium carbonate and accounts for 9 to 12 percent of the total weight of an egg. It is the egg's first line of defense against bacterial contamination. A protective coating called the cuticle, or bloom, covers the surface and serves to prevent microbial contamination of the contents by blocking the pores in the shell, which contains anywhere from seven thousand to seventeen thousand infinitesimal openings to permit moisture and carbon dioxide to escape and air to move in and form the air cell. The strength of the shell is greatly influenced by the vitamins and minerals in the hen's diet: The higher the content of calcium, phosphorus, manganese, and vitamin D, the stronger it is.

Brown eggs come from reddish-brown hens such as Rhode Island reds, Plymouth Rocks, and New Hampshires (obviously all New England favorites). White eggs are produced by white hens such as white leghorns (America's most common chicken). Rare breeds such as Araucana will produce eggs in an array of pastel blues and greens. No matter the color, the taste and nutrition will be equal.

The Internal Composition of an Egg

Air cell: The pocket of air found at the larger end of the egg. It is easily observed at the flattened end of a peeled, hard-boiled egg. When laid, the egg is quite warm and filled with liquid. As it cools, the contents contract, and the air cell is created. The air cell increases in size as the egg ages and air enters by way of the pores, replacing the original moisture and carbon dioxide that escape as time passes. The size of the air cell is one means used for determining the commercial grade of an egg.

Shell membranes: Immediately inside the shell, two membranes—inner and outer—surround the albumen (white) to provide a protective barrier against bacterial penetration. The air cell forms between these two membranes.

Albumen: The albumen, or egg white, is made up of four layers. Closest to the yolk is the thick, chalaziferous white; this is surrounded by the thin inner white; then the thick outer white; and, finally, the outer thin white, located nearest to the shell. In fresher, higher-quality eggs, the thicker layers stand higher and spread less than thin albumen, while in lower-grade eggs they may be indistinguishable from the thinnest layer. As the egg ages, chemical changes in the proteins of the albumen cause it to thin. The albumens of older eggs also look clearer than those of fresh eggs because they contain less carbon dioxide, which causes the cloudy appearance of fresh egg whites. The albumen accounts for about 67 percent of an egg's liquid weight, as well as half the protein and a good portion of niacin, riboflavin, chlorine, magnesium, potassium, sodium, and sulfur.

Chalazae: Twisted strands of egg white attached to opposite ends of the yolk to hold it in place at the center of the egg albumen. If you can see them when you crack the raw egg, it is a sign of freshness.

Although sometimes rather strange looking, chalazae are not beginning embryos and do not interfere with any cooking process; however, most chefs strain them out when making a smooth-textured egg dish such as custard.

Vitelline membrane: A transparent, superthin covering that keeps the egg yolk intact. This membrane tears more easily if the egg is older.

Germinal disc: This barely noticeable dent on the surface of the egg yolk is the entrance to the latebra, the channel through which the sperm enter when an egg is fertilized.

Yolk (vitelline): The interior yellow globe that accounts for about 33 percent of the egg's total liquid weight and includes all the fat and half the protein, as well as the higher proportion of minerals and vitamins (except niacin and riboflavin). The yolk provides phosphorus, manganese, iron, copper, iodine, calcium, and vitamins A, E, and D—it is one of the few foods with vitamin D. The yellow color varies, depending upon the type of feed given, but pale or deep, it is not indicative of nutritive value. The yolk is responsible for the emulsifying and enrichment properties of the egg. It 60 calories account for 90 percent of the total calories in an egg.

Egg Terms

Washing: The law requires that eggs be washed and sanitized before being packed for shipping. The natural protective layer, the bloom that coats the shell and seals the pores to prevent moisture loss and interior bacterial contamination is thus removed. Some producers then coat the eggs with a very thin layer of mineral oil to replace it for consumer assurance of safety.

Determining the Freshness of an Egg

Is a farm-fresh, just-laid egg the freshest you can buy? There is some debate on this issue, as so many other factors help determine the freshness of an egg: the temperature at which it has been held, the storage humidity, and the handling process, to name three. Proper handling translates to prompt gathering, wash-ing, and oiling within a few hours after being laid. Most commercially produced eggs are handled with extreme care from laying to market and reach the marketplace within a few days of leaving the laying house. So, if handled properly by the producer, the market, and the buyer, an egg should be "farm-fresh" when it reaches the table.

An egg deteriorates very rapidly at room temperature, as the warmth allows moisture and carbon dioxide to escape through the pores in the shell. This, in turn, causes the air cell to expand and the albumen to thin. The ideal storage temperature is one that does not go above 4°C (40°F), with a relative humidity of 70 to 80 percent. Consequently, a freshly laid egg held at room temperature for one day will age as much as a properly refrigerated egg will age in a week.

As an egg ages, the albumen becomes thinner and the yolk becomes flatter. These changes do not have any significant effect on the nutritional quality or the functional cooking properties of the egg. However, age will affect the appearance of a cooked egg; fresher eggs hold a tall, firm shape in a pan, while older ones spread out. This is particularly important when poaching, frying, or coddling. On the other hand, when boiled, older eggs are generally easier to peel than very fresh eggs.

As a general rule of thumb, when purchasing and storing eggs, choose a reputable market with high volume and rapid turnover, where eggs are kept in cartons in a refrigerated case. Before buying, open the carton and check for dirt and cracked shells and, of course, do not purchase eggs in anything less than pristine condition. If an egg is damaged after purchasing and leaks into the carton, discard it and wash and dry the remaining eggs before refrigerating them. Do not remove eggs from the storage carton, as it helps preserve their freshness and prevent both moisture loss and the absorption of odors from other foods stored alongside them.

Do not rely on old wives' tales to determine the freshness of an egg. For instance, freshness cannot be judged by placing an egg in saltwater to determine if it sinks or floats. A carefully controlled brine test is sometimes used in the commercial marketplace to judge shell thickness of eggs for hatching purposes, but it has no application to the freshness of table eggs.

Grading, Sizing, and Packaging of Eggs

In the grading process, eggs are judged on both their interior and exterior quality and are sorted according to weight. Grade and size are not related to each other. In descending order of quality, standard grades are AA, A, and B. The nutritional value of the different grades of eggs is the same.

	Grade AA	Grade A	Grade B
Breakout appearance	Covers a small area	Covers a moderate area	Covers a wide area
Albumen appearance	Thick and stands high; chalazae prominent	Reasonably thick, stands fairly high; chalazae prominent	Small amount of thick white; chalazae small or absent; appears weak
Yolk appearance	Firm, round, high	Firm and fairly high	Somewhat flattened and enlarged
Shell appearance	Approximates usual shape; generally clean; ridges or rough spots that do not affect strength are permitted	Same as for AA	Abnormal shape; some slight stained areas permitted; unbroken; ridges and thin spots permitted
Usage	Ideal for any use but especially desirable for poaching, frying, and cooking in shell	Same as for AA	Good for scrambling and baking, and in recipes

Several factors influence the size of an egg, including the breed of chicken, the age and weight of the laying bird, and the environmental conditions in which the hen was raised. Obviously, a healthy, drug-free, well-adjusted bird raised in a natural setting will produce more and better eggs than one raised in less-than-desirable conditions. And, in general, the older the hen, the larger the egg.

Eggs are sized based on their minimum weight per dozen, as follows: jumbo, extra large, large, medium, small, and peewee, with the most commonly available sizes being extra large, large, and medium.

Jumbo: 30 ounces per dozen, 56 pounds per standard 30-dozen case
Extra Large: 27 ounces per dozen, 50½ pounds per standard 30-dozen case
Large: 24 ounces per dozen, 45 pounds per standard 30-dozen case

Medium: 21 ounces per dozen, 39½ pounds per standard 30-dozen case
Small: 18 ounces per dozen, 34 pounds per standard 30-dozen case
Peewee: 15 ounces per dozen, 28 pounds per standard 30-dozen case

For commercial distribution, eggs are packed in flats. There are 30 eggs in one flat; 12 flats in one case to equal 30 dozen eggs; and 6 flats in a half-case to equal 15 dozen eggs. Sizes vary according to weight and are classified according to the minimum net weight expressed in ounces per dozen.

Egg Safety

Although very few eggs—about 1 in 20,000 eggs—carry internal bacterial infection when they are laid, eggs can become contaminated through improper handling or cooking. Most often, *Salmonella enteritidis* bacteria, which can cause severe gastrointestinal illness, are found to be the culprit. The yolk is generally the point of infection, with the white almost never infected. *Salmonella* rarely causes fatalities in healthy adults but it can make them sick—and it can be extremely serious for infants and small children, pregnant women, the infirm, those with compromised immune systems, or the elderly.

Because of the virulence of the *Salmonella* bacteria, kitchen sanitation is of the utmost importance when using eggs.

Dean's Tip

"A pinch of salt or sugar will stabilize egg whites that are being whipped."
Dean André Soltner

○ Eggs, raw or cooked, should always be refrigerated as quickly as possible and left unrefrigerated for as short a period as is sensible.

○ Hands, utensils, work surfaces, and pots and pans should be washed in very hot, soapy water after coming into contact with eggs.

○ Raw eggs should not be served to infants and small children, pregnant women, the infirm, those with compromised immune systems, or the elderly.

○ Before adding eggs to other ingredients, they should be checked for purity by breaking them, one at a time, into a small bowl. They should have no odor and no contaminants from the exterior.

○ If concerned about egg safety, bring poached, fried, coddled, baked, or soft-boiled eggs to 60°C (140°F) for 3½ minutes to kill any existing bacteria. This amount of heat and cooking time will cause the white to solidify and the yolk to become slightly firm but not hard.

Egg Wash

An egg wash is used to give a shiny finish to baked goods, such as Danish pastry, soft breads and rolls, puff pastry, and other pastry doughs. It can also be used as a "glue" to cement decorative sugars, candy décor, or nuts to the surface of baked goods and to hold dough pieces together during baking.

Egg wash may be made in two ways: whole egg or yolk only. The deepest, richest shine is obtained using yolks, but a yolk wash is quite thick and difficult to apply in a thin, even layer. It also tends to darken when the product is baked at high temperatures. To eliminate waste, most bakers use a whole-egg wash, even though it produces a paler sheen. Because it is thinner, it is easier to apply in an even layer. In commercial bakeries, egg wash is often applied with a spray gun, which reduces labor time and creates a perfect, even sheen.

Whole-egg wash: Whole eggs and a pinch of salt beaten together with a fork or whisk until the yolks and whites are completely combined. When refrigerated for 8 hours, the salt will break down and thin the egg whites somewhat, creating a thinner wash that's easier to apply.

Yolk-only egg wash: a combination of egg yolk, liquid (milk, cream, or water), and a pinch of salt. You will need about 1 teaspoon of liquid for every yolk used.

Blancs d'Oeufs et Meringues (Egg-White Foams and Meringues)

Egg whites are composed of several proteins and, when the correct amount of air is properly beaten into them to create an egg-white foam, the proteins will stay soft, moist, and elastic. This is a very important aspect of a great many pastry items, such as cakes, *soufflés*, and *mousses*, where the foam gives the finished product its light, airy texture. When sugar is added to the egg foam, the mixture is called a meringue.

Once a cake prepared using an egg-white foam is put into the oven, the heat causes the air bubbles to expand, giving the baked cake its desired rise. The heat then cooks and sets (or coagulates) the proteins around the bubbles. If the egg-white foam is solely responsible for leavening the cake, it is said that the cake rises due to mechanical leavening, i.e., by means of the air bubbles created during the action of beating or whisking egg whites. (There are some circumstances in which a cake is leavened by both mechanical and chemical action, an egg foam and a chemical leavener.) A meringue performs this same leavening action in *mousses* and *Chiboust* creams, often with the assistance of gelatin, to set the product if no baking is involved.

The most important condition for making a foam or meringue is a simple one: No yolk must taint the whites. Even the tiniest bit will prevent the foam from forming and render the whites useless for this purpose.

Overbeating is one of the most common mistakes when preparing an egg-white foam or meringue. When overbeaten, the proteins in egg whites become dry, the foam becomes grainy and loses volume, and the finished product will not achieve the desired rise. Meringues with a low sugar content are very easy to overbeat. If such a meringue is used to lighten a flavored base such as a *mousse* or pastry cream, it will be difficult to combine with the base mixture, which, in turn, causes it to be overfolded, deflating the mixture even more.

If the foam is to be used for lightening or leavening a product, it should be beaten until it forms a soft peak—a peak that, when lifted, falls over itself, forming a "hook." The beaten foam or meringue should be extremely smooth, with absolutely no trace of graininess. Whatever the consistency required, it is important to heed the directions stated in a specific recipe.

Meringues do not keep well in humid conditions, as the sugar soaks up moisture from the air, compromising its porous texture and making it limp and soggy. If made in advance of use, all meringues should be stored in absolutely airtight, dry conditions.

Necessary Tools and Ingredients for Successful Foams and Meringues

When preparing foams and meringues, all equipment must be pristine. There should be no trace of any fat on the bowl, beaters, or whisk, as this will inhibit the ability of the egg whites to foam. Egg whites beaten by hand will, for the most part, result in a more even texture. If possible, even when using an electric mixer, finish the beating by hand.

To beat by hand, use a large, flexible balloon whisk and a large copper or stainless-steel bowl. A copper bowl reacts with one of the proteins in the egg whites, causing the foam to remain soft, elastic, and moist for a longer period of time and coagulate at a higher temperature. This translates to a cake or *soufflé* that will rise higher because it has more time before it sets. Whites beaten in a copper bowl will also have a better consistency and will be more difficult to overbeat.

An acidic ingredient, such as cream of tartar or vinegar, increases stability in both a hand-beaten and electric mixer–made foam or meringue. The acid increases the holding power of the foam or meringue and decreases the possibility of overbeating. However, if beating in a copper bowl **do not** add an acid, as the acid may dissolve a larger amount of copper into the mix than is safe for human consumption.

Viscosity=Stability

One question to face when making an egg-white foam or meringue is, Does one egg give a better result than another? In answering this question, it is best to keep in mind that viscosity equals stability, but reduced viscosity equals greater volume. Very fresh eggs are more viscous, so the volume will not be as great as when using older egg whites. But the resultant foam or meringue will have more stability—it will resist breaking down. Using cold egg whites, rather than those at room temperature, also adds stability but

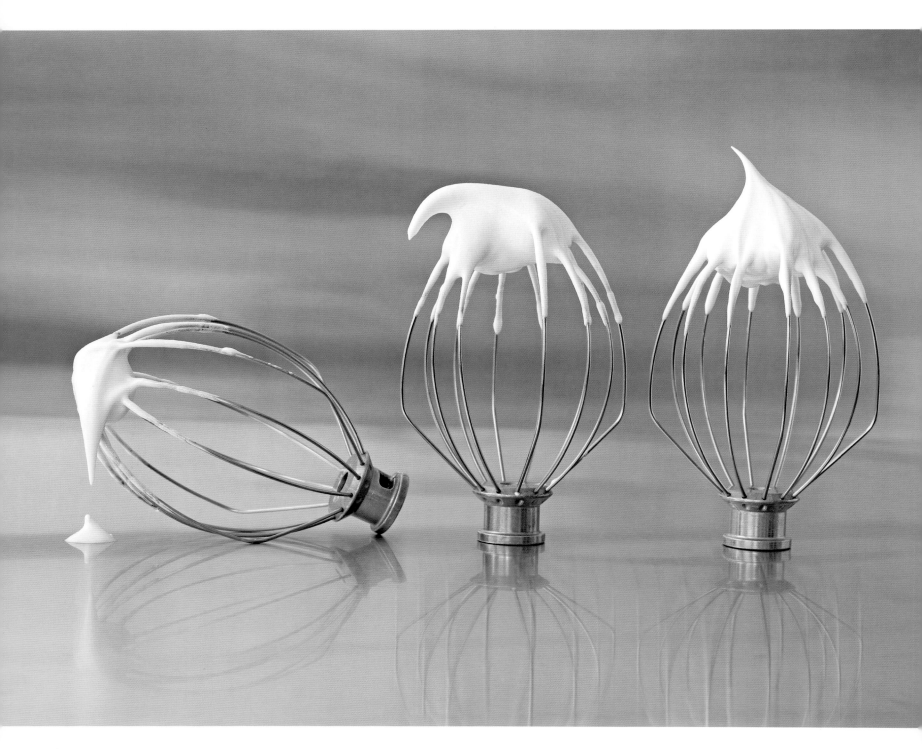

lessens volume. Adding a pinch of salt will reduce the viscosity of the whites, producing greater volume, but, again, stability will be reduced. The type of egg to use is very much the decision of the pastry chef as it relates to the result desired for a specific preparation.

Folding Foams and Meringues into Base Mixtures

Once a foam or meringue is properly beaten, it is either folded into a base mixture or the base mixture is folded into it. The only exception to this is a meringue with no other ingredients that will be piped out and baked.

Folding is extremely important because it incorporates two different preparations, generally one lighter than the other, into a homogeneous mixture. Folding is usually done with a rubber spatula to gently pull the heavier preparation (frequently a batter) from the bottom of the mixing bowl up and over the lighter one (most often whipped cream or egg whites). This motion continues as the bowl is turned slightly, to ensure that all of the heavier batter is pulled up from the bottom. The lighter preparation may or may not be added all at once. Often it is suggested that a small amount (no more than a quarter) of the lighter preparation be mixed into the heavier, which will lighten the mixture considerably and allow the folding to be accomplished more easily. All of this should be done quickly and with the greatest care, as you do not want to lose the airiness of the lighter preparation. Heavy or solid bits of chocolate, dried fruit, or fruit purées are other ingredients that can be folded into a batter. In these instances, it is not as necessary to fold gently; however, you do not want to overmix or the batter will toughen.

Types of Meringues

There are three basic types of meringue: French, Italian, and Swiss, each having a different use in pastry making.

The most delicate of the meringues, **French meringue** is most typically used in cake and cookie prepara-

tions. It is a simple combination of uncooked sugar beaten into egg whites. It must be baked to meet food safety requirements.

For an **Italian meringue**, a hot sugar syrup (114°C/238°F, soft-ball stage) is beaten into egg whites, allowing the whites to poach and producing a high-volume, stable meringue that is light and shiny. Italian meringues are used in preparations such as *mousses* and white buttercreams, since they do not have to be baked.

A **Swiss meringue** is a combination of egg whites and sugar, heated over a *bain-marie* until it reaches about 108°C (226°F) on a candy thermometer. The hot mixture is then beaten to a very stable and sturdy meringue. Swiss meringue has less volume and lightness than others because the sugar is added at the beginning. (And, in general, the more sugar used, the denser the meringue.) Since it is very firm, it is an excellent choice for baked decorations such as meringue mushrooms.

When preparing any meringue, it is important to remember that you are working with a very fragile entity that, even when made correctly, has a delicate constitution. Many factors can determine its ultimate quality.

The specific steps for the preparation of each type are:

French Meringue
- Place the egg whites in the mixer bowl.

- Turn the mixer on low speed to begin breaking up the egg whites and incorporating air.

- If using an acid, add it when the egg whites are just frothy.

- Raise the speed to medium.

- When the whites reach the soft-peak stage, add the sugar in a slow steady stream. Adding the sugar at this point ensures high volume and hastens the ability of the egg whites to foam.

° Beat on medium until the mixture reaches the desired consistency. Note that the more sugar added, the longer the meringue will need to be beaten to reach the desired consistency.

° "Sear" the meringue by beating it at a high speed for a few seconds at the very end of the beating period. This stabilizes the mix, preventing the meringue from expanding and then deflating.

° The finished meringue should be smooth and shiny. If it looks grainy or cottony, it has been overbeaten and should be discarded.

Italian Meringue

° Combine the sugar with enough water to just moisten it in a saucepan over medium heat.

° Bring it to a boil without stirring.

° Using a clean pastry brush, wash the sugar crystals from the interior sides of the pan.

° When the syrup comes to a full boil, begin whipping the egg whites on low speed.

° Increase the speed to medium while monitoring the progress of the syrup.

° When the syrup reaches 114°C (238°F), or the soft-ball stage, the whites should be forming soft peaks. If the whites are progressing at a faster rate than the syrup, slow down the mixer speed. If the sugar is nearing the soft-ball stage before the whites are ready, reduce the heat under the saucepan.

° When both the egg whites and sugar are ready, carefully drizzle the hot syrup down the side of the mixing bowl into the egg-white foam. Take care not to allow the hot syrup to hit the whip or it will splatter onto the sides of the bowl.

° Whip until the desired consistency is reached.

° "Sear" the meringue by beating at a high speed for a few seconds at the very end of the beating period.

° This stabilizes the mix, preventing the meringue from expanding and then deflating.

Swiss Meringue

○ Combine the egg whites and sugar in the mixing bowl, beating with a whisk.

○ When combined, place the bowl over a bain-marie of simmering water.

○ Slowly whisking, bring the mixture to 54°C (130°F) on a candy thermometer.

○ Remove the bowl from the heat.

○ Slowly begin beating the mixture.

○ When some volume has been reached, increase the speed and beat to the desired consistency.

○ Usually the meringue will have cooled by the time it reaches firm peaks because of its high ratio of sugar.

Baking Meringues

Any meringue can be baked, and you will find that many pastry preparations require this. Meringues may include other ingredients, such as nut flours, confectioners' sugar, food coloring, or liquid flavorings. Some are folded into a base mixture to add lightness, while others might be piped into decorative forms and baked.

Meringues with nut flour added are commonly used to make baked cake layers in classic French pastry making. *Dacquoises*, *vacherins*, *succés*, and *Japonais* are just a few of the traditional desserts that use this method. A French meringue is generally used for all of these. Occasionally, when preparing a French meringue for baking, part of the sugar (usually confectioners') is folded in after the meringue has reached is required consistency. This is done to produce a baked meringue with a crisp but tender texture. French meringue–based batters should be baked as soon as possible after being prepared, as they rapidly begin to deflate. The one exception to this rule is a specific type of macaroon (**Gerbet** or **French macaroon**) that has to sit after baking in order to develop an external skin.

Plain meringues are usually baked at a very low temperature for a long period of time which allows them to remain pale while turning crisp and dry on the interior. Nut-based meringues are often baked at medium temperatures to color slightly but remain a bit soft inside.

Dairy Products

Dairy products complete the tetrad that, with flour, sugar, and eggs, forms the basis for almost all pastry making. Milk and butter are the two most important, but other dairy products also impact on successful baking. Among other roles, the fat in milk and cream offers richness, creaminess, and deep flavor, while acidic products, such as yogurt and buttermilk, contribute their own depth of flavor as well as help activate baking soda in quick breads. Dairy products form the basic structure of custards and ice creams, and their sugars (lactose) not only assist in browning when baking but also feed the yeast in yeast-leavened products. Butter can give some baked products their distinct flakiness or crumbliness. Different cheeses have applications in both sweet and savory pastry making, adding richness, depth of flavor, texture, and lushness.

Milk

Although there are many different types of animal milk available, cow's milk is by far the most popular and readily available. Highly nutritional, most animal milk contains protein, calcium, phosphorus, vitamins A and D, lactose (milk sugar), and riboflavin. It is also relatively high in sodium. Unless purchased directly from a farm, almost all milk sold commercially has been pasteurized to destroy the microorganisms that can cause disease and speed spoilage. To ensure a uniform liquidity, most commercial milk products have also been homogenized, or emulsified, to prevent the fats from separating from the liquid.

Cow's milk is available in a number of forms:

Raw milk: Generally available only in certain states and through licensed raw milk distributors in health-food stores or directly from a dairy, raw milk is—pure and simple—milk that goes directly from the cow through a rapid cooling system to 2°C to 3°C (36°F to 38°F) and is then bottled. There is no pasteurization, homogenization, or addition of vitamins or minerals. It is not recommended for use in the commercial kitchen.

Whole milk: Containing about 3½ percent butterfat, whole milk is the most full-flavored milk product. Commercially, vitamins A and D will have been added and the milk will be homogenized, but otherwise this is just as it comes from the cow.

Lowfat milk: As its name indicates, this is milk from which almost all fat has been removed. Generally, it is sold as either 2 percent, meaning 98 percent of the fat has been removed, or 1 percent, indicating that 99 percent of the fat has been removed.

Nonfat or skim milk: These milks contain less than ½ percent of the total fat in whole milk. Since nonfat milk is usually quite pale and watery, some nonfat milks are fortified with protein to add body, richness, and flavor.

Buttermilk: Traditionally, this was the liquid remaining when cream was churned into butter. However, commercial buttermilk is, in fact, pasteurized skim milk that has been altered to replicate the original buttermilk. It is called "cultured" and has been thickened and had bacterial culture added, which transforms the lactose to lactic acid to create a sour flavor. Natural buttermilk is rather thin and only slightly sour, while cultured buttermilk is thick, with a pronounced tartness. Buttermilk's acidity hinders bacterial growth, adding to its ability to withstand long refrigeration. Buttermilk is also available in a dry, powdered form.

Ultra-pasteurized milk: This is milk that has been rapidly brought to 149°C (300°F) and then vacuum-packed to allow for long-term storage without refrigeration. Although the heat destroys any microorganisms that would precipitate spoilage, it also gives the milk a rather flat, cooked taste. Once the vacuum seal is broken, ultra-pasteurized milk must be refrigerated and dealt with as you would any other milk.

Dry or powdered milk (whole or nonfat): These packaged products are milk with all (or almost all) of its moisture removed. If whole milk, the dry mix must be refrigerated.

Nonfat dry milk is shelf-stable. Either one may or may not be fortified with vitamins A and D and, although inexpensive and convenient, will not have the taste of fresh milk.

Among the other types of animal milk, goat and sheep milk are the most common in the United States. They are sometimes available in specialty and health-food stores but are rarely seen in supermarkets, except in large urban areas. The milk of llamas, reindeer, camels, and water buffalo are widely used in other parts of the world, for both drinking and cheese-making.

Evaporated milk: Canned, slightly caramel-flavored milk made from fresh, homogenized whole milk from which 60 percent of the water has been removed. It is available in whole, lowfat, or skim varieties, generally with vitamin D added for a nutritional boost. It has quite a long shelf life, but once opened, it should be stored, tightly covered and refrigerated, for no longer than five days. Mixed half and half with water, evaporated milk can be used as a replacement for fresh milk in most recipes. Evaporated whole milk can also be frozen slightly and whipped as a replacement for whipped cream. Unlike whole milk, evaporated milk will not curdle when heated. It is often used to enrich custards, add a creamy texture to cooked dishes, and to add nutrition to the diets of infants and the infirm.

Sweetened condensed milk: This is a very thick, gummy, and sweet mixture of milk and sugar. As with evaporated milk, 60 percent of the water has been removed from sweetened condensed milk, but it is also about 40 to 45 percent sugar. It also has a long shelf life but once opened should be stored, tightly covered and refrigerated, for no longer than 5 days. Sweetened condensed milk is used in desserts and confectionery.

Cream

Left to its own devices, milk straight from the cow will separate into layers; a bottom layer of almost fat-free liquid and a top layer of almost solid-butterfat thick cream. Since straight-from-the-cow cream is rarely available, we are most familiar with commercially prepared creams, which have been separated from the milk by centrifugal force.

There are a number of different types of cream on the market:

Heavy (or heavy whipping) cream: This is the richest, highest-quality commercial cream, with 36 to 40 percent butterfat. It is used primarily to make whipped cream or *crème Chantilly*. Heavy cream will double in volume when whipped. Unlike the more widely available ultra-pasteurized heavy cream, this cream is generally only found in specialty-food stores or fine dairies.

Ultra-pasteurized cream: Also called whipping cream, this is cream that has been quickly heated to 149°C (300°F) to increase its shelf life by destroying any microorganisms that would create spoilage. It is not as cleanly flavored nor does it whip as easily as regular cream, due to changes in the molecular structure during pasteurization.

Light whipping cream: A lower-fat cream, light whipping cream has 30 to 36 percent butterfat. It may also have added emulsifiers and stabilizers to improve its whipping capabilities.

Light table or coffee cream: Light cream most frequently contains about 20 percent butterfat, although it can have up to 30 percent. It is, as its alternative names indicate, most often used to lighten hot beverages.

Half-and-half: Just as its name indicates, this is a mixture of equal parts whole milk and cream, with 10 to

12 percent butterfat. It is most often used in beverages. It cannot be whipped. (Also available in a nonfat form, which is simply nonfat milk thickened with a number of additives. We do not recommend it.)

Pressurized whipped cream: Today, many people only know the whipped creams that come from a pressurized can, available from the refrigerated dairy section of supermarkets. Most are not pure cream and instead contain a mixture of cream and sugar along with emulsifiers, stabilizers, and the gas that simulates the whipping action. It is not to be confused with other pressurized "nondairy" dessert toppings that contain absolutely no cream. It is not recommended for use in the pastry kitchen.

Butter

Butter is nothing more than highly concentrated milk: 20 liters (19 quarts) of milk are required to make 1 kilogram (2.2 pounds) of butter. Most butter used in America today comes from cow's milk, although it can be make from the milk of almost any milk-producing animal. Butter is made from the milk of horses in Mongolia, of goats in Eastern Europe, of sheep throughout the Mediterranean, and of camels in Ethiopia.

Traditionally, dairy butter was created by churning cream by hand to solidify the fat to a spreadable consistency. The modern process of commercial butter making remains almost the same, though it has been mechanized. The main difference is that the skim milk and buttermilk remaining after the churning process are now also used as commercial products, whereas they were once used primarily as animal feed.

Commercially prepared butter is, by governmental dictate, no less than 82.5 percent butterfat, no more than 16 percent water, and no more than 2 percent milk solids. It may or may not have added salt (no more than 2 percent), color, vitamins, and minerals. Today's specialty-food markets now feature many artisanal or imported butters that replicate the old-fashioned hand-churned texture and flavor. These very-high-fat (85 percent or more) butters are often called "European style" and are substantially more expensive than the supermarket varieties.

The distinct flavor of fresh butter comes from five principal sources: fatty acids, lactones, diacetyl and dimethyl sulfide, and methyl ketones. Butterfat is composed of a mixture of triglycerides, mainly those from fatty acids such as palmitic, stearic, oleic, and myristic acids. The diet of the animal from which the butter comes will determine the fatty-acid composition of the final product. Butter also contains protein, fat-soluble vitamins A, E, and D, calcium, and phosphorus.

Depending on how butter is stored, its flavor can vary dramatically. Tainted flavor may be the result of chemical or bacterial influences or of absorption. Chemical flavors can come from the degradation of the butterfat, illness or medication in the milk-producing animal, dairy disinfectants, and so forth. Rancidity is distinguished by sour taste and deepening color. Bacterial flavors arise through unsanitary equipment or storage, improper cooling, or external contamination. Absorption occurs when unwrapped butter takes on the flavors of other products stored with it. for these reasons, it is imperative that all butters be stored well wrapped and refrigerated or frozen.

Baking with Butter

Without question, butter is absolutely indispensable in the pastry kitchen. When butter is heated, the lactones and methyl ketones present in it are activated, providing the luscious flavor in baked goods prepared with butter. They also interact with the flavors created by the Maillard reactions to create the taste and aromas associated with caramelization. These compounds, along with others, work together to enhance the rich flavor, meltingly sweet taste, and wonderful aromas we associate with warm croissants, butter cakes, and cookies.

Dean's Tip

"Pastry cannot be superlative without superlative butter."

Dean Jacques Pépin

Dean's Tip

"To use butter in place of oil, first clarify the butter."

Dean André Soltner

Almost all bakery recipes use unsalted butter, also known as sweet butter (not to be confused with sweet creamery butter, which may or may not be salted). This is because it has the purest flavor and allows the baker to salt the dough to a specific taste. Salted butter may be used only if the recipe contains salt; however, if it is used, the active salt ingredient should be reduced by about 6 grams (⅕ ounce) for every 455 grams (1 pound) butter used. Whatever type of butter is used, it is usually brought to room temperature when being creamed into a recipe and chilled when being worked into a dough.

Types of Butter and Butter Substitutes

Unsalted (or sweet) butter is pure, unflavored butter made from pasteurized fresh cream. It is highly perishable and must be kept under refrigeration—or frozen for longer periods of storage.

Salted butter is butter to which either fine salt or brine has been added during the churning process. The salt not only flavors the butter but also acts as a preservative.

"European" butters are those with a higher fat content and lower moisture content, best used in laminated doughs such as croissant and puff pastry. Because of these two elements, they are also used to create a more stable buttercream.

Clarified butter can be made with either unsalted or salted butter. It is butter that has been slowly heated, evaporating the water and allowing the fat to separate from the milk solids. During the heating, the milk solids sink to the bottom of the saucepan and the clear, golden fat rises to the top. This clarified liquid is then either poured or ladled off. The finished prod-uct has a clean, rich taste and a very high smoke point, which allows it to be heated to very high temperatures. Also, without milk solids the butter does not turn rancid as quickly as regular butter. Ghee is an East Indian variation of clarified butter.

Margarine is a meat fat or vegetable oil–based product that has been chemically altered to a butterlike consistency. It is composed of 80 percent fat, 18 percent water, and 2 percent salt (unless unsalted). Cream or milk can be added to achieve a buttery taste and various additives are used to create color, texture, and aroma. Oleomargarine is made from beef fat and vegetable (or other) oil, and vegetable margarine is made with only vegetable oils, usually corn or soy. Oleomargarine was developed primarily for use in commercial bakeries to address issues of shelf life and stability. No margarine is used in a fine-quality bakery kitchen.

Vegetable shortening is a flavorless vegetable oil–based fat that has been chemically altered to achieve a smooth, solid texture. It is relatively inexpensive and can endure long periods of room-temperature storage. It is often used to make American-style pie pastry.

Lard is rendered pork fat that has been clarified to a smooth, solid texture. Unprocessed lard is strongly flavored and almost never used in a bakery setting. Processed lard, on the other hand, has a clean and delicate taste. It is quite rich and is often used to create tender doughs and pastries. When it is substituted for butter, the amount used is generally about 25 percent less.

Vegetable and nut oils can be created from a wide variety of plants, nuts, and seeds, such as corn, canola, grapeseed, cottonseed, peanuts, olives, and so forth. These oils can be used to create some cakes, sweet or tea breads, and cookies.

Cheese and Other Cultured Dairy Products

Historically, cheese was essentially a means of preserving milk. By the time this was no longer a necessary method of storage, a wide variety of cheeses had found their way into the culinary landscape. Cheeses are categorized in two broad groupings: fresh or unripened, and aged or ripened. No matter the type, all cheeses are created by shaping curdled milk through a variety of methods. Within each grouping, there are huge numbers of subdivisions that classify a specific cheese by its texture, terroir (the place from which it originated), the mechanics of its manufacture, the ripening process, and many other delineations. A classification may be altered by the aging process, too; a young, unripened cheese is an entirely different entity from the same cheese a few weeks later, when it has fully matured.

Almost all cheese are created by allowing milk (usually cow's, sheep's, or goat's) to thicken until it separates into whey (liquid) and curds (semisolids). Often the enzyme rennin (or another enzyme or bacterium) is added to speed the thickening process. Once separated, the liquid is drained. The curds are either left as they are to be used as fresh or unripened cheese, or pressed into a shape and cured according to the type of cheese being made. The curing process may include heating the curd, cutting the curd with a variety of cutting and shaping tools, molding and pressing to expel even more moisture, salting the exterior, immersion in brine, or a combination of some of these methods. The formed cheese may be seasoned with fat; wrapped in cheesecloth or leaves; coated in ash, herbs, or other natural products; smoked; pierced with needles; or in other ways encouraged to form a rind. Natural aged cheese must be ripened through controlled storage (usually uncovered) that guarantees the appropriate humidity and temperature for the creation of the desired texture and flavor.

Storing Cheese

All cheeses should be carefully stored under refrigeration, wrapped, airtight in plastic film, a plastic bag, or preferably both. Most cheeses keep up to four weeks, but some may be stored for longer periods. Some hard cheeses freeze quite well, but freezing will alter the texture and flavor of most cheeses. During refrigerated storage, a mold will often appear on ripened cheeses, but the cheese will remain edible if the moldy portion, along with a bit extra, is cut off and discarded. If mold appears on stored fresh cheese, the cheese should be discarded, as this signifies that it has deteriorated and is unsafe to consume. All cheeses are best consumed at room temperature.

Baking with Cheese

Fresh or unripened cheeses can be used in a variety of baked goods, and aged or ripened cheeses are often used in the preparation of quiches and custards. A cheese selection is often served in lieu of or in addition to a pastry course in a fine-dining restaurant, so it is important that a pastry chef be familiar with a selection of international cheeses.

Cheesecakes and cheese-flavored breads are the most familiar in the pastry kitchen. Fresh cheese is most often used, although some hard, aged cheeses are used to create savory breads or *petits fours*, such as the classic French *gougères*. Fresh cheeses are usually brought to room temperature before mixing for easy incorporation into a batter or dough. Hard, aged cheeses are always shredded or cubed before integrating into a batter or custard to ensure even melting into the baked product.

The most common fresh or unripened cheeses and related dairy products are:

Cream cheese: Smooth, spreadable, slightly tangy cow's milk cheese with a fairly long shelf life due to the addition of gum arabic (or carrageenan or xanthan gum), a commercial stabilizer. By law, cream cheese must contain 33 percent butterfat and no more than 55 percent moisture. An American invention, it is the primary ingredient for American-style cheesecake; it is also mixed with sour cream to make the classic French dessert *coeur à la crème*. Cream cheese is often sold with the addition of herbs, fruits, and vegetables. Other cream cheeses are **neufchâtel** (not to be confused with the aged French neufchâtel) and non-fat, lowfat, and whipped cream cheese; with the exception of the whipped version, these have less fat, and the neufchâtel has even less moisture. Whipped has less calories due to the fact that air has lightened it. All cream cheese should be stored refrigerated and tightly wrapped.

Cottage cheese: A fresh, unpressed cheese that comes in a number of small- or large-curd varieties (the curd being the visible pieces in the finished cheese). It has a bland flavor and a slightly loose texture because of the small portion of whey that remains after draining. It is best known as the "curds and whey" of Little Miss Muffet in the children's nursery rhyme. It can be made from whole, skim, or nonfat milk. Cottage cheese can be eaten plain, served with fruit or vegetables, or used as an ingredient in cakes, puddings, gelatin salads, or desserts; it can also replace ricotta or farmer cheese in recipes.

Farmer (or farmer's) cheese: Created by pressing all of the whey (or liquid) from cottage cheese. It is rather dry and crumbly, with a slightly tangy flavor, and is sold in either tubs or logs. It can be eaten plain, served with fruit or vegetables, or used in cooking, such as in a filling for blintzes, crêpes, or savory casseroles.

Pot cheese: Created by draining most, but not all, of the whey from cottage cheese. Like farmer cheese, it can be eaten plain, served with fruit or vegetables, or used in cooking, such as in fillings for blintzes or savory casseroles.

Ricotta cheese: A traditional Italian fresh sheep's or water buffalo's milk cheese made from the whey remaining from other types of cheese making. The American version is generally made from cow's milk. The Italian usually has a stronger flavor and drier texture than the American. Both are quite sweet, with a fine curd. Technically, ricotta is not a fresh cheese but rather a whey cheese or dairy product, as no rennet or starter is used to create it; it is manufactured through heating. Besides the fresh, soft form, ricotta is also sold salted, baked, and smoked. Fresh ricotta can be eaten plain, served with fruit or vegetables, or used as an ingredient in cakes, breads, puddings, and savory casseroles.

Mozzarella cheese: A traditional fresh Italian cheese made from water buffalo's or cow's milk. It is delicately flavored and creamy white. Traditionally served on the day it is made, mozzarella can also be stored in a light brine or vacuum-packed. It may or may not be pasteurized. Mozzarella is rarely used in baking, except as a topping for pizza.

Quark: A fresh, unripened curd cheese that is very moist (about 80 percent water), with a texture that

ranges from a smooth consistency like that of sour cream to a soft ricottalike curd. Rich in flavor, it is sold both as lowfat and nonfat. It is a common central European cheese that can be eaten plain or seasoned with herbs and spices, served with fruit or vegetables, or used in cheesecakes or fillings for pastries.

Crème fraîche: A traditional French unpasteurized, thickened cream. In America, it is made from pasteurized cream with an added fermenting ingredient, such as buttermilk. The result is similar to the French original, with a tangy, rich flavor and a thick, smooth texture that can be as loose as sour cream or as dense as soft cream cheese. Crème fraîche is a wonderful dessert topping and is also used to enrich hot sauces or soups, as it does not curdle when cooked.

Mascarpone: A traditional rich, double- or triple-cream Italian cheese made from unpasteurized cow's milk. It is created by adding citric acid to heavy cream and then draining off the whey, leaving a soft, spreadable cheese. American-made mascarpone is usually denser and tangier than that imported from Italy. Mascarpone is high in butterfat, usually 70 to 75 percent. Its soft, buttery texture and delicate flavor make it an excellent dessert cheese to serve with fresh fruit. It can also be used to make cheesecakes or fillings for pastries.

Sour cream: Sour cream was once simply heavy cream that had soured. Today, commercially made sour cream contains 18 to 20 percent butterfat that has been "soured" through the addition of lactic acid culture. It generally also contains stabilizers and emulsifiers. Reduced fat and nonfat sour creams are available also. Sour cream can be eaten plain, served with fruit or vegetables, or used as an ingredient in cakes, cookies, breads, or puddings.

Yogurt: One of nature's oldest foods, yogurt is made by fermenting and coagulating milk with nonharmful bacteria. Commercial yogurt is made by a controlled process in which the required bacteria (most often *Lactobacillus bulgaricus* and *Streptococcus thermophilus*) are added to the milk. Stabilizers may also be added to facilitate emulsification. In America yogurt is made from whole, lowfat, or nonfat cow's, sheep's, or goat's milk, and in other parts of the world it is also made from the milk of horses, buffalo, or camels. It is often sold flavored with fruits or other ingredients. Traditional Greek yogurt, now available in the United States, is usually thicker and richer than commercial American yogurts. Yogurt can be eaten plain, served with fruit or vegetables, or used as an ingredient in cakes, breads, or muffins to add moisture and stability.

The basic types of aged or ripened cheese are the following:

Hard cheese: Cheeses that have been processed (usually cooked and pressed) and then aged for long periods of time (generally at least 2 years) have a firm, dense texture and a saltier, often sharper flavor. Some hard cheeses are Parmigiano-Reggiano, Pecorino Romano, and dry Monterey Jack. These cheeses are often used for grating.

Semifirm cheese: These cheeses are firm, but not hard or crumbly. They are processed as with hard cheese, but not aged quite as long. Some familiar semifirm cheeses are the various American and English Cheddars, Jarlsberg, and Edam, all of which can be eaten out of hand or used in sauces, soups, or other cooked dishes.

Semisoft cheese: these cheeses may or may not be cooked, but they are always pressed into a specific shape. They can be sliced and eaten out of hand or used in cooked dishes. Some familiar semisoft cheeses are Gouda, Monterey Jack, and Port Salut.

Soft-ripened (or surface-ripened) cheese: These have not been cooked or pressed but have been formed into specific shapes that are then exposed to various bacteria to ripen them from the outside in. the bacteria may be applied through dipping or spraying, which allows the cheese to develop a rind. The rind will range in color from pale white to brilliant orange. The interior will range in texture from slightly soft to creamy and almost runny. **Blue-veined cheese** is a soft-ripened cheese that has been sprayed or inoculated with spores of the molds *Penicillium roqueforti* or *Penicillium glaucum* to create rich blue-gray or green veins of mold throughout the ripened cheese.

Pasta filata **(or spun-paste) cheese:** This Italian cheese is created through a special process whereby the curd is given a bath in hot whey and, once heated, is then manipulated through kneading and stretching until it reaches a specific pliable texture. This technique can be used to make both fresh and ripened cheeses.

Gelifiers, Thickeners, and Emulsifiers

An extensive array of thickening ingredients is available to pastry chefs and bakers. Each type is selected dependent upon its ability to marry with the other ingredients, as well as the desired texture of the finished product. Gelifiers are agents that, when married with a hot liquid (often water) and subsequently cooled, form a jelly or jelled substance without modifying taste. Thickeners are elements that, when added to a liquid, increase stability and density and control the suspension of added ingredients without affecting taste. Emulsifiers are used to bind together ingredients that will not normally blend, such as oil and water, by dispersing fine droplets of one ingredient into the other. Gelifiers and thickeners are used in *mousses*, sauces, jams, jellies, Bavarians, fruit fillings, glazes, and confections. Gelatin, eggs, pectin, and various starches are the most common of these ingredients, each with different strengths and thickening properties.

Gelatin

Gelatin is a colorless, odorless, tasteless, pure protein that is available from animals and a few plants and functions as a mechanical stabilizer. High-quality, animal-based, commercial gelatin is generally extracted from pig's skin. Vegetable-based gelatin is usually extracted from seaweed, either Japanese agar-agar or carrageenan (Irish moss). Agar-agar is extracted from a Japanese red seaweed of the genus Euchema, while carrageen is extracted from a red seaweed, *Chrondus crispus*, available on both sides of the Atlantic Ocean. Agar-agar-based gelatins can withstand heated temperatures near the boiling point and are recommended for use in the preparation of jellied dishes or aspics in tropical climates. Seaweed gelatins can be used interchangeably with animal-based ones, although agar-agar has about eight times more jelling strength than culinary gelatin, so less is required.

Gelatin is most commonly used to increase the viscosity of liquid mixes through the absorption of water. It will, consequently, turn liquids into solids when the gelatin-infused mix is dissolved, heated, and then chilled. The mix may also be returned to its liquid form by heating. Liquid mixes with added gelatin will set (firm up) at 20°C (68°F) and melt at 30°C (86°F).

Gelatin is sold in two forms, granular (or powdered) and in transparent sheets called leaf gelatin. They can be used interchangeably, with certain adjustments. Before use, all gelatin must be soaked, or "bloomed," in a cold liquid so that it softens. It is usually placed on the surface of the liquid and left to rest for a few minutes, after which it is heated until it completely dissolves. A recipe using granular gelatin will often specify the amount of liquid, as well as the exact time required to soften it.

Leaf gelatin comes in thin, transparent sheets that usually weigh 3 grams (¹⁄₁₀ ounce) each. Three sheets will absorb 45 millimeters (1½ ounces) of liquid, or five times its weight, when fully bloomed. Although an exact amount of liquid is not required, sheet gelatin must be completely submerged in a bowl of cold water for at least 5 minutes for it to sufficiently absorb the water.

After soaking, the softened gelatin can be combined with any liquid and then heated over a low flame to completely dissolve, or it can be placed in liquid that is already very to dissolve. The dissolved gelatin will have no graininess, nor will any solid pieces remain. It must be fully dissolved to properly do its job. Never allow gelatin to boil, as the high heat will damage the protein. Finally, the mixture must be chilled to allow the gelatin to increase its viscosity

and set it to a firm consistency.

There is a fine line in adding gelatin to a mix: too little, and the mixture will not set, too much, and the mixture will turn chewy and rubbery. When chilling a gelatined mixture, it is important to stir it occasionally during the first bit of chilling time to keep the gelatin from settling on the bottom. (We all can remember a bowl of Jell-O with a thick, rubbery bottom that peeled off the bowl!) When making a *mousse* or a Bavarian cream, allow the liquid to begin to set before folding in the required whipped cream or meringue. If the mixture has set too stiffly to easily fold in the lightening ingredient, place the mix on top of a *bain-marie* and gently heat until it reaches the correct consistency.

Enzymes, acids, and sugars in some fresh fruits, such as pineapple, papaya, guava, passion fruit, figs, and mangoes, acids, and sugars will interfere with the thickening properties of animal-based gelatin by breaking down its holding power. Neither of the seaweed gelling agents react adversely when used in combination with tropical fruits. If the fruit or fruit juice is heated to 79°C (175°F) before the gelatin is added, the enzyme is deactivated and the gelatin should hold.

Guidelines for Calculating Gelatin Substitutions

In his epic tome, *The Professional Pastry Chef*, the esteemed pastry chef and teacher, Bo Friberg, provides the following excellent advice for calculating substitutions between animal- and vegetable-based gelatins:

To substitute sheet gelatin in a recipe that calls for powdered, submerge the sheets in water, calculate the amount of liquid absorbed by each sheet, and figure that into your recipe. Then add the missing water to the gelatin sheets when you heat them to dissolve. For example: If the recipe instructs you to soften 2 tablespoons (18 grams) of powdered gelatin in ½ cup (4 ounces/120 ml) water, substitute 6 gelatin sheets (6 sheets at 3 grams each = 18 grams), softened in enough water to cover. But, since you know that they will have absorbed only 3 ounces (90 ml) of the water, add 1 ounce (30 ml) more water.

To substitute powdered gelatin in a recipe that calls for gelatin sheets, use an equal weight of powder dissolved in as much water as the sheet would have absorbed. For example: If the recipe uses 6 sheets of softened gelatin, you would substitute 18 grams (2 tablespoons) of powdered gelatin, softened in the same amount of water that the sheet would have absorbed; in this case 3 ounces (90 ml).

Pectin

Pectin is a water-soluble sugar derivative found in many fruits and plants that, in a proper environment offering heat, sugar, and acid, will thicken or gel. It is most often used to thicken jams, jellies, conserves, and compotes. Some fruits (such as apples, quince, citrus, and some berries) are high enough in natural pectin, acid, and sugar that, when they are cooked, the pectin is activated. Some fruits need the addition of sugar and acid to activate their natural pectin so that the mix will gel. Other fruits are so low in natural pectin that they require the addition of commercial pectin, along with sugar and acid. Commercial pectin is available in both liquid and powdered forms, both of which are derived from apple or citrus parings.

The same procedure is followed whether using fruits with adequate natural pectin or the addition of commercial pectin: The fruit is mixed with sugar, an acidic element is added if the fruit requires it, and the mixture is brought to a boil. With naturally occurring pectin, the fruit is cooked rapidly to prevent the pectin from breaking down. As the mixture thickens, a small amount is removed from the pot and tested for consistency by placing it on an ice-cold plate, which will cause it to firm. Cooking is continued until the proper consistency is reached. When using commercial pectin, defined instructions should be followed exactly or the mix will not gel properly.

Eggs as Thickeners and Emulsifiers

Eggs are the most commonly used thickeners in the pastry kitchen. Egg proteins coagulate over a wide temperature range, 62°C to 70°C (144°F to 158°F) with coagulation occurring gradually at low temperatures and almost immediately at high heat. Under high heat, there may be less than a degree's difference between thickening and curdling—obviously, curdling is less likely when a mixture is cooked over low heat.

Natural protein consists of individual molecules that are complex, folded, and coiled, with loose bonds across the fold and coils holding each protein in a separate, tight unit. When the protein is heated or exposed to acid, these bonds break. The protein molecules unfold and then, with their bonds exposed, approach and begin bonding to the other molecules. In essence, millions of protein molecules join in a three-dimensional network to coagulate, or thicken. This delicate process has to be expertly handled. Exposure to very low heat over too long a period of time or too much heat applied too quickly will cause the molecules to become too firm and rupture, thereby squeezing out the liquid within the molecular structure. In the pastry kitchen, this is known as "weeping" or "curdling."

Eggs can also be used to emulsify a mixture. The yolks, especially, contain a number of emulsifiers (among them lecithin and phospholipids) that serve to hold liquids and fats together in such mixtures as mayonnaise, salad dressings, or butter sauces. If an egg yolk is whisked into a hot liquid, it will bond the fats and liquids, producing a rich flavor and silky texture. A classic *sabayon* is created by whisking egg yolks with the other flavoring ingredients over a hot-water bath to produce an ethereal, airy emulsified sauce.

Starches as Thickeners

Although there are many starches that can be used to thicken or even gelatinize foods, the most common ones in the pastry kitchen are flour and cornstarch. Rice flour, potato starch, and arrowroot are also used, but infrequently. Starches thicken sauces, puddings, fruit fillings, and custards through their molecular ability to absorb water when mixed with liquids and heated. Before being heated, starch must always be made into a **slurry**—that is, it must be dissolved in cold liquid, whisking constantly, or the mixture will lump. It must then be cooked to eliminate a starchy taste and to begin the thickening process. Different starches require differing heats to thicken. When liquids are mixed with starch and heated, gelatinization generally begins to happen at about 60°C (140°F) and will reach the thickest level at about 93°C (200°F). Once removed from the heat, the liquid will continue to thicken as it cools, which makes it difficult to judge the amount of starch needed to appropriately thicken a mix. Interestingly, if the mix is cooked for too long, it will begin to lose its thickness and thin out. A safe way to judge thickness is to remove a small amount from the cooking mix and quickly cool it over an ice bath. The cooled texture will tell you whether more or less starch is needed.

Flour: Wheat flour is the most frequently used thickener, but it is not as strong as other starches. One and a half times more flour than cornstarch is required to thicken the same amount of liquid.

There are commercially made **instant wheat flours** that have been combined with a liquid, heated, dried, and ground to a fine powder. They are less starchy in flavor, finer in texture, less apt to lump,

absorb liquid quickly, and gelatinize rapidly. They are most useful in sauces.

Cornstarch: This fine, gluten-free powder has been created by soaking, washing, drying, and finally grinding the germ of corn. It has no distinct flavor and an extremely fine texture that does not easily lump. When used in sauces and gravies, it produces a silky, translucent, and slightly glassy finish. When sauces bound with cornstarch are stored for several days, the starch will begin to lose its strength and the liquid in the mix will begin to weep out and loosen the texture. However, this does not affect the flavor. Frozen products will also manifest weeping.

Potato starch: A fine, powdery starch made from cooked, dried, and ground white potatoes. It is almost flavorless, with more strength than wheat flour or cornstarch, so that products thickened with it do not break down easily. It has a low gelatinization temperature, which makes it useful when thickening a mix that cannot be boiled.

Arrowroot: Technically made from the roots of a tropical tuber, *Maranta arundinacea*, the powdered starch from a variety of other roots is also referred to as arrowroot. A very delicate thickener made by washing, drying, and pulverizing the root into extremely fine grains, arrowroot is lighter than cornstarch, with twice the thickening strength of wheat flour. It creates a light-textured, flavorless, translucent paste that sets to an almost-clear gel.

Chocolate

The enticingly rich chocolate so familiar to lovers of sweets is derived from the fruits (or beans) of the tropical cacao tree, through a long and complicated process beginning with the type of tree from which they are picked. There are three main species of cacao that yield the desirable fruit: *criollo, forastero,* and *trinitario. Criollo* is the rarest and most expensive bean. It is less acrid than the others and has an intense fragrance. *Forastero* is the most common bean used in the manufacture of cocoa and chocolate. It is hardy, full-flavored, and affordable for mass production. *Trinitario*, a mild-flavored hybrid of the other two beans, is not commonly used in commercial production. The fruit from each is a football-shaped pod that turns red, orange, or yellow when ripe and is hand-harvested at exactly the proper stage of ripeness. Each pod contains from thirty to fifty seeds held in a sticky, white pulp. The pods are split and the seeds are removed along with the pulp, then left to ferment for a few days. During fermentation, the white pulp decomposes, and the beans begin to lose their innate bitter-

ness and exhibit the color, taste, and aroma of chocolate. After the fermentation process is complete, the beans are sun-dried for about two weeks to reduce their water content and enhance their flavor. Once dried, the beans are cleaned, inspected, sorted according to their quality, and shipped to chocolate factories for processing. All these processes are done by hand usually within close proximity to the trees themselves.

At the processing station, the cacao beans are first roasted to develop their flavor and aroma. The husk (outer shell) is removed, leaving the small internal kernel called the nib. The nibs are then crushed, and the resulting paste—simply unsweetened chocolate—is called chocolate liquor. Chocolate liquor may be used as is, or it can be ground to a smoother consistency to make sweetened chocolate.

The different types of chocolate used in cooking are:

Unsweetened chocolate: 100 percent pure cocoa paste with no sweetener added. Also known as chocolate liquor, it is usually about 53 percent cocoa butter and 47 percent cocoa solids and is used in baking and candy making.

Bittersweet chocolate: Sweetened chocolate created by adding sugars, extra cocoa butter, vanilla, and an emulsifying agent. It consists of 35 percent cocoa paste and 27 percent cocoa butter, with less than 50 percent sugar added.

Semisweet chocolate: Sweetened chocolate with the same ingredients added to make bittersweet chocolate, but consisting of 27 percent cocoa butter, 15 percent cocoa paste, and more than 50 percent added sugar.

Milk chocolate: Milk chocolate requires all of the above ingredients, plus milk solids and lecithin. It consists of 10 to 20 percent chocolate.

White chocolate: Not actually chocolate, but extracted cocoa butter mixed with sugar, milk, vanilla, and an emulsifying agent. Compound white chocolates are made by adding fats other than cocoa butter.

Cocoa powder: A fine powder ground from the solid cake that is the result of pressing chocolate liquor to separate the butter from the solids. Cocoa powder that has been treated with potassium carbonate, an alkaline solution, is called Dutch-processed cocoa; the addition of alkaline darkens the color and softens the flavor. It is not to be confused with cocoa mix, which has sugars and other flavoring agents added.

Cocoa butter: This is the pale, almost creamy fat that is extracted from cacao beans during the chocolate-making process. It is a complex fat used for colored décor in candy making.

Melting Chocolate

Many baking recipes call for melted chocolate, a process that requires a certain amount of care. Assemble all utensils and make sure they are clean and dry. Even a tiny drop of liquid can cause the chocolate to seize—that is, cocoa solids suddenly stick together and clump into a grainy mass. At this point, the chocolate cannot be redeemed. More liquid can be stirred into the mass to bring it back to a smooth, flowing state, but it is now chocolate with added liquid. The recipe must be adjusted, or the chocolate used for other purposes.

1. If melting a solid block of chocolate, the chocolate should be chopped into small, even pieces with a strong, serrated knife or a chocolate-breaking fork before using.

2. Place chocolate bits or chopped chocolate in a clean, dry heat-proof bowl over a saucepan of gently simmering water or in the top half of a double boiler over gently simmering water. Stir the chocolate as it melts to ensure even melting.

3. Make sure that the water remains at a gentle simmer and that you stir from the edges in; otherwise, the chocolate at the sides will overheat and stick.

4. When the chocolate is approximately three-quarters melted, remove it from the simmering water and continue to stir until it is completely melted. Use as directed in a specific recipe.

Tempering Chocolate

If chocolate is being used for candy making or decorating, it must be tempered, because once chocolate is heated and melted, the molecules of fat separate and break up. To reunite them, you have to stabilize the chocolate through a process of heating and cooling called **tempering**. This can be done in a variety of ways, but the end result must always be a smooth chocolate that retains its texture and sheen once set. You should always temper more chocolate than you need, as a larger batch will hold its temperature for a longer period of time, allowing you more leeway in preparation. The three most common methods of tempering chocolate are:

1. *Tabliering*, the traditional French method whereby two -thirds of the amount of chocolate to be tempered is melted and poured out onto a cool surface (usually marble) and worked back and forth with a spatula until it reaches 27°C (81°F), then worked back into the remaining third of melted chocolate until in reaches a uniform temperature of 28°C (83°F).

2. Working over a hot-water bath.

3. Tempering in a microwave oven.

In the first two methods, the chocolate must reach and maintain an exact temperature, which necessitates using a perfectly calibrated thermometer.

The chocolate usually begins at a room temperature of about 23°C (75°F). During the melting process, the temperature is raised to between 43°C (110°F) and 49°C (120°F). It must then be lowered immediately to between 28°C (82°F) and 29°C (83°F) by adding finely chopped, room-temperature chocolate. Finally, the temperature of the chocolate is raised to between 31°C (88°F) and 32°C (90°F). The temperature must be checked continually to ensure proper tempering.

To temper chocolate using a microwave, finely chop all of the chocolate to be tempered and place it in a microwave-safe bowl, preferably glass. Melt on high for 20 seconds. This should result in a slightly lumpy mixture, with about one-third of the chocolate remaining solid. Remove the bowl from the microwave and, using a rubber spatula, scrape the chocolate into a clean, cold glass bowl. Beat the chocolate with a handheld immersion blender until it reaches 32°C (90°F).

Storing Chocolate

To keep chocolate fresh, it must be stored, airtight, in a dark spot with a cool temperature (76°C to 78°C/60°F to 65°F) and low humidity. Stored in such a manner, dark chocolate should keep for up to two years. White chocolate or chocolate with added milk stored in the same way will have a shelf life of up to seven months.

Flavoring

An Introduction to Vanilla

Vanilla is the most frequently used flavoring in the pastry kitchen—in fact, it is one of the most widely used flavors in the world. With its mellow accent that complements both sweet and savory products, it is used in baked goods and confections in America, in sauces in Mexico, on fruits in Polynesia, and in the famous perfumes of France. The long, thin pod is the fruit of a small group of flowered, climbing tropical orchids native to Mexico, the West Indies, Central and South America, and Tahiti. There are more than 20,000 varieties of fruit-bearing orchids in the world, and the vanilla bean is the only one that is edible. Most commercial vanilla comes from the *Vanilla planifolia Andrews* orchid. This particular type of orchid has only one natural pollinator, the melipone bee, and it was not until the intervention of science in the mid-1880s that commercial production was possible. Even now, pollination is still carried out by hand on family plantations.

Because it is labor-intensive and time-consuming to produce, pure vanilla is a very costly ingredient. The entire cultivation process, from planting to market, can take up to six years. For a start, each of the plant's blossoms only stay open for a day, which makes pollination more difficult.

Vanilla beans differ in chemical, physical, and organoleptic (affecting the senses) properties, depending upon their species, geographical source, and physical form (or grade). Each has a marked difference in aroma and taste having to do with the plant it came from, its maturity when picked, the curing method used, and the process used to obtain the extract.

Further definitions of these types are:

Bourbon-Madagascar vanilla: This type is considered to be the finest-quality pure vanilla available. The term "Bourbon" comes from the Bourbon Islands, Madagascar, Comoro, Seychelles, Mauritius, and Réunion off the east coast of Africa. The beans grown there are very thin, with a sweet, rich flavor that is described as creamy, smooth, sweet, and mellow.

Indonesian vanilla: Traditional Indonesian vanilla has been known as a mixed-quality vanilla, with minimal attention paid to its grading. Grown on Bali, South Java, Sulawesi, North and South Sumatra, Lomboc, Flores, and Timor, it possesses a deep, full-bodied flavor. With improved techniques, modern Indonesian vanilla can frequently be favorably compared to Bourbon vanillas.

Mexican vanilla: Mexican vanilla is described as creamy, sweet, smooth, and spicy. Considerably cheaper than many other imported vanillas, Mexican vanillas are sometimes suspect as they contain coumarin, a carcinogenic product outlawed in the United States for some time that can cause liver and kidney damage when consumed. However, when processed by a reputable manufacturer under proper guidelines, Mexican vanilla is considered to be very high quality.

South American and West Indian vanilla: Rarely available in the United States, this vanilla should be similar to Bourbon vanilla, but when imported it is generally of poor quality.

Tahitian vanilla: Tahitian vanilla beans are the thickest, darkest pods, and their seeds are fewer and stickier than those of other types. They come from the species *Vanilla tahitensis Moore* and have a fragrant but delicate aroma and taste and a lower vanillin content. They are generally less favored, as they have a relatively high volatile oil content, which results in cloudy extracts.

Common Forms of Vanilla

As a flavoring, vanilla adds potency and aroma to both sweet and savory dishes. Liquid extract is the most common form of vanilla used, but the seeds and pod are also employed.

Pure vanilla extract: Extract is made by macerating chopped pods in an alcohol-and-water solution to draw out the flavor. The mixture is aged for several months until the liquid is brown, clear, and very fragrant. The strength of the extract is measured in units called folds. Single-fold vanilla is sold for the home cook. Two-, three-, and four-fold vanilla is sold for food-processing purposes.

Pure vanilla extract must meet certain standards set by the United States Food and Drug Administration. Single-fold vanilla contains the extractive matter of 378 grams (13.35 ounces) of vanilla beans, containing less than 25 percent moisture in 3.8 liters (1 gallon) of 35 percent aqueous ethyl alcohol. Two-fold uses 756 grams (26.7 ounces) of vanilla beans, contains two times as much extractive matter, and is twice as strong. Three- and four-fold are, as one would imagine, three and four times as strong. Vanilla extract will keep indefinitely if stored, airtight, in a cool, dark spot.

Vanilla essence is also produced and is so strong that only a drop or two is necessary to adequately flavor a mix. It is available only by special order through specialty suppliers.

To retain the intensity of flavor, vanilla extract should be added to cooked mixtures after they have cooled slightly. When baking, the vanilla should be mixed in with the fat, which will encapsulate it and prevent it from volatilizing during the hot baking process.

Homemade vanilla extract may be made by placing split whole beans in a jar of vodka or cognac, sealing it airtight, and setting it aside in a cool, dark spot for six months.

Whole vanilla beans: Whole beans are frequently used in the pastry kitchen. To use the internal seeds only, the pod is split open lengthwise down the center, and the thousands of tiny seeds are scraped out. The seeds are added to a mix, often ice cream or custards, to infuse it with a rich, vanilla flavor. In cookies, cakes, or other doughs, they may be creamed into the butter. The pod itself may also be added to heighten the flavor of mixtures that are simmered, but it will be removed at some point before serving. Split pods, either with or without the seeds, can be placed in granulated or confectioners' sugar to create a beautifully scented vanilla sugar. Whole beans that have been used as a flavoring for cooked mixtures may also be removed, rinsed clean, dried, and stored, airtight, for reuse. All vanilla beans should be stored, tightly wrapped in an airtight container, in a cool, dark spot. Under these conditions, they will stay fragrant for about six months.

Imitation vanilla: Composed entirely of artificial flavorings (most of which are paper industry by-products that have been chemically treated), imitation vanilla has a harsh taste that will often leave a bitterness on the palate. Much cheaper than pure vanilla extract, it is not comparable to the real thing and much more will be needed to add flavor to a mix. It may also be called artificial vanillin.

Vanilla flavoring: A blend of pure and imitation vanilla used primarily for commercial products.

Vanilla sugar: Either confectioners' or granulated sugar that has been flavored by being stored, airtight, with a vanilla bean. Two beans are generally used to flavor 1 pound of sugar; the beans may be those that have been scraped of their seeds. The aromatic sugar is used to flavor baked products, ice creams, pudding, or other desserts.

Vanilla powder: Available in bakery or cake supply stores, vanilla powder is pure vanilla extract that has been dried on maltodextrin (a modified, all-natural cornstarch), with sugar added or not. It is used as a topping, for color, or for flavoring liquid-sensitive products.

Vanilla paste: With a consistency somewhere between syrup and molasses, vanilla paste is formulated to match pure extract in flavor, strength, and usage. Its consistency holds hundreds of vanilla seeds in suspension, which gives the finished product a natural vanilla look.

Liqueurs and Liquors as Flavoring

Liqueurs are extremely important flavoring agents in the pastry kitchen. These sweetened alcoholic spirits are made with a wide variety of seeds, herbs, fruits, flowers, plant roots, spices, nuts, and even the bark and leaves of trees and shrubs. They can be distilled, macerated, infused, or percolated to create an intensely flavored brew that will be defined by the flavoring agent. Some liqueurs are proprietary, that is, they are secret formulations that have been made by one producer for, often, centuries. Others are made from known recipes and can be made by any number of producers. As with other products, the finest liqueurs are made with the highest-quality ingredients.

Along with the standard liqueurs, **cream liqueurs**, **crème liqueurs**, and **liqueur brandies** are also produced. Cream liqueurs are flavored liqueurs that have been homogenized with heavy cream to make a thick, silky, sweet drink that can be consumed as is or added to mixed drinks. Crème liqueurs, most of which are produced in France, have no dairy product added but are extremely syrupy. They were originally only single-flavored. Generally fruit-based and colored appropriately, crème liqueurs are usually served as an after dinner drink. Liqueur brandies are made by combining brandy with a fruit liqueur. They are usually produced in France and are most often flavored with cherries, peaches, or apricots. Liqueurs are usually added at the end of a recipe, just prior to baking, setting, or freezing.

Some liqueurs are:

Advocaat, or Advokatt: Brandy, sugar, and egg yolks from the Netherlands.

Amaretto: Brandy, apricot pits, and bitter almond extract from Italy.

Anisette, or Anise: Neutral spirits with aniseed or star anise from France and Spain.

Aurum: Brandy with a blend of orange and other citrus fruits from Italy.

Bénédictine: A secret cognac-based formula that tastes of citrus peel, herbs, and spices, made for centuries by Benedictine monks in France and sold to a privately held company in the mid-1800s. The formula remains a secret.

Chartreuse: Only two Chartreuse monks at any time know the secret formula for the two naturally colored brilliant green and bright yellow chartreuses. Made in France by the infusion of 130 secret herbs and other unknown ingredients.

Chéri-Suisse: Liqueur flavored with chocolate and dark cherries from Switzerland.

Cointreau: Colorless, slightly herbal orange liqueur from France.

Curaçao: A bitter orange peel–flavored liqueur that may be clear or vibrant red, blue, green, or orange, from the island of the same name.

Drambuie: A blend of Scotch whiskey, heather honey, and herbs from Scotland.

Frangelico: A liqueur flavored with hazelnuts and vanilla bottled in a monk-shaped bottle in Italy.

Galliano: A bright yellow liqueur flavored with anise, licorice, and vanilla from Italy.

Glayva: A blend of Scotch whiskey, heather honey, orange peel, and herbs from Scotland.

Goldschlager: A cinnamon-flavored schnapps with edible gold leaf from Switzerland.

Goldwasser (Danziger Goldwasser): A strongly flavored root and herbal liqueur that contains small particles of gold leaf, originally from Germany, but now made in Poland.

Grand Marnier: Orange-flavored cognac from France.

Herbsaint: An anise-flavored liqueur from New Orleans, Louisiana.

Irish Mist: A blend of Irish whiskey, herbs, honey, and other spirits from Ireland.

Kahlua: A coffee-flavored liqueur from Mexico.

Kümmel: An aromatic liqueur flavored with caraway, anise, cumin, and fennel seeds, made in Holland and throughout Eastern Europe.

La Grande Passion: A passionfruit-infused liqueur from France.

Malibu: A rum-based, coconut-flavored drink from the Caribbean.

Mandarine Napoléon: A tangerine-flavored cognac from France.

Maraschino: A clear, dry, slightly bitter liqueur made from marasca cherries and their pits in Italy.

Midori: A tropical fruit liqueur made with honeydew melons in Japan.

Nocino (Nocciole or Nocello): A walnut-flavored liqueur from Italy.

Noisette: A hazelnut-flavored liqueur from France.

Ouzo: A strong anise-flavored liqueur from Greece.

Pastis: An anise-flavored liqueur that was formulated to replace the banned wormwood-based absinthe in France. **Pernod** is a popular brand.

Poire Williams: An eau-de-vie made from pears that originated in France.

Prunelle: A blend of brandy and wild blackthorn plums (sloes) from France.

Punsch: Rum blended with sweet spices such as cinnamon and cloves from Sweden.

Sabra: A chocolate and orange-flavored liqueur from Israel.

Sambuca: An Italian liqueur that is strongly scented with the essential oils from star anise.

Sloe Gin: A slightly sweet liqueur made from macerating pricked wild blackthorn plums (sloes) in gin for several months, from both the United States and Great Britain.

Southern Comfort: A blend of bourbon, oranges, and peaches made in the United States.

Strega: A very complex Italian herbal liqueur that gets its yellow color from saffron. It is almost always taken after a meal as a digestif.

Tia Maria: Rum that has been flavored with dark-roast coffee, made in Jamaica.

Triple Sec: A clear liqueur based on Curaçao that has been flavored with bitter orange peel. It is made in France.

Vandermint: A blend of chocolate and mint made in the Netherlands.

Cream Liqueurs

Irish Cream: A blend of Irish whiskey, coffee, chocolate, and cream from Ireland.

White Chocolate (such as Godiva brand): A blend of brandy, white chocolate, cream, and vanilla from the United States, as well as other countries.

Chocolate (such as Cadbury brand from Great Britain): A blend of brandy, chocolate, and cream.

Crème Liqueurs

Crème d'abricots: apricots

Crème d'amande: almonds

Crème d'ananas: pineapples and vanilla

Crème de banane: bananas

Crème de cacao: cocoa beans and vanilla

Crème de café: coffee

Crème de cassis: black currants

Crème de cerise: sweet cherries

Crème de fraise: strawberries

Crème de framboise: raspberries

Crème de mandarine: tangerines

Crème de menthe: mint

Crème de myrtille: bilberries or blueberries

Crème de noix: walnuts and honey

Crème de noyaux: apricot and other stone fruit kernel pits, tasting like almond

Crème de rose: rose petals and vanilla

Crème de thé, de rocco: black tea leaves and brandy

Crème de vanille: vanilla

Crème de violette: violet flower blossoms

Pastry Chef
Marisa Croce

Executive Pastry Chef, BR Guest Restaurant Group
The French Culinary Institute, Class of January 2002

Mascarpone Rice Pudding with Roasted Black Mission Figs and Port Wine Reduction

Serves 10

This is a rich and elegant rice pudding. If you want to go the extra distance, you can sprinkle the pudding with candied walnuts and serve some tiny brandy snap cookies (see page 466) on the side.

---

290 grams (10¼ ounces) long-grain rice

.95 liter (1 quart) whole milk

2 vanilla beans, split in half lengthwise

4 cinnamon sticks

¼ teaspoon ground cinnamon

⅛ teaspoon ground nutmeg

.95 liter (1 quart) heavy cream

335 grams (11¾ ounces) sugar

One 17.6-ounce container mascarpone cheese

Combine the rice with the milk in a medium heavy-bottomed saucepan. Using a paring knife, scrape the seeds from the vanilla beans into the rice. Then add the scraped beans, along with the cinnamon sticks, cinnamon, and nutmeg. Place over medium heat and, stirring frequently, bring to a simmer. Simmer, adjusting the heat, if necessary, for about 20 minutes, or until all the milk has been absorbed by the rice.

Add the cream, raise the heat, and bring to a simmer. Lower the heat and cook at a gentle simmer for about 30 minutes, or until all the cream has been absorbed by the rice.

Remove from the heat and stir in the sugar. When the sugar has dissolved, add the cheese, gently stirring to incorporate without breaking up the rice grains.

Scoop an equal portion of the rice pudding into each of 10 dessert bowls. Lay 3 roasted fig halves (see below), cut side up, around the pudding. Drizzle with a port reduction (see below) and serve.

Roasted Black Mission Figs

15 fresh Black Mission figs

30 grams (1 ounce) unsalted butter

21 grams (1 tablespoon) sugar

Preheat the oven to 205°C (400°F).

Using a small, sharp knife, trim the stem end of each fig. Slice the fruits in half, lengthwise. Set aside.

Place the butter in a small saucepan over low heat.

When melted, stir in the sugar until completely blended.

Pour the butter mixture into a 8-inch square baking dish, spreading it out to cover the bottom.

Place the figs into the pan, cut side down, in a single layer. Roast for about 10 minutes, or just until the juices begin to ooze.

Remove from the heat and serve immediately.

Port Wine Reduction

475 milliliters (16 ounces) ruby port wine

115 grams (4 ounces) sugar

Combine the port and sugar in a medium heavy-bottomed saucepan over low heat, stirring just until the sugar begins to dissolve.

Raise the heat and bring to a boil. Immediately lower the heat to medium and simmer for about 20 minutes or until the mixture is reduced to 115 milliliters (½ cup).

Remove from the heat and set aside to cool. The reduction should become thick and syrupy.

Session 3

Tartes: An Overview of Basic French Tart Doughs

Theory

A *pâte*, or pastry dough, is a flour-based preparation that, when rolled out into a thin sheet and molded, acts as a container for a filling. (Do not confuse *pâte*—which is pronounced PAHT—with *pâté*, pronounced pah-TAY, the French term for baked ground-meat preparations.) All pastry doughs are made with four basic ingredients: flour, fat, liquid, and salt. Occasionally, one will also call for sugar or either a raw egg or a hard-cooked egg yolk. The proportions of the four basic ingredients and the method by which they are combined determine the type and texture of the dough created. The word *pâte* can also refer to a batter, as well as to fresh pasta dough (*pâte fraîche*) and fresh noodle dough (*pâte à nouilles*).

A pastry dough that is rolled out, fitted into a mold, and baked is called a tart or pie shell. A tart generally refers to the French open-faced shell, whereas a pie usually refers to the traditional English two-crusted (top and bottom) pastry version. The fillings contained in a pastry dough tart or pie are many and varied. Fruit, meat, vegetables, fish, creams, custards, nuts, and chocolate are just some of the possibilities.

There is absolutely no mystery to making perfect pastry, but there is definitely a lot of fear associated with it. In fact, many cooks avoid pastry making, which limits them greatly in the kitchen. As with so many basic skills, pastry making is best mastered through practice. It is, therefore, a good plan to create menus around pastry-based dishes so that you have no waste as you learn.

Dough gets its strength from the gluten in the flour and its tenderness from the fat. The amount of water added to the basic mixture is crucial, as the water enables the gluten molecules to form when the flour is mixed with the liquid. Too much water and the dough will be hard and dry; with too little water, it will be crumbly and unworkable. In addition, the amount of water needed depends upon external factors such as temperature and humidity, as well as the moisture in the flour, the type of fat used, and how the fat and flour have been mixed together. As a general rule, just enough water should be added to allow the flour and fat mixture to hold together when pressed between your fingertips.

The basic pastry doughs are *pâte brisée*, *pâte sucrée*, *pâte sablée*, and *pâte feuilletée*. Another basic dough, *pâte à choux*, will be discussed on page 150. All of these doughs are essential, not only to pastry and baking, but to French cuisine in general.

Basic Components of Classic Pastry Doughs

Flour: For pastry making, it is generally recommended that a low-protein pastry or cake flour be used to create a tender dough. Cake flour has a smooth texture with an almost white color and, because it contains fewer gluten-producing proteins, creates a product that is light-textured and somewhat crumbly. The flour in France, however, has a somewhat higher protein content—it's closer to all-purpose flour in gluten strength, texture, and color. For that reason, a mixture of cake flour and all-purpose flour might be used.

Fat: Fat plays two very important roles in pastry dough: It tenderizes the dough, and it provides the desired flakiness in the finished pastry. Tenderization occurs as the fat in the dough prevents the buildup of gluten by separating and lubricating the proteins in the flour. Flakiness occurs because the fat keeps the components of the dough separate until the dough structure sets during the baking process. Although vegetable shortening, lard, or other fat can be used, unsalted butter is almost always the fat of choice for classic French pastry doughs. (In some regional French specialties, lard or poultry or game fat is used.) Whatever fat is used, it must always be well chilled. If it is too soft, it will break down too early and melt into the flour; if it is frozen, it will be too hard to combine easily.

Of all the fats that can be used, butter infuses the best flavor; however, it is also the most difficult to work with. Because of its low melting point, it must be thoroughly chilled before use, as well as when the baking process begins. The fact that it is also composed of at least 20 percent water allows it to easily— sometimes too easily—activate the gluten in the flour.

Vegetable shortening or lard are most often called for when making American pie doughs. Even when cold, these fats are soft and malleable, but since they have a very high melting point, they create a very flaky pastry.

Because it completely surrounds the flour proteins, preventing gluten development, oil can make an extremely tender crust. However, it will not produce the desired flakiness.

Liquid: Water is usually the liquid of choice in classic French tart doughs because it does not impart any residual flavor. However, due to its lack of fat, water does contribute to gluten development. Milk, eggs, juice, sour cream, or even cream cheese may also be used, each affecting the finished dough in a different way. Milk will add some flavor and heighten the color of the baked dough. Juices, especially acidic ones, will break down gluten, but will also prevent the desired browning during baking. Cream, sour cream,

and cream cheese all contain fats, acids, and sugars, which prohibit gluten development. A bit of acid also produces a very flaky finished product.

When adding the liquid ingredients to the flour-and-fat combination, keep in mind that the amount of liquid required varies depending on the moisture content of the flour, the kind of fat, and the temperature and humidity of the day. The liquid should be very cold, which helps retard the development of the gluten in the flour and prevents the fat from melting too quickly. Liquid should be added little by little and mixed in quickly and easily. Add just enough to hold the dough together when pressed lightly into a ball between your fingertips. If the dough is sticky or easily pulls into a mass, it is too wet. It will stick to the work surface, is almost impossible to roll, and shrinks when baked. A dry dough, on the other hand, is difficult to roll and will crack and fall apart.

When eggs are added to a pastry dough, they count toward the liquid portion of the basic ingredients. Since they contain fat and protein, they will prevent gluten development and heighten the color of the baked pastry. Because of their viscosity, they will not combine easily with flour if not thoroughly beaten, either by themselves or with other liquid ingredients before being added.

No matter the type of liquid used, learning to mix it in quickly and knowing how much to add are perhaps the most crucial skills involved in making a light and flaky pastry. Like many other kitchen techniques, it simply requires patience and practice to succeed.

Salt: Salt hinders gluten development in pastry doughs. To prevent this, it should always be mixed with the flour, never with the liquid. Salt also adds flavor to the dough.

Sugar: The addition of sugar to a pastry dough prevents gluten development and helps create a tender crust. Through caramelization during the baking process, sugar also adds golden color. And, of course, it adds sweetness. Granulated sugar is the form most commonly used in classic doughs, although confectioners' sugar can also be used.

Dean's Tip

"I love to scale [weigh] all of my ingredients, even liquids. This is the most precise way to accomplish a perfect recipe."
Dean Jacques Torres

Pâte Brisée, Pâte Sucrée, and Pâte Sablée

Of the three basic types of classic pastry dough, *pâte brisée* is used for all manner of tarts (both savory and sweet); *pâte sucrée* and the even sweeter *pâte sablée* are used solely with sweets. As with all pastry doughs, making them successfully requires the use of specific ingredients, the exact measurement of these ingredients, and careful adherence to the procedure outlined in the recipe. Never improvise or substitute ingredients until you have completely mastered the technique.

Pâte Brisée

Because of its versatility, *pâte brisée* is the most frequently made basic dough. It is very flaky and usually has little flavor other than that provided by the butter and the addition of salt. It is created with a low-protein (cake or pastry) flour, fat (butter, lard, or shortening), salt, and water (or other liquids substituted for flavor and appearance). A small amount of sugar can be added to increase its ability to take on color or to heighten its flavor when used with a sweet filling. When eggs are added to this dough, the result is a firmer, sturdier, and slightly less delicate finished pastry.

Literally translated, *pâte brisée* means "broken dough," which aptly describes the flaky, layered texture of the finished pastry. This is the result of incorporating fat into the flour in small fragments that eventually melt, leaving a void or pocket inside the dough.

The first rule to remember when making **pâte brisée**—or any pastry—is to use an easy hand. Work the dough as little as possible to keep from overdeveloping the gluten. This occurs when the protein molecules in the flour are moistened with liquid as the ingredients are worked together. A small amount of gluten is necessary to hold the dough together, but if the gluten is overexpanded, the pastry will be too elastic, shrink, and be hard and tough when baked.

To make *pâte brisée*, first combine the flour and salt. When blended, begin "cutting" the chilled fat into the mix, working until the pieces of fat are the size of dried lentils or split peas. The fat can be cut in with a pastry blender, two kitchen knives, or the paddle attachment of an electric mixer. Care must be taken that the fat particles are cut to the right size; too small and the dough will be crumbly, too large and, as the fat melts, it will create holes that go completely through the dough. Once the fat has been appropriately cut in, begin adding the water. Remember, work the dough as little as possible.

After mixing, the dough should rest for several hours in the refrigerator before being rolled out and molded. This allows some of the gluten to relax and, more importantly, causes the fat to firm up and allows the moisture to become evenly distributed throughout the dough.

Pâte Sucrée

Literally translated as "sugared dough," *pâte sucrée* is simply a *pâte brisée* with a higher proportion of sugar and (usually) eggs. This results in a tender dough that, when baked, is crumbly rather than flaky and has a lovely golden color. Because of the high sugar content, it burns faster than doughs containing a lesser amount of sweetener.

To make *pâte sucrée*, follow the procedure for *pâte brisée*, cutting the fat into the flour mix until it completely "covers" the flour. You do not want the relatively large pieces of fat needed for *pâte brisée*. *Pâte sucrée* can also be made using the creaming method, whereby the fat and sugar are first worked together until light and airy. The liquid (usually eggs) is then added and the flour is blended in as the final step. The high content of sugar and fat in a *pâte sucrée* prevents the development of gluten. As with *pâte brisée*, the dough should be rest, chilled, for several hours before being rolled out and molded.

Pâte Sablée

Literally translated as "sandy dough," *pâte sablée* is a delicate dough used exclusively for cookies and sweet

Dean's Tip

"For any recipe, flour should always be sifted before using. And before starting any recipe, be sure to have all of the necessary equipment at hand. If using the oven, be sure to preheat it."

Dean Alain Sailhac

tarts. It is a basically *pâte sucrée* with an even higher proportion of sugar and less liquid, which transforms it into something cookielike. The texture is so different from that of *pâte brisée* and *pâte sucrée* that it is often referred to as "shortbread" dough.

To make *pâte sablée*, either the cutting or creaming method may be used. The dough can be difficult to work with and should be very well chilled before being rolled out, shaped, and baked.

Working with Tart Doughs

Despite the differences between the three basic tart doughs, the basic steps for rolling and shaping them are much the same. All these doughs contain a fair amount of fat, so they require a deft hand to keep them from being overworked.

Once the pastry dough has been mixed, it should be formed into a ball or slightly flattened disk (make certain your hands are clean, cool, and dry), then wrapped in plastic film and chilled. Chilling, one of the most important steps in pastry making, allows the gluten to rest and assists in the creation of a flaky, tender pastry that does not shrink when baked. With the exception of *pâte à choux* (see page 150), all pastry dough should be refrigerated for at least 30 minutes after being made. It is even more beneficial to refrigerate it for 24 hours. In most cases, the dough should be chilled again after it has been rolled and shaped.

Rolling out the dough is where many cooks panic. Don't! Just remember the light hand. All doughs should be rolled out on a clean, cool surface—well-chilled marble is an exceptional anchor. (Some cooks have a piece of marble just for this purpose.) Prepare the rolling surface by lightly coating it with flour. Lightly press the chilled dough onto the floured surface, using the heel of your hand to flatten it slightly. If the dough is too firm, strike it a few times with the rolling pin to make it pliable. Lightly flour the rolling pin and, using quick, firm, consistent strokes, begin rolling the dough from the center outward, away from yourself, taking care not to roll all the way off the edge, as this will thin it out. Return to the center of the dough and repeat the rolling motion, this time rolling toward yourself. After rolling once in each direction, carefully lift and turn the dough 90 degrees, checking as you turn that the dough is not sticking to the surface or the rolling pin. If it is, carefully drag the slightly rolled dough through the flour on the rolling surface or lightly dust the top of the dough with a little flour to keep the pin from sticking. Again, roll away and toward yourself and turn the dough 90 degrees. Continue rolling and turning until the dough is a circle (or other shape specified) that is at least 2 inches greater than the diameter of the pan you plan to line. Always roll forward and backward, never side to side, as this will stretch the dough and cause it to shrink during baking. For a classic French tart, the dough should be approximately 3 millimeters (⅛ inch) thick.

After rolling, use a bench brush (see page 23) to gently brush off the top of the dough. Roll the dough around the rolling pin, unroll it in the opposite direction and brush the excess flour from the other side.

Once rolled and brushed clean, the dough is transferred to the pan.

There are three basic methods for doing this:

1. Lift the dough gently and fold it in half over the rolling pin and then slip it, still folded, into the pan. Unfold the circle to cover the bottom of the pan, and remove the rolling pin.
2. Carefully fold the dough in half and then in quarters and then place the point where the two folds meet into the center of the pan. Unfold the quartered dough to cover the bottom of the pan.
3. Slide both hands, fully opened, under the dough and gently and carefully lift it up and into the pan.

For each method, once positioned in the pan the dough must be worked into the edges. Slowly turning the pan, gently push the dough into the bottom and against the edges. Take care not to pull or stretch the dough or it will shrink and crack as it bakes. Smooth the pastry into the pan with quick, light, pressing movements,

making certain there are no holes from which the juices of the filling can escape. If using a bottom crust only, as for a tart, make sure the edges are neat. After the dough is completely pressed into the pan (or mold), trim the excess dough a bit at a time—it is better to remove too little than too much. If, at any point during the rolling and shaping, the dough becomes soft and sticky or too warm to work with easily, chill it for at least 15 minutes before continuing to work it.

Many recipes call for a pastry shell to be **docked**. This is a simple process of poking small holes in the raw dough, either before or after it is placed in the pan, to allow for the release of steam and trapped air during baking. The holes can be made by using either the tines of a table fork or a roller docker. Tart dough is docked when the filling to be used is not heavy enough to weigh it down and keep it from rising (see one-step-method tarts, below) and for blind-baked shells (see two-step-method tarts, below). The pricked dough will not usually allow any leakage. Tart dough is not docked if the filling is very liquid and might seep through the holes, causing sticking and burning in the bottom of the pan.

Tarts are filled and baked using different methods. The easiest to assemble and bake is the **one-step method**, whereby the raw shell is filled and the shell and filling are baked together. A good example would be a classic *Tarte aux Pommes* (see page 96). This method usually requires a long baking time to ensure that both the filling and the dough are cooked through.

The **two-step method** requires that the pastry shell be partially or completely baked and then cooled before any filling is added. For a soft filling such as a custard, that bakes quickly and therefore requires a

low temperature—examples include *Quiche Lorraine* (see page 261), *Tarte Alsacienne* (see page 101), and *Tartelettes au Citron* (see page 117)—or a filling that needs no further cooking, such as fresh fruit, *ganache*, or Bavarian cream, the pastry shell must be thoroughly baked beforehand to prevent it from becoming soggy. This process is called *cuire à blanc*, or blind-baking.

To blind-bake a tart shell, the molded, docked pastry shell is first refrigerated for at least 15 minutes, then lined with a piece of parchment paper cut to fit the bottom and come up the sides of the pan. The paper-coated pastry is then filled with dried beans or rice or pastry weights (small metal or ceramic rounds made for this purpose) or a necklace of metal pie weights or a heavy dog choke collar (both of which have the advantage of being an easy-to-handle single piece) to weight it down so that it does not form air pockets and will keep its shape during the initial baking. The prepared shell is placed in a preheated, fairly hot oven (usually 204°C/400°F) and baked until it looks chalky white. It is then removed from the oven, the weights and parchment paper are taken out, and the pastry is returned to a moderate oven (162°C /325°F) oven to be baked until golden and cooked through.

If a filling requires substantial cooking, the pastry shell can still be prepared in this fashion. In such a case, it should be baked just until cooked through without turning color, then allowed to cool before it is filled and returned to the oven for complete baking.

Blind-baked tart shells can be prepared up to a day in advance, but since they are fragile, there is always the risk of damage during storage.

Chef Melissa Murphy

Pastry Chef / Co-Owner, Sweet Melissa Patisserie
The French Culinary Institute, Class of October 1995

North Fork Peach-Raspberry Pie

Makes one 10-inch double-crust pie

My family used to have a summer house on Shelter Island, just off the North Fork on New York's Long Island. The car trip out was grueling on those late Friday afternoons. Once we exited the congested expressway, we'd crawl through miles and miles of potato farms. Briermere Farm was our beacon near the end of the road. We'd stop to stretch and pick up fresh vegetables and a couple of their handmade fruit pies for the weekend. Their peach-raspberry pie alone made the entire trip worthwhile. This is my homage to those pies of my childhood.

Flour for dusting
All Butter Pie Dough (recipe follows)
1 large egg, at room temperature
30 milliliters (2 tablespoons) heavy cream
⅛ teaspoon, plus pinch salt
180 grams (6⅓ ounces) sugar, plus more for
  sprinkling
34 grams (3 tablespoons) tapioca flour

14 grams (2 tablespoons) cornstarch
1.6 kilograms (6 cups, or about 3½ pounds) sliced,
  peeled ripe peaches
200 grams (1 pint) fresh raspberries
Juice and zest of 1 lemon
Whipped cream for serving (optional)

Position a rack in the bottom third of the oven and preheat the oven to 177°C (350°F).

Line a cookie sheet with parchment paper. Set aside.

Lightly flour a clean, flat work surface. Divide the pie dough into two equal pieces and, working with one piece at a time, roll each one out to a 36-centimeter (14-inch) circle about 6 millimeters (¼ inch) thick.

Fit one of the pieces into a 10-inch pie plate and lay the other one on the parchment paper–lined cookie sheet. Place both in the refrigerator to chill.

Combine the egg and heavy cream with a pinch of salt in a small bowl. Whisk together with a kitchen fork to make a combined egg wash. Set aside.

Combine the sugar with the tapioca flour, cornstarch, and remaining salt in a small bowl, whisking to blend.

Combine the peaches and raspberries with the lemon juice and zest in a large mixing bowl. Sprinkle the sugar mixture over the top and, using your hands, toss gently to combine.

Remove the pie shell and top from the refrigerator.

Pour the fruit mixture into the unbaked shell. Cover with the remaining dough circle. Fold the edges of the dough together and then, using your fingertips, crimp the edges together to make a neat, attractive edge.

Using a pastry brush, lightly coat the surface of the pie with the egg wash. Using a small, sharp knife, cut 4 steam vents in the top of the pie. Sprinkle the surface with sugar.

Bake for about 90 minutes, or until the juices are thick and bubbling out of the pie.

Remove from the oven and set on a wire rack to cool to room temperature before serving with whipped cream, if desired.

All Butter Pie Dough

320 grams (11¼ ounces) all-purpose flour

42 grams (2 tablespoons) sugar

¼ teaspoon baking powder

¼ teaspoon salt

225 grams (8 ounces) very cold unsalted butter, cut into 1.3-centimeter (½-inch) pieces

Combine the flour, sugar, baking powder, and salt in a large mixing bowl, whisking to blend.
Add the butter, in pieces, tossing to coat each piece with the flour mixture.

Using a pastry blender, cut the butter into the flour until the mixture resembles large peas.

Sprinkle 75 milliliters (5 tablespoons) of ice water over the mixture and, using a kitchen fork, toss to combine. The dough should hold together when squeezed in your hand. If not, add the additional 15 milliliters (1 tablespoon) ice water.

Use as directed in the above recipe.

Demonstration

Pâte Brisée ("Broken Dough" Tart or Pie Pastry)

Makes pastry for two 8-to 9-inch tarts
Estimated time to complete: 45 minutes

Ingredients	Equipment
250 grams (8¾ ounces) cake flour	Sifter
½ teaspoon salt	Metal or plastic pastry scraper (optional)
½ teaspoon sugar	Plastic film
125 grams (4½ ounces) very cold unsalted butter, cut into small pieces	
65 milliliters (¼ cup plus 1 teaspoon) very cold water, or 1 large egg mixed with 1 teaspoon very cold water, plus additional ice water, if needed	

Prepare your *mise en place*.

Sift the flour, salt, and sugar together directly onto the work surface.

Add the butter to the sifted flour mixture and cut it into the flour with a pastry scraper, working until the pieces of butter are the size of dried lentils or split

peas. There should be no large butter particles. This procedure is called *sablage* in French, from the verb *sabler*, meaning "to make sandy."

Form a well in the center of the butter-and-flour mixture and pour the water or the water-and-egg mixture into it. Working quickly and smoothly, incorporate the

liquid into the butter-and-flour mixture just until the dough holds together, adding ice water if necessary. Do not add too much liquid or the dough will be sticky and tough. Do not overwork the dough. Crush any lumps against the work surface with the heel of your hand or the pastry scraper, and press them back into the dough to combine. This process is called *fraisage*, from the verb *fraiser* ("to mill").

Alternatively, prepare the dough in an electric mixer fitted with the paddle attachment. Sift the flour, salt, and sugar directly into the mixer bowl. Cut the butter into 1.3-centimeter (½-inch) cubes and add it to the flour mixture. Turn the machine on low and mix the ingredients just until the butter pieces are approximately 3 millimeters (⅛ inch). Gradually add the cold liquid to the dough, mixing until it is soft and shaggy. Scrape the dough onto a lightly floured work surface and work it by hand until it is homogeneous (*fraisage*).

Gather the dough together, form it into a disk, wrap the disk in plastic, and refrigerate it for at least 30 minutes or up to 24 hours before rolling it into the shape required.

TIPS

This dough can also be made without the addition of sugar. If so, it will be flavored by the salt. This pastry is known as *pâte salée*.

Depending upon the amount of moisture in the flour and in the air, the amount of water needed to hydrate the dough will vary greatly.

The dough must be well chilled before rolling and shaping.

If preparing the dough in an electric mixer, stop and start the machine regularly to check on the size of the butter particles.

EVALUATING YOUR SUCCESS

When rolling out the dough, streaks of butter should be visible. If the butter pieces are so large that there is no dough sandwiching them, fold the dough several times and roll it out again. Large pieces of butter will form holes while the dough is baking. If no butter is visible, either the butter was cut too small and has melted into the dough or the dough was overworked. The baked pastry will not be tender and flaky.

If the dough is extremely crumbly and cracks when rolled, not enough water was added.

If the dough is extremely soft after thorough chilling, too much water was added.

If the dough is elastic when rolled, it was overworked. Resting and chilling may redeem it somewhat, but it will not be tender when baked.

The dough should be flaky and tender when baked.

Flakiness results when the butter pieces sandwiched between the dough melt and create steam during the baking process. This forces the dough apart and allows the butter to melt into it.

Demonstration

Pâte Sucrée (Sweet Tart Dough)

Makes pastry for two 8- to 9-inch tarts
Estimated time to complete: 45 minutes

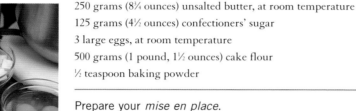

Ingredients	Equipment
250 grams (8¾ ounces) unsalted butter, at room temperature	Standing electric mixer fitted with paddle attachment
125 grams (4½ ounces) confectioners' sugar	Rubber spatula
3 large eggs, at room temperature	Plastic film
500 grams (1 pound, 1½ ounces) cake flour	
½ teaspoon baking powder	

Prepare your *mise en place*.

Place the butter in the bowl of a standing electric mixer fitted with the paddle attachment. Add the sugar and beat on low to just combine. Raise the speed to medium-high and beat until the mixture is light and creamy.

Add the eggs one at a time, mixing well after each addition. (Do not add them too quickly or the mixture will separate. If separation occurs, continue mixing until the mixture comes back together. If it does not homogenize after a period of mixing, add just a spoonful of flour to encourage the process.)

When the eggs are well incorporated, turn off the motor and add the cake flour and baking powder all at once. Return the machine to slow speed and, scraping down the sides of the bowl with a rubber spatula, beat until the flour is just incorporated. Do not overmix.

Using the spatula, scrape the dough from the bowl. Gather the dough together and form it into a disk. Wrap the disk in plastic film and refrigerate it for at least 30 minutes or up to 1 week before rolling it into the shape required. The dough may also be wrapped and frozen for up to 3 months.

TIPS

If all ingredients are at room temperature, the dough will come together quicker and easier.

This dough may be used for both tart shells and cookies.

Any dough scraps may be rerolled, but the dough will be slightly tougher.

EVALUATING YOUR SUCCESS

The dough should be light yellow.

The ingredients should be completely homogenized.

The dough should roll out easily with no cracking.

The dough should be tender and crumbly when baked.

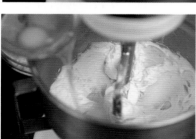

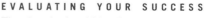

Demonstration

Pâte Sablée (Shortbread or Shortcrust Dough)

Makes pastry for two 8- to 9-inch tarts
Estimated time to complete: 45 minutes

Ingredients	Equipment

150 grams (5⅓ ounces) unsalted butter, at room temperature
90 grams (3¼ ounces) confectioners' sugar
Pinch salt
2 large egg yolks
255 grams (9 ounces) cake flour, sifted

Sifter
Electric mixer with paddle attachment
Rubber spatula
Plastic film

Prepare your *mise en place*.

Place the butter, sugar, and salt in the bowl of a standing electric mixer fitted with the paddle attachment. Beat at medium speed for about 4 minutes, or until the mixture is light and fluffy.

Add the egg yolks one at a time, beating to fully incorporate after each addition.

Turn off the motor and add the sifted cake flour all at once. Return the machine to slow speed and, scraping down the sides of the bowl with a rubber spatula, beat until the flour is just incorporated. If the dough seems dry or crumbly, add 15 to 30 milliliters (1 to 2 tablespoons) ice water to soften. Make the addition slowly and carefully so that the dough does not get too wet. Using the spatula, scrape the dough from the mixing bowl. Gather the dough together and form it into a disk. Wrap the disk in plastic film and refrigerate it for at least 1 hour or up to 1 week before rolling it into the shape required. Note that if the dough is not well chilled, it will be very difficult to roll.

The dough may also be stored, well wrapped and frozen, for up to 1 month. Unwrap and thaw before using.

TIPS
This dough may be used to make cookies as well as tart shells.

Pâte sablée is a very fragile dough, which should not be overworked. When rolling it out and transferring the rolled dough to a tart pan or ring, work quickly and carefully.

If the dough breaks when being rolled, just press it back together. It is a very forgiving dough that can be manipulated more easily than other doughs. Although frowned upon in a professional kitchen, when all else fails, don't hesitate to roll the dough between two pieces of plastic film.

When blind-baking, watch carefully to monitor the color. Remove the shell from the oven just as soon as it begins to change color, as it will quickly burn. Always cool a blind-baked shell before filling it. It will become soggy otherwise.

EVALUATING YOUR SUCCESS
The dough should be crumbly and buttery.

If the dough is tough and compacted, it was overworked.

The rolled dough should be of an even thickness.

The baked dough should be firm and golden brown.

Demonstration

Tarte aux Pommes (Apple Tart)

Makes one 9-inch tart

Estimated time to complete: 90 minutes

Ingredients	Equipment
Flour for dusting	Rolling pin
1 recipe *Pâte Brisée, Pâte Sucrée*, or *Pâte Sablée* (see pages 92, 94, and 95)	Pastry brush
	9-inch tart pan
For the apple compote	Vegetable peeler
370 grams (13 ounces) Golden Delicious apples	Paring knife
½ lemon	Melon baller, optional
75 grams (2⅔ ounces) sugar	Medium saucepan
1 vanilla bean, split lengthwise	Wooden spoon
	Rubber spaula
For the garnish	Baking sheet with sides
3 (about 1 pound) Golden Delicious apples	Plastic film
½ lemon	2 small bowls
	Metal spoon
For the *nappage*	Wire rack
100 grams (3½ ounces) apricot jam	Small saucepan
	Fine-mesh sieve
	Serving platter

Prepare your *mise en place*.

Lightly flour a clean, flat work surface. Place the dough in the center of the floured surface and, using a rolling pin, roll the dough out to a 25-centimeter (10-inch) circle about 3 millimeters (⅛ inch) thick. Using a pastry brush, lightly brush off excess flour.

Roll the circle up and over the rolling pin and carefully transfer it to the tart pan. Using your fingertips, gently press the dough into the pan to make a neat fit. Pinch off any excess dough around the edges to neaten. Transfer the shell to the refrigerator for 30 minutes to chill.

While the dough is chilling, prepare the apple compote.

Using a vegetable peeler, peel the apples. Using a paring knife, cut them in half lengthwise; remove the core with the paring knife or a melon baller. Generously rub the apples with the cut lemon to prevent discoloration. Do not put the apples in acidulated water or the natural juices and sugars will be leached out. Cut the apples into 6-millimeter (¼-inch) cubes, keeping the pieces as equal in size as possible so that they will cook evenly.

Combine the sugar and 50 milliliters (3 tablespoons plus 1 teaspoon) water in a medium saucepan over medium heat. Add the apples and, using a paring knife, scrape the seeds from the vanilla bean into the pan. Add the scraped bean, cover, and place over low

heat. Cook, stirring occasionally with a wooden spoon, for about 20 minutes, or until the apples are translucent and all the moisture has evaporated. Take care that the apples do not disintegrate—you want a chunky mixture. If the apples are cooked before the moisture has evaporated, uncover the pan and raise the heat to high to quickly dry them out. If the moisture evaporates before the apples are ready, add a tablespoon of water or the apples will begin to caramelize and burn.

Remove the pan from the heat and, using a rubber spatula, spread the compote out on a plastic film–wrapped sheet pan to stop the cooking. Cover with plastic film and let cool. While the compote is cooling, prepare the garnish.

Using a vegetable peeler, peel the apples. Using a paring knife, cut them in half lengthwise; remove the core with the paring knife or a melon baller. Generously rub the apples with the cut lemon to prevent discoloration. Do not put the apples in acidulated water or the natural juices and sugars will be leached out.

Using a chef's knife, cut each apple half lengthwise into very thin slices, no more than 3 millimeters (⅛ inch) thick. Place the apple slices in a small bowl and, using the lemon half, squeeze lemon juice over them, tossing to coat.

Preheat the oven to 177°C (350°F).

Remove the tart shell from the refrigerator. Spoon the

apple compote into the shell, spreading it out with a rubber spatula to make an even layer that fills the shell three-quarters full.

Starting with the outside edge, begin arranging the apple slices, slightly overlapping, in concentric circles over the top of the compote. Fill in any holes with apple scraps and then finish the center with a tight circle of apple slices.

Bake for about 1 hour, or until the crust is golden and the apple slices are beautifully caramelized and cooked through.

Remove from the oven and place on a wire rack to cool slightly.

To make the glaze, combine the apricot jam with 20 milliliters (3 tablespoons plus 1 teaspoon) water in a

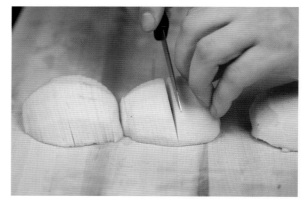

small saucepan over medium heat and cook for just about a minute to heat through. Remove from the heat and press through a fine-mesh sieve into a small bowl. Set aside.

Unmold the tart and place on a serving platter. Using a pastry brush, lightly coat the entire top with the warm apricot glaze.

Serve warm or at room temperature.

TIPS

The tart may be made ahead and refrigerated for up to 2 days before baking. If so, lightly coat the top with melted, unsalted butter and cover with plastic film before storing.

For additional sweetness and flavor, sprinkle the top of the tart with granulated sugar or vanilla sugar (see page 82) before baking.

EVALUATING YOUR SUCCESS

The apples should be uniform, even and very thin.

The apricot *nappage* should completely, but lightly, cover the apples.

The crust should have an even edge.

The apples should be uniformly browned when the tart has finished baking.

When properly baked, the crust will be completely cooked in the center.

Demonstration

Tartelettes Tatin façon Rapide (Quick Apple Tartlets)

Makes four 4-inch tarts

Estimated time to complete: 1 hour 10 minutes

Ingredients	Equipment
200 grams (7 ounces) sugar	Small saucepan
4 Granny Smith apples	Pastry brush
Flour for dusting	Four 4-inch round tartlet pans
240 grams (8½ ounces) *Pâte Sucrée* (see page 94)	Vegetable peeler
	Paring knife
	Melon baller, optional
	Rolling pin
	Small sharp knife or pastry cutter

Prepare your *mise en place*.

Place the sugar in a small saucepan with just enough cold water to cover and thoroughly moisten the sugar. Too much water will increase the cooking time dramatically. Using a wet pastry brush, clean the interior sides of the pan of any clinging sugar crystals. This will prevent crystallization.

Place the saucepan over high heat and cook for about 15 minutes, or until the sugar is the color of maple syrup and nicely caramelized (160°C/320°F) on a candy thermometer. Once the liquid begins to color, swirl the mixture around in the pan to even out the color as it cooks. (It is easier to distinguish the appropriate color when the mixture is not boiling. Simply remove the pan from the heat for a moment and let the bubbles subside. The desired color is really up to the cook; however, a too light caramel will be flavorless, and a too dark syrup will be bitter.)

Remove the syrup from the heat and pour an equal portion into each of the tartlet pans.

Preheat the oven to 177°C (350°F).

While the syrup is cooking, peel the apples. Cut them in half lengthwise and remove the core, using a melon baller, if desired. Cut each half lengthwise into 4 wedges.

Arrange an equal number of apple wedges in a decorative pattern in each tartlet pan.

Lightly flour a clean, flat work surface. Place the dough in the center of the floured surface and, using a rolling pin, roll the dough out to a 25-centimeter (10-inch) circle about 3 millimeters (⅛ inch) thick. Using a small, sharp knife or pastry cutter, cut four circles from the dough exactly the size of the tartlet pans. Place one circle on top of the apples in each pan. The tartlets may be made up to this point, covered with plastic film, and refrigerated for up to 3 days.

Bake the tartlets for about 30 minutes, or until the pastry is golden brown.

Remove the tartlets from the oven and carefully turn each one upside down, unmolding them onto individual plates. Serve warm.

The dough scraps can be saved and used for another purpose, such as cookies or other tart shells.

The *pâte sucrée* should be a thin, even disk that, when baked, is golden brown and cooked through with no burnt edges.

The tartlets must be unmolded while still hot or the caramel will harden and make it impossible to get them out of the pans.

When baked, the apples should retain their shape, but be tender and golden brown.

The tartlets should be served the day they are made.

In the unmolded dessert, the apples should completely cover the pastry.

The baked tartlets should have a distinct caramel flavor with no trace of bitterness.

Demonstration

Tarte Alsacienne (Alsatian Apple Tart)

Makes one 9-inch tart
Estimated time to complete: 1 hour

Ingredients	Equipment
Flour for dusting	Rolling pin
1 recipe *Pâte Brisée, Pâte Sucrée*, or *Pâte Sablée* (see pages 92, 94, and 95)	9-inch tart pan
2 Golden Delicious or other sweet, firm apples	Parchment paper
60 grams (2 ounces) sugar	Pastry weights or dried beans
1 teaspoon brandy	Vegetable peeler
1 large egg, at room temperature	Paring knife
50 milliliters (3 tablespoons plus 1 teaspoon) whole milk	Melon baller, optional
50 milliliters (3 tablespoons plus 1 teaspoon) heavy cream	Medium sauté pan
½ teaspoon pure vanilla extract	Wooden spatula
	Slotted spoon
	2 medium mixing bowls
	Chinois
	Baking sheet
	Wire rack

Prepare your *mise en place*.

Lightly flour a clean, flat work surface. Place the dough in the center of the floured surface and, using a rolling pin, roll it out to a 25-centimeter (10-inch) circle about 3 millimeters (⅛ inch) thick.

Roll the circle up and over the rolling pin and carefully transfer it the tart pan. Using your fingertips, gently press the dough into the pan to make a neat fit. Pinch off any excess dough around the edges to neaten. Transfer the shell to the refrigerator for 30 minutes to chill.

Preheat the oven to 177°C (350°F).

Cut a round piece of parchment paper large enough to cover the bottom of the shell and come up against the sides, leaving an edge with which you can lift it out of the shell when you need to. Place the parchment paper into the shell and add the pastry weights, spreading them out in an even layer.

Bake the shell for about 10 minutes, or until the pastry is dry and chalky white. Lift out the parchment paper and weights and continue to bake the shell for an additional 15 minutes, or until the pastry is lightly browned and cooked through. Remove the pastry shell from the oven and set it aside to cool.

Reduce the oven temperature to 121°C (250°F).

While the pastry is chilling and baking, prepare the apples and custard.

Peel the apples and cut them in half lengthwise. Core them, using a melon baller if desired. Cut each half lengthwise into 5 equal wedges.

Place a medium sauté pan over medium heat. When hot, add the apple wedges and, using a wooden spatula, turn and move the pieces around until they begin to color. Sprinkle the apple pieces with half of the sugar. Lower the heat and cook, stirring occasionally to prevent burning, for about 5 minutes, or until the sugar has caramelized the apples. Add the brandy,

ignite, and flambé for a minute to burn off the taste of the alcohol and to thicken the liquid.

Using a slotted spoon, transfer the apples to a plate to cool.

Combine the egg, milk, cream, and vanilla with the remaining 30 grams (1 ounce) sugar in a mixing bowl, whisking to combine well. When blended, pour the custard through a *chinois* into a clean mixing bowl.

When the pastry shell and the apples are cool, arrange the apple wedges in a decorative pattern over the bottom of the shell. Place the shell on a baking sheet in the preheated oven.

Carefully pour the custard over the apples. Bake for about 20 minutes, or until the custard is set.

Place on a wire rack to rest and cool for at least 5 minutes before cutting into wedges and serving warm or at room temperature.

TIPS

Make sure that there are no holes, tears, or cracks in the baked pastry shell before filling or the custard will leak through and the tart will stick to the pan. If needed, seal the pastry by brushing it with an egg wash or beaten egg white, or fill the holes with raw dough.

If, for any reason, the custard begins to leak during baking, prepare another recipe of the custard and add as much as is necessary to the baking tart to keep the level even with the edge of the tart shell. This will require some additional baking time.

As the baked tart cools, the apples will shrink away from the custard, so it should be served as soon after baking as possible.

EVALUATING YOUR SUCCESS
The blind-baked shell should be smooth, even, and golden brown, covering the entire bottom and sides of the pan.

The apples should be beautifully caramelized, with no trace of burning.

The custard should reach the top edge of the tart shell.

The baked custard should be smooth, with no evidence of curdling.

Pastry Chef Donna Sardella

Basilico Restaurant, Milburn, New Jersey
The French Culinary Institute, Culinary Program, August 1999

Pear Tarts with Chocolate Goat Cheese and Honey

Makes five 4-inch tarts or one 8-inch tart

5 Bosc or other firm pears, peeled
100 grams (3½ ounces) sugar
1 teaspoon ground cinnamon
Flour for dusting
Tart Dough (recipe follows)
2 logs chocolate goat cheese (see Note)
2 tablespoons honey
Vanilla ice cream, optional

Peel, core, and cut the pears into 2.5-centimeter (1-inch) cubes. Place the cubed pears in a medium heavy-bottomed saucepan. Stir in the sugar and place over low heat. Cover and cook, stirring occasionally, for about 15 minutes, or until the pears are just tender.

Stir in the cinnamon and cook for another minute or two to just infuse the spice into the pears.

Set aside to cool.

Lightly flour a clean, flat work surface. Place the dough in the center of the floured surface and, using a rolling pin, roll it out to about 3 millimeters (⅛ inch) thick. Cut the dough into 5 circles about 14 centimeters (5½ inches) in diameter.

Working with one piece at a time, roll the circles up and over the rolling pin and carefully transfer them to the individual tart pans. Using your fingertips, gently press the dough into the pan to make a neat fit. Pinch off any excess dough around the edges to neaten. Transfer the shells to the refrigerator for 30 minutes to chill.

Preheat the oven to 177°C (350°F).

Place a 13-centimeter (5-inch) round of parchment paper in the bottom of each shell and push it up against the sides, leaving an edge with which you can lift it out of the shell when you need to. Add pastry weights, spreading them out in an even layer over the bottom of each pan.

Bake the shells for about 10 minutes, or until the pastry is dry and chalky white. Lift out the parchment paper and weights and continue to bake for an additional 12 minutes, or until the pastry is lightly browned and cooked through.

Set aside to cool.

When ready to finish the tarts, return the oven to 177°C (350°F).

Spoon an equal portion of cooked pears into each baked tart shell. Cut the goat cheese logs crosswise into slices about 3 millimeters (⅛ inch) thick. Place 4 to 5 slices on top of each tart, completely covering the pears. Drizzle with a bit of the honey.

When all the tarts have been covered, bake them for about 5 minutes, or just until the cheese has melted and the honey has glazed the top.

Serve warm, with a small scoop of vanilla ice cream, if desired.

Tart Dough

250 (8¾ ounces) grams cake flour
100 grams (3½ ounces) sugar
200 grams (7 ounces) unsalted butter, cut into cubes
3 large eggs, at room temperature
1 teaspoon orange zest, optional

Sift the flour and sugar together directly on the work surface.

Add the butter to the sifted flour mixture and cut it into the flour with a pastry scraper, working until the pieces of butter are the size of dried lentils or split peas. There should be no large butter particles.

Form a well in the center of the butter-and-flour mixture and add the eggs and, if using, the orange zest. Working quickly and smoothly, incorporate the eggs into the mixture just until the dough holds together, adding ice water if necessary. Do not add too much liquid or overwork the dough.

Gather the dough together and form it into a disk. Wrap the disk in plastic film and refrigerate it for at least 30 minutes or up to 24 hours before rolling it into the shape required.

NOTE

Chocolate goat cheese is available from Westfield Farm, 28 Worcester Road, Hubbardston, Massachusetts 01452, (978) 928-5110, www.chevre.com.

Demonstration

Tarte aux Fruits Frais (Fresh Fruit Tart)

Makes one 9-inch tart

Estimated time to complete: 90 minutes

Ingredients	**Equipment**

Ingredients

Flour for dusting

1 recipe *Pâte Brisée, Pâte Sucrée,* or *Pâte Sablée*
   (see pages 92, 94, and 95)

100 grams (3½ ounces) *Crème d'Amandes* (see page 252)

100 grams (3½ ounces) *Crème Pâtissière* (see page 248)

15 milliliters (1 tablespoon) liqueur of choice, or similar
   flavoring (see Tips)

Fresh fruit of choice (see Tips)

For the *nappage*

100 grams (3½ ounces) apricot jam

Equipment

Rolling pin

9-inch tart pan

Standing electric mixer fitted with paddle attachment

Rubber spatula

Pastry bag fitted with large, plain tip

Docker or kitchen fork

Wire rack

Small mixing bowl

Whisk

Small saucepan

Fine-mesh sieve

Small bowl

Pastry brush

Prepare your *mise en place*.

Lightly flour a clean, flat work surface. Place the dough in the center of the floured surface and, using a rolling pin, roll it out to a 28-centimeter (11-inch) circle about 3 millimeters (⅛ inch) thick.

Lift the dough gently and fold it in half over the rolling pin and then slip it, still folded, into the tart pan. Unfold the circle to cover the bottom of the pan and remove the rolling pin.

Slowly turning the pan, gently push the dough into the bottom and against the edges, using quick, light pressing movements, taking care not to pull or stretch the dough. and making certain there are no holes. Make sure the edges are neat and pressed into the corners of the pan. Pinch off any excess dough around the edges to neaten. Transfer the shell to the refrigerator for 30 minutes to chill.

Preheat the oven to 177°C (350°F).

Place the almond cream in the bowl of a standing electric mixer fitted with the paddle attachment and beat until light and fluffy. Using a rubber spatula, scrape the cream into a pastry bag fitted with a large plain tip.

Using a docker or kitchen fork, dock the pastry shell.

Pipe the almond cream over the bottom of the shell and, using a rubber spatula, spread it out to a smooth, even layer.

Bake the tart for about 20 minutes, or until evenly browned, then place it on a wire rack to cool.

When the tart is cool, place the pastry cream in a small mixing bowl and whisk to lighten it slightly and smooth it out. Add the liqueur and whisk to blend.

Using the spatula, spread the pastry cream evenly over the almond cream, smoothing the top.

Arrange the fruit on the tart in a decorative pattern, taking care to cover the pastry cream completely.

Combine the apricot jam with 50 milliliters (3 tablespoons plus 1 teaspoon) water in a small saucepan over medium heat, stirring to melt. When melted, strain it through a small fine-mesh sieve into a small bowl and discard the solids.

Using a pastry brush, lightly coat the fruit with a thin layer of the warm jam.

Refrigerate until ready to serve, but for no longer than 1 day.

TIPS

You can use any type of fruit that is in season or that you prefer. A good combination is 10 strawberries, sliced; 3 oranges, cut into *suprêmes*; 200 grams (1 pint) blueberries; and 4 kiwis, peeled and thinly sliced crosswise.

Although Grand Marnier is a lovely flavoring for the pastry cream in this tart, you can also use kirschwasser or any cognac. Choose something that will enhance the flavor of the fruits used.

The apricot glaze not only adds sheen to the fruit, but also seals it to prevent oxidation.

Fresh fruit tarts must be made on the day they are to be served and kept refrigerated until service.

EVALUATING YOUR SUCCESS

The crust should be thoroughly baked with no bubbles on the bottom.

The *crème d'amandes* should be baked to a medium-brown color, but not burnt.

The fruit should be presented in a very attractive pattern and completely cover the pastry cream.

The glaze should completely cover the fruit in a thin, even layer.

Demonstration

Tarte aux Fruits (Fresh Fruit Tart with Pastry Cream)

Makes one 9-inch tart

Estimated time to complete: 90 minutes

Ingredients	Equipment
Flour for dusting	Rolling pin
1 recipe *Pâte Brisée, Pâte Sucrée,* or *Pâte Sablée* (see pages 92, 94, and 95)	Pastry brush
350 grams (12⅓ ounces) *Crème Pâtissière* (see page 248)	One 9-inch tart pan
50 grams (1¾ ounces) cake or graham cracker crumbs	Docker or kitchen fork
Fresh fruit of choice (see Tips)	Small mixing bowl
	Whisk
For the *nappage*	Rubber spatula
100 grams (3½ ounces) apricot jam	Wire rack
	Small saucepan
	Fine-mesh sieve

Prepare your *mise en place*.

Lightly flour a clean, flat work surface. Place the dough in the center of the floured surface and, using a rolling pin, roll it out to an 28-centimeter (11-inch) circle about 3 millimeters (⅛ inch) thick. Using a pastry brush, lightly brush off the excess flour.

Lift the dough gently and fold it in half over the rolling pin and then slip it, still folded, into the tart pan. Unfold the circle to cover the bottom of the pan and remove the rolling pin.

Slowly turning the pan, gently push the dough into the bottom and against the edges using quick, light pressing movements, taking care not to pull or stretch the dough and making certain there are no holes. Pinch off any excess dough around the edges to neaten.

Using a docker or kitchen fork, dock the bottom of the pastry shell. Transfer the shell to the refrigerator for 30 minutes to chill.

Preheat the oven to 177°C (350°F).

When the pastry shell has chilled, place the pastry cream in a small mixing bowl and whisk to lighten it slightly and smooth it out. Using a rubber spatula, scrape the cream into the pastry shell and spread it out to a smooth, even layer.

Sprinkle the top of the pastry cream with the crumbs. Arrange the fruit over the top in a decorative pattern, taking care to cover the pastry cream completely. Bake the tart for approximately 1 hour, or until the pastry is golden brown and the tart is baked through. Set on a wire rack.

Combine the apricot jam with 100 milliliters (3 tablespoons plus 1 teaspoon) water in a small saucepan over medium heat, stirring to melt. When melted, strain the glaze through a small fine-mesh sieve into a small bowl and discard the solids.

Using a pastry brush, coat the fruit with a thin layer of the warm jam.

Serve immediately, or within a few hours of baking.

TIPS

Do not add any alcohol-based flavoring to the pastry cream or it will not set during baking.

Do not use too many crumbs or the finished tart will have an unpleasant, chewy texture.

Any type of crumb may be used—cake, graham cracker, or unflavored bread. If not available, a nut flour can be substituted.

Plums, apricots, peaches, nectarines, cherries, and blueberries are excellent fruits to use for this tart. Even canned apricots and peaches can be used.

Whatever fruit you use should be very firm and not too ripe or it will release too much juice during the baking. You will need about 10 each of a stone fruit, 908 grams (2 pounds) of cherries, pitted, and 400 grams (2 pints) of blueberries or other berries.

If the fruit used lacks natural sweetness, a light dusting of sugar may be sprinkled over the surface before baking.

EVALUATING YOUR SUCCESS

The baked pastry should be even, smooth, and free of bubbles and completely line the entire pan.

The fruit should completely cover the pastry cream.

When baked, the fruit should be cooked through and tender.

The apricot glaze should cover the fruit in a thin, even layer.

Demonstration

Tartelettes aux Fruits Frais (Fresh Fruit Tartlets)

Makes four 4-inch tartlets
Estimated time to complete: 90 minutes

Ingredients	**Equipment**
Flour for dusting	Rolling pin
1 recipe *Pâte Brisée, Pâte Sucrée*, or *Pâte Sablée* (see pages 92, 94, and 95)	Pastry cutter or small knife
300 grams (11 ounces) *Crème Pâtissière* (see page 248)	Four 4-inch tartlet pans
15 milliliters (1 tablespoon) liqueur of choice or similar flavoring (see page 83)	Four 6-inch round pieces parchment paper
75 milliliters (2½ ounces) heavy cream	Pastry weights or dried beans
Fresh fruit of choice (see Tips)	2 small mixing bowls
	Whisk
For the *nappage*	Standing electric mixer fitted with whip attachment
100 grams (3½ ounces) apricot jam	Rubber spatula
	Pastry bag fitted with a small plain tip
	Offset spatula
	Small saucepan
	Small fine-mesh sieve
	Pastry brush

Prepare your *mise en place*.

Lightly flour a clean, flat work surface. Place the dough in the center of the floured surface and, using a rolling pin, roll it out to a 30-centimeter (12-inch) circle about 3 millimeters (⅛ inch) thick. Using a pastry cutter or a small, sharp knife, cut four circles about 15 centimeters (6 inches) in diameter from the dough.

Working with one circle at a time, lift the dough gently, fold it in half over the rolling pin, and slip it, still folded, into a tartlet pan. Unfold the circle to cover the bottom of the pan and remove the rolling pin. Slowly turning the pan, gently push the dough into the bottom and against the edges using quick, light pressing movements, taking care not to pull or stretch the dough and making certain there are no holes. Pinch off any excess dough around the edges to neaten.

Transfer the lined shells to the refrigerator for 30 minutes to chill.

Preheat the oven to 177°C (350°F).

Place a round piece of parchment paper in the bottom of each shell and push it up against the sides, leaving an edge with which you can lift it out of the shell when you need to. Add the pastry weights, spreading them out in an even layer over the bottom of each shell.

Bake the shells for about 10 minutes, or until the pastry is dry and chalky white. Lift out the parchment paper and weights, and continue to bake for an additional 15 minutes, or until the pastry is lightly browned and cooked through. Set the pastry shells aside to cool.

Place the pastry cream in a small mixing bowl and whisk vigorously to eliminate any lumps. It should be perfectly smooth. Add the liqueur and whisk to blend well.

Place the heavy cream in the bowl of a standing electric mixer fitted with the whip and beat until stiff peaks form (*crème fouettée*). Using a rubber spatula, gently fold the whipped cream into the smooth pastry cream to make a *crème légère*.

Using a rubber spatula, scrape the *crème légère* into a pastry bag fitted with a small, plain tip. Pipe an equal amount of the cream into each baked tartlet shell, smoothing the top with an offset spatula.

Arrange the fruit in a decorative pattern over the surface of each tartlet, taking care to completely cover the cream.

Combine the apricot jam with 50 milliliters (3 tablespoons plus 1 teaspoon) water in a small saucepan over medium heat, stirring to melt. Strain the melted mixture through a small fine-mesh sieve into a small bowl and discard the solids.

Using a pastry brush, coat the fruit with a thin layer of the warm jam.

Serve immediately, or refrigerate until ready to serve, but for no more than a few hours.

TIPS

The baked shells and the pastry cream can be made up to 3 days in advance of use. The shells should be stored, airtight, at room temperature, and the pastry cream should be covered and refrigerated.

Although Grand Marnier is a lovely flavoring for the pastry cream in this tart, you can also use kirschwasser or any cognac. Choose a flavoring that will enhance the flavor of the fruits used.

The *crème fouettée* must be whipped to stiff peaks before folding it into the pastry cream to make *crème légère* or the mixture will be too loose.

You can use any type of fruit that is in season or that you prefer. A good combination is 10 strawberries, sliced; 3 oranges, cut into *suprêmes*; and 200 grams (1 pint) blueberries. Whatever fruit is chosen, it should be colorful and, if a variety is used, the flavors should blend well.

If serving the tartlets immediately, the fruit may be left unglazed or sprinkled with confectioners' sugar.

The apricot *nappage* not only adds sheen to the fruit but also seals it to prevent oxidation.

Fresh fruit tartlets must be made on the day they are to be served and kept refrigerated until service.

EVALUATING YOUR SUCCESS

The dough should go all the way up the sides of the pan.

When baked, the pastry shells should be smooth, evenly colored, and crisp.

The *crème légère* should be smooth, and the flavoring agent used should be distinctly perceptible.

The apricot glaze should completely cover the fruit in a thin, even layer.

Demonstration

Tarte aux Bananes et Crème (Banana Cream Tart)

Makes one 9-inch tart
Estimated time to complete: 90 minutes

Ingredients	Equipment
Flour for dusting	Rolling pin
1 recipe *Pâte Brisée, Pâte Sucrée,* or *Pâte Sablée* (see pages 92, 94, and 95)	One 9-inch tart pan
300 grams (11 ounces) *Crème Pâtissière* (see page 248)	Parchment paper
150 milliliters (5 ounces) heavy cream	Pastry weights or dried beans
35 grams (1¼ ounces) confectioners' sugar	Small mixing bowl
1½ large, ripe but firm bananas	Whisk
¼ teaspoon pure vanilla extract	2 chilled mixing bowls
15 milliliters (1 tablespoon) rum	Rubber spatula
	Paring knife
	Offset spatula
For the *crème Chantilly*	Pastry bag fitted with decorative tip
200 milliliters (6¾ ounces) heavy cream	
35 grams (1¼ ounces) confectioners' sugar	
1 milliliter (¼ teaspoon) pure vanilla extract	

Prepare your *mise en place.*

Lightly flour a clean, flat work surface. Place the dough in the center of the floured surface and, using a rolling pin, roll it out to a 28-centimeter (11-inch) circle about 3 millimeters (⅛ inch) thick.

Lift the dough gently, fold it in half over the rolling pin, and slip it, still folded, into the tart pan. Unfold the circle to cover the bottom of the pan and remove the rolling pin.

Slowly turning the pan, gently push the dough into the bottom and against the edges using quick, light pressing movements, taking care not to pull or stretch the dough and making certain there are no holes. Do not trim off the excess dough, as it should chill so it does not shrink when baked. Transfer the pan to the refrigerator and allow the dough to chill for at least 30 minutes.

Preheat the oven to 177°C (350°F).

Remove the pastry shell from the refrigerator and trim the dough from the edge. Place a 28-centimeter (11-inch) round piece of parchment paper in the bottom of the shell and push it into the sides, leaving an edge with which you can lift it out of the shell when you need to. Add the pastry weights, spreading them out in an even layer.

Bake the shell for about 10 minutes, or until the pastry is dry and chalky white. Lift out the parchment paper and weights and continue to bake for an additional 15 minutes, or until the pastry is lightly browned and cooked through. Set aside to cool.

Place the pastry cream in a small mixing bowl and whisk vigorously to eliminate any lumps. It should be perfectly smooth.

Dean's Tip

"If you whip cream in a very cold bowl in a cool spot, it will gain more volume."
Dean André Soltner

Place the heavy cream in a well-chilled mixing bowl and begin whisking. When frothy, add the confectioners' sugar and continue to vigorously whisk until stiff peaks form (*crème fouettée*). (Alternatively, place the cream in the bowl of a standing electric mixer fitted with the whip and beat until stiff peaks form.)

Using a rubber spatula, gently fold the whipped cream into the smooth pastry cream to make a *crème légère*. Peel the bananas and, using a paring knife, cut them into 1.3-centimeter (½-inch) cubes. Place the bananas in a mixing bowl and add the vanilla and rum. Using a rubber spatula, carefully fold the bananas into the *crème légère*.

Pour the banana cream into the baked shell and, using an offset spatula, spread it out to a smooth, even layer.

Prepare the *crème Chantilly*. Place the heavy cream in a well-chilled mixing bowl and begin whisking. When frothy, add the confectioners' sugar and vanilla and continue to vigorously whisk until stiff peaks form. (Alternatively, place the cream in the bowl of a standing electric mixer fitted with the whip and beat as above.)

Using a rubber spatula, scrape the whipped cream into a pastry bag fitted with the star tip (or other decorative tip of choice). Pipe the *crème Chantilly* in a decorative pattern over the entire top of the tart, completely covering the banana cream.

Transfer to the refrigerator until ready to serve, but for no longer than 8 hours.

TIPS

Be sure to whip the cream for the *crème légère* to stiff peaks or the finished cream will be too soft.

Do not overwork when folding the whipped cream into the pastry cream or the whipped cream will begin to solidify and turn into butter.

If the surface of the tart is not completely covered with the *crème Chantilly,* the exposed bananas will discolor, and the tart will be unappealing.

The piped decoration may be any type you choose—rosettes, ropes, and seashells are just a few that work well, as long as they are piped neatly in an attractive pattern.

The tart must be served the day it is made.

EVALUATING YOUR SUCCESS

When baked, the pastry shells should be smooth, evenly colored, and crisp.

The sides of the pastry shell should be even with the rim of the pan.

The *crème légère* should be smooth, with the bananas evenly dispersed throughout, so that there is a piece of banana in every bite.

Demonstration

Tarte Bourdaloue (Pear and Almond Tart Bourdaloue Style)

Makes one 9-inch tart
Estimated time to complete: 90 minutes

Ingredients	Equipment
Flour for dusting	Rolling pin
1 recipe *Pâte Brisée* (see page 92)	Pastry brush
3 firm ripe pears, peeled	One 9-inch tart pan
2 liters (2¼ quarts) dry white wine	Medium saucepan
3 vanilla beans, split in half lengthwise	Paring knife
Juice of 5 lemons	Melon baller
1 kilogram (2¼ pounds) sugar	Small strainer or slotted spoon
250 grams (8¾ ounces) *Crème d'Amandes* (see page 252)	Plate
50 grams (1¾ ounces) slivered raw almonds	Docker or kitchen fork
	Standing electric mixer fitted with the paddle attachment
For the *nappage*	Rubber spatula
100 grams (3½ ounces) apricot jam	Pastry bag fitted with large, plain tip
	Offset spatula
	Cutting board
	Wire rack
	Small saucepan
	Small bowl
	Small fine-mesh sieve

Prepare your *mise en place*.

Lightly flour a clean, flat work surface. Place the dough in the center of the floured surface and, using a rolling pin, roll the dough out to a 28-centimeter (11-inch) circle about 3 millimeters (⅛ inch) thick.

Using a pastry brush, lightly brush off excess flour. Lift the dough gently, fold it in half over the rolling pin, and slip it, still folded, into the tart pan. Unfold the circle to cover the bottom of the pan and remove the rolling pin.

Slowly turning the pan, gently push the dough into the bottom and against the edges using quick, light press-ing movements, taking care not to pull or stretch the dough and making certain there are no holes. Do not trim off the excess dough, as it should chill so it does not shrink when baked. Transfer the pan to the refrigerator and allow the dough to chill for at least 30 minutes.

Meanwhile, prepare the pears.

Combine the wine with an equal amount of water in a medium saucepan. Using a small, sharp knife, scrape the seeds from the vanilla beans into the wine. Add the scraped beans along with the lemon juice and sugar. Place over medium-high heat and bring to a boil.

Using a paring knife, peel the pears and cut them in half lengthwise through the core. Using a mellon baller, carefully remove and discard the core from each half. You will need only 5 pear halves. Reserve the sixth for another use.

Add the pears to the poaching liquid and reduce the heat to a gentle simmer. Cook, gently stirring occasionally, for about 30 minutes, or until the point of a paring knife inserted into the thickest part meets little resistance. It is a good idea to test each pear for doneness, as each will cook at a different rate according to its size and ripeness.

Using a small strainer or slotted spoon, carefully transfer the pears to a plate to cool completely. Cool and reserve the poaching liquid, tightly covered and frozen, for future use. If not using the pears immediately, return the cooled pears to the cooled poaching liquid and store, tightly covered and refrigerated, for up to one week. The pears must be very cool before placing on the *crème d'amandes* or they will melt the cream and render the tart unusable.

Preheat the oven to 177°C (350°F).

Remove the pastry shell from the refrigerator and trim the dough from the edge. Using a docker or kitchen fork, dock the shell.

Place the almond cream in the bowl of a standing electric mixer fitted with the paddle attachment and beat until light and fluffy. Using a rubber spatula, scrape the almond cream into a pastry bag fitted with a large plain tip. Pipe the almond cream over the bottom of the shell and, using an offset spatula, spread it out to a smooth, even layer.

Place the cooled pears on a double layer of paper towel to drain well. If they remain very wet, their juices will ruin the tart.

Place the pear halves, cut side down, on a cutting board and, using the paring knife, cut the pears, crosswise, into very thin slices, keeping the entire pear half together as you slice.

Working with one at a time, place the complete pear halves, tops facing to the center, on top of the almond cream. Fan out the individual slices, covering as much of the surface of the tart as possible. Fill any uncovered areas with the almonds.

Bake the tart for about 50 minutes, or until the pastry is golden brown, the edges of the pears are caramelized, and the almond cream is cooked through.

Place on a wire rack to cool.

Combine the apricot jam with 50 milliliters (3 tablespoons plus 1 teaspoon) water in a small saucepan over medium heat, stirring to melt. Strain the glaze through a small fine-mesh into a small bowl and discard the solids.

Using a pastry brush, lightly coat the pears with a thin layer of the warm jam.

Serve immediately or refrigerate until ready to serve, but for no more than a few hours.

TIPS

This tart may also be made with raw cherries, plums, apricots, peaches, or blueberries.

The poaching liquid is a basic mix. Spices may be added, the citrus flavors and wine changed to suit various preparations. However, the flavorings should always work to enhance the fruit being poached. When properly stored, poaching liquid may be reused. After poaching, the pears should remain firm with no mushiness.

The almond cream must be very soft before piping into the pastry shell or it will be difficult to spread out evenly.

Use only raw almonds; if toasted, they will burn during the baking period.

The unbaked tart may be assembled and stored, covered and refrigerated, for up to 2 days, or frozen for up to 1 month. The baking time will increase accordingly.

EVALUATING YOUR SUCCESS

When baked, the pastry shell should be smooth, evenly colored, and crisp.

The sides of the pastry shell should be even with the rim of the pan.

The *crème d'amandes* should be soft in the center but not raw tasting.

The pears should all be fanned in the same direction.

The pears should be arranged so that, when cut, each slice of tart has an equal amount of fruit.

The apricot glaze should completely cover the fruit in a thin, even layer.

NOTE

This tart has its origins in a mixture of poached pears, almond paste, and crushed almond macaroons. The *tarte Bourdaloue* made its appearance at the beginning of the twentieth century created by an unknown pastry chef. It was named for the street—Rue Bourdaloue—where the pastry chef's shop was located. In turn, the street was named for a seventeenth-century theologian, Louis Bourdaloue, who, we imagine, would be surprised to find himself a part of culinary history.

Demonstration

Tartelettes au Citron (Lemon Tartlets)

Makes four 4-inch tart

Estimated time to complete: 2 hours

Ingredients	Equipment

Ingredients

Flour for dusting

1 recipe *Pâte Brisée, Pâte Sucrée*, or *Pâte Sablée* (see pages 92, 94, and 95)

For the candied lemon zest

2 large lemons, preferably organic

520 grams (18 ounces) sugar

200 milliliters (8 ounces) light corn syrup

For the lemon curd

3 large eggs, at room temperature

150 grams (5⅓ ounces) sugar

95 milliliters (3 ounces plus 1 teaspoon) fresh lemon juice

Grated zest of 3 lemons

180 grams (6⅓ ounces) unsalted butter, at room temperature

For the Swiss meringue

100 grams (3½ ounces) egg whites, at room temperature

125 grams (4½ ounces) sugar

Equipment

Rolling pin

Pastry cutter or small knife

Pastry brush

Four 4-inch tartlet pans

Vegetable peeler

Small saucepan

Fine-mesh sieve

Medium saucepan

Paring knife

Wire rack

Shallow bowl

Parchment paper

Pastry weights or dried beans

Heat-proof mixing bowl

Whisk

Saucepan with rim large enough to fit heat-proof bowl

Sheet pan

Plastic film

Offset spatula

Stainless-steel mixing bowl

Saucepan with rim large enough to fit stainless-steel bowl

Pastry bag fitted with small decorative tip

Handheld propane torch

Prepare your *mise en place*.

Lightly flour a clean, flat work surface. Place the dough in the center of the floured surface and, using a rolling pin, roll it out to a 30-centimeter (12-inch) circle about 3 millimeters (⅛ inch) thick. Using a pastry cutter or small knife, cut four circles about 15 centimeters (6 inches) in diameter from the dough. Using a pastry brush, lightly brush the excess flour from the dough.

Working with one circle at a time, lift the dough gently, fold it in half over the rolling pin, and slip it, still folded, into a tartlet pan. Unfold the circle to cover the bottom of the pan and remove the rolling pin. Slowly turning the pan, gently push the dough into the bottom and against the edges using quick, light pressing movements, taking care not to pull or stretch the dough and making certain there are no holes. Pinch off any excess around the edges to neaten.

Transfer the shells to the refrigerator for at least 30 minutes to chill.

Prepare the candied zest.

Using a vegetable peeler, carefully remove the zest from the lemons in large pieces, taking care not to remove any of the white pith. Using a paring knife, cut the zest into thin strips.

Place the strips in a small saucepan with cold water to cover over high heat. Bring to a boil. Immediately remove from the heat and drain well. Repeat this process three more times.

Combine the blanched zest with 475 milliliters (2 cups) of cold water in a medium saucepan. Add 400 grams (14 ounces) of the sugar along with the corn syrup and place over medium-high heat. Bring to a boil, then lower the heat and simmer for about 20 minutes or until the zest is translucent and tender.

Drain the zest well using a fine-mesh sieve and place the strips on a wire rack to cool.

When the zest is cool, but still tacky to the touch, place the remaining 120 grams (4 ounces) of sugar in a shallow bowl and roll each piece of zest in the sugar to give a crystallized finish. Return to the wire rack to dry completely.

Preheat the oven to 177°C (350°F).

Remove the pastry shells from the refrigerator. Place a 25-centimeter (10-inch) round piece of parchment paper in the bottom of each shell and push it up against the sides, leaving an edge with which you can lift it out of the shell when you need to. Add the pastry weights, spreading them out in an even layer over the bottom of each shell.

Bake the shells for about 10 minutes, or until the pastry is dry and chalky white. Lift out the parchment paper and weights, and continue to bake for an additional 15 minutes, or until the pastry is lightly browned and cooked through. Set the shells aside to cool.

Prepare the curd. Combine the eggs, sugar, and lemon juice with the grated zest in a heat-proof bowl, whisking to combine. Add the butter.

Fill a saucepan large enough to hold the bowl with water and place it over medium-high heat. Bring to a simmer and reduce the heat to medium.

Place the bowl over the simmering water, taking care that the bottom of the bowl does not touch the hot water and that the saucepan is centered over the heat so the flame does not burn the curd at the sides of the bowl. Cook, whisking frequently to ensure even cooking, for about 7 minutes, or until the mixture is quite thick and light. Great care must be taken when cooking the curd. If it gets too hot, the eggs will scramble and it will not be salvageable.

Remove the curd from the heat and pour it through a fine-mesh sieve onto a plastic film–lined sheetpan, discarding any solids. Place a piece of plastic film directly on the surface of the curd and refrigerate for about 1 hour, or until well chilled.

Pour an equal amount of curd into each baked pastry shell, smoothing the tops using an offset spatula.

Make a Swiss meringue. Combine the egg whites and sugar in a medium stainless-steel mixing bowl.

Fill a saucepan large enough to hold the bowl with water and place it over medium-high heat. Bring to a simmer and reduce the heat to medium.

Place the bowl over the simmering water set over medium heat, taking care that the bottom of the bowl does not touch the hot water. Cook, whisking frequently, until the mixture reaches 55°C (130°F) on an instant-read thermometer.

Remove the warm mixture from the heat and whisk vigorously until the meringue is cool and soft, but firm peaks will hold. (Alternatively, transfer the mixture to a standing electric mixer fitted with the whip attachment and beat to the same end.)

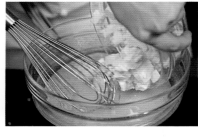

Scrape the meringue into a pastry bag fitted with a small decorative tip. Pipe a decorative design over the surface of the lemon curd in each tartlet to completely cover. Using a handheld propane torch, lightly brown the meringue.

Sprinkle some candied lemon zest in the center of each tartlet and serve immediately or refrigerate and serve within a few hours.

TIPS

The pastry shells, the zest, and the curd can be made and stored, tightly covered, and refrigerated, up to 3 days in advance.

If the zest to be candied is not cut so that it is absolutely free of pith, it will be bitter.

The peel of any citrus fruit can be candied. It can be used as a decorative garnish for desserts, as a confection or *mignardise* (a "delicacy," or another name for *petits fours*). In fact, the same method may be followed to candy almost any other firm fruit or vegetable, such as carrot disks or peels (see Tips, page 349).

If not crystallized, candied zest can be stored in its cooking syrup, tightly covered and refrigerated, almost indefinitely. If the syrup crystallizes during storage, simply bring it back to a boil with the addition of a couple of spoonfuls of water.

When making the curd, do not allow the sugar and eggs to sit together unmixed or they will "burn." Cooked lemon curd may be stored, tightly covered and refrigerated, for up to 4 days.

The Swiss meringue may be substituted with Italian meringue (see page 66) or *crème Chantilly* (see page 111).

If you do not have a handheld propane torch, the meringue may be browned under the broiler—but great care must be taken so that the curd doesn't get hot and soften or that the meringue itself does not burn.

EVALUATING YOUR SUCCESS

When baked, the pastry shells should be smooth, evenly colored, and crisp.

The sides of the pastry shells should be even with the rim of the pan.

When finished, the curd should be smooth in texture and appearance, slightly soft, and have a tart flavor.

The meringue should be piped in a neat, attractive design and evenly browned, with no trace of burning. The zest should be in thin, even pieces.

Demonstration

Tarte à l'Oignon (Rustic Onion Tart)

Makes one 9-inch tart

Estimated time to complete: 1 hour 10 minutes

Ingredients	Equipment
Flour for dusting	Rolling pin
240 grams (8½ ounces) *Pâte Brisée* (see page 92)	Pastry brush
50 grams (1¾ ounces) unsalted butter	One 9-inch tart pan
2 large onions, peeled and thinly sliced	Medium sauté pan
3 medium ripe tomatoes	Wooden spoon
50 grams (1¾ ounces) blue cheese, crumbled	Paring knife
30 grams (1 ounce) walnut pieces	Slicing knife
Coarse salt and freshly ground pepper to taste	Rubber spatula

Prepare your *mise en place*.

Lightly flour a clean, flat work surface. Place the dough in the center of the floured surface and, using a rolling pin, roll the dough out to an 28-centimeter (11-inch) circle about 3 millimeters (⅛ inch) thick. Using the pastry brush, remove any excess flour from the dough.

Lift the dough gently and fold it in half over the rolling pin and then slip it, still folded, into the tart pan. Unfold the circle to cover the bottom of the pan and remove the rolling pin.

Slowly turning the pan, gently push the dough into the bottom and against the edges using quick, light pressing movements, taking care not to pull or stretch the dough and making certain there are no holes. Do not trim off the excess dough. Transfer the pan to the refrigerator and allow the dough to chill for at least 30 minutes.

Place the butter in a medium sauté pan over low heat. Add the onions and cook, stirring often with a wooden spoon, for about 20 minutes, or until the onions are golden brown and nicely caramelized. Do not rush this process or the onions will turn dark and bitter. Set them aside to cool.

Preheat the oven to 177°C (350°F).

Peel and core the tomatoes. Using a slicing knife, cut them, crosswise, into thin slices. Set aside.
When the onions have cooled, remove the tart shell from the refrigerator.

Using a rubber spatula, scrape the onions onto the tart shell, spreading them out in an even layer. Fold the excess dough in to make a decorative edge around the onions. Place the tomato slices in a slightly overlapping pattern on the onions. Top with the crumbled cheese and walnut pieces. Season with salt and pepper.

Bake the tart for about 15 minutes, or until the pastry is baked through and golden brown and the cheese is bubbly.

Cut into wedges and serve warm.

TIPS

The tart may be decorated with any other ingredients that are not too liquid, such as any nut or hard cheese, or bell peppers.

Although at its most delicious this tart is served warm, it may also be eaten at room temperature. Either way, it is best served shortly after taken from the oven.

EVALUATING YOUR SUCCESS

The tart should be a neat circle.

The onion filling and the decorative topping should extend to the edge of the tart.

The pastry crust should be neat and even, but not too thick.

Once baked, the onions should be a rich brown with no trace of burned particles.

Demonstration

Tarte au Ganache Chocolat (Chocolate *Ganache* Tart)

Makes one 9-inch tart
Estimated time to complete: 1 hour

Ingredients	Equipment
Flour for dusting	Rolling pin
1 recipe *Pâte Brisée*, *Pâte Sucrée*, or *Pâte Sablée* (see pages 92, 94, and 95)	Pastry brush
170 grams (6 ounces) semisweet or bittersweet chocolate, chopped into small pieces	One 9-inch tart pan
30 grams (1 ounce) Trimoline (see page 499)	Parchment paper
70 grams (2½ ounces) unsalted butter, cut into small pieces, at room temperature	Pastry weights or dried beans
185 milliliters (6 ounces plus 2 teaspoons) heavy cream	Heat-proof mixing bowl
Chocolate shavings or curls (see page 407), optional	Heavy-bottomed saucepan
	Wooden spoon
	Small offset spatula

Prepare your *mise en place*.

Lightly flour a clean, flat work surface. Place the dough in the center of the floured surface and, using a rolling pin, roll it out to a 25-centimeter (10-inch) circle about 3 millimeters (⅛ inch) thick. Using a pastry brush, lightly brush the excess flour from the dough.

Roll the circle up and over the rolling pin and carefully transfer it to the tart pan. Using your fingertips, gently press the dough into the pan to make a neat fit. Pinch off any excess dough around the edges to neaten. Transfer the shell to the refrigerator for at least 30 minutes to chill.

Preheat the oven to 177°C (350°F).

Remove the pastry shell from the refrigerator. Place a 25-centimeter (10-inch) round piece of parchment paper in the bottom of the shell and push it up against the sides, leaving an edge with which you can lift it out of the shell when you need to. Add the pastry weights, spreading them out in an even layer.

Bake the shell for about 10 minutes, or until the pastry is dry and chalky white. Lift out the parchment paper and weights and continue to bake for an additional 15 minutes, or until the pastry is lightly browned and cooked through. Set the shell aside to cool.

opposite:

top: *Tarte Bavaroise au Chocolat*

bottom: *Tarte au Ganache Chocolat*

While the pastry is chilling and baking, prepare the *ganache*.

Place the chopped chocolate in a heat-proof mixing bowl. Add the Trimoline (or corn syrup) along with the butter. Set aside.

Place the cream in a heavy-bottomed saucepan over medium-low heat and bring to a boil. Watch very carefully, as once the cream reaches a boil, it will quickly overflow the pan.

Pour the hot cream over the chocolate mixture. Let stand for a few seconds and then begin stirring the cream into the chocolate with a wooden spoon. Do not beat vigorously or air bubbles will be created and mar the appearance of the *ganache*.

Pour the chocolate into the pastry shell, smoothing the top with a small offset spatula. Set aside to cool to room temperate and allow the *ganache* to firm.

Transfer the tart to the refrigerator until ready to serve, but for no longer than 8 hours. If desired, the top may be decorated with chocolate shavings or curls before serving.

TIPS

The blind-baked pastry shell may be brushed with melted chocolate before filling to keep it crisp once filled.

When preparing the *ganache*, do not set the bowl on a cold surface, as the low temperature will interfere with the melting process.

If the *ganache* separates, stir a small piece of cold butter or a bit of cold cream into it and it will come together.

The *ganache* may be made up to 3 days in advance. Warm it gently by placing the bowl over hot water and stirring to soften.

If air bubbles appear on the surface of the tart after filling, use a handheld propane torch to slightly warm the surface and the air bubbles will pop.

EVALUATING YOUR SUCCESS

When baked, the pastry shell should be smooth, evenly colored, and crisp.

The sides of the pastry shell should be even with the rim of the pan.

The chocolate in the *ganache* should be completely dissolved, and it should be smooth, shiny, and homogeneous with no air bubbles.

Demonstration

Tarte Bavaroise au Chocolat (Chocolate Bavarian Tart)

Makes one 9-inch tart
Estimated time to complete: 90 minutes

Ingredients	Equipment
Flour for dusting	Rolling pin
1 recipe *Pâte Brisée*, *Pâte Sucrée*, or *Pâte Sablée* (see pages 92, 94, and 95)	Pastry brush
1¼ sheets gelatin	One 9-inch tart pan
2 large egg yolks, at room temperature	Parchment paper
50 grams (1¾ ounces) sugar	Pastry weights or dried beans
125 milliliters (4 ounces) whole milk	3 mixing bowls
50 grams (1¾ ounces) semisweet, bittersweet, or unsweetened chocolate,	Whisk
chopped in small pieces	Medium saucepan
125 milliliters (½ cup plus 1½ teaspoons) heavy cream	Heat-proof spatula
	Wooden spoon
For the *crème Chantilly*	*Chinois*
200 milliliters (6¾ ounces) heavy cream	Ice-water bath
35 grams (1¼ ounces) confectioners' sugar	Standing electric mixer fitted with whip attachment
¼ teaspoon pure vanilla extract	Rubber spatula
	Small offset spatula
For the garnish	Chilled mixing bowl
Chocolate Curls (see page 407), optional	Pastry bag fitted with small decorative tip

Prepare your *mise en place*.

Lightly flour a clean, flat work surface. Place the dough in the center of the floured surface and, using a rolling pin, roll it out to a 25-centimeter (10-inch) circle about 3 millimeters (⅛ inch) thick. Using a pastry brush, lightly brush the excess flour from the dough.

Roll the circle up and over the rolling pin and carefully transfer it to the tart pan. Using your fingertips, gently press the dough into the pan to make a neat fit. Pinch off any excess dough around the edges to neaten. Transfer the shell to the refrigerator for at least 30 minutes to chill.

Preheat the oven to 177°C (350°F).

Place a 25-centimeter (10-inch) round piece of parchment paper in the bottom of the shell and push it up against the sides, leaving an edge with which you can lift it out of the shell when you need to. Add the pastry weights, spreading them out in an even layer.

Bake the shell for about 10 minutes, or until the pastry is dry and chalky white. Lift out the parchment paper and weights and continue to bake for an additional 15 minutes, or until the pastry is lightly browned and cooked through. Set aside to cool.

While the pastry is chilling and baking, prepare the filling.

Fill a mixing bowl with cold water. Add the gelatin sheets and, taking care that they are completely submerged to ensure proper softening, set them aside to soak until ready to use.

Place the egg yolks in a mixing bowl along with half of the sugar and, using a whisk, beat until the yolks are thick and fluffy.

Combine the milk with the remaining sugar in a medium saucepan and place it over medium heat. Cook, stirring constantly with a heat-proof spatula, for about 5 minutes, or just until the mixture comes to a boil.

Remove the milk from the heat and, whisking rapidly and constantly, slowly pour about one-third of the hot milk into the yolk mixture to temper it. Pour the tempered yolks into the hot milk and return the mixture to medium heat. Cook, stirring constantly with a wooden spoon, for about 4 minutes, or until the mixture

returns to a boil, taking care to scrape the bottom edges of the pan, as the custard will coagulate there and overcook.

When the custard naps (coats) the back of the spoon, draw a fingertip through the custard on the spoon; if the line you make holds its shape, the custard is ready (*nappant*). Watch carefully, as this is a small amount of custard that cooks quickly.

Immediately remove the pan from the heat, add the chopped chocolate, and beat to combine.

Squeeze the excess water from the gelatin sheets and add them to the hot custard, stirring to incorporate.

When the gelatin has melted into the custard, pour the mixture through a *chinois* into a clean mixing bowl, discarding any undissolved chocolate or pieces of curdled egg. The gelatin must be completely dissolved into the custard, or it will not set properly.

Place the bowl in an ice-bath. Cool, stirring occasionally to ensure an even temperature and to speed up the process. When properly chilled, the custard will begin to set up and resemble loose jam. If it remains too loose, it will not set properly. If it is too firm, it will be impossible to fold it into the whipped cream.

Place the heavy cream in the bowl of a standing electric mixer fitted with the whip and beat until stiff peaks form (*crème fouettée*). Using a rubber spatula, gently fold the whipped cream into the cooled custard. You have now made a Bavarian cream.

Pour the Bavarian cream into the baked pastry shell, spreading it out evenly with a small offset spatula. Place the filled tart in the refrigerator to chill thoroughly.

When the tart is well chilled, prepare the *crème Chantilly*. Place the heavy cream in a well-chilled mixing bowl and begin whisking. When frothy, add the confectioners' sugar and vanilla and continue to vigorously whisk until stiff peaks form. (Alternatively, place the cream in the bowl of a standing electric mixer fitted with the whip and beat until stiff peaks form.)

Using a rubber spatula, scrape the whipped cream into a pastry bag fitted with the star tip (or other decorative tip of choice). Just before serving, pipe the *crème Chantilly* in a decorative pattern over the surface of the tart. It is not necessary to completely cover the chocolate. If using, place chocolate curls in a decorative pattern in the center.

Transfer to the refrigerator until ready to serve, but for no longer than 8 hours.

TIPS
The blind-baked pastry shell may be brushed with melted chocolate before filling to keep it crisp once filled.

Do not allow the eggs and sugar to sit for too long a period without mixing, or they will "burn."
Bavarian cream may be made in a variety of flavors by replacing the chocolate with other flavorings, such as pure vanilla extract and liqueurs.

Mixing half the sugar with the milk when heating helps prevent scorching.

It is important to use a wooden spoon when making a custard, as metal can scrape bits of metal from the bottom of a pan and a whisk creates too much air and foam.

If curds appear during cooking, the custard is overcooked and unusable.

Once cooked, a custard must be cooled immediately, or it will continue to cook and will then curdle.

When adding the whipped cream, if it is too stiff, it will not fold into the custard and if too soft, the Bavarian will be loose and not fluffy.

The tart should be decorated *à la minute*, since the *crème Chantilly* will discolor as it sits.

The chocolate curls look best heaped in the middle of the tart so that, when the tart is cut, the curls will hide the cut marks.

EVALUATING YOUR SUCCESS
When baked, the pastry shell should be smooth, evenly colored, and crisp.

The sides of the pastry shell should be even with the rim of the pan.

The Bavarian cream should be light, fluffy, and smooth, with a distinct chocolate flavor.

The surface of the cream should be completely smooth and even.

The décor should be evenly and neatly applied.

Demonstration

Tarte aux Noix (Nut Tart)

Makes one 9-inch tart
Estimated time to complete: 90 minutes

Ingredients	**Equipment**
Flour for dusting	Rolling pin
240 grams (8½ ounces) *Pâte Brisée*, *Pâte Sucrée*, *Pâte Sablée* (see pages 92, 94, and 95)	Pastry brush
125 grams (4½ ounces) raspberry jam	9-inch tart pan
50 grams (1¾ ounces) sliced raw almonds	Metal spoon
60 grams (2⅛ ounces) *Crème d'Amandes* (see page 252)	Standing electric mixer with paddle and whip
2 large egg yolks, at room temperature	Rubber spatula
15 grams (½ ounce) granulated sugar	Mixing bowl
45 milliliters (3 tablespoons) heavy cream	Wire rack
60 grams (2⅛ ounces) almond flour	Small fine-mesh sieve
60 grams (2⅛ ounces) hazelnut flour	
Confectioners' sugar for dusting	

For the French meringue
2 egg whites, at room temperature
60 grams (2⅛ ounces) granulated sugar

Prepare your *mise en place*.

Lightly flour a clean, flat work surface. Place the dough in the center of the floured surface and, using a rolling pin, roll it out to a 25-centimeter (10-inch) circle about 3 millimeters (⅛ inch) thick. Using a pastry brush, lightly brush the excess flour from the dough.

Roll the circle up and over the rolling pin and carefully transfer it to the tart pan. Using your fingertips, gently press the dough into the pan to make a neat fit. Pinch off any excess dough around the edges to neaten. Transfer the shell to the refrigerator for at least 30 minutes to chill.

Preheat the oven to 177°C (350°F).

Remove the chilled shell from the refrigerator.

Spoon a thin layer of raspberry jam over the bottom of the pastry shell. Sprinkle the almonds over the jam.

Place the *crème d'amandes* in the bowl of a standing electric mixer fitted with the paddle attachment and beat until light and fluffy. Add the egg yolks and cream along with the granulated sugar, beating until well incorporated. Using a rubber spatula, scrape the mixture from the mixer bowl into a clean mixing bowl and set aside.

Wash the mixer bowl, dry it thoroughly, return it to the mixer, and attach the whip.

To make the French meringue, place the egg whites in the mixer bowl and beat on low to aerate. Add the granulated sugar, increase the speed to high, and beat for about 5 minutes, or until stiff peaks form. Set aside.

Fold the almond and hazelnut flours into the almond cream. When well incorporated, fold in the meringue.

Pour the batter into the prepared tart shell and bake for about 30 minutes, or until the surface is evenly browned and the center is firm to the touch.

Place the tart on a wire rack to cool slightly.

Place the confectioners' sugar in a small, fine-mesh sieve and, tapping the side of the sieve, lightly dust the tart with sugar.

Serve warm or at room temperature.

TIPS

Always have the shell completely ready to fill before making the filling; the meringue will quickly deflate if set aside.

Do not overmix when folding the meringue into the batter or the baked tart will not have a smooth top.

The baked tart may be stored, covered and refrigerated, for up to 3 days.

The pastry shell should be thoroughly baked and the bottom golden brown.

The almonds should remain crisp after baking.

The top of the baked tart should be smooth.

Demonstration

Tarte aux Noix Caramel (Caramel-Nut Tart)

Makes one 9-inch tart
Estimated time to complete: 90 minutes

Ingredients

Flour for dusting

240 grams (8½ ounces) *Pâte Brisée*, *Pâte Sucrée*, *Pâte Sablée* (see pages 92, 94, and 95)

125 grams (4½ ounces) granulated sugar

15 milliliters (1 tablespoon) light corn syrup

75 milliliters (2½ ounces) heavy cream

75 milliliters (2½ ounces) whole milk

128 grams (4.4 ounces) chopped walnuts

200 grams (7 ounces) *Crème d'Amandes* (see page 252)

For the optional *nappage*

100 grams (3½ ounces) apricot jam

Confectioners' sugar for dusting (see Tips)

For the French meringue

2 egg whites, at room temperature

60 grams (2⅛ ounces) granulated sugar

Equipment

Rolling pin

Pastry brush

9-inch tart pan

Medium heavy-bottomed saucepan

Candy thermometer

Wooden spoon

Ice-water bath

Offset spatula

Standing electric mixer fitted with paddle

Rubber spatula

Pastry bag fitted with #5 plain tip

Wire rack

Small saucepan, optional

Small bowl, optional

Small fine-mesh sieve

Prepare your *mise en place*.

Lightly flour a clean, flat work surface. Place the dough in the center of the floured surface and, using a rolling pin, roll it out to a 25-centimeter (10-inch) circle about 3 millimeters (⅛ inch) thick. Using a pastry brush, lightly brush the excess flour from the dough.

Roll the circle up and over the rolling pin and carefully transfer it to the tart pan. Using your fingertips, gently press the dough into the pan to make a neat fit. Pinch off any excess dough around the edges to neaten. Transfer the shell to the refrigerator for at least 30 minutes to chill.

Preheat the oven to 177°C (350°F).

While the pastry cools, make the filling.

Place the sugar in a medium heavy-bottomed saucepan. Add just enough cold water to cover the sugar.

Place the saucepan over high heat and cook for about 15 minutes, or until the sugar is the color of maple syrup and nicely caramelized (160°C/320°F on a candy thermometer). Once the liquid begins to color, swirl the mixture around in the pan to even out the color as it cooks. (It is easier to distinguish the appropriate color when the mixture is not boiling. Simply remove the pan from the heat for a moment and let the bubbles subside. The desired color is really up to the cook; however, a too light caramel will be flavorless and a too dark syrup will be bitter.)

Add the corn syrup, stirring with a wooden spoon to combine. Then stir in the cream, milk, and walnuts, watching carefully, as the added liquid will produce a large amount of steam and could cause the mixture to bubble and boil over. Continue to cook, stirring constantly, for about 5 minutes, or until the mixture reaches the consistency of pancake batter.

Place the caramel in an ice-water bath to cool. When cool, pour the caramel into the chilled pastry shell. Work carefully as you spread so that you don't tear the pastry. Smooth the top with an offset spatula. Place the almond cream in the bowl of a standing electric mixer fitted with the paddle attachment and beat until light and fluffy. Using a rubber spatula, scrape the almond cream into a pastry bag fitted with a #5 plain tip.

Pipe the almond cream over the caramel and, using a rubber spatula, spread it out to a smooth, even layer.

Bake the tart for about 30 minutes, or until evenly browned.

Place it on a wire rack to cool.

If glazing the tart, combine the apricot jam with 50 milliliters (3 tablespoons plus 1 teaspoon) water in a small saucepan over medium heat and cook for just about a minute to heat through. Remove from the heat and press through a fine-mesh sieve into a small bowl. Using a pastry brush, lightly coat the entire top of the tart with the warm apricot glaze.

If a shiny surface is not desired, simply dust the top of the tart with confectioners' sugar. Place the confectioners' sugar in a small, fine-mesh sieve and, tapping the side of the sieve, sprinkle it over the tart.

TIPS

If, after cooling, the caramel is too stiff to spread, add additional water or milk and reheat.

The apricot *nappage* is not necessary; it is only applied when a shiny surface is desired.

If desired, both the nappage and confectioners' sugar can be used. However, do not cover the *nappage* with the sugar or the sugar will melt. You might dust just the edges of the tart to make a neat decorative finish.

EVALUATING YOUR SUCCESS

The crust should be thin, even, thoroughly baked, and golden brown on the bottom.

The cream filling should have risen slightly and taken on a rich brown color.

No caramel should have bubbled up and through the cream during baking.

Every slice of the tart should have an equal amount of caramel filling and almond topping.

Demonstration

Clafoutis aux Cerises Limousin (Clafoutis, Limousin-style)

Makes one 9-inch tart
Estimated time to complete: 90 minutes

Ingredients	Equipment
Flour for dusting	Rolling pin
240 grams (8½ ounces) *Pâte Brisée, Pâte Sucrée, Pâte Sablée* (see pages 92, 94, and 95)	Pastry brush
125 milliliters (4 ounces plus 1 teaspoon) whole milk	9-inch tart pan
50 milliliters (1⅔ ounces) heavy cream	Parchment paper
½ vanilla bean, split in half lengthwise	Pastry weights or dried beans
2 large eggs, at room temperature	2 medium mixing bowls
100 grams (3½ ounces) granulated sugar	Small sharp knife
150 grams (5⅓ ounces) pitted cherries (or blueberries)	Whisk
Confectioners' sugar for dusting	Fine-mesh sieve
	Wire rack

NOTE

Traditionally, *clafoutis* was made with unpitted black cherries. In addition, it was usually made in a baking dish by pouring a batter, probably leftover crêpe batter, over the fresh fruit.

Prepare your *mise en place.*

Lightly flour a clean, flat work surface. Place the dough in the center of the floured surface and, using a rolling pin, roll it out to a 25-centimeter (10-inch) circle about 3 millimeters (⅛ inch) thick. Using a pastry brush, lightly brush the excess flour from the dough.

Roll the circle up and over the rolling pin and carefully transfer it to the tart pan. Using your fingertips, gently press the dough into the pan to make a neat fit. Pinch off any excess dough around the edges to neaten. Transfer the shell to the refrigerator for at least 30 minutes to chill.

Preheat the oven to 177°C (350°F).

Place a 25-centimeter (10-inch) round piece of parchment paper in the bottom of the shell and push it up against the sides, leaving an edge with which you can lift it out of the shell when you need to. Add the pastry weights, spreading them out in an even layer.

Bake the shell for about 10 minutes, or until the pastry is dry and chalky white. Lift out the parchment paper and weights and continue to bake for an additional 15 minutes, or until the pastry is lightly browned and cooked through. Set aside to cool.

Reduce the oven temperature to 121°C (250°F).

Combine the milk and cream in a medium mixing bowl. Using a small, sharp knife, scrape the seeds from the vanilla beans into the liquid. Add the scraped beans along with the eggs and sugar and whisk to blend well.

Pour the custard through a fine-mesh sieve into a clean bowl.

Arrange the fruit in the bottom of the baked pastry shell. Carefully pour the custard over the fruit.

Bake the tart for about 35 minutes, or until the custard is set in the center.

Place it on a wire rack to cool slightly.

Place the confectioners' sugar in a small fine-mesh sieve and, tapping the side of the sieve, lightly dust the edge of the tart.

Serve warm or within a few hours of being made.

TIPS

Both the pastry and the custard can be made one day in advance, then assembled and baked just before serving.

Any flavorful cherry can be used. If using frozen fruit, it must be very well drained and patted dry or the custard will not set.

EVALUATING YOUR SUCCESS

The pastry shell should be thin, even, free of holes or tears, thoroughly baked, and golden brown on the bottom.

The custard should completely fill the pastry shell. When baked, the custard should be firm but not stiff.

The fruit should retain its shape.

Demonstration

Tarte aux Tomates (Tomato Tart)

Makes one 9-inch tart
Estimated time to complete: 90 minutes

Ingredients	Equipment
Flour for dusting	Rolling pin
240 grams (8½ ounces) *Pâte Brisée*, *Pâte Sucrée*, *Pâte Sablée* (see pages 92, 94, and 95)	Pastry brush
1 stalk celery, washed, peeled, and cut into 6-millimeter (¼-inch) dice	9-inch tart pan
1 carrot, washed, peeled, and cut into 6-millimeter (¼-inch) dice	Parchment paper
1 red onion, peeled and cut into 6-millimeter (¼-inch) dice	Pastry weight or dried beans
1 clove garlic, peeled and crushed	Mixing bowl
8 sprigs flat-leaf parsley	*Rondeau* with lid
4 fresh basil leaves, plus additional for garnish	Food processor fitted with metal blade
45 milliliters (3 tablespoons) olive oil	Medium saucepan
40 grams (1⅓ ounces) unsalted butter	Wooden spoon
675 grams (1½ pounds) tomatoes, peeled, cored, seeded, and chopped	
Coarse salt and freshly ground pepper to taste	
3 large eggs, at room temperature, beaten slightly	
100 grams (3½ ounces) freshly grated Parmesan cheese	
Parmesan cheese curls, optional	

Prepare your *mise en place*.

Lightly flour a clean, flat work surface. Place the dough in the center of the floured surface and, using a rolling pin, roll the dough out to a 25-centimeter (10-inch) circle about 3 millimeters (⅛ inch) thick. Using a pastry brush, lightly brush the excess flour from the dough.

Roll the circle up and over the rolling pin and carefully transfer it to the tart pan. Using your fingertips, gently press the dough into the pan to make a neat fit. Pinch off any excess dough around the edges to neaten. Transfer the shell to the refrigerator for at least 30 minutes to chill.

Preheat the oven to 177°C (350°F).

Place a 25-millimeter (10-inch) round piece of parchment paper in the bottom of the shell and push it up against the sides, leaving an edge with which you can lift it out of the shell when you need to. Add the pastry weights, spreading them out in an even layer over the bottom.

Bake the shell for about 10 minutes, or until the pastry is dry and chalky white. Lift out the parchment paper and weights and continue to bake for an additional 15 minutes, or until the pastry is lightly browned and cooked through. Set aside to cool.

Combine the celery, carrot, and onion in a mixing bowl. Add the garlic, along with the parsley and basil, tossing to blend well.

Combine the olive oil and butter in a *rondeau* over low heat. When hot, add the tomatoes in an even layer. Add the vegetable-and-herb mixture in an even layer. Cover and cook, without stirring, for about 12 minutes, or until the vegetables are very tender.

Remove from the heat, uncover, and transfer to the bowl of a food processor fitted with the metal blade. Process to a smooth purée. (Alternatively, you can pulse to a rough chop for added texture in the finished tart.) This may have to be done in batches.

Scrape the purée into a clean medium saucepan and place over high heat. Cook, stirring constantly with a wooden spoon, for about 5 minutes, or until all the excess moisture has evaporated (*dessécher*). Remove from the heat and set aside to cool.

Preheat the oven to 121°C (250°F).

Season the cooled vegetable purée with salt and pepper to taste, noting that the cheese will add additional saltiness. Add the eggs and cheese, stirring to blend well.

Pour the mixture into the cooled pastry shell. Bake the tart for about 30 minutes, or until the filling is set in the center.

Serve warm, garnished with fresh basil leaves, Parmesan curls, or both, if desired.

This tart can also be served at room temperature or even cold. It will keep, wrapped airtight and refrigerated, for up to 2 days.

TIPS

When preparing the celery, it is a good idea to remove the tough, stringy fibers, as this helps release the aroma.

All the vegetables should be of an equal dice to ensure that they cook evenly.

The tomatoes can be either fresh or canned, according to the season. During the cooler months, canned will provide the best flavor. When using canned tomatoes, add a little of the juices to increase the flavor.

Make certain that the puréed mixture is completely cool before adding the eggs, as any heat will cook the eggs.

The filling can be made ahead and will keep, covered and refrigerated, for up to 2 days.

EVALUATING YOUR SUCCESS

The pastry shell should be thin, thoroughly baked, flaky, and golden brown on the bottom.

The filling should be very flavorful and well seasoned, with the cheese evenly distributed throughout.

The filling should be set without being stiff and over-cooked.

Theory
A Few Cookies Based on the Principles of French Tart Doughs

Because the methods of dough mixing used to create some specialty tarts and cookies are much the same as the techniques used to create *pâte brisée* and *pâte sucrée*, we include a few basic recipes. The most well-known of these doughs is that used to make the traditional Austrian Linzer Torte. Classically it is made as a tart, but it is now commonly made into small tarts or cookies.

Demonstration
Pâte à Linzer #1 (Linzer Dough #1)

Makes enough dough for one 8-inch tart
Estimated time to complete: 30 minutes

Ingredients	Equipment
250 grams (8¾ ounces) cake flour	Sifter
100 grams (3½ ounces) hazelnut flour	Plastic pastry scraper, optional
100 grams (3½ ounces) confectioners' sugar	Plastic film
½ teaspoon ground cinnamon	
Pinch ground cloves	
Pinch baking powder	
125 grams (4½ ounces) unsalted butter, cut into small cubes and chilled	
2 large eggs, at room temperature	
15 milliliters (1 tablespoon) rum	
1 teaspoon pure vanilla extract	

Prepare your *mise en place*.

Sift the cake flour, hazelnut flour, sugar, cinnamon, cloves, and baking powder together onto a clean work surface.

Make a well in the center and place the butter in the well.

Cut the butter into the flour mixture with your fingertips or a plastic pastry scraper, working until the pieces of butter are the size of dried lentils or split peas. There should be no large butter particles. Do not overwork or the dough will be tough.

Make a well in the center of the flour-and-butter mixture and place the eggs, rum, and vanilla into it. Using your fingertips, gradually combine ingredients, taking care not to overwork the dough. It should just hold together.

When the dry and liquid ingredients have come together, pull the mixture into a ball. Pull out walnut-size pieces of the dough and, using the heel of your hand, crush them into the work surface. Do this very systematically so that the dough is worked only one time. The technique is referred to as *fraisage*, and its purpose is to combine the components of the dough without overworking them.

When all of the dough has been worked, flatten it into a disk shape, wrap in plastic film, and refrigerate for at least 2 hours.

Use as directed in a specific recipe.

TIPS
Other sweet spices, such as nutmeg or mace, may be used in place of or in addition to the cinnamon and cloves.

When blending the butter into the dry ingredients, there must be no uncoated, large pieces remaining when the process is finished.

The dough may be refrigerated for up to 5 days or frozen for up to 1 month.

The dough should always be well chilled before you use it.

EVALUATING YOUR SUCCESS
The dough should be homogeneous, with a medium-brown color.

Demonstration

Pâte à Linzer #2 (Linzer Dough #2)

Makes enough dough for one 8-inch tart
Estimated time to complete: 30 minutes

Ingredients	Equipment
6 large hard-boiled egg yolks	Fine-mesh sieve
280 grams (9¾ ounces) unsalted butter, cut into pieces	Standing electric mixer fitted with paddle
300 grams (11 ounces) cake flour	Rubber spatula
50 grams (1¾ ounces) hazelnut flour	Plastic film
50 grams (1¾ ounces) confectioners' sugar	Fine-mesh sieve
1 teaspoon ground cinnamon	
15 milliliters (1 tablespoon) rum	

Prepare your *mise en place*.

Pass the egg yolks through a fine-mesh sieve into the bowl of a standing electric mixer fitted with the paddle. Add the butter along with the cake flour, hazelnut flour, confectioners' sugar, and cinnamon and mix until just combined. Stir in the rum, blending well but taking care not to overmix.

Using a rubber spatula, scrape the dough from the bowl and form it into disk shape. Wrap it in plastic film and refrigerate for at least 1 hour.

Use as directed in a specific recipe.

TIPS
Hard-boiled egg yolks give the dough a crumblier texture and add fat without liquid—liquid in this dough would toughen it.

This is an extremely delicate dough that breaks easily.

EVALUATING YOUR SUCCESS
The ingredients should be well combined, with no trace of any one ingredient evident.

The dough should be pliable, not elastic.

The dough should be malleable, but not too soft.

Demonstration

Linzer Torte

Makes one 8-inch tart
Estimated time to complete: 1 hour

Ingredients	Equipment
Pâte à Linzer #1 or #2 (see pages 134 and 135)	Baking sheet
Flour for dusting	Parchment paper
100 grams (3½ ounces) *Crème d'Amandes* (see page 252)	Rolling pin
200 grams (7 ounces) *Compote à la Framboise* (see page 139)	Pastry brush
Egg wash (see page 62)	8-inch tart pan
Confectioners' sugar for dusting	Standing electric mixer fitted with paddle
	Rubber spatula
	Pastry wheel
	Small bowl
	Wire rack
	Small fine-mesh sieve

Prepare your *mise en place*.

Line a baking sheet with parchment paper. Set aside.

Divide the dough into 2 halves.

Lightly flour a clean, flat work surface. Place one piece of dough in the center of the floured surface and, using a rolling pin, roll it out to a 23-centimeter (9-inch) circle about 3 millimeters (⅛ inch) thick. Using a pastry brush, lightly brush the excess flour from the dough.

Roll the circle up and over the rolling pin and carefully transfer it to the tart pan. Using your fingertips, gently press the dough into the pan to make a neat fit.

Again, lightly flour the surface and place the remaining piece of dough in the center. Roll the dough out to another circle about the same size as the first. Using a pastry brush, lightly brush the excess flour from the dough.

Roll the circle up and over the rolling pin and carefully transfer it to the prepared baking sheet.

Transfer both the pastry pieces to the refrigerator to chill for at least 30 minutes.

Preheat the oven to 177°C (350°F).

Place the almond cream in the bowl of a standing electric mixer fitted with the paddle and beat until light and fluffy.

Remove the pastry shell from the refrigerator and, using a rubber spatula, spread the almond cream over the bottom of the shell. Spread the raspberry compote over the almond cream in a smooth layer.

Remove the sheet of pastry from the refrigerator. Using a pastry wheel, cut the dough into strips about 6 to 12 millimeters (¼ to ½ inch) wide.

Weave the strips in a lattice design over the top of the torte.

Pinch the edges of the pastry together to seal, discarding any excess, or cut off the excess dough with a paring knife and place small balls of excess dough around the border as a decorative edge.

Place the egg wash in a small bowl.

Using a pastry brush, lightly coat the lattice strips with egg wash, taking care not to get compote on the brush in the process, as it will transfer to the pastry and the sugars will cause the pastry to burn.

Bake the tart for about 30 minutes, or until the dough is golden brown and cooked through. Place on a wire rack to cool.

When the tart is cool, place the confectioners' sugar in a small fine-mesh sieve and, tapping the side of the sieve, lightly dust the edge of the torte.

Cut into wedges and serve.

TIPS
The dough is very fragile and must be well chilled before rolling.

If the dough becomes too soft to roll, return it to the refrigerator and chill until firm.

Scraps of dough can also be used to make the lattice top.

If the almond cream is too soft, chill it until firm enough to spread easily.

If the raspberry compote is very soft, assemble the lattice top on a cake cardboard and then slide it onto the torte.

The unbaked torte may be wrapped, airtight, and refrigerated for up to 3 days or frozen for up to 1 month.

When removing the pan or tart ring from the baked torte, take care, as the filling might have boiled over and caused the pastry to stick to the pan or ring. The baked torte will keep, refrigerated, for up to 2 days. You might want to wait to dust the edge with sugar until just before serving.

EVALUATING YOUR SUCCESS
The dough should be very crumbly but should still hold together when worked.

The lattice strips should be of a consistent size, and the design should be even.

There should be no burned filling on the lattice or on the sides of the torte.

The almond cream should be thoroughly baked.

The compote should be soft, but not runny, with a strong, tart raspberry flavor.

Demonstration

Compote à la Framboise (Raspberry Compote)

Makes 500 grams (1 pound, 1½ ounces)
Estimated time to complete: 30 minutes

Ingredients	Equipment
250 grams (8¾ ounces) raspberries (see Tips)	2 medium heavy-bottomed saucepans
125 grams (4½ ounces) Apple Compote (see page 96)	Wooden spoon
125 grams (4½ ounces) sugar	Rubber spatula
14 grams (½ ounce) pectin	Fine-mesh sieve
	Container with lid
	Plastic film

Prepare your *mise en place*.

Combine the raspberries, compote, sugar, and pectin in a heavy-bottomed saucepan over medium heat. Cook, stirring frequently with a wooden spoon, for about 5 minutes, or until the raspberries have broken down.

Remove from the heat and, using a rubber spatula, press through a fine-mesh sieve into a clean heavy-bottomed saucepan. If the mixture is too thick to pass through the sieve easily, add a bit of water.

Place the strained mixture over high heat and bring to a boil, stirring frequently. Lower the heat and simmer, stirring constantly to prevent scorching, for about 10 minutes, or until thickened.

Remove from the heat and scrape into a clean container. Place plastic film directly on top of the compote to prevent a skin from forming as the mixture cools.

When cool, put the lid on the container and refrigerate until ready to use, or for up to a week.

Use as directed in a specific recipe.

TIPS
The raspberries may be fresh, frozen, or even a frozen purée.

The apple compote is used both as a filler and for its pectin content.

EVALUATING YOUR SUCCESS
The compote should be firm but not rubbery, with a defined, tart raspberry flavor.

The compote should be smooth and seedless.

Demonstration

Spritskakor (Scandinavian Butter Cookies)

Makes about 100 cookies
Estimated time to complete: 1 hour

Ingredients	Equipment
440 grams (15½ ounces) unsalted butter, at room temperature	3 baking sheets
160 grams (5⅔ ounces) confectioners' sugar	Parchment paper or silicone baking liners
Zest of 1 lemon	Standing electric mixer fitted with paddle
Pinch salt	Rubber spatula
2 large eggs, at room temperature	Pastry bag fitted with #5 rosette tip
1 teaspoon pure vanilla extract	Metal spatula
600 grams (1 pound, 5 ounces) cake flour	2 wire racks
Approximately 100 hazelnuts or nut pieces for finishing (see Tips)	

Prepare your *mise en place.*

Line 3 baking sheets with parchment paper or silicone liners and set aside. If you don't have 3 baking sheets, you can reuse a single sheet, but let it cool thoroughly before piping each batch of cookies onto it.

Preheat the oven to 177°C (350°F).

Place the butter in the bowl of a standing electric mixer fitted with the paddle. With the motor on low, begin mixing the butter. Add the sugar, lemon zest, and salt, raise the speed to medium, and beat until light and fluffy.

Add the eggs one at a time, followed by the vanilla, scraping down the sides of the bowl with a rubber spatula after each addition.

Add the cake flour all at once and beat just to combine.

Scrape the dough into a pastry bag fitted with a #5 rosette tip.

Begin piping out cookies into little rosettes, leaving at least 2.54 centimeters (1 inch) between each one to allow for spreading as the cookies bake.

Place a nut in the center of each cookie.

Bake the cookies for about 7 minutes, or until lightly browned around the edges.

Using a metal spatula, transfer them to wire racks to cool.

Store the cookies, airtight, for up to 1 week, or frozen for up to 1 month.

TIPS

The butter and sugar must be creamed to a very soft consistency or the dough will not pipe easily.

Adding the eggs slowly keeps the dough from separating.

There will be undesirable gluten development if the dough is overmixed after the flour has been added.

The dough may be flavored with sweet spices such as nutmeg or cinnamon, other citrus, or other natural flavorings.

The dough may be stored, well-wrapped and refrigerated, for several days, but it must be warmed before piping.

Any nut can be used to decorate the cookies, but choose either small nuts or nut pieces; large ones will overwhelm the small cookies.

EVALUATING YOUR SUCCESS

The flavor of the dough should be quite delicate.

The cookies should be uniformly brown around the edges.

The baked cookies should be tender and crumbly but not dry.

Demonstration

Vanille-Kipferl (Viennese Vanilla Crescents)

Makes about 60 cookies
Estimated time to complete: 1 hour

Ingredients	Equipment
300 grams (11 ounces) unsalted butter, at room temperature	3 baking sheets
180 grams (6⅓ ounces) confectioners' sugar	Parchment paper or silicone baking liners
½ teaspoon pure vanilla extract	Standing electric mixer fitted with paddle
Pinch salt	Rubber spatula
410 grams (14½ ounces) all-purpose flour	Shallow bowl
150 grams (5⅓ ounces) ground hazelnuts	
Vanilla sugar for finishing (see page 82)	

Prepare your *mise en place*.

Line the baking sheets with parchment paper or silicone liners. Set aside.

Preheat the oven to 177°C (350°F).

Place the butter in the bowl of a standing electric mixer fitted with the paddle. With the motor on low, begin mixing the butter. Add the sugar, vanilla, and salt, raise the speed to medium, and beat until light and fluffy.

Add the flour and ground hazelnuts, scrape down the sides of the bowl with a rubber spatula, and beat just to combine.

While the dough is still soft, using your hands, begin rolling 7.5-centimeter-long (3-inch-long) crescent-shaped cookies.

Place the cookies on the prepared baking sheets, leaving adequate space between each one to allow for spreading as the cookies bake.

Bake the cookies for about 12 minutes, or until baked through and lightly colored.

Place the vanilla sugar in a shallow bowl.

While the cookies are still warm, roll them in the sugar to completely, but lightly coat.

Serve warm or store, airtight, for up to 3 days, or frozen for up to 1 month.

TIPS

Hazelnut flour is simply ground hazelnuts. You can grind toasted hazelnuts yourself, using a food processor fitted with the metal blade; however, care must be taken not to purée them so they become a paste.

The raw dough may be wrapped, airtight, and refrigerated for up to 3 days or frozen for up to 1 month.

EVALUATING YOUR SUCCESS
The cookies should be uniform in size and shape.

The baked cookies should be firm but not crunchy or hard.

The vanilla sugar should just lightly coat the cookies.

Demonstration

Bourbon-Pecan Cookies

Makes about sixty 2½-inch round cookies
Estimated time to complete: 2 hours

Ingredients	Equipment
170 grams (6 ounces) pecans	Small baking sheet
170 grams (6 ounces) unsalted butter, at room temperature	Parchment paper or silicone baking liners
200 grams (7 ounces) sugar	Food processor fitted with metal blade
½ vanilla bean, split in half lengthwise	Standing electric mixer fitted with paddle
1 large egg yolk	Small sharp knife
30 milliliters (2 tablespoons) bourbon	Rubber spatula
¼ teaspoon salt	Plastic film
230 grams (8⅛ ounces) all-purpose flour	2 baking sheets
Egg wash (see page 62)	Small bowl
Pecan pieces for finishing	Sharp knife
	Pastry brush
	Metal spatula
	Wire racks

Prepare your *mise en place*.

Preheat the oven to 149°C (300°F).

Place the pecans on a small baking sheet lined with parchment paper and toast for about 7 minutes, or until very aromatic and lightly colored. Watch carefully, as the oil in the nuts will cause them to burn easily.

Set the pecans aside to cool.

When they are completely cool, place them in the bowl of a food processor fitted with the metal blade.

Process, using quick on and off turns, until the nuts resemble coarse cornmeal. Remove from the food processor and set aside.

Place the butter in the bowl of a standing electric mixer fitted with the paddle. With the motor on low speed, begin mixing the butter. Add the sugar, raise the speed to medium, and beat until light and fluffy.

Using a small, sharp knife, scrape the vanilla seeds into the creamed mixture.

Add the egg yolk, bourbon, and salt, along with the reserved ground nuts, scrape down the sides of the bowl with a rubber spatula, and beat until thoroughly combined.

Add the flour and mix just to incorporate.

Using a rubber spatula, scrape the dough from the bowl. Using your hands, shape the dough into a log about 6 centimeters (2½ inches) in diameter. Wrap in plastic film and refrigerate for at least 1 hour, or until well chilled.

Line 2 baking sheets with parchment paper or silicone liners. Set aside.

Preheat the oven to 177°C (350°F).

Place the egg wash in a small bowl.

Remove the dough log from the refrigerator. Unwrap and, using a sharp knife, cut the log, crosswise, into 6-millimeter-thick (¼-inch-thick) slices. Roll the log slightly after each cut to keep the log completely round so that the cookies will be of a uniform size.

Place the cookies on the prepared baking sheets, leaving room between each one so that they can hold their shape and don't stick together.

Using a pastry brush, coat the top of each cookie with egg wash, using just enough to wet the surface slightly.

Place a pecan piece in the center of each cookie.

Bake the cookies for about 7 minutes, or just until lightly browned on the edges.

Remove from the oven and, using a metal spatula, transfer the cookies to wire racks to cool.

Store, airtight, for up to 3 days, or frozen for up to 1 month.

There will be undesirable gluten development if the dough is overmixed after the flour has been added.

To easily shape the dough into a log, place the soft dough on a piece of parchment paper and roughly mold it into the desired shape. Then, fold the paper up and over the dough and tighten the log by holding one side with your hand and pushing the other edge with the side of a cutting board or sheet pan.

The raw dough may be wrapped, airtight, and refrigerated for up to 3 days or frozen for up to 1 month. For long-term freezer storage, first wrap the log in parchment paper and then in plastic film, making sure that both are airtight.

EVALUATING YOUR SUCCESS

The baked cookies should be completely round and uniform in size.

The tops of the baked cookies should be shiny from the egg wash.

The baked cookies should be golden brown, with slightly darker edges.

The cookies should be very crumbly but not dry.

The flavors of toasted nuts and bourbon should predominate.

Demonstration

Fig Newton–Style Cookies

Makes about 32 cookies
Estimated time to complete: 90 minutes

Ingredients

250 grams (8¾ ounces) unsalted butter, at room temperature
150 grams (5⅓ ounces) sugar
1 large egg, at room temperature
1 large egg yolk, at room temperature
440 grams (15½ ounces) all-purpose flour
Pinch salt
Flour for dusting
Egg wash (see page 62)

For the filling
450 grams (16 ounces) dried figs
100 grams (3.5 ounces) sugar
Juice of 1 lemon

Equipment

Standing electric mixer fitted with paddle
Rubber spatula
Plastic film
Chef's knife
Medium saucepan
Baking sheet
Parchment paper
Rolling pin
Small bowl
Pastry brush
Cutting board
Serrated knife

Prepare your *mise en place.*

Place the butter in the bowl of a standing electric mixer fitted with the paddle. With the motor on low speed, begin mixing the butter. Add the sugar, raise the speed to medium, and beat until light and fluffy. Add the egg and egg yolk, one at a time, frequently scraping down the sides of the bowl with a rubber spatula, and beat until thoroughly combined.

Add the flour and salt, mixing just to incorporate.

Using a rubber spatula, scrape the dough from the bowl. Wrap in plastic film and refrigerate for at least 1 hour, or until well chilled.

Meanwhile, prepare the filling.

Remove the woody stems from the figs and then, using a chef's knife, chop the figs into small pieces.

Place the chopped figs along with the sugar and lemon juice in a medium saucepan. Add 205 milliliters (7 ounces) of water and place over high heat. Bring to a boil. Lower the heat and cook, stirring frequently with a wooden spoon to prevent scorching, at a bare simmer for about 15 minutes, or until the figs are very tender. Watch carefully, as you may need to add additional water if the liquid evaporates before the figs are tender. Set aside to cool.

Line a baking sheet with parchment paper.

When the dough is well chilled, remove it from the refrigerator, unwrap it, and divide it into two halves. Set aside to warm slightly to allow for easier rolling.

Lightly flour a clean, flat work surface.

Working with one piece of dough at a time and using a rolling pin, roll each piece of the dough out to a rectangle about 15 centimeters by 60 centimeters (6 inches by 24 inches). Place each rectangle on a piece of parchment paper.

Place the egg wash in a small bowl. Using a pastry brush, lightly coat the edges of each rectangle with the wash.

Working with one piece at a time, spoon half of the cooled fig filling down the center of the rectangle. Carefully fold the sides up and over the filling, pressing the edges together to form a seam down the middle of the log.

Gently lift the parchment paper up and carefully roll the filled log over so that the seam side is facing down. Transfer the 2 logs to the parchment paper-lined baking sheet.

Brush the top of each log with egg wash, taking care that the wash does not drip down the sides or onto the paper. Place in the refrigerator to chill for 30 minutes.

Preheat the oven to 177°C (350°F).

Bake the logs for about 15 minutes, or until the pastry is golden brown and thoroughly baked.

Carefully transfer the logs to a cutting board. While they are still warm, using a serrated knife, cut each log, crosswise, into 4-centimeter-long (1½-inch-long) cookies.

Store, airtight, for up to 3 days, or frozen for up to 1 month.

TIPS
Fresh figs may be substituted for the dry, but the amount will have to be increased to 560 grams (1¼ pounds).

The cookie logs must be chilled before baking or the dough will melt, exposing the filling.

The unbaked logs may be wrapped, airtight, and refrigerated for up to 1 week.

EVALUATING YOUR SUCCESS
The fig filling should be very soft and tender.

The filling should be completely contained within the dough.

The finished cookies should be equal in size with a rich, golden brown color.

Demonstration

Gingersnaps

Makes 50 cookies

Estimated time to complete: 2 hours

Ingredients	Equipment
150 grams (5⅓ ounces) unsalted butter, at room temperature	Standing electric mixer fitted with paddle
400 grams (14 ounces) sugar	Rubber spatula
2 large eggs, at room temperature	Sifter
165 milliliters (5⅔ ounces) molasses	Plastic film
20 milliliters (1 tablespoon plus 1 teaspoon) white vinegar	2 baking sheets
525 grams (18½ ounces) white bread flour	Parchment paper or silicone baking liners

1 tablespoon baking soda
1 tablespoon ground ginger
¾ teaspoon ground cinnamon
¾ teaspoon ground cloves
¾ teaspoon ground cardamom
Granulated sugar for coating

Shallow bowl
Metal spatula
Wire racks
Small bowl
Pastry brush
Cutting board
Serrated knife

Prepare your *mise en place*.

Place the butter in the bowl of a standing electric mixer fitted with the paddle. With the motor on low, begin mixing the butter. Add the sugar, raise the speed to medium and, frequently scraping down the sides of the bowl with a rubber spatula, beat until light and fluffy.

Add the eggs one at a time, frequently scraping down the sides of the bowl, and beat until thoroughly combined.

Slowly add the molasses and vinegar. If you add these ingredients too rapidly, the mixture will separate.

Sift the flour, baking soda, ginger, cinnamon, cloves, and cardamom together.

Add the dry ingredients to the batter, mixing to just incorporate.

Using a rubber spatula, scrape the dough from the bowl. Shape into a flat rectangle, wrap in plastic film, and refrigerate for at least 1 hour, or until firm and very well chilled.

Preheat the oven to 177°C (350°F).

Line the baking sheets with silicone baking liners or parchment paper. Set aside.

Place the coating sugar in a shallow bowl. Set aside.

Remove the dough from the refrigerator, unwrap, and pull it into 50 equal pieces. Roll each piece into a small ball.

Working with one ball at a time and using your hands, roll each one in the coating sugar.

Place the cookies on the prepared baking sheets, leaving adequate space between each one to allow for spreading during baking.

Bake the cookies for about 7 minutes, or until they have spread, the sugar crust has cracked, and the dough is firm in the center.

Using a metal spatula, transfer the cookies to wire racks to cool.

Store, airtight, for up to 3 days, or frozen for up to 1 month.

TIPS
Chilling the dough prevents the cookies from spreading too much during baking.

Unbaked cookies may be wrapped, airtight, and refrigerated for up to 5 days or frozen for up to 1 month.

EVALUATING YOUR SUCCESS
The cookies should be equal in size and shape.

The baked cookies should be chewy, but not gummy and raw tasting.

Demonstration
Brownies

Makes 20 bars

Estimated time to complete: 1 hour

Ingredients	Equipment
90 grams (3¼ ounces) dried cherries	Small saucepan
115 milliliters (4 ounces) fresh orange juice	13-by-18-inch baking pan
Butter cube for pan	Parchment paper
380 grams (13 ounces) semisweet or bittersweet	*Bain-marie*
chocolate, chopped into small pieces	Wooden spoon
240 grams (8½ ounces) unsalted butter, cut into small pieces	Standing electric mixer fitted with paddle
6 large eggs	Sifter
480 grams (1 pound, 1 ounce) sugar	Rubber spatula
150 grams (5⅓ ounces) all-purpose flour	Offset spatula
30 grams (1 ounce) Dutch-process cocoa powder	Cake tester
90 grams (3¼ ounces) walnut (or other nut) pieces	Wire rack
45 grams (1½ ounces) chocolate bits	Heat-proof bowl
	Small heavy-bottomed saucepan
For the ganache	Cake comb
200 grams (7 ounces) bittersweet chocolate, chopped into small pieces	Serrated knife
200 milliliters (6¾ ounces) heavy cream	

Prepare your *mise en place.*

Combine the cherries and orange juice in a small saucepan over medium heat and bring to a boil. Immediately remove from the heat and set aside to cool.

Using a cube of butter, make a large X on the baking pan. Line the pan with a piece of parchment paper, pressing down so the butter holds the parchment paper in place.

Preheat the oven to 177°C (350°F).

Place the chopped chocolate and butter in a *bain-marie* over simmering water. Heat, stirring frequently, just until the chocolate and butter have melted. Do not allow the mixture to get very hot. Remove from the heat.

Place the eggs and sugar in the bowl of a standing electric mixer fitted with the paddle. Beat on medium until very light in color and fluffy (*blanchir*). Do not allow the egg-and-sugar mixture to sit without mixing or it will "burn."

Pour the chocolate mixture into the egg mixture, adding it all at once and immediately turning the mixer on low to combine. (Otherwise the batter will break up into little pieces.)

Sift the flour and cocoa together. Add to the batter, scraping down the sides of the bowl with a rubber spatula, and mix just to incorporate.

Remove the bowl from the mixer and fold in the reserved cherries along with their soaking liquid. When incorporated, fold in the nuts and chocolate bits.

Pour the batter into the prepared baking pan, spreading it out in an even layer with an offset spatula. Bake for about 15 minutes, or until a cake tester inserted in the center comes out clean.

Set the brownies on a wire rack to cool.

Meanwhile, make the *ganache*.

Place the chopped chocolate in a heat-proof bowl. Place the cream in a small heavy-bottomed saucepan over medium-low heat and bring to a boil.

Immediately remove the pan from the heat. Watch very carefully, as once the cream reaches a boil, it will quickly overflow the pan.

Pour the hot cream over the chocolate. Let stand for a few seconds and then begin stirring the cream into the chocolate with a wooden spoon. Do not beat vigorously or air bubbles will be created and mar the appearance of the *ganache*.

Pour the *ganache* over the top of the cooled brownies, spreading it out with a cake comb. Set aside to cool before cutting.

Using a serrated knife, cut the brownies into 20 equal-size bars.

Store, airtight and refrigerated, for up to 3 days, or frozen for up to 1 month.

TIPS

Boiling the cherries in liquid rehydrates them. If time permits, bring the cherries to a boil and refrigerate them overnight to allow them to absorb the maximum amount of liquid.

The nuts should be coarsely chopped to facilitate spreading the batter and cutting the baked cookies.

Chocolate bits can be replaced with coarsely chopped white, milk, semisweet, or bittersweet chocolate.

EVALUATING YOUR SUCCESS

The cherries, nuts, and chocolate pieces should be evenly distributed throughout the batter and finished brownies.

The cut brownies should be equal in size and shape.

The *ganache* should completely cover the top of the brownies.

The baked brownies should be moist and slightly chewy.

Session 4

Pâte à Choux: An Overview of Cream Puff Dough

Although *pâte à choux* is made from the basic flour-liquid-fat combination of other pastry doughs, unlike the other doughs, it is leavened through the addition of eggs and cooked before it is shaped. It falls somewhere between a batter and a dough. The initial dough is formed by beating flour into a heated mixture of water, butter, sugar, and salt. The heat causes the flour to swell and form a paste. The paste is then cooked on the stovetop, where it is beaten constantly to pull out moisture and dry the pastry enough to enable it to absorb the eggs. The French term for this process is *dessécher*. The paste is then removed from the heat and beaten to develop the gluten structure and to cool slightly so that the eggs can be added safely. If the eggs are added before the mixture has properly cooled, they will begin to cook and will not blend into the paste. The eggs are beaten in, one at a time, with the number dependent upon the size of the eggs, the amount of moisture in the air, and the amount of moisture that has been extracted from the paste during the cooking period. Using the correct amount of each of the basic ingredients is crucial in the formation of a successful *choux* paste.

Because of the extra moisture content—through the addition of eggs and more water than usual—*pâte à choux* behaves differently from other pastry doughs. When making *choux* pastry, the dough is usually transferred to a pastry bag and piped in a shape designated by the particular recipe onto baking sheets lined with parchment paper. The top of the shape is usually scored to help it rise evenly, then coated with an egg wash before baking. During baking, the excess moisture and the eggs in the dough expand and turn to steam, causing the pastry to puff up and form an internal hollow cavity with a dry, firm shell. If piped into small rounds, the resulting pastry puffs resemble the little cabbages from which the pastry gets its name, *choux* being French for "cabbage."

Pâte à choux can also be deep-fried or poached. It can be used for savory preparations as well as for desserts. The most familiar baked pastries are *choux à la crème* (cream puffs) and *éclairs*. It is used to make *beignets* (fritters), *gougères* (cheese puffs), *pommes dauphine* (deep-fried potato croquettes made from two parts mashed potato and one part *choux* paste), and *gnocchi parisienne* (small dumplings poached in water, drained, covered with Mornay sauce, and gratinéed). It is a most versatile pastry dough.

Many classic French desserts are prepared with *pâte à choux*:

Choux à la Crème Chantilly or Choux à la Crème Pâtissière: Puff pastry rounds filled with sweetened whipped cream (*crème Chantilly*, see page 111) or pastry cream (*crème pâtissière*, see page 248).

Profiteroles: Puff pastry rounds either filled with ice cream and served with warm chocolate sauce or filled with *crème Chantilly* or *crème pâtissière*. Profiteroles can be savory (filled, for example, with meat or poultry *mousses*) as well as sweet, and are often used as a soup garnish. According to *Larousse Gastronomique*, the name comes from the French word *profit* and originally meant "a small gratuity or tip."

Éclairs: Elongated puff pastries that are filled with *crème pâtissière* and dipped in *fondant* icing (see page 228), a glaze prepared by cooking sugar to the soft-ball stage and working it on a marble surface until it becomes opaque. Traditionally, the flavor of the *fondant* (generally chocolate, coffee, or vanilla) matches the flavor of the filling.

Paris-Brest: A dessert that consists of a ring of almond-topped *pâte à choux* filled with praline-flavored *crème mousseline* (see page 377).

Cygnes: *Choux* paste piped into the shape of swans, then baked and filled with *crème Chantilly*, *crème pâtissière*, or fruit.

Gâteau Saint-Honoré: A round of *pâte sucrée* (see page 94) encircled by caramel-dipped cream puffs filled with *crème Chiboust* (see page 174), which is also known as Saint-Honoré cream.

Croquembouche: A pyramid of pastry puffs held together by caramel that is a traditional centerpiece often featured at celebratory occasions.

Gougères: Baked savory *choux*, usually piped in a round or ring shape, flavored with cheese such as Gruyère, Comté, or Emmenthal. In the Burgundy region of France, *gougères* often accompany wine tastings.

Guidelines for Working with *Pâte à Choux*

° For maximum expansion of the dough and to create an adequate gluten structure to contain the air, fat, and steam during baking, bread flour or other high-protein flour must be used. Bread flour with its 13 percent protein content is the strongest of all flour types; other pastry flours have a protein content that falls between 6 and 9 percent. If a weaker flour is used, the dough will tear during baking.

° The water and fat should be brought to boil together. Never leave the boiling mixture unattended or water will evaporate from it and alter the proportions of the recipe.

° It is important to cut the fat into small pieces when combining it with the water so that it melts at the same time that the water comes to a boil. If the water boils before all the fat melts, evaporation may, again, alter the proportions of the recipe.

° Sugar and salt should be added to the water and fat to slightly flavor the dough. Sugar promotes color and crust in the baked pastry; salt helps intensify the gluten action of the flour, which contributes to the structural strength of the baked pastry.

° Using milk instead of water will produce a richer-tasting pastry and deeper color in the baked product.

° The flour should be added to the hot-water-and-fat mixture all at once so that the starch can swell instantly and evenly in the liquid.

° The stovetop stage of cooking a *choux* paste should not last too long or the baked pastry will have an unpleasant reddish tinge.

° If too little egg is beaten in, the dough will have a poor rise; if too much, the dough will not hold its shape.

° For a lighter, crisper baked pastry, replace one or two of the whole eggs with an equal volume of egg whites.

There are three methods for testing the proper consistency of *choux* paste:

° The batter should fall from a spoon or mixer paddle attachment in a ribbon.

° When a trench is made in the batter, it should close slowly.

° The batter should form a small hook or curl and flop over when pulled up.

Guidelines for Baking *Pâte à Choux*

° The batter should be piped out onto a baking sheet lined with parchment paper or a silicone baking sheet or on greased baking pans.

° To produce the best rise, *pâte à choux* items should be formed and baked while the initial batter is still fresh and slightly warm.

° The piped items should be positioned in alternating rows to allow heat to circulate freely between them.

° Since the pastry expands as it bakes, allow at least 2.54 centimeters (1 inch) between items to ensure even baking.

° All of the piped items should be evenly shaped and of the same size.

° To create the most attractive finished pastry, egg wash should be applied lightly just before baking; if applied too heavily it will inhibit the rise and cause the individual items to distort.

° For ease of application, egg wash can be efficiently applied using a spray bottle. If the egg wash is too thick to spray easily, thin it with a small amount of milk.

° Score the piped items with a fork or a star pastry tip to prevent the surface from cracking during baking. The pastry tip provides a more consistent score than a fork, with the pastry shape developing nicely along the mark of the score.

° Scoring prior to baking makes it easier to check for doneness, as you can see inside the pastry through the score marks. The color on the inside of the mark should be exactly the same as the color on the surface.

° To bake in a convection oven: Preheat to 260°C (500°F), place the *choux* in the oven, turn the oven off for 15 minutes, and then turn the oven on to 177°C (350°F). As the pastry expands, the hardening crust will force a crack to form, ideally at the base.

° To bake in a conventional or deck oven: Preheat to 233°C (450°F), place the *choux* in the oven, and bake for about 40 minutes, or until golden brown, crisp, and dry internally, with no white paste evident.

° No matter the type of oven used, *choux* must bake until they are completely dried out, or they will collapse as they cool. It is important to note that *choux* puffs often look fully baked before they are dry and crisp—properly and completely baked *choux* pastries will feel light and hollow.

° All *choux* pastries should be thoroughly cooled before filling.

Storing *Pâte à Choux*

° *Choux* batter may be made in large batches and stored, well covered and refrigerated, for up to 3 days.

° *Choux* batter can be piped out into the desired shape and frozen. Once frozen, the pastry should be wrapped airtight. It will last for up to 1 month.

° Frozen *choux* pastry should be removed from the freezer, brushed with egg wash, and baked as usual. This method produces crisp, fresh-tasting baked goods.

° *Choux* pastries may also be baked, cooked, left unfilled, and stored, airtight, at room temperature for up to 3 days or frozen for up to 1 month.

° To crisp refrigerated or frozen *choux* pastries, place them in a single layer on a parchment paper–lined baking sheet in a preheated 177°C (350°F) oven for a few minutes to dry them out.

Demonstration

Pâte à Choux (*Choux* Pastry or Cream Puff Dough)

Makes about 4 dozen *choux* puffs

Estimated time to complete: 90 minutes

Ingredients	Equipment

250 grams (8¾ ounces) unsalted butter, cut into small pieces

¾ teaspoon sugar

¾ teaspoon salt

340 grams (12 ounces) bread flour, sifted

10 to 12 large eggs, at room temperature

Egg wash (see page 62)

2 baking sheets

Parchment paper or silicone baking liners

Stainless-steel saucepan

Wooden spoon

Rubber spatula

Standing electric mixer fitted with paddle attachment

Small bowl

Pastry bag fitted with #5 plain tip

Pastry brush

Prepare your *mise en place*.

Preheat the oven to 260°F (500°C) for a convection oven or 233°C (450°F) for a conventional or deck oven.

Line the baking sheets with parchment paper or silicone baking sheets. Set aside.

Combine the butter, sugar, and salt with 475 milliliters (1 pint) water in a stainless-steel saucepan over high heat and bring to just a boil. Do not allow the

water to boil for any length of time or it will begin to evaporate, and the proportion of liquid to dry ingredients will change, compromising the final dough. Once boiling, immediately remove the pan from the heat and, using a wooden spoon, quickly beat in the flour.

Return the saucepan to medium heat and continue beating in the flour for 30 seconds. The mixture should begin to thicken, dry out (*dessécher*), and form a mass. A thin film should form on the bottom of the pan and the mixture should begin to pull away from the sides of

the pan. Take care that you do not overcook the mixture, as the fat might separate out and the final product will have an unappetizing reddish tint.

Using a rubber spatula, scrape the mixture into the bowl of a standing electric mixer fitted with the paddle. Begin beating the paste at medium-low speed to release some steam and to allow it to cool somewhat. This is very important because the eggs will begin cooking if they are added while the paste is too hot.

Working with one at a time, crack each egg into a small bowl and then add it to the paste, beating continuously until the paste is smooth and shiny. You will know you have added enough egg when 1) a ribbon of dough forms and does not break when the paddle is lifted out of the bowl; 2) a spoon run through the paste leaves a channel that fills in slowly; and 3) a dollop of paste lifted on a spatula curls over on itself and forms a hook.

The *pâte à choux* is now ready to be formed into whatever shape you need.

To make *choux* puffs, transfer the paste to the pastry bag and pipe it in alternating rows into 1.3-centimeter (½-inch) rounds on the prepared baking sheets, allowing sufficient room between each one to ensure even baking.

Using a pastry brush, lightly coat each piece with egg wash.

For convection ovens, place the *choux* in the preheated oven and immediately turn it off. Bake in the turned-off oven for 15 minutes. Then, turn the oven to 177°C (350°F) and bake for about 25 minutes, or until the *choux* are golden brown and baked through, with the color on the inside matching the color on the surface. You can also lift the pastries and check the cracks on the bottoms to make sure that they are done.

For conventional or deck ovens, place the *choux* in the preheated oven and bake for about 40 minutes, or until done.

Remove the baking sheets from the oven and allow the *choux* to cool for 20 minutes. Then proceed with the cutting and filling required for a specific recipe.

TIPS
Sifting the bread flour before adding it to the hot mixture ensures that it will not lump.

If the mixture seems to need only a bit more egg, lightly beat one egg and add just a part of it to the batter.

Using too much egg wash will inhibit the rise of the *choux* during baking.

EVALUATING YOUR SUCCESS
The *choux* paste should be smooth and shiny.

The piped pieces should be consistent in size and shape.

The egg wash should cover the top of the puffs only. It should not drip down the sides and settle on the baking sheet.

The baked *choux* should be golden brown, even in the cracks, as well as uniform in height and width.

The interior of the *choux* should be soft and hollow, and the center should not be wet or gooey.

The cracks in the baked *choux* should be along the base, not across the top.

Demonstration

Éclairs

Makes about forty-five 4-inch *éclairs*
Estimated time to complete: 2 hours

Ingredients	Equipment
1 recipe unbaked *Pâte à Choux* (see page 153)	2 baking sheets
Egg wash (see page 62)	Parchment paper or silicone baking sheets
	Pastry bag fitted with #5 plain tip
For the *crème légère*	Small bowl
910 grams (2 pounds) *Crème Pâtissière* (see page 248)	Pastry brush
300 milliliters (10 ounces) heavy cream, chilled	#3 star tip
Flavored *Fondant Décor façon Colette* (see page 403)	Small mixing bowl
Pâte à Glacer (see page 381), or confectioners' sugar	Whisk
	Standing electric mixer fitted with whip
	Rubber spatula
	#4 plain tip

Prepare your *mise en place*.

Preheat the oven to 260°C (500°F) for a convection oven or 233°C (450°F) for a conventional or deck oven.

Line the 2 baking sheets with parchment paper or silicone baking sheets.

Place the *choux* paste in a pastry bag fitted with the #5 plain tip and pipe it in alternating rows into 10-centimeter-long (4-inch-long) pieces on the prepared baking sheets, allowing sufficient room between each one to ensure even baking—the pastry will double or even triple in size.

Place the egg wash in a small bowl.

Using a pastry brush, lightly coat each piece with egg wash.

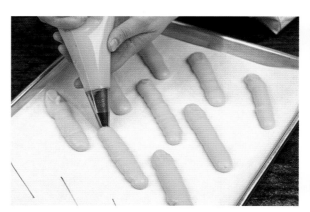

For convection ovens, place the pastries in the pre-heated oven and immediately turn it off. Bake in the turned-off oven for 15 minutes. Then, turn the oven to 177ºC (350ºF) and bake for about 25 minutes, or until the pastries are golden brown and baked through, with the color on the inside matching the color on the surface. You can also lift the pastries and check the cracks on the bottom to make sure that they are done.

For conventional or deck ovens, place the pastries in the preheated oven and bake for about 40 minutes, or until done.

Remove the baking sheets from the oven and allow them to cool for 20 minutes.

Using a #3 star tip, poke two holes in the bottom of each *éclair*. Set the pastry aside.

Place the pastry cream in a small mixing bowl and whisk vigorously to eliminate any lumps. It should be perfectly smooth.

Place the heavy cream in the bowl of a standing electric mixer fitted with the whip and beat until stiff peaks form (*crème fouettée*). Using a rubber spatula, gently fold the whipped cream into the smooth pastry cream to make a *crème légère*.

Using a rubber spatula, scrape the *crème légère* into a pastry bag fitted with a #4 plain tip. Pipe the cream through the holes in the bottom of the pastry shells, completely filling the inside. There should be no gaps or air spaces remaining.

Glaze the *éclairs* with flavored *fondant* or *Pâte à Glacer*, or simply dust them with confectioners' sugar.

TIPS

Always pipe the *éclair* pastry in pieces that are of the same size and shape otherwise the pastries will rise and bake unevenly.

You can also make miniature *éclairs*. Use the #3 plain tip and pipe the paste into 6-centimeter (2-inch) pieces.

Do not press down when applying the egg wash or the even shape of each pastry will be destroyed.

If not baked throughout, the pastry will collapse on itself when cool.

Baked, unfilled *éclair* pastries may be wrapped, air-tight, and frozen for up to 1 month.

The pastry must be completely cool before filling, or the heat will melt the *crème légère*.

EVALUATING YOUR SUCCESS

The piped *choux* paste should be consistent in size and shape.
The egg wash should cover the top only. It should not drip down the sides and settle on the baking sheet.

The baked pastry should be golden brown, even in the cracks, as well as uniform in height and width.

The interior of the *choux* should be soft and hollow, and the center should not be wet or gooey.

The cracks in the baked pastry should be along the base, not across the top.

The *crème légère* should be smooth and well flavored, and should completely fill the *éclairs*.

The glaze, if used, should be shiny and firm and just cover the top of the *éclairs*, with no drips down the sides.

Looking straight down at the finished pastries, a small amount of unglazed *choux* should be visible.

Demonstration

Profiteroles (Small Ice Cream–Filled Puffs)

Makes 4 servings
Estimated time to complete: 30 minutes

Ingredients	Equipment
Twelve 5-centimeter (2-inch) round *choux*, baked and cooled (see page 153)	Serrated knife
Twelve 4.5-centimeter (1¾-inch) round scoops vanilla ice cream	Small ice cream scoop
Sauce au Chocolat (recipe follows)	Attractive sauceboat
Confectioners' sugar	4 dessert plates
	Small fine-mesh sieve

Prepare your *mise en place*.

Using a serrated knife, carefully cut each *choux* in half crosswise, keeping each pastry together.

Working quickly, place a small scoop of ice cream in the bottom of each *choux*. Place the top piece of pastry over the ice cream.

Pour the chocolate sauce into an attractive sauceboat or pool an equal portion in the center of each dessert plate.

Place 3 profiteroles on each plate. Place the confectioners' sugar in a small fine-mesh sieve and, lightly tapping the side of the sieve, dust each plate with sugar.

Serve immediately, with the sauce passed on the side.

Demonstration

Sauce au Chocolat (Chocolate Sauce)

Makes 475 milliliters (2 cups)
Estimated time to complete: 20 minutes

Ingredients	Equipment
300 grams (11 ounces) semisweet or bittersweet chocolate, chopped	Medium stainless-steel bowl
265 milliliters (9 ounces) whole milk	Medium saucepan
125 milliliters (4 ounces) heavy cream	Rubber spatula
115 grams (4 ounces) sugar	Medium heavy-bottomed saucepan
30 grams (1 ounce) unsalted butter	Wooden spoon
	Bain-marie, optional
	Plastic film, optional
	Container with lid, optional

NOTE

Traditionally, *profiteroles* are filled with vanilla ice cream and served with a small pitcher of hot chocolate sauce at the side. However, almost any flavor ice cream and sauce may be used, as long as the flavor of each one is complementary to the other. The pleasure of the dessert is in the contrast between the cold ice cream and the hot sauce.

Prepare your *mise en place*.

Place the chopped chocolate in a medium stainless-steel bowl. Set aside.

Place the milk in a medium saucepan over medium heat and bring to just a boil. Pour the hot milk over the chocolate and let rest for about 30 seconds to allow the chocolate to begin to melt. Stir with a rubber spatula until the chocolate is completely melted. Set aside.

Combine the cream, sugar, and butter in a medium heavy-bottomed saucepan over medium heat. Bring to just a boil, watching carefully so that the mixture does not boil over.

As soon as the cream mixture comes to a boil, scrape the melted chocolate into it. Cook, stirring constantly with a wooden spoon, for about 3 minutes, or just until the mixture returns to the boil. Immediately remove it from the heat.

If you do not need the sauce right away, pour it into a *bain-marie*, cover with plastic film, and keep warm until ready to use. Alternatively, pour it into a container, cover, and refrigerate for up to 1 week. Reheat the sauce in a *bain-marie* when ready to use. (When reheating, always use a *bain-marie* because the sauce will scorch or burn if reheated over direct heat.)

TIPS
The ice cream may be scooped in advance and kept frozen on a sheet pan until ready to use.

The *profiteroles* may be attached to the serving plate with a small dot of the sauce. This will keep them from sliding around on the plate as they are being served.

Classically, three small *profiteroles* are served per person.

This chocolate sauce should always be served warm.

Enough sauce should be served so that some can accompany every bite of the *profiterole*.

The *profiteroles* should be consistent in size.

The ice cream should be soft but not melting.

The *profiteroles* should be not frozen when served.

Demonstration

Cygnes (Swans)

Makes twenty-four 3½-inch swans
Estimated time to complete: 2 hours

Ingredients	Equipment
1 recipe unbaked *Pâte à Choux* (see page 153)	4 baking sheets
Egg wash (see page 62)	Parchment paper or silicone baking liners
800 grams (1¾ pounds) *Crème Pâtissière* (see page 248)	Pastry bag fitted with #5 and #0 plain tips
24 small berries or pieces of fresh fruit	Small bowl
600 grams (1 pound, 5 ounces) *Crème Chantilly* (see Tips and page 111)	Pastry brush
	Wire rack
	Serrated knife or scissors
	Small mixing bowl
	Whisk
	Rubber spatula

Prepare your *mise en place.*

Preheat the oven to 260ºC (500ºF) for a convection oven or 233ºC (450ºF) for a conventional or deck oven.

Line the baking sheets with parchment paper or silicone baking sheets.

Place about two-thirds of the *choux* paste in a pastry bag fitted with the #5 plain tip and pipe it in large teardrop shapes on two of the prepared baking sheets, allowing sufficient room between each shape to ensure even baking—the pastry will double or even triple in size.

Place the egg wash in a small bowl.

Using a pastry brush, lightly coat each piece with egg wash.

For convection ovens, place the pastry in the preheated oven and immediately turn it off. Bake in the turned-off oven for 15 minutes. Then, turn the oven to 177ºC (350ºF) and bake for about 25 minutes, or until the pastries are golden brown and baked through, with the color on the inside matching the color on the surface. You can also lift the pastries and check the cracks on the bottom to make sure that they are done.

For conventional or deck ovens, place the pastry in the preheated oven and bake for about 40 minutes, or until done.

Remove the baking sheets from the oven, transfer the pastries to a wire rack, and allow them to cool for 20 minutes. Lower the oven temperature to 177°C (350°F).

Change the tip on the pastry bag to a #0 plain tip, fill the bag with the remaining *choux* paste, and pipe S shapes (for the swan necks) on the other two baking sheets, allowing sufficient room between each one to ensure even baking. Using a pastry brush, lightly coat each shape with egg wash.

Bake for 15 minutes. This is less time than normal because of the thinness of the necks. When the pastries feel dry, light, and hollow, transfer them to a wire rack to cool for 20 minutes.

When the pastry is completely cool, using a serrated knife or scissors, cut the teardrop shape in half crosswise. Cut the top piece in half lengthwise, to form two wing shapes.

Place the pastry cream in a small mixing bowl and whisk vigorously to eliminate any lumps. It should be perfectly smooth. Using a rubber spatula, scrape the cream into a pastry bag fitted with a #5 plain tip.

Working with one swan at a time, pipe a small amount of pastry cream into the hollow of the larger piece of the pastry teardrop—the swan's body. If desired, a small piece of fruit (such as a berry) can be placed on top of the cream.

Using a rubber spatula, scrape the *crème Chantilly* into a pastry bag fitted with the #5 star tip.

Pipe a large rosette of *crème Chantilly* on top of the pastry cream. Stick a wing piece onto each side of the rosette with the points at the narrow end of the teardrop. Stick the neck piece into the rosette of *crème Chantilly* at the rounded end of the teardrop.

Continue making swans until all are complete. Serve immediately, as the filling will quickly cause the pastry to get soggy.

NOTE
In France, *cygnes* are traditionally filled only with *crème Chantilly* and given a light dusting of confectioners' sugar. They are then served as a small treat with coffee or tea rather than as a dessert at the end of a meal.

TIPS
The *crème Chantilly* should be beaten very stiff so that it is strong enough to support the wings and neck. However, take care not to overbeat. The cream should just be firm and able to hold a stiff peak without breaking.

The swan body can be made with one large teardrop or two smaller ones that are piped and baked together.

The S pieces (the necks) should not be too thin or they will burn while baking or break easily once baked.

The unfilled baked pastry may be wrapped, airtight, and frozen for up to 1 month.

If desired, the pastry cream can be flavored (see page 249) with chocolate, liqueur, or any other flavor you like.

EVALUATING YOUR SUCCESS
The bodies and necks should be consistent in size and shape.

The baked pastry should be golden brown.

The *crème pâtissière* should be smooth and flavorful.

The *crème Chantilly* should be firm, but not over-whipped.

Demonstration

Popovers

Makes 6 popovers
Estimated time to complete: 1 hour

Ingredients	Equipment
30 grams (1 ounce) unsalted butter, softened	6 popover molds or large muffin cups
1 large whole egg	Medium mixing bowl
1 large egg yolk	Whisk
½ teaspoon salt	
150 milliliters (5 ounces) whole milk	
85 grams (3 ounces) all-purpose flour	

NOTE

Popovers are not technically *choux* paste, but they have evolved out of a similar combination of ingredients, and like *choux*, they rise and form hollow puffs. This is a quintessentially American recipe based on the batter used for England's famous Yorkshire pudding. Like Yorkshire pudding, popovers are often made in cups that have been greased with meat drippings for additional flavor.

Prepare your *mise en place*.

Using the softened butter, lightly grease the interior of each popover mold or large muffin cup, as well as around the edge of the surface of the pan.

Combine the whole egg, egg yolk, and salt with approximately one-fourth of the milk in a medium mixing bowl, whisking until very well blended. Whisking constantly, beat in the flour, taking care that the mixture is lump-free.

Whisking constantly, beat in the remaining milk. The mixture should be thick and smooth.

Pour an equal portion of the batter into each of the prepared molds, filling them only halfway—the batter will triple in height while baking.

Transfer the molds to a cold oven. Then, turn the oven temperature to 233°C (450°F).

Bake for about 25 minutes, or until the popovers are golden brown and well puffed.

Serve immediately. Popovers do not keep well.

TIPS

Buttering the top of the pan prevents the baked popovers from sticking.

Using a small amount of milk with the eggs facilitates transforming the flour and liquids into a lump-free batter.

You may add 14 grams (1 tablespoon) chopped fresh herbs, 28 grams (2 tablespoons) grated cheese, or any ground spice to taste to the batter.

Popovers get quite brown during baking, but they must be thoroughly baked; otherwise, they will collapse as soon as they are removed from the oven.

Always remove popovers from their baking pan as soon as they come out of the oven, as they tend to stick.

EVALUATING YOUR SUCCESS

The popovers should rise straight and tall.

The inside should be soft, but not gooey.

Although plain popovers have a very mild flavor, a hint of saltiness should be discernable.

Demonstration

Gougères (Cheese Puffs)

Makes approximately 40 *gougères*
Estimated time to complete: 1 hour

Ingredients	Equipment
120 grams (4¼ ounces) grated Gruyère cheese	2 baking sheets
⅓ recipe warm, unbaked *Pâte à Choux* (see page 153)	Parchment paper
Egg wash (see page 62)	Wooden spoon
	Rubber spatula
	Pastry bag fitted with #5 plain tip
	Small bowl
	Pastry brush

Prepare your *mise en place*.

Preheat the oven to 260°C (500°F).

Line the baking sheets with parchment paper. Set aside.

Using a wooden spoon, beat 100 grams (3½ ounces) of the cheese into the warm *choux* paste. The paste should not be too hot or it will immediately melt the cheese.

When well blended, using a rubber spatula, scrape the cheese mixture into a pastry bag fitted with the #5 plain tip.

Pipe the *gougères* out into rounds—they can be as large as a quarter or as small as a raisin. It is the chef's choice.

Place the egg wash in a small bowl.

Using a pastry brush, lightly coat the top of each pastry with egg wash. Sprinkle a bit of the remaining cheese on each one.

Transfer the baking sheets to the preheated oven. Immediately turn the oven off and bake the *gougères* for 15 minutes.

Turn the oven temperature to 177°C (350°F) and continue to bake the pastries for about 15 minutes (for smaller *gougères*, 7 to 8 minutes), or until golden brown and baked through. Look into the cracks on the bottom of the pastries to make sure they are done.

Remove the *gougères* from the oven and serve them hot. Alternatively, cool and then wrap, airtight, and freeze for up to 1 month. Reheat before serving.

TIPS

Larger *gougères* may be served plain as an accompaniment to wine, as they are in the Burgundy region of France, or filled with a savory filling and served as an hors d'oeuvre.

In the classic French culinary world, very tiny *gougères* are used to garnish *consommés*.

EVALUATING YOUR SUCCESS

The piped *gougères* should be round, without tails or points sticking up.

The cheese on top of the baked *gougères* should be lightly colored and not burned.

The baked *gougères* should be evenly colored and of the same size.

The interior of the baked *gougères* should be moist but not eggy.

The baked *gougères* should have a distinct, nutty, cheesy flavor, with pieces of cheese visible in the interior.

Demonstration

Österreichische Kirschknödeln (Austrian Cherry Dumplings)

Makes about 16 dumplings
Estimated time to complete: 2 hours

Ingredients	Equipment
For the compote	Medium saucepan
400 grams (14 ounces) sour cherries, pitted	Wooden spoon
50 grams (1¾ ounces) sugar	Small bowl
35 milliliters (2 tablespoons plus 1 teaspoon) kirschwasser	Saucer
40 grams (1⅓ ounces) cornstarch	Rolling pin
	Small, round metal cookie cutter plus a slightly
For the dumplings	larger cutter, or a small sharp knife
Confectioners' sugar for dusting	Baking pan
250 grams (8¾ ounces) marzipan (see page 401)	Large pot
16 pitted sweet cherries	Shallow bowl
Flour for dusting	Slotted spoon
½ recipe *Knödelteig aus Brandteig* (recipe follows)	Decorative serving platter
500 grams (1 pound, 1½ ounces) fresh bread crumbs	

100 grams (3½ ounces) unsalted butter, melted
Crème Chantilly (see page 111), *crème fraîche*, or vanilla ice
cream, optional

Prepare your *mise en place*.

Combine the cherries, sugar, and kirschwasser in a medium saucepan over medium heat. Bring to a boil, stirring occasionally with a wooden spoon.

Place the cornstarch in a small bowl and add just enough cold water to dissolve it.

Stirring the cherries constantly, add about half of the cornstarch slurry to the cherries. Continuing to stir, return the cherries to a boil. Once boiling, immediately test the thickness of the compote by spooning a bit of the cherry liquid onto a saucer and allowing it to cool. If it is of a saucelike consistency, remove the compote from the heat. If it is still too thin, add additional cornstarch slurry, a bit at a time, stirring constantly, until the compote reaches the desired consistency. Remove from the heat and set aside.

Lightly coat a clean, smooth work surface and a rolling pin with confectioners' sugar. Place the marzipan in the center and, using the rolling pin, roll the marzipan until it is a bit less than 3 millimeters (⅛ inch) thick. Using a small cookie cutter or a small, sharp knife, cut out the marzipan into 16 circles, each about 3 times the size of the sweet cherries you are using.

Place a cherry in the center of each marzipan circle. Working with one piece at a time, carefully pull the marzipan up and over the cherry and pinch it to completely enclose the fruit. Set aside.

Clean the work surface and rolling pin and lightly dust them both with flour.

Place the dumpling dough in the center of the floured surface and, rolling the pin from the center out, roll the dough until it is 6 millimeters (¼ inch) thick.

Using a round metal cookie cutter or a small, sharp knife, cut the dough into 16 circles just large enough to completely enclose the marzipan-covered cherries.

Working with one piece at a time, carefully pull the dough circle up and over the marzipan-covered cherry and pinch it closed. Roll the dumpling between the palms of your hand to create a smooth, round ball. At this point, the dumplings may be wrapped, airtight, and refrigerated for up to 2 days.

Preheat the oven to 205°C (400°F).

Toss the bread crumbs with the butter in a baking pan. Place in the preheated oven and bake, stirring occasionally, for about 5 minutes, or until the crumbs are dark brown and crunchy. Remove from the oven and keep warm while you cook the dumplings.

Bring a large pot of water to a simmer over high heat.

Carefully lower the dumplings into the simmering water without crowding them. Cook for about 4 minutes, or until the dumplings float to the top.

Place the warm, toasted bread crumbs in a shallow bowl.

Using a slotted spoon, carefully remove the dumplings from the water and immediately roll them in the bread crumbs.

Spoon the compote on a decorative serving platter. Place the warm dumplings in the compote and sprinkle with some of the bread crumbs. Serve immediately, accompanied by *crème Chantilly*, *crème fraîche*, or vanilla ice cream, if desired.

Demonstration

Knödelteig aus Brandteig (Austrian Dumpling Dough)

Makes about 16 dumplings
Estimated time to complete: 90 minutes

Ingredients	Equipment
265 milliliters (9 ounces) whole milk	Wooden spoon
Medium saucepan	Rubber spatula
20 grams (1 tablespoon) unsalted butter, cubed	Plastic film
Pinch salt	
150 grams (5⅓ ounces) all-purpose flour	
2 large egg yolks, at room temperature	

Prepare your *mise en place.*

Combine the milk, butter, and salt in a medium saucepan over high heat. Bring to a boil and immediately remove from the heat.

Using a wooden spoon, quickly beat in the flour.

When the flour is incorporated, return the mixture to medium-low heat and cook, beating constantly, for a couple of minutes to dry it out (*dessécher*). The mixture will form a film over the bottom of the pan.

Beating constantly, add the egg yolks one at a time. When the yolks are completely incorporated, remove the pan from the heat.

Using a rubber spatula, scrape the dough from the pan. Wrap it in plastic film and refrigerate for about 1 hour, or until well chilled.

When the dough is chilled, use as directed in the cherry dumpling recipe, or as specified in any other recipe.

TIPS
Different varieties of cherries can be used for this recipe, but a sour-cherry compote serves to balance the sweetness of the marzipan.

If using frozen cherries for the center of the dumpling, drain them exceedingly well or their liquid will melt the marzipan.

The dough can be made in advance of use and refrigerated, wrapped airtight, for up to 5 days. It is imperative that the package be airtight or a skin will form on the dough, rendering it useless.

The dough may be flavored, sparingly, with sweet spices such as cinnamon or nutmeg.

These are extremely rich and heavy, so no more than 3 should be served per person.

EVALUATING YOUR SUCCESS
The dough should be smooth with all ingredients well incorporated.

The dough should feel slightly soft and elastic, but should be firm enough to roll out easily and still hold its shape.

The dough surrounding the marzipan-covered cherries should be no more than 6 millimeters (¼ inch) thick.

Although technically not a *choux* paste, Austrian dumpling dough uses the same ingredients and follows the same preparation procedure as classic French dough. The dumpling dough, however, uses much less liquid, which makes it firm enough to roll and shape.

The dumplings should have no holes, which would allow the cherry juice to escape.

When cooked, the dumplings should be soft, but not falling apart from contact with the water.

The cooked dumplings should have a distinct almond flavor from the marzipan.

The bread crumbs should add a contrasting crunch to the soft dumplings.

When served, the dumplings should be very warm in the center.

Demonstration

Paris-Brest (Ring-shaped Cake)

Makes one 8-inch cake
Estimated time to complete: 2 hours

Ingredients	Equipment
¼ recipe *Pâte à Choux* (see page 153)	Baking sheet
Egg Wash (see page 62)	Parchment paper
50 grams (1¾ ounces) sliced almonds	Pencil
Crème Paris-Brest (recipe follows)	Small bowl
Confectioners' sugar for dusting	Pastry bag fitted with #5 plain tip and #5 star tip
	Pastry brush
	Wire rack
	Serrated knife
	Serving platter
	Small fine-mesh sieve

Prepare your *mise en place*.

Preheat the oven to 260°C (500°F) for a convection oven or 233°C (450°F) for a conventional or deck oven.

Line a baking sheet with parchment paper. Using a pencil, draw a circle, 20 centimeters (8 inches) in diameter, on the parchment paper to serve as your guide when piping the *choux* paste.

Place the egg wash in a small bowl.

Place the *pâte à choux* in a pastry bag fitted with the #5 plain tip and pipe a ring of paste on the parchment paper just on the inside of the circle. Pipe another ring just on the outside of the circle so that the two piped rings touch. Finally, pipe a third ring on top of the two bottom rings, covering the line where they meet. To keep the pastry high as it bakes, gently push on the bag to allow the *choux* to "fall" rather than be forced out. The rings should not overlap, yet there should be no gaps.

Using a pastry brush, lightly coat the piped *pâte à choux* with egg wash.

Sprinkle the almond slices over the top of the pastry

rings. Do not overload the pastry with almonds. If there are too many, they will just fall off during baking.

For convection ovens, place the pastry in the preheated oven and immediately turn it off. Bake in the turned-off oven for 15 minutes. Then, turn the oven to 177°C (350°F) and bake for about 25 minutes, or until the pastries are golden brown and baked through, with the color on the inside matching the color on the surface. You can also lift the pastries and check the cracks on the bottom to make sure that they are done.

For conventional or deck ovens, place the pastry in the preheated oven and bake for about 35 minutes, or until done.

Remove the pan from the oven, place it on a wire rack, and allow the pastry to cool completely.

Using a serrated knife, cut the cooled pastry ring in half crosswise. Place the bottom half on a serving platter. Set the almond-covered top half aside.

Transfer the *crème Paris-Brest* to a pastry bag fitted with the #5 star tip. Begin piping the cream along the outside edge of the ring and then pipe it along the inside edge. Fill in any gaps between the two to completely cover the pastry.

Pour the confectioners' sugar into a small fine-mesh sieve and, lightly tapping the side of the sieve, dust the pastry top with sugar.

Carefully place the pastry top over the cream-filled bottom.

Serve immediately or within a couple of hours.

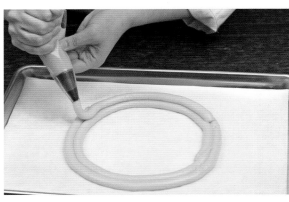

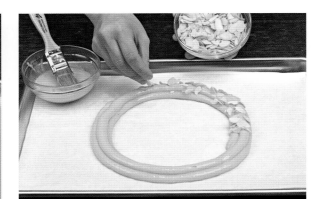

Crème Paris-Brest (Praline Cream for *Paris-Brest*)

Makes 575 grams (1¾ pounds)
Estimated time to complete: 1 hour

Ingredients	Equipment
175 grams (6⅛ ounces) unsalted butter, at room temperature	Standing electric mixer fitted with paddle
100 grams (3½ ounces) praline paste (see Tips)	Rubber spatula
300 grams (11 ounces) *Crème Pâtissière* (see page 248), cooled	
Liquor or liqueur to taste, optional	

Prepare your *mise en place*.

Combine the butter and praline paste in the bowl of a standing electric mixer fitted with the paddle. Mix on medium speed, scraping down the sides of the bowl with a rubber spatula, for about 5 minutes, or until the mixture is thoroughly creamed, light, and fluffy. The pra-

line paste should be completely blended into the butter.

Add the cool pastry cream and beat until very light and airy. It is extremely important that the cream be cool; otherwise, it will melt the butter. If the finished praline cream is too soft, refrigerate it for a few minutes and then beat it to smooth it out. If it is too firm,

NOTE

Paris-Brest was created in the round shape of a bicycle wheel by a pastry cook whose shop was on the route of a famous bicycle race between the cities of Paris and Brest. There is also a cake known as a *Paris-Nice*, honoring another city-to-city bicycle race, which is made in the same fashion but with a vanilla filling.

continue beating until it is soft enough to pipe easily. If using, fold in the alcohol and use as directed in the *Paris-Brest* recipe or in any other recipe.

TIPS

Praline paste is a commercially available product created by grinding caramelized nuts to a thick paste. It is used as a flavoring in pastry making.

Individual *Paris-Brest* pastries may also be made by simply reducing the size of the circles. If making very small ones, pipe only one ring of *choux* paste rather than three.

If, after being thoroughly baked, the interior of the pastry remains gooey, just scrape it out, leaving as dry a center as possible.

The baked, unfilled ring may be wrapped, airtight, and frozen for up to 1 month.

The cream should be visible from the side of the filled pastry, but it should not be dripping over the edge.

Hazelnut liqueur and brandy are excellent flavorings for this cream.

If the praline cream is refrigerated to thicken it before

piping, it must always be beaten with the electric mixer to smooth it out.

Use the praline cream as soon as it reaches the right consistency for piping.

EVALUATING YOUR SUCCESS

The pastry ring should be thoroughly baked, golden, dry, and crisp.

The interior of the pastry should be dry, not gooey.

When baked, the pastry ring should be evenly round.

The almonds should be baked into the *choux* paste, not lying on top of it.

The filling should be decoratively piped into the pastry.

The filling should be visible, but contained within the ring.

The finished praline cream should have a strong, nutty flavor and be lump-free, silky smooth, and soft enough to pipe easily, but firm enough to hold its shape.

The confectioners' sugar should lightly dust the cake, not overwhelm it.

Demonstration

Gâteau Saint-Honoré (Saint Honoré's Cake)

Makes one 8-inch cake
Estimated time to complete: 2 hours

Ingredients	Equipment
Flour for dusting	3 baking sheets
200 grams (7 ounces) *Pâte Brisée* (see page 92)	Parchment paper
½ recipe *Pâte à Choux* (see page 153)	Rolling pin
Egg wash (see page 62)	Pastry brush
	Docker or kitchen fork

For the caramel

300 grams (11 ounces) sugar

Crème Chiboust (recipe follows)

Pastry bag fitted with #5 plain tip

Plastic film

Ice-water bath

Heavy-bottomed saucepan

Wooden spoon

Shallow heat-proof container

Small star pastry tip

#4 plain tip

Offset spatula

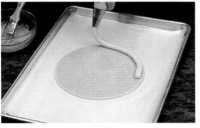

Prepare your *mise en place*.

Line two of the baking sheets with parchment paper.

Lightly flour a clean, flat work surface. Place the *pâte brisée* dough in the center of the floured surface and, using a rolling pin, roll the dough out to an 20-centimeter (8-inch) circle about 3 millimeters (⅛ inch) thick. Using a pastry brush, lightly brush the excess flour from the dough.

Roll the circle up and over the rolling pin and carefully transfer it to one of the parchment paper-lined baking sheets. Place it in the refrigerator for at least 1 hour, or until well chilled.

Using a docker or a kitchen fork, dock the entire surface of the chilled dough circle.

Preheat the oven to 177°C (350°F).

Transfer the *pâte à choux* to a pastry bag fitted with the #5 plain tip. Beginning from the outside edge, carefully pipe concentric circles of *choux* paste over the *pâte brisée*. Using a pastry brush, lightly coat the *choux* circles with egg wash.

Bake for 20 to 30 minutes, or until golden brown, then set aside to cool.

Raise the oven temperature to 260°C (500°F) for convection and 233°C (450°F) for conventional or deck ovens.

Still using the #5 plain tip, pipe the *choux* paste into about twelve 1.3-centimeter (½-inch) rounds onto the remaining baking sheet, allowing sufficient room between each one to ensure even baking.

Using a pastry brush, lightly coat each piece with egg wash.

For convection ovens, place the *choux* in the 260°C (500°F) oven and immediately turn it off. Bake in the turned-off oven for 15 minutes. Then, turn the oven to 177°C (350°F) and bake for about 25 minutes, or until the *choux* are golden brown and baked through. You can also lift the pastries and check the cracks on the bottom to make sure that they are baked completely through. (To bake in a conventional or deck oven, see page 152.)

For either oven, turn off the heat and leave the pastries inside with the door ajar, for 5 to 10 minutes to thoroughly dry them.

When the pastry feels dry, light, and hollow, remove the baking sheets from the oven and allow to cool for 20 minutes.

Line a baking sheet with plastic film. Set aside.

To make the caramel, place a heavy-bottomed saucepan over medium heat. When just hot, add the sugar and lower the heat. Cook, stirring with a wooden spoon to prevent lumps from forming, for about 5 minutes, or until the sugar melts, turns a warm amber color, and is quite clear. If the syrup is cloudy, the sugar needs to dissolve more.

Immediately remove the pan from the heat and place it in the ice-water bath to stop the cooking. If overcooked, the caramel will darken and turn bitter.

Transfer the caramel to a shallow heat-proof container (so that you don't have to reach down into a hot pan). Working quickly, dip the top of each *choux* into the caramel to just lightly coat. Immediately place the *choux*, caramel side down, on the plastic film–lined baking sheet.

When all of the *choux* have been dipped in caramel, using a small, star pastry tip and holding it upright, poke a hole in the center of each *choux*.

Transfer the *crème Chiboust* to a pastry bag fitted with the #4 plain tip and pipe the cream into each *choux* to fill it completely.

Working with one at a time, dip the uncoated side of each filled *choux* into the caramel and affix it to the outer edge of the *pâte brisée* round to create the *gâteau*. When almost all of the *choux* have been fitted along the edge, "dry fit" the remaining *choux*,

as a test to identify just how many more it will take to entirely cover the edge. Then, dip and affix the necessary number.

Pipe the remaining *crème Chiboust* into the center to completely cover the *pâte brisée*. Alternatively, spread the cream out with an offset spatula to completely cover.

Transfer to the refrigerator to chill thoroughly before serving.

NOTE

Gâteau Saint-Honoré is named in honor of the patron saint of bakers and pastry chefs, Saint Honoré or Honoratus, bishop of Amiens, who is often displayed carrying a baker's peel. It is said that the cake was first made by a pastry chef named Chiboust in 1846 in his shop located on the Rue-St. Honoré in Paris. The classic filling is referred to as Chiboust cream and a signature *Chiboust* or *Saint-Honoré* pastry tip is used to pipe it. It is still often served on Saint Honoré's Day, May 16, the purported day of the saint's death.

Crème Chiboust (also called Crème Saint-Honoré)

Makes enough filling for one 8-inch cake
Estimated time to complete: 30 minutes

Ingredients	Equipment
1 gelatin sheet	Shallow bowl
40 grams (1⅓ ounces) sugar	Medium heat-proof mixing bowl
3 large egg yolks, at room temperature	Whisk
15 grams (1 tablespoon) pastry cream powder (see Tips)	Medium saucepan
175 grams (6⅛ ounces) whole milk	Small sharp knife
½ vanilla bean, cut in half lengthwise	Heat-proof spatula

For the Italian meringue

150 grams (5⅓ ounces) sugar

75 grams (2⅔ ounces) egg whites

Plastic film

Medium heavy-bottomed saucepan

Pastry brush

Standing electric mixer fitted with whip

Rubber spatula

Pastry bag fitted with appropriate tip

Prepare your *mise en place.*

Place the gelatin in a shallow bowl with cold water to cover. Set aside to soften.

Combine half of the sugar with the egg yolks and pastry cream powder in a medium heat-proof mixing bowl, whisking to combine well. Set aside.

Combine the milk with the remaining sugar in a medium saucepan over medium heat. Using a small, sharp knife, scrape the seeds from the vanilla bean into the milk. Add the scraped bean and bring to a boil, watching carefully so that it does not boil over.

Remove the hot milk from the heat and, whisking constantly, pour about one-third of it into the egg yolk mixture to temper it.

Whisking constantly, pour the tempered egg yolks into the hot milk. Return to medium-high heat and cook, stirring constantly with a heat-proof spatula, until the mixture comes to a boil. Boil, stirring constantly, for 2 minutes.

Remove from the heat.

Squeeze the excess water from the softened gelatin sheet. Add the gelatin to the hot mixture, stirring to combine well.

Cover the surface of the hot cream with plastic film to keep a skin from forming and set it aside to cool slightly.

Meanwhile, make the meringue.

Place 115 grams (4 ounces) of the sugar in a medium heavy-bottomed saucepan. Add just enough cold water to cover. Place over high heat and bring to a boil. As the sugar cooks, using a wet pastry brush, brush down the interior of the pan to remove any crystallized sugar granules. Cook, stirring and brushing down the sides frequently, for about 10 minutes, or until the syrup reaches the soft-ball stage, 112°C to 116°C (234°F to 240°F) on a candy thermometer.

While the syrup is cooking, place the egg whites in the bowl of a standing electric mixer fitted with the whip and beat until soft peaks form. When the whip begins to leave a trail in the meringue, add the remaining sugar and beat to blend it into the whites.

With the motor running, carefully pour the hot syrup into the beaten egg whites, continuing to beat until stiff peaks form.

Using a rubber spatula, carefully fold the warm meringue into the still-warm cream, taking care that the mixture does not form lumps.

Transfer the cream to a pastry bag and pipe as directed in the recipe while still warm or at no more than room temperature. If refrigerated, the cream will firm up and be impossible to pipe.

TIPS

It is extremely important to completely prepare your *mise en place* before beginning this recipe, as time is of the essence in putting it all together.

Pastry cream powder is a commercially-produced bakery product that is simply cornstarch with vanilla flavoring and, occasionally, yellow food coloring added to ensure brightness in the finished pastry cream. It is used as a thickener and is available from cake and bakery supply stores. Cornstarch can be used as a substitute.

The ring of *pâte brisée* gives strength to the finished cake and offers a higher edge.

If the caramel begins to harden, it can be reheated in the oven or over very low heat on the stovetop.

The gelatin must be very soft before it is added to the custard.

Crème Chiboust is a very thick custard, and great care must be taken to keep lumps from forming.

If the cream seems too soft, refrigerate it briefly to firm it up; however, do not cool it for too long or the gelatin will set. If it becomes too firm, soften it slightly in a *bain-marie*.

The cream may be stored, tightly covered and refrigerated, for up to 3 days.

EVALUATING YOUR SUCCESS

The *choux* should be equal in size and height.

The caramel should be dark enough to have a distinct flavor, but it should not be burned and bitter and should form a hard and crunchy coating on the *choux*.

The cream should be smooth and lump-free, with a strong vanilla flavor.

The cream should be firm enough to hold a piped shape but not so firm that it tears when piped.

The *choux* should be completely filled with cream. When set, the cream should be light and airy.

The piped décor should be even and attractively placed.

Demonstration

Croquembouche

Makes one cone-shaped tower
Estimated time to complete: 5 hours

Ingredients	Equipment
Flour for dusting	3 or more baking sheets
1 recipe *Pâte Brisée* (see Note and page 92)	Parchment paper
½ recipe *Pâte à Choux* (see page 153)	Rolling pin
Egg wash (see page 62)	Pastry brush
600 grams (1 pound, 5 ounces) sugar	Docker or kitchen fork
1 recipe *Crème Patissière* (see page 248)	Tart pan large enough to cover the base of the *croquembouche*
1 recipe *Nougatine* (recipe follows)	Pastry weights or dried beans
	Pastry bag with #5 and #4 plain tips and small star tip
	Wire rack
	Plastic film
	Ice-water bath
	Heavy-bottomed saucepan
	Wooden spoon

Prepare your *mise en place*.

Line the baking sheets with parchment paper.

Lightly flour a clean, flat work surface. Place the *pâte brisée* dough in the center of the floured surface and, using a rolling pin, roll the dough out to a 3-millimeter (⅛-inch) thick circle to serve as the base for the *croquembouche*. Using a pastry brush, lightly brush the excess flour from the dough.

Roll the circle up and over the rolling pin and carefully transfer it to one of the parchment-lined baking sheets. Place it in the refrigerator for at least 1 hour, or until well chilled.

Preheat a convection or a conventional oven to 149°C (300°F).

Remove the dough from the refrigerator. Using a docker or a kitchen fork, dock the entire surface of the circle.

Place a piece of parchment paper large enough to cover the dough circle entirely over the dough. Set a tart pan large enough to cover the dough circle on top. Add the pastry weights to the pan, spreading them out in an even layer.

Bake the pastry for about 10 minutes, or until it is dry and chalky white. Remove the tart pan with the weights and the parchment paper, and continue to bake for an additional 15 minutes, or until the pastry is lightly browned and cooked through. Set aside to cool.

Increase the oven temperature to 260°C (500°F) for convection ovens or 233°C (450°F) for conventional or deck ovens.

Place the *choux* paste in a pastry bag fitted with the #5 plain tip and pipe it into 3.8-centimeter (1½-inch) rounds on the two remaining baking sheets, allowing sufficient room between each round to ensure even baking. Each round should be the exact same size as the others to facilitate proper construction of the *croquembouche's* cone shape. You will probably have to make the rounds in batches, as you will need about 100 of them to finish the cone shape (see sizing chart, page 181). Make a few extra rounds as well, in case you have any breakage or a *choux* (or two or three) gets stuck in the caramel when dipping.

Using a pastry brush, lightly coat each piece with egg wash.

For convection ovens, place the *choux* in the 260°C (500°F) oven and immediately turn it off. Bake in the turned-off oven for 15 minutes. Then, turn the oven to 177°C (350°F) and bake for about 25 minutes or until the *choux* are golden brown and baked through. You can also lift the pastries and check the cracks on the bottom to make sure that they are baked completely through. (To bake in a conventional or deck oven, see page 152.)

For either oven, turn off the heat and leave the pastries inside with the door ajar, for 5 to 10 minutes to thoroughly dry them.

Transfer to a wire rack to cool.

Line a baking sheet with plastic film. Set aside.

To make the caramel, place a heavy-bottomed saucepan over medium heat. When just hot, add the sugar and lower the heat. Cook, stirring with a wooden spoon to prevent lumps from forming, for about 5 minutes, or until the sugar melts, turns a warm amber color, and is quite clear. If the syrup is cloudy, the sugar needs to dissolve more.

Immediately remove the caramel from the heat and place the pan in the ice-water bath to stop the cooking. Overcooked caramel will darken and turn bitter.

Pour the caramel into a shallow heat-proof container. (The depth is important for safety, as you don't want

Croquembouche literally means "crunch in the mouth." The *pièce montée* is the traditional French wedding cake. Individual *choux* are broken off of the cone shape by a server, who plates and serves them to the guests.

Although a *croquembouche* may be served as is, it is traditionally elaborately decorated. The décor adds much—it serves to hide any deficiencies in the symmetry of the cone shape.

A croquembouche may be decorated in a delicate fashion in any of the following ways:

The top of each *choux* may be first dipped in caramel and then dipped in pearl or sanding sugar or chopped nuts before being set into the cone shape.

Thinly piped *choux* paste decorations may be attached to the *croquembouche* with caramel.

Hot caramel may be poured onto an oiled surface in decorative shapes and, when cooled and hardened, attached to the *croquembouche* with caramel.

Using the caramel as glue, dried or candied fruits may be attached to the *croquembouche* to add color.

Using the caramel as glue, whole or candied nuts may be stuck on the sides of the finished tower to add decorative interest.

A veil of spun sugar may be draped over the top.

A decorative pattern of royal icing (see page 381) can be piped on.

Marzipan or pulled-sugar flowers may be placed in a decorative fashion over the *croquembouche*.

to have to reach down into a hot pan.) If the caramel cools, reheat it over very low heat or in the oven—you don't want it to cook or get any darker in color. You may have to warm the caramel a few times during the dipping process.

Working quickly, dip the top of each *choux* into the caramel to just lightly coat. Immediately place the *choux*, caramel side down, on the plastic film–lined baking sheet.

When all of the *choux* have been dipped in caramel, using a small star pastry tip and holding it upright, poke a hole in the center of each *choux*.

Transfer the *crème pâtissière* to a pastry bag fitted with the #4 plain tip and pipe the cream into each *choux* to fill it completely.

Working with one at a time, dip the bottom of each filled *choux* into the caramel and affix it to the outer edge of the *pâte brisée* base round. Continue "gluing" choux onto the base until it is entirely covered.

If you are making the *croquembouche* freehand, begin making layers of *choux*, setting the pastries on their sides with the caramel tops facing outward. Glue each *choux* in place using caramel as you build. As the layers move upward, each should decrease in size to create a cone-shaped tower. Continue adding layers until the shape reaches a point at the top with a single *choux*. Be aware as the *croquembouche* is constructed that the caramel needs time to set before the next layer is added, or else the previous layer may shift. Simply

wait a bit between layers until the sugar hardens enough to hold. If a *choux* hardens out of place, gently break it off and put another *choux* in the proper spot.

To assemble a *croquembouche* using a cone-shaped mold, lightly grease the interior of the *croquembouche* mold. Place one caramel-topped *choux* in the point. Begin adding layers by attaching the next layer to the point with caramel, taking care that the caramel-covered top is resting against the mold. Continue making layers until the entire mold is lined on the inside with *choux*.

Drizzle the interior with caramel to further ensure that the *choux* will hold firmly together when unmolded.

Transfer the mold to the refrigerator to chill just long enough to harden the caramel.

Remove the *croquembouche* from the refrigerator and carefully unmold it onto a flat work surface. This should happen rather easily if the caramel has hardened properly.

Drizzle caramel around the edge of the base and firmly plant the cone shape on top of it. Set aside for a few minutes to allow the caramel to harden.

Decorate the *croquembouche* with small pieces of *nougatine*.

Serve the *croquembouche* within an hour or two of being made, as the *choux* will begin to soften very quickly.

TIPS

You may use *pâte sucrée* (see page 94) in place of the *pâte brisée* for the base.

Choux puffs and decorations can be baked in advance but not filled or dipped in caramel. The assembly and decoration of the *croquembouche* must be done shortly before it is served.

The pastry cream can be flavored, but it should not be lightened or the finished *choux* will quickly soften.

To reiterate: Prepare and fill a few more *choux* than you need to be prepared for any breakage or sticking.

Although the peaked shape is the most common *croquembouche* structure, other traditional shapes include cradles, churches, buildings, and containers for candies.

Before building a *croquembouche*, you must consider the number of choux puffs you will need and then calculate the construction needs. A well-built *croquembouche* decreases by one puff per layer. If using a mold, less skill is required; however, it will still need to be glued to the pastry base.

The chart below can be used to calculate the size of a *croquembouche*. The number on the left indicates the height of the *croquembouche* with the measurement given in individual puffs. This also indicates the number of puffs that must be used as the base. For example, a *croquembouche* that will include 76 puffs (at 2 per person, enough for 38 guests) will have a base of 12 puffs and will stand 11 puffs high.

Layer	Puffs per layer	Total
1	1	1
2	3	4
3	4	8
4	5	13
5	6	19
6	7	26
7	8	34
8	9	43
9	10	53
10	11	64
11	12	76
12	13	89
13	14	103
14	15	118

In damp or humid conditions, the entire structure may begin to melt and sag if it cannot be served soon enough. As a last resort, the chef can set the structure on a stiff form, but this is not recommended as it is neither attractive nor traditionally done.

EVALUATING YOUR SUCCESS

The *choux* puffs should be equal in size and height.

The *choux* puffs should be thoroughly baked and crunchy.

The caramel used on the tops of the *choux* and for cementing them together should be dark enough to have a distinct flavor, but not burned and bitter. The caramel coating should be hard and crackling on the *choux*.

The cream should be smooth and lump-free, with a strong vanilla flavor.

The cream should be firm enough to hold a piped shape but not so firm that it tears when piped.

The *choux* should be completely filled with cream.

The finished shape should be a tall, symmetrical cone, with no large gaps or holes visible.

Any decorations placed on the *croquembouche* should add interest and contrast, but should not overwhelm it

Demonstration

Nougatine

Makes 1 sheet pan
Estimated time to complete: 90 minutes

Ingredients	**Equipment**
600 grams (1 pound, 5 ounces) sugar	2 silicone baking liners
250 grams (8¾ ounces) lightly toasted sliced almonds, warm	Sheet pan
	Heavy-bottomed saucepan
	Wooden spoon
	Offset spatula
	Rolling pin
	Oiled marble slab or cutting board
	Chef's knife
	Molds (see Note)

Prepare your *mise en place*.

Place one of the silicone baking liners into the sheet pan.

Place a heavy-bottomed saucepan over medium heat.

When just hot, add the sugar and lower the heat. Cook, stirring with a wooden spoon to prevent lumps from forming, for about 5 minutes, or until the sugar melts, turns a warm amber color, and is quite clear. If the syrup is cloudy, the sugar needs to dissolve more.

NOTE

Nougatine is traditionally used as the base for a croquembouche, as well as to make a wide variety of pastry show-pieces and display stands. To mold *nougatine*, you can use almost anything made out of metal: bowls, pans, measuring cups, tuile molds, etc. The mold should be cool, dry, and very clean, as well as lightly coated in vegetable oil to facilitate unmolding. The *nougatine* can be either pushed into the mold or pressed over the exterior of it. It can also simply be cut into small squares, rounds, or triangles.

Add the warm almonds, stirring to incorporate. Immediately remove from the heat and pour the hot mixture into the sheet pan, spreading it out as thinly as possible with an offset spatula, without allowing any holes or spaces to open.

Place another silicone sheet on top and, using a rolling pin, roll the *nougatine* as thin and even as possible without tearing.

Remove the top silicone liner and carefully transfer the *nougatine* to a lightly oiled marble slab or a cutting board. If the *nougatine* sticks to the bottom silicone sheet when lifted, it is still too hot. Carefully transfer the bottom silicone liner along with the *nougatine* to a cooler spot, then attempt to transfer it after it cools a bit more. It should be cool enough to touch but warm enough to cut without cracking.

Using a chef's knife, cut and mold the warm *nougatine* into the desired shape or into the required shape for a specific recipe. Work quickly and neatly so that the mixture remains warm enough to shape (see Note).

If the *nougatine* cools too much to work with, return it to the silicone liner and place it in a preheated 177°C (350°F) oven for just a few minutes, until just soft enough to cut and mold. The reheated *nougatine*

pieces may be rerolled into one piece, but do not reroll it too often, as each time the mixture is rolled, the almonds break a bit more.

Allow the molded pieces to cool thoroughly so that they are firm enough to hold their shape when being handled before using them as decorative pieces for *croquembouche* or another recipe.

TIPS

Nougatine easily absorbs moisture and is therefore greatly affected by humidity in the work area. It should be made as close as possible to the time it will be used.

Any leftover pieces should be stored, airtight, with a chemical desiccant such as limestone or silica gel (available from cake and bakery supply stores) in the container to help absorb moisture. These pieces can be coarsely chopped and folded into mousses and ice creams for added flavor and texture.

Nougatine is often piped with elegant royal icing designs for added interest.

Session 5

Pâte Feuilletée: An Overview of Puff Pastry

Theory

Puff pastry, rich, light, and delicious, is the base for a wide variety of sweet and savory dishes in the classic French culinary repertoire. Having a nice, even rise, it is used for pies, tarts, *allumettes* (puff pastry strips), and *vols-au-vent* (puff pastry shells), as well as many other dishes. It has an elegant and refined image that, for generations, has been surrounded with mystique. Throughout its history, puff pastry has been known as time-consuming to prepare, complicated to master, and, with its luxurious use of butter, expensive to make. Although it is true that it is time-consuming and somewhat expensive, given the proper attention, puff pastry—contrary to its reputation—is not particularly difficult to make.

Literally translated, the French term *pâte feuilletée* or *feuilletage* means "leaved dough" and refers to its thin layers. The term itself goes back to fifteenth-century France, where pastry cooks and guildsmen prepared rolled and folded pastries from a layered dough made with butter. This early dough was probably quite primitive compared to the light, flaky pastry of today; however, through evolution, it has come down to us as flaky pastries, such as marzipan turnovers, and the butter-based pastries, croissants, and *brioches* that are so popular in contemporary pastry kitchens. The first recorded recipe for *pâte feuilletée* appeared in a book called *Pâtissier françois* in 1654. A recipe for *mille-feuilles* ("a thousand leaves," referring to the dough's many layers) first appeared in 1651 in a tome entitled *Le cuisinier français*; it is the pastry we Americans know as a Napoleon (see page 228).

Pastry guilds, established in the Middle Ages, were abolished by decree in 1776. However, late-eighteenth-century and early-nineteenth-century pastry chefs, including the renowned Antonin Carême, who is credited with the invention of *vols-au-vent* and *croquembouches*, would continue to refine and perfect *pâte feuilletée*. During this period, puff pastry was taken to new heights with elaborate and fanciful creations, many of them the delicate pastries of the classic French repertoire.

According to the culinarian's bible, *Larousse Gastronomique*, puff pastry was known and made as far back as ancient Greece and Rome, where it began as a phyllo-like layered pastry made with oil. A mention of puff pastry is found in a fourteenth-century charter drawn up by the Bishop of Amiens. However, it seems that its techniques were perfected by two seventeenth-century cooks, a chef named Feuillet, who served as pastry cook to an aristocratic family, and the renowned French landscape painter Claude Lorrain, who also happened to have served a pastry apprenticeship in his youth. Some historians credit Feuillet as the inventor, some credit Lorrain, but whoever it was, by the eighteenth-century *pâte feuilletée* was firmly entrenched in the French pastry kitchen.

Several specialized terms are associated with the making of puff pastry. The process begins with a simple dough composed of flour, salt, water, and melted butter called a *détrempe* and a block of butter called a *beurrage*. The *détrempe* is folded around the *beurrage* to form a package called a *pâton*. The *pâton* is then folded,

turned, rolled, and chilled many times, until a multilayered dough has been created. The more folds, turns, and rolls there are, the more layers in the finished pastry.

This process of folding, turning, and rolling is called *tourage*. Typically, the dough is rolled out at intervals of two turns at a time, followed by a substantial refrigerated resting period, which firms the fat and prevents it from melding into the dough. The classic number of turns is six, but four or five can also be done, depending on the final use of the pastry. The dough will not rise as much when fewer turns are done.

Since puff pastry has no leavening agent such as yeast, eggs, or baking powder, the layers created by *tourage* are necessary to buoy up the dough. Through *tourage*, the layers of fat and dough are each rolled thinner than a piece of paper but remain separate and intact. Because of this layered structure, *pâte feuilleté* is classified as a laminated dough. The lamination leavens the dough and creates height by stacking the layers and trapping pockets of air in between. When baked, the moisture in the dough and the melting (or boiling) of butter creates steam that forces the layers to rise, one by one, puffing up the pastry and causing it to become flaky and light. It is a remarkable dough in that, even without leavening agents, it can rise to eight to ten times its original height and can contain more than one thousand layers.

Types of Puff Pastry Doughs and Their Uses

Pâte feuilletée: The most well-known and frequently used classic French puff pastry dough, *pâte feuilletée* is suitable for any preparation requiring a light, flaky dough. Although time-consuming to prepare, the result is a crisp, buttery, layered pastry with a perfectly even rise.

Feuilletage rapide: As its name implies, quick or rapid puff pastry is faster to make than the classic variety. It does not rise as evenly or as high, and its texture is not nearly as tender and flaky. However, it is a useful alternative when time is of the essence or when the delicacy and height of the finished pastry is not of primary importance. The time savings is the result of eliminating the refrigerated resting period. Quick puff pastry is most frequently used to encase savory preparations, such as *salmon en croûte*. It is also useful when making quick tart bases and for small pastries, such as *palmiers* or *paillettes* (cheese straws).

Pâte feuilletée inversée: As its name indicates, inverse (or reverse) puff pastry is a dough in which the positions of the *détrempe* and the *beurrage* are reversed—whereby the *beurrage* is on the outside rather than on the inside. When using this method, less gluten is formed, and the dough develops very evenly without much shrinkage. This in turn, produces an extremely tender and flaky baked pastry. It is often used when delicacy and texture are important to the finished

dish. Chocolate puff pastry is created using the inverse method with, of course, the addition of cocoa powder to the flour. *Feuilleté inversé* has recently been popularized by the renowned French pastry chef, Pierre Hermé.

Leavening by Aeration

Aeration is the leavening action that occurs in *pâte feuilletée* when it bakes. It is a mechanical method that occurs in three ways:

1. **Enclosed or trapped air:** During the preparation of the puff pastry dough, a certain amount of air is trapped between each layer each time the dough is folded. During baking, these air cells expand and push the layers up and apart.

2. **Steam:** As *pâte feuilletée* is baked, steam is released from the melting butter and from the water contained in the dough layers. The steam created pushes on the leaves (layers) of dough, forcing them to rise. Concurrently, the starch contained in the flour coagulates on contact with the steam, strengthening the leaves of pastry and helping them remain separated.

3. **Fat:** As the fat (butter) held in the dough layers melts during baking, it leaves behind air pockets that can fill with steam and assist in the rising.

Using the Proper Ingredients for a Successful *Pâte Feuilletée*

Fat: When making *pâte feuilletée*, the fat used has a significant impact on the final quality of the baked product. Historically (and, in France, regionally) many types of fat have been used in its preparation, including lard, goose fat, vegetable shortening, and margarine, but the most classic and desirable fat is unsalted, premium-quality butter, as it provides the smoothest flavor. Whatever fat is used, it must be chilled and kept at roughly the same consistency as the dough throughout the preparation period.

Flour: When making *pâte feuilletée*, the choice of flour is almost as important as the fat type and quality. It should be high enough in protein to stretch without breaking as the dough bakes and low enough to remain tender and light. A mix of equal amounts of cake and bread flour or a simple all-purpose flour is the recommended choice for successful *pâte feuilletée*. The addition of an acid, such as cream of tartar, lemon juice, or vinegar, can help the protein in the flour become more elastic and allows the dough to stretch rather than break when being worked. However, if the dough must be refrigerated for a long period of time before baking, adding acid will have the opposite effect and will inhibit rising of the dough.

Guidelines for Making Perfect *Pâte Feuilletée*

Most types of puff pastry involve three stages: the preparation of a *détrempe* and then a *beurrage*, followed by *tourage* (a series of folds or turns). The only exception is the quick or rapid *feuilletage*, wherein the butter is mixed in with the *détrempe*.

In order to make a successful puff pastry of any type, it is important to keep the following points in mind:

Keep the work environment cool. The kitchen should be cool, and there should be a cool surface to work on, preferably marble. Otherwise, puff pastry can be very difficult to manage. It must be rechilled as soon as it starts to soften and before the butter begins to melt or it will be impossible to manipulate.

Do not overdevelop the gluten. When making the *détrempe*, mix the ingredients as little as possible—just enough to form a rough mass that holds together. Too much mixing will cause excessive development of gluten, making the dough difficult to turn. The long rest periods between the turns also aids in containing the gluten development by letting the dough relax.

Always consider the strength and quality of the flour relative to the product that you will be making. Some pastry chefs use combinations of different types of flour to adjust the gluten strength. For instance, adding cake flour to all-purpose flour lowers its gluten content and produces a dough that better tolerates the repeated working and rolling of the pastry.

Make sure that the *détrempe* has time to rest before proceeding with the *beurrage*. Always begin by resting the *détrempe* in the refrigerator before incorporating the butter. Form the *beurrage* just before incorporating it into the *détrempe*.

Carefully control the temperature and consistency of the *détrempe* and the *beurrage*. The *détrempe* and the *beurrage* should be as similar in consistency as possible so that they will easily roll together to form the *pâton*. If the *beurrage* is chilled, it will become much harder than the *détrempe*.

When shaping puff pastry, roll it out to the desired thickness and then chill it. This allows the dough to rest; resting prevents shrinkage during the baking period. Once firm, the *pâton* can be cut into the desired shapes and then chilled again before baking.

Use as little flour as possible when turning. The dough should be dusted as lightly as possible with just enough flour to ease handling. Brush off any excess before folding.

Keep the shape of the dough even during *tourage*. When incorporating the *beurrage* and rolling out and turning the *pâton*, keep the dough in an even rectangle of an even thickness as much as possible, continually squaring the sides with a rolling pin as you work. Even layers result in pastry that rises perfectly when baked.

Practice damage control. Do not damage the layered structure of the dough when rolling it out. Do not roll over the sides of the dough as this will compress the edges and interfere with the rising process.

Cut dough carefully. Do not cut *pâte feuilletée* in a sawing motion; always cut straight down. This will keep the edges of the dough even and will help the rise during baking.

Carefully apply egg wash. When applying egg wash to an uncooked puff pastry item, do not allow the liquid to run down the cut sides of the pastry dough. This will inhibit the rise during baking.

Make sure that the pastry is cooked completely before removing it from the oven. To be edible, crisp, and delicious, puff pastry must be cooked until it is brown throughout all layers. Unless the pastry is rolled very thin, the oven temperature may have to be lowered to ensure that this occurs. Unbrowned layers of dough inside the pastry will be heavy, somewhat gummy, and unpleasant on the palate.

Puff pastry scraps should never be wasted. Because it is so time-consuming to produce, even a bit of leftover puff pastry dough should be put to use. Scraps, also known as *demi-feuilletage* or *rognures*, are suitable for making many types of small pastries, such as cheese straws, tart bottoms, barquettes (small boat-shaped pastry shells), *palmiers* (strips of puff pastry dough formed into circular shape, sprinkled with sugar, and baked to golden crispness). In fact, any pastry item that does not need to rise much can be made with scraps. Never roll the scraps into a circle; they should be stored chilled, flat, and as even as possible to avoid destroying the delicate layers, before they are rolled out into the desired shape.

Points to Consider When Puff Pastry Making Is Unsuccessful

If your *pâte feuilletée* does not produce satisfactory results, the following may pinpoint the reason:

○ The flour was too weak and inhibited the development of the gluten and the structure of the dough.

○ The fat was too soft and prevented the proper formation of the layered structure.

○ The fat was too hard and broke through the layers.

○ The dough was not given enough turns, leaving large areas of fat that could not be absorbed by the dough layers. As a result, the fat ran out of the dough when baked, leaving it undeveloped.

○ The oven temperature was too low, preventing sufficient steam from developing to promote proper rising.

Guidelines Proceedure for Making *Pâte Feuilletée*

The *détrempe*: Mix the flours and salt. For every kilogram (2¼ pounds) of flour, add 28 grams (1 ounce) of salt. Soften a small amount of butter until it is the consistency of thick sour cream to make a *beurre en pommade* (softened butter that is cool but malleable). Add the *beurre en pommade* to the flour mixture. Add cold water and mix until the dough just comes together.

The amount of water should be 50 to 60 percent of the total weight of the flour, although this can vary depending upon the quality of the flours. Once mixed, refrigerate the dough to allow it to rest.

The *beurrage*: While the *détrempe* rests, soften the butter for the *beurrage* by pounding it with a rolling pin or working it by hand. In general, the amount of butter should equal 50 to 100 percent of the weight of the flours. The butter should be malleable, with the same consistency as the *détrempe* and shaped into a square of even thickness. The shaped butter should then be kept in a cool area.

Forming the *pâton*: Roll the chilled and rested *détrempe* to create a center square with a flap on each edge. The center square should be slightly thicker than the flaps and the same size as the *beurrage*.

Place the shaped butter in the center of the *détrempe*. First fold one set of opposite flaps over the butter and then fold the remaining two flaps up and over to completely enclose the *beurrage*. Pinch the dough together to lightly seal. This envelope of *détrempe* and butter is called a *pâton*. Once the butter has been enclosed in the *détrempe*, the *pâton* must be evened out. Using a rolling pin, lightly tap it in two directions. The *pâton* should now be a square. Lightly dust the *pâton* with flour to prevent sticking and roll it so that it forms a neat rectangle about 1.3 centimeters (½ inch) thick, with the length being about three times its width. Do not use too much flour or it will dry out the dough and prevent the layers from adhering when folded. Throughout this process be sure to keep the thickness of the dough very even and the corners square. Next, you will give the *pâton* either two single-letter turns or two double-book turns.

Turning the *Pâte Feuilletée*

Letter turn: Fold the rectangle into thirds—this completes the letter fold, or one turn. Now give the *pâton* a quarter turn. (This is necessary to do before each rolling so that the gluten is stretched in all directions, not just lengthwise. Otherwise the end product will shrink and bake unevenly.) Again, roll the rectangle and repeat the letter fold. The *pâte feuilletée* has now received two single-letter turns.

Wrap the *pâton* in plastic film and refrigerate for at least 1 hour to allow the dough to rest. Once rested, repeat the entire rolling and turning procedure to give the dough four complete turns. Again, wrap the dough tightly in plastic film and refrigerate for at least 1 hour to allow the dough to rest.

Once rested for the second time, repeat the entire rolling and turning procedure to give the dough six complete single-letter turns. Again, wrap the dough tightly in plastic film and refrigerate for at least 1 hour to allow the dough to rest before using.

Book turn: Once the butter has been enclosed in the détrempe, the pâton must be evened out. Using a rolling pin, lightly tap it in two directions. The pâton should now be a square. Lightly dust the pâton with flour to prevent sticking and roll it so that it forms a neat rectangle about 1.3 centimeters (½ inch) thick, with the length being about three times its width. Do not use too much flour or it will dry out the dough and prevent the layers from adhering when folded. Throughout this process be sure to keep the thickness of the dough very even and the corners square.

Fold the top edge down to the middle of the pâton and the bottom edge up to meet the top edge in the middle. Fold the pâton in half to make one complete double-book turn.

Give the pâton a quarter turn. Then, roll it back into a rectangle and repeat the book fold. Wrap the pâton in plastic film and refrigerate for at least 1 hour to allow the dough to rest.

Repeat the entire rolling and turning procedure to give the dough two more book or double turns, for a total of four turns. Again, wrap the dough tightly in plastic film and refrigerate for at least 1 hour to allow the dough to rest before using.

Storing *Pâte Feuilletée*

Pâte feuilletée must be wrapped airtight for storage to keep it from drying out. It freezes well for up to 1 month, both as a plain dough and in pastry products assembled for later baking. It can also be refrigerated, but if it is held for more than a couple of days, the dough will begin to ferment and turn an unappealing gray. This will render it useless, as both the taste and texture will be affected.

Dean's Tip

"The puff will rise correctly if you do not overwork the dough."

Dean Alain Sailhac

Among the sweet and savory classic French items using puff pastry as a base are the following:

Napoleon or **mille-feuilles**: A classic sweet pastry consisting of three crisp, paper-thin layers of puff pastry alternating with pastry cream and sprinkled with confectioners' sugar or iced with fondant (see page 229).

Pithiviers: A specialty of the French town of the same name, this large, round tart with scalloped edges is made by sandwiching almond cream between two layers of pastry and baking to a golden crispness.

Palmier: Small, palm-leaf-shaped pastry made from sugared, double-rolled puff pastry; often served with tea or as a garnish for cold desserts such as ice cream. *Palmiers* can be made with puff pastry scraps.

Sacristain: A classic pastry, usually made with puff pastry scraps, created by twisting thin strips of pastry together, sprinkling with almonds, and baking.

Tarte tatin: An upside-down apple tart made by caramelizing the apples then topping them with a layer of puff pastry and baking. The tart is inverted when served so that the apples are on top and the crisp pastry is at the bottom.

Chausson: A turnover formed by filling thin circles of puff pastry with a stewed fruit or savory filling and folding the circle over to created a half-moon shape.

Allumette: Rectangular puff pastry strips baked with a savory topping or baked and then covered with a sweet glaze or icing. Sometimes *allumettes* are also made by sandwiching a savory filling between two layers of baked puff pastry strips.

Vol-au-vent: Round puff pastry case, with or without a lid, used as a container for a savory or sweet filling.

Demonstration

Pâte Feuilletée (Classic Puff Pastry)

Makes about 340 grams (¾ pound)
Estimated time to complete: 4 hours

Ingredients	Equipment
For the *détrempe*	Sifter
125 grams (4½ ounces) cake flour	Pastry scraper
125 grams (4½ ounces) bread flour	Plastic film
1 teaspoon salt	Rolling pin
35 grams (1¼ ounces) *beurre en pommade* (see page 188)	Pastry brush
For the *beurrage*	
250 grams (8¾ ounces) cold, unsalted butter	
Flour for dusting	

Prepare your *mise en place*.

Sift the flours together with the salt onto a clean, cold work surface, preferably marble. Make a slight well in the center and add the *beurre en pommade*. Begin mixing with your fingertips, adding just enough cold water to make a rough dough; it should take 125 to 150 milliliters (4 to 5 ounces) or so. Form the dough into a square block shape, using a pastry scraper to carefully lift the dough from the work surface. Wrap it

in plastic film and refrigerate for at least 30 minutes to rest the dough.

While the *détrempe* rests, make the *beurrage*. Place the chilled butter between two pieces of plastic film and, using a rolling pin, pound on the butter to flatten it. The butter should become pliable and free of lumps and will take on the same consistency as the *détrempe*. Form the butter into a square block and keep it very cool.

Check to make sure that both the *détrempe* and the *beurrage* are as near the same consistency as possible. If not, return them both to the refrigerator until equal consistency is reached.

Lightly flour the cool work surface and, from this point onward, when rolling and turning the dough, make sure that the surface is coated with just enough flour to keep the dough from sticking. If it sticks, it will not form proper layers.

Unwrap and very gently roll the chilled and rested *détrempe* to create a thicker center square with a flap at each edge just large enough to enclose the *beurrage*.

Place the *beurrage* on the thicker center of the *détrempe* (it will look like a diamond in the middle of a square). First fold one set of opposite flaps over the butter and then fold the remaining two flaps up to completely enclose the *beurrage*. Pinch the dough together to lightly seal, creating the *pâton*.

Using a rolling pin, press on the *pâton* about four or five times along its length, or until it is about 23 centimeters (9 inches) long and 9 millimeters (⅜ inch) thick.

Again dust the work surface with flour and roll the dough out to a longer rectangle, this time about 56 centimeters (22 inches) long and 9 millimeters (⅜ inch) thick, keeping the sides even and square as you work. Roll only the length of the dough, not the width.

Using a pastry brush, brush off excess flour and begin the *tourage*. Fold one side of the dough piece over the center and then fold the other side over the top to make a neat letter fold. Again roll the dough out to a

long rectangle the same size as above. You have now rolled two turns; using your fingertips, make two marks in the dough (see Tips). Wrap the *pâton* in plastic film and refrigerate for at least 1 hour, or until very well chilled.

Remove the dough from the refrigerator and put in two additional turns as directed above. Using your fingertips, make four marks in the dough to indicate four turns. Again, wrap the *pâton* in plastic film and refrigerate for at least 1 hour before putting in two more turns. Then either rewrap, refrigerate for 1 hour, and proceed with your recipe, or wrap in freezer paper, date, and freeze. Thaw before using.

TIPS

Depending upon the requirements of a specific recipe, puff pastry can be turned four, five, or six times. The optimum number of turns is six. No matter the number of turns, the dough must be refrigerated to chill thoroughly after every two turns.

Using a combination of flours both controls the protein content in the *détrempe* and decreases the problems associated with gluten development.

If the texture of the *beurre en pommade* becomes too soft and liquid, small lumps will appear in the final product and inhibit the rise.

Use cold water to slow gluten development.

Add just enough water to create a dough that has the consistency of *pâte brisée*.

The butter for the *beurrage* must be cold or it will melt into the dough rather than create layers.

When softening a large amount of butter, it is imperative that it be the same consistency as the chilled *détrempe*.

Extra care should be taken when making the first turns, as the layers of butter are still very thick and can easily break.

When making turns with a dough that has come directly from the refrigerator, start out slowly and gently to avoid cracking the dough or breaking the layers of butter.

Make only two turns at a time to prevent the butter from melting into the dough.

Always mark the dough to remind yourself of the number of turns completed.

If the work environment is hot, chill the dough frequently as you work.

If freezing the dough, defrosting is easier if the dough is rolled into sheets.

EVALUATING YOUR SUCCESS
The *détrempe* should be smooth and not too elastic.

The *détrempe* should be slightly off-white, but not tinged with yellow.

The *beurre en pommade* should be the consistency of thick, cold sour cream.

The *beurrage* should be completely sealed by the *détrempe*.

The *pâton* should be square or rectangular.

When cut through, the laminate structure of the dough should be visible.

When baked, the *feuilletage* should rise evenly to about ten times its original height.

In a baked *feuilleté*, there should be many layers of crisp dough visible. If not, the dough did not receive enough turns.

The baked *feuilleté* should be crisp and flaky, with a buttery, slightly salty flavor.

When removed from the oven, a puddle of melted butter should not appear under the baked *feuilleté*. If it does, the *feuilletage* was too warm before baking and the butter melted out rather than helping to give the dough its desired rise.

Demonstration

Feuilletage Rapide (Quick Puff Pastry)

Makes 550 grams (1 pound, 3½ ounces)

Estimated time to complete: 3 hours

Ingredients	Equipment
125 grams (4½ ounces) cake flour	Sifter
125 grams (4½ ounces) bread flour	Pastry scraper
1 teaspoon salt	Plastic film
50 grams (1¾ ounces) *beurre en pommade* (see page 188)	Rolling pin
150 grams (5⅓ ounces) cold, unsalted butter, cut into	Pastry brush
1.3-centimeter (½-inch) cubes	
Flour for dusting	

Prepare your *mise en place*.

Sift the flours together with the salt and place it onto a clean, cold work surface, preferably marble. Make a slight well in the center and add the *beurre en pommade*. Begin mixing with your fingertips, adding just enough cold water to make a rough dough. (It should take 100 to 120 milliliters/3½ to 4½ ounces.)

Add the cold butter and mix just enough to integrate the butter into the dough.

Form the dough into a square block shape, using a pastry scraper to carefully lift the dough from the work surface. Wrap it in plastic film and refrigerate for at least 30 minutes to rest the dough.

Lightly flour a cool work surface and, when rolling and turning the dough, make sure that the surface is coated with just enough flour to keep the dough from sticking. If it sticks, it will not form proper layers.

Remove the dough from the refrigerator and unwrap. Using a rolling pin, press on the dough about four or

five times along its length, or until it is about 23 centimeters (9 inches) long and 9 millimeters (⅜ inch) thick.

Again dust the work surface with flour and roll the dough out to a longer rectangle about 56 centimeters (22 inches) long and 9 millimeters (⅜ inch) thick, keeping the sides even and square as you work. Roll only the length of the dough, not the width.

Using a pastry brush, brush off excess flour and fold one side of the dough piece over the center and then fold the other side over the top to make a neat letter fold. Again dust the work surface with flour and roll the dough out to a long rectangle as described above. You have rolled two turns; using your fingertips, make two marks in the dough (see Tips). Wrap the dough in plastic film and refrigerate for at least 30 minutes, or until very well chilled.

Again dust the work surface with flour and roll two turns of the dough as above. Using your fingertips, make four marks in the dough to indicate you have completed four turns. Wrap the dough in plastic film and refrigerate for at least 30 minutes, or until very well chilled.

Remove the dough from the refrigerator and proceed with your recipe, or wrap it in freezer paper, date, and freeze. Thaw before using.

TIPS

Remember that, although quick puff pastry takes less time to prepare than the classic version, it does not have the same high rise or flakiness. It is used primarily for baked items that do not require a high rise.

Using a combination of flours both controls the protein content in the dough and decreases the problems associated with gluten development.

The amount of water needed is dependent upon the moisture in the flour and the ambient humidity.

If the texture of the *beurre en pommade* becomes too soft and liquid, small lumps will appear in the final product and inhibit the rise.

Use cold water to slow gluten development.

The dough should be the consistency of *pâte brisée* before adding the cold butter.

The butter must be very cold or it will melt into the dough rather than create layers.

The first two turns require quite a bit of flour both on the work surface and the rolling pin to prevent sticking.

Make only two turns at a time to prevent the butter from melting into the dough.

Always mark the dough to remind yourself of the number of turns completed.

If the work environment is hot, chill the dough frequently as you work.

If freezing the dough, defrosting is easier if the dough is rolled into sheets.

EVALUATING YOUR SUCCESS

The *pâton* should be square or rectangular.

The *beurre en pommade* should be the consistency of thick, cold sour cream.

There should be no lumps or dark spots in the *feuilletage*; these indicate that the butter got too soft and liquid.

When baked, the *feuilletage* should rise evenly to several times its original height.

When removed from the oven, a puddle of melted butter should not appear under the baked *feuilleté*. If it does, the *feuilletage* was too warm before baking and the butter melted out during baking, rather than helping to give the dough its desired rise.

Demonstration

Pâte Feuilletée Inversée (Inverse Puff Pastry)

Makes about 16 dumplings
Estimated time to complete: 3 hours

Ingredients	Equipment
150 grams (5⅓ ounces) bread flour	Sifter
100 grams (3½ ounces) cake flour	Plastic film
1 teaspoon salt	Rolling pin
200 grams (7 ounces) cold, unsalted butter	Pastry brush
30 grams (1 ounce) *beurre en pommade* (see page 188)	
Flour for dusting	

Prepare your *mise en place*.

Sift the flours together with the salt onto a clean, cold work surface, preferably marble.

Combine 100 grams (3½ ounces) of the flour mixture with the cold butter, working the mixture together with your fingertips to blend well. Then, pat the *beurrage* into a square shape. Wrap in plastic film and refrigerate for at least 30 minutes.

Combine the remaining 150 grams (5⅓ ounces) of the flour mixture with the *beurre en pommade*. Add about 70 milliliters (¼ cup plus 2 teaspoons) cold water and, using your fingertips, work the mixture together to form a rough dough. Pat the *détrempe* into a square shape, wrap in plastic film, and refrigerate for at least 30 minutes.

Remove the *beurrage* and *détrempe* from the refrigerator. Check to make sure that they are both as near the same consistency as possible. If not, return them to the refrigerator until equal consistency is reached.

Lightly flour the cool work surface and, when rolling and turning the dough, make sure that the surface is coated with just enough flour to keep the dough from sticking. If it sticks, it will not form proper layers.

Unwrap the chilled and rested *beurrage* and, using a rolling pin, roll it to create a thicker center square with a flap on each edge just large enough to enclose the *détrempe*. The *beurrage* should be rolled very gently.

Place the *détrempe* on the thick center of the *beurrage* (it will look like a diamond in the middle of a square. First fold one set of opposing flaps over the *détrempe* and then fold the remaining two flaps up and over to completely enclose it. Pinch the flaps together to lightly seal, forming the *pâton*.

Using a rolling pin, press on the *pâton* about four or five times along its length, or until it is a rectangle about 23 centimeters (9 inches) long and 9 millimeters (⅜ inch) thick.

Again dust the work surface with flour and roll the *pâton* out to a piece about 56 centimeters (22 inches) long and 9 millimeters (⅜ inch) thick, keeping the sides even and square as you work. Roll only along the length of the dough, not the width.

Using a pastry brush, brush off excess flour and fold the dough into thirds. Again roll the dough out to a long rectangle as above. You have rolled two turns; using your fingertips, make two marks in the dough (see Tips). Wrap the *pâton* in plastic film and refrigerate it for at least 30 minutes, or until very well chilled.

Remove the dough from the refrigerator and put in two additional turns as directed above. Using your fingertips, make four marks in the dough to indicate four turns. Again, wrap the *pâton* in plastic film and refrigerate for at least 30 minutes.

Remove the dough from the refrigerator and put in two more turns as above. Then either rewrap, refrigerate for 1 hour, and proceed with your recipe, or wrap in freezer paper, date, and freeze. If freezing the dough, roll it into sheets to speed thawing before use.

TIPS

Be sure to completely integrate the butter and flour in the *beurrage* or it will remain firmer than the *détrempe* and make rolling out difficult.

Using a combination of flours both controls the protein content in the dough and decreases the problems associated with gluten development.

The butter should not be room temperature. It has to be soft enough to be able to work it into the dough, but cold enough to layer in the dough rather than melt into it.

The amount of water needed is dependent upon the moisture in the flour and the ambient humidity.

Using cold water slows gluten development, although that is less necessary with this dough because little or no gluten can develop when the flour is mixed with a *beurrage*.

The first two turns require quite a bit of flour both on the work surface and the rolling pin to prevent sticking.

The dough will be pale yellow during the first turns, but will lighten as more turns are completed.

Make only two turns at a time to prevent the butter from melting into the dough.

Always mark the dough to remind yourself of the number of turns completed.

In this recipe, the turns can often be done rapidly, allowing only 15 to 20 minutes for the dough to chill between them.

If the work environment is hot, chill the dough frequently.

If freezing the dough, defrosting is easier if the dough is rolled into sheets.

EVALUATING YOUR SUCCESS

The *pâton* should be square or rectangular.

The *beurre en pommade* should be the consistency of thick, cold sour cream.

The *feuilletage* should have a smooth, even texture and appearance.

When baked, the *feuilletage* should rise evenly to about ten times its original height.

In a baked *feuilleté*, there should be many layers of crisp dough visible. If not, the dough did not receive enough turns.

The baked *feuilleté* should be crisp and flaky with a buttery, slightly salty flavor.

When removed from the oven, a puddle of melted butter should not appear under the baked *feuilleté*. If it does, the *feuilletage* was too warm before baking and the butter melted out during baking rather than helping to give the dough its desired rise.

Demonstration

Pâte Feuilletée au Chocolat (Chocolate Puff Pastry)

Makes approximately 560 grams (1¼ pounds)
Estimated time to complete: About 3 hours

Ingredients	Equipment
150 grams (5⅓ ounces) bread flour	Sifter
100 grams (3⅓ ounces) cake flour	Plastic film
1 teaspoon salt	Rolling pin
30 grams (1 ounce) Dutch-process cocoa powder	Pastry brush
200 grams (7 ounces) cold, unsalted butter	
30 grams (1 ounce) *beurre en pommade* (see page 188)	
Flour for dusting	

Prepare your *mise en place*.

Sift the flours together with the salt onto a clean, cold work surface, preferably marble.

Combine 100 grams (3½ ounces) of the flour mixture with the cocoa powder and the cold butter, working the mixture together with your fingertips to blend well. Then, pat the *beurrage* into a square shape. Wrap in plastic film and refrigerate for at least 30 minutes.

Combine the remaining flour mixture with the *beurre en pommade*. Add about 70 milliliters (¼ cup plus 2 teaspoons) cold water and, using your fingertips, work the mixture together to form a rough dough. Pat the *détrempe* into a square shape, wrap in plastic film, and refrigerate for at least 30 minutes.

Remove the *beurrage* and *détrempe* from the refrigerator. Check to make sure that they are both as near the same consistency as possible. If not, return them both to the refrigerator until equal consistency is reached.

Lightly flour the cool work surface and, when rolling and turning the dough, make sure that the surface is coated with just enough flour to keep the dough from sticking. If it sticks, it will not form proper layers.

Unwrap and roll the chilled and rested *beurrage* to create a thicker center square the same size as the *détrempe*, with a flap on each edge. The dough should be rolled very gently.

Place the *détrempe* in the middle of the *beurrage* so that it looks like a diamond in the middle of a square. Fold one set of opposing flaps over the butter and then fold the remaining two flaps up and over to completely enclose the *beurrage*. Pinch the dough together to lightly seal to make the *pâton*.

Using a rolling pin, press on the *pâton* four or five times along its length, or until it is a rectangle about 23 centimeters (9 inches) long and 9 millimeters (⅜ inch) thick.

Again, dust the work surface with flour and roll the dough out to a longer rectangle, about 56 centimeters (22 inches) long and 9 millimeters (⅜ inch) thick, keeping the sides even and square as you work. Roll only along the length of the dough, not the width.

Using a pastry brush, brush off excess flour and fold the dough into thirds. Again roll the dough out to a long rectangle as above. You have rolled two turns.

Using your fingertips, make two marks in the dough (see Tips). Wrap the *pâton* in plastic film and refrigerate for at least 30 minutes, or until very well chilled.

Remove the dough from the refrigerator and put in two additional turns as directed above. Using your fingertips, make four marks in the dough to indicate four turns. Again, wrap the *pâton* in plastic film and refrigerate for at least 30 minutes.

Remove the dough from the refrigerator and put in two more turns as above. Then either rewrap, refrigerate for 30 minutes, and proceed with your recipe, or wrap in freezer paper, date, and freeze. If freezing the dough, roll it into sheets to speed thawing before use.

TIPS

Depending upon the requirements of a specific recipe, puff pastry can be turned four, five, or six times. The optimum number of turns is six. No matter the number of turns, the dough must be refrigerated to chill thoroughly after every two turns.

Using a combination of flours both controls the protein content in the *détrempe* and decreases the problems associated with gluten development.

The butter should not be room temperature. It has to be soft enough to be able to work it into the dough but cold enough to form layers rather than melt into the dough.

Cold water slows gluten development, although this is somewhat less critical with this dough, as little or no gluten can develop when the flour has been mixed with a *beurrage*.

Add just enough water to create a dough that has the consistency of *pâte brisée*.

The feuilletage will be slightly marbled during the first turns but will become more uniform in color.

Always mark the dough to remind yourself of the number of turns you have completed.

In this recipe, the turns can often be done rapidly, allowing only 15 to 20 minutes for the dough to chill between them.

If the work environment is hot, chill the dough frequently as you work.

EVALUATING YOUR SUCCESS

The *détrempe* should be smooth and not too elastic.

The *détrempe* should be slightly off-white but not tinged with yellow.

The *beurre en pommade* should be the consistency of cold cream.

The *beurrage* should be completely sealed by the *détrempe*.

The *pâton* should be square or rectangular.

When cut through, the laminate structure of the dough should be visible.

When baked, the *feuilletage* should rise evenly to about ten times its original height.

Demonstration

Vols-au-Vent (Round Puff Pastry Cases)

Makes eight to ten 4-centimeter (1½-inch) or four 10-centimeter (4-inch) *Vols-au-Vent*
Estimated time to complete: If *feuilletage* is on hand, 1 hour

Ingredients	Equipment
Flour for dusting	Baking sheet
1 recipe unbaked *Pâte Feuilletée* (see page 190)	Parchment paper or silicone baking liner
Egg wash (see page 62)	Rolling pin 1½-inch or 4-inch round cookie cutter

NOTE

Marie-Antoine Carême, known as the "king of chefs" and the "chef of kings" is credited with, among many other important items and techniques in the classic French culinary repertoire, the invention of the *toque*, or chef's hat, as well as these puff pastry cases that can wear their own "hats." When all the pastry pieces are baked and the cases filled and covered, classic *vols-au-vent* do, in fact, resemble little, round boxes filled to the brim with jaunty lids covering the filling.

Vols-au-vent can be filled with almost any savory or sweet filling and, depending upon their size, used for hors d'oeuvre, appetizers, entrées, petits fours, or desserts. In classic cuisine, the filling is usually a cream-based mixture of poultry, fish or shellfish, white meats, or mushrooms. The case itself may be made, as we do here, in individual sizes or as one large shell. The lids may or may not be used at the discretion of the chef.

Prepare your *mise en place*.

Lightly flour a cool work surface and, when rolling and turning the dough, make sure that the surface is coated with just enough flour to keep the dough from sticking. If it sticks, it will not form proper layers.

Preheat the oven to 177°C (350°F).

Line a baking sheet with parchment paper or a silicone liner. Set aside.

Place the dough on the floured surface and, using a rolling pin, roll it to a 3- to 6-millimeter (⅛- to ¼-inch) thickness.

Using a round metal ring or cookie cutter, cut out 16 to 20 disks. Using a small sharp knife, remove the centers from half of the disks, leaving a ring about 6 millimeters (¼ inch) wide. If you wish, save the smaller disks to be used as "hats" for the filled pastry cases.

Place the egg wash in a small bowl. Using a docker or a kitchen fork, dock the full disks. Using a pastry brush, lightly coat each disk with egg wash. Place a pastry ring on the top of each disk and, using a pastry brush, lightly coat it with egg wash. Add just enough egg wash to slightly wet the surface without dripping down the sides. Excess egg inhibits the rise and makes the pastry more susceptible to burning.

If you are using them, dock the smaller disks and brush them with egg wash too.

Place the completed *vols-au-vent* (and smaller disks, if using) on the prepared baking sheet. Place a piece of parchment paper over the surface of the pastry. This helps to ensure an even rise and to prevent the pastry ring from distorting or tumbling over during baking. Bake for about 20 minutes, or until nicely browned and baked through.

Remove from the oven and use as directed in a specific recipe. If not using immediately, baked *vols-au-vent* should be stored, airtight, at room temperature for no longer than a day or two.

TIPS

When a high rise is desired, use only fresh *feuilletage*.

The bottom disks can be made from any type of *feuilletage*, including scraps.

When making *vols-au-vent*, take care that the pastry remains very well chilled throughout. This will ensure easier assembly and help them hold their shape during baking.

Unbaked *vols-au-vent* may be stored, tightly wrapped and frozen, for up to 1 month.

The rings should not be too thick or the baked pastry will have too much *feuilleté* in proportion to the filling. On the other hand, they should not be too thin or they will be unable to achieve a full rise.

The egg wash should be lightly and evenly applied.

The center of each pastry case should be even in size and large enough to adequately hold a creamy filling.

Each *vol-au-vent* should be equal in size and rise.

Due to docking, the bottom disks should have minimal rise, while the sides should have the optimum.

Every surface of the baked pastry should be nicely browned, with no visible unbaked or white areas.

The multiple layers of *feuilleté* should be visible from the sides of the baked pastry.

Demonstration

Feuilleté Assemblage Rapide (Quick Puff Pastry Cases)

Makes two 12.5-centimeter (5-inch) cases

Estimated time to complete: If *feuilletage* is on hand, 1 hour

Ingredients	Equipment
Flour for dusting 100 grams (3½ ounces) unbaked *Pâte Feuilletée* (see page 190) Egg wash (see page 62)	Baking sheet Parchment paper or silicone baking liner Rolling pin Small sharp knife Small bowl Pastry brush

Prepare your *mise en place*.

Lightly flour a cool work surface and, when rolling and turning the dough, make sure that the surface is coated with just enough flour to keep the dough from sticking. If it sticks, it will not form proper layers.

Line a baking sheet with parchment paper or a silicone liner. Set aside.

Place the dough on the floured surface and, using a rolling pin, roll it to a 3- to 6-millimeter (⅛- to ¼-inch) thickness.

Using a small sharp knife, cut out two 12.5-centimeter (5-inch) squares.

Fold each square, corner to corner, to make a triangle.

Place each triangle with the long side in front of you and, using a small sharp knife, cut a slit along one short side approximately 9 millimeters (⅜ inch) in from the edge to within 20 millimeters (¾ inch) of the long side. Make an identical cut on the remaining short side. Then unfold each triangle and place it on the prepared baking sheet.

Place the egg wash in a small bowl.

Using a pastry brush, lightly coat each triangle with egg wash. Then, lift the loose corners and fold each one over to the opposite corner. Do not discard the egg wash.

Cover lightly with plastic film and refrigerate for at least 1 hour to chill thoroughly.

When ready to bake, preheat the oven to 177°C (350°F).

Using a pastry brush, lightly coat the top surface with egg wash. Add just enough egg wash to slightly wet the surface without dripping down the sides. Excess egg inhibits the rise and makes the pastry more susceptible to burning.

Bake the pastry for about 25 minutes, or until golden brown and baked through.

Remove from the oven and use as directed in a specific recipe. If not using immediately, the baked pastry should be stored, airtight, at room temperature for no longer than a day or two.

When a high rise is desired, use only fresh *feuilletage*.

Chill and rest the dough often for ease in cutting and folding and to ensure that, during baking, the cases will hold their shape.

The sides of the cases should not be too wide or the baked pastry will have too much *feuilleté* in proportion to the filling. If too narrow, the pastry will be unable to achieve an adequate rise.

Unbaked pastry cases may be stored, tightly wrapped and frozen, for up to 1 month.

The baked pastry cases may be used with almost any sweet or savory filling to create hors d'oeuvre, appetizers, entrées, *petits fours*, and desserts.

The egg wash should be lightly and evenly applied.

The center of each pastry case should be even in size and large enough to adequately hold the filling.

The pastry cases should be equal in size and rise.

Every surface of the baked pastry should be nicely browned, with no visible unbaked or white areas.

The multiple layers of *feuilletée* should be visible from the sides of the baked pastry.

Demonstration

Palmiers (Palm Leaves)

Makes 25 to 30 cookies
Estimated time to complete: 1 hour

Ingredients	Equipment
Granulated sugar for dusting	Rolling pin
1 recipe unbaked *Pâte Feuilletée* (see page 190)	Ruler, optional
	Small baking sheet
	Plastic film
	2 or more large baking sheets
	Parchment paper or silicone baking liners
	Sharp knife
	Metal spatula
	Wire racks

Prepare your *mise en place*.

Liberally coat a cool work surface with sugar. Use plenty of sugar so that it can work its way into the dough and leave enough on the surface to cause good caramelization.

Place the dough on the sugared surface and liberally sprinkle the top with more sugar. Using a rolling pin, roll it out to a 30.5-by-35.5-centimeter (12-by-14-inch) rectangle 3 millimeters (⅛ inch) thick. The long side should be directly in front of you. Lightly brush the surface with water and liberally sprinkle with more sugar.

Carefully fold the top sixth of the length in toward the center. Then, fold the bottom sixth of the length in toward the center. Fold the top section in and over to make another layer, then do the same with the bottom section. At this point, there should only be a tiny gap between the folds. Fold the long piece in half so that the two folded parts meet. Take care that you do not stretch the dough as you work. If the sides do not meet evenly, unfold the entire sheet and repeat the process to make them even. If necessary, use a ruler to divide the rectangle into even folds.

Using a rolling pin, gently push the layers together.

Try to work quickly so that the *feuilletage* remains cold.

Transfer the dough to a small baking sheet, cover with plastic film, and refrigerate for at least 1 hour, or until very well chilled. It is ideal if the dough can be refrigerated for between 8 hours and 3 days, as the humidity of the refrigerator will help the sugar melt during baking.

Preheat the oven to 177°C (350°F).

Line the large baking sheets with parchment or silicone liners. Set aside.

Using a sharp knife, cut the chilled *feuilletage* crosswise, into 9-millimeter (⅜-inch) slices. Place each slice on the prepared baking sheets, allowing plenty of space between each one—the cookies will double or triple in size as they bake.

Bake for about 10 minutes, or until the bottoms are golden. Using a metal spatula, flip each cookie and continue to bake for an additional 10 minutes, or until golden.

Remove the cookies from the oven and transfer them to wire racks to cool.

If not using immediately, store, airtight, at room temperature. If not airtight, the cookies will get soggy very quickly.

TIPS
Any type of *feuilleté* may used to make *palmiers*.

Cinnamon or vanilla sugar may replace plain granulated sugar.

The long sides of the rolled-out dough must be straight and even before you fold it. If necessary, trim them to achieve this.

EVALUATING YOUR SUCCESS
Each of the dough folds should be of the same size.

During baking, both sides of the *palmiers* should open up to be equal in size.

During baking, the sugar should completely melt, and no crystals should be visible once the cookies are fully baked.

The baked cookies should be completely golden with a very sweet, slightly caramel flavor and a crunchy texture.

Demonstration

Paillettes (Cheese Straws)

Makes 25 to 30 straws
Estimated time to complete: 2 hours

Ingredients	Equipment
Flour for dusting	2 baking sheets
335 grams (11¾ ounces) unbaked *Pâte Feuilletée* (see page 190)	Parchment paper or 2 silicone baking liners
150 grams (5⅓ ounces) grated Parmesan cheese	Rolling pin
Paprika to taste	Small bowl
Cayenne pepper to taste	Pastry wheel
	Plastic film
	Small sharp knife

Prepare your *mise en place*.

Line the baking sheets with parchment or silicone liners. Set aside.

Lightly flour a cool work surface and, when rolling and turning the dough, make sure that the surface is coated with just enough flour to keep the dough from sticking. If it sticks, it will not form proper layers.

Place the dough on the floured surface. Using a rolling pin, roll it out to a 25-by-30.5-centimeter (10-by-12-inch) rectangle about 3 millimeters (⅛

inch) thick, dusting the rolling pin with flour if necessary to prevent sticking.

Combine the cheese with paprika and cayenne to taste in a small bowl. Keep in mind that too much of either will make the finished pastry too dark and too spicy.

Sprinkle the entire surface of the dough with the cheese mixture. Using a rolling pin, lightly force the cheese into the dough.

Using a pastry wheel, cut the dough into strips about 1.3 centimeters (½ inch) wide. Working with one

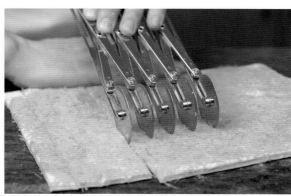

strip at a time and holding each end, twist the strips into *paillettes*.

Place the *paillettes* on the prepared baking sheets, leaving sufficient space in between each one to allow for expansion during baking. Cover with plastic film and refrigerate for at least 1 hour, or until very well chilled. It is important to chill them on the baking sheets as this eases the transition to the oven.

Preheat the oven to 177°C (350°F).

Bake the *paillettes* for about 20 minutes, or until golden brown on all sides.

Remove from the oven and, using a small sharp knife, immediately and carefully trim each end to make all the paillettes equal in size.

Serve warm or at room temperature.

If you do not plan to serve the cheese straws immediately, store them airtight at room temperature. Exposure to air will make them soggy very quickly.

TIPS

Any type of plain *feuilletage*, including scraps, is appropriate for this recipe.

Although Parmesan cheese is the cheese of choice, the ends and rinds of other strongly flavored cheeses may also be used in this recipe.

Unbaked *paillettes* may be covered with plastic film and refrigerated for up to 2 days, or wrapped, airtight, and frozen for up to 1 month. If frozen, the baking time will increase slightly.

EVALUATING YOUR SUCCESS

The cheese mixture should completely cover the pastry.

There should be only the slightest hint of heat from the cayenne.

After being baked, the *paillettes* should be golden brown and tightly twisted.

The *paillettes* should be uniform in width and length.

Demonstration

Bande de Tarte aux Fruits (Fresh Fruit Strip)

Makes one 15-by-46-centimeter (6-by-18-inch) strip
Estimated time to complete: 2 hours

Ingredients	Equipment
Flour for dusting	Baking sheet
225 grams (8 ounces) *Pâte Feuilletée* (see page 190)	Parchment paper or silicone baking liner
Egg wash (see page 62)	Rolling pin
100 grams (3½ ounces) *Crème Pâtissière* (see page 248)	Pastry wheel
2 small bowls	Docker or kitchen fork
Grand Marnier or other liqueur to taste	Pastry brush

40 milliliters (2 tablespoons plus 2 teaspoons) heavy cream, chilled

Fresh fruit (see tips)

For the *nappage*

100 grams (3½ ounces) apricot jam

Confectioners' sugar for dusting

Plastic film

Small mixing bowl

Whisk

Standing electric mixer fitted with whip

Rubber spatula

Pastry bag fitted with medium plain tip

Offset spatula

Small saucepan

Small fine-mesh sieve

Small sharp knife (optional)

Prepare your *mise en place*.

Line a baking sheet with parchment or a silicone liner. Set aside.

Lightly flour a cool work surface and, when rolling and turning the dough, make sure that the surface is coated with just enough flour to keep the dough from sticking. If it sticks, it will not form proper layers.

Place the egg wash in a small bowl.

Place the dough on the floured surface. Using a rolling pin, roll it out to a large rectangle at least 46 centimeters (18 inches) long and 3 millimeters (⅛ inch) thick, dusting the rolling pin with flour if necessary to prevent sticking. Using a pastry wheel, cut a 15-centimeter-wide (6-inch-wide) strip as long as the rectangle. Then, cut two 1.5-centimeter-wide (1-inch-wide) strips of the same length.

Transfer the large strip to the prepared baking sheet and, using a docker or kitchen fork, dock the surface.

Use a pastry brush to lightly coat the long edges of the strip with egg wash. This is extremely important, as you do not want the pastry to rise. Do not discard the egg wash.

Carefully place one small strip on top of each long side of the large strip as a border.

Wrap the entire pan with plastic film and place it in the refrigerator for 30 minutes, or until well chilled.

Preheat the oven to 177°C (350°F).

Using a pastry brush, lightly coat the top of each of the small strips with the egg wash. Use just enough egg wash to slightly wet the surface without dripping down the sides. Excess egg will inhibit the rise and make the pastry more susceptible to burning. Place a piece of parchment paper on top of each of the small strips, leaving the center of the dough uncovered.

Bake the pastry for about 25 minutes, or until golden brown with no white areas visible. Set aside to cool completely.

Place the pastry cream in a small mixing bowl and whisk vigorously to eliminate any lumps. It should be perfectly smooth. Add the liqueur and whisk to blend well.

Place the heavy cream in the bowl of a standing electric mixer fitted with the whip and beat until stiff peaks form (*crème fouettée*). Using a rubber spatula, gently fold the whipped cream into the smooth pastry cream to make a *crème légère*.

Using a rubber spatula, scrape the *crème légère* into a pastry bag fitted with a medium, plain tip. Pipe the cream over the center of the baked, cooled pastry shell, smoothing the top with an offset spatula. Arrange the fruit in a decorative pattern over the surface, taking care to completely cover the cream.

Combine the apricot jam with 45 milliliters (3 table-spoons) water in a small saucepan over medium heat, stirring to melt. Pour the melted mixture through a small fine-mesh sieve into a small bowl and discard the solids.

Using a pastry brush, lightly coat the fruit with a thin layer of the warm glaze, taking care not to get it on the pastry. Allow the glaze to cool and set.

Place the confectioners' sugar in a small, fine-mesh sieve and, lightly tapping on its edge, dust the border pastry to frame the fruit. If the ends are not neat and even, use a small sharp knife to trim them.

Serve immediately or refrigerate until ready to serve, but for no more than a few hours.

TIPS

Any type of fresh fruit may be used (or even canned stone fruits). A good, classic combination is 6 sliced strawberries, 2 oranges cut into *sûpremes*, 4 sliced kiwis, and about 100 grams (½ pint) blueberries; however, one type or a combination of many types may be used.

The bottom, larger strip of pastry may be made from scraps.

Because a high rise must be achieved, the smaller strips should be made from either classic or inverse puff pastry.

Attaching parchment paper to the egg-washed edges before baking prevents the sides from flopping over before setting and ensures that they both rise at the same rate and height.

If the center strip rises during baking, gently push it down flat, or cut the raised part out with a parking knife after baking so that the center is completely flat. Take care that you leave enough pastry to support the cream and fruit.

Cover the bottom strip with just enough *crème légère* to moisten it and to create a base that will hold the fruit in place.

The fruit should be placed evenly and attractively so that each cut piece receives a similar amount and variety.

EVALUATING YOUR SUCCESS

The bottom *feuilleté* should not have risen, and the sides should have a straight, even, high rise.

Every surface of the baked pastry should be nicely browned, with no visible unbaked or white areas.

The multiple layers of *feuilleté* should be visible from the sides of the baked pastry.

The *crème légère* should be well flavored and firm.

The fruit should cover the cream in an attractive design.

The glaze should completely cover the fruit to seal it and give it sheen, but it should not touch the edges of the pastry.

Demonstration

Tarte Feuilletée (Fruit Strip or Bar Tart)

Makes one 15-by-46-centimeter (6-by-18-inch) tart
Estimated time to complete: 90 minutes

Ingredients	Equipment
Flour for dusting	2 baking sheets
225 grams (8 ounces) *Pâte Feuilletée* (see page 190)	Parchment paper
240 milliliters (1 cup) light corn syrup	Rolling pin
75 grams (2⅔ ounces) *Crème d'Amandes* (see page 252)	Plastic film
Fresh fruit (see Tips)	2 small bowls
	Docker or kitchen fork
For the *nappage* and finish	Pastry brush
100 grams (3½ ounces) apricot jam	Small sharp knife
80 grams (2¾ ounces) toasted nuts (such as slivered almonds	Offset spatula
or chopped pistachios) for decoration	Small saucepan
	Small fine-mesh sieve

Prepare your *mise en place.*

Line a baking sheet with parchment paper. Set aside.

Lightly flour a cool work surface and, when rolling and turning the dough, make sure that the surface is coated with just enough flour to keep the dough from sticking. If it sticks, it will not form proper layers.

Place the dough on the floured surface. Using a rolling pin, roll it out to a large rectangle at least 46 centimeters (18 inches) long and a bit less than 3 millimeters (⅛ inch) thick, dusting the rolling pin with flour if necessary to prevent sticking.

Transfer the pastry rectangle to the prepared baking sheet. Wrap the entire pan with plastic film and place in the refrigerator for 30 minutes, or until well chilled.

Preheat the oven to 177°C (350°F).

Place the corn syrup in a small bowl. Set aside.

Unwrap the pastry and, using a docker or kitchen fork, dock the chilled dough. Cover it with a piece of parchment paper and then place another baking sheet on top to hold the pastry down.

Bake the weighted pastry for about 20 minutes, or until golden brown. Remove the top pan and parchment paper and, using a pastry brush, lightly coat the surface with corn syrup. Return the pastry to the oven and bake for an additional 5 minutes, or until the pastry is dark brown and the corn syrup has stopped bubbling.

Remove from the oven and set aside to cool slightly. Do not turn off the oven.

While the pastry is still warm, using a small sharp knife, trim the edges slightly to make a neat rectangle. Allow it to cool completely on the baking sheet. Using an offset spatula, carefully spread a thin layer—less than 3 millimeters (⅛ inch) thick—of almond cream over the cooled pastry.

Arrange the fruit in a decorative pattern over the almond cream, taking care that it doesn't overlap the sides.

Return the tart to the oven and bake for about 15 minutes, or until the almond cream is set and the fruit has caramelized on the edges. Set the tart aside to cool slightly.

Combine the apricot jam with 45 milliliters (3 table-spoons) water in a small saucepan over medium heat, stirring to melt. Pour the melted glaze through a small fine-mesh sieve into a small bowl and discard the solids.

Using a pastry brush, lightly coat the fruit and the edges of the tart with a thin layer of the warm glaze. Neatly sprinkle toasted nuts along the edges to make an even trim. Allow the glaze to cool and set.

Cut the tart into slices while it is still warm. Serve immediately or refrigerate until ready to serve, but for no more than a few hours.

TIPS

Any type of *feuilleté*, including scraps, may be used in this recipe.

Any type of fresh fruit may be used (or even canned stone fruits). Some possibilities are ¼ fresh pineapple, sliced; 6 apricots, halved; 6 peaches, halved; 4 pears, sliced; or 8 plums, halved; however, one type or a combination of many other types may be used.

Baking the pastry between two pans prevents a rise. The corn syrup glaze on the pastry adds sweetness and seals the dough to prevent it from getting soggy if not used immediately. The syrup must be thoroughly baked and caramelized or it will be sticky.

It is best to cut the baked pastry while still warm, as it tends to break into pieces.

Any fruit that is firm enough to hold its shape during the long baking period can be used.

Classically, the almond garnish is an indication that either almonds or almond flavoring will be in the pastry. However, other nuts, such as pistachios, may be used for their added color.

EVALUATING YOUR SUCCESS

The pastry should be evenly and thoroughly baked.

There should be just enough almond cream to lightly coat the pastry and hold the fruit in place.

The fruit should completely cover the cream. The apricot glaze should completely cover the fruit in a light, even coating.

Demonstration

Galettes aux Fruits de Saison (Seasonal Fruit *Galettes*)

Makes six 10-centimeter (4-inch) *galettes*
Estimated time to complete: 2 hours

Ingredients	Ingredients
Flour for dusting	Baking sheet
160 grams (5⅔ ounces) *Pâte Feuilletée* (see page 190)	Parchment paper

For the compote

500 grams (1 pound, 1½ ounces) fruit (see Tips)

½ lemon

50 grams (1¾ ounces) granulated sugar

1 teaspoon ground spice, optional (see Tips)

For the finish

Confectioners' sugar for dusting

Rolling pin

Plastic film

Vegetable peeler

Paring knife

Sautoir or *russe*

Wooden spoon

5-inch round metal ring

Metal spoon

Wire rack

Small fine-mesh sieve

Prepare your *mise en place*.

Line a baking sheet with parchment paper. Set aside.

Lightly flour a cool work surface and, when rolling and turning the dough, make sure that the surface is coated with just enough flour to keep the dough from sticking. If it sticks, it will not form proper layers. Place the dough on the floured surface. Using a rolling pin, roll it out until it is about 3 millimeters (⅛ inch) thick, dusting the rolling pin with flour if necessary to prevent sticking.

Transfer the pastry to the prepared baking sheet. Wrap the entire pan with plastic film and place it in the refrigerator for 30 minutes, or until well chilled. Meanwhile, make the compote.

If necessary, peel and core (or pit) the fruit. Then, cut the fruit into 2.5-centimeter (1-inch) cubes Sprinkle with lemon juice.

Combine the sugar and 30 milliliters (2 tablespoons) water in a *sautoir* or *russe* over medium heat. Add the fruit and, if using, the spice, and cook, stirring frequently with a wooden spoon, for about 15 minutes, or until all the moisture has evaporated, taking care that the fruit does not disintegrate—you want a chunky mixture that is almost dry. Set the fruit aside to cool.

Transfer the pastry to a cool, floured work surface. Using the metal ring, cut out six disks. Place them on the parchment-lined baking sheet.

Spoon an equal portion of the cooled fruit compote into the center of each disk, leaving at least 2.5 centimeters (1 inch) of uncovered pastry around the edge. Carefully fold the edges of each pastry up and over toward the center and then gently pleat the dough to make a finished edge. Wrap the entire pan with plastic film and chill thoroughly, for at least 30 minutes or up to 24 hours.

When ready to bake the *galettes*, preheat the oven to 177°C (350°F).

Unwrap the *galettes* and bake them for about 20 minutes, or until the pastry is golden brown. Transfer them to a wire rack to cool.

Place the confectioners' sugar in a small, fine-mesh sieve and, lightly tapping on its edge, dust the tops of the cooled *galettes*.

Serve immediately or refrigerate until ready to serve, but for no more than a few hours.

TIPS

Any type of *feuilleté*, including scraps, may be used in this recipe.

Although we have made these into individual-serving-size rounds, you can make any size you choose, including one large *galette*. No matter the size, the pastry should be formed in a neat round.

Any type of fresh or dried fruit may be used to make

the compote. Plums, pears, quince, or any stone fruit are excellent choices.

The fruit compote should be very flavorful and, if fresh fruit is used, the fruit should be seasonal.

You can add any ground spice that marries well with the specific fruit. Vanilla or other extracts can also be used.

The pastry pleats should sit high, as they will open and slump as the *galettes* bake.

The pastry pleats should be well-sealed prior to baking or they will open too much as the pastry cooks. If you have trouble holding the pleats together, apply a small amount of egg wash (see page 62).

The *galettes* should be well chilled before baking so that they will hold their shape.

If desired, extra sweetness and crunch can be added by sprinkling the *galettes* with granulated sugar, cinnamon sugar, or vanilla sugar just before baking.

EVALUATING YOUR SUCCESS
During baking, the compote should not ooze out of the center or bubble onto the edge, nor should any heavy skin form on its surface.

The compote should be cooked until very dry or it will ooze during baking.

During baking, the pleats should remain closed but rise high enough to create sides for the *galette*.

The finished pastry should be golden brown, thoroughly baked, crispy, and flaky.

Demonstration

Conversations (Almond Tartlets)

Makes four 4-inch tartlets
Estimated time to complete: 2 hours

Ingredients	Equipment
Flour for dusting	Baking sheet
500 grams (1 pound, 1½ ounces) *Pâte Feuilletée* (see page 190)	Parchment paper
300 grams (11 ounces) *Crème d'Amandes* (see page 252)	Rolling pin
Egg wash (see page 62)	Plastic film
200 grams (1 cup) Royal Icing (see page 381)	Small sharp knife
	Docker or kitchen fork
	Four 4-inch tartlet pans
	Small bowl
	Pastry brush
	Offset spatula
	Wire rack

Prepare your *mise en place*.

Line a baking sheet with parchment paper. Set aside.

Lightly flour a cool work surface and, when rolling and turning the dough, make sure that the surface is coated with just enough flour to keep the dough from sticking. If it sticks, it will not form proper layers.

Place the dough on the floured surface. Using a rolling pin, roll it out until it is about 3 millimeters (⅛ inch) thick, dusting the rolling pin with flour if necessary to prevent sticking.

Transfer the pastry to the prepared baking sheet. Wrap the entire pan with plastic film and place in the refrigerator for 30 minutes, or until well chilled. Using a small sharp knife, cut out four 15-centimeter (6-inch) squares, reserving the remaining pastry for later use.

Using a docker or a kitchen fork, dock each square. Fit each pastry square into a tartlet mold, carefully fitting it into the sides. Do not cut off the excess dough. When all of the molds are lined with pastry, fill each halfway with almond cream (the cream will expand as it bakes).

Place the egg wash in a small bowl and, using a pastry brush, lightly coat the exposed pastry with the wash. Make sure that you do not use too much or it will cause the pastry to separate rather than holding it together.

Using a small sharp knife, cut a piece of the remaining *feuilleté* to fit over the surface of the almond cream in each tartlet. Fold over enough of the excess bottom pastry to completely seal the tartlets. Trim off any excess pastry, leaving a neat top. Reserve any remaining pastry in the refrigerator for later use.

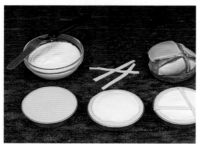

Place the filled tartlets in the refrigerator for at least 30 minutes, or up to 3 days. For the longer storage, wrap them with plastic film. The wrapped tartlets may also be frozen for up to 1 month.

Preheat the oven to 177°C (350°F).

Using an offset spatula, cover the top of each tartlet with a thin layer of the icing.

Using the remaining *feuilleté*, cut thin strips of pastry and place them in neat rows across the top of the icing. Running from side to side across the tartlet, these strips will act as expansion joints for the icing as it bakes. Their positioning allows the chef to dictate where the icing will split and break during baking.

Bake the tartlets for about 30 minutes, or until golden brown and cooked through. Transfer them to a wire rack to cool slightly before serving.

Serve warm or at room temperature on the same day as baked. The tartlets do not hold well.

TIPS

Any type of *feuilleté*, including scraps, may be used in this recipe. However, scrap dough must be allowed additional time to relax before using.

The pastry in the bottom of the tartlet must be thoroughly docked to keep it from rising during baking. The royal icing should be just stiff enough to spread easily.

EVALUATING YOUR SUCCESS

The almond cream should not bubble out of the tartlets.

The *feuilleté* should be golden brown, crispy, and flaky.

The icing should be a blond color and should adhere to the top of the tartlets.

The icing should not bubble and run off the top of the tartlet; it should break only along the lines of the decorative pastry.

Demonstration

Tarte Tatin (Upside-down Apple Tart)

Makes one 9-inch tart
Estimated time to complete: 2 hours

Ingredients	Equipment
Flour for dusting	Baking sheet
80 grams (2¾ ounces) *Pâte Feuilletée* (see page 190)	Parchment paper
75 grams (2⅔ ounces) unsalted butter	Rolling pin
6 Golden or Red Delicious apples (see Tips)	Plastic film
300 grams (11 ounces) sugar	Vegetable peeler
60 milliliters (2 ounces) Calvados	Small sharp knife
Vanilla ice cream, *crème fraîche*, or *Crème Chantilly*	Melon baller
(see page 111) for serving, optional	9-inch heavy-bottomed ovenproof skillet

Prepare your *mise en place*.

Line a baking sheet with parchment paper. Set aside.

Lightly flour a cool work surface and, when rolling and turning the dough, make sure that the surface is coated with just enough flour to keep the dough from sticking. If it sticks, it will not form proper layers.

Place the dough on the floured surface. Using a rolling pin, roll it out until it is about 3 millimeters (⅛ inch) thick, dusting the rolling pin with flour if necessary to prevent sticking.

Transfer the pastry to the prepared baking sheet. Wrap the entire pan with plastic film and place in the refrigerator for 30 minutes, or until well chilled.

Meanwhile, prepare the apples. Peel and halve the apples. Using a melon baller, carefully remove the core from each half.

Melt the butter in the skillet over medium heat. Add the apples, cut side down, packing them in as tightly as possible. You may not be able to use all the apples at first, but once they begin to cook, releasing their juices and shrinking, you will be able to fit in the remainder. You need to have a tight, compact layer of apples that will hold together when the tart is inverted for serving.

Turn the apples cut side up and sprinkle the sugar over them and into the pan. Cook, covered in foil, frequently shaking and moving the pan gently to ensure that the apples don't stick to the pan, for about 30 minutes, or until the apples are cooked and the sugar has caramelized to a beautiful brown color. You must watch the caramel carefully so that it does not get too dark and bitter. Add more apple halves when you can fit them in. Remove from the heat and remove the foil. Add the Calvados and place back on the heat.

Dean's Tip

"To glaze a Tarte Tatin after baking, reduce any excess apple juice to a fine glaze and brush it over the apples."
Dean André Soltner

One story goes that *tarte Tatin* was created by a French cook, Stéphanie Tatin who, with her sister Caroline, ran a small hotel, Hotel Tatin, in Lamotte-Beuvron. The year was 1889 and, as usual, Stéphanie was overwhelmed with work, running both the kitchen and the hotel. It is said that she was making an apple tart for lunch, but got distracted and forgot about the cooking apples. Only the smell of the burning sugar and butter brought her back to the stove, where she tried to save the dish by immediately putting the pastry she had prepared over the pan of caramelized apples. She threw the whole pan in the oven and baked her upside-down tart. To her surprise, when she inverted the dish onto a serving platter, not only did it look extremely appetizing, but her guests loved it. It became a signature dish of the hotel where it is said, it was experienced by the Parisian restaurateur, Louis Vaudable, who "stole" it and made it the signature dessert at his world-famous restaurant, Maxim's. All these years later, the tart is still available at the Hotel Tatin and is often referred to as *tarte des demoiselles Tatin*.

Quickly ignite the Calvados to flambé. Leave on the heat for 1 minute to reduce the liquid. Remove from the heat and set aside to cool.

Preheat the oven to 177°C (350°F).

When the apples are cool enough that they will not melt the pastry when it is applied, prepare the dough.

Using a small sharp knife, cut out a round of pastry large enough to completely cover the top of the skillet.

Place the dough circle on top of the apples, fitting it tightly around the edges of the pan. It is extremely important to make a tight seal to trap the steam inside the tart as it bakes.

Bake the tart for about 30 minutes, or until the pastry is golden brown and baked through.

Remove it from the oven and immediately place a serving plate over the top. Invert the pan and lift it to unmold the tart onto the plate. It should come out in one complete piece with a tight layer of caramelized apples on top.

Serve immediately or no more than a few hours after baking.

When serving, cut the tart into wedges and, if desired, serve with a scoop of vanilla ice cream, *crème frâiche*, or *crème Chantilly* (see page 111).

TIPS
Any type of *feuilleté*, including scraps, may be used in this recipe. Scrap dough must be allowed additional time to relax before using.

It is important to use either Golden or Red Delicious apples, as their high starch content allows them to hold their shape, rather than turn to mush, during the long cooking required for this recipe.

When making the caramel, take care that it does not get too dark or it will be bitter instead of sweet.

EVALUATING YOUR SUCCESS
The pastry should be golden brown, thoroughly baked, and flaky.

The apples should all be round side up with no core showing and evenly browned.

The apples and the *feuilleté* should both be completely cooked.

The caramel should be a medium brown with no trace of bitterness.

Demonstration

Tartes aux Bananes et Chocolat (Banana and Chocolate Tarts)

Makes four 10-centimeter (4-inch) tarts

Estimated time to complete: 1 hour

Ingredients	Equipment
240 milliliters (1 cup) light corn syrup	2 baking sheets
Flour for dusting	Parchment paper
100 grams (3½ ounces) *Pâte Feuilletée* (see page 190)	Small bowl
2 ripe but firm bananas	Rolling pin
50 grams (1¾ ounces) granulated or turbinado sugar	Docker or kitchen fork
475 milliliters (2 cups) *Sauce au Chocolat* (see page 159)	Small sharp knife
Vanilla or peanut butter ice cream to finish, optional	Pastry brush
	Wire rack
	Handheld propane torch
	Metal spoon
	4 dessert plates

Prepare your *mise en place.*

Line a baking sheet with parchment paper. Set aside.

Place the corn syrup in a small bowl. Set aside.

Preheat the oven to 177°C (350°F).

Lightly flour a cool work surface and, when rolling and turning the dough, make sure that the surface is coated with just enough flour to keep the dough from sticking. If it sticks, it will not form proper layers.

Place the dough on the floured surface. Using a rolling pin, roll it out until it is about 3 millimeters (⅛ inch) thick, or even a bit thinner, dusting the rolling pin with flour if necessary to prevent sticking. The pastry can be rolled this thin because no rise is required.

Using a docker or a kitchen fork, dock the entire surface of the pastry. Then, using a small sharp knife, cut out four 12.5-centimeter (5-inch) circles. Transfer the circles to the prepared baking sheet.

Place a piece of parchment paper over the top and another baking sheet on top of the paper to hold the pastry down as its cooks. Bake for 15 minutes, or until nicely colored and almost cooked through.

Remove the top pan and parchment paper and, using a pastry brush, lightly coat the surface with corn syrup. Return the pastry to the oven and bake for an additional 5 minutes, or until it is dark brown and the corn syrup has stopped bubbling. Transfer it to a wire rack to cool. If desired, the cooled pastry may be wrapped, airtight, and stored up for to 3 days before using.

Peel the bananas and, using a small sharp knife, cut them crosswise or on the bias into 3-millimeter (⅛-inch) slices.

Place the banana slices in a slightly overlapping pattern on top of each pastry round.

Sprinkle the bananas with the sugar and with a torch lightly caramelize the sugar until it turns golden and the bananas are slightly charred around their edges.

When ready to serve, spoon an equal portion of the chocolate sauce over the center of each dessert plate.

Place a tart in the center of the sauce, pushing it down lightly to spread the sauce. If desired, add a small scoop of vanilla or peanut butter ice cream at the side.

TIPS

Any type of *feuilleté*, including scraps, may be used in this recipe. Scrap dough must be allowed to relax and rest for at least 45 minutes before using.

The corn syrup glaze on the pastry adds sweetness and seals the dough to prevent it from getting soggy if not used immediately. The syrup must be thoroughly baked and caramelized or it will remain sticky.

Since the pastry expands a bit while baking, to ensure even circles, first bake the entire sheet of pastry and then very carefully cut out the circles.

EVALUATING YOUR SUCCESS

The pastry rounds should be of the same size and golden brown, crisp, and flaky.

The bananas should completely cover the pastry.

The sugar should be completely melted and caramelized, with no apparent graininess.

Demonstration

Tartes aux Poires en Cage (Individual Pear Tarts with Lattice)

Makes 4 pear-shaped tarts

Estimated time to complete: 2½ hours

Ingredients	Equipment
Flour for dusting	2 baking sheets
160 grams (5⅔ ounces) *Pâte Feuilletée* (see page 190)	Parchment paper
2 ripe but firm pears	Rolling pin
2 liters (2 quarts, 3½ ounces) dry white wine	Plastic film
2 vanilla beans, split in half lengthwise	Melon baller
Juice of 3 lemons	Medium shallow pot
1 kilogram (2¼ pounds) sugar	Paring knife
Egg wash (see page 62)	Slotted spoon
50 grams (1¾ ounces) *Crème d'Amandes* (see page 252)	Plate
	Lattice cutter
	Paper towel
	Small bowl
	Rubber spatula
	Pastry bag fitted with small plain tip
	Pastry brush
	Wire rack

Prepare your *mise en place*.

Line a baking sheet with parchment paper. Set aside.

Lightly flour a cool work surface and, when rolling and turning the dough, make sure that the surface is coated with just enough flour to keep the dough from sticking. If it sticks, it will not form proper layers.

Place the dough on the floured surface. Using a rolling pin, roll it out until it is about 3 millimeters (⅛ inch) thick, dusting the rolling pin with flour if necessary to prevent sticking.

Transfer the pastry to the prepared baking sheet.

Wrap the entire pan with plastic film and place it in the refrigerator for 30 minutes, or until well chilled.

Meanwhile, prepare the pears.

Peel and halve the fruits and, using a melon baller, core each pear half.

Combine the wine with an equal amount of water in a medium shallow pot. Using a paring knife, scrape the seeds from the vanilla beans into the wine. Add the scraped bean along with the lemon juice and sugar.

Place over medium heat and bring to a boil. Add the pear halves and reduce the heat to a gentle simmer.

Cook, gently stirring occasionally, for about 20 minutes, or until the point of a paring knife inserted into the thickest part meets little resistance. It is a good idea to test each pear half for doneness, as each will cook at a different rate according to its size and ripeness.

Using a slotted spoon, carefully transfer the pears to a plate to cool. (If not using the pears immediately, cool the poaching liquid and, when it is cooled, return the cooled pears to it until ready to use. Store, tightly covered and refrigerated, for up to 1 week. If using the pears immediately, you can store the cooled poaching liquid, tightly covered and frozen, to be reused for poaching fruit in the future.) The pears

must be completely cool before using or they will melt the butter in the pastry and render the tarts unusable.

While the pears are cooling, prepare the pastry shapes.

Remove the pastry from the refrigerator and cut 4 pear-shaped pieces at least 2.5 centimeters (1 inch) larger than each pear half. Return the pear shapes to the parchment paper-lined baking sheet.

Using a lattice cutter, carefully roll the cutter over the remaining pastry, cutting 4 lattice pieces large enough to completely cover the top of the pears. Carefully transfer the lattice pieces to the baking sheet.

Cover the entire baking sheet with plastic film and refrigerate for at least 30 minutes, or until well chilled.

Place the cooled pears on a double layer of paper towel to drain well. If they remain very wet, their juices will ruin the tarts.

Preheat the oven to 177°C (350°F).

Line another baking sheet with parchment paper.

Place the egg wash in a small bowl.

Transfer the pear-shaped pastry pieces to the clean parchment paper-lined baking sheet. Return the lattice pieces to the refrigerator to keep cold until ready to use.

Using a rubber spatula, place the almond cream into a pastry bag fitted with a small plain tip. Pipe just enough of the almond cream to fill the hollowed core of the pear half into the center of each pear-shaped pastry piece. Place a well-drained pear on top of the almond cream, fitting the core over the cream.

Remove the lattice tops from the refrigerator and carefully place one over the pear on each tart. Press down gently around the edges to seal the lattice to the bottom crust and then fold and pinch a decorative edge all around the rim. If desired, you can cut 4 leaf shapes out of the dough scraps and place one at the stem end of each tart. At this point, the tarts may be wrapped, airtight, and frozen for up to 1 month.

Using a pastry brush, lightly coat the dough of each tart with egg wash. Take care that you don't brush the pears; the brush would transfer sugar from the pears to the pastry, which would then darken or burn during baking.

Bake the tarts for about 20 minutes, or until the pastry is golden brown and cooked through.

Transfer them to a wire rack to cool slightly. Serve immediately or no more than a few hours after baking.

If desired, the tarts may be dusted with confectioners' sugar before serving.

TIPS
Any type of *feuilleté*, including scraps, may be used in this recipe. Scrap dough must be allowed to relax and rest for at least 45 minutes before using.

EVALUATING YOUR SUCCESS
The *feuilleté* should be golden brown, evenly risen, crispy, and flaky.

The lattice top should be evenly open and risen slightly above the pear to give the impression of a cage.

The decorative edge should remain sealed during baking.

There should be no almond cream visible.

The pears should be tender, flavorful, evenly colored, and slightly shiny.

Demonstration

Dartois aux Pommes (Apple *Dartois*)

Makes one 20-centimeter (8-inch) square tart
Estimated time to complete: 90 minutes

Ingredients	Equipment
Flour for dusting	2 baking sheets
300 grams (11 ounces) *Pâte Feuilletée* (see page 190)	Parchment paper
Egg wash (see page 62)	Rolling pin
400 grams (14 ounces) Apple Compote (see page 96)	Plastic film
	Pastry wheel
	Lattice cutter
	Pastry brush
	Metal spoon
	Wire rack

Prepare your *mise en place*.

Line the baking sheets with parchment paper. Set aside.

Lightly flour a cool work surface and, when rolling and turning the dough, make sure that the surface is coated with just enough flour to keep the dough from sticking. If it sticks, it will not form proper layers.

Place the dough on the floured surface. Using a rolling pin, roll it out to a rectangle approximately 20

by 36 centimeters (8 by 14 inches) and 3 millimeters (⅛ inch) thick, dusting the rolling pin with flour if necessary to prevent sticking.

Transfer the pastry to one of the prepared baking sheets. Wrap the entire pan with plastic film and place it in the refrigerator for 30 minutes, or until well chilled.

Preheat the oven to 177ºC (350ºF).

Using a pastry wheel, cut the chilled dough into a 20-centimeter (8-inch) square and a 20-by-15-centimeter (8-by-6-inch) rectangle.

Place the square on the remaining parchment paper-lined baking sheet.

Lift the rectangle from the baking sheet and carefully roll a lattice cutter over length of the pastry. Return the cut lattice piece to the baking sheet and refrigerate to keep cold.

Using a pastry brush, lightly coat the edges of the square with egg wash. Spoon the compote onto the pas-

try square, spreading it out in all directions, leaving a 1-inch border all around. Do not discard the egg wash.

Carefully place the lattice over the compote-filled square. Press down gently around the edges to seal the lattice to the square and then fold and pinch a decorative edge all around the rim. At this point, the tart may be wrapped, airtight, and refrigerated for up to 2 days, or frozen for up to 1 month.

Using a pastry brush, lightly coat the lattice with egg wash, taking care that you don't touch the compote. The brush would transfer sugar from the compote to the pastry, causing darkening or burning during baking.

Bake the tart for about 40 minutes, or until golden brown.

Place it on a wire rack to cool slightly before serving.

TIPS
In this recipe, it is particularly important that the *feuilletage* be well chilled after being rolled out or it will not hold its shape when cut and baked.

The compote should be very thick and dry so that it does not ooze out of the pastry during baking.

EVALUATING YOUR SUCCESS
The *feuilleté* should be golden brown, evenly risen, crispy, and flaky.

The lattice top should be evenly open and risen slightly above the compote to give the impression of a cage.

The decorative edge should remain sealed during baking.

Demonstration

Mille-Feuilles (Napoleon Strip)

Makes one 15-by-38-centimeter (6-by-15-inch) strip
Estimated time to complete: 90 minutes

Ingredients	Equipment
Flour for dusting	2 baking sheets
300 grams (11 ounces) *Pâte Feuilletée* (see page 190)	Parchment paper
240 milliliters (1 cup) light corn syrup	Rolling pin
500 grams (1 pound, 1½ ounces) *Crème Pâtissière* (see page 248)	Docker or kitchen fork
30 milliliters (1 ounce) Grand Marnier or liqueur of choice	Pastry brush
100 milliliters (3½ ounces) chilled heavy cream	Pastry wheel
	Small mixing bowl
For the *fondant*	Whisk
30 grams (1 ounce) sugar	Standing electric mixer fitted with whip
50 grams (1⅓ ounces) couverture chocolate, melted	Rubber spatula
150 grams (5¼ ounces) *fondant glacé* (see Tips)	Offset spatula
Toasted slivered almonds to finish, optional	Small saucepan
	Bain-marie
	Wooden spoon
	Pastry bag fitted with small plain tip
	Wooden skewer

Prepare your *mise en place*.

Line a baking sheet with parchment paper. Set aside.

Lightly flour a cool work surface and, when rolling and turning the dough, make sure that the surface is coated with just enough flour to keep the dough from sticking. If it sticks, it will not form proper layers.

Preheat the oven to 177°C (350°F).

Place the dough on the floured surface. Using a rolling pin, roll it out to a large rectangle that is no more than 3 millimeters (⅛ inch), dusting the rolling pin with flour if necessary to prevent sticking.

Transfer the pastry to the prepared baking sheet.

Using a docker or kitchen fork, dock the entire surface of the pastry. Cover it with a piece of parchment paper and then place another baking sheet on top to hold the pastry down.

Bake the pastry for about 15 minutes, or until almost baked through. Remove the top pan and parchment paper and, using a pastry brush, lightly coat the surface with corn syrup. Return the pastry to the oven and bake for an additional 5 minutes, or until the pastry is golden brown and the corn syrup has stopped bubbling.

Using a pastry wheel, immediately cut the pastry into three 15-centimeter-wide (6-inch-wide) strips of even length. If the pastry cools, it will break into pieces when cut. Save the crumbs to decorate the finished pastry, if desired.

Set aside to cool completely on the baking sheet. The pastry can be wrapped, airtight, and stored at room temperature for a day or two.

Place the pastry cream in a small mixing bowl and whisk vigorously to eliminate any lumps. It should be perfectly smooth. Add the liqueur and whisk to blend well.

Place the heavy cream in the bowl of a standing electric mixer fitted with the whip and beat until stiff peaks form (*crème fouettée*). Using a rubber spatula, gently fold the whipped cream into the smooth pastry cream to make a thick *crème légère*.

Place one of the pastry strips on a clean work surface. Using an offset spatula, carefully coat the strip with the *crème légère*. Place a second strip on top of the cream and carefully coat it with an equal amount of the *crème légère*. Top with the final pastry strip. Smooth the long sides of the strips to make a neat finish.

To prepare the *fondant*, combine the sugar with 60 milliliters (¼ cup) water in a small saucepan over low heat. Cook for about 4 minutes, or until a clear liquid forms. Remove from the heat and set aside.

Place the *fondant* in a *bain-marie* over low heat. Cook, stirring frequently with a wooden spoon, until the *fondant* reaches 36°C (97°F). The temperature is best tested by touching the *fondant* to your lip; it should feel neither hot or cold.

Begin adding the syrup to the *fondant* a bit at a time, stirring and adding syrup until the *fondant* forms a short ribbon when lifted on the spoon and held over the bowl.

Using a rubber spatula, scrape the chocolate into a pastry bag fitted with a small plain tip.

Working quickly, as you don't want the *fondant* to harden, using an offset spatula, coat the top of the pastry with the white *fondant* to make a neat, even glaze. Immediately pipe thin lines of chocolate, lengthwise, over the *fondant*.

Gently drag a wooden skewer crosswise through the *fondant* in 1.3-centimeter (½-inch) intervals, alternating directions each time, to make a decorative, marbleized pattern.

Cover the long sides of the Napoleon with either crumbs left over from the *feuilleté* or with toasted slivered almonds.

Serve immediately.

TIPS

Any type of *feuilleté*, including scraps, may be used in this recipe. If scrap is used, you will need to roll out larger-than-normal pieces, as the dough will shrink during baking. It must also be allowed to relax and rest for at least 45 minutes before baking.

The *feuilletage* can be rolled very thin, as almost no rise is required.

Fondant glacé is a commercially prepared pastry product available from cake and bakery supply stores. It should not be confused with rolled *fondant* (see page 403).

The corn-syrup glaze on the pastry adds sweetness as well as sealing the dough to prevent it from getting soggy. The syrup must be thoroughly baked and caramelized, or it will remain sticky.

The pastry is cut after baking, while hot, to prevent it from breaking and to ensure that all strips are all of equal size. This is very important.

The *crème légère* must be very thick so that it remains on the pastry without oozing out the sides. To make smoothing the sides easier, when spreading the *crème légère* between the pastry layers, push it slightly inward off the edges.

NOTE

To make *Mille-Feuilles de Forme Rond* (Round Mille-Feuilles), cut the pastry into three 15-centimeter (6-inch) disks and proceed as for the traditional version, up to the glazing step.

To finish the pastry, simply coat the top with a thin layer of confectioners' sugar and make a crosshatch design over the top by dragging a very hot metal skewer through the sugar in neat even lines. The skewer can be heated on the stovetop; it has to be kept very hot or the sugar will not caramelize.

Finish the sides with crumbs or toasted almonds as directed in the recipe.

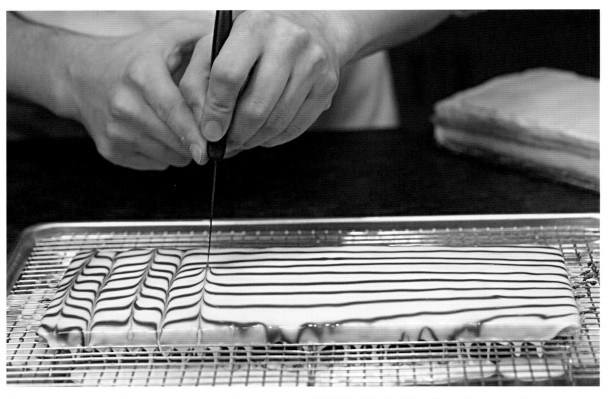

The crumbs or almonds are put on last so that they do not attract any wet fondant.

Finished *mille-feuilles* cannot be kept for a long period of time; they are never held overnight.

EVALUATING YOUR SUCCESS

The *feuilleté* should be golden brown, evenly risen, crispy, and flaky.

The strips should be of the same size, shape, thickness, and color.

The *crème légère* should be light, smooth, and firm, and the layers should be equal in depth.

The fondant should completely cover the top of the pastry.

The marbleized pattern in the *fondant* should be distinct and evenly spaced.

The crumbs or almonds should cover the sides only.

Demonstration

Mille-Feuilles au Chocolat (Chocolate Napoleon)

Makes one 30-centimeter (12-inch) strip
Estimated time to complete: 90 minutes

Ingredients	Equipment

Ingredients

Flour for dusting
300 grams (11 ounces) *Pâte Feuilletée au Chocolat* (see page 198)
240 milliliters (1 cup) light corn syrup

For the *crème d'or*
400 grams (14 ounces) bittersweet chocolate, chopped into small pieces
400 milliliters (13½ ounces) chilled heavy cream

For the finish
125 milliliters (4 ounces plus 1 teaspoon) chilled heavy cream
128 grams (4½ ounces) bittersweet chocolate, chopped into small pieces
50 grams (1¾ ounces) white chocolate, chopped into small pieces

Equipment

2 baking sheets
Parchment paper
Rolling pin
Docker or kitchen fork
Pastry brush
Pastry wheel
Standing electric mixer fitted with whip
Offset spatula
Small saucepan
Wooden spoon
Double boiler
Rubber spatula
Pastry bag fitted with small plain tip
Wooden skewer

Prepare your *mise en place*.

Line a baking sheet with parchment paper. Set aside.

Lightly flour a cool work surface and, when rolling and turning the dough, make sure that the surface is coated with just enough flour to keep the dough from sticking. If it sticks, it will not form proper layers.

Preheat the oven to 177°C (350°F).

Place the dough on the floured surface. Using a rolling pin, roll it out to a large rectangle that no more than 3 millimeters (⅛ inch) thick, dusting the rolling pin with flour if necessary to prevent sticking.

Transfer the pastry to the prepared baking sheet. Using a docker or kitchen fork, dock the entire surface of the pastry. Cover it with a piece of parchment paper and then place another baking sheet on top to hold the pastry down.

Bake for about 15 minutes, or until almost baked through. Remove the top pan and parchment paper and, using a pastry brush, lightly coat the surface with corn syrup. Bake for an additional 5 minutes, or until the pastry is golden brown and the corn syrup has stopped bubbling.

Using a pastry wheel, immediately cut the pastry into three 15-centimeter-wide (6-inch-wide) strips of even length. If the pastry cools, it will break into pieces when cut. Save the crumbs to decorate the finished pastry. At this point, the pastry can be wrapped, airtight, and stored at room temperature for 2 or 3 days.

Place the chocolate in the top half of a double boiler over simmering water. Heat, stirring frequently, until melted. Let cool slightly.

Place the heavy cream in the bowl of a standing electric mixer fitted with the whip and beat until stiff peaks form (*crème fouettée*). Quickly fold the melted chocolate into the whipped cream to make a *crème d'or*.

Place one of the pastry strips on a clean work surface. Using an offset spatula, carefully spread half of the *crème d'or* over the top of the pastry strip. Place a second strip on top of the cream and carefully coat it with the remaining *crème d'or*. Top with the final pastry strip. Wipe the spatula clean and then smooth the long sides of the strips to make a neat finish.

Make a *ganache* by heating the heavy cream in a small saucepan over medium heat just until faint bubbles appear around the edge of the pan. Remove from the heat and add the bittersweet chocolate pieces. Let rest for about 30 seconds and then begin beating with a wooden spoon. Beat until the mixture is completely homogenized and smooth.

Place the white chocolate in the top half of a double boiler set over simmering water. Cook, stirring frequently, for about 3 minutes, or just until the chocolate has melted.

Using a rubber spatula, scrape the melted white chocolate into a pastry bag fitted with the small, plain tip.

Using an offset spatula, carefully coat the top of the pastry with a thin layer of the *ganache*. Immediately pipe thin, straight lines of white chocolate lengthwise over the *ganache*.

Gently drag a wooden skewer crosswise through the white piping at 1.3-centimeter (½-inch) intervals to make a decorative, marbleized pattern.

Cover the long sides of the Napoleon with crumbs left over from the *feuilleté*.

Serve immediately.

TIPS

Any type of *feuilleté*, including scraps, may be used in this recipe. If scrap dough is used, you will need to roll out larger-than-normal pieces, as the dough will shrink during baking. It must also be allowed to relax and rest for at least 45 minutes before baking.

The *feuilletage* can be rolled very thin, as almost no rise is required.

The corn-syrup glaze on the pastry adds sweetness as well as sealing the dough to prevent it from getting soggy. The syrup must be thoroughly baked and caramelized, or it will remain sticky.

The pastry is cut immediately after baking, while hot, to prevent it from breaking and to ensure that all strips are of equal size. This is very important.

The *crème d'or* must be very thick so that it remains on the pastry without oozing out the sides.

To make smoothing the sides easier, when spreading the *crème d'or* between the pastry layers, push it slightly inward off the edges.

The crumbs are put on last so that they do not stick to the *ganache*.

Finished *mille-feuilles* cannot be kept for a long period of time; they are never held overnight.

EVALUATING YOUR SUCCESS

The *feuilleté* should be golden brown, evenly risen, crispy, and flaky.

The strips should be of the same size, shape, thickness, and color.

The *crème d'or* should be light, smooth, and firm, and the layers should be equal in depth.

The *ganache* should completely cover the top of the pastry.

The marbleized effect should be distinct and evenly spaced.

The crumbs should cover the sides only.

Demonstration

Gâteau Pithiviers (Puff Pastry Cake with Almond Cream in the Style of Pithiviers)

Makes one 20-centimeter (8-inch) cake
Estimated time to complete: 90 minutes

Ingredients	Equipment
Flour for dusting	2 baking sheets
225 grams (8 ounces) *Pâte Feuilletée* (see page 190)	Parchment paper
Egg wash (see page 62)	Rolling pin
75 grams (2⅔ ounces) *Crème Pâtissière* (see page 248)	Pastry wheel
150 grams (5⅓ ounces) *Crème d'Amandes* (see page 252)	Plastic film
	Small mixing bowl
	Whisk
	Wooden spoon
	Small bowl
	Pastry brush
	Pastry bag fitted with medium plain tip
	Small round cookie cutter
	Paring knife
	Wire rack

NOTE

This cake is named for the French town of Pithiviers. The classic filling is always frangipane, but it may be combined with fruit. It is traditionally served on Twelfth Night, when it is also called *Gâteau du Roi* (king's cake) because a coin, whole almond, or dried bean is baked into it, and whoever gets this bonus in their slice is crowned king (or queen) for a day, with the privilege of wearing a paper crown in celebration.

Prepare your *mise en place*.

Line the baking sheets with parchment paper. Set aside.

Lightly flour a cool work surface and, when rolling and turning the dough, make sure that the surface is coated with just enough flour to keep the dough from sticking. If it sticks, it will not form proper layers.

Place the dough on the floured surface. Using a rolling pin, roll it out to a large rectangle that is no more than 3 millimeters (⅛ inch) thick, dusting the rolling pin with flour if necessary to prevent sticking.

Using a pastry wheel, cut one 20-centimeter (8-inch) circle and one 23-centimeter (9-inch) circle from the pastry.

Transfer the pastry circles to one of the prepared baking sheets. Wrap the entire pan with plastic film and place in the refrigerator for 30 minutes, or until well chilled.

Place the pastry cream in a small mixing bowl and whisk vigorously to eliminate any lumps. It should be perfectly smooth. Add the almond cream, beating to blend well. This is a *frangipane*.

Preheat the oven to 177°C (350°F).

Place the egg wash in a small bowl.

Transfer the smaller pastry to the other prepared baking sheet. Leave the larger disk in the refrigerator until ready to use.

Place the *frangipane* in a pastry bag fitted with a medium plain tip and then pipe the *frangipane* over the pastry, leaving 4 centimeters (1½ inches) uncovered around the edge of the circle.

Using a pastry brush, lightly coat the edge of the small circle with egg wash. Do not discard the egg wash.

Carefully place the larger circle over the *frangipane*. Lightly press on the top to push out any air and then press gently around the edges to seal the bottom and top together. Using a paring knife or a plain pastry tip, make a small vent in the center of the cake.

Using a small round cookie cutter, scallop the edge to make a delicate finish.

Using the pastry brush, lightly coat the entire cake with egg wash. Then, using the back of the knife, make curving lines on the top, working from the center out. Do not go deeply into the pastry or the filling will push out. Refrigerate for at least 1 hour before baking.

Place the pastry in the preheated oven and bake for about 40 minutes or until golden brown. Remove from

the oven and transfer to a wire rack to cool slightly before serving.

TIPS
The cake must be carefully sealed or the *frangipane* will run out during baking.

The pastry must be kept well chilled throughout the assembling process or it will not hold its shape during baking.

The cake must be baked until no white doughy spots are visible in the pastry.

EVALUATING YOUR SUCCESS
The *feuilleté* should rise evenly, with little or no rise around the edges, and be flaky and tender.

The cake should be golden brown and slightly shiny.

The baked *feuilleté* should be golden brown throughout, except for a thin layer of white next to the *frangipane*.

The *frangipane* should be light and moist.

The score marks on the top of the cake should be evenly spaced and even in their curve.

Demonstration

Jalousie (Venetian Blind Cake)

Makes one 46-centimeter (18-inch) cake
Estimated time to complete: 90 minutes

Ingredients	Equipment
Flour for dusting	2 baking sheets
300 grams (11 ounces) *Pâte Feuilletée* (see page 190)	Parchment paper
Egg wash (see page 62)	Rolling pin
250 grams (8¾ ounces) raspberry jam (see Note)	Plastic film
80 grams (2¾ ounces) toasted sliced almonds	Small bowl
250 grams Traditional Almond Cream (see page 252)	Pastry wheel
	Pastry brush
	Metal spoon
	Paring knife
	Wire rack

NOTE

Jalousie gets its name from the French word for Venetian blinds, because the slits over the top resemble the slats in the blinds. Although classically filled with jam or *frangipane*, it can be made with a fruit compote or a savory filling. Whichever filling is used, it must be thick and fairly dry so that it does not ooze out during baking.

Prepare your *mise en place*.

Line the baking sheets with parchment paper. Set aside.

Lightly flour a cool work surface and, when rolling and turning the dough, make sure that the surface is coated with just enough flour to keep the dough from sticking. If it sticks, it will not form proper layers.

Place the dough on the floured surface. Using a rolling pin, roll it out to a rectangle that is approximately 25 by 46 centimeters (10 by 18 inches) and 3 millimeters (⅛ inch) thick, dusting the rolling pin with flour if necessary to prevent sticking.

Transfer the pastry to one of the prepared baking sheets. Wrap the entire pan with plastic film and place in the refrigerator for 30 minutes, or until well chilled.

Place the egg wash in a small bowl.

Using a pastry wheel, cut the pastry rectangle in half lengthwise.

Place one of the pastry strips on the remaining parchment paper-lined baking sheet. Using a pastry brush, lightly coat its edges with egg wash. Do not discard the egg wash.

Using a piping bag with a #10 plain tip, pipe 2 strips of jam alternating with 3 strips of almond cream down the length of the dough, leaving a 2.5-centimeter (1-inch) border all around.

Fold the remaining strip in half lengthwise and, using a paring knife, carefully cut 4-centimeter (1½-inch) slits, 2.5 centimeters (1 inch) apart, across the middle of the pastry. Do not cut all the way to the edges of the folded pastry. You need to have enough of an uncut border to prevent the filling from running out.

Unfold the pastry strip and carefully place it over the jam and almond cream. Press gently around the edges

to seal the bottom and top together, fluting slightly to make a decorative edge. Cover with plastic film and refrigerate for at least 1 hour, or until well chilled. At this point, the cake may be wrapped, airtight, and refrigerated for up to 2 days, or frozen for up to 1 month.

Preheat the oven to 177°C (350°F).

Using the pastry brush, lightly coat the pastry with egg wash. Sprinkle the almonds along the edges.

Bake the cake for about 40 minutes, or until golden brown and cooked through. Transfer it to a wire rack to cool slightly before serving.

TIPS

The pastry must be kept well chilled throughout the assembling process or it will not hold its shape during baking.

A decorative seal is important to the final look of the baked cake.

EVALUATING YOUR SUCCESS

The baked *feuilleté* should be evenly puffed, golden brown, and slightly shiny.

The sealed edge of the baked cake should be even, with little or no rise.

The filling should be thoroughly cooked, moist, and visible through the cuts in the top layer—the way the light reflects through the slats of a Venetian blind.

The slits should be evenly opened and no filling should have oozed through.

Session 6

Crèmes et Flans: An Overview of Creams and Custards

Theory

Creams and custards are nothing more than a combination of eggs, milk or cream, and sugar. Done well, they are silky smooth, just sweet enough to please, and eminently satisfying. They can be used as dessert on their own or, to quote *Larousse Gastronomique*, "as fillings, toppings, or accompaniments to pastries." Whether custard or cream, they are referred to as *crèmes* in classic French pastry making.

As we know them today, *crèmes* date back to the Middle Ages, when they were used as fillings for flans or tarts. The word *custard* is derived from *croustade*, a flaky pastry crust. After the sixteenth century, fruit creams became popular, and at about the same time, custards were being served in individual dishes rather than as a filling enclosed in a pastry crust.

A *crème* can be as straightforward as a simple cup custard or as elegant as a crackling *crème brûlée*. Almost all creams and custards are cooked, although they may be eaten either warm or cold. No matter the type, the technique to master is the heating of the milk and eggs. When the perfect temperature is achieved, the result is a creamy, satiny texture. If the mixture becomes too hot, the protein in the eggs turns into lumps and cancels the egg mixture's ability to hold moisture. When the heat is prolonged, the lumps become desiccated chunks floating in a watery bath.

A custard thickens and sets by the coagulation of egg proteins mixed with liquid. The custards with which we are most familiar usually contain cream, milk, or both. They can be made with whole eggs, whole eggs plus egg yolks, or just yolks. They frequently contain sugar and sweet flavoring, but they can be savory as well, flavored by salt, herbs, cheeses, meats, and so forth. Technically, creams and custards can be made with liquids other than cream or milk, as with fruit curds and *sabayons* (see page 76). The consistency of a custard is determined by the ratio of eggs to liquid.

The Eggcyclopedia prepared by the American Egg Board tells us, "Coagulation occurs as the result of the joining of protein molecules. Natural protein consists of complex folded and coiled individual molecules. Loose bonds across the folds and coils hold each protein molecule in a tight, separate unit. When the protein is heated, the loose bonds, which hold the protein together in a wad, break, and the protein unfolds, or denatures, and changes its natural form. These unfolded molecules now have their bonds exposed. When two unfolded molecules with their bonds sticking out approach each other, the molecules unite. Essentially, millions of protein molecules join in a three-dimensional network, or coagulate." Simple egg proteins, when cooked by themselves, coagulate over a relatively wide temperature range from 62°C to 70°C (144°F to 158°F).

Coagulation in the preparation of creams and custards is a delicate process, as the ingredients are extremely sensitive to time and temperature, as well as to one another. Too much heat applied too quickly or low heat applied for too long will cause the protein molecules to overcoagulate. Once this occurs, they become firm and rupture, squeezing out the liquid that has been held within their molecular structure. Scientifically, this process is referred to as syneresis. It is evident in custards with tiny liquid-filled holes, a grainy texture, or a separated or curdled sauce.

Coagulation occurs gradually in a custard cooked at a low temperature. At a high temperature, coagulation takes place almost instantly. Unfortunately, there is often only a degree of difference between the thickening point and curdling action. This risk is lessened when a stovetop custard is stirred constantly as it cooks over very low heat. The stirring promotes the distribution of heat, allowing the mixture to cook evenly.

Another method to prevent curdling is insulating the custard from direct heat. This can be done by cooking the custard in the top half of a double boiler or using a heavy-bottomed saucepan over direct heat. Baked custards are generally cooked at a very low oven temperature in a *bain-marie* (water bath), for which the water serves as insulator. Custard or cream fillings such as those used in quiches or cream tarts or pies have the surrounding pastry crust to serve as insulation from direct heat.

Gentle heat not only safeguards against curdling, it is also an important factor in food safety. When a product is cooked at a constant low temperature, it benefits from even heat penetration, which also destroys any harmful bacteria.

All custards are fragile and susceptible to bacterial growth. Precautions must be taken to ensure that they are free from contamination. Pans and utensils should be extremely clean and dry. Only pasteurized milk should be used, and it should always be boiled before incorporating it into the custard mix. The eggs must be fresh and their shells pristine—residue on a shell can contaminate the egg when it is cracked open. It is highly recommended that an instant-read thermometer always be used to test custard doneness. Basic egg-based projects (those without added liquid) are pasteurized by maintaining a temperature of 60°C (140°F) for 3½ minutes. When eggs are diluted with liquid, or sugar is added (as for quiches, custards, and bread puddings), the temperature must be brought to 71°C (160°F) to eliminate the possibility of bacterial development.

Other Ingredients and Their Effect on Creams and Custards

All creams and custards have eggs as their base. The way the other ingredients in a specific recipe combine with the egg protein sets the formula. It is, therefore, important to understand the role of each one.

Liquids: When you combine milk, water, or any other liquid with beaten eggs, it dilutes and separates the protein molecules, which makes it difficult for them to join. In turn, this raises the coagulation temperature and slows the thickening process. When the eggs are combined with milk (with the possible addition of sugar), a stirred custard can be brought to 71°C (160°F) before it will curdle. One whole egg or 2 egg yolks will barely set 240 milliliters (1 cup) of milk. Making a firmer custard requires more protein, usually 3 whole eggs per 475 milliliters (2 cups) of milk. The rate at which a liquid conducts heat also affects the cooking time. For instance, homogenized whole milk conducts heat more slowly than skim or nonfat milk and therefore takes longer to cook.

Starches: The addition of almost any starch—flour, cornstarch, potato starch, arrowroot, tapioca—will prevent eggs and other proteins from curdling, even when the mixture is brought to a boil. The exact reason for this is not known, but it is assumed that the starch swells and blocks the egg protein molecules from finding each other and bonding before they have had the opportunity to unwind. Because of this, starchbound creams can be exposed to much higher heat. In fact, a starchbound custard must be reheated after the eggs have been added to inactivate an enzyme (alpha-amylase) in the yolks that destroys starch gels. In addition, the more sugar the mixture contains, the higher the temperature needed to do this. If this enzyme is not inactivated before refrigerated storage, even the thickest, firmest custard will become liquid once chilled.

Sugar: The addition of sugar of any type to a custard mix also serves to separate the egg protein molecules, which, in turn, raises the coagulation temperature and delays the rate of thickening. As a result, a sweet custard will require longer cooking than a savory one.

Salt: All salts, including those occurring naturally in milk, change the electrical makeup of egg protein molecules and, as a result, accelerate the coagulation.

Acids: All acidic elements will change the electrical environment of a custard mix, lower the coagulation temperature, and accelerate thickening. As a result, citrus-based curds as well as custards that contain fruits or vegetables (all of which contain some acid), will set more quickly than mixes containing no acidic elements.

The basic recipes for creams and custards can be divided into three categories. Each contains essentially the same ingredients but is different in the method of preparation:

- stirred custards such as custard cream (*crème anglaise*)

- starchbound custards such as pastry cream (*crème pâtissière*)

- baked custards such as *crème caramel, pot de crème, and crème brûlée*

Stirred Custards

Stirred custards are cooked on top of the stove and are stirred constantly, usually with a wooden spoon or a heat-proof rubber spatula. The continuous motion keeps the mixture liquid by preventing the bonding of the eggs, which results in a pudding that is poured as a sauce rather than solidified. The stirring should be steady, with regular sweeps over the bottom and sides of the pan to keep the mixture homogenized and prevent it from sticking. It is important that stirred custards not be heated to more than 77°C (170°F) or they will curdle. It is equally important that they be gently stirred, as aggressive stirring upsets the egg bonding and will result in a runny custard. The slower the custard heats and the more gently it is stirred, the creamier it will be.

The most basic example of a stirred custard is the classic French dessert sauce, *crème anglaise*. Sometimes called boiled custard or vanilla sauce, it is used not only as a sweet sauce, but as the base for French-style ice creams and Bavarian creams (see page 395). *Crème anglaise* is a simple combination of milk or cream, eggs or egg yolks, sugar, and flavoring that is cooked until thickened.

When making a stirred custard, the objective is to thicken it by gently poaching the egg yolk and sugar mixture in hot milk, without allowing it to form a solid mass. To achieve this, the custard must be kept in constant motion by stirring in a Z or figure-8 pattern. The constant movement breaks the bonds of the proteins as they attempt to set, allowing the yolks to coagulate evenly.

There is little room for error: The egg yolks and sugar for the custard must be whisked together until very pale (*blanchir*). This cannot be done too far in advance of combining them with the hot milk or cream, as it will then be difficult to achieve a smooth texture. A pastry chef might choose to add part of the sugar to the hot liquid and the remainder to the egg yolks. This leaves a smaller amount to *blanchir*, helps prevent scorching during the stirring process, and creates less foam.

This combining step is one of the most crucial parts of the process. Once the milk or cream reaches the boiling point, a small amount of it is slowly whisked into the egg-and-sugar mixture to temper it. In the process, the eggs are gently heated, which avoids cooking or scrambling them—which would occur if they were swiftly and immediately combined. When the eggs have been tempered, the ingredients can be completely combined. The mixture is then place over low, direct heat and cooked, stirring constantly. As the temperature reaches 74°C (165°F), the custard will be quite thick and will coat the back of the spoon (*nappant*). Holding it at 79°C (175°F) for one minute will sterilize it. If the mixture goes above 82°C (180°F), is heated too quickly or for too long, or is not constantly stirred, the yolks will hard-cook, thereby curdling and turning the mixture grainy. Should this happen, immediately remove it from the heat and add cold cream to halt the cooking process.

As soon as the custard reaches the desired consistency and temperature, strain it through a chinois (see page 23) and place it in an ice bath. (The internal heat of the custard mixture and the residual heat of the saucepan will continue to cook the custard if you do not work quickly.) Once the custard is in the ice bath, it should be stirred occasionally to release steam and ensure that it cools evenly.

As a stirred custard cools, it will continue to thicken and a skin will form over the top. This occurs as a result of evaporation on the surface of a hot milk or cream mixture, which causes casein—a protein found in milk—to dry out. If the mixture remains hot, no matter how many times you remove the skin, it will reappear. Applying a bit of butter to the surface prevents this (the French term for this is *tamponner*), as does placing a piece of plastic film directly on the surface.

If the custard is not used immediately, it must be refrigerated as soon as it has cooled. The refrigerated shelf life is approximately 48 hours.

Making Ice Cream

Basic *crème anglaise* may be flavored with any number of different ingredients and flavorings and made into ice cream. To do this, milk (or cream or a mixture of both) is heated, and the flavoring agent is added and left to infuse for a time, often overnight, under refrigeration. The infused milk may then be strained, if needed, before following the specific ice cream recipe.

Some common flavorings include:

° Chocolate: melted bittersweet chocolate added to the infusion

° Cinnamon: either ground or whole sticks

° Citrus: finely grated orange, lemon, or tangerine zest

° Coconut: toasted

° Coffee: roasted espresso beans

° Dried fruits: poached, puréed, and added to finished, cool custard

° Liqueurs: added to finished, cool custard

° Nuts: toasted, ground, or grated almonds, hazelnuts, or other aromatic nuts

° Praline: praline paste added to finished, cool custard or crushed praline folded into finished ice cream

° Vanilla: extract, paste, or split bean infused in milk

Starchbound Custards

Starchbound custards are cooked over direct heat or baked in a moderate oven and made even more stable by the addition of a starch. Unlike stirred custards, they are cooked to temperatures above 82°C (180°F), as they must be boiled for at least 2 minutes to eliminate the raw starch taste, destroy the alpha-amylase enzyme, and thicken to the desired consistency. They may be made with or without the addition of eggs. When eggs are a component, they are beaten together with the starch and sugar before cooking. The starch coats the eggs and prevents curdling. Starchbound custards are denser than the other custards and can withstand higher and more prolonged cooking periods. Overheating may cause the corners of the pan to burn, and both overheating and overstirring might cause a starchbound custard to become runny; undercooking results in an unpleasant raw starch taste. As with stirred custards, the cooking time and stirring process is crucial to a perfect ending.

Crème pâtissière, or pastry cream, is the primary starchbound custard. It is not meant to be served on its own, but rather to be used as a filling for cakes, fruit tarts, or pastries or as the basis for other dessert preparations. It is the workhorse of custards, an all-purpose cream used frequently throughout French pastry making, most famously as a filling for Napoleons and *pâte à choux*. It is also the base for dessert soufflés, *crème légère* (pastry cream lightened with whipped cream), *crème Chiboust* (pastry cream lightened with beaten egg whites and stabilized with gelatin), and *frangipane* (pastry cream combined with almond cream).

In the pastry kitchen, pastry cream powder is often used as a thickener for pastry cream; it consists of cornstarch with vanilla flavoring and, occasionally, yellow food coloring to ensure brightness in the finished pastry cream. It is generally available from cake and bakery supply stores; if it is unavailable, cornstarch can be used as a substitute.

Some points to remember about crème pâtissière are:

° It is very fragile and susceptible to bacterial growth. Extreme caution should be taken to avoid contamination.

° Use only pasteurized milk and be sure to bring it to a boil.

° Make sure that the eggs are fresh and the eggshells are clean, as residue on the shell can contaminate the eggs when they are cracked open.

° Cook the pastry cream for at least 2 minutes after it has come to a boil.

° After cooking is completed, cool the cream as quickly as possible by transferring it to a shallow container.

° Always refrigerate pastry cream until needed.

Some common flavorings include:

° Chocolate
° Rum
° Coffee
° Praline

Baked Custards

There are two types of baked custards: those that are served in the dishes in which they were baked and those that are served unmolded. Within these two types there are many varieties. Classic examples in French dessert making are *crème brûlée* (caramelized custard), *crème caramel* (caramel custard), *crème renversée* (unmolded caramel custard), and *pots de crème* (individual custards baked in a little, lidded ceramic or porcelain pot). American bread puddings and some cheesecakes may also qualify as baked custards. As with other custards, baked varieties can be sweet or savory.

A baked custard that is unmolded must be firmer than one that remains in its container. For that reason, it usually contains whole eggs or a combination of whole eggs and egg yolks—inclusion of the egg whites is important because they stiffen during cooking, helping the custard to retain its shape. As a general rule, at least six whole eggs per liter (quart) of milk are used.

Most baked custards are cooked in a *bain-marie*, or water bath, to keep an even heat around each container and prevent overbaking. An oven water bath is made by placing the filled custard cups or molds in a hotel pan large enough to hold them without the containers touching each other or the edges of the pan, and then adding boiling water to come halfway up the sides of the containers. The pan is usually lined with parchment paper, a wire rack, or a kitchen towel to insulate the custards from direct contact with the hot bottom. Water is most easily added to the pan once it is positioned in the oven: Pull out the oven rack, place the pan on the rack, place the molds in the pan, fill the pan with the boiling water, and then very carefully slide the rack back into the oven.

Baked custards can be considered done as soon as a skewer inserted near the middle comes out clean. The very center should still be a little quivery, a bit like set gelatin. Once the custard is out of the oven, the residual heat finishes the cooking process. To ensure that a custard is ready, tilt the container to about a 45-degree angle; if the center of the custard stays put, it is done. An overbaked custard will separate, or the edges will pull away from the mold. It will also toughen and take on an unpleasant, slightly grainy texture.

The ingredients for a baked custard are simply mixed together, but the following points are very important:

° To reduce cooking time and ensure even cooking, scald the milk (heat to just below the boiling point) before beating it into the eggs.

° When filling the mold, carefully skim off any foam or bubbles—they will mar the appearance of the baked product.

° Always bake the custard at a low temperature for a long period of time. The recommended heat is 149°C (300°F); higher temperatures increase the risk of overcooking and curdling.

° Most starchbound custards are baked in a *bain-marie* so that the outside edges do not over cook before the interior sets. (This is not necessary for custards with an especially high starch content.)

° To prepare a *bain-marie*, choose a pan large and deep enough to provide even temperature around all sides of the mold. Before placing the mold in the pan, line the bottom with insulating material to provide even heat.

° When done, immediately remove the custards from the oven and *bain-marie* or they will continue cooking.

° A custard is considered overbaked when holes appear on the top, the mixture has a curdled appearance, or the top begins to weep and the sides appear watery.

° Baked custards that are to be unmolded, such as *crème renversée*, must be allowed to cool and then refrigerated to chill thoroughly before being unmolded. Chilling causes the custard to congeal slightly and pull away from the sides of the mold. This allows the syrup that has formed during baking to act as a lubricant and aid in releasing the fairly solid custard from the dish.

° If the custard is to be served in its container, choose the appropriate one. There are specific dishes made for *crème brûlée* and *pots de crème*.

Crème Caramel

This custard dish is one of the best known and most loved French baked custard preparations. A ramekin or *charlotte* mold is coated with caramel and then the custard is poured into the mold and baked in a *bain-marie*. The custard is then chilled and unmolded just before serving. The caramel is soft and runny and makes a saucelike coating over the custard.

Crème Brûlée: Another classic baked custard that consists of cream, egg yolks, and sugar baked in a *bain-marie* in a shallow serving dish made specifically for it. After it has been baked and chilled, a thin layer of brown sugar is placed over the top and then burned with a blowtorch or placed under a salamander or broiler until it forms a warm, brittle crust that entirely covers the smooth, satiny cold custard. When a spoon is dipped into the custard, the crust snaps and shatters.

Pots de Crème: Richer than American pudding, this is the French version of a basic cup custard. It gets its name from the traditional lidded porcelain dish in which it is prepared. The name translates from the French as "pots of cream." The pots themselves may also be called *pots de crème* as well as *petits pots*. The lineage of the dish is not well documented, but it has been known from the eighteenth century.

The 90-millilliter (3-ounce) dishes are typically made of porcelain with a single wee handle. The lids may be decorated with an ornate detail, such as an acorn, a piece of fruit, or a bird. The design may range from very rustic to gilt or lavish floral embellishment, although the traditional pots are white porcelain with gold trim.

Demonstration

Crème Anglaise (Custard Cream)

Makes about 1 liter (4 cups)
Estimated time to complete: 40 minutes

Ingredients	Equipment
500 milliliters (2 cups plus 2 tablespoons) whole milk	*Russe*
½ vanilla bean, split lengthwise, seeds scraped and reserved	2 mixing bowls
5 large egg yolks, at room temperature	Whisk
100 grams (3½ ounces) sugar	Wooden spatula
	Metal spoon
	Candy thermometer
	Chinois
	Ice-water bath
	Wooden spoon
	Plastic film

Prepare your *mise en place*.

Place the milk in a *russe*. Add the vanilla bean and its seeds and place the pan over medium heat. Bring to a boil, then immediately remove the pan from the heat and allow the milk to cool for 1 minute.

Combine the egg yolks with the sugar in a mixing bowl, whisking until the mixture is very pale yellow (*blanchir*).

Whisking constantly, pour half the hot milk into the egg mixture to temper it, then, continuing to whisk, slowly pour the tempered mixture into the *russe*.

Cook, stirring constantly with a wooden spatula, for about 12 minutes, or until the custard coats the back of a metal spoon (*nappant*) and a finger drawn through it leaves a clean, stable line. While stirring, pay special attention to the bottom corners of the pan, as the egg will tend to coagulate there.

To pasteurize the pastry cream, bring it to 79°C (175°F) on a candy thermometer and hold it, stirring constantly, at that temperature for 5 minutes. Do not exceed 82°C (180°F) or the cream will curdle.

Remove the cream from the heat and pour it through a *chinois* into a mixing bowl set over an ice-water bath.

Stir constantly with a wooden spoon until the mixture stops steaming.

Cover the cooled cream with plastic film and refrigerate until chilled. Use as directed in a specific recipe.

TIPS
Do not let the eggs stand after adding the sugar, as the sugar will dehydrate the egg yolk, reducing its ability to incorporate into the mix. This is referred to as "burning" the eggs.

EVALUATING YOUR SUCCESS
The cream should be smooth and silky, with no lumps or burned bits.

Demonstration

Crème Pâtissière (Pastry Cream)

Makes about .5 liter (2 cups)
Estimated time to complete: 30 minutes

Ingredients	Equipment
2 large egg yolks, at room temperature	Mixing bowl
1 large whole egg	Whisk
50 grams (1¾ ounces) pastry cream powder (see page 244)	*Russe*
128 grams (4½ ounces) sugar	Small sharp knife
473 milliliters milk (2 cups) whole milk	Large shallow pan
½ vanilla bean, split lengthwise	Spatula
Unsalted butter for coating surface, optional	Plastic film

Prepare your *mise en place*.

Combine the egg yolks, whole egg, and pastry cream powder with half of the sugar in a mixing bowl, whisking until the mixture is well blended and lightly colored.

Place the milk in a *russe*. Using a small sharp knife, scrape the seeds from the vanilla bean into the milk. Add the bean, along with the remaining sugar, and place over high heat. Bring to a boil, then remove the pan from the heat.

Whisking constantly, pour about one-third of the hot milk into the egg mixture to temper it. Whisk the tempered mixture into the hot milk in the *russe*.

Place the mixture over high heat and, whisking constantly, return it to a boil. Boil, stirring constantly with a whisk and taking care to scrape the bottom and lower inner edges of the pan for 2 minutes, or until thick and smooth.

Remove the cream from the heat and pour it into a large shallow pan, spreading it out with a spatula to hasten cooling. Remove and discard the vanilla bean.

NOTE

Crème Pâtissière can be made in many different flavors. The flavorings—such as 100 grams (3½ ounces) melted bittersweet chocolate or nut paste. or 30 milliliters (1 ounce) liqueur, or 10 milliliters (2 teaspoons) of any pure extract—are added just before the cream is fully cooked.

Cover the surface of the pastry cream with a piece of plastic film placed directly over the top. Alternatively, brush the surface with melted, unsalted butter to prevent the formation of skin (*tamponner*). Set aside to cool, then refrigerate until ready to use.

TIPS

Do not let the eggs stand after adding the sugar, as the sugar will dehydrate the egg yolk, reducing its ability to incorporate into the mix. This is referred to as "burning" the eggs.

Once milk and eggs are combined and placed over heat they will burn easily; therefore, it is essential that the mixture be stirred constantly.

Boiling the cream activates the starch as a thickener and eliminates any raw starch taste.

Once cooked and cooled, pastry cream can be held in the refrigerator for up to 4 days.

The cream should be smooth, without lumps, dried skin, or "burnt" eggs.

The cooked cream should have no raw starchy taste. When cooked, the pastry cream should be firm, but it should soften when whisked.

Demonstration

Crème Pâtissière II (Pastry Cream II)

Makes about .7 liter (3 cups)
Estimated time to complete: 30 minutes

Ingredients	Equipment
4 large egg yolks, at room temperature	Mixing bowl
45 grams (1½ ounces) pastry cream powder (see page 244)	Whisk
100 grams (3½ ounces) sugar	*Russe*
475 milliliters milk (2 cups) whole milk	Small sharp knife
½ vanilla bean, split lengthwise	Large shallow pan
75 grams (2⅔ ounces) unsalted butter, at	Spatula
room temperature, cut into pieces	Plastic film
Unsalted butter for coating surface, optional	

Prepare your *mise en place*.

Combine the egg yolks and pastry cream powder with half of the sugar in a mixing bowl, whisking until the mixture is well blended and lightly colored.

Place the milk in a *russe*. Using a small sharp knife, scrape the seeds from the vanilla bean into the milk. Add the bean, along with the remaining sugar, and place over high heat. Bring to a boil, then remove the pan from the heat.

Whisking constantly, pour about one-third of the hot milk into the egg mixture to temper it. Whisk the tempered mixture into the hot milk in the *russe*.

Place the pan over high heat and, whisking constantly, return to a boil. Boil, stirring constantly with a whisk and taking care to scrape the bottom and lower inner edges of the pan for 2 minutes, or until thick and smooth.

Add the butter, whisking until well blended. Remove the cream from the heat and pour it into a large shallow pan, spreading it out with a spatula to hasten cooling. Remove and discard the vanilla bean.

Cover the surface of the pastry cream with a piece of plastic film placed directly over the top. Alternatively, brush the surface with melted, unsalted butter to prevent the formation of skin (*tamponner*). Set aside to cool, then refrigerate until ready to use.

TIPS

Do not let the eggs stand after adding the sugar, as the sugar will dehydrate the egg yolk, reducing its ability to incorporate into the mix. This is referred to as "burning" the eggs.

Once milk and eggs are combined and placed over heat, they burn easily; therefore, it is essential that the mixture be stirred constantly. If not, lumps will appear and the custard will scorch.

Boiling the mixture activates the starch as a thickener and eliminates any raw starch taste.

Once cooked and cooled, pastry cream can be held in the refrigerator for up to 4 days.

The cream should be smooth, without lumps, dried skin, or "burnt" eggs.

The cooked cream should have no raw starchy taste.

The finished cream should have a definite vanilla flavor.

When cooked, the pastry cream should be firm, but it should soften when whisked.

Demonstration

Crème Pâtissière III (Pastry Cream III)

Makes about .7 liter (3 cups)
Estimated time to complete: 30 minutes

Ingredients	Equipment
5 large egg yolks, at room temperature	Mixing bowl
40 grams (1⅓ ounces) cornstarch	Whisk
100 grams (3½ ounces) sugar	*Russe*
475 milliliters milk (2 cups) whole milk	Small sharp knife
½ vanilla bean, split	Large shallow pan
Unsalted butter for coating surface, optional	Spatula
	Plastic film

Prepare your *mise en place*.

Combine the egg yolks and cornstarch with half of the sugar in a mixing bowl, whisking until the mixture is well blended and lightly colored.

Place the milk in a *russe*. Using a small sharp knife, scrape the seeds from the vanilla bean into the milk. Add the bean, along with the remaining sugar, and place the pan over high heat. Bring to a boil, then remove the pan from the heat.

Whisking constantly, pour about one-third of the hot milk into the egg mixture to temper it. Whisk the tempered mixture into the hot milk in the *russe*.

Place the mixture over high heat and, whisking constantly, return it to a boil. Boil, stirring constantly with a whisk and taking care to scrape the bottom

and lower inner edges of the pan, for 2 minutes, or until thick and smooth.

Remove the cream from the heat and pour it into a large shallow pan, spreading it out with a spatula to hasten cooling. Remove and discard the vanilla bean. Cover the surface of the pastry cream with a piece of plastic film placed directly over the top. Alternatively, brush the surface with melted, unsalted butter to prevent the formation of skin (*tamponner*). Set aside to cool, then refrigerate until ready to use.

TIPS
Do not let the eggs stand after adding the sugar, as the sugar will dehydrate the egg yolk, reducing its ability to incorporate into the mix. This is referred to as "burning" the eggs.

Once milk and eggs are combined and placed over heat, they will burn easily; therefore, it is essential that the mixture be stirred constantly. If not, lumps will appear and the custard will scorch.

Boiling the mixture activates the starch as a thickener and eliminates any raw starch taste.

Once cooked and cooled, pastry cream can be held in the refrigerator for up to 4 days.

The cream should be smooth, without lumps, dried skin, or "burnt" eggs.

The cooked cream should have no raw starchy taste.

The finished cream should have a definite vanilla flavor.

Demonstration

Crème d'Amandes (Traditional Almond Cream)

Makes about 800 grams (28 ounces)
Estimated time to complete: 20 minutes

Ingredients	Equipment
250 grams (8¾ ounces) unsalted butter, at room temperature	Standing electric mixer with paddle attachment
250 grams (8¾ ounces) granulated sugar	Rubber spatula, optional
250 grams (8¾ ounces) almond flour	Container with lid, optional
3 large whole eggs, at room temperature	
30 grams (1 ounce) pastry cream powder (see page 244)	

Prepare your *mise en place*.

Combine the butter, sugar, and almond flour in the bowl of a standing electric mixer fitted with the paddle attachment. Beat on medium speed for about 5 minutes, or until very light and fluffy. This step is extremely important to a successful cream.

Adding one at a time, beat in the eggs, thoroughly incorporating each one before adding the next.

When the eggs are well incorporated, add the pastry cream powder, beating to blend well.

Use as directed in a specific recipe or scrape the almond cream from the mixing bowl into a clean container, cover, and refrigerate for up to a week.

TIPS
Thirty milliliters (1 ounce) of rum or other alcohol may be added for additional flavor.

If almond flour is unavailable, you can grind raw almonds with a bit of granulated sugar in a food processor fitted with the metal blade using quick on-and-off turns. You will need 30 grams (1 ounce) of sugar for every 454 grams (1 pound) of almonds.

If pastry cream powder is unavailable, substitute cornstarch or flour, increasing the amount by one-third.

EVALUATING YOUR SUCCESS
The finished cream should be completely smooth, with light color and soft texture.

The finished cream should have a strong almond aroma.

Demonstration

Crème d'Amandes II (Almond Cream II)

Makes about 900 grams (2 pounds)
Estimated time to complete: 20 minutes

NOTE

Crème d'Amandes and *Crème d'Amandes II* are not traditional custards, but are often used in place of custards as fillings for tarts and other pastries.

Ingredients	Equipment
250 grams (8¾ ounces) unsalted butter, at room temperature	Standing electric mixer with paddle attachment
500 grams (1 pound, 1½ ounces) almond paste	Rubber spatula, optional
3 large whole eggs, at room temperature	Container with lid, optional
30 grams (1 ounce) pastry cream powder (see page 244)	
30 milliliters (1 ounce) rum, optional	

Prepare your *mise en place*.

Combine the butter and almond paste in the bowl of a standing electric mixer fitted with the paddle attachment. Beat on medium speed for about 5 minutes, or until very light and fluffy. This step is extremely important to a successful cream.

Adding one at a time, beat in the eggs, thoroughly incorporating each one before adding the next.

When the eggs are well incorporated, add the pastry cream powder and, if using, the rum, beating to blend well.

Use as directed in a specific recipe or scrape the almond cream from the mixing bowl into a clean container, cover, and refrigerate for up to a week.

TIPS

The rum may be replaced with 30 milliliters (1 ounce) of any alcohol you like.

If pastry cream powder is unavailable, substitute cornstarch or flour, increasing the amount by one-third.

EVALUATING YOUR SUCCESS

The finished cream should be completely smooth, with light color and soft texture.

The finished cream should have a strong almond aroma.

Demonstration

Pots de Crème au Chocolat (Chocolate Custards)

Serves 6
Estimated time to complete: 4 hours

Ingredients	Equipment
1 large egg, at room temperature	6 *pots de crèmes* or 90-milliliter (3-ounce) ramekins
1 large egg yolk, at room temperature	Aluminum foil
30 grams (1 ounce) sugar	Hotel pan
Pinch salt	Kitchen towel
170 milliliters (5¾ ounces) whole milk	2 mixing bowls
115 milliliters (3¾ ounces) heavy cream	Whisk
85 grams (3 ounces) semisweet or bittersweet	Whipped cream, optional
chocolate, chopped into small pieces	Heavy-bottomed saucepan
6 candied violets or chocolate shavings, optional	Wooden spoon
	Chinois
	Ladle or paper towel
	Paring knife, optional
	Tray
	Pastry bag fitted with small star tip, optional

Prepare your *mise en place*.

Preheat the oven to 149°C (300°F).

If your porcelain *pots de crème* dishes do not have their own lids, or if you are using ramekins, cut 6 pieces of aluminum foil large enough to cover them.

Line a hotel pan (or other deep baking pan large enough to hold the dishes) with a clean kitchen towel. Place the dishes in the lined pan. Set aside.

Combine the egg, egg yolk, sugar, and salt in a mixing bowl, whisking vigorously until the mixture turns a very pale yellow (*blanchir*).

Combine the milk and cream in a heavy saucepan over medium-high heat and bring to a boil. Add the

chocolate, stirring with a wooden spoon until it dissolves completely. Remove the pan from the heat.

Whisking constantly, pour half of the hot chocolate milk into the egg mixture to temper it. Then, whisking constantly, return the tempered egg mixture to the saucepan.

Pour the well-blended mixture through a *chinois* into a clean mixing bowl. Using a ladle, skim off and discard any foam that forms on the top of the mixture. (Alternatively, lay a piece of paper towel over the surface, then remove it. The foam will come off with the towel.) This is an important step, as the surface of the cooked custard should be very smooth.

Transfer the hotel pan to the middle rack of the oven. Pour an equal amount of the chocolate cream into each dish in the prepared hotel pan. Add enough boiling water to come halfway up the sides of the dishes. Cover the entire pan with a piece of aluminum foil.

Bake for about 40 minutes, or until the custard just jiggles slightly in the center or a paring knife inserted into the center comes out clean. Check the custards about every 10 minutes to make sure that the water does not come to a boil. If it does, lower the oven temperature. If the custards get too hot, they will pit or curdle, which will make the finished dessert unpalatable.

Transfer the *pots de crème* to a tray and refrigerate for a couple of hours, or up to 2 days.

Serve well chilled. If desired, you can pipe a small rosette of whipped cream onto the center of each custard and then garnish the rosette with a candied violet or a shaving of bittersweet chocolate.

TIPS

Do not let the eggs stand after adding the sugar, as the sugar will dehydrate the egg yolk, reducing its ability to incorporate into the mix. This is referred to as "burning" the eggs.

EVALUATING YOUR SUCCESS

The custard should be smooth and firm enough to stand on its own.

The surface should be shiny and almost black.

The baked creams should have a deep chocolate flavor.

If decorated, the rosette and garnish on the custard should be in proportion to the surface area of the dish.

Demonstration

Crème Brûlée façon Le Cirque (Baked Custard with a Caramel Crust, Le Cirque Style)

Serves 4
Estimated time to complete: 1 hour

Ingredients	Equipment
4 large egg yolks, at room temperature	Hotel pan
50 grams (1¾ ounces) granulated sugar	Kitchen towel
500 milliliters (16 ounces plus 2 tablespoons) heavy cream	Four 178-millileter (6-ounce) fluted *crème brûlée* dishes
1 vanilla bean, split lengthwise	2 mixing bowls
Pinch salt	Whisk
Sugar for finishing	Heavy-bottomed saucepan
	Small sharp knife
	Chinois
	Ladle or paper towel
	Boiling water
	Aluminum foil
	Metal spatula
	Wire rack
	Handheld propane torch, optional
	Pastry bag fitted with small star tip, optional

Prepare your *mise en place*.

Line a hotel pan (or other deep baking pan large enough to hold the dishes) with a clean kitchen towel. Place the *crème brûlée* dishes in the lined pan. Set aside.

Preheat the oven to 149°C (300°F).

Combine the egg yolks with half of the granulated sugar in a mixing bowl, whisking until the mixture is pale yellow and thick (*blanchir*).

Place the cream in a heavy-bottomed saucepan. Using a small sharp knife, scrape the seeds from the vanilla bean into the cream. Add the bean along with the salt and remaining granulated sugar. Place over high heat and bring to a boil, then remove the pan from the heat.

Whisking constantly, pour about one-third of the hot cream into the egg mixture to temper it. Pour the tempered mixture into the hot milk in the saucepan, whisking to thoroughly combine.

Pour the custard through a *chinois* into a clean mixing bowl. Using a ladle, skim off and discard any foam that forms on the top. (Alternatively, lay a piece of paper towel over the surface, then remove it.) This is an important step, as the surface of the cooked custard should be very smooth.

Dean's Tip

"Glazing a crème brûlée with dark brown sugar will give a more intense flavor."
Dean Alain Sailhac

NOTE
Owned by the Maccioni family, Le Cirque is one of New York City's most acclaimed restaurants. Chef Alain Sailhac, Dean Emeritus and Executive Vice President of The French Culinary Institute, featured this dessert early in his tenure as the first chef at this legendary restaurant. From there, *crème brûlée* made its presence known on restaurant menus all across the United States.

Transfer the hotel pan to the middle rack of the oven. Pour an equal amount of the custard into each dish, filling to just under the rim.

Add enough boiling water to come halfway up the sides of the dishes. Carefully cover the entire pan with aluminum foil.

Bake for about 40 minutes, or until the custard is softly set but still jiggles slightly in the center. Check the custards about every 10 minutes to make sure that the water does not come to a boil. If it does, lower the oven temperature. If the custards get too hot, they will pit or curdle, which will make the finished dessert unpalatable.

Using a metal spatula, carefully transfer each dish to a wire rack to cool. Don't be concerned if the custards remain slightly soft—they will firm up as they chill.

When the custards have cooled to room temperature, transfer them to the refrigerator and chill for at least 3 hours, or up to 1 day. They must be very cold when served.

When ready to serve, if you are not using a handheld propane torch to caramelize the puddings, preheat the broiler.

Remove the custards from the refrigerator. Spread a thin layer of sugar over the surface of each one. Using the torch, caramelize (*brûler*) the sugar. It should take just a few seconds for it to melt and form a glassy crust. Alternatively, place the custards under the broiler for 15 seconds, or until golden brown.

Serve immediately.

EVALUATING YOUR SUCCESS
The baked custard should be silky smooth, with a deep vanilla flavor.

The burned sugar covering should be glasslike, very even, and a warm golden-brown color.

Demonstration

Crème Caramel (Caramel Custard)

Serves 4

Estimated time to complete: 1 hour

Ingredients	Equipment
	2 kitchen towels
For the caramel	Four 175-milliliter (6-ounce) ramekins
200 grams (6¾ ounces) sugar	Hotel pan
	Stainless-steel saucepan or copper *poêlon*
For the custard	Pastry brush
500 milliliters (2 cups plus 2 tablespoons) whole milk	Spoon
½ vanilla bean, split lengthwise, seeds scraped and reserved	Small heat-proof plate
3 large eggs, at room temperature	Ice cube
75 grams (2⅔ ounces) sugar	Medium heavy-bottomed saucepan
	Small bowl
	Whisk
	Chinois
	Medium bowl
	Ladle
	Boiling water
	Ice-water bath
	Paring knife
	4 dessert plates

Prepare your *mise en place*.

Preheat the oven to 162°C (325°F).

Using a clean kitchen towel, wipe the ramekins so that they are very clean and dry. Set aside.

Line a hotel pan or other deep baking pan large enough to hold the ramekins with a clean kitchen towel. Set aside.

To prepare the caramel, combine the sugar and 50 milliliters (3½ tablespoons) water in a stainless-steel saucepan or copper *poêlon* over medium heat and

bring to a boil.

As the syrup begins to cook, dip a pastry brush in cold water and brush down the sugar crystals that form on the inside of the pan.

When the sugar begins to turn golden, swirl the pot so that it caramelizes evenly. To test for correct color, spoon a bit of the caramel onto a heat-proof plate and add an ice cube to stop the cooking. If the color holds at a clear, light brown, remove the saucepan from the heat. If not, continue to cook until the proper color is achieved.

Pour a thin layer of the caramel syrup into each of the ramekins. Place the ramekins in the prepared pan and set aside.

To prepare the custard, place the milk in a medium heavy-bottomed saucepan. Add the vanilla bean and its seeds and place over medium heat. Bring to a boil, then immediately remove the pan from the heat.

Combine the eggs with the sugar in a small bowl, whisking until the mixture is very pale yellow and thick (*blanchir*).

Whisking constantly, pour half the hot milk into the egg mixture to temper it, then slowly pour the tempered mixture into the saucepan, continuing to whisk constantly.

When the custard is well combined, pour it through a *chinois* into a clean medium bowl. Using a ladle, skim off any foam that forms on the surface.

Pour an equal amount of the custard into each of the prepared ramekins in the hotel pan, filling to just under the rim.

Transfer the hotel pan to the middle rack of the oven.

Add enough boiling water to come halfway up the sides of the dishes. Bake for about 40 minutes, or until the custard no longer moves when the edge of a ramekin is tapped. Check the custards about every 10 minutes to make sure that the water does not come to

a boil. If it does, lower the oven temperature. If the custards get too hot, they will pit or curdle, which will make the finished dessert unpalatable.

Remove the pan from the oven and immediately transfer the ramekins to an ice-water bath to chill.

Crème caramel is always served cold. You may serve it as soon as it has chilled in the ice-water bath or refrigerate it for up to 2 days.

When ready to serve, run a paring knife around the inside of each ramekin and invert it onto a dessert plate. Carefully lift off the ramekin so that the custard remains intact, with the caramel layer on top gently drizzling down the sides.

EVALUATING YOUR SUCCESS
The baked custard should be smooth and silky but firm enough to stand on its own when unmolded. The surface should be shiny, with an even layer of loose caramel.

Demonstration

Quiche Lorraine (Savory Tart in the Style of Lorraine)

Makes one 9-inch tart
Estimated time to complete: 2 hours

Ingredients	Equipment
Flour for dusting	9-inch tart pan
Butter for greasing	Rolling pin
1 recipe *Pâte Brisée* (see page 92), chilled	Pastry brush
1 teaspoon vegetable oil	*Sautoir*
50 grams (1¾ ounces) bacon, cut into *lardons*	Wooden spoon
50 grams (1¾ ounces) Gruyère cheese, grated	Slotted spoon
2 large eggs, at room temperature	Paper towel
125 milliliters (4¼ ounces) whole milk	Parchment paper
125 milliliters (4¼ ounces) heavy cream	Pastry weights or dried beans
Pinch freshly grated nutmeg	Mixing bowl
Pinch coarse salt	Whisk
Pinch freshly ground pepper	Paring knife
	Wire rack

Prepare your *mise en place*.

Butter and flour the tart pan and set it aside.

Lightly dust a clean, flat work surface and the rolling pin with flour. Place the chilled *pâte brisée* in the center of the floured surface and lightly dust it with flour. Begin rolling the dough, using more flour as needed. Working from the center outward, as directed on page 89, roll until the dough is a fairly even circle 28 centimeters (11 inches) in diameter and about 3 millimeters (⅛ inch) thick. Using a pastry brush, lightly remove excess flour.

Carefully fold the dough in half and transfer it to the prepared pan, snugly fitting it into the sides and bottom. Trim off the excess dough, leaving an even edge all around. Transfer the pastry to the refrigerator to chill for at least 30 minutes.

Heat the oil in a large *sautoir* over medium-low heat. Add the bacon and cook, stirring frequently with a wooden spoon, for about 7 minutes, or until golden brown. Using a slotted spoon, transfer the bacon to a double layer of paper towels to drain.

Preheat the oven to 205°C (400°F).

Remove the pastry shell from the refrigerator. Place a 25-centimeter (10-inch) round piece of parchment paper in the bottom of the shell and push it into the sides, leaving an edge with which you can lift it out of the shell when you need to. Add the pastry weights, spreading them out in an even layer.

Bake the shell for about 10 minutes, or until the pastry is dry and chalky white. Remove it from the oven, lift out the parchment paper and weights, and continue to bake for an additional 15 minutes, or until the pastry is lightly browned and cooked through. Set aside to cool slightly.

Reduce the oven temperature to 162°C (325°F).

Spread the cheese over the bottom of the baked pastry shell and sprinkle the bacon over the top of the cheese.

Combine the eggs with the milk, cream, nutmeg, salt, and pepper in a mixing bowl, whisking to blend well. Add salt sparingly, remembering that both the bacon and cheese will add a fair measure of saltiness to the custard. Do not beat too much, as this will result in an excess of air bubbles in the custard.

Place the pastry shell on the middle rack of the hot oven. Carefully pour the egg mixture over the cheese and bacon, filling the shell completely.

Bake for about 30 minutes, or until the custard is set and a paring knife inserted into the middle comes out clean. Do not allow the custard to blossom and rise up—this means that it has baked too long and the eggs have begun to scramble.

Place the quiche on a wire rack to cool for 5 minutes before cutting it into wedges. Serve hot or at room temperature.

TIPS

If, after blind-baking, there are small holes in the pastry, make an egg wash (see page 62) and, using a pastry brush, lightly coat the bottom of the shell with it. Return the shell to the oven and bake for a couple of minutes to just seal the holes.

If, after blind-baking, there are large holes in the pastry, fill them with raw dough and proceed with the recipe.

Do not allow the filling to sit in the crust without immediately baking, as it will turn the pastry soggy.

The base custard may be combined with a variety of ingredients other than bacon and cheese. Some exam-

ples are ham, shrimp, lobster, spinach, broccoli, and any food that stands up to the custard.

A quiche is best eaten shortly after it comes from the oven.

EVALUATING YOUR SUCCESS

The pastry crust should be thoroughly baked and even, with no holes in the surface.

The custard should have no surface coloration.

Some bits of bacon and cheese should be visible on the top.

The custard should be firm, with no curdling.

NOTE

Although quiche is served throughout France, the regions of Alsace and Lorraine are home to extraordinary tarts. The Lorraine, in particular, is noted for its *charcuterie*, and it is the delicately smoked bacon combined with the rich cream and farm-fresh eggs of the area that created the classic and now world-famous *Quiche Lorraine*. It is said that these rich custard tarts evolved from a variation on the German *kuchen* of the sixteenth century.

Session 7

Pains et Viennoiseries:
An Overview of Breads and Pastries

Bread baking is one of man's oldest kitchen crafts, with some type of grain-and-water mix being a source of basic sustenance for thousands of years. From the Stone Age, when cooks made hard cakes from ground barley and water, through biblical references (including the oft-quoted "loaves and fishes" and the still-celebrated unleavened bread of the Exodus of the Israelites), to the sweet, soft, presliced white bread of mid-twentieth-century America—and even on to the contemporary revival of artisanal baking, bread has remained the staff of life for the world's population. Loaves have been found in Egyptian tombs and, in fact, the remains of some 5,000-year-old loaves can still be seen in the Egyptian galleries of the British Museum and other museums. Archeologists have also located bakeries in the remains of long-buried cities such as Pompeii. So important were the bread bakers of the region that, by 168 B.C., they had formed their own guild in Rome, a guild of craftsmen that still exists today.

Clearly, the oldest form of bread was a mix of ground grain and water. But, since yeast occurs naturally in the air and on the surface of most plants, there must have been incidents of intentionally leavened dough even in prehistoric periods. However, the earliest evidence that we have of leavened dough is the loaves found in Egyptian tombs. It was not until many years later, sometime around the late 1600s, that yeasted doughs were used to make the first sweet pastries.

A leavened bread or pastry dough is made of a mix of flour, water, and yeast, but this basic mix can be expanded with rich and flavorful additions. The ingredients chosen will vary the taste and texture, and the method of mixing will greatly influence the final result. Like everything else in the pastry kitchen, great breads and yeast-based pastry doughs begin with great ingredients, most of which have been discussed on pages 38 though 84. Without fresh, lively ingredients, breads and pastries will fall flat!

Basic Methods Making Leavened Bread Dough

There are two primary methods of making bread; the straight-dough, or direct-mix, method and the pre-ferment method. Within the pre-ferment method, there are four different types of doughs: sponge, old dough (or *pâte fermentée*), poolish, and sourdough (also called liquid *levain*). Each style of pre-ferment is used to create a particular type of bread with different crumb structure and flavor.

A bread composed of just flour, water, and yeast is known as a "lean" dough. Once other ingredients are added to this base, it becomes a "rich" dough. The addition of sugar and fat affects the crust, color, crumb, and taste of the baked bread. This will also alter the oven temperature required, as well as the baking time.

Straight-dough Method: This is the simplest way of making bread. It is a one-step process combining yeast, flour, and water that requires only a short period of fermentation. This basic dough lacks the more complex taste, texture, crust, and long shelf life of breads produced by a pre-ferment method. To improve those qualities, the fermentation process can be slowed by cooling down the dough. This is accomplished by using cold ingredients and allowing the dough to ferment and develop in a cold environment.

Pre-ferment Method: Using this method, prior to the mixing of the complete dough, a partial amount of the total yeast, flour, and water from the recipe's basic formula is mixed together to begin the fermentation process. Each pre-ferment type has different formulations and creates different types of crumb structure and taste characteristics.

A description of each type of pre-ferment dough is as follows:

- **Sponge method:** Flour, water, and most, if not all, of the yeast are mixed together and allowed to ferment. This method is used with enriched doughs, that is, those doughs to which butter, sugar, eggs, fruit and nuts will be added. Since the enriching ingredients will slow down the division and fermentation process of yeast, this method allows the yeast to begin its work before coming in contact with them—it "jump starts" the activity, helping to speed up the fermentation time once the final dough is fully combined.

  Dough that has been allowed 3 to 5 hours of fermentation, usually saved from the previous day's batch, is added to the basic yeast, flour, and water mix. Because of the ease of preparation and the superior taste, texture, crust, and shelf life of the baked product, this method has recently gained in popularity. The slow fermentation of the leftover dough contributes to the exceptional quality as well as requires that the baker reduce the amount of yeast needed to create the final dough since the "old dough" retains some leavening ability.

- **Poolish (or biga) method:** A poolish is made from some of the flour, water, and yeast taken from the basic dough. It is generally a mixture of equal amounts of flour and water and a small pinch of yeast, which is then allowed to develop at room temperature for between 3 and 18 hours. This particular pre-ferment method primarily adds to the flavor and crumb characteristics of the baked bread.

- **Sourdough method:** This is the oldest pre-ferment method and requires the longest period of fermentation, ranging anywhere from days to weeks. This long, slow process gives the baked bread a strong, slightly acidic flavor; a large, irregular crumb; a dark, crunchy crust; and a very long shelf life. It involves catching and cultivating wild yeast. A sourdough starter can be created with just wheat flour, water, and a bit of rye flour to kick-start the fermentation. The process encourages the yeast present in the air to begin to ferment with the flour-and-water mixture. The baker must go through a process of growing the yeast and building up the strength and amount of starter. The starter must be fed with flour and water at least once a day at first. When the starter has developed enough to make bread, a portion is mixed into the day's batch of bread dough. The remaining starter is fed with flour and water to build it up for the next time you bake. If the starter is not used regularly, a large amount will need to be discarded as, through constant feedings, it will continue to grow. Some sourdough starters have been kept alive for hundreds of years or through generations of one family, gaining a very distinctive flavor over time.

- **Autolyse method:** This is a full-production technique that can be applied to either the straight-dough method or any of the pre-ferment methods. In this process, the salt and yeast is omitted in the first mix, giving the dough a 10- to 15-minute rest period to allow gluten to develop through hydration. This saves time during the kneading-and-mixing stage, which is a valuable asset in high-production settings.

The Basic Steps to the Proper Execution of Great Yeast-Leavened Bread Doughs

1. Organize and weigh all your ingredients, taking care to select the finest available. This particularly applies to flour, butter, and eggs. Be certain that your yeast is active and that the required liquids are of the proper temperature.

2. Mix the ingredients together following the exact order and method described in the recipe. If this is not done, the dough may not rise properly. You can mix by hand, use a wooden spoon, use a heavy-duty standing electric mixer fitted with the paddle attachment, use a heavy-duty food processor fitted with the metal blade, or follow manufacturer's directions for an electric bread machine.

3. Knead in the style and for the length of time required in the recipe. This may be accomplished using a heavy-duty standing mixer fitted with the dough hook, a heavy-duty food processor fitted with the metal blade, an electric bread machine following manufacturer's directions, or by hand. When kneading by hand, the dough is worked by pressing it down, then folding and turning it (usually by about a quarter turn) for anywhere from 5 to 20 minutes, until the dough is smooth and elastic. Whatever method of mixing and kneading is used, these processes serve to properly distribute the ingredients, develop the gluten in the flour through hydration, and set fermentation in motion.

    The most reliable method for checking the proper development of gluten is known variously as the "windowpane test," finding a "good window," the membrane test, and "pulling a window." A very small piece of dough is cut off from the main batch and is pulled, turned, and stretched to determine whether or not the dough can maintain an almost paper-thin, translucent sheet (or membrane). If it does not, then the dough should be mixed for another couple of minutes and tested again.

4. Begin the first fermentation using the method and for the length of time called for in the specific recipe. A dough might receive its primary fermentation (or raising) covered, in an oiled bowl at room temperature (or warmer) for 1 to 2 hours. Or it might be immediately chilled to slow the fermentation process. Generally, the leaner the dough, the longer the fermentation required.

5. Upon completion of the first fermentation, the dough must be punched down to expel the gases and relax the gluten. This is known as degassing. This may either be gently done with a simple transfer of the dough from the bowl to a work surface, or the dough may be manipulated for a period of time. The process you use to degas will determine the desired crumb of the baked product.

6. The degassed dough is then neatly divided and scaled (weighed) into the exact proportions required by the recipe.

7. The divided dough is shaped into the exact form required by the recipe such as loaf, ball, or round. This is not necessarily the final shape.

8. The shaped dough may now be allowed to rest for a short period or it may immediately be formed into the final shape. If it is allowed to rest, the term used is "to bench" the dough, and the process will further relax the gluten.

9. The final shaping of the dough is done in the style determined by the type of bread or pastry being made. There are an infinite number of prescribed shapes in classic baking techniques.

10. The shaped dough is then given its second period of fermentation, which is known as proofing. (The primary fermentation is often called proofing too, but in the professional setting, the term usually

applies only to the second fermentation.) During this final period of fermentation, the dough either rises to its final size and shape or to a near approximation of it. Proofing may take place in the pans in which the dough will be baked, in proofing baskets (known as *bannetons* or Brotform baskets), on or under a proofing cloth (known as a *couche*), or with the shaped dough placed on parchment or silicone-lined sheet pans. For any of these methods, the proofing will be completed for a specific amount of time in temperature- and moisture-controlled proofing boxes, in a refrigerated dough retarder (as in most professional pastry kitchens or bakeries), or for a period of up to 2 hours at a constant room temperature.

11. The proofed dough is first marked or scored, if desired, and then baked in the style and for the length of time required. It is essential that the baker achieve the required degree of doneness necessary for the proper color and texture of the finished product.

12. Once the bread is baked to perfection, it should be cooled in the exact method and for the period of time called for in the recipe.

The Basic Elements of Leavened Doughs

Flour: A full discussion of flours can be found on pages 38 through 41; however, it is important to remember that you must use the exact type and amount designated in your recipe, as ingredients have a critical impact on the end result. As a general rule, high-gluten flours are used for yeast-leavened doughs and lower-gluten flours, such as cake flour, are used for chemically leavened doughs. Flour provides the starch and protein necessary for the creation of fine doughs, and the character and amount of protein will determine the worth of the finished product. It is most always the primary ingredient in leavened doughs, with all other components being added in varying lesser percentages to the total amount of flour.

Liquids: Liquid is necessary for dissolving the water-soluble proteins, glutenin and gliadin, in the flour. Water is most often the liquid of choice, but milk, cream, fruit juices, or alcoholic beverages can also be used. The common ratio of liquid to flour in yeast-leavened doughs is one part liquid to three parts flour; however, this can vary widely, depending upon the specific type of dough being made and the desired end result.

Leavenings: Leavening occurs with one of three elements: air, steam, or carbon dioxide. It is accomplished mechanically, chemically, or organically (naturally), and each type requires the addition of heat. A full examination of leavening agents and their properties can be found on pages 41 and 42.

Mechanical Leavening: Air is physically incorporated into a mixture to allow it to rise, or is already present, and the expansion increases when it turns to steam under heated conditions. This can occur regardless of other types of leavening agent used.

Chemical Leavening: These agents, usually baking soda or baking powder, cause a chemical reaction that produces gases during baking, causing the product to rise.

Organic Leavening: Yeast is used to produce carbon dioxide, which, in turn, causes the dough to rise. There are many types of yeast, but the most commonly used for leavening in baking (and brewing) is that known as *Saccharomyces cerevisiae*. Yeast requires food, moisture, oxygen, and a warm environment, and dough provides the best of all possible worlds for these organisms to thrive.

Sourdoughs make use of organic leavening, most often with a sourdough starter that is a natural culture of lactobacillus and yeast.

Fats: In some doughs, fat is introduced, both for its richness and for its ability to tenderize the finished product. It also affects the development of gluten. Any fat may be used, but the most common are butter, vegetable oils, and eggs.

Demonstration

Orange-Cinnamon Swirl Breads and Pecan Sticky Buns

Makes two 9-inch loaves and 8 buns
Estimated time to complete: 2½ to 3 hours

Ingredients	Equipment
	Medium mixing bowl
For the sponge	Wooden spoon
100 grams (3½ ounces) unbleached white flour	Standing electric mixer fitted with dough hook
30 grams (1 ounce) active dry yeast	Large, oiled bowl
	Plastic film
For the dough	Proofing box, optional
40 grams (1⅓ ounces) dry milk powder	Bowl scraper
Zest of 1 orange	Bench scraper
200 grams (7 ounces) orange juice	2 small bowls
800 grams (1¾ pounds) bread flour	Two 9-inch loaf pans
100 grams (3½ ounces) sugar	Rolling pin
60 grams (2 ounces) unsalted butter, at room temperature	Pastry brush
3 large eggs, at room temperature	Instant-read thermometer
14 grams (2 teaspoons) salt	Wire rack
	Small sauté pan
To finish the cinnamon loaves	Angel food cake pan
100 grams (3½ ounces) granulated sugar	Serrated knife
1 teaspoon ground cinnamon	Baking sheet
30 grams (1 ounce) melted unsalted butter, plus more for greasing the pans	Parchment paper
Egg wash (see page 62)	

Topping for the sticky buns

120 grams (4¼ ounces) dark brown sugar

60 grams (2 ounces) unsalted butter, at room temperature

50 grams (1¾ ounces) honey

100 grams (3½ ounces) chopped pecans

50 grams (1¾ ounces) Tennessee whiskey, optional

To finish the sticky buns

100 grams (3½ ounces) light brown sugar

1 teaspoon ground cinnamon

¼ teaspoon ground cloves

¼ teaspoon ground allspice

Pinch ground nutmeg

30 grams (1 ounce) melted unsalted butter, plus more for greasing the pan

Prepare your *mise en place*.

To make the sponge, combine the flour and yeast with 100 grams (3½ ounces) room-temperature water in a medium mixing bowl, stirring with a wooden spoon until a stiff dough forms. Sprinkle a pinch of flour on top of the sponge. The sponge should immediately begin to rise, and when cracks begin to show in the flour on the surface, cover the sponge 10 to 15 minutes.

Combine the milk powder and orange zest with the orange juice and 180 milliliters (6⅛ ounces) room-temperature water in the bowl of a standing electric mixer fitted with the dough hook. Add the raised sponge and mix on the lowest speed for 1 minute.

Add the flour, sugar, and butter and mix to just blend. Add the eggs, one at a time, and autolyse (see page 265) for 10 minutes.

Add the salt and mix on medium for 4 to 5 minutes, or until a very soft but stringy and elastic dough (similar to a *brioche*) with a good window (see page 266) has developed.

Place the dough in a large, oiled bowl, turning to lightly coat all surfaces with oil. Cover with plastic film and place in a warm, draft-free spot or in a 24°C (75°F) proofing box for 20 minutes.

Remove the plastic film, turn, fold, degas (see page 266), and flip the dough over in the bowl. Again, cover with plastic film and let rise in a warm, draft-free spot or in a 24°C (75°F) proofing box for another 20 minutes.

Lightly flour a clean, flat work surface. Using a bowl scraper, gently scrape the dough onto the prepared surface. Carefully and gently degas the dough and, using a bench scraper, divide it into two 600-gram (21-ounce) pieces for the breads and one 530-gram (19-ounce) piece for the sticky buns. Wrap the smaller piece in plastic film and refrigerate while you prepare the loaves.

Form each of the remaining pieces of dough into a loaf shape, cover with plastic film, and bench rest on the work surface for 10 minutes to allow the gluten to relax.

Combine the sugar and cinnamon in a small bowl. Set aside.

Lightly coat the interior of the loaf pans with melted butter. Set aside.

Uncover and, using a rolling pin, roll each piece of dough into an 18-by-23-centimeter (7-by-9-inch) rectangle. Using a pastry brush, lightly coat each piece with melted butter and then sprinkle with an equal portion of the cinnamon sugar. Beginning from the longest side, gently roll the dough into a neat log shape. Carefully seal the seam by pressing with the heel of your hand.

Preheat the oven to 191°C (375°F).

Fit each dough log into a buttered pan seam side down. Cover with plastic film and proof in a warm, draft-free spot or in a 24°C (75°F) proofing box for 15 to 20 minutes, or until doubled in size.

Using a pastry brush, lightly coat the top of each loaf with the egg wash. Bake the loaves for 25 minutes, until the internal temperature reaches 85°C (185°F) on an instant-read thermometer, or until a cake tester inserted into the center comes out clean and hot.

Tip the loaves from the pans and place them on a wire rack to cool.

Prepare the Pecan Sticky Buns.

First, make the topping. Combine the dark brown sugar with the butter and honey in a small sauté pan over low heat. Add the pecans and cook, stirring frequently with a wooden spoon, for about 5 minutes, or until the butter has melted and blended into the sugar. Remove from the heat and, if adding the whiskey, stir it in. Set aside to cool slightly.

Combine the light brown sugar with the cinnamon, cloves, allspice, and nutmeg in a small bowl. Set aside.

Lightly coat the interior of an angel food cake pan with a bit of melted butter. Set aside.

Preheat the oven to 191°C (375°F).

Degas the dough for the buns by gently patting the surface with the palm of your hand.

Lightly flour a clean, flat work surface.

Place the dough on the prepared surface and, using a rolling pin, roll the dough into a 20-by-30.5-centimeter (8-by-12-inch) rectangle. Using a pastry brush, lightly coat the dough with melted butter and then sprinkle with the spiced sugar. Beginning from the longest side, gently roll the dough into a neat log shape. Carefully seal the seam by pressing with the heel of your hand.

Using a serrated knife, cut the log crosswise into 8 equal pieces.

Pour the cooled caramel mixture into the bottom of the prepared angel food cake pan. Then, gently place the buns, sides touching, over the caramel mixture.

Cover the pan with plastic film and proof in a warm, draft-free spot or in a 24°C (75°F) proofing box for 15 minutes.

Bake the buns for 30 minutes, until the internal temperature reaches 85°C (185°F) on an instant-read thermometer, or until a cake tester inserted into the center comes out clean and hot.

Line a baking sheet with parchment paper. Set aside.

Remove the buns from the oven and let rest for 5 minutes. Then turn the pan over onto the prepared baking sheet, carefully unmolding the buns in one circular piece. This must be done while they are still warm or the caramel mixture will begin to harden and stick to the pan.

Place the baking sheet on a wire rack and allow the buns to cool completely.

TIPS

Sprinkling flour on the sponge helps to demonstrate the activity of the yeast. As the sponge rises, cracks appear in the flour, indicating that the yeast is active and the sponge is ready.

If some of the caramel remains in the pan after the pastry is removed, scoop it up and pour it over the pastry.

EVALUATING YOUR SUCCESS

The baked buns should be a rich caramel color.

If the whiskey is used, there should be just a subtle hint of the alcohol flavor.

Demonstration

Danish Pastry Dough

Makes 25 to 30 pastries
Estimated time to complete: 3 hours

Ingredients	Equipment
240 milliliters (1 cup) whole milk	Small bowl
30 grams (1 ounce) active dry yeast	Wooden spoon

340 grams (12 ounces) bread flour

225 grams (8 ounces) cake flour

50 grams (1¾ ounces) sugar

1 teaspoon salt

Pinch ground cardamom

50 grams (1 ¾ ounces) *beurre en pommade* (see page 188)

2 large eggs, at room temperature

Flour for dusting

340 grams (12 ounces) unsalted butter, softened

Standing electric mixer fitted with dough hook

Bowl scraper

Plastic film

Rolling pin

Offset spatula

Prepare your *mise en place*.

Place the milk in a small bowl. Stir in the yeast and set aside for a few minutes to allow it to dissolve into the milk.

Place the bread and cake flours along with the sugar, salt, and cardamom in the bowl of a standing electric mixer fitted with the dough hook. Add the *beurre en pommade*, eggs, and yeast mixture. Mix on low for 2 or 3 minutes, just to combine the ingredients. Do not overmix, as you do not want to develop the gluten at this point.

Using a bowl scraper, scrape the dough from the bowl and gently pat it into a square shape. Wrap in plastic film and refrigerate for 25 minutes, or until well chilled.

Lightly flour a clean, flat work surface and place the dough on it. Using a rolling pin, roll the dough out to a 1.3-centimeter-thick (½-inch-thick) rectangle. Do

not make too large a rectangle, or the butter will be spread too thinly to create the layers necessary for a flaky dough.

Using an offset spatula, spread the softened butter over one half of the dough rectangle. Fold the other half up and over the buttered half to make a *pâton* (see page 296). Carefully seal the edges.

Turn the *pâton* 90 degrees and, using the rolling pin, roll the dough out to a 6-millimeter-thick (¼-inch-thick) rectangle.

Make a single turn, carefully wrap the dough rectangle in plastic film, and refrigerate for 30 minutes. Repeat this process twice more.

At this point, the dough can be stored, well-wrapped and refrigerated, for 2 to 3 days, or frozen for up to 1 week.

Use the dough as directed in a specific recipe.

TIPS

The milk should be cold, because the dough will warm as it is turned.

Cardamom is a spice that is used in traditional Scandinavian baking.

With this dough, the turns can be made in relatively rapid sequence, as the butter will firm and the gluten relax during the 30-minute rest periods.

Do not roll the dough too thinly when making the turns or the butter will melt into the dough.

If you plan to freeze the dough for more than a week, the yeast should be increased to 35 to 40 grams (1¼ to 1⅓ ounces).

EVALUATING YOUR SUCCESS

The dough should be soft, yellow, smooth, and elastic.

When the unbaked dough is cut open, the many layers of butter should be visible.

Demonstration

Cinnamon-Nut Danish

Makes 25 to 30 pastries
Estimated time to complete: 3 hours

Ingredients	Equipment
140 grams (5 ounces) raisins	Small, heat-proof bowl
Flour for dusting	2 baking sheets
1 recipe Danish Pastry Dough (see page 271)	Parchment paper or silicone baking liners
200 grams (7 ounces) *Crème d'Amandes* (see page 252)	Rolling pin
50 grams (1¾ ounces) Cinnamon Sugar (see page 268)	Offset spatula
60 grams (2 ounces) chopped walnuts	Serrated knife
Egg wash (see page 62)	Plastic film
	Proofing box, optional
For the apricot *nappage*	2 small bowls
100 grams (3½ ounces) apricot jam	Pastry brush
	Small saucepan
For the sugar glaze	Fine-mesh sieve
115 grams (4 ounces) confectioners' sugar	Tablespoon
1 teaspoon pure vanilla extract	Wooden spoon
Up to 105 milliliters (3½ ounces) milk	Wire rack

Prepare your *mise en place*.

Place the raisins in a small, heat-proof bowl. Add just enough hot water to cover and set aside for about 10 minutes, or until the raisins are nicely plumped.

Drain well and set aside.

Line the baking sheets with parchment paper or silicone liners. Set aside.

Lightly flour a clean, flat work surface. Place the dough in the center and, using a rolling pin, roll the dough out into a 6-millimeter-thick (¼-inch-thick) rectangle. Be precise about this because dough that is thinner or thicker will not produce a neat, evenly baked finished pastry.

Using an offset spatula, spread a very thin layer of the almond cream over the dough, leaving about 2.5 centimeters (1 inch) uncovered on one of the long sides of the rectangle. Make certain that the almond cream layer is very thin or the baked pastry will separate from the cream. The uncovered edge will facilitate the process of wrapping the end of the dough under the filled pastry.

Sprinkle the almond cream with an even, light layer of cinnamon sugar, a layer of walnuts, and, finally, the reserved plumped raisins. Carefully roll the dough from the covered long side toward the uncovered edge to make a long log.

Using a sharp knife, carefully cut the log crosswise into 2.5-centimeter (1-inch) pieces. Carefully fold the end piece of each roll under one side and place each roll, wrapped end-piece-side down, on the prepared baking sheets.

When all of the pastries are on the baking sheets, lightly cover with plastic film and proof in a warm, draft-free spot or in a 24°C (75°F) proofing box for 20 to 25 minutes, or until airy and puffed.

Preheat the oven to 177°C (350°F).

Place the egg wash in a small bowl.

Using a pastry brush, lightly coat the top of each pastry with egg wash. At this point, the pastries may be covered in plastic film and refrigerated for up to 2 days, or frozen for 1 week.

Bake the pastries for 12 to 18 minutes, or until golden brown and nicely risen.

Meanwhile, prepare the glazes.

Combine the apricot jam with 50 milliliters (3 tablespoons plus 1 teaspoon) water in a small saucepan over medium heat and cook for just about a minute to heat through. Pour it through a fine-mesh sieve into a small bowl. Set aside.

Combine the confectioners' sugar and vanilla in a small bowl. Begin adding milk, a tablespoon at a time. Continue adding, stirring constantly with a wooden spoon, until the glaze has the consistency of white glue.

Remove the pastries from the oven and place on a wire rack.

While they are still hot, use a pastry brush to lightly coat the top of each pastry with the apricot mixture. Allow to set for a minute and then, using the pastry brush, lightly coat with the sugar glaze.

Let cool slightly before serving. The pastries should be served as soon after baking as possible, and will not keep well for longer than 1 day.

The walnuts should be chopped to the size of dried lentils so that they do not cut the dough.

The walnuts and raisins can be replaced with other nuts and chopped dried fruit of your choice.

Apply the egg wash with gentle strokes so that the dough is not deflated.

The apricot *nappage* not only adds sheen, it also seals the pastry to keep it from turning stale as quickly.

The glazes should be applied while the pastries are still hot to achieve a shiny finish.

If the pastries are to be baked and reheated to be served at a later time, the sugar glaze should not be applied until just before serving.

To make fruit-filled Danish pastries, prepare the individual pastries as directed. Indent a small area in the center of the proofed pastries and fill the depression with jam or fruit compote.

EVALUATING YOUR SUCCESS

During proofing, the pastries should remain tightly wrapped so that they retain their symmetry.

Each pastry should contain an equal amount of cinnamon sugar, nuts, and raisins.

During baking, the pastries should hold the same shape they had during proofing.

The baked pastry should be deep golden brown, flaky, sweet, and buttery, without a yeasty or sour taste.

The baked pastries should be about 2.5 centimeters (1-inch) high and should all be of the same diameter.

When baked, the dough should rise evenly and be extremely flaky. Many layers of pastry should be evident. If only a couple of definite layers of pastry are seen, the dough was not turned enough.

When the pastries are removed from the oven, melted butter should not pool underneath. If it does, the dough got too warm before being baked, so the butter melted out instead of giving the dough its risen layers.

When baked, the pastry should have a buttery, slightly sweet-spicy flavor.

The *nappage* should completely cover the pastries in a thin, almost invisible layer.

The sugar glaze should completely cover the pastries in an almost transparent layer. It should be dry, not sticky.

Every bite should contain both nuts and raisins.

Demonstration

Danish Pastry Dough, Austrian Variation

Makes 25 to 30 pastries
Estimated time to complete: 3 hours

Ingredients	Equipment

For the *détrempe* — Large mixing bowl
500 grams (1 pound, 1½ ounces) all-purpose flour — Wooden spoon
60 grams (2 ounces) sugar — Medium mixing bowl
10 grams (1½ teaspoons) salt — Bowl scraper
60 grams (2 ounces) *beurre en pommade* (see page 188) — Plastic film
Zest of 1 lemon — Rolling pin
15 grams (½ ounce) vanilla paste (see page 82)
225 grams (8 ounces) milk
3 large egg yolks, at room temperature
30 grams (1 ounce) active dry yeast

For the *beurrage*
400 grams (14 ounces) cold unsalted butter
40 grams (1⅓ ounces) all-purpose flour
Flour for dusting

Prepare your *mise en place*.

To make the *détrempe*, combine the flour, sugar, and salt in a large mixing bowl. Add the *beurre en pommade*, followed by the lemon zest and vanilla paste. Using a wooden spoon, mix together to just combine.

Pour the milk into a medium mixing bowl. Add the egg yolks and yeast and, using a wooden spoon, stir to combine. Pour the milk mixture into the dry ingredients and mix to just combine. Do not overmix.

Using a bowl scraper, scrape the dough from the bowl and wrap it in plastic film. Refrigerate for 30 minutes.

Make the *beurrage*. Knead the cold butter into the flour, using your hands, until well combined. Wrap in plastic film and refrigerate until ready to use.

Lightly flour a clean, flat work surface.

Using a rolling pin, roll the *détrempe* out to a rectangle about 6 millimeters (¼ inch) thick and 30.5 by 51 centimeters (12 by 20 inches).

Unwrap the *beurrage* and place it on a large piece of plastic film. Cover it with another piece of plastic film and, using a rolling pin (or cool hands), lightly pound it into a rectangle about half the size of the *détrempe*. Work quickly so that the butter stays very cold.

Place the *beurrage* on one side of the *détrempe* and fold the remaining side over it. Turn the dough so that the fold is on the left and the opening is on your right. Using a rolling pin, roll the dough to a long rectangle about the same size as before. Fold the dough into one single-letter fold. Make a quarter turn and gently press the dough together. Wrap it in plastic film and refrigerate for 30 minutes.

Remove the dough from the refrigerator and again place it on a lightly floured surface. Make one double or book turn. Wrap it in plastic film again and refrigerate for 30 minutes, or up to 24 hours, or freeze for up to 1 week. If you plan to freeze it for longer than 1 week, the yeast should be increased to 35 to 40 grams (1¼ to 1⅓ ounces). Use as directed in a specific recipe.

TIPS
The milk should be very cold, as the dough should stay cold until the final proofing. This will also keep the yeast from activating immediately.

The dough should not be too thinly rolled when making the turns or the butter will melt into the dough. The thickness should be an even 6 millimeters (¼ inch).

With this dough, the turns can be made in relatively rapid sequence, as the butter will firm and the gluten relax during the 30-minute rest periods.

EVALUATING YOUR SUCCESS
The dough should be smooth but not extremely elastic.

When the unbaked dough is cut open, there should be many visible layers of butter.

Demonstration

Fruit and Custard Danish Pastries

Makes 12 to 16 pastries
Estimated time to complete: 90 minutes

Ingredients	Equipment
Flour for dusting	2 baking sheets
Half recipe Danish Pastry Dough (see page 271)	Parchment paper or silicone baking liners
Egg wash (see page 62)	Rolling pin
Half recipe *Crème Pâtissière* (see page 248)	Pastry wheel or sharp knife
24 to 32 small pieces of fruit, such as apricots or berries (see Tips)	3 small bowls
	Pastry brush
For the apricot *nappage*	Offset spatula
100 grams (3½ ounces) apricot jam	Pastry bag fitted with #4 or #5 tip
	Plastic film
For the sugar glaze	Proofing box, optional
115 grams (4 ounces) confectioners' sugar	Small saucepan
Up to 105 milliliters (3½ ounces) whole milk	Fine-mesh sieve
1 teaspoon pure vanilla extract	Tablespoon
	Wooden spoon
	Wire rack

Prepare your *mise en place*.

Line the baking sheets with parchment paper or silicone liners. Set aside.

Lightly flour a clean, flat work surface.

Place the dough on the floured surface and, using a rolling pin, roll it out to about 6 millimeters (¼ inch) thick. Using a pastry wheel (or knife), cut the dough into twelve to sixteen 10-centimeter (4-inch) squares and an equal number of strips 6 millimeters (¼ inch) wide by 12.5 centimeters (5 inches) long.

Place the egg wash in a small bowl.

Using a pastry brush, lightly coat the edges of each square with egg wash. Do not discard the egg wash. Using an offset spatula, carefully transfer the squares to the prepared baking sheets, leaving plenty of room between each piece.

Place the pastry cream in a pastry bag fitted with the #4 or #5 tip and pipe about a teaspoonful of the cream into the center of each piece of dough. Take care not too put too much cream in the center as it will expand during baking and could spill out. Place two pieces of fruit on top of each dollop of cream.

Carefully fold each corner into the center so that the corners meet and slightly overlap one another, covering the fruit and cream.

Using the pastry brush, lightly coat the surface of each pastry with egg wash. Reserve the egg wash. Lay a thin strip of dough across the top of each pastry. These strips serve as a belt, firmly holding the pastry's neat shape during baking.

Cover the pastries with plastic film and proof in a warm, draft-free spot or in a 24°C (75°F) proofing box for 15 minutes. The pastries may be made up to this point and stored, covered and refrigerated, for up to 2 days, or frozen for up to 1 week.

Preheat the oven to 177°C (350°F).

Again, using a pastry brush, lightly coat the surface of each pastry with egg wash.

Bake the pastries for about 20 minutes, or until golden brown and nicely risen.

Meanwhile, prepare the *nappage* and glaze.

To make the *nappage*, combine the apricot jam with 20 milliliters (4 teaspoons) water in a small saucepan over medium heat and cook for just about a minute to heat through. Press through a fine-mesh sieve into a small bowl. Set aside.

Combine the confectioners' sugar and vanilla in a small bowl. Begin adding milk, a tablespoon at a time. Continue adding, stirring constantly with a wooden spoon, until the glaze has the consistency of white glue.

Remove the pastries from the oven and place them on a wire rack.

While they are still hot, use a pastry brush to lightly coat the top of each pastry with the apricot *nappage*. Allow to set for a minute and then, using the pastry brush, lightly coat the *nappage* with the sugar glaze.

Let cool slightly before serving. The pastries should be served as soon after baking as possible, and will not keep well for longer than 1 day.

TIPS

Pastry cream made with pastry cream powder (see page 244) is best for this purpose, as it does not get runny when baked.

Almost any type of fresh or canned fruit or fruit compote can be used to fill these pastries. If using small stone fruits, such as apricots or plums, one half may be used.

Do not roll the dough too thick or too thin or the pastries will not hold their shape when baked.

Apply the egg wash very gently so that you don't deflate the dough.

The apricot *nappage* not only adds sheen, it also seals the pastry to keep it from turning stale as quickly.

The glaze should be applied while the pastries are still hot so that it will dry to a shiny finish.

If the pastries are to be baked and then reheated to be served at a later time, the sugar glaze should not be applied until just before serving.

EVALUATING YOUR SUCCESS

The pastries should be of a uniform size and remain tightly closed during baking.

The baked pastry should be flaky, sweet, and buttery, with no sour or yeasty flavor.

The baked pastry should be medium brown, almost dark brown.

The baked filling should be lump-free.

The *nappage* should completely cover the pastries in a thin, almost invisible layer.

The sugar glaze should completely cover the rolls in an almost transparent layer. It should be dry, not sticky.

When baked, the dough should rise evenly and be extremely flaky. Many layers of pastry should be evident. If only a couple of definite layers of pastry are seen, the dough was not turned enough.

When the pastries are removed from the oven, melted butter should not pool underneath. If it does, the dough got too warm before being baked, so the butter melted out instead of giving the dough its risen layers.

When baked, the pastry should have a buttery, slightly sweet-spicy flavor.

Demonstration

Cheese Danish

Makes 12 to 16 pastries
Estimated time to complete: 90 minutes

Ingredients	Equipment
For the cheese filling	Standing electric mixer fitted with paddle attachment
200 grams (7 ounces) cream cheese	Rubber spatula
30 grams (1 ounce) granulated sugar	Container with lid, optional
1 large egg yolk, at room temperature	2 baking sheets
10 grams (1 tablespoon plus 1 teaspoon) pastry cream powder or 14 grams (2 tablespoons) cornstarch	Parchment paper or silicone baking liners
Zest of ½ lemon	Rolling pin
½ teaspoon pure vanilla extract	Pastry wheel or sharp knife
	3 small bowls
For the pastries	Pastry brush
Flour for dusting	Offset spatula
Half recipe Danish Pastry Dough (see page 271)	Pastry bag fitted with #4 tip
Egg wash (see page 62)	Plastic film
	Proofing box, optional

For the apricot *nappage*
100 grams (3½ ounces) apricot jam

For the sugar glaze
115 grams (4 ounces) confectioners' sugar
1 teaspoon pure vanilla extract
Up to 105 milliliters (3½ ounces) milk

Small saucepan
Fine-mesh sieve
Tablespoon
Wooden spoon
Wire rack

Prepare your *mise en place*.

Place the cream cheese and sugar in the bowl of a standing electric mixer fitted with the paddle attachment. Beat on low until just combined. Raise the speed to medium and beat for about 2 minutes, or until very smooth. Add the egg yolk and mix to blend. Turn off the motor, scrape down the sides of the bowl with a rubber spatula, and add the pastry cream powder (or cornstarch) along with the lemon zest and vanilla. Beat on medium for a minute, or until well combined. Set aside until ready to use or, alternatively, transfer the cheese filling to a clean container, cover, and refrigerate it until ready to use, or for up to 3 days.

Line the baking sheets with parchment paper or silicone liners. Set aside.

Lightly flour a clean, flat work surface. Place the dough on the surface and, using a rolling pin, roll it out to about 6 millimeters (¼ inch) thick. Using a pastry wheel (or knife), cut the dough into twelve to sixteen 10-centimeter (4-inch) squares and a double

number of strips about 6 millimeters (¼ inch) wide by 12.5 centimeters (5 inches) long.

Place the egg wash in a small bowl.

Using a pastry brush, lightly coat the edges of each square with egg wash. Do not discard the egg wash.

Using an offset spatula, carefully transfer the squares to the prepared baking sheets, leaving plenty of room between each piece.

Place the cream cheese filling in a pastry bag fitted with the #4 tip and pipe about a teaspoonful of the cream into the center of each piece of dough. Take care not too

put too much filling, as it will expand during baking and could spill out, causing the pastries to open.

Carefully fold each corner up into the center so that the corners meet and slightly overlap one another, covering the cheese filling.

Using the pastry brush, lightly coat the surface of

each pastry with egg wash. Lay two thin strips of dough across the top of each pastry, creating an X. These strips serve as a belt, firmly holding the pastry's neat shape during baking. Reserve the egg wash.

Cover the pans with plastic film and proof in a warm, draft-free spot or in a 24°C (75°F) proofing box for 15 minutes. The pastries may be made up to this point and stored, covered and refrigerated, for up to 2 days, or frozen for up to 1 week.

Preheat the oven to 177°C (350°F).

Again, using a pastry brush, lightly coat the surface of each pastry with egg wash.

Bake the pastries for about 20 minutes, or until golden brown and nicely risen.

Meanwhile, prepare the *nappage* and glaze.

To make the *nappage*, combine the apricot jam with 50 milliliters (3 tablespoons plus 1 teaspoon) water in a small saucepan over medium heat and cook for just about a minute to heat through. Press through a fine-mesh sieve into a small bowl. Set aside.

Combine the confectioners' sugar and vanilla in a small bowl. Begin adding milk, a tablespoon at a time. Continue adding, stirring constantly with a wooden spoon. until the glaze has the consistency of white glue.

Remove the pastries from the oven and place them on a wire rack.

While they are still hot, using a pastry brush, lightly coat the top of each pastry with the apricot *nappage*. Allow to set for a minute and then, using the pastry brush, lightly coat the *nappage* with the sugar glaze.

Let cool slightly before serving. The pastries should be served as soon after baking as possible, and will not keep well longer than 1 day.

TIPS

Approximately 30 grams (1 ounce) raisins can be added to the cream cheese filling.

Do not roll the dough too thick or too thin or the pastries will not hold their shape when baked.

Apply the egg wash very gently so that you don't deflate the dough.

The apricot *nappage* not only adds sheen, it also seals the pastry to keep it from turning stale as quickly. The glaze should be applied while the pastries are still hot so that it will dry to a shiny finish.

If the pastries are to be baked and then reheated to be served at a later time, the sugar glaze should not be applied until just before serving.

EVALUATING YOUR SUCCESS

The pastries should be of a uniform size and remain tightly closed during baking.

The baked pastry should be flaky, sweet, and buttery with no sour or yeasty flavor.

The baked pastry should be medium to almost dark brown.

The baked filling should be lump-free with a strong lemon-vanilla flavor.

The *nappage* should completely cover the pastries in a thin, almost invisible layer.

The sugar glaze should completely cover the rolls in an almost transparent layer. It should be dry, not sticky.

When baked, the dough should rise evenly and be extremely flaky. Many layers of pastry should be evident. If only a couple of definite layers of pastry are seen, the dough was not turned enough.

When the pastries are removed from the oven, melted butter should not pool underneath. If it does, the dough got too warm before being baked, so the butter melted out instead of giving the dough its risen layers.

When baked, the pastry should have a buttery, slightly sweet-spicy flavor.

Demonstration

Pâte à Brioche (*Brioche* Dough)

Makes 1 kilogram (2.2 pounds) dough
Estimated time to complete: About 6 hours

Ingredients	Equipment
Melted butter or vegetable oil for bowl	Large bowl
500 grams (1 pound, 1½ ounces) bread flour	Standing electric mixer fitted
70 grams (2½ ounces) sugar	with paddle
15 grams (½ ounce) yeast	Rubber spatula
5 large eggs, at room temperature	Clean kitchen towel
14 grams (2 teaspoons) salt	
250 grams (8¾ ounces) cold, tempered butter (see Tips)	

Prepare your *mise en place*.

Generously coat a large bowl with melted butter or vegetable oil. Set aside.

Combine the flour, sugar, and yeast with the eggs and 50 milliliters (3 tablespoons plus 1 teaspoon) water in the bowl of a standing electric mixer fitted with the paddle attachment. Mix on low speed for about 2

minutes, or just until the mixture has hydrated (moistened). Autolyse (see page 265) for 10 minutes.

Add the salt and mix on low speed for 5 to 8 minutes, or until the dough is fully developed. To check on the gluten development, pull gently at a small section of the dough and look for stretchy gluten fibers. The dough should be elastic, and should not break when pulled.

NOTE

One of the most frequently quoted remarks related to French history is the statement attributed to Queen Marie-Antoinette, referring to the rioting peasants during the French Revolution, "*S'ils n'ont plus de pain, qu'ils mangent de la brioche*." This is normally translated to mean "If they have no more bread, let them eat cake." It is now felt that the expression has been incorrectly attributed to her, but it seems it will forever be linked to her.

Brioche dough is often used in the contemporary pastry kitchen to wrap whole fruits that are going to be baked, for a plated French toast–style dessert served with a fruit compote, or to create sophisticated bread puddings.

With the motor running on low, begin adding the butter in gradual but steady increments. When all the butter has been incorporated, raise the speed to medium and beat until the dough is satin-smooth, scraping down the sides of the bowl with a rubber spatula from time to time. The final dough should have a smooth texture and well-developed elasticity; it should completely pull away from the bowl.

Transfer the dough to the buttered bowl. Cover with a clean kitchen towel and set aside in a warm spot to ferment and rise for 1 hour. It is important that the spot not be too warm or the butter will melt in the dough.

Lift the dough from the bowl, then turn and fold it into a ball shape and return it to the oiled bowl. Note that the high butter content of this dough makes it quite sticky when warm.

Cover the dough and refrigerate it for at least 4 hours, or up to 2 days, before proceeding with your chosen recipe. At this point, the dough may be wrapped, airtight, and frozen for up to 1 week. (If you plan to freeze it for a longer period of time, increase the yeast to 20 grams (¾ ounce).

TIPS

Because butter inhibits the development of gluten in the dough, it is extremely important to make sure that the gluten has been worked up before adding the fat.

Tempered butter is butter that is soft enough to incorporate easily but still very cold. Totally enclose the butter in plastic film and, using a rolling pin, pound on it until it softens. Work quickly and handle it as little as possible to avoid warming it. Otherwise, it will melt before integrating into the dough.

Chilling the mixed dough allows both the butter and the dough to firm, which makes shaping the dough an easier task.

If time is of the essence, the dough can be given its first rise at room temperature, but it cannot be shaped without a minimum 4-hour refrigerated period.

EVALUATING YOUR SUCCESS

The dough should be yellow, smooth, and very soft when mixed.

There should be no visible lumps of butter.

The chilled dough should be firm.

Demonstration

Brioche à Tête Parisiennes (Individual *Brioche* Rolls)

Makes 15 rolls
Estimated time to complete: 2½ hours

Ingredients	Equipment
Butter for greasing pans	15 small *brioche* molds
750 grams (1 pound, 1½ ounces) *Pâte à Brioche* (see page 282)	Clean kitchen towels
Flour for dusting	Small bowl
Egg wash (see page 62)	Pastry brush
	Instant-read thermometer
	Wire racks

Prepare your *mise en place*.

Lightly butter the *brioche* molds. Set aside.

Divide the dough into 50-gram (1¾-ounce) pieces and place them on a well-chilled surface to keep the butter from melting into the dough.

Roll each piece into a short *bâton*. Push the edge of your hand back and forth in a very gentle motion (to keep the dough from softening) about one-third of the way from one end of the dough piece to form a bowling pin shape. Work quickly and carefully so that the work surface does not warm.

Pull off the larger section of a dough piece and place it, torn side down, in one of the prepared molds. Flour a finger and, aiming straight down, poke it into the center of the dough, pushing outward to form a crater. Place the small piece of dough, torn side down, into the crater. The surface of the dough should be very smooth. Continue making *brioches* until all of the molds are filled.

Cover the *brioches* with clean kitchen towels and set them aside to proof for 1 hour, taking care that the resting spot is not too warm, which would cause the butter in the dough to melt.

About 10 minutes before you are ready to bake, preheat the oven to 177°C (350°F).

Place the egg wash in a small bowl.

Uncover the breads and, using a pastry brush, lightly coat the tops with egg wash.

Bake the *brioches* for about 18 minutes, or until the internal temperature has reached 85°C (185°F) on an instant-read thermometer and the crust is golden brown. Immediately unmold the *brioches* and set on a wire rack to cool.

TIPS
The dough should be well chilled before shaping.

Keep the scaled pieces of dough in the order in which they have been cut to allow each one to rest the same amount of time between the scaling process and shaping.

If you use too much pressure when forming the bowling pin shapes, the dough will become sticky.

NOTE
The *tête* ("head" in French) in this recipe refers to the little knot that forms when the smaller piece of dough pressed into the center crater of the larger piece rises on the baked bread.

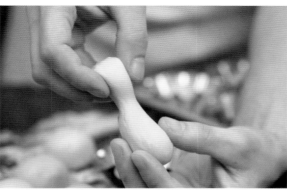

The egg wash is necessary to add the beautiful color and high gloss characteristic of *brioche*.

Brioches à tête can also be made in large *brioche* molds.

EVALUATING YOUR SUCCESS
When baked, the rolls should be distinct and remain centered in the mold, not falling to the side.

Each *brioche* should be consistent in size and shape. The crumb should be even and tight, with no large holes.

The crust should be soft, but not soggy or wet.

The taste and aroma of the rolls should be slightly sweet, neither yeasty nor sour.

Demonstration

Brioche Nanterre (*Brioche* Loaf)

Makes one 9-by-5-by-3-inch loaf
Estimated time to complete: 2 hours

Ingredients	Equipment
Butter for greasing pan	9-by-5-by-3-inch loaf pan
400 grams (14 ounces) *Pâte à Brioche* (see page 282)	Small bowl
Egg wash (see page 62)	Pastry brush
	Instant-read thermometer
	Wire rack

Prepare your *mise en place*.

Lightly butter the loaf pan. Set aside.

Divide the dough into eight 50-gram (1¾-ounce) pieces and place them on a well-chilled surface to keep the butter from melting into the dough.

Roll each piece into a very smooth ball and fit the balls in even rows into the buttered pan.

Cover with a clean kitchen towel and set aside to proof for 1 hour, taking care that the resting spot is not too warm, which would cause the butter in the dough to melt.

About 10 minutes before you are ready to bake, preheat the oven to 177°C (350°F).

Place the egg wash in a small bowl.

Uncover the bread and, using a pastry brush, lightly coat the top with egg wash.

Bake the loaf for about 30 minutes, or until the internal temperature has reached 85°C (185°F) on an instant-read thermometer and the crust is golden brown. Immediately unmold and set on a wire rack to cool.

TIPS
The dough should be well chilled before shaping.

Keep the scaled pieces of dough in the order in which they have been cut to allow each one to rest for the same amount of time between the scaling process and shaping.

The egg wash is necessary to add the beautiful color and high gloss characteristic of *brioche*.

EVALUATING YOUR SUCCESS
The baked loaf should have eight distinct, even rounds that are golden brown and shiny.

The cracks between the peaks in the baked loaf should be yellow.

The crumb should be even and tight, with no large holes.

The crust should be soft but not soggy or wet.

The taste and aroma of the loaf should be slightly sweet, neither yeasty nor sour.

Assorted *viennoiseries*

Demonstration

Ruche (Beehive)

Makes one 15-centimeter (6-inch) beehive
Estimated time to complete: 4 hours

Ingredients	Equipment

Ingredients

400 grams (14 ounces) *Pâte à Brioche* (see page 282)
Egg wash (see page 62)
350 grams (12⅓ ounces) *Crème Pâtissière* (see page 248)

For the honey syrup
150 milliliters (5 ounces) dry white wine
100 grams (3½ ounces) honey
Juice of ½ lemon
Herbs and spices as desired (such as lavender, cinnamon, vanilla)

For the Italian meringue
200 grams (7 ounces) sugar
150 grams (5⅓ ounces) egg whites

For the décor
Toasted almonds
Marzipan Bees (recipe follows)

Equipment

Paper *panettone* mold (see Sidebar)
Small bowl
2 pastry brushes
Baking sheet
Wire rack
Medium saucepan
Wooden spoon
Serrated knife
Mixing bowl
Whisk
Offset spatula
Serving platter
Medium heavy-bottomed saucepan
Candy thermometer
Standing electric mixer fitted with whip
Spatula
Pastry bag fitted with #4 plain tip
Handheld butane kitchen torch

Prepare your *mise en place*.

Place the dough on a well-chilled surface to keep the butter from melting into the dough and form it into a round that will cover the bottom of the paper *panettone* mold.

Flatten the dough down into the mold, cover, and set aside to proof for 1 hour.

Preheat the oven to 177°C (350°F).

Place the egg wash in a small bowl.

Uncover the *brioche* and, using a pastry brush, lightly coat the top of the dough with the egg wash.

Place the mold on a baking sheet and bake for about 25 minutes, or until baked through and golden brown. Set the loaf on a wire rack to cool.

Meanwhile, prepare the honey syrup.

Combine the wine, honey, and lemon juice with the herbs and spices in a medium saucepan over medium heat. Bring to a boil. Lower the heat and cook, stirring occasionally with a wooden spoon, until the mixture is syrupy and has reached the desired level of flavor.

Although you can use a traditional metal or ceramic *panettone* pan to make the beehive, the disposable paper molds work very well. The greaseproof paper is usually decorated so that bread can be served right in the paper wrapping. These disposable molds are generally available in three sizes, 2¾ inches, 6 inches, and 8¼ inches in diameter.

When the *brioche* has cooled, using a serrated knife, cut it crosswise into 4 round slices of equal thickness. Carefully remove and discard the exterior paper from each slice.

Place the pastry cream in a mixing bowl and, using a whisk, beat to smooth out.

Using a pastry brush, generously coat the bottom layer of the *brioche* with honey syrup. You want to almost soak the bread with syrup. Then, using an offset spatula, spread an even layer of pastry cream over the soaked *brioche*. Place the next layer of *brioche* on top of the pastry cream and soak with syrup and make a layer of pastry cream. Make another layer and top with the final slice of *brioche*.

Place the beehive on a serving platter and set aside while you make the Italian meringue.

Place 175 grams (6 ounces) of the sugar in a medium heavy-bottomed saucepan. Add just enough cold water to cover. Place over high heat and bring to a boil. As the sugar cooks, using a wet pastry brush, brush down the interior sides of the pan to remove any crystallized sugar granules. Cook, stirring and brushing down the sides frequently, for about 10 minutes, or until the syrup reaches the soft-ball stage, 112°C to 116°C (234°F to 240°F), on a candy thermometer.

While the syrup is cooking, place the egg whites in the bowl of a standing electric mixer fitted with the whip and beat until soft peaks form. When the whip begins to leave a trail in the meringue, add the remaining sugar and beat to blend it into the whites.

With the motor running, carefully pour the hot syrup into the beaten egg whites, beating until stiff peaks form.

Using a spatula, coat the entire exterior of the beehive with an even layer of meringue.

Place the remaining meringue in a pastry bag fitted with the #4 plain tip and, beginning from the bottom, pipe concentric rings around the meringue-coated form.

Place a generous ring of almonds around the base.

Using a handheld butane kitchen torch, caramelize the meringue (*brûler*).

Trim the beehive with marzipan bees and serve as soon as possible.

TIPS

If the dough round rises unevenly when baking, these imperfections can easily be disguised with the meringue coating.

If desired, the pastry cream may be lightened with whipped cream (*crème légère*, see page 155) or flavored with liqueur.

To loosen slightly grainy meringue, whisk it by hand.

The meringue is caramelized solely to enhance the appearance. It is not done to cook it.

EVALUATING YOUR SUCCESS

The finished shape should be a domed cylinder.

The meringue coating should be smooth and even.

The piped meringue should be in neat, even rings.

The caramelized areas of the meringue should just highlight the edges of the rings.

When cut, the brioche should have a tight crumb and be well soaked with the syrup, which should have a sweet aroma and a strong honey taste.

The pastry cream should be in thin, even layers.

The toasted almonds should be placed evenly and be only at the base.

Demonstration

Marzipan Bees

Makes 28 bees
Estimated time to complete: 30 minutes

Ingredients	Equipment
100 grams (3½ ounces) marzipan (see page 401)	Pastry bag fitted with #1 plain tip
56 toasted almond slices	
30 grams (1 ounce) melted bittersweet chocolate	

Prepare your *mise en place*.

Pull the marzipan into 28 equal pieces, each about the size of a hazelnut. Roll each piece into a small oval to resemble a bee's body.

Stick an almond slice into each side of the oval to resemble a bee's wings.

When all the bees are made, place the chocolate in a pastry bag fitted with the #1 plain tip and pipe lines over the top of each bee to make stripes.

Use the bees as décor on a *Ruche* or for other confections.

Demonstration

Tarte de Brioche aux Fruits (*Brioche* Fruit Tart)

Makes one 23-centimeter (9-inch) tart
Estimated time to complete: 2½ hours

Ingredients	Equipment
Flour for dusting	Baking sheet
150 grams (5½ ounces) *Pâte à Brioche* (see page 282)	Parchment paper or silicone baking liner
200 grams (7 ounces) *Crème Pâtissière* (see page 248)	Rolling pin
20 grams (¾ ounce) cake crumbs	Offset spatula
20 to 24 pieces fresh fruit	Clean kitchen towel
	Metal spatula
For the apricot *nappage*	Small saucepan
100 grams (3½ ounces) apricot jam	Fine-mesh sieve

For the optional finish
Confectioners' sugar for dusting
50 grams (1¾ ounces) toasted slivered almonds

Small bowl
Wire rack
Pastry brush

Prepare your *mise en place*.

Line a baking sheet with parchment or a silicone liner. Lightly flour a clean, flat work surface.

Place the dough on the floured surface and, using a rolling pin, roll it out to a circle about 23 centimeters (9 inches) in diameter. Carefully transfer the circle to the prepared baking sheet.

Using an offset spatula, spread a 6-millimeter-thick (¼-inch-thick) layer of pastry cream over the circle, leaving about 1.3 centimeters (½ inch) of dough uncovered around the edge. Sprinkle with an even layer of cake crumbs. Lay the fruit over the crumb-covered pastry cream in a decorative pattern. The fruit should cover the cream completely and overlap slightly, as it will shrink during baking. At this point, the tart may be stored, covered and refrigerated, for up to 1 day, or frozen for up to 1 week. It must be proofed before baking.

Cover the tart with a clean kitchen towel and set it aside in a draft-free, warm spot to proof for 1 hour. Take care that the resting spot is not too warm, which would cause the butter in the dough to melt.

About 10 minutes before you are ready to bake, preheat the oven to 177°C (350°F).

Bake the tart for about 20 minutes, or until the edges and the bottom are nicely browned and the fruit is tender. To check the bottom for proper color, gently lift it up with a metal spatula.

Meanwhile, prepare the *nappage*.

Combine the apricot jam with 20 milliliters (4 teaspoons) water in a small saucepan over medium heat and cook for just about a minute to heat through.

Press it through a fine-mesh sieve into a small bowl. Set aside.

Remove the tart from the oven and place it on a wire rack.

While it is still hot, using a pastry brush, lightly coat the surface of the tart with the *nappage*, completely covering the fruit in a thin, even coat. If desired, the edges may be sprinkled with confectioners' sugar or covered with toasted slivered almonds. Serve immediately or not more than a few hours after baking.

TIPS
For this recipe, the pastry cream should not be lightened with cream or liqueur, or it will become loose during baking and leak out of the tart.

The cake crumbs are used to absorb the juices that leach from the cooking fruit.

If cake crumbs are not available, they can be replaced with graham cracker crumbs.

Ideal fruits are soft stone fruits such as apricots, peaches, nectarines, cherries, or plums, as well as thinly sliced pineapple or whole blueberries.

If the tart will be served immediately after baking, it is not necessary to use the *nappage*.

EVALUATING YOUR SUCCESS
The layer of pastry cream should be thin and even.

The fruit should be applied in a neat, decorative pattern that holds through the baking process.

The baked tart should be a neat circle.

The exposed edges of the baked tart should be even and consistent in height and width.

The tart bottom should be evenly browned.

Neither the pastry cream nor the crumbs should be visible under the fruit once the tart is baked.

The baked fruit should be tender.

Blackened or caramelized edges on the fruit are acceptable and often desirable.

Demonstration

Brioche de Pomme de Terre Douce (Sweet Potato Brioche)

Makes 28 rolls or two 9-inch loaves
Estimated time to complete: 3 hours

Ingredients	Equipment
For the sponge	Standing electric mixer fitted with paddle and hook attachments
100 grams (3½ ounces) milk, at room temperature	Plastic film
12 grams (½ tablespoon) dry active yeast	Large bowl
100 grams (3½ ounces) bread flour	Bowl scraper
	2 baking sheets lined with parchment paper or silicone baking liners
For the dough	OR
4 large eggs, at room temperature	Two 9-inch loaf pans
500 grams (1 pound, 1½ ounces) bread flour	Small bowl
225 grams (8 ounces) sweet potato purée	Pastry brush
60 grams (2 ounces) sugar	Wire racks
14 grams (2 teaspoons) salt	
180 grams (6⅓ ounces) cold, tempered butter (see page 283)	
Butter for greasing bowl	
For the finish	
Egg wash (see page 62)	

Prepare your *mise en place*.

Combine the milk and yeast with the flour in the bowl of a standing electric mixer fitted with the paddle attachment. Beat on low speed until a sponge forms. Remove the bowl from the mixer, cover with plastic film, and let rise for 10 to 15 minutes.

Fit the mixer with the dough hook.

Return the bowl to the standing mixer. Add the eggs, flour, sweet potato purée, sugar, and salt and mix on the lowest speed for 1 minute. Raise the speed to medium and mix for 4 to 5 minutes, or until the dough is smooth and satiny and pulls away from the sides of the bowl. Test for a window (see page 266).

Add the cold, tempered butter and mix on medium for about 3 minutes, or until thoroughly combined. If the butter begins to melt out of the dough while mixing, add a small amount of additional cold butter to bring it back together.

Lightly coat a large bowl with butter.

Using a bowl scraper, scrape the dough into the greased bowl. Cover with plastic film and set aside in a draft-free, warm spot to proof for 1 hour. Take care that the resting spot is not too warm, which will cause the butter in the dough to melt.

Lightly flour a clean, flat work surface.

Place the proofed dough on the floured surface and turn, fold, and shape it into a ball. Wrap the ball in plastic film and refrigerate for 4 hours, or up to 2 days, or freeze it for up to 1 week. If you plan to keep it frozen for a longer period of time, the yeast must be increased to 15 to 18 grams (¾ tablespoon).

To make rolls, line 2 baking sheets with parchment paper or silicone liners. For loaves, lightly coat the interior of the 2 loaf pans with butter.

Divide and shape the dough into either twenty-eight 40-gram (1⅓-ounce) balls or 2 equal loaf-shaped pieces. Place the balls on the prepared baking sheets, leaving at least 5 centimeters (2 inches) between each one, or place the dough into the prepared loaf pans. Cover with plastic film set in a draft-free, warm spot, and proof the small rolls for 15 minutes or the loaves for 40 minutes. The dough should double in size.

About 10 minutes before you are ready to bake, pre-heat the oven to 177°C (350°F).

Place the egg wash in a small bowl. Using a pastry brush, lightly coat the surface of each roll or loaf with egg wash.

Bake for 15 to 18 minutes, or until perfectly risen and medium to dark brown in color.

Place on wire racks to cool. Serve immediately or no more than a few hours after baking.

TIPS

The room-temperature milk used to make the sponge will help speed the initial rise.

The sweet potatoes for the purée should be peeled, cooked, and puréed before weighing to ensure that the proper amount is added. In addition, the purée should be cool before being added to the dough.

It is extremely important to work up the gluten in the dough before adding the butter, which inhibits gluten development.

The tempered butter must be very cold but still soft. If it is too warm, it can melt before incorporating into the dough.

Chilling after mixing allows the dough and butter to firm up, making the dough easier to shape.

If the dough gets too warm, the high butter content will make it very sticky.

The egg wash is essential to give the baked dough the appropriate color and sheen.

EVALUATING YOUR SUCCESS

After mixing, the dough should be orange-colored, smooth, and very soft, with no lumps of butter showing.

After chilling, the dough should be firm to the touch.

The surface of the shaped dough should be smooth and tightly stretched.

The baked bread should be evenly browned and shiny.

The crumb should be very tight and even, with a soft orange color.

The baked bread should be sweet, with no sour or yeasty taste.

Demonstration

Pâte à Croissant (Croissant Dough)

Makes 2 dozen croissants
Estimated time to complete: 3½ hours

Ingredients

For the *détrempe*
500 grams (1 pound, 1½ ounces) all-purpose flour
60 grams (2 ounces) sugar
1 teaspoon salt
60 grams (2 ounces) *beurre en pommade* (see page 188)
12 grams (½ tablespoon) dry active yeast
125 grams (4½ ounces) milk, at room temperature
Flour for dusting

For the *beurrage*
300 grams (11 ounces) unsalted butter

Equipment

Standing electric mixer fitted with hook
Wooden spoon
Medium mixing bowl
Bowl scraper
Plastic film
Rolling pin
2 baking sheets
Parchment paper or silicone baking liners
Chef's knife

Prepare your *mise en place*.

To make the *détrempe*, combine the flour, sugar, and salt in the bowl of a standing electric mixer. Add the *beurre en pommade* and, using a wooden spoon, mix together to just combine.

Combine the yeast and 125 grams (4½ ounces) water in a medium mixing bowl. Add the milk and whisk to just combine. Pour the milk mixture into the dry ingredients and combine using the hook attachment. Do not overmix, or the dough will be difficult to roll and shape.

Using a bowl scraper, scrape the dough from the bowl and wrap it in plastic film. Place in the refrigerator for 30 minutes.

Make the *beurrage*. Wrap the cold butter in plastic film and, using the rolling pin, pound on it to soften it. Wrap in plastic film and refrigerate until ready to use.

Lightly flour a clean, flat work surface and place the *détrempe* on it.

Using a rolling pin, roll the dough out to a rectangle

about 30.5 by 46 centimeters (12 by 18 inches) and 9 millimeters (⅜ inch) thick.

Unwrap the *beurrage* and place it on a large piece of plastic film. Cover it with another piece of plastic film and, using a rolling pin (or cool hands), lightly pound it into a square about two thirds the size of the *détrempe*. Do this quickly so that the butter stays very cold.

To make the *pâton*, place the *beurrage* on the *détrempe*, leaving the top one-third uncovered.

Fold the top third of the uncovered *détrempe* over the middle third of the *beurrage*. Fold the bottom third of the butter-covered dough up, over, and onto the top of the other two sections of folded dough. The dough should now look like a folded business letter.

Turn the dough 90 degrees. Using a rolling pin, gently press the dough together. This is the end of the first single turn.

Wrap the dough in plastic film and refrigerate it for 30 minutes. If refrigerated longer, the butter will become too hard and brittle for you to be able to turn it properly.

Repeat the above process for 3 additional single-letter turns, chilling the dough for 30 minutes between each turn. Afterward, the dough may be wrapped in plastic film and refrigerated for up to 3 days, or frozen for up to 10 days.

Line the baking sheets with parchment paper or silicone liners.

Lightly flour a clean, flat work surface.

Unwrap the dough and, using a rolling pin, roll it to a long rectangle about 30.5 by 61 centimeters (12 by 24 inches) and 6 millimeters (¼ inch) thick. Using a chef's knife, cut the dough into 24 triangles with a 7.5-centimeter (3-inch) base and 30.5-centimeter (12-inch) sides.

Make a small slit with a chef's knife about 1.3 centimeters (½ inch) up the center of the base of each triangle. Fold the two tabs that are formed by the slit up and out toward the outside edges. Using your fingertips, roll the bottom one turn up toward the apex of the triangle. Then, roll further toward the apex, putting the pressure on the ends. By the time you finish rolling, the croissant should be at least twice the length of the original base and should taper off at the ends. Carefully bend the finished croissant into a soft, even half-moon shape. Work as quickly as possible to keep the dough from getting too warm.

Place the finished croissants on the prepared baking sheets.

Cover them with plastic film and place them in a draft-free, warm spot to proof for about 1 hour, or until doubled in size. Take care that the dough does not get too warm or the butter will leach out.

About 10 minutes before you are ready to bake, preheat the oven to 177°C (350°F).
Bake the proofed croissants for about 20 minutes, or until golden brown and serve them immediately, or no more than a few hours after being made.

TIPS

The *beurre en pommade* should be the consistency of cold cream.

Depending upon the humidity and flour, the dough may require more or less liquid than specified to reach the appropriate consistency.

When rolling out the rectangle of dough, do not make it too large, or the butter will be spread too thinly to create the required layer.

If the butter does get too hard during the chilling, allow the dough to sit at room temperature for a few minutes.

If the turns are done too rapidly or in a too-warm environment, the layers of butter will melt in the dough, altering its structure and the quality of the baked croissants.

EVALUATING YOUR SUCCESS

The dough should be smooth and creamy white.

There should be no pieces of butter visible.

When the raw dough is cut, alternating layers of butter and dough should be apparent.

The baked croissants should be golden brown and feel very light.

A cross-section of the baked croissant should reveal a flaky, cooked dough, not one filled with gaping holes.

Demonstration

Pains au Chocolat (Chocolate-Filled Croissants)

Makes 24
Estimated time to complete: 3½ hours

Ingredients	Equipment
Egg wash (see page 62)	Parchment paper or silicone baking liners
Flour for dusting	Small bowl
One recipe *Pâte à Croissant* (see page 295)	Rolling pin
48 chocolate *bâtons* (see Tips)	Pastry wheel
	Pastry brush
	Sharp knife
	Plastic film

Prepare your *mise en place*.

Line the baking sheets with parchment paper or silicone liners. Set aside.

Preheat the oven to 177°C (350°F).

Place the egg wash in a small bowl.

Lightly flour a clean, flat work surface.

Place the dough on the floured surface and, using a rolling pin, roll it out to a rectangle about 41 by 61 centimeters (16 by 24 inches) and 6 millimeters (¼ inch) thick. Using a pastry wheel, cut the dough into 24 equal squares. Trim off each end to expose the layers of dough.

Using a pastry brush, lightly coat one long side of the dough with egg wash. Reserve the egg wash.

Arrange a row of chocolate *bâtons* slightly in from the edge on the long side of the dough without egg wash. Fold the uncoated edge up and over the chocolate. Then, place another row of *bâtons* along the seam of the folded-over dough. Begin rolling the dough to meet the egg-washed edge and form a neat, even log.

Make definite, slightly loose folds to avoid stretching the dough. If it is stretched, the *pains au chocolat* may unroll during the baking process.

Using a sharp knife, cut the log crosswise, between the *bâtons*, into 24 even pieces. Place the pieces on lined baking sheets, seam-side down, leaving adequate room between each one. At this point, they may be wrapped in plastic film and refrigerated for up to 2 days, or frozen for up to 1 week.

Cover the pastries with plastic film and place them in a draft-free, warm spot to proof for 1 hour, or until doubled in size. Take care that the dough does not get too warm or the butter will leach out.

About 10 minutes before you are ready to bake, preheat the oven to 177°C (350°F).

Uncover the *pains au chocolat* and, using the pastry brush, lightly coat each one with egg wash. Do not allow the egg wash to spill or pool onto the pans or it will burn during baking.

Bake the pastries for about 20 minutes, or until medium brown and serve immediately, or no more than a few hours after baking.

Use very little flour on the work surface when shaping, as excess flour will reduce the quality of the baked product.

The dough must be kept well chilled when working with it.

When rolling, put any small scraps on the center of the rectangle so that you don't lose valuable dough.

Do not roll the dough out too thinly or the desired layers will be destroyed.

Chocolate *bâtons* are chocolate sticks about 1.3 centimeters (½ inch) wide and 7.5 centimeters (3 inches) long that are used to make *pains au chocolat*. They are a commercially produced and are available from cake and bakery supply stores. They may be replaced with about 60 grams (2 ounces) of semisweet or bittersweet chocolate bits for each roll.

Each *pain au chocolat* should be a slightly flattened cylinder, with the same width along its entire length.

The seam should remain underneath and not unroll during baking.

The appropriate layers of dough and butter should be visible on all exposed edges, and the interior of the baked product should have defined layers.

The two chocolate *bâtons* should be evenly spaced inside the dough and should be pointed toward the outside edge.

The baked *pains au chocolat* should be flaky on the outside and slightly chewy on the interior. The flavor and aroma should be sweet and buttery, with no sour or yeasty taste or smell.

Chef | Chef/Owner, Silver Moon Bakery, New York City
Judith Norell | The French Culinary Institute Bread Program 1999

Espresso Bread

Makes 1 bread ring or 5 rolls

At Silver Moon Bakery, I love to celebrate all holidays because they give me a chance to be especially creative. This bread was originally devised for Valentine's Day, when I thought a little caffeine would go a long way to make a heart race. I formed it in the shape of a heart for the occasion, but after Valentine's Day was over, everyone decided that it was too delicious to put away for a year. So now I knot it into rolls or shape it into a ring every weekend. It has turned out to be one of our all-time customer favorites!

225 grams (8 ounces) high-gluten flour

30 grams (1 ounce) sugar

Scant 1 teaspoon salt

8 grams (1 heaping teaspoon) fresh yeast, or ⅓ teaspoon instant yeast

1 large egg yolk, at room temperature

50 grams (1¾ ounces) espresso coffee

30 grams (1 ounce) milk

40 grams (1⅓ ounces) unsalted butter, softened

42.5 grams (1½ ounces) semisweet chocolate bits

Flour for dusting

Egg wash (see page 62)

Sanding sugar (see page 44) for garnish, optional

Combine the flour, sugar, and salt with the yeast in a large mixing bowl, stirring with a wooden spoon to blend. Add the egg yolk, espresso, and milk and continue to stir until the mixture turns into a shaggy dough. Add the butter and continue mixing until it is completely incorporated into the dough. Stir in the chocolate bits. When they are thoroughly blended into the dough, cover the bowl with a clean kitchen towel, and set aside to rise for 15 minutes.

Lightly flour a clean, flat work surface. Using a bowl

scraper, scrape the dough out onto the floured surface and knead for about 10 minutes, or until the dough becomes almost too difficult to work. Cover and let rest for 15 minutes.

Again lightly flour the surface and knead the dough for another 10 minutes, or until it is smooth and shiny.

Lightly oil a large mixing bowl and transfer the dough to it. Cover it with a clean kitchen towel and set aside in a warm, draft-free spot to ferment for 90 minutes, or until doubled in bulk.

Line a baking sheet with parchment paper. Set aside.

To make a ring, divide the dough into halves. To make rolls, divide it into 5 equal pieces. Cover the dough with a clean kitchen towel and let rest for 5 minutes.

Lightly flour the work surface.

For the ring: Roll each piece of dough out to a strip about 36 centimeters (14 inches) long. Roll each piece into a long rope and then carefully twist the two pieces around each other. Form the twisted rope into a circle, gently squeezing the ends together to make a ring.

For the rolls: Form each piece of dough into a rope about 15 centimeters (6 inches) long. Tie each rope into a knot by folding one end over the other. Alternatively, each piece may be rolled into a ball.

Carefully transfer the ring or the rolls to the parchment paper-lined baking sheet. Cover with a clean kitchen towel and set aside in a warm, draft-free spot to ferment for 90 minutes, or until very light and doubled in bulk.

About 30 minutes before you are ready to bake, place a rack in the middle of the oven and preheat it to 191°C (375°F).

Uncover the dough ring or rolls and, using a pastry brush, lightly coat the surface with the egg wash. If desired, sprinkle sanding sugar over the top.

Bake the bread for 15 minutes for the ring or 10 minutes for the rolls. Turn the baking sheet 180 degrees and continue to bake for another 15 minutes for the ring or 10 minutes for the rolls, or until nicely browned and cooked through.

Serve warm or at room temperature.

Demonstration

Kugelhopf (Austrian Bowl Cake)

Makes one 10-inch kugelhopf
Estimated time to complete: 3 hours

Ingredients	Equipment
	Medium mixing bowl
For the sponge	Wooden spoon
150 grams (5⅓ ounces) warm milk	Plastic film
15 grams (½ ounce) dry active yeast	Small heat-proof bowl
150 grams (5⅓ ounces) all-purpose flour	Standing electric mixer fitted with paddle attachment
	Rubber spatula
For the dough	Paper towel
150 grams (5⅓ ounces) raisins	Large mixing bowl
140 grams (5 ounces) unsalted butter, at room temperature	Bowl scraper
4 grams (1 tablespoon) confectioners' sugar	Kugelhopf mold (see Tips)
4 grams (1 tablespoon) vanilla sugar	Small bowl
1 teaspoon salt	

Zest of ½ lemon

2 large eggs, at room temperature

250 grams (8¾ ounces) bread flour

Pinch ground nutmeg

50 grams (1¾ ounces) warm milk

Butter for greasing bowl and mold

15 to 20 whole blanched almonds

Egg wash (see page 62)

Pastry brush

Wire rack

Fine-mesh sieve

For the finish

12 grams (3 tablespoons) confectioners' sugar

Prepare your *mise en place.*

Combine the milk and yeast with the flour in a medium mixing bowl, stirring with a wooden spoon until a sponge forms. Cover with plastic film and set aside to rest for 10 minutes, or until the sponge doubles in volume.

To plump the raisins, place them in a small heat-proof bowl with very hot water to cover by 2.5 centimeters (1 inch). Set them aside while you prepare the dough.

Place the butter in the bowl of a standing electric mixer fitted with the paddle attachment. Beat on low speed until very soft. Add the confectioners' sugar, vanilla sugar, and salt along with the lemon zest and raise the speed to medium. Beat, occasionally scraping down the sides of the bowl with a rubber spatula, for about 4 minutes, or until very light and fluffy.

Begin adding the eggs, one at a time, beating well to fully incorporate the first before adding the second.

Add the doubled sponge to the creamed mixture, beating to incorporate. Add the flour and nutmeg alternately with the milk. Beat, frequently scraping down the sides of the bowl with a rubber spatula, for about 4 minutes to fully develop the gluten.

Drain the soaking raisins and pat them dry with paper towel.

Remove the bowl from the mixer and, using a wooden

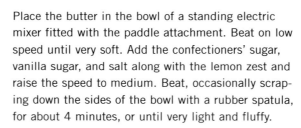

spoon, stir the raisins into the dough, mixing to just combine.

Lightly coat the interior of a large mixing bowl with butter. Using a bowl scraper, scrape the dough into the greased bowl. Cover with plastic film and set aside in a warm, draft-free spot to rise for 40 minutes, or until doubled in volume.

Lightly coat the interior of a *kugelhopf* mold with butter. Arrange the almonds in a neat circle around the bottom of the mold with the pointed ends all facing the same direction.

Turn the proofed dough and place it into the prepared mold. Cover with plastic film and set aside in a warm, draft-free spot to ferment for about 40 minutes. The dough should rise to within 1.3 centimeters (½ inch) of the top of the mold.

About 10 minutes before you are ready to bake, preheat the oven to 177°C (350°F).

Place the egg wash in a small bowl.

Uncover the dough and, using a pastry brush, lightly coat its surface with egg wash.

Bake the cake for 40 minutes, or until it is a warm brown color.

Immediately unmold the *kugelhopf* onto a wire rack to prevent it from getting soggy.

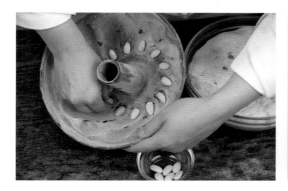  

When the bread has cooled slightly, place the confectioners' sugar in a fine-mesh sieve and lightly dust the top.

TIPS

A *kugelhopf* mold is a heavy-duty tube pan that has sloping, swirled sides. It is only used to bake this bread.

It will take several minutes for the gluten to develop once the sponge and bread flour have been added to the dough.

The dough will remain very loose, but the gluten structure should be apparent.

The raisins are stirred in by hand to keep them from breaking apart and discoloring the dough.

The bread is very fragile when hot, so take great care when unmolding it.

EVALUATING YOUR SUCCESS

The baked bread should be dark golden brown and in the perfect shape of the mold.

The almonds should make a neat, decorative pattern over the top of the unmolded bread.

When the bread is cut, the crumb should be fine and even.

The confectioners' sugar finish should be very light, just enough to highlight the top.

Demonstration

Stollen (German Christmas Bread)

Makes 2 loaves about 30.5 centimeters (12 inches) long
Estimated time to complete: 2½ to 3½ hours

Ingredients	Equipment
For the sponge	Medium mixing bowl
100 milliliters (3½ ounces) whole milk	Wooden spoon
25 grams (1 ounce) dry active yeast	Plastic film
110 grams (3¾ ounces) bread flour	Large mixing bowl

For the dough

150 grams (5⅓ ounces) softened unsalted butter,
   plus more for greasing bowl

230 grams (8⅛ ounces) bread flour

45 grams (1½ ounces) sugar

Zest of ½ orange

Zest of ½ lemon

1 teaspoon salt

Flour for dusting

225 grams (8 ounces) soft raisins

50 grams (1¾ ounces) whole almonds

35 grams (1¼ ounces) candied orange peel

30 grams (1 ounce) whole pecan halves

30 grams (1 ounce) whole walnut halves

Egg wash (see page 62)

For the finish

55 grams (2 ounces) vanilla sugar

55 grams (2 ounces) confectioners' sugar

115 grams (4 ounces) melted unsalted butter

Standing electric mixer fitted with paddle attachment

Rubber spatula

Bowl scraper

Proof box, optional

Baking sheet

Parchment paper or silicone baking liner

Wooden dowel or thin rolling pin

Small bowl

Pastry brush

Instant-read thermometer

Wire rack

Prepare your *mise en place*.

Combine the milk and yeast with the flour in a medium mixing bowl, stirring with a wooden spoon until a sponge forms. Cover with plastic film and set aside to rise for 10 minutes, or until the sponge doubles in volume.

Lightly coat the interior of a large mixing bowl with butter. Set aside.

Place the softened butter in the bowl of a standing electric mixer fitted with the paddle attachment. Beat on low speed until very soft. Add the sponge, along with the flour, sugar, and orange and lemon zests, and beat for 2 minutes to hydrate. Sprinkle the salt over the top and autolyse (see page 265).

Continue to beat on low speed, occasionally scraping down the sides of the bowl with a rubber spatula, for about 4 minutes, or until the gluten has developed. Test for a window (see page 266).

When the dough pulls a window, using a bowl scraper, scrape it into the greased bowl, cover it with plastic

film, and set aside in a proof box or a warm, draft-free spot to rise for 20 minutes.

Uncover the dough, turn, fold, and flip it over. Return the dough to the greased bowl, cover it with plastic film, and let rise a second time for 20 minutes.

Lightly flour a clean, flat work surface.

Uncover the dough and gently turn and fold it. Place it on the floured surface and degas (see page 266). Add the raisins, almonds, candied orange peel, pecans, and walnuts and knead them into the dough using your hands. Although it is difficult to work this much product into the dough by hand, it is important to do, as you want to keep the fruit and nuts as whole as possible.

When the fruit and nuts are well incorporated, divide the dough into halves. Bench rest (see page 266) for 5 minutes.

Using your hands, form each piece of dough into a loaf shape, about 15 by 25 centimeters (6 by 10

inches). Cover with plastic film and bench rest for 5 minutes.

Using your hands, mold each piece of dough into a rectangle about 10 by 20 centimeters (4 by 8 inches). Then, form each piece into a football shape by folding the top third down to the middle. Fold the dough again so that the edges meet and then seal the bottom by pressing the seams together. Bench rest for another 5 minutes.

Line a baking sheet with parchment paper or a silicone liner.

Working with one loaf at a time, make the final traditional shape by using a wooden dowel or narrow rolling pin to form two channels down the length of the loaf—there should be 3 bumps of dough and 2 channels. Lift the top bump up and place it in the channel closest to you, then fold the dough edge backward to create a loaf that now has 3 ridges, a high center ridge with a lower ridge on each side. Place the loaves on the lined baking sheet, leaving at least 3 inches between them.

Cover the loaves with plastic film and either place them in a proof box or in a warm, draft-free spot for 45 minutes.

Preheat the oven to 177°C (350°F).

Place the egg wash in a small bowl.

Using a pastry brush, lightly coat the surface of each loaf with egg wash.

Bake for about 40 minutes, or until an internal temperature of 85°C (185°F) is reached on a instant-read thermometer, or a cake tester inserted into the center comes out hot and clean.

Transfer the loaves to a wire rack to cool slightly. Carefully remove and discard any dark or burned raisins from the exterior of the stollen.

While the loaves are still warm, combine the vanilla sugar and confectioners' sugar on a clean, flat work surface. Using a pastry brush, lightly coat the entire surface of the stollen with melted butter. Then, roll the warm breads in the sugar mixture to make a light, even coating.

The stollen can be tightly wrapped and sealed in waxed paper and stored, at room temperature, for many weeks. It can also be wrapped in plastic film and then freezer paper and stored, frozen, for up to 3 months.

TIPS
To speed up the rise of the sponge, use lukewarm milk.

The raisins don't have to be soaked, but they should be fresh and soft.

The almonds can also be slivered or sliced.

Any combination of nuts may be used, as long as they come to the same total amount.

The candied orange peel should be chopped into raisin-size pieces.

When shaping the final loaves, remove any exposed fruit and nuts from the surface of the dough and tuck them inside the fold.

The warm, baked loaves are very fragile, so finish them with great care.

The melted-butter coating adds flavor and moisture and helps to seal the stollen, keeping it fresh for a longer period of time.

EVALUATING YOUR SUCCESS
The baked loaves should be a rich brown color.

The sugar coating should be even.

Demonstration

Panettone (Italian Fruit Bread)

Makes two 6-inch breads

Estimated time to complete: 3 hours

Ingredients	Equipment
	2 medium mixing bowls
For the sponge	Wooden spoon
Butter for greasing bowl	Bowl scraper
100 milliliters (3½ ounces) whole milk, at room temperature	Plastic film
30 grams (1 ounce) dry active yeast	Standing electric mixer fitted with dough hook
200 grams (7 ounces) bread flour	Rubber spatula
	Large mixing bowl
For the dough	Proof box, optional
500 grams (1 pound, 1½ ounces) bread flour	Scale
160 grams (5⅔ ounces) sugar	Two 6-inch *panettone* molds
14 grams (2 teaspoons) salt	Small bowl
Zest of 2 oranges	Pastry brush
Zest of 2 lemons	Instant-read thermometer
6 large whole eggs	2 wire racks
4 large egg yolks	
200 grams (7 ounces) cold, tempered butter (see page 283)	
Butter for greasing bowl	
All-purpose flour for dusting	
200 grams (7 ounces) raisins	
Egg wash (see page 62)	

Prepare your *mise en place.*

Lightly coat the interior of a medium mixing bowl with butter. Set aside.

To make the sponge, combine the milk and yeast with the flour in a second medium mixing bowl, stirring with a wooden spoon until a sponge forms. Using a bowl scraper, scrape the sponge into the greased bowl. Cover with plastic film and set aside to rise for 15 minutes, or until the sponge doubles in volume.

To make the dough, place the flour, sugar, salt, and orange and lemon zests in the bowl of a standing elec-

tric mixer fitted with the dough hook. Beat on low speed to just combine. Add the eggs and egg yolks, one at a time, beating to incorporate after each addition. Scrape down the sides of the bowl with a rubber spatula from time to time, and beat for 2 minutes to hydrate.

Raise the speed to medium and continue to beat for about 4 minutes, occasionally scraping down the sides of the bowl with a rubber spatula, until the gluten has developed. Check for gluten development by lifting up the dough hook—long strands should be visible. This is extremely important, as the addition of the butter will inhibit gluten development.

When the gluten has developed fully, add the cold, tempered butter and continue to beat on medium for about 3 minutes, or until the dough becomes a smooth, satiny ball.

Lightly coat the interior of a large mixing bowl with butter.

Using a bowl scraper, scrape the dough from the mixer bowl into the greased bowl. Cover with plastic film and place in a proof box or in a warm, draft-free spot to rise for 20 minutes.

Lightly flour a clean, flat work surface.

Uncover the dough, turn, and fold it. Very gently lift the dough from the bowl and carefully scale (weigh) it into two equal pieces.

Set each piece on the lightly floured surface and place an equal amount of the raisins on each one. Knead the raisins into each piece of dough, taking care that you do not mash them, which would discolor the dough.

Pat each piece of dough into a circle. Then, pull the outside edges into the middle, holding them down with one hand.

Flip the dough over and finish shaping it by using your hands to move it around in a circular motion on the floured surface, stretching the outside of the dough to form a tight ball.

Place a ball of dough into the middle of each of the *panettone* molds, cover with plastic film, and place in a proof box or in a warm, draft-free spot to proof for about 1 hour, or until doubled in volume. At this point, the dough may be stored, covered and refrigerated, for up to 2 days, or frozen for up to 1 week. If you plan to freeze them, increase the amount of yeast to 35 to 40 grams (1¼ to 1⅓ ounces).

About 10 minutes before you are ready to bake, preheat the oven to 177°C (350°F).

Place the egg wash in a small bowl.

Uncover the breads and, using a pastry brush, lightly coat the surface of each one with egg wash.

Bake them for about 40 minutes, or until an internal temperature of 85°C (185°F) is reached on an instant-read thermometer.

Invert each bread onto a wire rack, remove the mold, and let cool. Store, well wrapped, at room temperature for up to 1 week.

TIPS

If metal, ceramic, or paper *panettone* molds are not available, a collar of aluminum foil or parchment paper can be tied around a 15-centimeter (6-inch) cake pan or *charlotte* mold.

The butter must be cold but softened by tempering.

If the butter begins to melt out of the dough while mixing, add a small amount of additional cold butter to bring it back together.

EVALUATING YOUR SUCCESS

The baked loaves should be a rich brown color.

The tops should be an even dome shape.

Demonstration

Fruitcake

Makes one 9-by-5-by-2½-inch loaf
Estimated time to complete: 90 minutes

Ingredients	Equipment
Butter for greasing	One 9-by-5-by-2½-inch loaf pan
All-purpose flour for dusting and dredging	2 medium mixing bowls
300 grams (11 ounces) chopped, mixed dried fruit	Sifter
150 grams (5⅓ ounces) nut pieces	Standing electric mixer fitted with paddle attachment
150 grams (5⅓ ounces) bread flour	Rubber spatula
Pinch baking powder	Cake tester
Pinch ground mace	Wire rack
150 grams (5⅓ ounces) unsalted butter, at room temperature	Pastry brush, optional
150 grams (5⅓ ounces) sugar	Plastic film, optional
Zest of ½ orange	Cheesecloth, optional
Zest of ½ lemon	
2 large eggs, at room temperature	
1 large egg yolk	
1 teaspoon pure vanilla or other extract	

For the finish
210 milliliters (7 ounces) brandy, rum, or other liquor, optional
Sugar glaze, optional (see page 273)

Prepare your *mise en place*.

Lightly coat the interior of the loaf pan with butter and then with a thin coating of flour. Set aside.

Place the dried fruits and nuts in a medium mixing bowl. Add enough all-purpose flour to lightly coat and toss. This helps to keep the fruits and nuts suspended in the batter. Set aside.

Preheat the oven to 177°C (350°F).

Sift the bread flour, baking powder, and mace together into a medium mixing bowl.

Place the butter in the bowl of a standing electric mixer fitted with the paddle attachment and beat on low until very soft. Add the sugar, along with the orange and lemon zest, and beat on medium speed until light and fluffy. Occasionally, scrape down the sides of the bowl with a rubber spatula.

Add the eggs and egg yolk, one at a time, beating well after each addition to incorporate well, then beat in the extract.

Add the sifted ingredients, beating to just combine. When blended, add the reserved dredged fruit and nuts and mix to just incorporate.

Using a rubber spatula, scrape the batter into the prepared pan. Bake for about 20 minutes, or until the top is nicely browned. Reduce the oven temperature to 149°C (300°F) and continue to bake for another 40 minutes, or until a cake tester inserted into the center comes out clean.

Cool the cake in its pan on a wire rack for 10 minutes. Then, invert the pan and unmold it. Continue to cool.

Serve immediately or drizzle with the rum or brandy, allowing the liquid to soak in. This will add moisture and flavor. While still warm, the cake can also be brushed with a plain sugar glaze to add sheen and sweetness.

The cake may be stored, tightly wrapped in plastic film and refrigerated, for up to 1 week, or frozen for up to 3 months. Alternatively, the cake can be wrapped in a double or triple layer of cheesecloth that has been soaked in brandy or rum. Then, wrap it in plastic film and store at room temperature for up to 1 month.

TIPS
The ingredients will combine faster if they are all at about room temperature.

You can use any type or combination of dried fruits, but they should be fresh and soft. If they are hard, they can be rehydrated in hot water for a few minutes, or soaked in brandy or rum for 8 hours or overnight.

If the fruits or nuts are in large pieces, chop them into small ones before adding them to the batter.

Any extract can be used. Vanilla, orange, lemon, and almond are some of the recommended ones. Whatever type you choose, adding it with the eggs increases the flavor in the baked cake.

Do not overmix the batter once the flour has been added or the gluten will develop and the cake will be tough and tunneled.

Do not overmix when adding the fruit and nuts, or they will break apart and discolor the batter.

The moisture in the fruit and nuts gives the cake a long shelf life.

The cake takes quite a long time to bake. If the surface gets too dark before it has finished, cover the top with aluminum foil and lower the oven temperature to complete the baking.

If you choose to soak the cake with brandy, rum, or other alcohols, make sure to pour it over the cake while it is still warm so the liquid will be absorbed rapidly.

EVALUATING YOUR SUCCESS
The cake should rise in the center during baking.

The split or crack on the baked cake should run down the length of the loaf.

The surface should be dark brown but not burned.

The fruit should be evenly distributed throughout the baked cake.

The crumb should be yellow, not gray from the fruit and nuts breaking down.

The baked cake should be moist and not crumbly.

Demonstration

Banana Crumb Bread

Makes one 9-by-5-by-2½-inch loaf or 12 muffins

Estimated time to complete: 2 hours

Ingredients	Equipment
For the topping	Standing electric mixer fitted with paddle attachment
32 grams (1⅛ ounces) brown sugar	Bowl scraper
32 grams (1⅛ ounces) unsalted butter, at room temperature	9-by-5-by-3-inch loaf pan or 12-cup muffin pan
15 grams (2 teaspoons) almond paste	Rubber spatula
½ teaspoon ground cinnamon	Spoon, optional
½ teaspoon pure vanilla extract	Cake tester
65 grams (2¼ ounces) all-purpose flour	Wire rack
For the bread	
Butter and flour for coating pan	
125 grams (4½ ounces) unsalted butter, at room temperature	
250 grams (8¾ ounces) sugar	
2 large eggs, at room temperature	
350 grams (12⅓ ounces) ripe bananas, mashed	
225 grams (8 ounces) all-purpose flour	
1 teaspoon baking soda	
1 teaspoon salt	

Prepare your *mise en place*.

Prepare the crumb topping. This can be made up to a week in advance of use and stored, tightly covered and refrigerated. It must be done before making the bread batter because the baking soda in the batter will lose its leavening power if not baked immediately after mixing.

Place the brown sugar, butter, and almond paste in the bowl of a standing electric mixer fitted with the paddle attachment. Beat on low speed for 1 minute; then, raise the speed and beat on medium until very light. Add the cinnamon and vanilla and beat to incor-

porate. Add the flour, a bit at a time, beating just until large crumbs form. Set aside.

Preheat the oven to 177°C (350°F).

Lightly coat the interior of the loaf pan or the muffin cups with butter and then with a thin coating of flour. Set aside.

Place the butter in the clean bowl of a standing electric mixer fitted with the paddle attachment and beat on low until very soft. Add the sugar and beat on medium speed until light and fluffy. Occasionally scrape down the sides of the bowl with a rubber spatula.

Add the eggs, one at a time, beating well after each addition and frequently scraping down the sides of the bowl.

Add the bananas and beat on medium to incorporate. Add the flour, baking soda, and salt and beat to blend well.

Scrape the batter into the prepared loaf pan or spoon it into the muffin cups.

Sprinkle the crumbs in an even layer over the batter.

Bake for about 1 hour for the loaf or 30 minutes for the muffins, until the top is golden brown and a cake tester inserted into the center comes out clean.

Invert the bread onto a wire rack to cool. Store, tightly covered and refrigerated, for up to 5 days, or frozen for up to 3 months.

TIPS

If the crumb mixture is overmixed, the texture will be too fine. If this occurs, squeeze handfuls of the topping into big lumps and break them into crumbs.

Very ripe or even overripe bananas give the best flavor to this bread. Overripe bananas can be held frozen until you are ready to use them.

Do not overmix the batter once the flour has been added; this will develop the gluten, toughen the finished product, and cause tunneling in the baked bread.

The moisture in the bananas gives this bread long shelf life.

EVALUATING YOUR SUCCESS

The crumb should be fine, with no tunneling evident in the baked bread.

Executive Pastry Chef | *The Water Club, New York City*
Victoria Love | *The French Culinary Institute, Class of December 1998*

Pumpkin Quick Bread

Makes two 9-inch loaves

I created this recipe to add to the Viennoiserie selection for the brunch bread baskets at the Water Club in New York City. I already had a pumpkin muffin that was laden with nuts and raisins, so a wanted a quick bread that would be lighter. The spices in the bread are a delicate mix, so if you prefer a more assertive flavor, feel free to increase the amounts. Just make sure that you go light on the cloves—a little bit goes a long way!

The warm bread is especially delicious sliced and topped with a dollop of whipped cream and a sprinkle of freshly ground nutmeg.

Butter for the pans
540 grams (1 pound, 3 ounces) all-purpose flour, sifted
10 grams (2½ teaspoons) baking powder
6 grams (1½ teaspoons) ground cinnamon
1 teaspoon salt
½ teaspoon ground ginger
½ teaspoon ground nutmeg
½ teaspoon ground allspice
½ teaspoon ground cloves
225 grams (8 ounces) unsalted butter, at room temperature
650 grams (1 pound, 7 ounces) sugar
4 large eggs, at room temperature
455 grams (1 pound) solid-pack canned pumpkin purée

Preheat the oven to 149°C (300°F) with a rack in the middle position.

Lightly butter two 9-by-5-inch loaf pans. Line the bottom of each pan with a piece of parchment paper cut to fit.

Sift the flour, baking powder, cinnamon, salt, ginger, nutmeg, allspice, and cloves together. Set aside. Place the butter in the bowl of a standing electric mixer fitted with the paddle attachment. Beat on low to soften and then raise the speed to medium and beat until fluffy.

Gradually add the sugar and beat until light and fluffy. Add the eggs, one at a time, beating well after each addition. Using a rubber spatula, scrape down the sides of the bowl from time to time.

Add the pumpkin purée and beat to incorporate. The mixture will look separated.

Remove the bowl from the mixer and slowly add the sifted dry ingredients, mixing with a wooden spoon. You don't want to overmix, as this will develop the gluten in the flour and make the bread tough.

Pour an equal portion of the batter into each of the prepared pans and bake for about 1 hour, or until a cake tester inserted into the center comes out clean.

Place the pans on a wire rack to cool slightly. Unmold them onto the racks while they are still warm. The breads may be stored, well wrapped and refrigerated, for 4 days, or frozen for up to 1 month.

Serve warm or at room temperature.

Demonstration

Savoy Scones

Makes 12 to 15 scones
Estimated time to complete: 1 hour

Ingredients	Equipment
325 grams (11½ ounces) bread flour	Baking sheet
45 grams (1½ ounces) sugar	Parchment paper or silicone baking liner
20 grams (1 tablespoon plus 2 teaspoons) baking powder	Large mixing bowl
Pinch salt	Pastry blender or 2 kitchen knives
110 grams (3¾ ounces) chilled butter, cut into small cubes	Measuring cup
100 grams (3½ ounces) dried currants	Kitchen fork
1 large egg, at room temperature	Wooden spoon
1 large egg yolk, at room temperature	Bowl scraper
100 to 145 milliliters (3½ to 5 ounces) heavy cream	Biscuit cutter or other shaped cutter or small sharp knife
Flour for dusting	Small bowl
	Pastry brush

For the finish
80 milliliters (2¾ ounces) heavy cream, or egg wash (see page 62)
Granulated sugar for sprinkling, optional

Prepare your *mise en place*.

Preheat the oven to 177°C (350°F).

Line a baking sheet with parchment paper or a silicone liner. Set aside.

Combine the flour, sugar, baking powder, and salt in a large mixing bowl, stirring to blend. Add the butter

and, using a pastry blender or two kitchen knives, cut the butter into the dry ingredients until the mixture forms pieces the size of dried lentils. Don't overcut or the scones will be dense instead of flaky.

Add the currants, tossing to combine.

Combine the egg and egg yolk in a measuring cup. Add enough cream to bring the measurement to 200

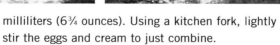

milliliters (6¾ ounces). Using a kitchen fork, lightly stir the eggs and cream to just combine.

Add the egg mixture to the dry ingredients and, using a wooden spoon, mix just until a dough forms. The dough should be quite soft and just barely come together.

Lightly flour a clean, flat work surface.

Using a bowl scraper, scrape the dough onto the floured surface. Lightly flour your hands and pat the dough out to about 2 centimeters (¾ inch) thick.

Using a biscuit cutter, cut the dough into circles. (Alternatively, using a sharp knife, or any other shaped cutter, cut the dough into squares, triangles, or any shape you wish.) Place the scones on the prepared baking sheet, leaving a bit of space between each one. At this point, the scones may be stored, covered and refrigerated, for up to 2 days, or frozen for up to 3 months.

Place the cream or egg wash in a small bowl.

Using a pastry brush, lightly coat the surface of each scone with the liquid. If desired, sprinkle the tops with granulated sugar for extra color and sweetness. Bake the scones for about 15 minutes, or until lightly browned on the bottom and around the edges.

Serve them immediately, or within a few hours of being baked.

TIPS

The currants should be fresh and plump. If not, rehydrate them in hot water, drain well, and pat dry.

Any dough scraps can be pulled together and reused, but the scones made from them will not be as delicate in texture because the dough has been handled more.

Any burned currants appearing on the exterior of the baked scone may be gently brushed off before serving.

Scones, a specialty of England and Scotland, are usually served at teatime, hot, split, and covered with butter or clotted cream and jam.

The baked scones should retain a perfect shape.

Baked scones should be sweet, tender, flaky, and golden brown on the bottom and around the edges.

There should be no taste of baking powder.

The crumb should be white.

Baked scones should be moist, but not wet on the inside.

Pastry Chef | Owner, Tompkins Square Bakery, New York City
Matthew Hutchins | The French Culinary Institute, March 1999

Fruit Scones

Makes 16

I created this recipe for scones because I wanted to offer my customers a treat that was sugar-free. I chose scones, as I had found that most scones were just too sweet for my taste, and I do appreciate a warm one with my morning coffee. I use whatever fresh fruit is in season, but I have found that my customers prefer strawberry and cranberry.

510 grams (1 pound, 3 ounces) all-purpose flour

10 grams (2½ teaspoons) baking powder

16 grams (1 tablespoon) coarse salt

340 grams (12 ounces) unsalted butter, cubed and chilled

4 large eggs, at room temperature

225 milliliters (8 ounces) heavy cream

200 grams (1 pint) fresh fruit such as blueberries, cranberries, or chopped strawberries (see Note)

Egg wash (see page 62)

Prepare your *mise en place*.

Preheat the oven to 177°C (350°F).

Line a baking sheet with parchment paper or a silicone liner.

Combine the flour, baking powder, and salt in a large mixing bowl. Using your hands, blend in the butter until the mixture resembles coarse meal.

Whisk the eggs and cream together in a medium bowl. When well blended, using a wooden spoon, gently stir the egg mixture into the flour mixture to just incorporate.

Add the fruit, stirring gently to blend. Do not beat or overmix.

Lightly flour a clean, flat work surface.

Using a bowl scraper, scrape the dough onto the floured surface. Using your hands, gently press the dough down until it is about 2 centimeters (¾ inch) thick. Do not overwork the dough.

Using a chef's knife, cut the dough into 16 triangle shapes of even size.

Place the egg wash in a small bowl and, using a pastry brush, lightly coat each scone with the egg wash. Transfer the scones to the prepared baking sheet as finished.

Bake the scones for about 20 minutes, or until they turn a light, golden brown. Serve warm.

TIPS

Almost any berry or fruit can be used in this recipe. If you use firmer fruits, such as apples or pears, they should be cooked until just slightly tender before being added to the dough.

Demonstration

Blueberry Muffins

Makes 12 muffins

Estimated time to complete: 45 minutes

Ingredients	Equipment
Butter or nonstick vegetable spray for pan, optional	12-cup muffin pan
265 grams (9⅓ ounces) all-purpose flour	Paper muffin cups, optional
12 grams (1 tablespoon) baking powder	2 medium mixing bowls
½ teaspoon salt	Wooden spoon
200 grams (7 ounces) sugar	Metal spoon or scoop
290 grams (10¼ ounces) sour cream	Cake tester
60 grams (2 ounces) cooled, melted butter	
1 large egg, at room temperature	
200 grams (7 ounces) fresh blueberries, well washed and dried	

Prepare your *mise en place*.

Preheat the oven to 177°C (350°F).

Either line the muffin pan with paper liners or lightly coat the interior of each cup with butter or nonstick vegetable spray.

Combine the flour, baking powder, and salt in a medium mixing bowl, stirring to blend with a wooden spoon.

In another medium mixing bowl, combine the sugar with the sour cream, stirring with a wooden spoon to blend well. Add the melted butter and again stir to blend. Add the egg and stir to incorporate fully.

Gently toss the blueberries into the flour mixture. Add the sugar mixture to the flour mixture, gently stirring with the wooden spoon and using as few strokes as possible to quickly combine. Do not beat.

Spoon an equal portion of the batter into each prepared muffin cup.

Bake the muffins for about 25 minutes, or until they are golden brown and a cake tester inserted in the center comes out clean.

Allow them to cool in the pan for 10 minutes before serving.

TIPS

Add the blueberries gently so that they don't get mashed.

Do not overmix or the muffins will be tough.

EVALUATING YOUR SUCCESS

The baked muffins should be evenly browned and of equal size, with an even rise in the center.

The crumb should be small and cakelike.

The muffins should be moist, but with no wet interior. If they are wet, they were underbaked or the leavener lost its power, perhaps due to age.

Demonstration

Lemon Poppy Seed Muffins: Creamed Butter Method

Makes 12 muffins

Estimated time to complete: 30 minutes

Ingredients	Equipment
Butter or nonstick vegetable spray for pan, optional	12-cup muffin pan
250 grams (8¾ ounces) all-purpose flour	Paper muffin cups, optional
1 teaspoon baking soda	Medium mixing bowl
1/4 teaspoon salt	Wooden spoon
115 grams (4 ounces) unsalted butter	Standing electric mixer fitted with paddle attachment
175 grams (6⅛ ounces) sugar	Rubber spatula
2 large eggs, at room temperature	Metal spoon or scoop
200 grams (7 ounces) sour cream	Cake tester
50 grams (1¾ ounces) lemon juice	Wire racks
Zest of 1 lemon	Small saucepan
14 grams (2 tablespoons) poppy seeds	Pastry brush

For the finish

150 milliliters (5 ounces) lemon juice

50 grams (1¾ ounces) sugar

Prepare your *mise en place*.

Either line the muffin pan with paper liners or lightly coat the interior of each cup with butter or nonstick vegetable spray.

Preheat the oven to 177°C (350°F).

Combine the flour, baking soda, and salt in a medium mixing bowl, stirring with a wooden spoon to blend. Set aside.

Combine the butter with the sugar in the bowl of a standing electric mixer fitted with the paddle attachment. Beat on low speed to just blend; then, raise the speed to medium and beat for about 4 minutes, or until light and fluffy, frequently scraping down the

sides of the bowl with a rubber spatula.

Add the eggs, one at a time, beating well after each addition.

Add the sour cream and lemon juice and beat to incorporate, frequently scraping down the sides of the bowl with a rubber spatula.

Add the reserved flour mixture and mix to just combine.

Remove the bowl from the mixer stand. Add the lemon zest and poppy seeds and, using a wooden spoon, stir to incorporate.

Spoon an equal portion of the batter into each prepared muffin cup.

Bake the muffins for about 15 minutes, or until they are golden brown and a cake tester inserted in the center comes out clean.

Transfer them to wire racks to cool slightly.

To finish the muffins, combine the lemon juice and sugar in a small saucepan over medium heat. Cook, stirring frequently with a wooden spoon, for about 2 minutes or just until the sugar has dissolved and the mixture comes to a boil.

Using a pastry brush, liberally coat each muffin with the glaze, coating until all of the glaze is used. Serve the muffins immediately or within a few hours of being baked.

TIPS
Once the dry and wet ingredients have been combined, the batter must be baked immediately or the baking soda will quickly react with the acids in the lemon juice and sour cream. This will cause the chemical leavener to be spent and the batter will deflate.

Make the glaze just before you remove the muffins from the oven so that you can apply it while both muffins and glaze are very hot.

EVALUATING YOUR SUCCESS
The baked muffins should be evenly browned and of equal size, with an even rise in the center.

The crumb should be small and cakelike.

The muffins should be moist, but with no wet interior. If they are wet, they are underbaked or the leavener lost its power, perhaps due to age.

The muffins should have a strong lemon aroma and flavor.

The finished surface should be evenly and thoroughly soaked with the glaze.

Demonstration

Cream Biscuits

Makes 12 biscuits
Estimated time to complete: 30 minutes

Ingredients	Equipment
135 grams (4¾ ounces) cake flour	Baking sheet
135 grams (4¾ ounces) bread flour, plus additional for dusting	Parchment paper or silicone baking liner
14 grams (2 teaspoons) sugar	Medium mixing bowl
1 teaspoon baking powder	Wooden spoon
1 teaspoon salt	Bowl scraper
Up to 250 milliliters (8¾ ounces) heavy cream	Biscuit cutter
	Small bowl
For the finish	Pastry brush
75 grams (2⅔ ounces) melted, unsalted butter	

Prepare your *mise en place*.

Line a baking sheet with parchment paper or a silicone liner. Set aside.

Preheat the oven to 177°C (350°F).

Combine the cake and bread flours with the sugar, baking powder, and salt in a medium mixing bowl, stirring with a wooden spoon to blend.

Add about three-quarters of the cream to the dry ingredients (the dough may not require all of the liquid).

Mix with the wooden spoon to just pull the dough together, adding the remainder of the cream, if necessary, to make a soft dough.

Lightly flour a clean, flat work surface.

Using a bowl scraper, scrape onto the floured surface. Lightly flour your hands and pat the dough out to a 2.5-centimeter-thick (1-inch-thick) square.

Using a biscuit cutter, cut the dough into circles. Place the biscuits on the prepared baking sheet, leaving a good amount of space between each one.

Place the melted butter in a small bowl. Using a pastry brush, lightly coat the surface of each biscuit with the melted butter. At this point, the biscuits may be stored, covered and refrigerated, for up to 2 days, or frozen for up to 3 months.

Bake the biscuits for about 12 minutes, or until golden brown.

Serve hot, or within a few hours of baking.

TIPS
Avoid overmixing or kneading the dough or the baked biscuits will be tough.

The biscuits can be cut into any shape or size you wish.

Dough scraps can be pulled together and reused, but the biscuits made from them will not be as delicate because the dough has been handled more.

EVALUATING YOUR SUCCESS
The dough should be smooth, soft, and neither crumbly or wet.

The baked biscuits should be tender, flaky, and golden brown all over, with a buttery flavor.

The baked biscuits should be even in size and thickness.

If dark brown spots appear in the baking biscuits, the sugar was not fully incorporated into the dough.

There should be no strong flavor of baking powder in the baked biscuits.

Session 8

Gâteaux: An Overview of Cakes

Theory

French *gâteaux* are among the richest, sweetest, and most flavorful of all desserts. They range from the simple *quatre-quarts* (pound cake, see page 356) to the elaborately decorated *Marjolaine* (see page 411). It is the skill of the *pâtissier* that allows the creation of a beautifully light, delicate confection from the basic elements of flour, sugar, eggs, and butter. The achievement of a perfect cake with a delicate crumb, sweet, buttery aroma, and delicious flavor is the baker's dream. When it is decorated with artistry, it becomes the creator's crowning glory.

As with all other pastry, the selection and use of high-quality ingredients is of primary importance. It is also essential to follow the mixing and baking procedures exactly to achieve the desired result. There are essentially three goals to mixing a cake batter, no matter the type: The batter should be smooth and even, air cells must be created and incorporated into it, and the appropriate texture must be reached to give the desired final result.

A smooth and even batter can only be reached when all the ingredients are of the designated type and specified amount, the right type and temperature of fat is used, the eggs or egg yolks or whites are correctly incorporated into the batter, all ingredients are incorporated at the appropriate temperature, the butter and sugar are well creamed, and the liquids are added as directed.

The fine, delicate texture of a baked cake is mainly the result of the formation of small, uniform air cells in the batter. These air cells also help leaven the cake as they expand in the heat of the oven. To create the desired air cells, the ingredients must be of the proper temperature, and the mixing speed should be moderate. Cold ingredients and high-speed mixing will produce fewer air cells that are not uniform in size, resulting in a finished cake that is tough and chewy.

The proper texture is achieved through the use of the appropriate flour, usually one that is low in gluten. The exception to this is cakes that contain heavy ingredients, such as candied or glazed fruit, for which some high-gluten flour may be introduced into the mix. Again, the length and speed of the mixing and the temperature of the batter while being mixed will affect gluten development and, subsequently, the texture of the baked cake.

Cakes in the French pastry kitchen are primarily made from a base of *génoise* (see page 328), a classic egg-foam cake made with a large quantity of whipped eggs, little fat, and no chemical leavening agent, and finished with other flavorful components such as *crème au beurre* (buttercream, see page 372) or *mousses* (see page 382). The *génoise* is usually cut into layers and brushed or soaked with a flavored syrup before being filled.

The finished cakes generally require time, patience, and skill to put together. However, *génoise* can be baked ahead and stored, well wrapped, and either refrigerated or frozen. The syrups and fillings can usually be made ahead of time also, so that the cake can be assembled after all the components have been prepared over the course of a few days.

Even the most skilled baker occasionally creates a cake that does not measure up to the industry standard. Sometimes this occurs from inattention to detail and sometimes because an ingredient was not up to par.

Following are three hints that will help minimize the risk of this happening.

1. Follow the recipe instructions to the tee—measure, sift, beat, cream, whip, stir, fold, and so forth as directed.

2. Use utensils and pans as directed. The wrong utensil or the wrong size pan can result in disaster.

3. Use ingredients at the directed temperature. Melted butter or chocolate (or other ingredients) that are too hot will ruin a batter as effectively as ingredients that are too cold.

The Possible Causes of Problems in a Finished Cake

Improperly risen cake

° Strength of leavening agent diminished

° Improperly sifted dry ingredients

° Batter overmixed

° Too much or too little fat, liquid, or sugar

° Oven too hot

° Collapsed center: too much fat, sugar, or leavening

° Collapsed edges: too little flour or too much liquid

Surface appearance of baked cake

° Baked color dull, mottled, or dark: too much sugar or leavening, too little fat, or the wrong oven temperature

° Surface too dark or covered in dark spots: too much sugar

° Cracked surface: too little sugar or fat, too much flour or the wrong type, overmixed batter, or the wrong oven temperature

Interior appearance and texture of baked cake:

° Large holes: too much sugar or leavening agent

° Tunnel-like holes: too little fat, wrong flour, or overmixed batter

° Uneven color: strength of leavening agent diminished or improperly mixed batter

° Tough and chewy: too little sugar or fat or too many eggs

° Dry and crumbly: too little liquid, fat, or sugar, or the cake baked too long

Theory
About Egg-Foam Cakes

Almost all egg-foam cakes (also known as sponge and egg-white-foam cakes, depending on how the eggs are used and mixing technique) contain very little fat and rely on the eggs for their light texture. No other leavening agent, such as baking powder or baking soda, is used to create the desired airiness. Although the batter can be fragile, a baked egg-foam cake generally has a very springy texture and can be easily handled, which makes it an excellent choice for use as the base for more complex *gâteaux* or desserts. The most best known of classic French egg-foam cakes is *génoise* (see page 328), a whole-egg-foam cake that is the workhorse of the pastry kitchen.

Egg-foam cakes that are to be used for a rolled cake (such as a jelly roll or a *bûche de Noël*, see page 429) will often have no fat, as the addition of fat would weaken the gluten in the flour and cause the cake to crack during rolling. In addition, cake flour is almost always used, occasionally with added cornstarch, to ensure that the cake will not be tough.

Separated-egg-foam cakes are made from whipped egg whites and have no fat added. The whites are whipped until soft, not stiff, peaks form, as overwhipped whites lose their lightness and ability to leaven the cake during baking. Softly whipped egg whites will create the desired light, airy texture.

Some classic cakes are made from a combination of the creamed-butter method (see page 326) and the sponge method. The butter and sugar are first creamed until light and fluffy, then made into a batter. Whipped egg whites are then folded into the batter.

There is a category of cakes called liquid fat cakes, for which the fat called for is either vegetable oil or melted butter. For these cakes, all the liquids are usually mixed together and then the dry ingredients are stirred in. An example of this type of cake would be a traditional carrot cake (see page 346).

About *Génoise* (French Sponge Cake)

Génoise (French sponge cake) differs from traditional American sponge cake, as well as the classic French *biscuit*, in that the eggs are heated and beaten whole rather than whipped separately. The cake rises as the heat of the oven causes the air that was trapped in the whipped eggs and the air produced as the water in the butter turns to steam to expand.

The technique for making *génoise* is not easy to master. It uses a hot process that relies entirely on whipped whole eggs for the cake's light, spongy texture. The method requires that the eggs be heated to 43°C (110°F) and beaten until tripled in volume. The cake contains no chemical leavener, such as baking powder or baking soda.

Dean's Tip

"Do not overheat the egg mixture when making a génoise batter or the cake will dry out as it bakes. About 39°C (102°F) is the temperature you should look for."

Dean Jacques Torres

The whole eggs and sugar are heated gently over a *bain-marie*. If the mixture becomes too hot, the eggs will scramble and be rendered unusable. The protein in the eggs must just partially coagulate, transforming them into an elastic mass. The heat also helps to dissolve the sugar. The warm egg mixture is continually beaten until it forms a thick ribbon when lifted from the bowl. It is now capable of holding large quantities of air, which, in turn, results in a batter with high volume and a cake that bakes higher and lighter.

Once the egg-and-sugar mixture has reached maximum volume, sifted flour (with any dry flavorings) is folded into it in several additions. You must make sure that the flour does not clump as it is added. Each addition is folded in while the batter is still streaky from the previous one. The folding must be done quickly, but very gently. The butter is then quickly folded in to complete the batter. Great care must be taken to retain the air in the batter. It must be handled gently and baked immediately after mixing. Although a properly made *génoise* is light and delicious on its own, the ways in which it can be decorated or finished are myriad. It is most often cut into layers, brushed with a flavored syrup, and layered with jams, *crème au beurre* (buttercream, see page 372), *bavarois* (see page 395), *mousses* (see page 382), or other fillings.

In order to provide maximum versatility in the pastry kitchen, a *génoise* batter is not normally flavored. The flavoring is done after baking by soaking or brushing the cake with flavored syrup. Some dry flavorings, however, such as almond flour or cocoa powder, do not lend themselves to incorporation in liquid form, so they are sifted into the dry ingredients should be sifted along with the cake flour and incorporated into the batter.

General Procedure for Preparing *Génoise*

Preheat the oven to 177°C (350°F).

Prepare the pans for baking.
a. If using round cake pans, using a pastry brush, lightly coat them with softened (not melted) unsalted butter. Then add a little flour and swirl it around—use just enough to ensure that all the butter is lightly coated with flour. Invert the pans and lightly bang on the bottom to remove any excess flour. If you wish, you can line the bottom of the pans with parchment paper cut to fit after buttering. Place it in the bottom and then flour the pan.
b. If using sheet pans, draw a large X on the bottom of each one with softened butter and then line it with a piece of parchment paper. The butter will prevent the parchment from moving about when the batter is spread into the pan. It is not necessary to butter the edges of the pan because you run a paring knife around the edges to unmold the baked cake.

Sift the flour through a fine-mesh sieve, such as a drum sieve, to ensure that all lumps and impurities have been eliminated. Set it aside.

Melt the butter and set it aside.

Combine the eggs with the sugar, whisking to blend. Do not allow the eggs and sugar to sit without blending or they will "burn."

Stirring constantly and evenly, warm the egg-and-sugar mixture over hot water (using either a *bain-marie* or a heat-proof bowl over a saucepan), until it reaches 43°C (110°F).

Once the mixture has reached the appropriate temperature, remove it from the heat and, using a large wire whisk, whisk vigorously until it has tripled in volume. The egg foam should be pale yellow and, when lifted by the whisk from the bowl, should fall in a wide ribbon without disappearing back into the batter. This step can also be done using a standing electric mixer fitted with the whisk attachment.

When beating the egg foam in an electric mixer, watch the inside of the bowl to judge the batter's rise. When it stops rising, it is ready, and continuing to beat will reduce the quality of the batter.

Fold the sifted cake flour into the egg mixture in several additions, making sure that the flour does not clump. Fold in each addition while the batter is still streaky from the previous addition.

When all the flour has been incorporated and the batter is still streaky, fold in the melted butter. The butter should be liquid, but not hot. To easily incorporate the butter into the batter, stir a small amount of batter into the warm butter so that the mixture becomes a consistency closer to that of the airy batter. Then fold the butter mixture into the batter.

Immediately transfer the batter to the prepared pans and into the preheated oven. If allowed to sit for even a couple of minutes, either in the bowl or in a pan, the batter will begin to deflate.

Depending upon the size of the cake, baking time can vary from 10 to 25 minutes.

During baking, avoid opening and closing the oven door or hitting or banging against the oven, as this can cause the baking cake to deflate. Avoid testing a *génoise* too early for doneness. This too can cause the cake to deflate.

A *génoise* is completely baked when
a. it pulls away from the sides of the pan (The exception to this is when the cake is baked in a sheet pan where the sides were not buttered. The sides will remain close to the pan edges and will have to be loosened with a paring knife.)
b. the top is a dark, medium brown;
c. the center springs back when the surface is gently touched; and
d. a cake tester inserted into the center comes out clean with no crumbs sticking to it.

Once removed from the oven, a *génoise* must be immediately inverted and unmolded onto a wire rack to allow air to circulate around all sides of the cake. If the cake is left in the pan, trapped steam from the hot batter will cause the cake to become soggy and the sides to cave inward.

If the cooled cake will not be used immediately, it should be tightly wrapped in plastic film to keep it from drying out and turning stale. It can be refrigerated for up to 1 day, or frozen for up to 2 weeks.

About *Quatre-Quarts* (Pound Cake or Creamed-Butter Cake)

The creamed-butter method of making cakes is used in a wide variety of both French and American cakes. Because of its high fat and sugar content, a creamed-butter cake is usually served "as is," without a filling or icing, although it may be given a light glaze. Variations to the flavor and texture may include the addition of citrus zests, extracts, and liquids such as milk, fruit juices, and liquors or liqueurs.

 Quatre-quarts (translated to "four quarters"), or pound cake, is the best-known example of the creaming-method cakes. Traditionally, a pound cake is made with an equal amount of butter, sugar, flour, and eggs, but these proportions have been adjusted in recipes for many contemporary variations.

 Creamed-butter cakes are leavened by air incorporated when the butter and sugar are creamed together. Classically, no other leaveners were used, but it is now common to add a small amount of a chemical leavening agent such as baking powder or baking soda to produce a lighter cake. As the butter is creamed with the sugar, the sharp edges of the sugar crystals cut into the fat, which allows air to become trapped inside the batter. The use of extra-fine sugar, with its higher number of edges, and butter that has first been brought to 21°C (70°F) by beating (most effectively in the bowl of a standing electric mixer fitted with the paddle attachment), incorporates additional air. In some creamed-butter cakes, a French meringue is folded in to add more leavening and produce a lighter cake.

 Unlike most egg-foam cakes, creamed-butter cake batters are quite stable after mixing. This allows larger batches to be mixed without the fear of them falling or not rising during baking. The exception is any cake that relies on baking soda as the leavening agent; this cake must be baked directly after mixing, as the baking soda activates immediately upon being combined with an acid.

General Procedure for Preparing Creamed-Butter Cakes

Preheat the oven to 177°C (350°F).

Prepare the pans for baking by lightly coating them with softened (not melted) unsalted butter. Add a little flour—just enough to lightly coat the butter—and swirl it around to create an even, thorough coating. Invert the pan and lightly bang it on the bottom to remove excess flour. To further facilitate unmolding, you can line the bottom of the pan with a piece of parchment paper cut to fit after buttering. Place it in the bottom of the pan, then coat with flour. Creamed-butter cakes are often baked in loaf pans, but they

can be baked in almost any type of cake pan.

Sift the dry ingredients together and set them aside. Begin creaming the butter in the bowl of a standing electric mixer fitted with the paddle attachment, scraping down the sides of the bowl with a rubber spatula from time to time. The butter should warm to about 21°C (70°F), and the texture should be smooth and even.

Add the granulated sugar and continue to beat the mixture until it is light in color and soft and fluffy. The mixing time will vary, especially if the kitchen or ingredients are cold, or if the butter was not creamed for long enough initially.

Add the eggs one at a time, occasionally scraping down the sides of the bowl with a rubber spatula. It is important that, as each egg is added, the mixture is beaten for a couple of minutes until it is completely emulsified. If the eggs are very cold, it may take longer to incorporate them, so make sure they are at room temperature to start with.

If you use vanilla or liquid flavoring, it may be added with the eggs as long as the total amount of liquid, including the eggs, is not more than one and a half times the amount of butter. If at any point during this step the mixture looks curdled, continue to beat until it is homogenous.

Add the sifted dry ingredients to the creamed butter mixture all at once and mix just until combined. If overmixed, the gluten will develop, resulting in a tough cake.

If the specific recipe calls for a large amount of liquid that cannot be easily incorporated into the butter-and-sugar mixture along with the eggs, it should be added alternately with the dry ingredients.

Pour the batter into the prepared pans and bake for 45 minutes to 1 hour, depending upon the pan and type of cake.

After 15 to 20 minutes of baking, the top of the cake may be scored by running a small sharp knife from end to end to allow the cake to rise more evenly. *Quatre-quarts* is a very dense cake and requires a long baking period. The surface of the cake will often reach the desired dark brown color long before the center is baked. After scoring, lower the oven temperature to 162°C (325°F). If the cake still darkens too rapidly, cover the top loosely with aluminum foil.

The cake is completely baked when a cake tester (or skewer or paring knife) inserted into the center comes out clean and dry. If unsure of doneness, test the cake in several places.

Unmold the baked cake onto a wire rack. Some recipes call for syrup to be brushed onto the cake while it is still warm to add flavor and moisture. The cake will absorb the liquid more easily if the syrup and the cake are both warm.

Once cooled, the cake should be tightly wrapped in plastic film to prevent staling. The high fat content of creamed-butter cakes gives them a relatively long shelf life. They can be stored, tightly wrapped, at room temperature for up to 1 week, or frozen for up to 1 month.

Demonstration

Basic Cake Recipes

Before proceeding to the more complex *gâteaux*, it is a good idea to master a few basic cake recipes. In the following pages, you will find cakes that either stand on their own or are used as a component of more elaborate rolled, filled, frosted, glazed, or decorated confections.

Demonstration

Génoise (French Sponge Cake)

Makes one 18-by-26-inch sheet cake (or two half-sheet pans)
Estimated time to complete: 1 hour

Ingredients	Equipment
Butter and flour for pan	One 18-by-26-inch sheet pan
12 large eggs, at room temperature	Parchment paper
300 grams (11 ounces) sugar	Sifter
300 grams (11 ounces) cake flour	Saucepan
60 grams (2 ounces) unsalted butter, melted and cooled slightly	Heat-proof bowl to fit saucepan
	Large wire whisk
	Instant-read thermometer
	Rubber spatula
	Large wire rack

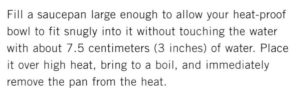

Prepare your *mise en place*.

Preheat the oven to 177°C (350°F).

Prepare the sheet pan for baking as directed on page 325.

Fill a saucepan large enough to allow your heat-proof bowl to fit snugly into it without touching the water with about 7.5 centimeters (3 inches) of water. Place it over high heat, bring to a boil, and immediately remove the pan from the heat.

Combine the eggs with the sugar in the heat-proof bowl and, using a wire whisk, whisk to blend. Quickly place the bowl into the pan, checking to make sure that the bottom is not resting in the hot water. Immediately begin whisking and continue to do so for about 10 minutes, or until the mixture reads 43°C (110°F) on an instant-read thermometer. (Do not allow the temperature to exceed 49°C/120°F or the cake will be dry and tough.)

Remove the bowl from the heat and continue to whisk

vigorously for about another 10 minutes, or until the mixture has tripled in volume and forms a ribbon when lifted from the bowl.

Using a rubber spatula, begin folding the flour into the whipped mixture in several additions, making sure that it does not clump. Fold in each addition while the batter is still streaky from the previous one.

When all the flour has been incorporated and the batter remains streaky, fold in the melted butter.

Pour the batter into the prepared pan, taking care that it forms an even layer.

Bake the cake for about 25 minutes, or until the top is golden brown, the sides pull away from the pan, the center springs back when gently touched, and a cake tester inserted into the center comes out clean.

Immediately invert the cake onto a large wire rack to cool completely. The baked cake must immediately be removed from the oven and from the pan. If it is left to sit for even a couple of minutes, the steam from the

batter will be trapped in the cake pan and cause the cake to become soggy and the sides to cave inward.

When the cake is cool, wrap it in plastic film and store refrigerated for up to 1 day, or frozen for up to 2 weeks.

Use as directed in a specific recipe.

TIPS

To make one 6-inch round cake, you will need 75 grams (2⅔ ounces) cake flour, sifted; 14 grams (1 tablespoon) unsalted butter, melted and cooled slightly; 3 large eggs; and 75 grams (2⅔ ounces) sugar. A 9-inch round cake will require 125 grams (4½ ounces) cake flour, sifted; 35 grams (1¼ ounces) unsalted butter, melted and cooled slightly; 5 large eggs; and 125 grams (4½ ounces) sugar. Bake for 20 to 25 minutes.

Be sure to blend the eggs and sugar before vigorously whisking or they will "burn" and be unusable.

When whisking the warmed egg-and-sugar mixture in an electric mixer, watch the inside of the bowl to judge the batter's rise. When the level of the mixture stops rising, it is ready. Do not overbeat.

To allow the warm butter to be easily incorporated into the batter, stir a small amount of the batter into it so that the butter becomes a consistency closer to that of the airy batter. Then fold the butter mixture into the batter.

To assure a light, airy texture in the baked cake, as soon as the batter is mixed, place it in the prepared pan and transfer it quickly to the preheated oven. Any delay will allow the batter to deflate.

Try not to open and close the oven door or bang into the oven while the cake is baking, as this will cause the cake to deflate.

Take care when testing the cake for doneness, as testing too early can cause it to deflate.

EVALUATING YOUR SUCCESS

The baked cake should be evenly browned on all sides with no residual flour evident.

The baked cake should rise slightly more in the center than on the sides.

The crumb should be a light yellow color with no large holes or tunnels in it.

The interior texture should look the same from top to the bottom.

There should be no wet or soggy areas in the baked cake.

There should be no unincorporated flour lumps in the baked cake.

The finished cake should be very tender with a slightly sweet aroma and no eggy taste.

Demonstration

Génoise au Chocolat (Chocolate *Génoise*)

Makes one 18-by-26-inch sheet cake (or 2 half-sheet pans)
Estimated time to complete: 1 hour

Ingredients	Equipment
Butter and flour for pan	18-by-26-inch sheet pan
300 grams (11 ounces) cake flour	Parchment paper, optional
60 grams (2 ounces) Dutch-process cocoa powder	Sifter
Pinch baking soda	Saucepan
12 large eggs, at room temperature	Heat-proof bowl to fit saucepan
300 grams (11 ounces) sugar	Large wire whisk
60 grams (2 ounces) unsalted butter, melted and cooled slightly	Instant-read thermometer
	Rubber spatula
	Large wire rack

Prepare your *mise en place*.

Preheat the oven to 177°C (350°F).

Prepare the sheet pan for baking as directed on page 325.

Sift the cake flour, cocoa powder, and baking soda together. Set aside.

Fill a saucepan large enough to allow your heat-proof bowl to fit snugly into it without touching the water with about 7.5 centimeters (3 inches) of water. Place it over high heat, bring to a boil, and immediately remove the pan from the heat.

Combine the eggs with the sugar in the heat-proof bowl and, using a wire whisk, whisk to blend. Quickly place the bowl into the pan, checking to make sure that the bottom is not resting in the hot water. Immediately begin whisking and continue to do so for about 10 minutes, or until the mixture reads 43°C (110°F) on an instant-read thermometer. (Do not allow the temperature to exceed 49°C/120°F or the cake will be dry and tough.)

Remove the bowl from the heat and continue to whisk vigorously for about another 10 minutes, or until the mixture has tripled in volume and forms a ribbon when lifted from the bowl.

Using a rubber spatula, begin folding the flour mixture into the whipped mixture in several additions, making sure that the dry ingredients do not clump. Fold in each addition while the batter is still streaky from the previous one.

When all the flour mixture has been incorporated and the batter remains streaky, fold in the melted butter.

Pour the batter into the prepared pan, taking care that it forms an even layer.

Bake the cake for about 25 minutes, or until the top is golden brown, the sides pull away from the pan, the center springs back when gently touched, and a cake tester inserted into the center comes out clean.

Immediately invert the cake onto a large wire rack to cool completely. Peel off and discard the parchment paper. The baked cake must immediately be removed from the oven and from the pan. If it is left to sit for even a couple of minutes, the steam from the batter will be trapped in the cake pan and cause the cake to become soggy and the sides to cave inward.

When the cake is cool, wrap it in plastic film and store refrigerated for up to 1 day, or frozen for up to 2 weeks.

Use as directed in a specific recipe.

TIPS

To make one 6-inch round cake, you will need 75 grams (2⅔ ounces) cake flour, sifted; 8 grams (1 tablespoon) Dutch-process cocoa powder; 14 grams (1 tablespoon) unsalted butter, melted and cooled slightly; 3 large eggs; and 75 grams (2⅔ ounces) sugar. One 9-inch round cake will require 125 grams (4½ ounces) cake flour, sifted; 30 grams (1 ounce) Dutch-process cocoa powder; 35 grams (1¼ ounces) unsalted butter, melted and cooled slightly; 5 large eggs; and 125 grams (4½ ounces) sugar.

Be sure to blend the eggs and sugar before vigorously whisking or they will "burn" and be unusable.

When whisking the warmed egg-and-sugar mixture in an electric mixer, watch the inside of the bowl to judge the batter's rise. When the level of the mixture stops rising, it is ready. Do not overbeat.

To allow the warm butter to be easily incorporated into the batter, stir a small amount of the batter into it so that the butter becomes a consistency closer to that of the airy batter. Then fold the butter mixture into the batter.

To assure a light, airy texture in the baked cake, as soon as the batter is mixed, place it in the prepared pan and transfer it directly to the preheated oven. Any delay will allow the batter to deflate.

Try not to open and close the oven door or bang into the oven while the cake is baking, as this will cause the cake to deflate.

Take care when testing the cake for doneness, as testing too early can cause it to deflate.

EVALUATING YOUR SUCCESS

The baked cake should be evenly browned on all sides, with no residual flour evident.

The baked cake should rise slightly more in the center than on the sides.

The crumb should be a light brown color, with no large holes or tunnels in it.

The interior texture should look the same from top to the bottom.

There should be no wet or soggy areas in the baked cake.

There should be no unincorporated flour lumps in the baked cake.

The finished cake should be very tender, with a slightly sweet aroma and no eggy taste.

Demonstration

American Milk-Sponge Cake

Makes one 17¼-by-11½-by-1-inch cake
Estimated time to complete: 50 minutes

Ingredients	Equipment
110 grams (3¾ ounces) cake flour	One 17 ¼-by-11 ½-by-1-inch pan
1 teaspoon baking powder	Parchment paper
60 milliliters (2 ounces) whole milk	Sifter
30 grams (1 ounce) unsalted butter, at room temperature	Small saucepan
3 large whole eggs, at room temperature	Medium saucepan
3 large egg yolks, at room temperature	Heat-proof bowl to fit saucepan
175 grams (6⅛ ounces) sugar	Large wire whisk
	Rubber spatula
	Wire rack

Prepare your *mise en place*.

Line the pan with parchment paper. Set aside.

Preheat the oven to 177°C (350°F).

Sift the flour and baking powder together. Set aside.

Combine the milk and butter in a small saucepan over low heat. Heat for a minute or two, or just until the butter has melted.

Fill a saucepan that is large enough to allow your heat-proof bowl to fit snugly into it without touching the water with about 7.5 centimeters (3 inches) of water. Place over high heat, bring to a boil, and immediately remove the pan from the heat.

Combine the eggs and egg yolks with the sugar in the heat-proof bowl and, using a wire whisk, whisk to blend. Quickly place the bowl into the pan, checking to make sure that the bottom is not resting in the hot water. Immediately begin whisking and continue to do so for about 10 minutes, or until the mixture reads 43°C (110°F) on an instant-read thermometer. (Do not

allow the temperature to exceed 49°C/120°F or the cake will be dry and tough.)

Remove the bowl from the heat and continue to whisk vigorously for about another 10 minutes, or until the mixture has tripled in volume and forms a ribbon when lifted from the bowl.

Using a rubber spatula, begin folding the reserved sifted flour mixture into the whipped mixture in several additions, making sure that the dry ingredients do not clump. Fold in each addition while the batter is still streaky from the previous one.

When all of the flour mixture has been incorporated and the batter remains streaky, fold a bit of the batter into the milk-butter mixture to create a consistency similar to the batter. Then, using the spatula, carefully fold the liquid mixture into the batter. Do not overfold or the batter will deflate.

Pour the batter into the prepared pan and, using the spatula, carefully smooth the top. Immediately place it in the preheated oven and bake for about 10 minutes, or until the top is golden brown and the cake springs back when gently touched in the center.

Set the cake on a wire rack to cool, then invert the pan and carefully remove the parchment paper.

Store, tightly wrapped and refrigerated, for 1 day, or frozen for up to 1 month.

Serve as is or use as directed in a specific recipe.

TIPS

Be sure to blend the eggs, egg yolks, and sugar before vigorously whisking or they will "burn" and be unusable.

The egg mixture is properly whipped when it does not rise any higher in the bowl and falls in a ribbon from the whisk, and when a small amount drizzled on top takes several seconds to melt back into the batter.

EVALUATING YOUR SUCCESS

The batter should completely fill the pan.

The baked cake should be lump-free with no large air pockets in the interior.

The cake should be moist, soft, light, and fluffy with a tight crumb.

Demonstration

Biscuit Dobos (Dobos Sponge)

Makes twelve 15-centimeter (6-inch) rounds (enough for two cakes)
Estimated time to complete: 45 minutes

Ingredients	Equipment
For the French meringue	Parchment paper
8 large egg whites, at room temperature	2 sheet pans or 4 half-sheet pans
100 grams (3½ ounces) sugar	Pencil
	Standing electric mixer fitted with whip attachment
For the batter	Saucepan
10 large egg yolks, at room temperature	Heat-proof bowl to fit saucepan
100 grams (3½ ounces) sugar	Wire whisk
150 grams (5¼ ounces) sour cream	Instant-read thermometer
200 grams (7 ounces) cake flour, sifted	Small bowl
	Rubber spatula
	Sifter
	Pastry bag fitted with #5 plain tip
	Wire racks

Prepare your *mise en place*.

Cut parchment paper to fit the pans and, using a pencil, draw twelve 15-centimeter (6-inch) circles

on them. The circles will serve as your pattern for piping the batter. Invert the parchment paper onto the pans so the pencil will not touch the batter. The circles should still be visible.

333

Preheat the oven to 177°C (350°F).

To make the meringue, place the egg whites in the bowl of a standing electric mixer fitted with the whip attachment. Beat on low to aerate. Add the sugar, raise the speed to high, and beat for about 5 minutes, or until soft peaks form. Set aside.

Fill a saucepan large enough to allow your heat-proof bowl to fit snugly into it without touching the water with about 7.5 centimeters (3 inches) of water. Place it over high heat, bring to a boil, and immediately remove the pan from the heat.

Combine the egg yolks with the sugar in the heat-proof bowl and, using a wire whisk, whisk to blend. Quickly place the bowl into the pan, checking to make sure that the bottom is not resting in the hot water. Immediately begin whisking and continue to do so for about 10 minutes, or until the mixture registers 43°C (110°F) on an instant-read thermometer. (Do not allow the temperature of the mixture to exceed 49°C/120°F or the cake will be dry and tough.)

Remove the bowl from the heat and continue to whisk vigorously for about another 10 minutes, or until the mixture has tripled in volume and forms a ribbon when lifted from the bowl.

Place the sour cream in a small bowl and stir enough of the egg yolk mixture into it to bring it to a smooth consistency equal to the egg yolks. There should be no lumps of sour cream remaining.

Using a rubber spatula, fold the sour cream into the egg yolks. Immediately fold the meringue into the egg yolk mixture, leaving the batter a bit streaky (it will receive further mixing with the addition of the flour). This process should happen very quickly, as the egg yolk mixture will rapidly break down as soon as the whipping stops.

Still using a rubber spatula, begin folding the sifted cake flour into the egg yolk mixture in several additions, making sure that the flour does not clump. Fold in each addition while the batter is still streaky from the previous one.

Once the batter is mixed, immediately transfer it to a pastry bag fitted with the #5 plain tip. Pipe the batter onto the parchment paper-lined pans, forming each circle by spiraling from the center out and stopping just inside the lines, as the batter will slightly spread during baking.

Bake the rounds for about 12 minutes, or until evenly browned, then carefully transfer them to wire racks to cool.

When the rounds are cool, use as directed in a specific recipe.

TIPS

Be sure to blend the eggs and sugar before vigorously whisking or they will "burn" and be unusable.

Always pipe a round shape by working from the center out.

EVALUATING YOUR SUCCESS

There should be no lumps of sour cream, flour, or unmixed meringue.

The baked rounds of batter should be distinct and of an even size, and there should be minimal spreading during baking.

The edges of the baked rounds should be light brown.

The baked sponge should be soft and moist.

Demonstration

Biscuit Joconde (Almond Sponge Cake)

Makes one 18-by-26-inch sheet cake (or 2 half-sheet pans)
Estimated time to complete: 1 hour

Ingredients	Equipment
Butter for pan	18-inch by 26-inch sheet pan
185 grams (6½ ounces) almond flour	Parchment paper
85 grams (3 ounces) sugar	Standing electric mixer fitted with paddle and whip attachments
45 grams (1½ ounces) all-purpose flour, sifted	Rubber spatula
5 large whole eggs, at room temperature	Medium mixing bowl
	Wire rack

For the French meringue

125 grams (4½ ounces) large egg whites, at room temperature

100 grams (3½ ounces) sugar

Prepare your *mise en place*.

Preheat the oven to 177°C (350°F).

Prepare a sheet pan with butter and parchment paper as directed on page 325. Set aside.

Combine the almond flour, sugar, and all-purpose flour in the bowl of a standing electric mixer fitted with the paddle attachment. Beat on low to just blend.

Add the eggs, one at a time, occasionally scraping down the sides of the bowl with a rubber spatula. It is important that as each egg is added, the mixture is beaten for a couple of minutes until it is completely emulsified. After all of the eggs have been added, beat for about 4 minutes to ensure that as much air as possible has been incorporated. Scrape the mixture from the electric mixer bowl into another clean bowl.

Wash the mixer bowl and return it to the stand. Fit the mixer with the whip attachment. Place the egg whites in the bowl and beat on low to aerate. Add the sugar, raise the speed to high, and beat for about

4 minutes, or until soft peaks form. Keep a close eye on the meringue; you can overmix it very quickly. If the egg whites do form dry, stiff peaks, discard the meringue and make a new one.

Remove the bowl from the mixer and, using the spatula, carefully fold the meringue into the batter. Work quickly and carefully so that the batter is not overworked, which will create a tough cake.

Gently spread the batter out in a thin layer in the parchment paper-lined pan and bake for about 7 minutes, or until the surface is an even golden brown and the center springs back when lightly touched.

Carefully invert the cake onto a wire rack. Peel off and discard the parchment paper and let cool.
Use as directed in a specific recipe (see Tips).

TIPS

Biscuit is the French word for sponge or sandwich cake. This particular *biscuit* can be used to make decorations for two types of cold confections. It may be stacked, layered with jam, and sliced to decorate the

335

NOTE
The world-famous painting *Mona Lisa*, Leonardo da Vinci's masterpiece, is thought to be the portrait of the wife of an Italian merchant, Francesco di Bartolomeo del Giocondo. It is, therefore, also known as *La Gioconda* (*La Joconde* in French). Da Vinci visited France in 1516 or 1517 as the guest of King François I and then remained there for the rest of his life. The *Mona Lisa* was still in the artist's possession and was held in very high esteem by the French. The name of this cake, *joconde*, was given to indicate how highly regarded the cake was among pastry chefs.

outside of a cake (see *Miroir aux Fruits*, page 424), or it may be made into a roll, filled with jelly, and used to decorate a *charlotte royale* (see page 427). It can also be used as a component in layered cakes and *petits fours* such as *opéra* cake (see page 453).

Great care must be taken when mixing the batter; if it is overworked, it will deflate and there will not be enough to cover the entire pan.

If the baked *biscuit* is crispy, place it in the refrigerator for about an hour and it will soften.

EVALUATING YOUR SUCCESS

The batter should display no unmixed ingredients.

The baked *biscuit* should be a thin, even layer across the entire sheet pan.

The baked *biscuit* should be soft and pliable, with no dark or crispy sections.

Demonstration

Biscuit Chocolat Noisette (Chocolate-Hazelnut *Biscuit*)

Makes one sheet cake or two 17¼-by-11½-by-1-inch cakes
Estimated time to complete: 45 minutes

Ingredients	Equipment
Butter for pan	Sheet pan or two 17¼-by- 11½-by-1-inch pans
	Parchment paper
For the batter	Medium mixing bowl
155 grams (5½ ounces) unsweetened hazelnut paste (see Tips)	Wooden spoon
155 grams (5½ ounces) confectioners' sugar	Standing electric mixer fitted with whip attachment
40 grams (1⅓ ounces) Dutch-process cocoa powder, sifted	Rubber spatula
105 grams (3⅔ ounces) egg whites, at room temperature	Cold sheet pan or wire rack
For the French meringue	
300 grams (11 ounces) egg whites, at room temperature	
30 grams (1 ounce) powdered egg whites (see Tips)	
100 grams (3½ ounces) confectioners' sugar, sifted	

Prepare your *mise en place*.

Preheat the oven to 177°C (350°F).

Prepare the pan with butter and parchment paper as directed on page 325. Set aside.

Combine the hazelnut paste and confectioners' sugar with the cocoa powder in a medium mixing bowl, stir-

ring with a wooden spoon to blend. Beat in the egg whites and, when well blended, set aside.

To make the French meringue, combine the fresh and powdered egg whites in the bowl of a standing electric mixer fitted with the whip attachment. Beat on low to blend and aerate. Add the sugar, raise the speed to high, and beat for about 5 minutes, or until stiff peaks form.

Using a rubber spatula, combine enough of the meringue with the hazelnut mixture to bring it to a smooth consistency almost equal to the meringue. There should be no lumps in the mixture, but do not overmix or the batter will quickly deflate and there won't be enough to fill the pan.

Carefully pour the batter into the prepared pan, smoothing it out into an even layer.

Bake the cake for 3 minutes, rotate the pan, and continue to bake for another 4 minutes, or until the surface is an even golden brown and the center springs back when lightly touched. Watch carefully, as the *biscuit* bakes very quickly.

Carefully invert the *biscuit* onto a clean, cold sheet pan or a wire rack. Carefully peel off and discard the parchment paper and let cool.

Use as directed in a specific recipe.

TIPS

Unsweetened hazelnut paste is available from cake and bakery supply stores. To make it, grind toasted, skinless hazelnuts in a food processor using the metal blade until a paste forms. Unsweetened hazelnut paste should not be confused with praline paste, which is sweetened. They cannot be used interchangeably.

Powdered egg whites are available from baking supply stores, many specialty food stores, and some supermarkets.

The cake is very thin, so great care must be taken not to overwork the batter when spreading it in the pan.

EVALUATING YOUR SUCCESS

The batter should display no unmixed ingredients or lumps of meringue.

The baked *biscuit* should be about 6 millimeters (¼ inch) thick in an even layer with no thin spots.

The baked *biscuit* should be soft and tender, with a strong hazelnut aroma and flavor.

Demonstration

Biscuit d'Amandes (Almond Biscuit)

Makes one sheet cake or two 17¼-by-11½-by-1-inch cakes
Estimated time to complete: 45 minutes

Ingredients	Equipment
Butter for pan	Sheet pan or two 17¼-by- 11½-by-1 inch pans
	Parchment paper
For the batter	Large mixing bowl
150 grams (5.2 ounces) almond flour	Wooden spoon
40 grams (1½ ounces) cake flour	Standing electric mixer fitted with whip attachment
80 grams (2¾ ounces) sugar	Rubber spatula
5 large eggs, at room temperature	Cold sheet pan or wire rack
30 grams (1 ounce) unsalted butter, melted and cooled slightly	

For the French meringue

135 grams (4¾ ounces) egg whites, at room temperature
100 grams (3½ ounces) sugar

Prepare your *mise en place*.

Preheat the oven to 177°C (350°F).

Prepare a sheet pan with butter and parchment paper as directed on page 325. Set aside.

Combine the almond and cake flours with the sugar in a large mixing bowl, stirring with a wooden spoon to blend. Beat in the whole eggs and, when well blended, set aside.

To make the meringue, place the egg whites in the bowl of a standing electric mixer fitted with the whip attachment. Beat on low to blend and aerate. Add the sugar, raise the speed to high, and beat for about 5 minutes, or until stiff peaks form.

Using a rubber spatula, combine enough of the meringue with the flour mixture to bring it to a smooth consistency almost equal to the meringue. There should be no lumps in the mixture.

Using the rubber spatula, fold the remaining meringue into the flour mixture, folding to just combine. Then, carefully fold the melted butter into the meringue. The butter should be liquid, but not hot or it will deflate the batter.

Carefully pour the batter into the prepared pan, smoothing it out into an even layer.

Bake the cake for 3 minutes, rotate the pan, and continue to bake for another 4 minutes, or until the surface is an even golden brown and the center springs back when lightly touched. Watch carefully, as the *biscuit* bakes very quickly.

Carefully invert the *biscuit* onto a clean, cold sheet pan or a wire rack. Peel off and discard the parchment and let cool.

Use as directed in a specific recipe.

TIPS

Great care must be taken when mixing the batter; if it is overworked, it will deflate and there will not be enough to cover the entire pan.

If the baked *biscuit* is crispy, place it in the refrigerator for about an hour and it will soften.

EVALUATING YOUR SUCCESS

The batter should display no unmixed ingredients or lumps of meringue.

The baked *biscuit* should be about 6 millimeters (¼ inch) thick in an even layer, with no thin spots or dark or crispy sections.

The baked *biscuit* should be soft and pliable.

The baked *biscuit* should be soft and tender, with a light almond aroma and flavor.

Demonstration

Biscuit au Chocolat pour Forêt Noire (Sponge for Black Forest Cake)

Makes two 6-inch cakes
Estimated time to complete: 45 minutes

Ingredients	Equipment
Butter and flour for the pans	Two 6-inch round cake pans
	Sifter
For the batter	Standing electric mixer fitted with paddle and whip attachments
200 grams (7 ounces) cake flour	Rubber spatula
50 grams (1¾ ounces) Dutch-process cocoa powder	Medium mixing bowl
130 grams (4½ ounces) unsalted butter, at room temperature	Cake tester
100 grams (3½ ounces) confectioners' sugar	Wire racks
140 grams (5 ounces) egg yolks, at room temperature	
For the French meringue	
270 grams (9½ ounces) egg whites, at room temperature	
190 grams (6 ¾ ounces) granulated sugar	

Prepare your *mise en place*.

Butter and flour the cake pans. Set aside.

Preheat the oven to 177°C (350°F).

Sift the cake flour and cocoa powder together. Set aside.

Combine the butter with the confectioners' sugar in the bowl of a standing electric mixer fitted with the paddle attachment. Beat on low to just combine. Raise the speed to medium and beat, scraping down the sides of the bowl with a rubber spatula from time to time, for about 4 minutes, or until light and fluffy.

Add the egg yolks one at a time, beating well and scraping down the sides of the bowl after each addition. Transfer the mixture to another bowl and clean the electric mixer bowl. Fit the mixer with the whip attachment.

To make the meringue, place the egg whites in the bowl of the standing electric mixer and beat on low to aerate.

Add the granulated sugar, raise the speed to high, and beat for about 5 minutes, or until stiff peaks form.

Using a rubber spatula, fold enough of the meringue into the butter mixture to lighten it so that the complete folding will be easier. Fold the remaining meringue into the butter mixture, until it is just blended. There should be no lumps, but the batter should be streaky.

Fold the sifted flour mixture into the meringue mixture in several additions; do not overmix.

Pour an equal portion of the batter into each of the prepared pans and bake for about 20 minutes, or until the surface is an even brown, a cake tester inserted into the center comes out clean, and the center springs back when lightly touched.

Invert the cakes on wire racks to cool.

Use as directed in the Black Forest cake (see page 417) recipe or any other suitable cake.

Great care must be taken when mixing the batter; if it is overworked, it will deflate and there will not be enough to cover the entire pan.

If the baked *biscuit* is crispy, place it in the refrigerator for about an hour and it will soften.

The batter should display no unmixed ingredients or lumps of meringue.

The cake should dome up in the center while baking.

The finished cake should be soft and moist, with an intense chocolate flavor and aroma.

Demonstration

Roulade de Biscuit (Sponge Cake Roll)

Makes 1 half-sheet cake or 17¼-by-11½-by-1-inch cake
Estimated time to complete: 45 minutes

Ingredients	Equipment
Butter for pan	Half-sheet pan or 17¼-by-11½-by-1-inch pan
	Parchment paper
For the French meringue	Standing electric mixer fitted with whip attachment
4 large egg whites, at room temperature	Rubber spatula
125 grams (4½ ounces) sugar	Cold sheet pan or wire rack
For the batter	
4 large egg yolks, at room temperature, beaten	
125 grams (4½ ounces) cake flour, sifted	
60 grams (2 ounces) unsalted butter, melted and cooled slightly	

Prepare your *mise en place*.

Preheat the oven to 177°C (350°F).

Prepare the pan with butter and parchment paper as directed on page 325. Set aside.

To make the meringue, place the egg whites in the bowl of a standing electric mixer fitted with the whip attachment. Beat on low to aerate. Add the sugar, raise the speed to high, and beat for about 5 minutes, or until stiff peaks form.

Beat the egg yolks and, using a rubber spatula, carefully fold them into the meringue. Fold the sifted cake flour into the meringue. Finally, carefully fold the butter into the meringue. The butter should be liquid but not hot, or it will deflate the batter.

Carefully pour the batter into the prepared pan, smoothing it out into an even layer.

Bake the cake for 3 minutes, rotate the pan, and continue to bake for another 4 minutes, or until the surface is an even golden brown and the center springs back when lightly touched.

Carefully invert the cake onto a clean, cold sheet pan or a wire rack. Peel off and discard the parchment paper and let the cake cool.

Use as directed in a specific recipe.

TIPS

Great care must be taken when mixing the batter; if it is overworked, it will deflate and there will not be enough to cover the entire pan.

If the baked *biscuit* is crispy, refrigerate it for about an hour and it will soften.

EVALUATING YOUR SUCCESS

The batter should not display unmixed ingredients.

The baked *biscuit* should be a thin, even layer across the entire sheet pan.

The baked *biscuit* should be soft and pliable, with no dark or crispy sections.

Demonstration

Roulade de Biscuit au Chocolate (Chocolate Roll)

Makes one full-sheet cake or two 17¼-by-11½-by-1-inch cakes
Estimated time to complete: 45 minutes

Ingredients	Equipment
Butter for pan	Full-sheet pan or two 17¼ by-11½-by-1-inch pans
	Parchment paper
For the batter	Sifter
150 grams (5⅓ ounces) cake flour	Standing electric mixer fitted with whip attachment
70 grams (2⅓ ounces) Dutch-process cocoa powder	Rubber spatula
½ teaspoon baking powder	Clean sheet pan or wire rack
½ teaspoon baking soda	
10 large egg yolks, at room temperature, beaten	
For the French meringue	
10 large egg whites, at room temperature	
200 grams (7 ounces) sugar	

Prepare your *mise en place.*

Preheat the oven to 177°C (350°F).

Prepare the pans with butter and parchment paper as directed on page 325. Set aside.

Sift the flour, cocoa powder, baking powder, and baking soda together. Set aside.

Beat the egg yolks and set them aside.

Place the egg whites in the bowl of the standing electric mixer fitted with the whip attachment. Beat on low to aerate. Add the sugar, raise the speed to high, and beat for about 4 minutes, or until soft peaks form. Keep a close eye on the meringue. You do not want to overmix it, which can happen very quickly. If dry, stiff peaks form, discard the meringue and make a new one.

Remove the bowl from the mixer and, using a rubber spatula, carefully fold the egg yolks into the meringue.

Fold the sifted dry ingredients into the meringue mixture in two segments, mixing as little as possible. The mixture should still be streaky from the first addition before you fold in the second amount. You do not want to deflate the batter.

Pour the batter into the prepared pan and, using the spatula, carefully smooth the top. Do not press down or the batter will deflate.

Immediately, place the cake in the preheated oven and bake for about 7 minutes, or until the surface is an even golden brown and the center springs back when lightly touched.

Carefully invert the cake onto a clean, cold sheet pan or a wire rack. Peel off and discard the parchment paper and let cool.

Use as directed in a specific recipe.

TIPS

Great care must be taken when mixing the batter; if it is overworked, it will deflate and there will not be enough to cover the entire pan.

If the baked *biscuit* is crispy, refrigerate it for about an hour and it will soften.

EVALUATING YOUR SUCCESS

The batter should not display unmixed ingredients.

The baked *biscuit* should be a thin, even layer across the entire sheet pan.

The baked *biscuit* should be soft and pliable, with no dark or crispy sections.

Demonstration

Biscuits à la Cuillère (Ladyfingers)

Makes two 66-centimeter-long (26-inch long) strips
Estimated time to complete: 45 minutes

Ingredients	Equipment
Butter for pan	Sheet pan
	Parchment paper
For the French meringue	Standing electric mixer fitted with whip attachment
5 large egg whites, at room temperature	Small mixing bowl
125 grams (4½ ounces) confectioners' sugar	Whisk
	Rubber spatula
For the batter	Pastry bag fitted with #5 plain tip
5 large egg yolks, at room temperature	Fine-mesh sieve
½ teaspoon pure vanilla extract, optional	
125 grams (4½ ounces) cake flour	
For the finish	
Confectioners' sugar for dusting	

Prepare your *mise en place*.

Preheat the oven to 177°C (350°F).

Prepare a sheet pan with butter and parchment paper as directed on page 325. Set aside.

Place the egg whites in the bowl of the standing electric mixer fitted with the whip attachment. Beat on low to aerate. Add the sugar, raise the speed to high, and beat for about 4 minutes, or until stiff peaks form.

Combine the egg yolks and vanilla in a small mixing bowl and whisk to blend well.

Using a rubber spatula, carefully fold the egg yolks into the meringue. Then carefully fold the flour into the meringue. You do not want to deflate the batter. Immediately transfer the batter to a pastry bag fitted with the #5 plain tip. Pipe 2 strips of batter down the length of the sheet pan. Alternatively, to bake the ladyfingers as individual cookies, pipe the batter into 7.5-centimeter-long (3-inch-long) strips, leaving about 2.5 centimeters (1 inch) between each one.

Place the confectioners' sugar in a fine-mesh sieve and coat the strips with a light dusting.

Bake the ladyfingers, watching carefully to prevent burning, for about 7 minutes, or until they are light brown around the edges and the center springs back when lightly touched.

Place them on a wire rack to cool.

Use as directed in a specific recipe.

Store in layers, tightly covered, for up to 3 days.

TIPS
This batter cannot sit at all, as it deflates very rapidly. If you need more ladyfingers, do not increase the recipe. Instead, always make them in small batches.

The vanilla flavoring can be replaced with any other extract.

When preparing ladyfingers for use in a *charlotte* (see page 433), you can pipe them next to each other to form a pliable, attached band that can be used in one piece to line the *charlotte* mold.

If desired, or if required in a specific recipe, food coloring may be added to the egg yolks to make a more colorful presentation.

EVALUATING YOUR SUCCESS
The batter should display no lumps of meringue or unmixed ingredients.

The baked ladyfingers should be consistent in size and shape.

The baked ladyfingers should be soft and pliable, with no dark or crispy sections.

Demonstration

Flourless Chocolate Cake

Makes two 6-inch cakes

Estimated time to complete: 1 hour

Ingredients	Equipment
Butter and flour for pans	Two 6-inch round cake pans
	Saucepan
For the batter	Heat-proof bowl to fit saucepan
115 grams (4 ounces) unsalted butter, at room temperature	

80 grams (2¾ ounces) semisweet or bittersweet chocolate, chopped into small pieces

80 grams (2¾ ounces) almond flour

4 large egg yolks, at room temperature

For the French meringue

4 large egg whites, at room temperature

150 grams (5⅓ ounces) sugar

Wooden spoon

Standing electric mixer fitted with whip attachment

Rubber spatula

Cake tester

Wire racks

Prepare your *mise en place.*

Preheat the oven to 177°C (350°F).

Butter and flour the cake pans.

Fill a saucepan large enough to allow your heat-proof bowl to fit snugly into it without touching the water with about 7.5 centimeters (3 inches) of water. Place over high heat and bring to a boil. Immediately remove the pan from the heat.

Combine the butter and chocolate in the heat-proof bowl and place the bowl into the pan, checking to make sure that the bottom is not resting in the hot water. Using a wooden spoon, stir to blend as the butter melts.

When the butter and chocolate have melted and the mixture is homogeneous, stir in the almond flour. Then stir in the egg yolks. The mixture will be warm, but should not be hot. If it is too hot, the yolks will cook and congeal and render the mixture unusable.

Remove the bowl from the heat and set it aside.

Place the egg whites in the bowl of a standing electric mixer fitted with the whip attachment. Beat on low to aerate. Add the sugar, raise the speed to high, and beat for about 5 minutes, or until firm peaks form. The peaks should not be too stiff or dry.

Using a rubber spatula, carefully fold the meringue into the chocolate batter.

Carefully pour the batter into the prepared pans, smoothing it into an even layer.

Bake the cakes for 20 to 30 minutes, or until a cake tester inserted into the center comes out clean. The tester can be moist or shiny, but it should have no crumbs attached.

Place the cake pans on wire racks to cool completely before unmolding. The cake will fall as it cools.

Serve as is, with *crème Chantilly* (see page 111), or as directed in a specific recipe.

TIPS

This recipe can be used to make a 17¼-by-11½-by-1-inch cake.

Do not attempt to unmold the cake before it has cooled, as it is very fragile when hot and will fall apart.

EVALUATING YOUR SUCCESS

The batter should display no lumps or unincorporated meringue.

The finished cake should be very moist, with a tight, dense crumb and a strong chocolate aroma and flavor.

Demonstration

Lemon Chiffon Cake

Makes two 6-inch cakes or one 9-inch cake
Estimated time to complete: 1 hour

Ingredients	**Equipment**
Butter for pan	Two 6-inch cake pans or one 9-inch cake pan
	Medium mixing bowl
For the batter	Wire whisk
5 large egg yolks, at room temperature	Sifter
80 milliliters (2¾ ounces) vegetable oil	Wooden spoon
Juice and zest of 1 lemon	Standing electric mixer fitted with whip attachment
150 grams (5⅓ ounces) cake flour	Rubber spatula
60 grams (2 ounces) sugar	Wire rack
6 grams (1⅓ teaspoons) baking powder	
For the French meringue	
5 large egg whites, at room temperature	
150 grams (5¼ ounces) sugar	

NOTE

Chiffon cakes are an American invention (credited to Henry Baker, 1927), with vegetable oil as the most significant ingredient. They are very light, airy cakes made by folding beaten egg whites into a batter composed of flour, oil, and egg yolks.

Prepare your *mise en place*.

Preheat the oven to 177°C (350°F).

Lightly coat *only* the bottom of the pans with softened butter. Do not butter the sides or the cake will collapse inward when baked. Set aside.

Combine the egg yolks and oil with the lemon juice and zest in a medium mixing bowl, whisking to blend well.

Sift the flour, sugar, and the baking powder together and, using a wooden spoon, stir the dry ingredients into the egg yolk mixture, taking care that it remains lump-free.

To make the meringue, place the egg whites in the bowl of a standing electric mixer fitted with the whip attachment. Beat on low to aerate. Add the sugar, raise the speed to high, and beat for about 5 minutes, or until firm peaks form. The peaks should not be too stiff or dry.

Using a rubber spatula, carefully fold the meringue into the batter.

Carefully pour the batter into the prepared pans, smoothing it out to make it even.

Bake for 35 to 45 minutes, or until the surface is an even golden brown and the center springs back when lightly touched.

Place the pans on a wire rack to cool completely before unmolding.

Use as directed in a specific recipe.

Lemon Chiffon Cake may be served as is, with a dusting of confectioners' sugar, or lightly glazed with a lemon glaze (64 grams/1 cup confectioners' sugar blended with 45 milliliters/3 tablespoons fresh lemon juice).

The large amount of liquid fat in the recipe keeps chiffon cake soft and moist and provides a long shelf life.

The baked cake should be golden brown on the exterior and bright yellow on the interior.

The cake should be moist and flavorful, with a tight crumb.

No dark or wet spots should appear on the interior. The cake should hold its rise after baking.

Demonstration

Carrot Cake

Makes two 6-inch cakes
Estimated time to complete: 90 minutes

Ingredients	Equipment
Butter and flour for pans	Two 6-inch round cake pans
	Sifter
For the batter	Saucepan
125 grams (4½ ounces) cake flour	Heat-proof bowl to fit saucepan
1 teaspoon ground cinnamon	Wire whisk
½ teaspoon baking powder	Instant-read thermometers
½ teaspoon baking soda	Rubber spatula
½ teaspoon salt	Cake tester
2 large eggs, at room temperature	Wire racks
220 grams (7¾ ounces) sugar	Standing electric mixer fitted with paddle attachment
170 grams (6 ounces) vegetable oil	Wooden spoon
165 grams (5¾ ounces) grated carrots	Serrated knife
60 grams (2 ounces) chopped walnuts	2 cake plates
	Offset spatula
For the icing	
455 grams (1 pound) cream cheese, at room temperature	
180 grams (6⅓ ounces) unsalted butter, at room temperature	
350 grams (12⅓ ounces) confectioners' sugar	
20 grams (2 tablespoons) sour cream	
1 teaspoon pure vanilla extract	
Zest of ½ lemon	

For the finish
50 grams (1¼ ounces) chopped walnut
12 marzipan carrots, optional (see Tips)
Candied carrots, optional (see Tips)

Prepare your *mise en place*.

Butter and flour the cake pans. Set aside.

Preheat the oven to 177°C (350°F).

Sift the flour, cinnamon, baking powder, baking soda, and salt together. Set aside.

Fill a saucepan large enough to allow your heat-proof bowl to fit snugly into it without touching the water with about 7.5 centimeters (3 inches) of water. Place over high heat and bring to a boil. Immediately remove the pan from the heat.

Combine the eggs with the sugar in the heat-proof bowl and, using a wire whisk, whisk to blend. Quickly place the bowl into the pan, checking to make sure that the bottom is not resting in the hot water. Immediately begin whisking and continue to do so for about 10 minutes, or until the mixture registers 43°C (110°F) on an instant-read thermometer. (Do not allow the temperature of the mixture to exceed 49°C/120°F or the cake will be dry and tough.)

Remove the bowl from the heat and continue to whisk vigorously for about another 10 minutes, or until the mixture has tripled in volume and forms a ribbon when lifted from the bowl.

Slowly pour in the oil in a steady stream and, using a rubber spatula, gently stir to combine. Work slowly and steadily or the mixture will separate.

Add the sifted dry ingredients and, using the spatula, mix slowly to just barely combine. Do not overmix.

Stir in the carrots and nuts to just incorporate, then pour an equal portion of the batter into each of the prepared pans.

Bake the cakes for about 35 minutes, or until a cake tester inserted into the center comes out clean.

Immediately invert each pan onto a wire rack. Unmold the cakes and let cool completely.

While the cakes are cooling, make the icing.

Combine the cream cheese and butter in the bowl of a standing electric mixer fitted with the paddle and mix on low to just blend. Add the confectioners' sugar and beat on medium for about 4 minutes, or until very smooth.

Beat in the sour cream and vanilla. When well blended, remove the bowl from the mixer and stir in the zest.

When the cakes are completely cool, using a serrated knife, cut each one in half crosswise. (At this point, the cakes can be stored, tightly wrapped and refrigerated, for up to 2 days, or frozen for up to 1 month.)

Place the bottom layer, cut side up, on each of 2 cake plates. Using an offset spatula, lightly coat the surface of each bottom with an equal portion of the icing. Place a top layer over the icing, cut side down. Using the remaining icing, completely cover each cake with about a 6-millimeter-thick (⅛-inch-thick) coating of icing. Note that the cake itself is quite sweet, so you don't want to frost it too thickly.

Using your hands, apply chopped walnuts about 1.3 centimeters (½ inch) up the side of each cake.

Place 6 small marzipan or candied carrots on top of each cake in a decorative pattern that will yield one carrot per slice when the cakes are cut.

Serve immediately or within a few hours of being frosted.

The egg-and-sugar mixture should be very light before the oil is added.

Once the dry ingredients are added, the batter should be barely mixed or the baked cake will be tough.

The cakes are easier to frost if they are cut in half, tightly wrapped, and frozen overnight. Frost while still frozen.

Marzipan carrots may be created using commercially made marzipan colored with food coloring or they may be purchased ready-made.

Candied carrot disks—fresh carrots cut crosswise into 3-millimeter-thick (⅛-inch-thick) slices—or candied carrot strips—carrots cut lengthwise with a vegetable peeler into very thin strips—can be made following the directions for Candied Lemon Zest on page 118.

EVALUATING YOUR SUCCESS

The baked cake should be very moist and have a distinct cinnamon flavor and aroma.

The carrots and nuts should be visible in the baked cake.

The icing should be very smooth with a sharp edge.

Demonstration

Meringue pour Vacherin (Meringue Nests)

Makes forty 2.5-centimeter (1-inch) meringues
Estimated time to complete: 2 hours

Ingredients	Equipment
250 grams (8¾ ounces) egg whites, at room temperature	Parchment paper
Pinch cream of tartar	Pencil
Pinch salt	Sheet pan
300 grams (11 ounces) granulated sugar	Standing electric mixer fitted with whip attachment
150 grams (5⅓ ounces) confectioners' sugar	Rubber spatula
	Pastry bag fitted with #1 plain tip
	Airtight container, optional

NOTE

A *vacherin* is a meringue-based cake that is, traditionally, filled with ice cream and then covered with whipped cream.

Prepare your *mise en place*.

Preheat the oven to 107°C (225°F).

Draw forty 2.5-centimeter (1-inch) circles on parchment paper using a pencil. The circles will serve as your patterns for piping the batter. Invert the parchment paper onto a sheet pan so that the pencil marks will not touch the batter. The circles should still be visible.

Combine the egg whites with the cream of tartar and salt in the bowl of a standing electric mixer fitted with the whip attachment. Beat on low for about 2 minutes, or until foamy.

Raise the speed to medium and add the granulated sugar in a slow, steady stream. Whip for about 5 minutes or until stiff peaks form. Do not overwhip or the meringue will separate and become grainy.

Remove the bowl from the mixer and, using a rubber spatula, fold in the confectioners' sugar, until just blended.

Once the batter is mixed, immediately transfer it to a pastry bag fitted with the #1 plain tip. Pipe the batter onto the parchment paper-lined pans, piping each circle pattern from the center out. Pipe another roll of meringue around the outside edge of each circle to form a 2.5-centimeter-high (1-inch high) wall all around.

Bake the meringues for about 90 minutes, or until they feel very light and dry but have taken on absolutely no color.

Use them immediately as directed in a specific recipe or store them, *absolutely airtight*, in a dry spot. Take care—baked meringues are very fragile.

TIPS

The cream of tartar acts as a stabilizer. If it is unavailable, you can replace it with a few drops of lemon juice or white vinegar.

The salt is essential for achieving greater volume, as it helps break down the proteins in the egg whites.

Watch the oven temperature carefully because if the meringues are baked in a too-hot oven, they will puff up quickly but then deflate when removed from the heat.

EVALUATING YOUR SUCCESS

Both the interior and exterior of the baked meringue nests should be dry and crunchy.

The baked meringues should be consistent in size and shape, with no color or caramelization.

Demonstration

Meringues au Chocolat (Chocolate Meringues)

Makes about ten 66-centimeter-long (26-inch-long) strips
Estimated time to complete: Up to 8 hours

Ingredients	Equipment
For the batter	Sheet pan, half sheet pans, or baking sheets
150 grams (5⅓ ounces) confectioners' sugar	Parchment paper
25 grams dutch process cocoa powder	Sifter
	Standing electric mixer fitted with whip attachment
For the French meringue	Rubber spatula
170 grams (6 ounces) egg whites, at room temperature	Pastry bag fitted with appropriate tip
150 grams (5⅓ ounces) granulated sugar	Airtight container, optional

Prepare your *mise en place.*

Line the pans with parchment paper.

Preheat the oven to 107°C (225°F).

Sift the confectioners' sugar and cocoa powder

together and set aside.

Place the egg whites in the bowl of a standing electric mixer fitted with the whip attachment. Beat on low to aerate. Add the granulated sugar, raise the speed to high, and beat for about 5 minutes, or until stiff peaks form.

Using a rubber spatula, carefully fold the dry ingredients into the meringue. Do not overfold or the meringue will deflate.

Once the batter is mixed, immediately transfer it to a pastry bag fitted with whatever tip is specified by the recipe.

Working quickly, so that the meringue does not begin to deflate, pipe it onto the parchment paper-lined pans into whatever shape is required. The shapes can be piped quite close together, as the meringue will not spread during baking.

Bake the meringues for about 2 hours, or until they feel very light and dry but have taken on absolutely no color. Turn the oven off and let the meringues cool and dry. It is difficult to give a specific time—it can take up to 8 hours for the meringues dry out sufficiently.

Use the meringues immediately as directed in a specific recipe or store *absolutely airtight* in a dry spot. Take care—baked meringues are quite fragile.

TIPS

The meringue batter can be piped into any shape you desire. In many bakeries, it is baked in strips that can be broken up or crumbled to use as cake décor. It is also used to make mushrooms, logs, rounds, and other decorative pieces.

Watch the oven temperature carefully because if the meringues are baked in a too-hot oven, they will puff up quickly during baking and then deflate when removed from the heat.

Since the drying process takes so long, rather than baking them in a hot oven, it is most convenient to place the meringues in the oven overnight with just the heat of the pilot light to dry them.

Baked meringues must be stored, airtight, as even the slightest amount of humidity will cause them to soften and become gooey.

EVALUATING YOUR SUCCESS

The meringue batter should not be flat or runny.

When piped, the unbaked meringue should sit nicely above the parchment paper.

The baked meringues should be crispy, with no soft parts, and should be even in color and size

---

Demonstration

Pâte à Dacquoise (Nut Meringues)

Makes five 15-centimeter (6-inch) disks or four 10-by-30.5-centimeter (4-by-12-inch) strips
Estimated time to complete: Up to 8 hours

Ingredients	Equipment
300 grams (11 ounces) egg whites, at room temperature	Pencil
300 grams (11 ounces) sugar	Parchment paper
300 grams (11 ounces) almond flour	Sheet pan or 2 half-sheet pans
	Standing electric mixer fitted with whip attachment
	Rubber spatula
	Pastry bag fitted with #5 plain tip

Prepare your *mise en place*.

Using a pencil, draw five 15-centimeter (6-inch) circles or four 10-by-30.5-centimeter (4-by-12-inch) rectangles on parchment paper. The circles or rectangles will serve as your pattern for piping the batter. Invert the parchment paper onto a sheet pan so that the pencil marks will not touch the batter. The images should still be visible.

Preheat the oven to 107°C (225°F).

Place the egg whites in the bowl of a standing electric mixer fitted with the whip attachment. Beat on low to aerate. Add the sugar, raise the speed to high, and beat for about 5 minutes, or until stiff peaks form.

Using a rubber spatula, carefully fold the almond flour into the meringue. Do not overfold or the meringue will deflate.

Once the batter is mixed, immediately transfer it to a pastry bag fitted with the #5 plain tip. The meringue cannot sit or it will break down and become watery.

Pipe the batter onto the patterns on the parchment paper-lined pans. The meringue expands slightly during baking, so make sure that you stay just inside of the lines.

Bake the meringues for about 2 hours, or until they feel very light and dry, but have taken on no color. Turn the oven off and let the meringues cool and dry.

It is difficult to give a specific time—it can take up to 8 hours for the meringues dry out sufficiently. Use the meringues immediately as directed in a specific recipe or store *absolutely airtight* in a dry spot. Take care—baked meringues are quite fragile.

TIPS

Since the drying out process takes so long, it is most convenient to place the meringues in the oven overnight with just the heat of the pilot light to dry them.

Watch the oven temperature carefully because if the meringues are baked at too high a temperature, they will puff up quickly and then deflate when removed from the heat.

Baked meringues must be stored, airtight, as even the slightest amount of humidity will cause them to soften and become gooey.

EVALUATING YOUR SUCCESS

The meringue batter should not be flat or runny. When piped, it should sit nicely above the parchment paper.

There should be no lumps of egg white or flour in the batter.

Whatever the shape of the meringue, it should be distinct before and after baking.

The baked meringues should be completely dried out, even in size, light golden brown, and crispy, with no soft parts.

Demonstration

Angel Food Cake

Makes one 10-inch cake

Estimated time to complete: 1 hour

Ingredients	Equipment
145 grams (5⅛ ounces) cake flour	Sifter
100 grams (3½ ounces) confectioners' sugar	Small bowl
200 grams (7 ounces) granulated sugar	Wooden spoon
1 teaspoon cream of tartar	Standing electric mixer fitted with whip attachment
400 grams (14 ounces) large egg whites	Rubber spatula
(about 14 egg whites), at room temperature	Ungreased 10-inch angel food cake pan
Pinch salt	(or a *kugelhopf* mold or regular tube pan)
½ teaspoon pure vanilla extract	Metal spatula or kitchen knife
	Wire rack
	Long, thin
	knife
	Serving plate

Prepare your *mise en place*.

Preheat the oven to 162°C (325°F).

Sift the flour and confectioners' sugar together. Set aside.

Combine the granulated sugar with the cream of tartar in a small bowl, stirring with a wooden spoon to combine. Set aside.

Place the egg whites in the bowl of a standing electric mixer fitted with the whip attachment. Stir in the salt. Beat on low until foamy.

Raise the speed to medium and begin adding the granulated sugar mixture, a bit at a time, allowing the meringue to stiffen after each addition. Beat for about 7 minutes, or until stiff peaks form.

Turn off the motor and, using a rubber spatula, fold in the vanilla. It is okay if the extract streaks the

batter; when the flour mixture is folded in, it will be fully incorporated.

Using the rubber spatula, carefully fold in the flour mixture in a few additions. The batter can be left streaked after each addition, as the egg whites will deflate if it is folded too much. The finished batter should be quite stiff.

Spoon the batter into pan. Run a metal spatula or kitchen knife through the batter to release trapped air pockets and to help fill in any voids.

Bake the cake for about 40 minutes, or until the surface is golden brown and the top is firm to the touch.

Invert the pan onto a wire rack and allow the cake to cool completely before unmolding. Otherwise, it will collapse.

When the cake is cool, unmold it by inserting a long, thin knife down the sides of the pan and, pressing the knife to carefully loosen the cake from the sides without tearing it. Repeat the process around the center tube. Invert the pan and carefully tap the sides and bottom of the pan to release the cake. Holding the tube, carefully lift the cake from the pan. Then use the knife to loosen the cake from the bottom piece. Invert the cake onto a serving plate and lift the pan bottom off.

Use as directed in a specific recipe or serve as is, dusted with confectioners' sugar, if desired.

Store the cake, tightly covered and refrigerated, for up to 2 days, or frozen for up to 1 month.

TIPS
The cream of tartar acts as a stabilizer in the meringue. If it is unavailable, substitute a few drops of lemon juice or white vinegar.

The salt breaks down the protein in the whites, helping them achieve greater volume.

Any other extract, such as orange, almond, or lemon, may be added in addition to or in place of the vanilla.

The mold is not greased because the cake needs its support as it cools and sets. The cake would pull away from greased pan sides and collapse.

EVALUATING YOUR SUCCESS
The cake batter should completely fill the mold, with no large voids or air pockets.

The finished cake should be golden brown on all outer surfaces.

The bottom should be flat and not curved upward.

The crumb should be tight but soft, slightly moist, and bright white.

The finished cake should be spongy, slightly chewy, and sweet, with just a hint of vanilla.

Demonstration

Quatre-Quarts (Pound Cake)

Makes two 9-by-5-by-2½-inch loaves
Estimated time to complete: 90 minutes

Ingredients	Equipment
Butter and flour for pans	Two 9-by-5-by-2 ½-inch loaf pans
455 grams (1 pound) all-purpose flour	Sifter
4 grams (1 tablespoon) baking powder	Standing electric mixer fitted with paddle attachment
455 grams (1 pound) unsalted butter, at room temperature	Rubber spatula
450 grams (16 ounces) granulated sugar	Cake tester
9 large eggs, at room temperature	Wire rack
Zest of 1 orange	Plastic film
Zest of 1 lemon	
1 teaspoon extract of choice, optional	

For the finish
125 grams (4½ ounces) confectioners' sugar, optional

Prepare your *mise en place*.

Preheat the oven to 177°C (350°F).

Butter and flour the pans as directed on page 326.

Sift the flour and baking powder together. Set aside.

Place the butter in the bowl of a standing electric mixer fitted with the paddle attachment. With the speed on low, begin creaming the butter, scraping down the sides of the bowl with a rubber spatula from time to time. The butter should warm to about 21°C (70°F), and the texture should be smooth and even.

Add the granulated sugar and continue to beat the mixture until it is light in color and very soft and fluffy.

Add the eggs, one at a time, occasionally scraping down the sides of the bowl with a rubber spatula. It is important that, as each egg is added, the mixture is beaten for a couple of minutes until it is completely emulsified.

Add the sifted dry ingredients to the creamed mixture all at once and continue to beat until just combined.

Remove the bowl from the mixer stand. Using the spatula, fold the zests and extract, if using, into the batter.

Pour the batter into the prepared pans and bake for 15 minutes. Reduce the heat to 148°C (300°F) and continue to bake for another 45 minutes, or until a cake tester inserted into the center comes out clean and dry.

Unmold the cakes onto a wire rack.

Serve as is or lightly dust with confectioners' sugar.

Store the cooled cake, tightly wrapped in plastic film, refrigerated for up to 1 week, or frozen for up to 1 month.

TIPS
Do not overmix the batter once the flour has been added or gluten will develop; the baked cake will be tough and may have tunneling.

To get an even split in the top of the cake, run a knife down the center of the surface of the loaf after it has baked for 20 minutes.

If the surface of the cake gets too dark before it has finished baking, cover it loosely with aluminum foil.

A chocolate marbled pound cake can be created by separating out one-third of the batter and adding 200 grams (7 ounces) melted unsweetened chocolate. When filling the pans, fill them one-half to two-thirds with the plain batter and then spoon some of the chocolate batter on top. Cover with the remaining plain batter, then gently swirl a metal spoon two or three times around the batter to create a marbled effect.

Pound cake may be sliced and served with *crème Chantilly* (see page 111) and fresh fruit or berries or a cooked fruit compote.

EVALUATING YOUR SUCCESS

The loaf should rise in the center during baking.

The split or crack on the top surface should run almost end-to-end in the finished cake.

The top surface should be nicely browned but not burned.

The cake should be moist and not too crumbly.

Demonstration

Cheesecake

Makes one 6-inch cake
Estimated time to complete: 90 minutes

Ingredients	Equipment
Butter for pan	6-inch round cake pan
	Standing electric mixer fitted with paddle attachment
For the batter	Rubber spatula
335 grams (11¼ ounces) cream cheese at room temperature	Bowl scraper
60 milliliters (2 ounces) sugar	Ovenproof pan at least 7.5 centimeters
35 grams (1¼ ounces) sour cream	(3 inches) larger than the cake pan
2 large eggs, at room temperature	Wire rack
60 grams (2 ounces) heavy cream	Small bowl
Zest of ½ orange	Wire whisk
Zest of ½ lemon	Handheld kitchen torch, optional
½ teaspoon pure vanilla extract	15-centimeter (6-inch) cardboard cake circle
	Offset spatula
For the finish	
70 grams (2½ ounces) sour cream	
4 grams (1 tablespoon) confectioners' sugar	
14 grams (2 tablespoons) cake or cookie crumbs, finely chopped toasted nuts, or chocolate curls (see page 407)	

Dean's Tip

"To neatly cut any cream cake, warm your knife in hot water and then dry it with a clean kitchen towel."

Dean André Soltner

Prepare your *mise en place*.

Preheat the oven to 149°C (300°F). Butter the interior of the pan. Set aside.

Combine the cream cheese and sugar in the bowl of a standing electric mixer fitted with the paddle attachment. Beat on low to just blend. Raise the speed to medium and beat for about 4 minutes, or until smooth and creamy. This is important; otherwise the baked cake will have undesirable lumps of cream cheese.

Add the sour cream and continue to beat, scraping down the sides of the bowl with a rubber spatula from time to time to ensure that the sour cream is completely incorporated and that the batter remains very smooth.

Reduce the speed to low and add the eggs one at a time, occasionally scraping down the sides of the bowl with a rubber spatula. The batter should be completely emulsified but not overmixed. If it is overmixed, particularly at higher speeds, too much air will be incorporated into the batter and the cake will rise as it bakes and fall as it cools.

Add the cream along with the orange and lemon zests and vanilla, beating to just combine.

Using a bowl scraper, scrape the batter into the prepared pan.

Place the cake pan in a larger pan on the middle rack of the preheated oven. Add enough warm water to come halfway up the sides of the filled cake pan.

Bake for about 1 hour, or until set in the center.

Place the cake pan on a wire rack to cool completely before unmolding. It can also be helpful to place the cooled cake in the refrigerator for about 1 hour to chill slightly before unmolding.

To finish the cake, combine the sour cream and confectioners' sugar in a small bowl, whisking to blend well.

Unmold the cake by warming the bottom of the pan,

either on the stovetop, with a handheld kitchen torch, or by placing it in warm water. At this point, the cake may be stored, well wrapped and refrigerated, for up to 1 week.

Place the cardboard cake circle on the top of the cake to completely cover it. Invert the cake onto the cardboard and gently tap to unmold.

Using an offset spatula, lightly coat the top of the cake with the sweetened sour cream, smoothing it to an even layer.

Coat the sides of the cake with crumbs, nuts, or chocolate curls.

Serve immediately or cover and refrigerate for no longer than 2 days.

TIPS
You may replace the citrus zest and vanilla with any flavoring you desire. A small amount—about 30 milliliters (2 tablespoons)—of alcohol such as amaretto works very well.

The cake should be completely cooled before unmolding. It is quite fragile and will fall apart if unmolded too quickly after baking.

To slice the cake, tightly hold a thin piece of fine string by each end and push the taut string down through the cake. Pull the string out of one side—*do not* lift it back up through the top.

To make marbled cheesecake, add approximately 100 grams (3½ ounces) cooled, melted unsweetened chocolate to one-third of the plain batter, stirring to combine well. Fill the pan with the plain batter, add the chocolate batter, and swirl it with a metal spoon.

EVALUATING YOUR SUCCESS
The top of the baked, unfinished cake should be smooth, with just a hint of color.

The interior of the baked cake should be smooth, with no large air pockets.

The baked cake should have a strong citrus flavor and a very creamy mouthfeel.

The sour cream topping should be very white and extremely smooth.

There should be just enough sweetener in the sour cream topping to cut the acidity.

The sides of the cake should be completely covered with the crumbs, nuts, or curls.

Demonstration

Neapolitan Cheesecake

Makes two 6-inch cakes
Estimated time to complete: 90 minutes

Ingredients	Equipment
Flour for dusting	Pastry cutter
	Two 6-inch round cake pans
For the batter	Standing electric mixer fitted with paddle attachment
1 recipe *Pâte Sucrée* (see page 94)	Rubber spatula
500 grams (1 pound, 1½ ounces) fresh ricotta cheese	Wooden spoon
165 grams (5¼ ounces) mascarpone cheese	Small bowl
110 grams (3¾ ounces) sugar	Pastry brush
3 large eggs, at room temperature	Wire racks
¾ teaspoon pure vanilla extract	
½ teaspoon orange-flower water	
55 grams (2 ounces) all-purpose flour	
100 grams (3½ ounces) raisins, soaked and well-drained	
50 grams (1¼ ounces) wheat berries, soaked for 24 hours and well drained	

For the finish
Egg wash (see page 62)

NOTE

Wheat berries are whole, hull-less wheat kernels. They may be either hard or soft processed grain and are composed of the bran, germ, and endosperm. When used in breads, muffins, salads, or other dishes, they are generally presoaked or even parboiled to soften. Otherwise, they are cooked as a whole-grain cereal or side dish.

Prepare your *mise en place*.

Preheat the oven to 149°C (300°F).

Lightly flour a clean, flat work surface. Using a pastry cutter, cut two 15-centimeter (6-inch) circles from the *pâte sucrée*. Reserve the remaining pastry for the lattice top.

Line the cake pans with the *pâte sucrée* circles. Set aside.

Combine the ricotta and mascarpone cheeses with the sugar in the bowl of a standing electric mixer fitted with the paddle attachment. Beat on low to just blend. Raise the speed to medium and beat for about 4 minutes, or until smooth and creamy. This is important; otherwise the baked cake will have undesirable lumps of cheese.

Reduce the speed to low and add the eggs one at a time, occasionally scraping down the sides of the

359

bowl with a rubber spatula. When the all the eggs have been added, blend in the vanilla and orange-flower water. The batter should be completely emulsified, but not overmixed. If it is overmixed, particularly at higher speeds, too much air will be incorporated into the batter and the cake will rise as it bakes and fall as it cools.

Remove the bowl from the mixer and, using a wooden spoon, stir in the flour. When blended, stir in the raisins and wheat berries.

When well combined, pour an equal portion of the cheese batter into each of the lined cake pans.

Using the pastry cutter, cut 19-millimeter-wide (¾-inch-wide) strips from the remaining *pâte sucrée*. Carefully make a lattice weave across the top of each cake, gently pressing the edges into the sides of the pan. Discard the excess pastry dough.

Place the egg wash in a small bowl and, using a pastry brush, lightly coat the latticed pastry with the egg wash. Do not allow the wash to drip onto the cake batter.

Bake the cakes for about 40 minutes, or until the pastry is golden brown and they are set in the center.

Place them on wire racks to cool completely. Cut the cooled cheesecakes into wedges or store, covered and refrigerated, for up to 2 days.

TIPS
If ricotta cheese is unavailable, substitute cottage cheese.

If mascarpone cheese is unavailable, substitute cream cheese.

You may replace the vanilla and orange-flower water with any flavoring you desire. A small amount—about 30 milliliters (2 tablespoons)—of alcohol such as amaretto works very well.

Other small pieces of dried or candied fruits may be substituted for the raisins.

EVALUATING YOUR SUCCESS
The lattice weave should be evenly spaced.

The interior of the baked cake should be smooth, with no large air pockets.

The baked cheesecake should have a creamy mouth-feel, with a slight hint of the ricotta curds and a strong citrus flavor.

Pastry Chef | Owner, DessertTruck, New York City
Jerome Chang | The French Culinary Institute, Class of October 2004

Goat Cheesecake with Rosemary, Caramel, Pistachio Crumble, and *Tuile*

Makes 15 single-serving cakes

I was inspired to create this dessert for DessertTruck after attending a fantastic goat cheese tasting at Murray's Cheese in New York City. My customers kept requesting a cheesecake, but I had always found the traditional one too heavy for my personal taste, especially during the steamy days of summer. The brightness, tanginess, and citrusy flavor of goat cheese offered the lightness that I was looking for in a new spring dessert. The rosemary caramel adds just a hint of spiciness and helps create a clean finish.

510 milliliters (16½ ounces) heavy cream
375 milliliters (12⅔ ounces) whole milk
315 grams (11⅛ ounces) sugar
¼ teaspoon salt
4½ sheets gelatin
900 grams (2 pounds) fresh goat cheese

Juice of 1½ lemons
Pistachio Crumble (recipe follows)
Rosemary Caramel (recipe follows)
200 grams (1 pint) blackberries
Pistachio *Tuiles* (recipe follows)

Combine the cream, milk, sugar, and salt in a large heavy-bottomed saucepan over medium heat. Bring to a simmer and immediately remove from the heat.

Place the gelatin in a small bowl. Add .95 liters (1 quart) water and allow the gelatin to soften.

Add the goat cheese to the warm cream mixture, allowing it to sit for a few minutes to soften. Then, using a handheld immersion blender, beat until very smooth.

Add the lemon juice along with the softened gelatin and blend to incorporate.

Pour an equal portion of the mixture into each of fifteen 210-milliliter (7-ounce) flexible silicone molds. Transfer the cakes to the freezer for 4 hours, or until firm.

About 30 minutes before you are ready to serve, place a Pistachio Crumble round on each of 15 dessert plates. Unmold the cheesecakes and place one on top of each round. Set aside to allow the cheesecake to thaw.

When ready to serve, drizzle each cake and the plate with the caramel, place a few blackberries around the plate, and stick a *tuile* in the top of each one.

Pistachio Crumble

200 grams (7 ounces) all-purpose flour
120 grams (4¼ ounces) sugar
50 grams (1¾ ounces) ground pistachios
1 teaspoon salt
225 grams (8 ounces) unsalted butter, chilled and cut into cubes

Place the flour, sugar, ground pistachios, and salt in the bowl of a food processor fitted with the metal blade. Add the butter and, using quick on and off turns, process to just combine. Add a teaspoon or two of cold water, if necessary.

Preheat the oven to 149°C (300°F).

Lightly flour a clean, flat work surface.

Using a rubber spatula, scrape the mixture from the processor bowl onto the floured surface. Use a rolling pin to lightly roll the mixture out to about 3 millimeters (⅛ inch) thick. Transfer it to a baking sheet and place it in the freezer for about 10 minutes, or until very firm.

Line a second baking sheet with parchment paper or a silicone baking liner.

Using a round ring mold or cookie cutter the same size as the diameter of your flexible molds, cut 15 dough rounds.

Using an offset spatula, carefully transfer the dough rounds to the prepared baking sheet. Bake for about 15 minutes, or until lightly browned around the edges and set in the center.

Transfer to wire racks to cool.

Rosemary Caramel

270 grams (9½ ounces) sugar
30 grams (1 ounce) light corn syrup
3½ sprigs fresh rosemary

Combine the sugar and corn syrup with 370 milliliters (12½ ounces) cold water in a medium heavy-bottomed saucepan. Bring to a boil and immediately remove from the heat. Add 3 sprigs of the rosemary, cover, and set aside to infuse for at least 8 hours, or overnight.

Place the remaining ½ sprig of rosemary in a bowl with 125 grams (4½ ounces) water and let infuse for at least 8 hours, or overnight.

Return the rosemary-infused sugar syrup to the stove over medium-high heat. Bring to a boil and then lower the heat and simmer for about 15 minutes, or until the syrup is a light amber color.

Slowly whisk in the rosemary-infused water and when it is incorporated, remove the syrup from the heat.

Set aside to cool. The caramel syrup may be stored at room temperature, covered, for 2 to 3 months.

Pistachio *Tuiles*

250 grams (8¾ ounces) egg whites
375 grams (13¼ ounces) confectioners' sugar
200 grams (7 ounces) all-purpose flour, sifted
250 grams (8¾ ounces) melted, unsalted butter
Approximately 50 grams (1¾ ounces) chopped
  pistachios

Prepare your *mise en place*.

Preheat the oven to 162°C (325°F).

Line 2 baking sheets with silicone liners. Set aside.

Choose a saucepan large enough to hold a medium heat-proof bowl snugly into it and fill it with about 7.5 centimeters (3 inches) of water. Place it over high heat and bring to a boil. Immediately remove the pan from the heat.

Place the egg whites in the heat-proof bowl. Whisk in the sugar and place the bowl over the hot water, taking care that the bottom doesn't touch the water and whisking until the egg white mixture is warm to the touch.

Remove from the heat and whisk in the flour.

Transfer the mixture to the bowl of a standing electric mixer fitted with the paddle attachment. With the motor on low, gradually add the melted butter.

Using a metal spoon, drop the batter by the tablespoonful onto the lined baking sheets, leaving about 5 centimeters (2 inches) between each cookie to allow for spreading.

Sprinkle the top of each *tuile* with chopped pistachios.

Bake the *tuiles* for 7 to 10 minutes, or until paper-thin and nicely browned.

Transfer them to wire racks to cool.

Alternatively, using an offset spatula, transfer the hot cookies to a *tuile* mold or rolling pin so that they drape over to form a rounded tile shape. As soon as the cookie sets, transfer it to a wire rack to cool completely. Handle the baked *tuiles* carefully, as they are very fragile.

If the *tuiles* harden on the baking sheet before being shaped, return them to the oven for a minute or so to soften.

Demonstration

Chocolate Cupcakes

Makes 12 cupcakes
Estimated time to complete: 1 hour

Ingredients	Equipment
Butter and flour for molds	12-cup cupcake mold or muffin tin
	Sifter
For the batter	Large mixing bowl
225 grams (8 ounces) sugar	Medium saucepan
200 grams (7 ounces) cake flour	Wire whisk
¾ teaspoon baking soda	Wooden spoon
¼ teaspoon salt	Metal spoon
80 grams (2¾ ounces) unsalted butter, at room temperature	Cake tester
80 grams (2¾ ounces) vegetable oil	Wire racks
65 grams (2¼ ounces) Dutch process-cocoa powder	Small saucepan
1 large whole egg, at room temperature	
1 large egg yolk, at room temperature	
175 grams (6⅛ ounces) buttermilk	
1 teaspoon pure vanilla extract	
For the icing	
110 grams (3¾ ounces) unsalted butter, at room temperature	
40 milliliters (1⅓ ounces) heavy cream	
100 grams (3½ ounces) confectioners' sugar	
6 grams (2 teaspoons) Dutch-process cocoa powder	

Prepare your *mise en place*.

Preheat the oven to 177°C (350°F).

Butter and flour the muffin pan.

Sift the sugar, flour, baking soda, and salt together into a large mixing bowl. Set aside.

Combine the butter, oil, and cocoa powder with 175 milliliters (6⅛ ounces) water in a medium saucepan over medium heat. Cook, whisking constantly with a wire whisk, for about 3 minutes, or until the butter has melted and the cocoa powder has completely dissolved into the liquid. Do not let the mixture get too hot or boil or the eggs will cook when added to the batter.

Pour the warm liquid over the dry ingredients and, using a wooden spoon, stir to blend well. Stir in the egg and egg yolk, along with the buttermilk and vanilla. Do not overmix or the baked cupcakes will be tough.

Spoon an equal portion of the batter into each of the prepared muffin cups.

Bake the cupcakes for about 10 minutes, or until a cake tester inserted into the center comes out clean and the top springs back when gently touched.

Immediately unmold the cupcakes and turn them right side up onto wire racks to cool. At this point, they may be stored, covered and refrigerated, for up to 2 days, or frozen for up to 1 month.

While the cupcakes are cooling, make the icing.

Combine the butter and cream with the confectioners' sugar and cocoa powder in a small saucepan over medium heat. Cook, stirring constantly with a wooden spoon, for about 4 minutes or until well blended.

Set the icing aside to cool until it is thick enough to hold together. Stir occasionally to speed the cooling and to test for consistency.

Holding the cooled cupcakes by the bottom, gently dip the top of each one into the cooled icing to just cover the domed top. Do not allow the icing to drip down over the sides.

Serve immediately or within a few hours.

TIPS
Alternatively, the cupcakes may be baked in tins lined with paper muffin cups.

Dipping the cupcakes into the icing is a time-efficient technique for finishing.

If you want to spread the icing instead, refrigerate it for about 15 minutes, then beat vigorously with a wire whisk until thick enough to spread.

The cupcakes may be decorated with cocoa nibs, colored sprinkles, chopped nuts, grated toasted coconut, or in fact with whatever décor you prefer.

EVALUATING YOUR SUCCESS
The baked cupcakes should have an even rise, with a domed center.

The crumb should be tight, moist, and dark brown.

There should be no large holes or air pockets in the interior of the cupcakes.

The baked cupcakes should have a strong, sweet chocolate flavor.

Demonstration

Pecan Coffee Cake

Makes one 9-inch cake
Estimated time to complete: 1 hour

Ingredients	Equipment

Ingredients

Butter and flour for the pan

For the topping

130 grams (4⅔ ounces) pecans, coarsely chopped

110 grams (3¾ ounces) light brown sugar

65 grams (2¼ ounces) all-purpose flour

10 milliliters (2 teaspoons) pure vanilla extract

50 grams (1¾ ounces) unsalted butter, at room temperature

For the batter

330 grams (11⅔ ounces) all-purpose flour

1 teaspoon baking powder

½ teaspoon baking soda

Pinch salt

150 grams (5⅓ ounces) sugar

2 large eggs, at room temperature

220 grams (7¾ ounces) sour cream

150 grams (5⅓ ounces) unsalted butter, melted and cooled slightly

1 teaspoon pure vanilla extract

For the finish

Confectioners' sugar for dusting, optional

Equipment

9-inch round cake pan

2 medium mixing bowls

Pastry cutter or kitchen fork

Sifter

Wooden spoon

Cake tester

Wire rack

Prepare your *mise en place*.

Preheat the oven to 162°C (325°F).

Butter and flour the pan. Set aside.

Place the pecans, brown sugar, flour, and vanilla in a medium mixing bowl. Add the butter and, using a pastry cutter or kitchen fork, cut the butter into the pecan mixture until coarse crumbs form. Set aside. The crumb topping may be stored, tightly covered and refrigerated, for up to 4 days.

Sift the flour, baking powder, baking soda, and salt together. Set aside.

Combine the sugar with the eggs, sour cream, melted butter, and vanilla in a medium mixing bowl, and, using a wooden spoon, stir to just combine. Add the reserved flour mixture, stirring just to blend; do not overmix.

Pour the batter into the prepared pan. Top with the reserved crumb mixture and bake for about 45 minutes, or until a cake tester inserted in the center comes out clean.

Set the cake on a wire rack to cool slightly before cutting.

If desired, the cake may be lightly dusted with confectioners' sugar before serving.

TIPS

Do not combine the wet and dry ingredients until just before you are ready to bake. Chemical leaveners such as baking powder and baking soda immediately react when exposed to an acid ingredient like sour cream. If that happens too soon, the leavening agents will be spent and the baked cake will be dense and tough.

EVALUATING YOUR SUCCESS

The crumbs should be fairly large and crunchy.

The pecans should taste fresh and lightly toasted.

The interior of the cake should be moist with a medium crumb, but not tough and dense.

The finished cake should be completely baked through but not dry.

The cake should have a distinct vanilla flavor and aroma.

Demonstration
Lemon Cake

Makes one 9-by-5-by-2½-inch loaf
Estimated time to complete: 90 minutes

Ingredients	Equipment
Butter and flour for the pan	9-by-5-by-2½-inch loaf pan
	Sifter
For the batter	Medium mixing bowl
220 grams (7¾ ounces) cake flour	Wooden spoon
1 teaspoon baking powder	Kitchen knife
4 large eggs, at room temperature	Cake tester
200 grams (7 ounces) granulated sugar	Small bowl
105 milliliters (3½ ounces) heavy cream	Small heavy-bottomed saucepan
100 grams (3½ ounces) unsalted butter, melted and cooled slightly	Wire rack
Zest and *suprêmes* (see page 37) of 2 lemons	Small baking pan
For the glaze	
200 grams (7 ounces) fresh lemon juice, strained	
180 grams (6⅓ ounces) confectioners' sugar	
100 grams (3½ ounces) *fondant glacé* (see page 229)	

Prepare your *mise en place*.

Preheat the oven to 162°C (325°F).

Butter and flour the loaf pan. Set aside.

Sift the flour and baking powder together. Set aside. Combine the eggs and sugar in a medium mixing bowl and, using a wooden spoon, stir to blend well. Stir in the cream.

Add the reserved flour mixture, stirring to just combine; do not overmix. Quickly stir in the melted butter, along with the lemon *suprêmes* and zest.

Pour the batter into the prepared pan and bake for 20 minutes. Open the oven door and run a kitchen knife down the center of the loaf. This will create an even split down the center of the baked cake. Continue baking for about 40 minutes, or until the top is golden brown and a cake tester inserted in the center comes out clean. Just before the cake has finished baking, prepare the glaze.

Combine the lemon juice and confectioners' sugar in a small bowl, stirring with a wooden spoon to dissolve the sugar. Set aside.

Place the fondant in a small heavy-bottomed saucepan over low heat. Cook, stirring constantly, for about 3 minutes, or until melted.

Remove the fondant from the heat and stir the reserved lemon juice mixture into it. Set aside.

Place the cake on a wire rack to cool for about 10 minutes. Do not turn the oven off.

Unmold the cake and place it in a small baking pan. Slowly pour the warm fondant glaze over the cake, allowing it to soak in.

When all the glaze has soaked in, return the cake to the hot oven. Bake for 10 minutes to set the glaze. Remove it from the oven and serve warm, or return it to the wire rack to cool. The cooled cake can be stored, tightly wrapped and refrigerated, for up to 1 week, or frozen for up to 1 month.

TIPS

Do not whip the eggs and sugar, as too much air will be incorporated into the batter giving the baked cake an undesirable texture.

Since the cake takes a long time to bake, the top may get too brown before the cake is finished. If so, loosely cover the top with aluminum foil until the cake is baked through.

EVALUATING YOUR SUCCESS

The loaf should have an even rise in the center.

The surface of the baked cake should be golden brown but not burned.

The split or crack down the center of the baked cake should run almost end to end.

The interior of the cake should be moist and not too crumbly.

Demonstration

White Cake

Makes two 6-inch cakes
Estimated time to complete: 90 minutes

Ingredients

Flour and butter for pans
90 grams (3¼ ounces) egg whites, at room temperature
170 milliliters (5⅔ ounces) whole milk
8 milliliters (1½ teaspoons) pure vanilla extract
200 grams (7 ounces) cake flour, sifted
200 grams (7 ounces) sugar
13 grams (1 tablespoon) baking powder
½ teaspoon salt
115 grams (4 ounces) unsalted butter, softened

Equipment

Two 6-inch round cake pans
Two 6-inch round pieces parchment paper
Small mixing bowl
Wooden spoon
Standing electric mixer fitted with paddle attachment
Bowl scraper
Cake tester
Wire racks

Prepare your *mise en place*.

Arrange two oven racks toward the center of the oven with about 7.5 centimeters (3 inches) between them.

Preheat the oven to 177°C (350°F).

Butter and flour the cake pans. Line the bottom of each with a circle of parchment paper. Set aside.

Combine the egg whites with the milk and vanilla in small mixing bowl and, using a wooden spoon, stir to blend.

Combine the flour, sugar, baking powder, and salt in the bowl of a standing electric mixer fitted with the paddle attachment. Beat on low to just blend. Add the butter and one-third of the egg white mixture and beat on low just until the batter has moistened and gathers into a paste. Raise the speed to medium and beat for 90 seconds to develop structure. Using a bowl scraper, scrape down the sides of the bowl.

Add the remaining egg white mixture in 3 batches, beating for 20 seconds and scraping down the sides of the bowl after each addition.

Pour an equal portion of the batter into each of the prepared pans.

Place the pans in the preheated oven so that they do not touch each other and air can move freely around them as they bake. Bake for about 30 minutes, or until the cakes are golden brown and a cake tester inserted into the center comes out clean. The cakes will also shrink away slightly from the edges of the pans.

Place the pans on wire racks to cool for 10 minutes. Then, invert the pans and unmold the cakes onto the racks to finish cooling.

When they are completely cool, use them as directed in a specific recipe or store, tightly wrapped and refrigerated, for up to 5 days, or frozen for up to 2 months.

TIPS
This is an adaptation of a cake featured in *The Cake Bible*, by Rose Levy Berenbaum.

If you plan to create a finished cake that will be assembled in advance, sprinkle the cake with simple syrup (see page 499) to keep it moist.

EVALUATING YOUR SUCCESS
The cake should dome in the center during baking.

The baked cake should be sweet and moist, with a very fine, white crumb.

There should be no wet or dark portions in the interior of the cake.

Pastry Chef Michelle Doll | *Owner, Michelle Doll Cakes, New York*
The French Culinary Institute, Class of December 2004

Moist Pumpkin Cake

Makes one 8-inch layer cake

I always get the same reaction when I make this cake: a lukewarm "oh" when I say what it is, then people try it and it's "OHHHHHHH." Pumpkin cake may not sound super sexy, but the amazing texture and moisture in this one makes it a cake to die for. Add the cream cheese frosting and you have a sensation!

Butter and flour for pans
250 grams (8¾ ounces) cake flour
10 grams (2 teaspoons) baking powder
1½ teaspoons ground cinnamon

½ teaspoon ground cardamom
½ teaspoon ground allspice
½ teaspoon baking soda
½ teaspoon salt

390 grams (13¾ ounces) solid-pack canned pumpkin
60 milliliters (2 ounces) buttermilk
170 grams (6 ounces) unsalted butter, at room temperature
300 grams (11 ounces) sugar

3 large eggs, at room temperature
1 vanilla bean, split lengthwise
Cream Cheese Frosting (recipe follows)

Preheat the oven to 177°C (350°F).

Butter and flour two 20-centimeter (8-inch) round cake pans. Set aside.

Sift the flour, baking powder, cinnamon, cardamom, allspice, baking soda, and salt together. Set aside.

Combine the pumpkin and buttermilk in a small mixing bowl, stirring to blend completely.

Place the butter in the bowl of a standing electric mixer fitted with the paddle attachment. Beat on low to soften and then raise the speed to medium and beat until fluffy.

Gradually add the sugar and beat until light and fluffy. Add the eggs one at a time, beating well after each addition. Using a rubber spatula, scrape down the sides of the bowl from time to time.

Stop the mixer and, using a paring knife, scrape the seeds from the vanilla pod into the butter-and-sugar mixture. Beat to blend.

With the mixer on the lowest speed, add the sifted dry ingredients alternately with the pumpkin mixture, beginning and ending with the dry ingredients. Using a rubber spatula, scrape down the sides of the bowl from time to time.

Scrape an equal portion of the batter into each of the prepared pans, smoothing down the surface with the spatula.

Bake the cakes for about 30 minutes, or until a cake tester inserted into the center comes out clean.

Remove the cakes from the oven, invert them onto wire racks, and lift off the pans. Let cool.

Cut each cooled cake crosswise through the center to make two equal layers.

Place one layer, cut side up, on a cake plate. Using an offset spatula, spread about 115 milliliters (½ cup) frosting over the cut side. Top with a second cake layer and spread about 115 milliliters (½ cup) frosting over it. Top with the third layer and again spread frosting over the surface. Top with the final cake layer and, using the remaining frosting, coat top and sides of the entire cake with an even layer of frosting.

Cover the cake with a cake dome and refrigerate until ready to serve, or for up to 1 day. Remove the cake from the refrigerator and let it stand for 1 hour before cutting into wedges and serving.

Cream Cheese Frosting
Makes 700 grams (1½ pounds)

560 grams (1¼ pound) cream cheese, at room temperature
250 grams (8¾ ounces) confectioners' sugar
60 grams (2 ounces) unsalted butter, at room temperature
½ teaspoon ground cinnamon
¼ teaspoon ground allspice
¼ teaspoon ground cardamom

Combine the cream cheese and sugar in the bowl of a standing electric mixer fitted with the paddle attachment. Beat on low to just combine. Then, raise the speed to medium and beat until very light and fluffy. Add the butter along with the cinnamon, allspice, and cardamom and continue to beat until well incorporated.

Use as directed in the recipe.

Theory

Decorating and Filling Cakes

Although many cakes are delicious on their own or with just a dollop of *crème Chantilly*, there is nothing more enticing than a beautifully iced, filled, and decorated *gâteau*. It is with these that the pastry chef can display creativity, artistry, and style.

There are many, many variations on the types of icings (also called frostings), fillings, and decorations that can be used to finish a cake. Some are classically defined, while others are innovative ideas from contemporary pastry chefs.

In the following pages, you will find some of the classic products used to finish and decorate French *gâteaux*. Once you have mastered them, only the limits of your imagination will define the beauty of your cake.

An Introduction to *Crème au Beurre* (Buttercream)

Crème au beurre, or buttercream, is a smooth, light icing that is used over and over again in the pastry kitchen. It is an essential element, not only as an icing but also as a filling or decoration for all types of cakes and pastries. Generally made from a mixture of fat and sugar, buttercreams may also contain eggs, which will further increase their lightness. They can be easily varied with the addition of many different flavorings and colorings, which are always added last. The flavoring is usually done according to the personal preference of the pastry chef.

Unsalted, or sweet, butter is preferred when making a buttercream. Obviously, the higher the quality, the better the finished product. Many pastry chefs substitute vegetable shortening or margarine to increase stability and shelf life; however, because of their higher melting point these products leave an unpleasant coating on the palate when eaten and have no place in fine pastry making.

In almost all cases, buttercreams can be made in advance of use and stored, tightly covered and refrigerated, for up to a couple of weeks, or frozen for longer periods of time. The high sugar content inhibits bacterial growth. Cold buttercream must be brought to room temperature before using. It will also often need to be beaten in a *bain-marie* over heat to restore its sheen and creaminess.

Although there are many variations on the basic formula of butter, sugar, eggs, and flavorings for making buttercream, in this text we cover only three:

Crème au Beurre I (*Pâte à Bombe*–based Buttercream)

This type of buttercream is also known as French or common buttercream. It is made by beating hot syrup into eggs or egg yolks to create a base mix known as *pâte à bombe*. Butter is then whipped into it to create a very luxe, light icing. It has a pale yellow tinge and is the richest of all buttercreams.

Crème au Beurre II (Buttercream II, or Italian Buttercream)

This simple, extremely light mixture of butter and meringue is often called a meringue-based buttercream. It is made by whipping softened, unsalted butter into an Italian meringue. It is very white and lighter than a yolk-based buttercream. Another meringue-based buttercream can be made with Swiss meringue, following the same procedure.

Crème Mousseline (Light Buttercream)

In its most basic form, this is a buttercream created by whipping an equal amount of softened, unsalted butter into *crème pâtissière*. In some recipes, a lesser amount of butter may be added and gelatin may be used to ensure the necessary stability to the finished icing. Confectioners' sugar is sometimes added for additional sweetness.

You may also find that some pastry chefs refer to "decorator's icing" or "decorator's buttercream." Sometimes these terms describe the *pâte à bombe*–based buttercream, but as often as not, it refers to an icing made from vegetable shortening and confectioners' sugar that is used to make extremely stable cake decorations such as flowers and leaves, for mass-produced cakes or for cakes that might have to stand for a long period of time at room temperature. It may also be called "rose paste."

Demonstration

Crème au Beurre I (*Pâte à Bombe*–based Buttercream)

Makes 1 kilogram (2¼ pounds)

Estimated time to complete: 30 minutes

Ingredients	Equipment
400 grams (14 ounces) sugar	Heavy-bottomed saucepan
5 large egg yolks, at room temperature	Wooden spoon

1 large whole egg, at room temperature

700 grams (1½ pounds) unsalted butter, cut into pieces,
 at room temperature

Pastry brush

Candy thermometer

Standing electric mixer fitted with whip and paddle attachments

Prepare your *mise en place*.

Combine the sugar with 150 milliliters (5 ounces) water in a medium heavy-bottomed saucepan, stirring with a wooden spoon until the mixture is the consistency of wet sand.

Using a wet pastry brush, clean all the sugar crystals from the sides of the pan to prevent the sugar syrup from crystallizing during cooking.

Place the saucepan over medium heat and cook, without stirring, for about 10 minutes or until the syrup reaches 116°C (240°F/soft-ball stage) on a candy thermometer. It is important that the syrup cook, undisturbed, as stirring might cause it to crystallize.

Prepare a *pâte à bombe*. Combine the egg yolks and egg in the bowl of a standing electric mixer fitted with the whip attachment. Beat on low to blend. Then, raise the speed and beat on medium until thick and pale yellow.

As soon as the syrup reaches the soft-ball stage, carefully and slowly and with the motor running, pour the hot syrup down the sides of the sides of the bowl. Do not let the syrup hit the whip or it may splatter and burn your skin. Beat for a few minutes, or until the mixture is cool, very smooth, and thick.

Remove the whip attachment and replace it with the paddle attachment. Add the butter, a bit at a time, and beat until all of it has been incorporated and the mixture is very smooth.

If a flavoring is required, beat it in after the butter has been incorporated.

Use the buttercream as directed in a specific recipe or store it, airtight, for up to 2 weeks in the refrigerator, or for up to 1 month in the freezer.

Buttercream may be stored, airtight, for a long period of time as the high sugar content inhibits bacterial growth.

TIPS

Since the eggs cannot be overbeaten, it is a good idea to start whipping before cooking the sugar.

The butter may be softened in the mixing bowl using the paddle attachment before preparing the *pâte à bombe*. If you do this, whip the *pâte à bombe* until it is body temperature before adding the butter.

If the butter is not softened, cube the cold butter and add it to the still-warm *pâte à bombe*. Be aware, however, that if the *pâte à bombe* is too hot, it will melt the butter and render the final buttercream soupy and unusable. If it is too cold, the butter will not incorporate properly, and the final buttercream will be unusable.

The finished buttercream may be flavored with a small amount of extracts, melted chocolate, nut pastes, or alcohol. All flavorings should be added to the baker's taste. Take care when flavoring with alcohol because if too much is added to the finished buttercream, it will break the emulsification.

If the finished buttercream is too soft or soupy, try chilling it for several minutes and then beating it again with the paddle attachment to see if it will reach the proper consistency.

If the finished buttercream is too stiff or appears separated and grainy, try heating the bowl containing it with a handheld propane torch over a *bain-marie* or an open flame. When it is slightly warm, again beat it with the paddle attachment to see if it will reach the proper consistency.

EVALUATING YOUR SUCCESS

The finished buttercream should be sweet and rich,

with a light yellow color (prior to the addition of any flavoring).

The finished buttercream should be shiny, easy to spread,

and smooth, with no sugar crystals or butter lumps.

There should be no visible air pockets. Any added flavoring should be distinct and strong.

Demonstration

Crème au Beurre II (Buttercream II or Italian Buttercream)

Makes 700 grams (1½ pounds)
Estimated time to complete: 30 minutes

Ingredients	Equipment
For the buttercream	Heavy-bottomed saucepan
300 grams (11 ounces) sugar	Wooden spoon
	Pastry brush
For the French meringue	Candy thermometer
150 grams (5⅓ ounces) egg whites, at room temperature	Standing electric mixer fitted with paddle attachment
75 grams (2⅔ ounces) sugar	
455 grams (1 pound) unsalted butter, cut into pieces, at room temperature	

Prepare your *mise en place*.

Combine the sugar with 150 milliliters (5⅓ ounces) water in a medium heavy-bottomed saucepan, stirring with a wooden spoon until the mixture is the consistency of wet sand.

Using a wet pastry brush, clean all the sugar crystals from the sides of the pan to prevent the sugar syrup from crystallizing during cooking.

Place the saucepan over medium heat and cook without stirring for about 10 minutes, or until the syrup reaches 116°C (240°F/soft-ball stage) on a candy thermometer. It is important that the syrup cooks undisturbed, as stirring might cause it to crystallize.

Meanwhile, prepare the French meringue.

Place the egg whites in the bowl of a standing electric mixer fitted with the whip attachment. Beat on low to aerate. Add the remaining sugar, raise the speed to high, and beat for about 5 minutes or until soft peaks form. Set aside.

As soon as the syrup reaches the soft-ball stage, carefully and slowly and with the motor running, pour the hot syrup down the sides of the sides of the bowl. Do not let the syrup hit the whip or it may splatter and burn your skin. Beat for a few minutes or until the mixture is cool and very smooth and thick.

Remove the whip attachment and replace it with the paddle attachment. Add the butter, a bit at a time, and beat until all of it has been incorporated and the mixture is very smooth.

If a flavoring is required, beat it in after the butter has been incorporated.

Use the buttercream as directed in a specific recipe or store it, airtight, for up to 2 weeks in the refrigerator, or for up to 1 month in the freezer.

TIPS
The butter may be softened in the mixing bowl using the paddle attachment before preparing the meringue. If you do this, whip the meringue until it is body temperature before adding the butter.

If the butter is not softened, cube it and add it to the still-warm meringue. Be aware, however, that if the egg mixture is too hot, it will melt the butter and render the final buttercream soupy and unusable. If it is too cold, the butter will not incorporate properly, and the final buttercream will be unusable.

The finished buttercream may be flavored with a small amount of extracts, melted chocolate, nut pastes, or alcohol. All should be added to the baker's taste. Take care when flavoring with alcohol because if too much is added to the finished buttercream, it will break the emulsification.

If the finished buttercream is too soft or soupy, try chilling it for several minutes and then beating it again with the paddle attachment to see if it will reach the proper consistency.

If the finished buttercream is too stiff or appears separated and grainy, try heating the bowl containing it with a handheld propane torch over a *bain-marie* or an open flame. When it is slightly warm, again beat it with the paddle attachment to see if it will reach the proper consistency.

EVALUATING YOUR SUCCESS
The finished buttercream should be sweet and rich, with a light yellow color (prior to the addition of any flavoring).

The finished buttercream should be shiny, easy to spread, and smooth, with no sugar crystals or butter lumps.

There should be no visible air pockets.

Any added flavoring should be distinct and strong.

Demonstration

Crème Mousseline (Light Buttercream)

Makes 1.5 kilograms (3¼ pounds)
Estimated time to complete: 40 minutes

Ingredients	Equipment
1,135 grams (2½ pounds) freshly made, still-warm *Crème Pâtissière* (see page 248) 340 grams (12 ounces) unsalted butter, cut into pieces, at room temperature	Standing electric mixer fitted with paddle attachment Rubber spatula

Prepare your *mise en place*.

If the pastry cream is very warm, place it in the bowl of a standing electric mixer fitted with the paddle attachment and beat on medium for a few minutes to cool it slightly.

With the motor running, add the butter, a bit at a time, beating until it is completely incorporated and the mixture is very light and fluffy, scraping down the sides of the bowl occasionally with a rubber spatula.

Use the buttercream as directed in a specific recipe as soon as possible after it is prepared—it is best when used immediately.

TIPS
Crème mousseline, a lightened buttercream, is the filling used in a classic French *fraisier* (see page 422), a sponge cake filled with the buttercream and decorated with fresh strawberries.

Only make as much *mousseline* as will be used immediately. If you do have any left over, it will have to be refrigerated, heated, and beaten again with the paddle until light and fluffy before being used.

The butter cannot be added if the pastry cream is still very hot, or it will melt and separate. If this does occur, finish beating, then refrigerate the *mousseline* until it is well chilled and beat again to emulsify.

If the pastry cream is too cold, the butter will not incorporate. If this occurs, warm the pastry cream and then beat until the butter blends into it.

Once chilled, *crème mousseline* becomes very firm. This makes it an excellent choice as a filling for cakes that must be left unrefrigerated for a long time or that are to be served in a warm environment.

Fruit-flavored *mousseline* may be made by substituting fruit purée for the milk in the pastry cream recipe. Follow the above instructions as written.

EVALUATING YOUR SUCCESS
The finished *mousseline* should be light and fluffy.

A Few Words about Ganache

Ganache is nothing more than hot heavy cream and fine-quality chocolate, known as *couverture*, with no more than 32 percent butterfat beaten to a luscious, velvety smoothness. Occasionally, flavorings or butter are added to this basic blend. *Ganache* is used as an icing or filling for cakes, pastries, and tarts, as well as a filling for bonbons. When applied while still warm, it can also be used to glaze cakes or pastries.

As with all pastry items, the better the quality of your ingredients, the better the finished product, so it is recommended that you choose only the finest-quality chocolate.

Demonstration

Ganache

Makes 1 kilogram (2¼ pounds)
Estimated time to prepare: 90 minutes

Ingredients	Equipment
500 grams (1 pound, 1½ ounces) semisweet or bittersweet chocolate, chopped into small pieces	Medium heavy-bottomed saucepan
	Wooden spoon
500 milliliters (16½ ounces) heavy cream	Rubber spatula
	Plastic film
	Standing electric mixer fitted with paddle attachment

Prepare your *mise en place*.

Place the chocolate in a medium stainless-steel bowl. Set aside.

Place the cream in a medium heavy-bottomed saucepan over medium-low heat. Bring it to a bare boil, watching carefully. Bubbles should form around the edge of the pan, but the cream should not vigorously bubble.

Remove the cream from the heat and pour it over the chocolate. Let stand for a minute or two to allow the hot cream to soften the chocolate.

Using a wooden spoon, stir the chocolate into the cream, beating until the mixture is completely smooth and homogeneous. Scrape down the sides of the bowl with a rubber spatula.

Allow the bowl to sit for about an hour to come to room temperature, stirring occasionally to ensure that the chocolate is completely melted.

When it is cool, cover with plastic film and refrigerate for 8 hours or up to 5 days, or freeze for up to 1 month. Thaw frozen *ganache* before beating it to finish.

When you are ready to use the *ganache*, place the chilled mixture in the bowl of a standing electric mixer fitted with the paddle attachment and beat for about 5 minutes, or until light and fluffy. Do not beat too much or the *ganache* will become grainy, or too firm to spread, or it may separate.

Use as directed in a specific recipe.

Chopping the chocolate into small pieces (or using *pistoles* or chocolate bits), hastens the melting process.

It is best to make the *ganache* at least one day in advance of use so it has the opportunity to chill thoroughly. If you make it at the last minute, pour it into a large, flat pan or container and refrigerate for an hour or two, until well chilled.

If the beaten *ganache* seems too loose, beat for an additional couple of minutes.

Ganache Pour l'Opéra (Opéra Cake Ganache): Follow the directions above using 400 grams (14 ounces) bittersweet or semisweet chocolate and 342 milliliters (11⅓ ounces) heavy cream.

EVALUATING YOUR SUCCESS
The finished *ganache* should be firm enough to easily spread and set on a cake.

The finished *ganache* should be smooth, with no discrete pieces of chocolate; it should not be grainy or curdled.

The finished *ganache* should be dark brown and airy in texture, with a very strong chocolate flavor.

Demonstration

Ganache Légère (Light *Ganache*)

Makes 1.4 kilograms (3 pounds)
Estimated time to complete: Up to 2 hours

Ingredients	Equipment
455 grams (1 pound) semisweet or bittersweet chocolate, chopped into small pieces	Medium stainless-steel bowl
940 milliliters (1 quart) heavy cream	Medium heavy-bottomed saucepan
	Wooden spoon
	Rubber spatula
	Plastic film
	Standing electric mixer fitted with paddle attachment

Prepare your *mise en place*.

Place the chocolate in a medium stainless-steel bowl. Set aside.

Place the cream in a medium heavy-bottomed saucepan over medium-low heat. Bring it to a bare boil, watching carefully. Bubbles should form around the edge of the pan, but the cream should not vigorously bubble.

Remove the cream from the heat and pour it over the chocolate. Let stand for a minute or two to allow the hot cream to soften the chocolate.

Using a wooden spoon, stir the chocolate into the cream, beating until the mixture is completely smooth and homogeneous. Scrape down the sides of the bowl with a rubber spatula.

Allow the bowl to sit for about an hour to come to room temperature, stirring occasionally to ensure that the chocolate is completely melted.

Use as directed in a specific recipe, or cover the cooled *ganache* with plastic film and refrigerate for

8 hours or up to 5 days, or freeze for up to 1 month. Thaw frozen *ganache* before beating it to finish.

When you are ready to use it, place the chilled *ganache* in the bowl of a standing electric mixer fitted with the paddle attachment and beat for about 5 minutes, or until light and fluffy. Do not beat too much or the *ganache* will become grainy or too firm to spread, or it may separate.

Use as directed in a specific recipe.

TIPS

Chopping the chocolate into small pieces (or using *pistoles* or chocolate bits), hastens the melting process.

It is best to make the *ganache* at least one day in advance of use so it has the opportunity to chill thoroughly. If you make it at the last minute, pour it into a large, flat pan or container and refrigerate for an hour or two, or until well chilled.

If the beaten *ganache* seems too loose, beat it for an additional couple of minutes.

EVALUATING YOUR SUCCESS

The finished *ganache* should be firm enough to easily spread and set on a cake.

The finished *ganache* should be smooth, with no discrete pieces of chocolate; it should not be grainy or curdled.

The finished *ganache* should be light brown and airy in texture, with a strong chocolate flavor.

Demonstration

Glaçage au Chocolat (Chocolate Glaze)

Makes 795 grams (1¾ pounds)
Estimated time to complete: 45 minutes

Ingredients	Equipment
455 grams (1 pound) semisweet or bittersweet chocolate, chopped into small pieces	Heat-proof bowl
330 grams (11⅔ ounces) unsalted butter, at room temperature	Saucepan large enough to hold the bowl
30 milliliters (2 tablespoons) light corn syrup	Wooden spoon

Prepare your *mise en place*.

Fill a saucepan large enough to allow your heat-proof bowl to fit snugly into it without touching the water with about 7.5 centimeters (3 inches) of water. Place it over high heat and bring to a boil. Immediately remove the pan from the heat.

Combine the chocolate, butter, and corn syrup in the heat-proof bowl and, using a wooden spoon, stir to blend. Quickly place the bowl into the pan, checking to make sure that the bottom is not resting in the hot water and immediately begin stirring. Heat just until the chocolate is partially melted.

Remove the bowl from the heat and continue to stir until the glaze is perfectly blended, with no evidence of separation and no lumps.

Set aside to cool to body temperature. This is important, because if the glaze is too hot, it will not only be too thin to use, it will melt the icing on the cake. If it is too cool, it will set too quickly and drips will form on the sides of the cake.

Use the glaze as directed in a specific recipe, or store it, covered and refrigerated, for up to 5 days. Reheat and stir to blend before using.

TIPS

Chopping the chocolate into small pieces (or using pistoles or chocolate bits), hastens the melting process.

When melting chocolate, always use a *bain-marie*, the glaze burns easily when exposed to direct heat.

Any excess glaze that runs off the cake can be remelted and reused.

Glacé au Chocolat Pour L'Opéra (**Chocolate Glaze for *Opéra* Cake**): Follow the directions above using 300 grams (11 ounces) *pâte à glacer* (a commercially prepared chocolate glaze available from cake supply stores that adds a very smooth texture and glossy sheen to a glaze), 90 grams (3 ¼ ounces) semisweet chocolate, 60 grams (2 ounces) unsweetened chocolate, and 45 milliliters (3 tablespoons) vegetable oil.

EVALUATING YOUR SUCCESS

The finished glaze should be dark brown, shiny, and just thick enough to be opaque.

A Few Words about Royal Icing

Royal icing is used as a decorating medium, as it hardens to a dry consistency. It can be tinted with and used to create long-lasting flowers, birds, leaves, and other decorative cake and pastry garnishes.

Demonstration

Royal Icing

Makes 455 grams (1 pound)
Estimated time to complete: 20 minutes

Ingredients	Equipment
455 grams (1 pound) confectioners' sugar, sifted	Sifter
1 large egg white, at room temperature	Medium mixing bowl
15 milliliters (1 tablespoon) white vinegar or strained lemon juice	Whisk

Prepare your *mise en place*.

Combine the sugar, egg white, and vinegar in a mixing bowl, whisking to blend well.

Use as called for in a specific recipe.

TIPS

The consistency required will be dependent upon the use. This recipe makes a fairly thick icing. For a thinner consistency, add egg white, a bit at a time, until desired consistency is reached.

Theory

A Word About *Mousses*

A *mousse* is a creamy, light, velvety dessert or cake filling made from a base of meringue, whipped cream, and flavorings, often with gelatin added for stability. In French, the term *mousse* means "froth" or "foam," which focuses on the airiness of this classic confection. The creaminess comes from the whipped cream, the lightness from the ethereal meringue, and the flavor from the chocolate or fruit that is combined with the basic ingredients. (Fruit *mousses* must almost always have gelatin added to help them set evenly and properly.)

Chocolate *mousses* can be made from semisweet, bittersweet, milk, or white chocolate using *pâte à bombe*, *ganache*, or *crème anglaise*. Although most chocolate *mousses* do not require gelatin for stability, since the chocolate will act as the binding agent, it can be added for extra insurance. In the *pâte à bombe* method, the chocolate is melted while the egg yolks are whipped. Soft-ball sugar syrup is poured over the whipping yolks. If gelatin is to be added, it is melted and poured into the warm *pâte à bombe*. The chocolate is then folded in, followed by an Italian meringue and, finally, the whipped cream.

To make a *ganache*-based *mousse*, the process begins with the making of a *ganache* (see page 378). If gelatin is to be added, the soaked gelatin is stirred into the warm *ganache*. An Italian meringue or whipped cream is then folded into the cooling *ganache*.

To make a chocolate *mousse* with a *crème anglaise* base, the custard (see page 246) is flavored with chocolate, an Italian meringue is folded in, and then the whipped cream is added.

Fruit *mousses* are frequently made in the same manner as a fruit-based Bavarian cream with the addition of meringue. As a fruit purée and gelatin mixture sets, an Italian meringue is prepared and then folded in. Whipped cream is folded in at the end to keep it from being overworked, which would deflate the *mousse*. *Crème anglaise* can also be used as a base for a fruit *mousse*. Gelatin is added to the custard, then a meringue is folded in, followed by whipped cream.

Mousses can be used in many, many ways. They can be piped into dessert cups, glasses, or crisp *tuiles*, chilled in molds, or used as cake fillings or components in plated dessert presentations. A *mousse* that is to be piped or will stand alone should be fairly thick. If, as for a *charlotte russe* (see page 433), cake or ladyfingers will be used in conjunction with the *mousse*, it can be looser, as the cake will prevent the *mousse* from shifting about. In general, the softer and looser the *mousse*, the airier and more pleasant the texture.

Dean's Tip

"Adding one teaspoon of instant coffee powder to a chocolate mousse will reinforce the rich flavor."

Dean André Soltner

Demonstration

Mousse au Chocolat (Chocolate *Mousse*)

Makes 985 grams (about 2 pounds)
Estimated time to complete: 45 minutes

Ingredients	Equipment
455 grams (1 pound) semisweet or bittersweet chocolate, chopped into small pieces	Heat-proof bowl Saucepan large enough to hold the bowl

375 milliliters (12⅔ ounces) chilled heavy cream
1 gelatin leaf or 1 teaspoon unflavored granulated gelatin
25 milliliters (1 tablespoon plus 2 teaspoons) liqueur or
    eau de vie of choice
75 grams (2⅔ ounces) sugar
1 large whole egg, at room temperature
1 large egg yolk, at room temperature

Wooden spoon
Standing electric mixer fitted with whip attachment
Rubber spatula
Medium container or bowl
Plastic film
Small bowl
Small heavy-bottomed saucepan
Pastry brush
Candy thermometer
Pastry bag fitted with decorative tip optional
Dessert dishes or glasses, optional

Prepare your *mise en place.*

Fill a saucepan large enough to allow your heat-proof bowl to fit snugly into it without touching the water with about 7.5 centimeters (3 inches) of water. Place it over high heat, bring to a boil, and immediately remove the pan from the heat.

Place the chocolate in the heat-proof bowl. Quickly set the bowl into the pan, checking to make sure that the bottom is not resting in the hot water, and immediately begin stirring with a wooden spoon. Heat just until the chocolate is partially melted.

Remove the bowl from the heat and continue to stir until the chocolate has melted completely. The chocolate should be liquid but not hot.

Place the cream in the bowl of a standing electric mixer fitted with the whip attachment. Beat on low to aerate and then raise the speed and beat until soft peaks form. Using a rubber spatula, scrape the whipped cream from the mixer bowl into a clean container. Cover with plastic film and refrigerate until ready to use.

Wash and dry the mixer bowl and whip attachment and return them to the mixer.

Place the gelatin in a small bowl with cold water to cover and let soak for a minute or two to soften. Drain the soft gelatin and melt it with the alcohol. This dilutes the gelatin and keeps it from sticking to the

bowl when added to the *mousse* mixture. Set aside until ready to use.

Combine the sugar with 25 milliliters (1 tablespoon plus 2 teaspoons) water in a small heavy-bottomed saucepan, stirring with a wooden spoon until the mixture is the consistency of wet sand.

Using a wet pastry brush, clean all the sugar crystals from the sides of the pan to prevent the sugar syrup from crystallizing during cooking.

Place the saucepan over medium heat and cook without stirring for about 5 minutes, or until the syrup reaches 116°C (240°F/soft-ball stage) on a candy thermometer. This small amount of sugar will cook quickly, so watch carefully. It is important that the syrup cook undisturbed, as stirring might cause it to crystallize.

Prepare a *pâte à bombe.* Combine the egg and egg yolk in the bowl of the standing electric mixer fitted with the whip attachment. Beat on low to blend. Raise the speed and beat on medium until the eggs are thick and pale yellow. This mixture cannot be overbeaten.

As soon as the sugar syrup reaches the soft-ball stage, carefully and slowly and with the motor running, pour the hot syrup down the sides of the sides of the bowl. Do not let the syrup hit the whip or it may splatter and burn your skin. Beat for a few minutes, or until just warm.

Add the reserved melted gelatin mixture and continue

to beat until the *pâte à bombe* is very smooth and thick. It should be a bit above body temperature.

Remove the bowl from the mixer and pour all the melted chocolate over the *pâte à bombe*. Using a rubber spatula, fold in the chocolate.

When the chocolate has been incorporated, remove the whipped cream from the refrigerator and, using the spatula, fold it into the chocolate mixture. At this point, the *mousse* should be smooth, light, and airy, with the consistency of soft-peak whipped cream.

If you plan to serve it as a stand-alone dessert, scrape the mixture into a pastry bag fitted with a decorative tip and pipe it into dessert bowls, glasses, or chocolate cups. For use as a cake filling, follow the instructions in the specific recipe.

TIPS
When soaking the gelatin, make certain that it is completely submerged in the water. If it remains the slightest bit dry, it will not melt into the mixture.

Pouring the chocolate into the *pâte à bombe* all at once prevents lumps from forming, as it does not give the chocolate the opportunity to set.

This *mousse* is fairly firm once set, which makes it an excellent choice for decorative, piped applications.

The *mousse* can be stored, covered and refrigerated, for up to 5 days, or frozen for up to 1 month. However, once stored, it will have less volume and be much denser than the fresh product.

EVALUATING YOUR SUCCESS
The finished *mousse* should be thoroughly combined, with no streaks of chocolate, *pâte à bombe*, or whipped cream and no lumps of sugar or chocolate.

The finished *mousse* should be very smooth, with no graininess or curdling.

The finished *mousse* should have a strong chocolate flavor and be airy, with small holes visible.

The finished *mousse* should not be overly sweet.

Demonstration

Mousse au Chocolat Blanc (White Chocolate *Mousse*)

Makes 795 grams (1¾ pounds)
Estimated time to complete: 45 minutes

Ingredients	Equipment
225 grams (8 ounces) white chocolate, chopped into small pieces	Heat-proof bowl
375 milliliters (12⅔ ounces) chilled heavy cream	Saucepan large enough to hold the bowl
2 gelatin leaves or 6 grams (2 teaspoons) unflavored granulated gelatin	Wooden spoon
	Standing electric mixer fitted with whip attachment
25 milliliters (1 tablespoon plus 2 teaspoons) liqueur or *eau de vie* of choice	Rubber spatula
	Medium container or bowl
75 grams (2⅔ ounces) sugar	Plastic film
1 large whole egg, at room temperature	Small bowl
1 large egg yolk, at room temperature	Small heavy-bottomed saucepan

Pastry brush
Candy thermometer
Pastry bag fitted with decorative tip, optional
Dessert dishes or glasses, optional

Prepare your *mise en place*.

Fill a saucepan large enough to allow your heat-proof bowl to fit snugly into it without touching the water with about 7.5 centimeters (3 inches) of water. Place over high heat, bring to a boil, and immediately remove the pan from the heat.

Place the white chocolate in the heat-proof bowl. Quickly set the bowl into the pan, checking to make sure that the bottom is not resting in the hot water, and immediately begin stirring with a wooden spoon. Heat just until the chocolate is partially melted.

Remove the bowl from the heat and continue to stir until the chocolate has melted completely. The white chocolate should be liquid but not hot.

Place the cream in the bowl of a standing electric mixer fitted with the whip attachment. Beat on low to aerate and then raise the speed and beat until soft peaks form. Using a rubber spatula, scrape the whipped cream from the mixer bowl into a clean container. Cover with plastic film and refrigerate until ready to use.

Wash and dry the mixer bowl and whip attachment and return them to the mixer.

Place the gelatin leaves in a small bowl with cold water to cover and let soak for a minute or two to soften. Drain the soft gelatin and melt it with the alcohol. This dilutes the gelatin and keeps it from sticking to the bowl when added to the *mousse* mixture. Set aside until ready to use.

Combine the sugar with 25 milliliters (1 tablespoon plus 2 teaspoons) water in a small heavy-bottomed saucepan, stirring with a wooden spoon until the mixture is the consistency of wet sand.

Using a wet pastry brush, clean all the sugar crystals from the sides of the pan to prevent the sugar syrup from crystallizing during cooking.

Place the saucepan over medium heat and cook without stirring for about 5 minutes, or until the syrup reaches 116°C (240°F/soft-ball stage) on a candy thermometer. This small amount of sugar will cook quickly, so watch carefully. It is important that the syrup cook undisturbed, as stirring might cause it to crystallize.

Prepare a *pâte à bombe*. Combine the egg and egg yolk in the bowl of the standing electric mixer fitted with the whip attachment. Beat on low to blend. Raise the speed and beat on medium until the eggs are thick and pale yellow. This mixture cannot be overbeaten.

As soon as the sugar syrup reaches the soft-ball stage, carefully and slowly and with the motor running, pour the hot syrup down the sides of the sides of the bowl. Do not let the syrup hit the whip or it may splatter and burn your skin. Beat for a few minutes, or until just warm.

Add the reserved melted gelatin mixture and continue to beat until the *pâte à bombe* is very smooth and thick. It should be a bit above body temperature.

Remove the bowl from the mixer and pour all the melted chocolate over the *pâte à bombe*. Using a rubber spatula, fold in the chocolate.

When the chocolate has been incorporated, remove the whipped cream from the refrigerator and, using the spatula, fold it into the chocolate mixture. At this point, the *mousse* should be smooth, light, and airy, with the consistency of soft-peak whipped cream.

If you plan to serve it as a stand-alone dessert, scrape the mixture into a pastry bag fitted with a decorative tip and pipe it into dessert bowls, glasses, or chocolate cups. For use as a cake filling, follow the instructions in the specific recipe.

TIPS

When soaking the gelatin, make certain that it is completely submerged in the water. If it remains the slightest bit dry, it will not dissolve into the mixture.

Pouring the chocolate into the *pâte à bombe* all at once prevents lumps from forming, as it does not give the chocolate the opportunity to set.

This *mousse* is fairly firm once set, which makes it an excellent choice for decorative, piped applications.

The *mousse* can be stored, covered and refrigerated, for up to 5 days, or frozen for up to 1 month. However, once stored, it will have less volume and be much denser than the fresh product.

EVALUATING YOUR SUCCESS

The finished *mousse* should be thoroughly combined, with no streaks of chocolate, *pâte à bombe*, or whipped cream and no lumps of sugar or chocolate.

The finished *mousse* should be very smooth, with no graininess or curdling.

The finished *mousse* should have a strong chocolate flavor and be airy, with small holes visible.

The finished *mousse* should not be overly sweet.

Demonstration

Mousse au Chocolat Noisette (Chocolate-Hazelnut *Mousse*)

Makes795 grams (1¾ pounds)
Estimated time to complete: 45 minutes

Ingredients	Equipment
225 grams (8 ounces) semisweet or bittersweet chocolate, chopped into small pieces	Heat-proof bowl
150 grams (5⅓ ounces) *gianduja* (see Tips), chopped into small pieces	Saucepan large enough to hold the bowl
750 milliliters (25 ⅓ ounces) heavy cream	Wooden spoon
210 grams (7⅓ ounces) sugar	Standing electric mixer fitted with whip attachment
9 large egg yolks, at room temperature	Rubber spatula
1 large whole egg, at room temperature	Medium container or bowl
25 milliliters (1 tablespoon plus 2 teaspoons) hazelnut liqueur	Plastic film
	Medium heavy-bottomed saucepan
	Pastry brush
	Candy thermometer
	Pastry bag fitted with decorative tip, optional
	Dessert dishes or glasses, optional

Prepare your *mise en place*.

Fill a saucepan large enough to allow your heat-proof bowl to fit snugly into it without touching the water with about 7.5 centimeters (3 inches) of water. Place it over high heat, bring to a boil, and immediately remove the pan from the heat.

Combine the chocolate and *gianduja* in the heat-proof bowl. Quickly place the bowl into the pan, checking to make sure that the bottom is not resting in the hot water, and immediately begin stirring with a wooden spoon. Heat just until the chocolate is partially melted.

Remove the bowl from the heat and continue to stir until the chocolate has melted completely. The mixture should be liquid but not hot.

Place the cream in the bowl of a standing electric mixer fitted with the whip attachment. Beat on low to aerate and then raise the speed and beat until soft peaks form. Using a rubber spatula, scrape the whipped cream from the mixer bowl into a clean container. Cover with plastic film and refrigerate until ready to use.

Wash and dry the mixer bowl and whip attachment and return them to the mixer.

Combine the sugar with 25 milliliters (1 tablespoon plus 2 teaspoons) water in a small heavy-bottomed saucepan, stirring with a wooden spoon until the mixture is the consistency of wet sand.

Using a wet pastry brush, clean all the sugar crystals from the sides of the pan to prevent the sugar syrup from crystallizing during cooking.

Place the saucepan over medium heat and cook without stirring, for about 5 minutes, or until the syrup reaches 116°C (240°F/soft-ball stage) on a candy thermometer. This small amount of sugar will cook quickly, so watch carefully. It is important that the syrup cook undisturbed, as stirring might cause it to crystallize.

Prepare a *pâte à bombe*. Combine the egg yolks and egg in the bowl of the standing electric mixer fitted with the whip attachment. Beat on low to blend, then raise the speed and beat on medium until the eggs are thick and pale yellow. This mixture cannot be overbeaten.

As soon as the syrup reaches the soft-ball stage, carefully and slowly and with the motor running, pour the hot syrup down the sides of the sides of the bowl. Do not let the syrup hit the whip or it may splatter and burn your skin. Beat for about 4 minutes, or until the *pâte à bombe* is very smooth and thick. It should be a bit above body temperature.

Remove the bowl from the mixer and pour all the melted chocolate mixture over the *pâte à bombe*. Using a rubber spatula, fold in the chocolate mixture.

When the chocolate mixture has been incorporated, remove the whipped cream from the refrigerator and, using the spatula, fold it into the chocolate mixture. At this point, the *mousse* should be smooth, light, and airy, with the consistency of soft-peak whipped cream.

If you plan to use it as a stand-alone dessert, scrape the mixture into a pastry bag fitted with a decorative tip and pipe it into dessert bowls, glasses, or chocolate cups. For use as a cake filling, follow the instructions in the specific recipe.

TIPS

Gianduja is a Swiss- or Italian-made sweet chocolate flavored with a mixture of hazelnut and almond pastes.

Pouring the chocolate into the *pâte à bombe* all at once prevents lumps from forming, as it does not give the chocolate the opportunity to set. This *mousse* is fairly firm once set, which makes it an excellent choice for decorative, piped applications.

The *mousse* can be stored, covered and refrigerated, for up to 5 days, or frozen for up to 1 month. However, once stored, it will have less volume and be much denser than the fresh product.

EVALUATING YOUR SUCCESS

The finished *mousse* should be thoroughly combined, with no streaks of chocolate, *pâte à bombe*, or whipped cream and no lumps of sugar or chocolate.

The finished *mousse* should be very smooth, with no graininess or curdling.

The finished *mousse* should have a strong chocolate-hazelnut flavor and be airy, with small holes visible.

The finished *mousse* should not be overly sweet.

Demonstration

Mousse aux Fruits (Fruit *Mousse*)

Makes 1 kilogram (2¼ pounds)
Estimated time to complete: 45 minutes

Ingredients	Equipment
4 gelatin leaves or 12 grams (4 teaspoons) unflavored granulated gelatin	Small bowl
335 grams (11¾ ounces) fruit purée (see page 58)	Medium saucepan
350 milliliters (11¾ ounces) chilled heavy cream	Wooden spoon
135 grams (4¾ ounces) sugar	Small heavy-bottomed saucepan
65 grams (2¼ ounces) light corn syrup	Standing electric mixer fitted with whip attachment
120 grams (4¼ ounces) egg whites, at room temperature	Plastic film
	Small heavy-bottomed saucepan
	Pastry brush
	Candy thermometer
	Pastry bag fitted with decorative tip, optional
	Dessert dishes or glasses, optional

Prepare your *mise en place*.

Place the gelatin leaves in a small bowl with cold water to cover and let soak for a minute or two to soften.

Place half of the fruit purée in a medium saucepan over medium heat. Heat, stirring with a wooden spoon, for just a minute or two or until hot. Do not cook.

Remove the purée from the heat. Squeeze the excess water from the gelatin and add the gelatin to the hot purée, stirring to dissolve the gelatin.

When the gelatin is dissolved, add the remaining fruit purée, stirring to blend. Set aside to cool.

(Alternatively, the purée may be chilled in an ice bath or covered and chilled in the refrigerator, but it must be carefully watched and stirred frequently as you don't want it to set unevenly or completely.)

Place the cream in the bowl of a standing electric mixer fitted with the whip attachment. Beat on low to aerate, then raise the speed and beat until soft peaks form. Using a rubber spatula, scrape the whipped cream from the mixer bowl into a clean container. Cover with plastic film and refrigerate until ready to use.

Combine the sugar and corn syrup with 50 milliliters (3 tablespoons plus 1 teaspoon) water in a small heavy-bottomed saucepan, stirring with a wooden spoon until the mixture is the consistency of wet sand.

Using a wet pastry brush, clean all the sugar crystals from the sides of the pan to prevent the syrup from crystallizing during cooking.

Place the saucepan over medium heat and cook without stirring for about 5 minutes, or until the syrup reaches 116°C (240°F/soft-ball stage) on a candy thermometer. This small amount of sugar will cook quickly, so watch carefully. It is important that the syrup cook undisturbed, as stirring might cause it to crystallize.

While the syrup is cooking, place the egg whites in the bowl of the standing electric mixer fitted with the whip and beat until soft peaks form. As soon as the syrup reaches the soft-ball stage, carefully and slowly and with the motor running, pour the hot syrup into the beaten egg whites, beating until stiff peaks form. This meringue should be firm but not dried out, or it will be difficult to fold into the fruit.

Remove the bowl from the mixer and pour all the cooled fruit purée over the meringue. Using a rubber spatula, fold in the purée.

When the purée has been incorporated, remove the whipped cream from the refrigerator and, using the spatula, fold it into the fruit mixture to just blend evenly. At this point, the *mousse* should be smooth, light, and airy, with the consistency of soft-peak whipped cream.

If you plan to use it as a stand-alone dessert, it into a pastry bag fitted with a decorative tip and pipe it into molds, dessert bowls, glasses, or chocolate cups. For use as a cake filling, follow the instructions in the specific recipe.

TIPS

When soaking the gelatin, make certain that it is completely submerged in the water. If it remains the slightest bit dry, it will not melt into the mixture.

Depending upon the sweetness of the fruit purée used, the amount of sugar in the recipe may be increased or decreased. Any additional sugar should be dissolved into the hot purée.

Warming only half the fruit purée allows the unheated portion to cool the hot mixture rapidly.

The purée and gelatin mixture should begin to set before being added to the meringue.

The *mousse* can be stored, covered and refrigerated, for up to 4 days, or frozen for up to 1 month. Be aware, however, that once stored, the *mousse* will have less volume and be much denser than the fresh product.

EVALUATING YOUR SUCCESS

The finished *mousse* should be thoroughly combined, with no streaks of fruit or meringue. The finished *mousse* should be very smooth, with no graininess or curdling.

The finished *mousse* should have a strong fruit flavor and be airy, with small holes visible.

The finished *mousse* should not be overly sweet.

Demonstration

Mousse au Mascarpone (Mascarpone *Mousse*)

Makes 2 kilograms (4⅓ pounds)
Estimated time to complete: 45 minutes

Ingredients	Equipment
700 milliliters (23⅓ ounces) chilled heavy cream	Standing electric mixer fitted with whip and paddle attachments
6 gelatin leaves or 18 grams (2 tablespoons) granular gelatin	Rubber spatula
125 milliliters (4¼ ounces) whole milk	Container or bowl
300 grams (11 ounces) sugar	Plastic film
6 large egg yolks, at room temperature	Small bowl
350 grams (12⅓ ounces) mascarpone cheese	Medium saucepan
150 grams (5⅓ ounces) cream cheese	Medium heat-proof bowl
Juice of 1 lemon	Wooden spoon
1 teaspoon pure vanilla extract	Fine-mesh sieve
	Medium bowl
	Ice bath
	Pastry bag fitted with decorative tip, optional
	Dessert dishes or glasses, optional

Prepare your *mise en place*.

Place the cream in the bowl of a standing electric mixer fitted with the whip attachment. Beat on low to aerate and then raise the speed and beat until soft peaks form. Using a rubber spatula, scrape the whipped cream from the mixer bowl into a clean container. Cover with plastic film and refrigerate until ready to use.

Wash and dry the mixer bowl and return it to the mixer.

Place the gelatin leaves in a small bowl with cold water to cover and let soak for a minute or two to soften.

Combine the milk with half of the sugar in a medium saucepan over medium heat and bring to a boil. Remove from the heat.

Combine the remaining sugar with the egg yolks in a medium heat-proof bowl. Whisking constantly, add about one-third of the hot milk to temper the egg yolk mixture.

Continuing to whisk constantly, pour the egg yolk mixture into the saucepan with the hot milk. Return to medium heat and cook, stirring constantly with a wooden spoon for about 5 minutes, or until the custard coats the back of a metal spoon. Note that this is a very small amount of custard and will cook quickly, so watch carefully.

While stirring, pay close attention to the bottom inner edges of the pan as the egg will coagulate and over-cook there first. When the custard coats the spoon, draw your fingertip across the coated spoon. If a distinct line appears and holds, the custard is done (*nappant*). Pour it through a fine-mesh sieve into a clean bowl and place the bowl over an ice bath to stop the cooking process.

Squeeze the excess water from the gelatin and add the gelatin to the still-warm custard, stirring to dissolve the gelatin. Continue cooling, stirring frequently to speed the process, for about 5 minutes, or until the custard is cool but still fluid.

While the custard is cooling, combine the mascarpone and cream cheese in the bowl of the standing electric mixer fitted with the paddle attachment. Beat on low to just combine. Add the lemon juice and vanilla and beat, occasionally scraping down the sides of the bowl with a rubber spatula, for about 3 minutes, or until light and fluffy.

Remove the bowl from the mixer. Add the cooled custard and, using the spatula, fold the two mixtures together.

When they are well blended, remove the whipped cream from the refrigerator and, using the spatula, fold it into the cheese mixture to just blend in evenly. At this point, the *mousse* should be smooth, light, and airy with the consistency of soft-peak whipped cream.

If you plan to use it as a stand-alone dessert, scrape it into a pastry bag fitted with a decorative tip and pipe it into molds, dessert bowls, glasses, or chocolate cups. For use as a cake filling, follow the instructions in the specific recipe.

TIPS
When soaking the gelatin, make certain that it is completely submerged in the water. If it remains the slightest bit dry, it will not dissolve into the mixture.

Do not allow the eggs and sugar to sit without blending or they will "burn."

Mixing half of the sugar with the milk while heating, it helps prevent the milk from scorching.

Only use a wooden spoon or heat-proof spatula to stir custard, metal spoons can scrape metal from the bottom of the pan, and whisks will cause too much aeration.

Passing the custard through the sieve removes any small bits of curdled egg that might have formed when cooking.

If the custard completely sets, it will be impossible to fold the whipped cream into it. If this occurs, warm it over a *bain-marie* until the desired consistency is reached.

If the custard overcooks, it will curdle and become unusable. The *mousse* can be stored, covered and refrigerated, for up to 4 days, or frozen for up to 1 month. Be aware, however, that once stored, it will have less volume and be much denser than the fresh product.

EVALUATING YOUR SUCCESS
The finished *mousse* should be thoroughly combined, with no streaks of cheese or custard.

The finished *mousse* should be light, smooth, and fluffy, with no coagulated gelatin.

The finished *mousse* should have a strong cheese flavor and be airy, with small holes visible.

The finished *mousse* should not be overly sweet.

Chef Jason Licker | *Consulting Pastry Chef, Nobu Restaurants, New York*

The French Culinary Institute, Class of 1999

Lemon Chiffon, Yogurt, and Raspberry Cake

Makes one 8-inch cake

I first made this cake when I was the pastry chef at the Westin Hotel in Shanghai. I wanted something well balanced and not overly sweet, as I had found that the Chinese do not favor sweet desserts. Fresh fruit cakes seemed to be quite popular—layer cakes filled with whipped cream and lots of fresh fruit. This cake was my version of the favorite. The balance of lemon, yogurt, and raspberry give it the sweet-sour refreshing flavor so appreciated in a hot climate. For extra excitement, I would often add white chocolate décor, along with fresh raspberries and caramelized almonds.

300 grams (11 ounces) sugar

300 grams (11 ounces) cake flour

1 teaspoon baking powder

1 teaspoon salt

6 large eggs, separated, at room temperature

125.5 milliliters (4¼ ounces) corn oil

96.5 milliliters (3¼ ounces) whole milk

96.5 milliliters (3¼ ounces) fresh lemon juice, strained

Zest of 2 lemons

Raspberry *Mousse* (recipe follows)

Yogurt *Mousse* (recipe follows)

White Chocolate Curls (see page 407) for garnish, optional

Fresh raspberries for garnish, optional

Caramelized almonds for garnish, optional

Preheat the oven to 177°C (350°F).

Butter and flour three 20-centimeter (8-inch) round cake pans. Set aside.

Sift 100 grams (3½ ounces) of the sugar together with the flour, baking powder, and salt. Set aside.

Place the egg yolks, oil, and milk in a large mixing bowl, stirring with a wooden spoon to blend. Stir in the lemon juice, then add the sifted dry ingredients along with the zest, beating until a thick pastelike batter forms.

Make a French meringue: Place the egg whites in the bowl of a standing electric mixer fitted with the whip attachment. Beat on low to blend and aerate. Add the remaining sugar, raise the speed to high, and beat for about 5 minutes, or until stiff peaks form.

Carefully fold the meringue into the batter, just until the dry ingredients are incorporated—you don't want to deflate the meringue.

Carefully pour the batter into the prepared pans, gently smoothing it into an even layer.

Bake the cakes for 10 minutes, rotate the pans, and continue to bake for another 10 minutes, or until the surface is an even golden brown and the center springs back when lightly touched.

Carefully invert the cakes onto wire racks.

When they are cool, place a 23-centimeter (9-inch) round cardboard cake circle on a clean, flat surface. Place a 23-by-7.5-centimeter (9-by-3-inch) cake ring over the circle. Then, position one of the cake layers inside the ring.

Using an offset spatula, carefully cover the top of the cake with a 13-centimeter-thick (½-inch-thick) layer of the raspberry *mousse*, coming exactly to the edge of the cake to make a neat layer. Stack another cake layer on top and cover it with a second layer of the *mousse*. Top with the final cake layer. Each layer should be perfectly lined up, even, and centered inside the cake ring.

Remove the cake ring and, using the spatula, carefully coat the entire cake with the yogurt *mousse*.

If desired, decorate the cake with white chocolate curls and fresh raspberries.

Refrigerate until ready to use, but for no longer than 1 day.

Raspberry *Mousse*

22.5 grams (¾ ounce) gelatin leaves
1 kilogram (2½ pounds) raspberry purée
60 grams (2 ounces) sugar
840 milliliters (28 ounces) chilled heavy cream

Place the gelatin leaves in a small bowl with cold water to cover and let soak for a minute or two to soften.

Place the fruit purée and sugar in a medium saucepan over medium heat. Heat, stirring with a wooden spoon, for about 5 minutes, or until hot. Do not cook.

Remove the purée from the heat. Squeeze the excess water from the gelatin and add it to the hot purée,

stirring to dissolve the gelatin. Set aside to cool.

When the purée has cooled, place the cream in the bowl of a standing electric mixer fitted with the whip attachment. Beat on low to aerate and then raise the speed and beat until firm peaks form. The cream should be firm, but not dried out or it will be difficult to fold into the fruit purée.

Remove the bowl from the mixer and pour all the cooled fruit purée over the whipped cream. Using a rubber spatula, fold in the purée.

Refrigerate until ready to use.

Yogurt *Mousse*

40 milliliters (2 tablespoons plus 2 teaspoons) rum
32.5 grams (1⅓ ounces) gelatin leaves
250 grams (8¾ ounces) egg yolks, at room temperature
250 grams (8¾ ounces) sugar
1 liter (1 quart, 2 ounces) heavy cream
500 grams (1 pound, 1 ½ ounces) plain whole-milk yogurt

Heat the rum in a small saucepan over low heat. Add the gelatin and let it dissolve.

Fill a saucepan large enough to allow your heat-proof bowl to fit snugly into it without touching the water with about 7.5 centimeters (3 inches) of water. Place over high heat and bring to a boil.

Combine the egg yolks with the sugar in the heat-proof bowl and, using a wire whisk, whisk to blend. Quickly place the bowl into the pan, checking to make sure that the bottom is not resting in the hot water. Immediately begin whisking, and continue to do so for about 10 minutes, or until the mixture has thickened, has gained volume, and reads 52°C (126°F) on an instant-read thermometer. Remove from the heat.

Stir the gelatin-and-rum mixture into the whipped egg yolks.

Place the heavy cream in the bowl of a standing electric mixer fitted with the whip attachment. Beat on low to aerate. Raise the speed to high and beat for about 4 minutes, or until firm peaks form.

Using a rubber spatula, fold the whipped cream and yogurt into the egg yolks.

Refrigerate until ready to use.

Theory

A Word About *Crème Bavaroise* (Bavarian Cream)

Crème bavaroise is a classic French creamy dessert custard. *Bavarois*, as it is often called, is usually chilled in a mold or used as a filling for cakes such as *charlotte russe*. There are two basic types: *crème anglaise*–based and fruit-based. In both types, the base is thickened with gelatin and lightened by folding in whipped cream. Bavarian creams are easier to make, but slightly denser than *mousses*.

The process for creating a *crème anglaise*–based *bavarois* is quite simple. The custard is prepared and infused or flavored as desired. The gelatin is soaked in cold water, squeezed, and stirred into the cooked and still-warm custard. The mixture is then cooled until it begins to set. This can be done at room temperature or hastened over an ice bath. The cream to be added is whipped to a firm peak and folded into the base with a rubber spatula. The mixture is then placed into a mold and chilled until completely set.

The process by which a fruit-based *bavarois* is made is quite similar. The fruit purée is warmed to slightly above body temperature. The soaked and squeezed gelatin is stirred into the warm purée. The mixture is removed from the heat and allowed to begin setting. This too can be done at room temperature or hastened over an ice bath. Meanwhile, the cream to be added is whipped to firm peaks. The purée mixture is folded into the whipped cream. The mixture is then placed into a mold and chilled until completely set.

In addition to the *charlotte russe*, Bavarian cream is also used as the filling for other *charlottes* in contemporary pastry making. The mold may be lined with slices of jelly roll or sponge cake, *madeleines*, meringue products, sliced fruits, or slices of bread. It is then filled with either *crème anglaise*–based or fruit-based *bavarois*, chosen to provide complementary flavors. The shape of the mold, the cake lining, and the filling used determine the name of the *charlotte*. For instance, a *charlotte royale* (see page 427) is made in a dome-shaped mold (or bowl) lined with slices of jelly roll. A *charlotte urbane* is a ribbonlike *charlotte* with the mold lined in ladyfingers and chocolate and strawberry Bavarian cream layered in the center.

To remove a Bavarian cream from a mold, slightly warm the mold by either dipping it in warm water or using a handheld kitchen torch. Then invert the dessert onto a serving plate, cake cardboard, or other appropriate dish and lift off the mold. Do not warm the mold too much or the *bavarois* will melt. Any Bavarian may be stored, tightly covered and refrigerated, for up to 2 days.

Demonstration

Bavarois à la Crème Anglaise (*Crème Anglaise*–based Bavarian Cream)

Makes 600 grams (1 pound, 5 ounces)
Estimated time to complete: 40 minutes

Ingredients	**Equipment**
250 milliliters (8 ounces) chilled heavy cream	Standing electric mixer fitted with whip attachment
2½ gelatin leaves or 8 grams (2 ½ teaspoons) unflavored granulated gelatin	Rubber spatula
	Container
250 milliliters (8 ounces) whole milk	Plastic film
100 grams (3½ ounces) sugar	Small bowl
3 large egg yolks, at room temperature	Medium saucepan
	Medium heat-proof bowl
	Wire whisk
	Wooden spoon
	Metal spoon
	Fine-mesh sieve
	Medium bowl
	Ice bath

Prepare your *mise en place*.

Place the cream in the bowl of a standing electric mixer fitted with the whip attachment. Beat on low to aerate and then raise the speed and beat until soft peaks form. Using a rubber spatula, scrape the whipped cream from the mixer bowl into a clean container. Cover with plastic film and refrigerate until ready to use.

Place the gelatin leaves in a small bowl with cold water to cover and let soak for a minute or two to soften.

Combine the milk with half the sugar in a medium saucepan over medium heat and bring to a boil. Remove from the heat.

Combine the remaining sugar with the egg yolks in a medium heat-proof bowl. Whisking constantly, add about one-third of the hot milk to temper the egg yolk mixture.

Continuing to whisk constantly, pour the egg yolk mixture into the saucepan with the hot milk. Return to medium heat and cook, stirring constantly with a wooden spoon, for about 5 minutes, or until the custard coats the back of a metal spoon. Note that this is a very small amount of custard and it will cook quickly, so watch carefully. While stirring, pay close attention to the bottom inner edges of the pan, as the egg will coagulate and overcook there first. When the custard coats the spoon, draw your fingertip across the coated spoon. If a distinct line appears and holds, the *crème anglaise* is done (*nappant*).

Squeeze the excess water from the gelatin and add it to the *crème anglaise*, stirring to dissolve the gelatin.

Pour the *crème anglaise* through a fine-mesh sieve into a clean bowl and place the bowl over an ice bath to stop the cooking process. Cool, stirring frequently to speed the process, for about 5 minutes, or until the custard is very cool but still fluid, similar to loose jam.

Remove the whipped cream from the refrigerator and, using the spatula, fold it into the cooled *crème anglaise* to blend in evenly.

Use the Bavarian cream as directed in a specific recipe.

TIPS

When soaking the gelatin, make certain that it is completely submerged in the water. If it remains the slightest bit dry, it will not dissolve into the mixture. Do not allow the eggs and sugar to sit without blend Mixing half of the sugar with the milk while heating prevents the milk from scorching.

Only use a wooden spoon or heat-proof spatula to stir custard; metal spoons can scrape metal from the bottom of the pan, and whisks will cause too much aeration.

Passing the *crème anglaise* through the sieve removes any small bits of curdled egg or unmelted gelatin.

If the *crème anglaise* is overcooked, it will curdle and be unusable.

If the gelatin has not begun to set when the whipped cream is added, the finished Bavarian cream will be loose and watery, rather than fluffy.

If the *crème anglaise* has set too much, it will be impossible to fold the whipped cream into it.

Likewise, if the whipped cream is too stiff, it will be difficult to fold into the custard.

If the custard is not cool enough when the whipped cream is added, it will deflate the cream, and the *bavarois* will not be fluffy.

The flavor of this Bavarian cream may be varied by the addition of 500 grams (1 pound, 1½ ounces) melted bittersweet, semisweet, milk, or white chocolate, or 15 to 30 milliliters (1 to 2 tablespoons) of pure extracts such as vanilla or almond.

EVALUATING YOUR SUCCESS

The finished Bavarian cream should be well-flavored and smooth, light, and fluffy, with the consistency of just-whipped cream.

There should be no lumps or streaks in the finished cream.

There should be no graininess or curdled appearance.

Demonstration

Bavarois aux Fruits (Classic Fruit Bavarian Cream)

Makes 680 grams (22⅔ ounces)

Estimated time to complete: 40 minutes

Ingredients	Equipment
2½ gelatin leaves or 7.5 grams (2½ teaspoons) unflavored granulated gelatin	Small bowl
	Medium saucepan
250 grams (1 cup plus 1 tablespoon) fruit purée (see page 58)	Wooden spoon

100 grams (3½ ounces) sugar

250 milliliters (8 ounces) chilled heavy cream

Standing electric mixer fitted with whip attachment

Rubber or plastic spatula

Prepare your *mise en place*.

Place the gelatin leaves in a small bowl with cold water to cover and let soak for a minute or two to soften.

Combine half of the fruit purée with the sugar in a medium saucepan over medium heat. Heat, stirring with a wooden spoon, for just a minute or two, or until hot. Do not boil.

Remove the purée from the heat. Squeeze the excess water from the gelatin and add it to the hot purée, stirring to dissolve the gelatin.

When the gelatin is dissolved, stir in the remaining fruit purée. Set aside to cool.

Place the cream in the bowl of a standing electric mixer fitted with the whip attachment. Beat on low to aerate and then raise the speed and beat until soft peaks form.

Using a rubber or plastic spatula, fold the whipped cream into the chilled fruit purée, blending them completely.

Use the Bavarian cream immediately as directed in a specific recipe or transfer it to a clean bowl, cover, and refrigerate until needed, or for up to 4 days. You can also freeze it for up to 1 month; thaw it before using.

TIPS

When soaking the gelatin, make certain that it is completely submerged in the water. If it remains the slightest bit dry, it will not dissolve into the mixture.

Depending upon the sweetness of the fruit purée used, the amount of sugar in the recipe may be increased or decreased. Any additional sugar should be dissolved into the hot purée.

Warming half the fruit purée allows the unheated portion to help cool the hot mixture more rapidly.

The fruit mixture should begin to set before the whipped cream is folded in.

EVALUATING YOUR SUCCESS

The finished Bavarian cream should have a strong fruit flavor and be smooth, light, and fluffy, with the consistency of just-whipped cream.

There should be no lumps or streaks in the finished cream.

There should be no graininess or curdled appearance. The finished cream should be well balanced in flavor, neither too sweet nor too sour.

Demonstration

Crème aux Pistaches (Pistachio Cream)

Makes 1.5 kilogram (3⅓ pounds)

Estimated time to complete: 1 hour

Ingredients

Equipment

---

100 milliliters (3½ ounces) whole milk

60 grams (2 ounces) sugar

Medium heavy-bottomed saucepan

Heat-proof spatula

35 grams (1¼ ounces) pistachio paste
4 large egg yolks, at room temperature
1 teaspoon pastry cream powder (see page 244)
320 grams (11¼ ounces) unsalted butter, at room temperature

For the Italian meringue
200 grams (7 ounces) egg whites, at room temperature
200 grams (7 ounces) sugar

Small stainless-steel mixing bowl
Whisk
Rubber spatula
Plastic film
Standing electric mixer fitted
with paddle and whip attachments
Medium mixing bowl

Prepare your *mise en place*.

Combine the milk, sugar, and pistachio paste in a medium heavy-bottomed saucepan over high heat. Bring to a boil, stirring frequently with a heat-proof spatula. Remove from the heat.

Combine the egg yolks and pastry cream powder in a small stainless-steel mixing bowl, whisking until completely smooth. Whisk in one-third of the hot milk mixture to temper the egg yolks.

Using a rubber spatula, scrape the tempered egg yolk mixture into the saucepan with the hot milk. Return the mixture to medium heat and cook, stirring constantly with the heat-proof spatula, for about 3 minutes, or until the mixture returns to a boil. Boil, stirring constantly, for 2 minutes to allow the mixture to be fully cooked and to reach its full thickening power.

Remove the custard from the heat. Immediately cover it with plastic film, pressing it against the surface of the custard to prevent a skin from forming as it cools.

Set aside to cool to room temperature.

When the pastry cream has cooled, place the butter in the bowl of a standing electric mixer fitted with the paddle attachment. Beat on medium until very light and fluffy. Add the cooled cream to the butter and beat to blend. Scrape the mixture into a medium mixing bowl.

Wash and dry the mixer bowl and return it to the mixer.

Make the meringue: Place the egg whites in the bowl of the standing electric mixer fitted with the whip attachment. Beat on low to aerate. Raise the speed to

medium and add the sugar in a slow, steady stream. Whip for about 5 minutes, or until stiff peaks form; do not overwhip.

Using a rubber spatula, fold the meringue into the cool pistachio cream.

Use the pistachio cream immediately as directed in a specific recipe or transfer it to a clean bowl, cover, and refrigerate until needed, or for up to 4 days. You can also freeze it for up to 1 month; thaw it before using.

TIPS
If pastry cream powder is not available, it may be replaced with 1½ teaspoons flour or cornstarch.

Do not allow the eggs and pastry cream to sit without blending or they will "burn."

Mixing half the sugar with the milk while heating prevents the milk from scorching.

Once combined and placed over the heat, the egg mixture must be stirred constantly or it will stick and burn.

Only use a wooden spoon or heat-proof spatula to stir custard; metal spoons can scrape metal from the bottom of the pan, and whisks will cause too much aeration.

Boiling the mixture activates the starch in the pastry cream powder as a thickener and eliminates any starchy taste.

When making a large batch of pistachio cream, allow the milk to return to a rolling boil before adding the tempered eggs.

The cream should be very firm when cooled but should soften when whisked.

The finished cream should be vibrant green in color, with a soft texture and a strong pistachio flavor.

There should be no lumps of pistachio paste or pastry cream powder.

There should be no starchy taste.

Demonstration

Lemon Curd Cake Filling

Makes 960 grams (2 pounds, 1½ ounces)

Estimated time to complete: 30 minutes

Ingredients	Equipment
3 gelatin leaves or 9 grams (3 tablespoons) unflavored granulated gelatin	Small bowl
4 large eggs, at room temperature	Bowl to fit saucepan
Zest of 4 lemons	Wooden spoon
280 grams (9¾ ounces) sugar	Heat-proof spatula
240 milliliters (8½ ounces) fresh lemon juice	Fine-mesh sieve
220 grams (7¾ ounces) unsalted butter, cubed, at room temperature	Medium bowl
	Plastic film

Prepare your *mise en place.*

Place the gelatin leaves in a small bowl with plenty of cold water and let soak for a minute or two to soften.

Fill a saucepan large enough to allow your heat-proof bowl to fit snugly into it without touching the water with about 7.5 centimeters (3 inches) of water. Place it over high heat and bring to a boil. Lower the heat so that the water continues at a low simmer.

Combine the eggs with the lemon zest, sugar, and lemon juice in the heat-proof bowl and, using a wooden spoon, stir to blend. Quickly place the bowl into the pan, checking to make sure that the bottom is not resting in the hot water and that the bowl is centered over the heat. Immediately begin stirring with a wooden spoon, and when the mixture begins to warm, stir

in the butter. Cook, stirring occasionally with a heat-proof spatula, for about 5 minutes, or until the mixture has thickened. It should be the consistency of hollandaise sauce or ketchup.

Remove the bowl from the heat, squeeze the excess water from the gelatin, and add it to the lemon mixture, stirring to dissolve the gelatin.

When the gelatin has dissolved, pour the mixture through a fine-mesh sieve into a clean bowl. Immediately cover the lemon curd with plastic film pressed directly onto the surface to prevent a skin from forming as it cools.

When cool, the lemon curd can be used as directed in a specific recipe or stored, tightly covered and refrigerated, for up to 4 days.

TIPS

Do not allow the eggs and sugar to sit without blending them or they will "burn."

The butter incorporates more easily when the mixture is a bit warm.

EVALUATING YOUR SUCCESS

The finished curd should be smooth and of a uniform color, with a strong, tart lemon flavor.

Once cool, the curd should be still somewhat soft, not stiff and firm.

Demonstration

Passion Fruit Curd

Makes 700 grams (1½ pounds)

Estimated time to complete: 30 minutes

Ingredients	Equipment
3 large eggs, at room temperature	Saucepan to fit bowl
210 grams (7⅓ ounces) sugar	Medium stainless-steel bowl
175 grams (6⅛ ounces) passion fruit purée (see page 58)	Wooden spoon
165 grams (5¾ ounces) unsalted butter, cut into small pieces,	Wire whisk
at room temperature	Fine-mesh sieve
	Medium bowl or container
	Plastic film

Prepare your *mise en place*.

Fill a saucepan large enough to allow your stainless-steel bowl to fit snugly into it without touching the water with about 7.5 centimeters (3 inches) of water. Place it over high heat and bring to a strong simmer.

Combine the eggs with the sugar and purée in a medium stainless-steel bowl, stirring with a wooden spoon to blend. Add the butter and quickly place the bowl into the pan, checking to make sure that the bottom is not resting in the hot water and that the bowl is centered over the heat. Immediately begin whisking with a wire whisk to blend the ingredients. Continue cooking and occasionally whisking for about 5 min-

utes, or until the mixture has blended completely and is the consistency of hollandaise sauce.

Remove the curd from the heat and strain it through a fine-mesh sieve into a clean bowl or container. Immediately cover the curd with plastic pressed directly onto the surface to prevent a skin from forming as it cools.

When cool, passion fruit curd can be used as directed in a specific recipe or stored, tightly covered and refrigerated, for up to 4 days.

TIPS

Do not allow the eggs and sugar to sit without blending them or they will "burn."

The butter incorporates more easily once the mixture is a bit warm.

If the curd is too loose for a particular application, add 3 sheets of soaked and squeezed gelatin to the hot mixture before straining it.

The finished curd should be smooth and of a uniform color with a strong, tart passion fruit flavor.

Once cool, the curd should still be somewhat soft, not stiff and firm.

Demonstration

Marzipan

Makes 455 grams (1 pound)

Estimated time to complete: 20 minutes

Ingredients	Equipment
225 grams (8 ounces) almond paste	Sifter
55 grams (2 ounces) light corn syrup	Plastic film
170 grams (6 ounces) confectioners' sugar or more if needed	
Liquid or paste food coloring, optional	

Prepare your *mise en place*.

Place the almond paste on a clean, flat work surface, pressing it out slightly. Pour the syrup on top and, using your hands, knead it into the almond paste until blended. Do not overknead. If overworked, the oil in the almonds will activate and begin to ooze out and make the finished product oily and unusable.

Add the confectioners' sugar and continue to knead until the sugar is completely incorporated into the marzipan, which should be pale brown and pliable, but not oily or sticky. Depending upon the consistency of the almond paste, additional sugar may be needed to create the consistency required for the recipe.

If coloring is desired, the appropriate liquid or paste food color should now be kneaded into the marzipan until a uniform color is reached.

Form the mixture into a round, tightly wrap it in plastic film, and refrigerate until ready to use for a specific recipe. It must be well wrapped or it will dry out and be unusable.

TIPS

Marzipan is used to cover cakes and *petits fours*, modeled for decorative pieces such as flowers, fruits, and figures, or flavored and colored and used as candy.

Marzipan can be kept almost indefinitely. Because of its high sugar content, marzipan will not spoil if stored at room temperature. However, if it is to be held for a long period of time, it should be refrigerated to inhibit bacterial growth.

When shaping marzipan, sprinkle confectioners' sugar to keep it from sticking to the work surface or to tools.

When using a small amount of marzipan, immediately rewrap the remainder to keep it from drying out.

When rolling large sheets of marzipan (as for wrapping a cake), work quickly; creating such a large surface area will speed the drying process.

If marzipan dries out or develops a crust, wrap it in a damp towel and refrigerate for 8 hours or overnight, then unwrap and knead it to the desired consistency.

EVALUATING YOUR SUCCESS
Well-kneaded marzipan should be of a consistent, smooth texture, pale beige, and pliable.

Marzipan should not be oily or sticky.

Marzipan should not crack when being worked.

Demonstration

Fondant Décor façon Colette (Colette's Rolled Fondant)

Makes 1 kilogram (2¼ pounds)
Estimated time to complete: 30 minutes

Ingredients	Equipment
3 gelatin leaves or 9 grams (1 tablespoon) unflavored granulated gelatin	Small heat-proof bowl
170 grams (6 ounces) light corn syrup	Saucepan small enough to fit the bowl
23 milliliters (1½ tablespoons) glycerin	Wooden spoon
910 grams (2 pounds) confectioners' sugar	Plastic film
Liquid or paste food coloring, optional	
150 grams (5 ounces) melted chocolate, optional	

Prepare your *mise en place*.

Place the gelatin leaves in a small heat-proof bowl with 60 milliliters (1/4 cup) cold water and let soak for a few minutes to soften completely.

Fill a saucepan small enough to allow your heat-proof bowl to fit snugly into it without touching the water with about 7.5 centimeters (3 inches) of water. Place over high heat and bring to a boil. Lower the heat so that the water continues at a low simmer.

Quickly place the bowl into the pan, checking to make sure that the bottom is not resting in the hot water and that the bowl is centered over the heat. Immediately begin stirring with a wooden spoon and heat until the gelatin has dissolved completely.

Stir in the corn syrup and glycerin and heat until well blended and very hot.

Place the confectioners' sugar on a clean, flat work surface. Make a well in the center and pour the hot gelatin mixture into the well. Begin stirring from the outside in and continue stirring until the mixture comes together and forms a dense mass.

Using your hands, knead the mixture until it is smooth and malleable.

If coloring or chocolate flavoring is desired, the appropriate liquid or paste food coloring or melted chocolate should now be kneaded into the fondant until a uniform color is reached.

NOTE
Colette Peters is the owner of
Colette's Cakes, a specialty cake
company in New York City. She is
famous for her cake replicas of
famous buildings as well as for
her inventive cake designs and
decorations.

Use the fondant as directed in a specific recipe, or form it into a round, tightly wrap it in plastic film, and set aside at room temperature until ready to use. If stored well wrapped or in an airtight container, fondant will keep almost indefinitely. Do not refrigerate it or the humidity will cause the sugar to dissolve, and the fondant will become too stiff to work with.

TIPS
It is usually best to make fondant the day before it is needed.

If the gelatin mixture is not hot enough, the fondant will require an excessive amount of kneading to come together.

If the fondant is very stiff and does not want to come together, it can be warmed slightly in a microwave, or a small amount (about ½ to 1 teaspoon) vegetable shortening can be kneaded into it.

If the fondant seems loose, knead in more confectioners' sugar, a bit at a time, until it no longer feels sticky.

EVALUATING YOUR SUCCESS
The finished (uncolored) fondant should be pure white and smooth, with no lumps or dry spots.

The finished fondant should be soft and malleable, so that it can be rolled and bent without cracking.

Demonstration

Pâte à Cornet (Design Paste for Cake Finishing)

Makes 225 grams (8 ounces)
Estimated time to complete: 2 hours

Ingredients	Equipment
45 grams (1½ ounces) cake flour	Sifter
8 grams (1 tablespoon) Dutch-process cocoa powder	Medium mixing bowl
70 grams (2½ ounces) confectioners' sugar, sifted	Wooden spoon

35 grams (1¼ ounces) unsalted butter, melted and cooled slightly

50 grams (1¾ ounces) egg whites, at room temperature

½ recipe *Biscuit* batter of choice (see pages 333 through 342)

Offset spatula
Silicone baking sheet liner
Cake comb
Sheet pan
Wire rack

Prepare your *mise en place*.

Sift the cake flour and cocoa together. Set aside.

Combine the sugar with the melted butter in a medium mixing bowl. Using a wooden spoon, stir to blend well. Add the egg whites alternately with the flour mixture, stirring until well blended.

Using an offset spatula, spread the *pâte* into a thin, even layer on a silicone sheet. Run a cake comb through the *pâte* to make a wavy decoration.

Place the whole silicone sheet in the freezer for about 30 minutes, or until the *pâte* has hardened.

Preheat the oven to 177°C (350°F).

Place the silicone sheet on a sheet pan. Cover the entire layer of hardened *pâte* with a thin layer of *biscuit* batter.

Bake according to the recipe instructions for whatever type of *biscuit* batter is used.

Cool the *pâte à cornet* on a wire rack, then remove the silicone sheet and use as directed in a specific recipe.

TIPS

If a color other than brown is desired, eliminate the cocoa powder and add 5 drops liquid or paste food

coloring to the sugar-and-butter mixture.

If the mixture is too thick to spread easily, add more egg white, a bit at a time, until spreading consistency is reached.

When creating a design with the cake comb, it is important to remember how you plan to use the *pâte à cornet*. For example, only a thin strip will be seen if it is used to line a cake ring.

To preview a design before baking, lift the silicon

sheet and look at the *pâte* from the bottom. Then, correct the design or proceed with the recipe.

A *pâte à cornet* may be piped or drizzled instead of being combed.

The *pâte à cornet* must be frozen; otherwise when the *biscuit* batter is spread onto it, the design will be destroyed.

EVALUATING YOUR SUCCESS

The *pâte* should make a perfectly even layer in the pan.

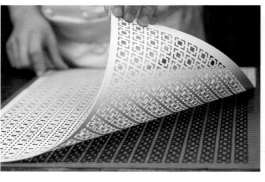

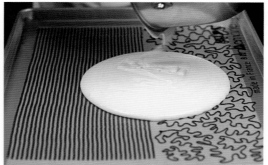

Demonstration

Chocolate Curls and Shavings

As needed
Estimated time to complete: 1 or 2 minutes

Ingredients	**Equipment**
One 450-gram (1-pound) block bittersweet, semisweet, milk, or white chocolate, at room temperature	Vegetable peeler or long sharp knife

Prepare your *mise en place*.

Holding the block of chocolate in one hand, slowly scrape the vegetable peeler along a flat side, allowing the chocolate to form itself into a curl. The wider the side you choose, the bigger the curls. A narrow side will produce thin strips or shavings.

TIPS

Although it is unlikely that the whole amount of chocolate will be used at one time, the large piece adds necessary weight and eases the making of curls.

If you hold the chocolate block in front of a pre-heated oven for a few minutes, it will soften just enough to speed the curling process. Do not allow it to begin to melt.

The best vegetable peeler for this job is an inexpensive, small plastic peeler with a short handle and triangular-shape section holding the blade.

EVALUATING YOUR SUCCESS

The curls should be fairly tight at the center, with frayed edges.

The shavings can be as random in size as you desire.

Theory
Putting Together Classic *Gâteaux*

Now that we have learned many of the basic cakes along with fillings, icings, and glazes, we can put together some of the more elaborate *gâteaux* of the classic French pastry repertoire.

Procedure for Covering a Cake with Marzipan or Rolled Fondant

You will find that many of the more elegant or elaborate cakes require being covered not with a simple icing or glaze, but with a smooth, refined sheet of marzipan or rolled fondant. The following instructions will help ease the process.

1. Cover the cake with a layer (or "crumb coat") of buttercream—make sure that this layer is very thin; otherwise, the buttercream will spill out from under the sides of the cake. This buttercream layer will help the coating adhere to the cake surface, as well as cover any blotches that might be on it.

2. Lightly dust a clean, flat work surface with confectioners' sugar. Place the marzipan or fondant on the sugared surface and, using a rolling pin, roll it out to a thin, even layer.

3. Throughout the process of shaping marzipan or fondant, work quickly and carefully. Both substances dry out very quickly, which will cause cracking and tearing.

4. Using a pastry brush, brush off any excess sugar, then carefully roll the marzipan or fondant onto the rolling pin.

5. Carefully unroll the marzipan or fondant onto the cake, gently removing any air bubbles beneath the surface. The coating should hang down over the sides of the cake.

6. If the marzipan or fondant rips when laying it over the cake or when smoothing it out, push the pieces together and smooth the area with the palm of your hand.

7. Using a sharp knife or pastry wheel, cut off any excess marzipan or fondant.

8. The coating should now cover the sides of the cake completely, sealing the cake.

9. Ragged edges, if any are visible, can be covered with piped decorations or a border, braided rope design, or frieze of leaves made out of marzipan or fondant. On a fondant-covered cake, piped decorations are usually done using royal icing (see page 381).

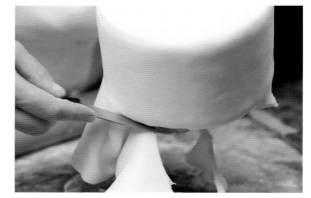

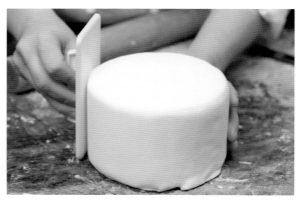

Demonstration

Génoise au Chocolat Glacée (Chocolate *Ganache* Cake)

Makes one 6-inch cake
Estimated time to complete: 3 hours

Ingredients	Equipment
For the cake	Serrated knife
6-inch *Génoise* (see Tips, page 331)	Standing electric mixer fitted with paddle attachment
½ recipe *Ganache Légère au Chocolat* (see page 379)	Small bowl
Simple syrup, flavored with alcohol of choice (see page 499)	6-inch cake ring
	6-inch round cake cardboard
For the finish	Parchment paper
½ recipe *Glaçage au Chocolat* (see page 380)	Offset spatula
Milk or White Chocolate Curls (see page 407)	Pastry brush
	Pastry bag fitted with #4 plain tip, plus other decorative tips
	Long metal spatula or chef's knife
	Handheld kitchen torch
	Cake decorating turntable

Prepare your *mise en place*.

Using a serrated knife, even off the top surface of the cake. Then cut the cake crosswise into 3 layers of equal size.

Place the *ganache* in the bowl of a standing electric mixer fitted with the paddle attachment and beat for a couple of minutes, or until soft peaks form. Pour the simple syrup into a small bowl or measuring cup.

Place the cake ring on the cake cardboard on a piece of parchment paper.

Using an offset spatula, spread a thin layer of the *ganache* onto the cardboard inside the cake ring, taking care that you leave no air pockets.

Place one cake layer on top of the *ganache*. Using a pastry brush, generously coat the cake surface with the simple syrup, allowing it to soak into the cake.

Place about half of the remaining *ganache* in a pastry bag fitted with the #4 plain tip and pipe the *ganache* to fill any voids between the *génoise* and the cake ring. Then, pipe a layer of *ganache* over the surface of the cake.

Place a second layer of *génoise* into the cake ring and, using a pastry brush, lightly coat the cake surface with some of the remaining syrup. Pipe a layer of *ganache* over the surface of the cake to equal the depth of the previous layer of *ganache*.

Place the final layer of *génoise* on top of the previous layers. Again lightly coat the cake surface with the syrup and pipe on a layer of *ganache*.

Using a long spatula or the back of a chef's knife, smooth the *ganache* across the top surface to make it even with the top of the cake ring.

Chill the cake for a couple of hours or until completely set.

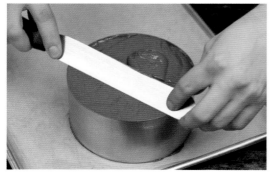

Remove the cake from the refrigerator and, using a handheld kitchen torch, warm the outside of the ring slightly to make it easier to lift the cake ring off.

Remove the cake ring. At this point, the cake (still sitting on the cake cardboard) can be tightly wrapped and stored, frozen, for up to 1 month.

Place the cake on a cake decorating turntable.

Using an offset spatula, cover the cake with a generous amount of the glaze, starting on the sides and then glazing the top. Make one pass across the top surface of the cake with the spatula immediately after glazing to make it smooth.

Arrange the chocolate curls around the base of the cake, carefully pressing them against the glaze to hold them in place.

If desired, use the remaining *ganache* to pipe decorative designs on top of the cake.

Refrigerate until ready to serve. Serve within 24 hours of being made.

TIPS

The layered *génoise* and *ganache* should be equal to the height of the cake ring.

The glaze should be kept as close to body temperature as possible to prevent it from melting the *ganache* or from setting too quickly and causing unattractive drips on the sides of the cake.

The light-colored chocolate curls contrast nicely with the dark chocolate glaze.

EVALUATING YOUR SUCCESS

The *génoise* should be moist and flavorful from the syrup.

The *ganache* should be light brown and smooth, with a strong, deep chocolate flavor.

The finished top surface should be perfectly smooth.

The top edge of the finished cake should be sharp.

The glaze should be even and just thick enough to be opaque, with no thin areas.

There should be no visible drips down the sides of the finished cake.

The band of chocolate curls around the base of the cake should be about 2.5 centimeters (1 inch) tall and evenly spaced all around.

Demonstration

Marjolaine (Marjolaine)

Makes two 10-by-30.5-centimeter (4-by-12-inch) cakes
Estimated time to complete: 1 to 2 days

Ingredients	Equipment
For the *crème d'or*	Standing electric mixer fitted with whip attachment
220 milliliters (7 ounces) chilled heavy cream	Medium saucepan to fit heat-proof bowl
200 grams (7 ounces) semisweet or bittersweet chocolate, chopped into bits	
For the stabilized whipped cream	Medium heat-proof bowl
350 milliliters (11 ounces) chilled heavy cream	Rubber spatula
75 grams (2⅔ ounces) confectioners' sugar	Small stainless-steel bowl
1½ gelatin leaves or 4.5 grams (1½ teaspoons) unflavored granulated gelatin	Small saucepan to fit small bowl
	Serrated knife
20 milliliters (1 tablespoon plus 1 teaspoon) alcohol-based flavoring of choice	Parchment paper or 2 cake cardboard strips
	Offset spatula
	Metal spatula

For the cake

1 recipe Chocolate *Génoise* (see page 330), baked as a sheet cake

Eight 10-by-30.5-centimeter (4-by-12-inch) *Pâte à Dacquoise* strips (see page 351)

1 recipe *Crème au Beurre* (see page 373), flavored with praline paste (see page 170)

For the finish

Glaçage au Chocolat (see page 380)

55 grams (2 ounces) chopped toasted hazelnuts

NOTE

The *Marjolaine* was created by the esteemed chef Fernand Point, for his restaurant, *La Pyramide*, in Vienne. Located halfway between Paris and the Côte d'Azur, *La Pyramide* featured many classic dishes, as well as Chef Point's revolutionary "modern" French cuisine. The cake was named for a special woman in the chef's life who remains unknown. It was, and still is, considered one of Chef Point's masterpieces. Years of trial and error went into its creation before he achieved the desired combination of flavors and textures. His original recipe created a cake large enough to serve both luncheon and dinner guests at the restaurant on an average day. Since its presentation to the culinary world in the mid twentieth century, myriad versions have been created by pastry chefs the world over. The *Marjolaine* is a time-consuming *gâteau* to put together; there are many steps involved, with many components. For this reason, the *mise en place* is especially important. Advance planning is crucial, and tight organization must be followed.

Prepare your *mise en place*.

To make the *crème d'or*, place the cream in the bowl of a standing electric mixer fitted with the whip attachment. Beat on medium for about 4 minutes, or until firm peaks form. Set aside to come to room temperature.

Fill a saucepan small enough to allow your medium heat-proof bowl to fit snugly into it without touching the water with about 7.5 centimeters (3 inches) of water. Place it over high heat and bring to a boil. Immediately remove the pan from the heat.

Quickly place the medium bowl into the pan, checking to make sure that the bottom is not resting in the hot water. Add the chocolate and let stand for a minute to start the melting. Heat, stirring frequently with a rubber spatula, for about 3 minutes, or until the chocolate has melted completely and is very hot.

Remove the bowl from the heat and fold the hot chocolate into the room temperature whipped cream.

Wash and dry the mixer bowl and whip and return them to the mixer.

To make the stabilized whipped cream, place the cream in the bowl of the standing electric mixer fitted with the whip attachment. Beat on low to aerate. Add the confectioners' sugar, raise the speed to medium-high, and beat until soft peaks form. Set aside to come to room temperature.

Place the gelatin in a small stainless-steel bowl with cold water to cover and let soak for a minute or two to

soften. When soft, drain the gelatin and add the flavoring. This begins to melt the gelatin, which speeds up the process.

Fill a saucepan small enough to allow your small stainless-steel bowl to fit snugly into it without touching the water with about 7.5 centimeters (3 inches) of water. Place it over high heat and bring to a boil. Quickly place the bowl holding the gelatin into the pan, checking to make sure that the bottom is not resting in the hot water. Heat, stirring, until the gelatin has dissolved completely.

Remove the bowl from the heat and pour the gelatin mixture into the whipped cream, stirring with a rubber spatula to blend well.

Using a serrated knife, cut two 10-by-30.5-centimeter (4-by-12-inch) strips of *génoise*.

Place each strip on a piece of parchment paper or cake board of an appropriate size.

Using an offset spatula, spread a 1.3-centimeter-thick (1-inch-thick) layer of *ganache* over one strip of *génoise*. Top with a *dacquoise* strip and then, using an offset spatula, spread a 1.3-centimeter-thick (1-inch-thick) layer of *crème d'or* over the *dacquoise*. Top with another *dacquoise* strip. Spread another layer of the buttercream over the *dacquoise* and top with another *dacquoise* strip. Using a clean offset spatula, cover the top of the layers with the stabilized whipped cream. Top with a final strip of *dacquoise*.

Repeat these steps to assemble the second cake. Reserve the remaining buttercream.

Transfer the cakes to the refrigerator to chill for 8 hours or overnight. This allows the cakes to absorb moisture and makes the *dacquoise* layers soft and chewy.

When the cakes are well chilled, using a serrated knife, neatly trim the longer sides, tapering the cake so it is narrower at the top.

Using an offset spatula, cover each cake with the remaining buttercream, smoothing to make a neat surface. At this point, the cakes can be wrapped and stored refrigerated for up to 3 days, or frozen for up to 1 month.

Glaze with the chocolate glaze as directed on page 380. Just as the glaze begins to set, using the edge of a metal spatula, make a neat crosshatch design over the top.

Using your hands, press the nuts along the base of the long sides of the cake.

Before serving, use the serrated knife to trim off the end pieces and reveal the many layers.

TIPS

The *crème d'or* should not be made in advance or it will get too firm to spread smoothly. If it is too loose, chill it for several minutes before spreading.

When assembling, keep the layers of filling thin; if they are too thick, the cake will be too tall and much too rich.

Trim only the long sides, not the ends, before glazing. The ends are trimmed after the glazing to reveal the many layers of the cake to diners.

EVALUATING YOUR SUCCESS

The *crème d'or* should be medium brown and airy.

The whipped cream should be smooth, with no pieces of unmelted gelatin.

The buttercream should have a very strong hazelnut flavor.

The *dacquoise* should be soft, chewy, and nutty in flavor.

The *ganache* should taste of deep chocolate and be dark and dense.

The filling layers should be of a consistent size.

The long sides of the cakes should be smooth and taper slightly at the top of the cake.

The glaze should be shiny, with no drips down the side of the cake.

The crosshatch should be neat and even in depth and distance between each line.

Demonstration

Dacquoise au Café (*Dacquoise* with Coffee Buttercream)

Makes one 15-centimeter (6-inch) cake

Estimated time to complete: 1 hour

Ingredients	Equipment
Five 15-centimeter (6-inch) *Pâte à Dacquoise* rounds (see page 351)	Round cake cardboard
½ recipe coffee-flavored *Crème au Beurre* (see page 373)	Offset spatula
Coffee beans	Pastry bag fitted with #5 star tip

Prepare your *mise en place*.

Place a meringue round on the cardboard round.

Using an offset spatula, lightly coat the meringue with just enough buttercream that it oozes out slightly when the next meringue layer is placed on top. Continue stacking meringues and coating with buttercream until the final disk has been placed on top.

Place the remaining buttercream in a pastry bag fitted with the #5 star tip and pipe rosettes around the edge

of the cake so that, when cut, each slice will have some décor. Decorate with the coffee beans.

Serve within a few hours.

TIPS

The cake cardboard should be slightly larger than the meringue disks, so that it is suitable for presentation.

The buttercream should be well flavored with coffee extract, or it will not stand up to the nutty flavor of the meringues.

If the buttercream oozes out between the layers, it is easier to square off the final coating.

EVALUATING YOUR SUCCESS

The meringue rounds should be crunchy with a slightly nutty flavor.

The buttercream should have a strong coffee flavor.

The buttercream should completely cover the meringues.

The rosettes should be consistent in size and shape.

Dacquoise au café

Demonstration

Forêt Noire (Black Forest Cake)

Makes two 15-centimeter (6-inch) cakes
Estimated time to complete: 2 hours

Ingredients	Equipment

For the cake

1 recipe *Biscuit au Chocolat pour Forêt Noire* (see page 339)
240 milliliters (1 cup) kirschwasser-flavored simple syrup
  (see page 499)

For the cherry compote

400 grams (14 ounces) pitted Bing cherries (see Tips)
100 grams (3½ ounces) sugar
20 milliliters (1 tablespoon plus 1 teaspoon) kirschwasser
12 grams (1 tablespoon) cornstarch

For the *crème d'or*

270 milliliters (8¾ ounces) chilled heavy cream
250 grams (8¾ ounces) semisweet or bittersweet chocolate,
  chopped into bits

For the *crème Chantilly*

500 milliliters (16 ounces) chilled heavy cream
100 grams (3½ ounces) confectioners' sugar

For the finish

Fresh, candied, or maraschino cherries, well dried
Chocolate Shavings (see page 407)

Equipment

Serrated knife
2 small bowls
Medium heavy-bottomed saucepan
Kitchen fork
Wooden spoon
Standing electric mixer fitted with whip attachment
Heat-proof bowl
Saucepan to fit heat-proof bowl
Rubber spatula
Two 15-centimeter (6-inch) cake cardboards
Pastry brush
Pastry bag fitted with #4 or #5 plain or star tip
Offset spatula

NOTE

This cake has its origins in the Black
Forest area of Germany, where it is
known as *Schwarzwälder Kirschtorte*.

Prepare your *mise en place*.

Using a serrated knife, even off the top surface of each cake, then cut it crosswise into 3 layers of equal size. Set aside.

Place the simple syrup in a small bowl and set it aside.

To make the compote, combine the cherries with the sugar and kirschwasser in a medium heavy-bottomed saucepan over medium heat. Bring to a boil.

Combine the cornstarch with 15 milliliters (1 tablespoon) cold water in a small bowl, stirring with a kitchen fork to dissolve the cornstarch. Immediately stir the cornstarch mixture into the boiling cherries. Return the mixture to a boil, stirring constantly with a wooden spoon. Lower the heat to a bare simmer and cook, stirring frequently, for about 3 minutes, or until the sauce has thickened and the starchy taste has

cooked out. Remove from the heat and set aside.

To make the *crème d'or*, place the cream in the bowl of a standing electric mixer fitted with the whip attachment. Beat on medium for about 4 minutes, or until firm peaks form. Set aside to come to room temperature.

Fill a saucepan small enough to allow your heat-proof bowl to fit snugly into it without touching the water with about 7.5 centimeters (3 inches) of water. Place over high heat, bring to a boil, and immediately remove the pan from the heat.

Quickly place the bowl into the pan, checking to make sure that the bottom is not resting in the hot water. Add the chocolate and let stand for a minute to start the melting. Heat, stirring frequently with a rubber spatula, for about 3 minutes, or until the chocolate has melted completely and is very hot.
Remove the bowl from the heat and fold the hot chocolate into the room-temperature whipped cream.

Wash and dry the mixer bowl and whip and return them to the mixer.

Make the *crème Chantilly*: Place the heavy cream in the standing electric mixer fitted with the whip attachment. Beat on medium for 1 minute. Add the confectioners' sugar and continue beating for about 4 minutes, or until firm peaks form.

Place one cake layer, cut side up, on each of the cake cardboards.

Using a pastry brush, generously coat the surface of each cake layer with the syrup, allowing it to soak into the cake.

Place the *crème d'or* in a pastry bag fitted with the #4 or #5 plain or star tip. Pipe 3 concentric rings onto each cake layer. Using about one quarter of the compote for each cake, fill in the spaces between the rings of cream.

Place a second cake layer on top of each cake and repeat the process described above.

Place the final cake layers, cut side down, on top of each cake and generously coat the surface of each with the syrup, allowing it to soak in. The cake may be made up to this point and stored, covered and refrigerated, for 1 day.

Use the remaining *crème Chantilly* to cover each cake, neatening the edges with an offset spatula.

Place a star tip in the pastry bag and pipe rosettes of cream around the top edge of each cake. Top each rosette with a cherry. Using your fingertips, press chocolate shavings all around the bottom edge of the cake.

Serve immediately or within a few hours. Refrigerate the cake until ready to serve.

TIPS
The compote may be made with fresh, canned, or frozen Bing cherries.

The *crème d'or* cannot be made in advance, as it will get too firm to pipe.

You can add 5 to 10 milliliters (1 to 2 teaspoons) of vanilla extract or kirschwasser to the *crème Chantilly* for more flavor.

You can fold in two leaves of melted gelatin to the soft-peak *crème Chantilly* for greater stability.

EVALUATING YOUR SUCCESS
The thickened compote should have a clear sauce, with no lumps of cornstarch.

The cake and the filling layers should be consistent in depth, so that there is perfect symmetry when viewing the cake from the side.

The *crème d'or* should be medium brown and airy.

The *crème Chantilly* should be smooth, with no graininess.

The filling should not show through the cream used to cover the cake.

The rosettes should be evenly spaced along the out-side edge of the top of the cake.

The shavings should be in an even row covering only the bottom 1.3 centimeters (½ inch) of the cake.

Demonstration

Dobos (Dobos Torte)

Makes two 15-centimeter (6-inch) cakes

Estimated time to complete: 2 hours

Ingredients	Equipment
For the caramel	Small heavy-bottomed saucepan
200 grams (7 ounces) sugar	Wooden spoon
	Ice bath
For the cake	Hot knife
1 recipe *Biscuit Dobos* (see page 333)	Two 15-centimeter (6-inch) cake cardboards
Rum-flavored simple syrup (see page 499)	Small bowl
½ recipe chocolate *Crème au Beurre* (see page 373)	Pastry brush
	Offset spatula
	Cake comb
	Pastry bag fitted with #5 star tip

NOTE

Created by an Austrian pastry chef, Josef Dobos, after whom it is named, Dobos Torte is an extremely rich cake.

Prepare an your *mise en place*.

To make the caramel, place a small heavy-bottomed saucepan over medium heat. When it is just hot, add the sugar and lower the heat. Cook, stirring with a wooden spoon to prevent lumps from forming, for about 5 minutes, or until the sugar melts, turns a warm amber color, and becomes quite clear. As long as the syrup is cloudy, the sugar needs to dissolve more.

Immediately remove the pan from the heat and place it in the ice bath to stop the cooking and keep the caramel from darkening and turning bitter.

Working quickly, dip the top of 2 of the sponge rounds into the hot caramel. Do not allow the

caramel to drip over the sides. Place the rounds, caramel side up on a piece of parchment paper to set slightly.

Using a heated knife, cut each caramel-coated round into single-serving-sized wedges. This is best done while the caramel is still warm and pliable rather than when you serve the cake.

Place one of the remaining rounds on each of the cake cardboards.

Pour the simple syrup into a small bowl. Using a pastry brush, generously coat the surface of each of the 10 rounds (those with no caramel) with the syrup, allowing it to soak in.

Using an offset spatula, spread a thin layer of buttercream on each of the two rounds sitting on the cardboards. Begin layering, adding one syrup-soaked round at a time and covering each with a thin layer of buttercream. When the final syrup-soaked layer has been placed on top, cover each cake with a coating of buttercream.

Using a cake comb, create a decorative pattern on the sides of each cake while the buttercream is still soft. Place the remaining buttercream in a pastry bag fitted with the star tip. Pipe rosettes around the top edge of the cake so that each slice of cake will include a rosette when sliced.

Angle a caramel-coated cake triangle into each rosette and serve.

EVALUATING YOUR SUCCESS

The caramel should be even and thin, and cover the entire top of the cake round, but not drip over the sides.

The caramel wedges should not be cracked or broken. There should be no burn marks from the hot knife in the cut caramel.

The caramel wedges should be of an even size.

The sponge rounds should be soft and moist.

The buttercream should have a strong chocolate flavor.

The caramel wedges should sit at even angles around the cake.

Demonstration

Fraisier Victoria (Strawberry *Génoise* Cake)

Makes two 6-inch cakes

Estimated time to complete: 2 hours

Ingredients	Equipment
For the cake	Paring knife
20 large fresh strawberries, washed, dried, and hulled	Paper towel
1 recipe American Milk Sponge Cake (see page 332)	6-inch cake cardboard
Simple syrup (see page 499)	Two 6-inch cake rings
1 recipe *Crème Mousseline* (see page 377)	Small bowl
	Pastry brush
For the finish	Pastry bag fitted with #5 and #0 or #1 plain tips
Confectioners' sugar for dusting	Offset spatula
100 grams (3½ ounces) pale-green Marzipan (see page 401)	Rolling pin
55 grams (2 ounces) Royal Icing (see page 381)	
Marzipan or glazed strawberries, optional	

Prepare your *mise en place*.

Using a paring knife, cut each strawberry in half lengthwise. Try to choose berries of a similar size and shape so all the pieces will be equal. Place them cut side down on a double layer of paper towel to drain.

Using a cake cardboard as a guide, cut 4 circles of sponge slightly smaller than the round so that they can fit easily into a the cake rings.

Place one of the sponge circles into each of the cake rings.

Place the simple syrup in a small bowl. Using a pastry brush, generously coat the surface of each of the two cake circles in the rings with the syrup, allowing it to soak in.

Place about half the *mousseline* in a pastry bag fitted with the #5 plain tip and pipe it any voids between the cake and the cake ring.

Place halved strawberries stem end up and cut side against the inside of the cake ring. Pipe a layer of *moussseline* to come halfway up the center of the cake so it is surrounded by the strawberries. Place a

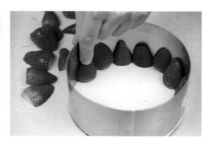

layer of strawberries, cut side down, on top of the *mousseline*, so that the *mousseline*-and-strawberry layer is equal in height to the outer line of strawberries. Cover the strawberries with more *mousseline*, smoothing out the layer with an offset spatula.

Using a pastry brush, generously coat the surface of each of the remaining cake circles with the syrup, allowing it to soak in. Place a soaked circle on top of the *mousseline* in each cake ring. The cake should come up to just below the top of the cake rings.

Using the remaining *mousseline*, cover the top of each cake. At this point, the cake may be wrapped and stored refrigerated for up to 2 days.

Sprinkle a flat work surface with confectioners' sugar and roll out the marzipan to 3 millimeters (⅛ inch) thick. The marzipan should be lightly tinted green.

Carefully unmold each cake.

Using the cake ring as a guide, cut out two circles of green marzipan to fit precisely on top of each cake.

Fill a pastry bag fitted with the #0 or #1 tip with the royal icing and pipe delicate decorations over the top of the marzipan.

Serve the cake immediately, or no more than 2 hours after it is finished. If refrigerated, the marzipan will begin to melt and render the cake unusable.

TIPS
This cake should never be frozen.

If strawberries are out of season, fresh clementine segments can be used; however, the cake would no longer be called *fraisier*.

EVALUATING YOUR SUCCESS
The outer border of strawberries should be composed of berries that are of equal size, shape, and height.

There should be no cream on the outside of the outer strawberries.

The *mousseline* should be smooth, with no lumps of butter or pastry cream.

The *mousseline* should have a strong vanilla flavor and a light off-white color.

There should be enough fruit in the center of the cake that each bite contains some.

The marzipan should be pale green, not bright or garish.

The marzipan should just reach the edge of the cake but not go over or remain inside the edge.

The piped design should be neat and clean.

NOTE
A *gâteau fraisier* is a classic cake that is traditionally made with layers of *génoise*, flavored buttercream, and fresh strawberries *(fraises)*. This variation is an adaptation of the classic using American sponge cake filled with light buttercream *(crème mousseline)*. It was created by a talented FCI pastry chef, Victoria Wells, who made it her signature cake.

Demonstration

Miroir aux Fruits (Fruit *Mousse* Miroir)

Makes two 6-inch cakes

Estimated time to complete: 24 hours

Ingredients	Equipment

Ingredients

1 recipe *Biscuit Joconde* (see page 335)

100 grams (3½ ounces) raspberry jam

Two 6-inch *Génoise* rounds (see Tips, page 329)

1 recipe *Mousse aux Fruits* (see page 388)

For the *miroir* glaze

200 grams (7 ounces) apricot jam

50 grams (2 ounces) raspberry purée

Equipment

Serrated knife

Offset spatula

Two 6-inch-round by 3-inch- deep cake rings

Small container with lid

Metal spoon

Plastic film

Small saucepan

Fine-mesh sieve

Small bowl

Handheld immersion blender

Paper towel, if needed

Hot kitchen towel

Prepare your *mise en place*.

Using a serrated knife, cut the *joconde* into quarters.

Using an offset spatula, lightly coat the surface of one of the squares with raspberry jam. Top with another cake square and coat it with jam. Repeat the process with the third layer and top with the final cake layer.

Using the serrated knife, cut the stacked *joconde* into 5-centimeter-wide (2-inch-wide) strips. Cut the strips into 6-millimeter-thick (¼-inch-thick) slices.

Working carefully, gently press the stacked strips, jam lines facing outward, against the interior of the two cake rings to come halfway up the sides of each ring.

When the bottom half of the interior of each ring has been covered with *joconde* strips, carefully fit a *génoise* round into the bottom of each ring.

Carefully spoon the *mousse* into the center of each ring to completely fill the cake ring. Using the offset spatula, carefully scrape any excess *mousse* from the surface by sliding the spatula across the ring. This will allow the *mousse* to settle evenly within the ring and create a smooth surface for finishing.

Place a piece of plastic film over the surface and transfer the cakes to the freezer for at least 8 hours, or until solidly frozen. At this point, they can be kept frozen for up to 1 month.

When ready to finish, make the *miroir* glaze.

Combine the apricot jam with the raspberry purée in a small saucepan over medium heat and cook for just about a minute to heat through, then purée with handheld immersion blender. Remove from the heat and press through a fine-mesh sieve into a small bowl. Set aside to cool.

Remove the cakes from the freezer. Remove and discard the plastic film. If condensation appears, carefully blot with a paper towel.

Using the offset spatula, carefully cover the surface of each frozen cake with an equal amount of the glaze, smoothing it out to an even layer.

Wrap each cake ring with a hot kitchen towel to warm it and carefully lift the ring off to unmold the cakes.

Refrigerate them until ready to serve, or for up to 4 days. Serve cold.

TIPS

The *joconde* strips can be positioned inside the ring vertically, horizontally, or in a slanted pattern. They can also be placed in an alternating pattern to create a woven effect.

The *joconde* strips go into the ring before the *génoise* so that the cake bottom is an even display of the strips.

If desired, a middle layer of *génoise* can be placed in between two layers of *mousse*.

If desired, pieces of fruit may be folded into the *mousse* for added texture.

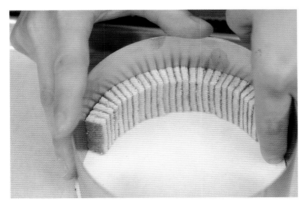

NOTE
Miroir is the French word for "mirror." In this instance, it is used to describe the glazed topping on the cake.

The *mousse* will sink slightly during freezing.

The *mousse* needs to be completely frozen before being covered with the *nappage* or the two components will mix.

EVALUATING YOUR SUCCESS
The *joconde* pieces should be even in height, with no gaps.

The *joconde* pieces should go approximately halfway up the sides of the cake ring.

There should be no *mousse* seeping between the cake ring and the *joconde*.

The *nappage* should be even, with no lumps or spatula lines.

The *nappage* should be a color that is complementary to the *mousse*.

There should be no *nappage* running down the sides of the cake or into the center when the cake is cut.

Demonstration

Charlotte Royale (Royal *Charlotte*)

Makes one 6-inch cake

Estimated time to complete: 6 hours

Ingredients	Equipment
1 recipe *Biscuit Joconde* (see page 335)	Baking sheet
100 grams (3½ ounces) apricot or raspberry jam	Parchment paper
One recipe *Bavarois à la Crème Anglaise* (see page 395)	Offset spatula
1 round *Génoise* (see Tips, page 329), slightly smaller than 6 inches in diameter	Parchment paper-lined baking sheet
	Plastic film
For the *nappage*	Serrated knife
200 grams (7 ounces) apricot jam	6-inch dome mold or stainless-steel bowl
	Small saucepan
For the finish	Fine-mesh sieve
100 grams (3½ ounces) toasted, sliced almonds	Small bowl
	8-inch round cake cardboard
	Warm kitchen towel, if needed
	Pastry brush

Prepare your *mise en place*.

Line a baking sheet with parchment paper. Set aside.

Place the *biscuit* on a sheet of parchment paper.

Using an offset spatula, lightly coat the surface of the *biscuit* with a thin layer of jam.

Carefully begin forming the cake into a tight roll, using the parchment paper to help keep it neat. Transfer the cake roll carefully to the parchment-lined baking sheet, seam side down. Cover with plastic film and refrigerate for at least 1 hour, or until set.

Using a serrated knife, cut the roll crosswise into 6-millimeter-thick (¼-inch-thick) slices.

Line the dome mold with plastic film.

Carefully press the cake slices into the film-lined mold in one layer, fitting them as tightly together as possible while still keeping each slice intact.

Fill the remaining space in the mold with *crème anglaise*.

Place the circle of *génoise* on top of the cream, patting it down to avoid forming air pockets. Cover the mold with plastic film and refrigerate for 3 hours, or until set. At this point, the *charlotte* may be refrigerated for up to 3 days, or frozen for up to 1 month.

To make the *nappage*, combine the apricot jam with 45 milliliters (3 tablespoons) of water in a small saucepan over medium heat and cook for just about a minute to heat through. Press the glaze through a fine-mesh sieve into a small bowl. Set aside.

When you are ready to finish the *charlotte*, invert the mold onto the cake cardboard carefully unmold the

charlotte. If necessary, wrap a wet, warm towel around the mold to loosen it.

Using a pastry brush, lightly glaze the *charlotte* with the apricot *nappage*.

Using your fingertips, press the almonds around the bottom edge of the *charlotte*. Serve immediately or within a few hours.

TIPS

A *charlotte royale* is a more elaborate version of the *charlotte russe*.

The cake roll may be made with any *biscuit* that is thin, pliable, and soft.

The type of jam used should complement the flavor of the Bavarian cream used.

Candied or fresh fruits, nuts, or chocolate bits may be mixed into the Bavarian cream to add interest and texture.

If you only have a mold larger than this recipe calls for, you can place an additional layer of *génoise* in the middle of the mold when it is half filled, then cover it with additional Bavarian cream and finish it with the final layer of *génoise*.

EVALUATING YOUR SUCCESS

The *biscuit* should be covered with just enough jelly to hold the roll together when cut.
The jelly roll circles should be completely round and tight, so that there are no holes or breaks.

When lining the mold, the cake circles should not be pressed out, but they must be placed close together so that there are no gaps.

The Bavarian cream should be smooth, with all ingredients thoroughly incorporated (unless fruit or nuts have been added).

The *nappage* should be thin and evenly applied to cover the entire mold.

Demonstration

Bûche de Noël (Yule Log)

Makes one 25-centimeter (10-inch) log
Estimated time to complete : 2 hours

Ingredients	Equipment
1 recipe *Roulade de Biscuit* (see page 340), baked in a half-sheet pan	Parchment paper
Simple syrup (see page 499)	Small bowl
½ recipe coffee- or chocolate-flavored	Pastry brush
Crème au Beurre I or *II* (see page 373 or 374)	Offset spatula
	30.5-centimeter (12-inch) cake cardboard strip
For the finish	Serrated knife
Any meringue, marzipan, or chocolate décor desired	Cake comb

Prepare your *mise en place.*

Place the *biscuit* on a sheet of parchment paper.

Place the simple syrup in a small bowl. Using a pastry brush, generously coat the cake surface with the syrup, allowing it to soak in.

Using an offset spatula, lightly coat the surface of the *biscuit* with a thin layer of buttercream.

Carefully begin forming the cake into a tight roll, using the parchment paper to help keep it neat. Transfer the roll carefully, seam side down, to the cardboard strip. At this point, the cake can be stored, tightly wrapped and refrigerated, for up to 2 days, or frozen for up to 1 month.

Using the offset spatula, carefully cover the entire log with a smooth layer of buttercream.

Using a cake comb, score the log in long even lines to resemble tree bark.

Using a serrated knife, cut 1.3 centimeters (½ inch) off each end of the log. Place the end pieces cut side up on top of the log to resemble cut branches.

Using the spatula, carefully cover the cut ends with buttercream.

The log may be served as it is or decorated with myriad decorations such as meringue mushrooms and snowmen, marzipan figures or berries, and chocolate trees or pinecones.

Serve within a few hours of finishing it.

TIPS
A *bûche de Noël* can be made with many other fillings, such as *mousses*, ice creams, or *ganache*. Buttercream is the classic filling and is most commonly used for this traditional Christmas cake, which is served throughout the holiday season in France.

If one side of the cake is a bit overcooked, roll the log so that the overcooked part is on the inside.

EVALUATING YOUR SUCCESS
The *biscuit* should be soft and moist.

The buttercream should have a strong coffee or chocolate flavor.

There should be no holes or gaps inside the rolled cake.

The buttercream should completely cover the log.

The "branch" cuts should lie on top of the log, not slip down the sides.

Demonstration

Gâteau de Mousse aux Deux Chocolats avec Pâte à Cornet
(White and Dark Chocolate *Mousse* Cake with Design Paste)

Makes two 8-inch cakes
Estimated time to complete: 6 hours

Ingredients	Equipment
1 recipe *Pâte à Cornet* made with 1 recipe *Biscuit d'Amandes* (see pages 404 and 337)	Two 8-inch oval cake rings
Confectioners' sugar for dusting, optional	Acetate or parchment paper, optional
½ recipe *Génoise au Chocolat* (see page 330)	Pastry wheel
1 recipe Dark Chocolate *Mousse* (see page 382)	Serrated knife
1 recipe White Chocolate *Mousse* (see page 384)	2 pastry bags fitted with #5 tips
	Plastic film

For the finish
Glaçage au Chocolat (see page 380), optional
Crème Chantilly (see page 111), optional
Chocolate Curls (see page 407), optional

Prepare your *mise en place*.

As you prepare the *biscuit* with the *pâte à cornet* decorations, keep in mind that the designs in the *pâte à cornet* should be busy enough to disguise the joints when they are placed inside the cake rings.

Line the cake rings with a strip of acetate or parchment paper cut to fit or lightly dust the *pâte à cornet* with confectioners' sugar to keep it from sticking to the ring.

Using a pastry wheel, cut 2 strips of the *biscuit* a bit longer than the diameter and a bit shorter than the height of the cake rings. Press the strip against the inside of the cake ring; it should fit tightly against it. The added length and height will give the finished cake a cleaner edge.

Using a serrated knife, cut a piece of the *génoise* to fit the bottom of each cake ring.

Place the dark chocolate *mousse* in one pastry bag fitted with the #5 plain tip and the white chocolate *mousse* in another pastry bag fitted with the #5 plain tip. Begin piping the two *mousses* into the cake rings to fill each ring completely. You can pipe in layers, stripes, or concentric circles. You want an attractive pattern to appear when the cake is sliced.

Cover the cakes with plastic film and refrigerate for 3 hours, or until set. At this point, they can be kept, tightly wrapped and refrigerated, for up to 4 days, or frozen for up to 1 month.

The cakes can now be finished in many different ways, and the decoration chosen should reflect the flavors of the two *mousses*. Possible finishes are:

Pipe the remaining *mousse* over the top in a decorative pattern.

Smooth the top and cover it with a coating of chocolate glaze.

Pipe *Crème Chantilly* over the top in a decorative pattern.

Heap chocolate curls on top (these may be added to the top of any of the other coverings as well).

Serve the cakes within a few hours of finishing them.

TIPS

When piping in the *mousse*, note that each slice of cake should be composed of the same amount of the two flavors.

If desired, you can add small pieces of fruit to one or both of the *mousses*.

EVALUATING YOUR SUCCESS

The *pâte à cornet* decorations should be neat and make a smooth surface.

The bottom layer of *génoise* should be approximately 9 millimeters (⅜ inch) thick.

The *mousses* should be firm enough that they do not mix together when the cake is finished.

Each *mousse* should be the consistency of freshly whipped cream—smooth, light, and airy, with no lumps or streaks.

Both *mousses* should be strongly flavored and not overly sweet.

Whatever the surface décor, it should completely cover the top of the cake and reflect the interior flavors.

NOTE

Named for the wife of King George III of England, the original *charlotte* was created at the end of the eighteenth century and consisted of an apple compote baked in a mold lined with toast slices. In the next century, the great chef Marie-Antoine Carême adapted the recipe as a result of a near disaster before a banquet celebrating the return of King Louis XVIII to Paris in 1815. The kitchen's supply of gelatin was insufficient for the Bavarian cream that Carême was preparing, so to solve the problem of a sagging dessert, he added ladyfingers to the sides and called it *charlotte parisienne*. The name was changed to *charlotte russe* during the Second Empire, when Russian-style table service became fashionable among French aristocrats.

Demonstration

Charlotte Russe (Russian *Charlotte*)

Makes two 15-centimeter (6-inch) cakes

Estimated time to prepare: 6 hours

Ingredients	Equipment
1 recipe *Biscuits à la Cuillère* (see page 342), prepared as 9-centimeter (3-inch) ladyfingers and one 15-centimeter (6-inch) round	Serrated knife
	7-inch *charlotte* mold
	Plastic film
1 recipe *Bavarois à la Crème Anglaise* (see page 395)	Metal spoon
	Serving plate

For the finish

Fresh fruit or berries, *Crème Chantilly* (see page 111), Chocolate Curls (see page 407), or nuts, optional

Prepare your *mise en place*.

When the ladyfingers are cool, using a serrated knife, cut each one in half lengthwise.

Line the *charlotte* mold with plastic film, pressing it neatly against the bottom and sides.

Using the cut ladyfingers, carefully line the inside of the mold. Press them tightly against the sides, leaving no gaps or holes.

Place the *biscuit* round in the bottom of the mold, easing it in to fit around the ladyfingers.

Spoon the Bavarian cream into the center to fill it to a point just slightly below the ends of the ladyfingers. Cover the mold with plastic film and refrigerate for 4 hours, or until completely set. At this point, the *charlotte* may be stored, tightly wrapped and refrigerated, for up to 2 days, or frozen for up to 1 month.

When you are ready to serve the *charlotte*, invert it onto a serving plate. Carefully remove the mold and the plastic film.

The *charlotte* may be presented as is or decorated with fresh fruit or berries, *crème Chantilly*, chocolate curls, or toasted or candied nuts.

TIPS

Almost any flavor of Bavarian cream may be used. If you choose a fruit Bavarian, you can mix in pieces of ripe, fresh fruit just before filling the cake.

EVALUATING YOUR SUCCESS

The ladyfingers should be consistent in length and width and light brown on the edges.

There should be no gaps or holes between the ladyfingers.

There should be no unmixed ingredients in the Bavarian cream.

The filling should be just below the height of the ladyfingers.

Demonstration

Sachertorte

Makes two 6-inch cakes

Estimated time to complete: 90 minutes

Ingredients	Equipment
Butter and flour for the pans	Two 6-inch round cake pans
	Saucepan to fit heat-proof bowl
For the cake	Heat-proof bowl
110 grams (3¾ ounces) unsweetened	Wooden spoon
chocolate, chopped into bits	Standing electric mixer fitted with whip and paddle attachments
110 grams (3¾ ounces) unsalted butter,	Rubber spatula
at room temperature	Medium bowl
55 grams (2 ounces) confectioners' sugar	Cake tester
6 large egg yolks, at room temperature	2 wire racks
110 grams (3¾ ounces) cake flour, sifted	2 baking sheets
	Serrated knife
For the French meringue	Small saucepan
6 large egg whites, at room temperature	Fine-mesh sieve
100 grams (3½ ounces) granulated sugar	Medium heavy-bottomed saucepan
	Metal spatula
For the finish	2 6-inch cake cardboards or serving plates
500 grams (1 pound, 1½ ounces) apricot jam	
30 milliliters (2 tablespoons) rum	
1 recipe *Fondant Décor façon Colette* (see page 403)	
300 grams (11 ounces) unsweetened chocolate, melted	

Prepare your *mise en place*.

Preheat the oven to 177°C (350°F).

Butter and flour the cake pans. Set aside.

Fill a saucepan large enough to allow your heat-proof bowl to fit snugly into it without touching the water with about 7.5 centimeters (3 inches) of water. Place over high heat, bring to a boil, and immediately remove the pan from the heat.

Place the chocolate in the heat-proof bowl and place the bowl into the pan, checking to make sure that the bottom is not resting in the hot water. Let stand for a minute and then, using a wooden spoon, stir to melt the chocolate. Set aside to cool slightly.

To make the French meringue, place the egg whites in the bowl of a standing electric mixer fitted with the whip attachment. Beat on low to aerate. Add the granulated sugar, raise the speed to high, and beat for about 5 minutes, or until soft peaks form.

Using a rubber spatula, scrape the meringue into a medium bowl and set aside.

This cake takes its name from Vienna's famous Sacher Hotel. It came into prominence during the time of the Austro-Hungarian Empire, when the emperor requested a pastry that he could easily ship to his embassies. The Sachertorte, with its hard glaze and long shelf life, was the one. There are only two bakeries in Vienna that are legally allowed to call this confection by its original name, the eponymous hotel and the Konditorei Demel. Austrian law also specifies that a Sachertorte must be made with butter (not margarine or vegetable shortening), fresh eggs, apricot jam, and chocolate (not cocoa powder).

Wash and dry the mixer bowl and return it to the mixer.

Place the butter in the bowl of the standing electric mixer fitted with the paddle attachment. Beat on low to just soften. Add the confectioners' sugar and beat on medium for about 4 minutes, or until light and fluffy.

Add the egg yolks, one at a time, beating well and scraping down the sides of the bowl with a rubber spatula after each addition.

With the motor on low, pour in the melted chocolate all at once to keep it from setting up before it is incorporated into the batter.

When the chocolate is completely incorporated, remove the bowl from the mixer and, using the spatula, fold the meringue into the batter, leaving the mixture slightly streaky, as it will be further blended in the next step.

Using the spatula, carefully fold the flour into the batter, taking care that the meringue and flour are completely incorporated.

Pour an equal portion of batter into each of the prepared pans and bake for about 30 minutes, or until a cake tester inserted into the center comes out clean and the surface springs back when the center is gently touched.

Invert each cake onto a wire rack placed on a baking sheet. Remove the pan and let cool.

Using a serrated knife, carefully trim the top of each cooled cake to make a flat surface. Then cut each cake crosswise into 2 equal layers.

Combine the apricot jam with the rum in a small saucepan over medium heat and cook for just 2 minutes, or until very hot but not boiling. Remove from the heat and press through a fine-mesh sieve into a medium bowl.

Pour the hot apricot mixture over the cut side of each layer. Place the 2 layers of each cake together and then pour the apricot mixture over the outside of each cake. Set them aside for about 15 minutes, or until the apricot glaze has cooled and set. As it cools, it will form a skin to which the fondant can adhere.

While the apricot glaze is cooling, place the fondant in a medium heavy-bottomed saucepan over low heat. Cook, stirring constantly, for about 3 minutes, or until melted. Do not let the temperature rise above body temperature.

Remove the fondant from the heat and stir the melted chocolate into the warm fondant until they are completely blended. Slowly pour the warm fondant glaze over the apricot-coated cakes, allowing it to completely cover them. Carefully skim a metal spatula over the surface of each cake to remove excess fondant.

Allow the fondant to harden before transferring the cakes to cardboards or serving plates.

Because they are encased in hardened fondant, the cakes can be stored, wrapped, at room temperature for weeks. Do not refrigerate them or the humidity will dissolve the fondant.

TIPS
If the fondant is too thick, it can be thinned with a bit of simple syrup (see page 499).

EVALUATING YOUR SUCCESS
The cake batter should be thoroughly mixed.

The cake should be baked through.

The fondant glaze should be hard and even, with no bare spots or drips down the sides. It should not be too thick over the top of the cake.

The interior of the baked cake should be moist and soft.

Demonstration

Panama Torte (Panama *Roulade* Cake)

Makes two 6-inch cakes

Estimated time to complete: 4 hours

Ingredients	Equipment
Butter for pan	Sheet pan
	Parchment paper
For the cake	Small bowl
190 grams (6¾ ounces) almond flour	Saucepan large enough for heat-proof bowl
55 grams (2 ounces) cake flour	Heat-proof bowl
180 grams (6⅓ ounces) chocolate, cut into bits	Wooden spoon
140 grams (5 ounces) egg yolks, at room temperature	Standing electric mixer fitted with whip and paddle attachments
30 grams (1 ounce) sugar	Rubber spatula
30 milliliters (2 tablespoons) rum	Medium bowl
	Cold sheet pan or wire rack
For the French meringue	Small saucepan
210 grams (7⅓ ounces) egg whites, at room temperature	Small mixing bowl
150 grams (5⅓ ounces) sugar	Wire whisk
	Plastic film
For the *mousseline* filling	Pastry brush
260 milliliters (8⅔ ounces) whole milk	Offset spatula
150 grams (5⅓ ounces) sugar	Serrated knife
40 grams (1⅓ ounces) egg yolks, at room temperature	Serving platter
7.5 grams (1 tablespoon) pastry cream powder (see page 244)	
200 grams (7 ounces) chocolate, cut into bits	
400 grams (14 ounces) unsalted butter, cut into small cubes, at room temperature	
For the finish	
100 milliliters (3½ ounces) simple syrup (see page 499)	
50 milliliters (1⅔ ounces) rum	
½ recipe chocolate buttercream (see page 372)	

Prepare your *mise en place*.

Preheat the oven to 177°C (350°F).

Prepare a sheet pan for baking with butter and parchment as directed on page 325 and set aside.

Combine the almond and cake flours in a small bowl and set aside.

Fill a saucepan large enough to allow your heat-proof bowl to fit snugly into it without touching the water with about 7.5 centimeters (3 inches) of water. Place

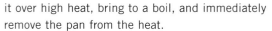

it over high heat, bring to a boil, and immediately remove the pan from the heat.

Place the chocolate in the heat-proof bowl and place the bowl into the pan, checking to make sure that the bottom is not resting in the hot water. Let stand for a minute and then, using a wooden spoon, stir to melt the chocolate. Set aside to cool slightly.

Make a French meringue: Place the egg whites in the bowl of a standing electric mixer fitted with the whip attachment. Beat on low to aerate. Add the sugar, raise the speed to high, and beat for about 5 minutes, or until soft peaks form.

Using a rubber spatula, scrape the meringue into a medium bowl and set aside.

Wash and dry the mixer bowl and return it to the mixer.

Place the egg yolks in the bowl of a standing electric mixer fitted with the whip attachment. Beat on low to aerate. Add the sugar and beat on medium for about 4 minutes or until very light and pale yellow. Slowly add the rum.

With the motor on low, pour in the melted chocolate all at once to keep it from setting up before it is incorporated into the batter.

Remove the bowl from the mixer and, using the spatula, fold the meringue into the chocolate mixture.

When the meringue has been incorporated, fold in the reserved flours. Do not overwork the batter or it will deflate and there will not be enough to completely cover the baking pan.

Pour the batter into the prepared pan, gently smoothing it into an even layer.

Bake the cake for 7 minutes, or until the surface springs back when the center is gently touched. Slide the cake onto a cold sheet pan or a wire rack and let it cool.

Meanwhile, make the *mousseline* filling. Combine the milk and sugar in a small saucepan over medium-high heat. Cook, stirring constantly, for about 3 minutes, or until the sugar has dissolved. Remove the pan from the heat.

Combine the egg yolks and pastry cream powder in a mixing bowl, whisking until well blended, pale, and light. Whisking constantly, add a bit of the hot milk to temper the eggs. Then, whisking constantly, pour the egg yolk mixture into the hot milk.

Return to medium-high heat and, stirring constantly with a wooden spoon, bring to a boil. Continue to stir, taking care to scrape the bottom and lower inner edges of the pan to prevent sticking and lumps from forming, for 2 minutes, or until thick and smooth.

Using a rubber spatula, scrape the hot mixture into the bowl of a standing electric mixer fitter with the paddle attachment. Add the chocolate and beat on medium until it has melted and blended into the cream and the mixture has begun to cool.

While the chocolate cream is still slightly warm but not hot, add the butter, a couple of pieces at a time, and beat on medium until it is fully incorporated into the cream, and the mixture is light and fluffy. If the cream is too hot, the butter will melt and separate. If this happens, chill the cream and then beat it until light and fluffy. (Conversely, if the cream is too cold, the butter will not incorporate into it. If this occurs, warm the cream slightly and then beat.)

Remove the bowl from the mixer, cover the surface with plastic film, and set aside to cool completely.

Combine the simple syrup with the rum in a small saucepan over low heat. Heat just until slightly warm, then set aside.

To finish the cake, unmold the cooled cake onto a piece of parchment paper. Peel off and discard the piece of parchment that lined the pan.

Using a pastry brush, generously coat the surface of the cake with the rum syrup, allowing it to soak in.

Using an offset spatula, lightly coat the cake with the *mousseline* filling.

Using a serrated knife, cut the cake into 7-centimeter-wide (2½-inch-wide) strips (use a cake ring or pan as a guide).

Roll one strip into a tight roll. Then begin wrapping the remaining *mousseline*-covered strips around the tightly rolled center strip until the cake is 15 centimeters (6 inches) across. Repeat to make the second cake.

Finish the cake using the chocolate buttercream.

Refrigerate until ready to use, or up to 2 days.

TIPS

If the *biscuit* is crispy, place it in the refrigerator for an hour to soften.

If the *mousseline* is refrigerated before being spread on the cake, it will need to be heated and beaten until light and fluffy.

EVALUATING YOUR SUCCESS

The batter should display no unmixed ingredients.

The baked *biscuit* should be a thin, even layer across the entire sheet pan.

The baked *biscuit* should be soft and pliable, with no dark or crispy sections.

The *crème mousseline* should be light brown and smooth, with no lumps of pastry cream or butter.

Pastry Chef
Lisbeth Rawl

Owner, Lulu's Bakery, Atlanta, Georgia

The French Culinary Institute, Class of July 2003

Coconut Cake

Makes one 9-inch cake

A coconut cake always takes me back to my grandma's kitchen. She was an unbelievable baker (and cook) who I like to think inspired me. I wanted to pay homage to her and the traditional southern cake, but I also just had to add my own twist.

540 grams (1 pound, 3 ounces) all-purpose flour

12 grams (1 tablespoon) baking powder

1 teaspoon salt

340 grams (12 ounces) unsalted butter, at room temperature

600 grams (1 pound, 5 ounces) sugar

340 grams (12 ounces) egg whites

355 milliliters (12 ounces) unsweetened coconut milk

15 milliliters (1 tablespoon) pure vanilla paste or extract

160 milliliters (5⅓ ounces) sweetened coconut milk, such as Coco Lopez

Cream Cheese Frosting (recipe follows)

Sautéed Pineapple (recipe follows)

Prepare your *mise en place*.

Preheat the oven to 177°C (350°F).

Lightly butter and flour two 23-centimeter (9-inch) round cake pans. Set aside.

Sift the flour, baking powder, and salt together. Set aside.

Place the butter in the bowl of a standing electric mixer fitted with the paddle attachment. With the speed on low begin creaming the butter, scraping down the sides of the bowl with a rubber spatula from time to time.

Add the granulated sugar and continue to beat the mixture until it is light in color and very soft and fluffy.

Whisk the egg whites, coconut milk, and vanilla together in a mixing bowl.

With the motor running on low, alternately add the dry ingredients and the egg white mixture to the butter mixture, beating and scraping down the bowl from time to time until well blended.

Pour the batter into the prepared pans and bake for 15 minutes. Rotate the pans and continue to bake for another 12 minutes, or until a cake tester inserted into the center comes out clean and dry.

Unmold the cakes onto a wire rack to cool.

Using a serrated knife, cut each cooled cake in half crosswise.

Place one half, cut side up, on a cake board. Using a pastry brush, lightly coat the cake with the sweetened coconut milk. Using an offset spatula, lightly coat with frosting. Spread about a third of the pineapple over the frosting. Repeat this process for the next 2 layers.

Brush the cut side of the final layer with sweetened coconut milk. Then place it cut side down on top and completely cover the entire cake with frosting.

Serve immediately or refrigerate until ready to serve, or for up to 2 days.

Cream Cheese Frosting

510 grams (1 pound, 2 ounces) cream cheese, at room temperature
225 grams (8 ounces) unsalted butter, at room temperature
150 grams (5¼ ounces) confectioners' sugar

Place the cream cheese and butter in the bowl of a standing electric mixer fitted with the paddle attachment. Beat on low to just blend. Then, raise the speed and beat until well blended and light. Add the sugar and beat until fluffy.

Use as directed.

Sautéed Pineapple

1 fresh pineapple, peeled, eyes removed, cored, and cut into medium dice
Approximately 70 grams (2½ ounces) sugar
1 vanilla bean, split lengthwise

Combine the pineapple with the sugar and vanilla bean in a nonstick sauté pan over low heat. Cook, stirring frequently, for about 10 minutes or until the pineapple is just tender.

Remove from the heat, allow to cool, and discard the vanilla bean before using.

The pineapple may be made up to 5 days in advance of use and stored (with the vanilla bean), tightly covered and refrigerated.

Session 9

Petits Fours: An Overview of Small Fancy Cookies, Cakes, and Confections

Theory

Classic Small Cakes

In America, when *petits fours* are mentioned, we immediately think of the delicate, ornately decorated, iced individual layer cakes served at teatime or at the end of an elegant meal. Although this is accurate, in the classic pastry kitchen these cakes are only a small part of the *petits fours* repertoire. Not only can they be small fancy cakes, they can also be cookies and other confections—they can even be savory tidbits served with cocktails or aperitifs or at receptions or cocktail parties.

According to the renowned French chef and author Antonin Carême, the term *petits fours* dates from the eighteenth century, when brick ovens were used and small items had to be baked after large items had been removed and the ovens had cooled slightly. This was called cooking *à petit four* ("at low heat").

Petits fours play an important role in the contemporary pastry kitchen. They are served not only at cocktail time, on buffets, and at luncheons, but also with tea, ice cream, and other desserts. In France, an assortment of them may accompany or follow the dessert course at an elegant dinner. In America, a small tray of tiny confections might be sent to the diners' table, with the chef's compliments, at the end of a restaurant meal.

Sweet *petits fours* are usually divided into two categories: *sec* and *frais*—dry and fresh.

Petits fours secs encompass a wide variety of small cookies, macaroons, puff pastry items, and baked meringues that, when properly stored, have a long shelf life. They are most often served with ice creams, sorbets, and custards, as well as with after-dinner drinks, such as liqueurs or dessert wines. They might include *tuiles*, *bâtonnets*, *palets*, *langues de chat*, *macarons*, individual meringues, ladyfingers, tiny *galettes*, and *milanais*. They may or may not contain a small of amount of filling, such as jam, buttercream, or *ganache*.

Petits fours frais fall into three basic groups:

1. miniature reproductions of specific cakes (miniature *éclairs*, *duchesses*, *choux*, *tartelettes*, *barquettes*, and *babas*);

2. iced or glazed *petits fours* (small geometric shapes made from *génoise* or other cakes filled with buttercream, *ganache*, pastry cream, or jam, glazed and then iced, coated with chocolate, or coated with fondant and decorated with piped icing); and

3. sugar-coated fruits, crystallized citrus rinds, or glazed fruits.

All of these have a very short shelf life and should be served as soon as possible after being prepared.

On restaurant or banquet menus, the words *friandises* and *mignardises* ("little precious things") are often used to describe both types of *petits fours*, as well as other confections such as bonbons, chocolate truffles, *pâtes de fruit,* nougat, and other candies or small treats. **Petits fours salés**—which are not covered in this book—are savory tidbits generally served with aperitifs or cocktails, often on passed trays at receptions, cocktail parties, or luncheons. They may also be referred to as *amuses-bouches* or *amuses-gueules* and, in many fine dining establishments, are presented to diners, with the chef's compliments, at the beginning of a meal. In the classic repertoire, these delicate enticements are usually made of a pastry base (matchsticks, straws, miniature turnovers, *croissants, barquettes, bouchées,* quiches, and pizzas being some) and filled with savory items, such as anchovy paste, flavored butters, shellfish, foie gras, *mousses,* cheeses, and smoked fish.

Most *petits fours* are quite simple to make, but because they are so small with a large number required to serve each diner, they take an enormous amount of the pastry chef's time to prepare. And, because they are delicate, the work requires great patience. It is estimated that one quarter to one third of a pastry kitchen's time is devoted to preparing and arranging *petits fours.*

When preparing a selection of *petits fours,* plan for four to five varieties per person should. When making your selection, in order to save time at service, choose items that can be made in advance in large quantities and stored, or components that can be used to create several different items. For an interesting and inviting presentation, it is also important to make use of a variety of flavors, textures, shapes, and colors. Almost any pastry can be used, as long as it is prepared in the smallest form or can be cut into attractive small pieces. *Petits fours* should always be presented in an appealing arrangement on a doily-lined silver tray or pretty serving plate.

Demonstration

Petits Fours Glacés Biscuit (Glazed Sponge Cake for *Petits Fours*)

Makes 1 half-sheet pan or
44-by-29-by-2.5-centimeter (17¼-by-11½-by-1-inch) cake
Estimated time to complete: 30 minutes

Ingredients	Equipment
Butter and flour for pan	Half-sheet pan
115 grams (4 ounces) almond paste	Parchment paper
40 grams (1⅓ ounces) sugar	Standing electric mixer fitted with paddle and whip attachments
6 large egg yolks, at room temperature	Rubber spatula
Zest of ½ lemon	Large bowl
½ teaspoon pure vanilla extract	Offset spatula
1 drop bitter almond extract	Wire rack
Pinch salt	

For the French meringue
3 large egg whites, at room temperature
55 grams (2 ounces) sugar
100 grams (3½ ounces) cake flour, sifted

Prepare your *mise en place.*

Preheat the oven to 177°C (350°F).

Butter and flour the pan, then line it with a piece of parchment paper. Set aside.

Combine the almond paste and sugar in the bowl of a standing electric mixer fitted with the paddle attachment. Beat on low to just blend. Raise the speed to medium and beat for about 2 minutes, or until the mixture resembles coarse sand.

Add the egg yolks one at a time, occasionally scraping down the sides of the bowl with a rubber spatula. Cream the mixture for a bit after adding the first couple of yolks so that any lumps of almond paste can break down into the mix.

Add the lemon zest, vanilla, almond extract, and salt and beat to blend.

Scrape the mixture from the mixing bowl into another clean large bowl.

Wash the mixer bowl and return it to the stand.

To make the meringue, place the egg whites in the bowl of the standing electric mixer fitted with the whip attachment. Beat on low to aerate. Add the sugar, raise the speed to high, and beat for about 4 minutes, or until soft peaks form. Keep a close eye on the meringue, as you do not want to overmix—that can happen very quickly, caus-

ing dry, stiff peaks to form and requiring you to discard the meringue and make a new one.

Remove the bowl from the mixer and, using the spatula, carefully fold the meringue into the batter. Carefully and quickly fold in the sifted flour.

Using an offset spatula, spread the batter very evenly into the parchment paper-lined pan.

Bake the cake for about 15 minutes, or until the surface is an even golden brown and the center springs back when lightly touched.

Carefully invert the cake onto a wire rack. Peel off and discard the parchment and let cool.

Use as directed in a specific recipe.

TIPS
Do not beat the almond paste without the addition of sugar; if you do, the heat from mixing can cause the oil to separate out.

This particular *biscuit* freezes well, so it can be made in large quantities and stored, tightly covered and frozen, for up to 3 months for use when needed.

EVALUATING YOUR SUCCESS
The finished cake should have a strong almond flavor and be light brown, soft, and moist.

There should be no lumps of almond paste, unmixed meringue, or flour in the batter or baked cake.

Demonstration

Petits Fours Glacés (Stacked Glazed Petits Fours)

Makes 30 to 35 *petits fours*
Estimated time to complete: 3 hours

Ingredients	Equipment
½ recipe *Petits Fours Glacés Biscuit* (see page 445)	Serrated knife
100 grams (3½ ounces) apricot jam, puréed	Parchment paper
Confectioners' sugar for dusting	3 to 4 baking sheets
200 grams (7 ounces) Marzipan (see page 401)	Offset spatula
500 grams (1 pound, 1½ ounces) *Pâte à Glacer* (see page 381)	Rolling pin
500 grams (1 pound, 1½ ounces) fondant *glacé* (see page 229)	Plastic film
100 grams (3½ ounces) piping chocolate (see Tips)	Half-sheet pan
or Royal Icing (see page 381), optional	Two 28-ounce cans (as for fruit or tomatoes) for weights
	Container for hot water
	Clean kitchen towel
	Wire racks
	Sharp knife
	Medium heavy-bottomed saucepan
	Wooden spoon
	Rubber spatula
	Small pastry bag or paper *cornet* with fine tip, optional

Prepare your *mise en place*.

Using a serrated knife, cut the *biscuit* down the center into 2 equal pieces. Place half on a parchment-lined baking sheet.

Using an offset spatula, spread a thin, even layer of apricot jam over the surface. Then place the other half on top, pressing down lightly to cause the two cake layers to stick together.

Sprinkle confectioners' sugar on a flat work surface and roll out the marzipan to 3 millimeters (⅛ inch) thick.

Cut the marzipan to precisely fit the top of the cake. Carefully cover the top of the cake with the marzipan.

Cover the cake with plastic film and then invert it onto another baking sheet. Cover the bottom with plastic film, wrapping to seal completely. Set a heavier baking sheet (such as a half-sheet pan) on top of the plastic film-wrapped cake. Place a couple of 28 ounce cans on top to weight the cake down. Refrigerate the cake for 8 hours or overnight.

Unwrap the cake and, using an offset spatula, lightly coat the non-marzipan-covered surface with the *pâte à glacer*. Set aside for about 10 minutes to allow the chocolate to harden. Reserve the remaining glaze.

Invert the cake onto a parchment paper-lined baking sheet so that the marzipan-coated side faces upward.

Place a container of hot water and a clean kitchen towel next to the cake.

Line a baking sheet with parchment paper. Place 1 large or 2 small wire racks on top of the parchment paper.

Dip a sharp knife into the hot water, wipe it dry, and begin cutting the cake into neat, even 2.5-centimeter (1-inch) squares, taking care that you cut all the way through.

Transfer the *petits fours* to the racks, leaving room between each one.

Combine the fondant with 60 grams (2 ounces) water in a medium heavy-bottomed saucepan over very low heat. Heat, stirring constantly with a wooden spoon, for about 2 minutes, or until softened—the fondant just needs to be loosened, not cooked. It should not heat above body temperature or it will be unusable.

Pour the fondant over the *petits fours*, taking care to cover each cake. Excess fondant will drip through the racks onto the parchment paper.

When all the excess fondant has dripped off, lift the racks from the paper. Using a rubber spatula, scrape up the fondant and return it to the pan. Place it over very low heat and add about 100 grams (3½ ounces) of the reserved glaze. This will darken the color and add a chocolate flavor. Heat, stirring constantly with a wooden spoon, for about a minute, or just until blended and softened.

Again pour fondant over the *petits fours*, taking care that each cake is completely covered.

Line another baking sheet with parchment paper. Using an offset spatula, carefully transfer the coated *petits fours* to the parchment. Do not touch them, as this will make unsightly fingerprints on the coating. Set them aside for about 30 minutes, or until thoroughly dry.

If desired, when dry, pipe decorations on the top of each *petit four* using piping chocolate (see Tips) or royal icing (see page 381).

TIPS

The stacked cake may be left, tightly wrapped, at room temperature, for 1 to 2 days. The fondant will then be very dry and easier to touch.

Keep in mind that the fondant should be loose enough that the layers inside the *petits fours* are visible through it after they have been coated.

Piping chocolate is a commercially made fluid chocolate used in cake decorating that is available from cake supply stores. It can also be made by adding 15 milliliters (1 tablespoon) light corn syrup to 100 grams (3½ ounces) melted chocolate. Tempered chocolate can also be used to pipe décor.

A very fine piping point is needed for piping designs on the surface of the finished *petits fours*.

EVALUATING YOUR SUCCESS

The *biscuit* should be very moist and have a strong almond flavor.

The piped designs, if used, should be neat, consistent, and very fine.

Demonstration

Dôme de Petits Fours Glacés (Domed Glazed *Petits Fours*)

Makes 30 to 35 *petits fours*
Estimated time to complete: 3 hours

Ingredients	Equipment
¼ recipe *Petits Fours Glacés Biscuit* (see page 445)	2 to 3 baking sheets
100 grams (3½ ounces) flavored simple syrup (see page 499)	Parchment paper
500 grams (1 pound, 1½ ounces) flavored *Crème au Beurre* (see pages 373 through 377)	Small bowl
	Pastry brush
500 grams (1 pound 1½ ounces) *Fondant Décor façon Colette* (see page 403), optional	1-inch-round biscuit or cookie cutter
	Pastry bag fitted with #4 plain tip
	Offset spatula
	1 large or 2 small wire racks
	Medium heavy-bottomed saucepan
	Wooden spoon
	Dipping fork
	Small pastry bag or paper *cornet* with fine tip, optional

Prepare your *mise en place*.

Line a baking sheet with parchment paper. Set aside.

Place the *biscuit* on a piece of parchment paper on a clean, flat work surface.

Place the syrup in a small bowl. Using a pastry brush and about 30 milliliters (2 tablespoons) of the syrup, generously coat the surface of the cake, allowing the syrup to soak in.

Using a biscuit or cookie cutter, cut the cake into as many circles as you can (you should be able to make up to 35).

Place the buttercream into a pastry bag fitted with the #4 plain tip and carefully pipe buttercream onto each cake circle, completely covering the surface. Using an offset spatula, transfer the cake circles to the parchment-lined baking sheet. Place in the refrig-

erator for about 1 hour or until the buttercream is chilled and firm.

Line another baking sheet with parchment paper. Place 1 large or 2 small wire racks on top of the parchment paper.

When the buttercream is well chilled, combine the fondant with the remaining syrup in a medium heavy-bottomed saucepan over very low heat. Heat, stirring constantly with a wooden spoon, for about 2 minutes, or until softened. The fondant just needs to be loosened, not cooked—it should not heat above body temperature or it will be unusable.

Working with one piece at a time, stick a dipping fork into the bottom of each cake circle and carefully dip it into the fondant, taking care that each cake is completely coated. Place the *petits fours* on the wire racks and allow any excess fondant to drip off.

Line another baking sheet with parchment paper and, using an offset spatula, carefully transfer the coated *petits fours* to it. Do not touch them, as this will make unsightly fingerprints on the coating. Set them aside for about 30 minutes, or until thoroughly dry.

If desired, when dry, pipe decorations on the top of each one using piping chocolate or royal icing (see page 381).

TIPS

The syrup used should not be too sweet, as both the buttercream and fondant are very sweet.

The syrup and the buttercream should be of complementary flavors.

The buttercream may be flavored with liqueurs, nuts, chocolate, or extracts.

When dipping the cakes into the fondant, take care that the fondant is no hotter than body temperature or the buttercream will melt.

A very fine piping point is needed for piping designs on the surface of the finished *petits fours*.

The assembled cakes can be stored, tightly wrapped and refrigerated, for up to 5 days. They can also be frozen for up to 1 month.

EVALUATING YOUR SUCCESS

The *biscuit* should be very moist and have both a strong almond flavor and the flavor of the syrup or liqueur used.

The buttercream should be strongly flavored and piped in an even, consistent mound.

The fondant should be shiny, not sticky, and translucent enough to just reveal the layers of the cake inside the *petits fours*.

The piped designs, if used, should be neat, consistent, and very fine.

Demonstration

Petits Fours Glacés Pyramide (Pyramid-Shaped Glazed *Petits Fours*)

Makes 30 to 35 *petits fours*

Estimated time to complete: 3 hours

Ingredients	Equipment
¼ recipe *Petits Fours Glacés Biscuit* (see page 445)	2 to 3 baking sheets
100 milliliters (3½ ounces) flavored simple syrup (see page 499)	Parchment paper
200 grams (7 ounces) vanilla-flavored	Serrated knife
Crème au Beurre (see page 373)	Small bowl
200 grams (7 ounces) chocolate-flavored	Pastry brush
Crème au Beurre (see page 373)	3 pastry bags fitted with #4 plain tips
200 grams (7 ounces) raspberry-flavored	Offset spatula
Crème au Beurre (see page 373)	1 large or 2 small wire racks
500 grams (1 pound, 1½ ounces) *Pâte à Glacer* (see page 381)	Cutting board
	Container for hot water
	Clean kitchen towel
	Sharp knife

Prepare your *mise en place*.

Line a baking sheet with parchment paper and set aside.

Place the *biscuit* on a piece of parchment paper on a clean, flat work surface. Using a serrated knife, cut the cake into 3 strips, each approximately 4 centimeters (1½ inches) wide.

Place the syrup in a small bowl. Using a pastry brush, generously coat the surface of the cake with the syrup, allowing the syrup to soak in.

Place each of the buttercream flavors into a pastry bag fitted with a #4 plain tip. Carefully pipe a rope of one of the flavors of buttercream along one of the long sides of each cake strip. Pipe a rope of another flavor next to the first rope. Follow this with a rope of the final buttercream flavor. The ropes should be close to one another, with no gaps or holes.

Using an offset spatula, transfer the buttercream-covered cake strips to the parchment paper-lined baking sheet. Refrigerate for about 1 hour, or until the buttercream is firm. At this point, the strips may be stored, well-wrapped and refrigerated, for up to 4 days, or frozen for up to 1 month.

Line another baking sheet with parchment paper. Place one large or 2 small wire racks on top of the parchment paper.

Using a serrated knife, carefully trim any excess *biscuit* from the long sides of each strip. Place the strips on the wire racks.

Pour the *pâte à glacer* over the strips, taking care that each one is completely covered. Set them aside for about 30 minutes, or until the glaze hardens.

Using an offset spatula, carefully transfer the strips to a cutting board.
Place a container of hot water and a clean kitchen towel next to the cake.

Dip a sharp knife into the hot water, wipe it dry, and begin cutting the strips into neat, even 1.3-centimeter-thick (½-inch-thick) pieces, taking care to cut all the way through.

TIPS
The syrup used should not be too sweet, as the buttercream is very sweet.

The buttercream may be further flavored with liqueurs, nuts, or extracts.

We have suggested buttercream flavors; however, you can use whatever flavors you prefer. Just take care that the colors and flavors are complementary.

When glazing the cakes, take care that they are well chilled or the buttercream will melt.

EVALUATING YOUR SUCCESS
The *biscuit* should be very moist and have both a strong almond flavor and the flavor of the syrup used.

The buttercreams should be strongly flavored and piped in even, consistent ropes.

The buttercream rope designs should look completely round on the cut sides.

451

Demonstration

Petits Fours au Chocolat et aux Noisettes (Chocolate-Hazelnut Cakes)

Makes 20 to 30 *petits fours*
Estimated time to complete: 45 minutes

Ingredients	Equipment

Ingredients

55 grams (2 ounces) all-purpose flour

115 grams (4 ounces) toasted hazelnuts, finely ground

180 grams (6⅓ ounces) semisweet or bittersweet chocolate, cut into small bits

115 grams (4 ounces) unsalted butter, at room temperature

5 large egg yolks

155 grams (5½ ounces) sugar

For the French meringue

5 large egg whites, at room temperature

155 grams (5½ ounces) sugar

Equipment

Thirty 1-inch foil cups or small molds

Baking sheet

Small bowl

Medium heat-proof bowl

Saucepan to fit heat-proof bowl

Wooden spoon

Medium bowl

Wire whisk

Standing electric mixer fitted with whip attachment

Rubber spatula

Pastry bag fitted with #4 tip

Wire racks

Prepare your *mise en place*.

Preheat the oven to 191°C (375°F).

Arrange the foil cups on a baking sheet and set aside. Combine the flour and hazelnuts in a small bowl and set aside.

Combine the chocolate and butter in a medium heat-proof bowl.

Fill a saucepan large enough to allow your heat-proof bowl to fit snugly into it without touching the water with about 7.5 centimeters (3 inches) of water. Set it over high heat and bring to a simmer.

Quickly place the bowl into the pan, checking to make sure that the bottom is not resting in the hot water. Using a wooden spoon, immediately begin stirring and continue to do so for about 4 minutes, or until the chocolate and butter have melted and blended. Remove

the bowl from the heat and set it aside to cool slightly. The chocolate should not be hot when added to the egg mixture or the eggs will cook and curdle.

Combine the egg yolks and sugar in a medium bowl, whisking to aerate and lighten. Whisking constantly, add the melted chocolate mixture, and, when the ingredients are combined, set the bowl aside.

Make a French meringue: Place the egg whites in the bowl of the standing electric mixer fitted with the whip attachment. Beat on low to aerate. Add the sugar, raise the speed to high, and beat for about 4 minutes, or until soft peaks form. Keep a close eye on the meringue—you do not want to overmix, and that can happen very quickly. If dry, stiff peaks form, discard the meringue and make a new one.

Remove the bowl from the mixer and, using a rubber spatula, carefully fold the meringue into the chocolate mixture. Carefully fold the flour-and-nut mixture into the batter. Work quickly and carefully.

Scrape the batter into a pastry bag fitted with the #4 plain tip. Pipe the batter into the foil cups, filling each one about three quarters full.

Immediately transfer the baking sheet to the preheated oven and bake for about 7 minutes, or until the *petits fours* are set and nicely risen. Do not allow the batter to sit or it will begin to deflate.

Place the little cakes on wire racks to cool before serving.

TIPS
The hazelnuts must be allowed to cool after toasting and before being ground or they will quickly turn to paste.

If foil cups are not available, the cakes may be baked in any small, well-buttered mold.

EVALUATING YOUR SUCCESS
The cake batter should be well mixed, with no lumps or unincorporated meringue.

The baked cakes should rise above the tops of the foil cups.

The finished cakes should be very moist, with a strong chocolate flavor.

Demonstration

Opéra Cake

Makes one 30.5-by-20-centimeter (12-by-8-inch) cake
Estimated time to complete: 3 hours

Ingredients	Equipment

Ingredients

Butter for pan
175 grams (6⅛ ounces) confectioners' sugar
40 grams (1⅓ ounces) cake flour

For the meringue
300 grams (11 ounces) egg whites, at room temperature
100 grams (3½ ounces) confectioners' sugar
250 grams (8¾ ounces) unsweetened hazelnut paste (see page 337)

For the finish
100 milliliters (3½ ounces) flavored simple syrup (see page 499)
1 recipe *Ganache Pour l'Opéra* (see page 379)
½ recipe coffee-flavored *Crème au Beurre I* (see page 373)
½ recipe vanilla-flavored *Crème au Beurre I* (see page 373)
1 recipe *Glacé au Chocolat Pour l'Opéra* (see page 381)

Equipment

Sheet pan
Parchment paper
Sifter
Standing electric mixer fitted with whip attachment
Rubber spatula
Cold sheet pan or wire rack
Serrated knife
Small bowl
Pastry brush
Offset spatula
Container for hot water
Clean kitchen towel
Sharp knife

Prepare your *mise en place*.

Preheat the oven to 177ºC (350ºF).

Prepare the sheet pan for baking with butter and parchment paper as directed on page 325. Set aside.

Sift the confectioners' sugar and cake flour together. Set aside.

To make the meringue, place the egg whites in the bowl of the standing electric mixer fitted with the whip attachment. Beat on low to aerate. Add the sugar, raise the speed to high, and beat for about 4 minutes, or until stiff peaks form.

Using a rubber spatula, combine enough of the meringue with the hazelnut paste to bring it to a smooth consistency almost equal to the meringue.

Remove the bowl from the mixer and, using the spatula, carefully fold the hazelnut paste mixture into the meringue. Do not attempt to completely incorporate the hazelnut mixture; the batter should be streaky. Working quickly and carefully, fold the sifted flour-and-sugar mixture into the batter.

Carefully pour the batter into the prepared pan, smoothing it into an even layer. Do not press down or the batter will lose volume and the cake will be tough.

Bake the cake for 7 minutes, or until the surface is an even golden brown and the center springs back when lightly touched. Watch carefully; it will bake very quickly.

Invert the *biscuit* onto a clean, cold sheet pan or a wire rack. Remove and discard the parchment paper and let cool.

Using a serrated knife, cut the cake crosswise into four equal pieces.

Place the syrup in a small bowl.

Place 1 cake layer on the parchment paper-lined baking sheet.

Using a pastry brush, generously coat the surface of the cake layer with the syrup, allowing it to soak in.

Using an offset spatula, spread a 6-millimeter-thick (¼-inch-thick) layer of the *ganache* over the cake, applying it as evenly and smoothly as possible. Top this with a cake layer, pressing down lightly to help the new layer to adhere to the *ganache*. Again, generously coat the surface with syrup, allowing it to soak in.

Coat the second cake layer with a smooth, even 6-millimeter-thick (¼-inch-thick) layer of the coffee buttercream. Top with the third cake layer, again pressing lightly and soaking with syrup.

Carefully spread smooth, even 6-millimeter-thick (¼-inch-thick) layer of the vanilla buttercream over the cake.

Cover with the final cake layer and press down lightly.

Transfer the cake to the refrigerator for about 1 hour, or until the *ganache* and buttercream have set and the cake is well chilled.

When the cake is chilled, pour the glaze over it to cover completely. Lightly bang the sheet pan on the counter to remove any air bubbles that might have formed when the glaze was poured.

Set the cake aside for about 30 minutes, or until the

NOTE

Opéra cake became a classic in the early part of the twentieth century. It is not known if this occurred when the cake was featured by pastry chef Louis Clichy at the 1903 Exposition Culinaire in Paris, with his name scrolled across the top, or if its fame was generated by the Parisian pastry shop Dalloyau, where a similar cake was known as *l'Opéra*, in honor of the Paris Opera. Either way, it remains a very rich cake featuring layers of almond sponge highlighted with coffee and chocolate buttercream and dark, luscious *ganache*.

glaze has set. At this point, the cake may be stored, tightly wrapped and refrigerated, for up to 4 days, or frozen for up to 1 month.

When you are ready to finish the *petits fours*, place a container of hot water and a clean kitchen towel next to the cake.

Dip a sharp knife into the hot water, wipe it dry, and begin cutting the cake into neat, even shapes, taking care to cut all the way through and leave no ragged edges.

Serve within a few hours.

TIPS

Classically, an *opéra* cake is made with coffee buttercream, but you could also use praline, pistachio, or peanut butter flavoring.

Do not overfold the batter or it will deflate.

There should be just enough batter to cover the sheet pan in a thin, even layer.

If the baked *biscuit* is overcooked or slightly dry or stale, place it in the refrigerator for several hours and the humidity will soften it. Alternatively, soak it with a coffee-flavored simple syrup (see page 499).

To check on the consistent depth of buttercream, gently push the tip of a metal spatula into various points on the buttercream.

It is best to use the *ganache* within 30 minutes of making it. If it is too loose, pour a thin layer on the cake and refrigerate for 10 minutes or until it has set. Then add the remaining *ganache*.

EVALUATING YOUR SUCCESS

The batter should be light and airy.

There should be no unmixed ingredients visible in the baked cake.

The *biscuit* should have a very strong hazelnut flavor and be golden brown and moist.

The buttercream should have a strong coffee flavor and be spread in smooth, even layers.

The *ganache* should be smooth, thick, and shiny, with no airiness and no unmelted pieces of chocolate.

The glaze should be dark brown and very shiny, as well as just thick enough to be opaque.

No matter the shape, all of the cut pieces of the cake should be neat and consistent in size and shape.

About Macaroons

Macaroons, known the world over, are among the most elegant *petits fours*. They can be made in one of two ways—by creaming the batter or by the sponge method, which involves incorporating a meringue into a nut-, seed- or fruit-based mixture. For the most part, egg whites are used to bind the batter together, but chocolate or puréed fruit can also be used. In America, we are most familiar with a very dense and extremely sweet macaroon made from a simple mix of shredded coconut, egg whites, and sugar. In France, a macaroon is often an almond confection that is crisp on the exterior and soft and chewy on the interior, generally made from almond paste or flour and meringue.

The most enticing of all macaroons are *macarons Gerbet* (see page 459). Named after a nineteenth-century French pastry chef, these delicate cookies are highly regarded in Parisian pastry making. In fact, Gerbet macaroons are considered to be the ultimate in contemporary macaroons. Most often filled with jam, in their most sumptuous form, they are filled with a richly flavored buttercream.

Demonstration

Macarons aux Noix de Coco (Coconut Macaroons)

Makes 10 to 15 cookies
Estimated time to complete: 30 minutes

Ingredients	Equipment
150 grams (5⅓ ounces) sweetened shredded coconut	Baking sheet
75 grams (2⅔ ounces) sugar	Parchment paper
50 grams (1¾ ounces) egg whites, at room temperature	Large mixing bowl
	Wooden spoon
	Small scoop or spoon
	Wire rack

Prepare your *mise en place*.

Preheat the oven to 121°C (250°F).

Line a baking sheet with parchment paper. Set aside. Combine the coconut with the sugar and egg whites in a large mixing bowl. Using a wooden spoon, stir the ingredients together until well blended. At this point, the batter may be stored, tightly covered and refrigerated, for several days.

Using a small scoop or spoon, form the mixture into tightly packed balls or pyramids. (They must be compact or they will crumble while baking.) Place on the parchment paper-lined baking sheet and bake for about 20 minutes, or until lightly browned.

Transfer the macaroons to a wire rack to cool. They may be stored, airtight, at room temperature for a day or two.

TIPS
Unsweetened, desiccated coconut may be used in place of the sweetened coconut.

A small amount (about 30 milliliters/2 tablespoons) rum may be added to the batter to give an extra dimension to the baked flavor.

The baked, cooled macaroons may be dipped about halfway in tempered chocolate or *pâte à glacer* (see page 381) for additional flavor, as well as to enhance their appearance.

EVALUATING YOUR SUCCESS
The baked macaroons should be consistent in size and shape, golden brown on the exterior and white on the interior.

The baked macaroons should be chewy and sweet with a distinct taste and aroma of coconuts.

Demonstration

Macarons au Chocolat (Chocolate Macaroons)

Makes 25 macaroon sandwich cookies
Estimated time to complete: 2 hours

Ingredients	Equipment

Ingredients

240 grams (½ ounces) granulated sugar
100 grams (3½ ounces) almond flour
8 grams (1 tablespoon) Dutch-process cocoa powder

For the meringue
120 grams (4¼ ounces) egg whites, at room temperature
40 grams (1⅓ ounces) confectioners' sugar

For the *ganache*
110 grams (3¾ ounces) semisweet or bittersweet chocolate,
  chopped into bits
60 milliliters (2 ounces) heavy cream

Equipment

Baking sheet
Parchment paper
Sifter
Standing electric mixer fitted with whip attachment
Rubber spatula
Pastry bag fitted with #4 plain tip
Wire racks
Medium stainless-steel bowl
Medium heavy-bottomed saucepan
Wooden spoon
Offset spatula

Prepare your *mise en place*.

Preheat the oven to 162°C (325°F).

Line a baking sheet with parchment paper. Set aside.

Sift the granulated sugar, almond flour, and cocoa powder together. Set aside.

To make the meringue, place the egg whites in the bowl of the standing electric mixer fitted with the whip attachment. Beat on low to aerate. Add the confectioners' sugar, raise the speed to high, and beat for about 4 minutes, or until stiff peaks form. Take care not to overwhip the meringue or it will be dry, and it will be difficult to fold in the dry ingredients.

Remove the bowl from the mixer and, using a rubber spatula, fold the sifted dry ingredients into the meringue until well blended.

Transfer the batter to a pastry bag fitted with the #4 plain tip.

Carefully pipe fifty 2.5-centimeter (1-inch) rounds of macaroon batter onto the parchment paper-lined baking sheet.

Bake the macaroons for about 10 minutes, or until firm and very lightly colored around the edges. (Macaroons should not color much during baking.) Watch carefully, as the high sugar content may cause the cookies to burn quickly.

Immediately transfer the macaroons to wire racks to cool.

Place the chocolate in a medium stainless-steel bowl. Set aside.

Pour the cream into a medium heavy-bottomed saucepan over medium-low heat and bring to just a

bare boil, watching carefully—bubbles should form around the edge of the pan, but the cream should not vigorously boil.

Pour the hot cream it over the chocolate. Let stand for a minute or two.

Using a wooden spoon, stir the softened chocolate into the cream, beating until the mixture is completely smooth and homogeneous. Scrape down the sides of the bowl with a rubber spatula.

Set aside, stirring occasionally to ensure that the chocolate is completely melted, for about an hour to allow the mixture to come to room temperature.

When the macaroons are cool and the *ganache* has thickened somewhat, using an offset spatula, lightly coat the flat bottom of 25 of the macaroons with *ganache*. Set another macaroon on top of the *ganache*, pressing to make a sandwich cookie.

Serve immediately or store, airtight in layers, at room temperature for a day or two.

TIPS

For a smoother texture, the sugar, almond flour, and cocoa powder can be ground in a food processor fitted with the metal blade until very fine. Sift the mixture and proceed as directed.

If the macaroons overbake and become crisp, place them in the refrigerator, uncovered, for 8 hours or overnight to soften.

EVALUATING YOUR SUCCESS

The baked macaroons should be soft in the center, but not wet.

The baked macaroons should be an even color and have a strong chocolate flavor.

The finished macaroons should be consistent in size and shape.

Demonstration

Macarons Gerbet (Gerbet Macaroons)

Makes 25 macaroon sandwich cookies
Estimated time to complete: 2 hours

Ingredients	Equipment
115 grams (4 ounces) almond flour	Baking sheet
200 grams (7 ounces) confectioners' sugar	Parchment paper
	Food processor fitted with the metal blade
For the meringue	Sifter
90 grams (3¼ ounces) egg whites, at room temperature	Standing electric mixer fitted with whip attachment
8 grams (2 tablespoons) confectioners' sugar	Rubber spatula
	Pastry bag fitted with #2 tip
For the finish	Wire racks
100 grams (3½ ounces) raspberry or other jam	Offset spatula

Prepare your *mise en place*.

Preheat the oven to 162°C (325°F).

Line a baking sheet with parchment paper. Set aside.

Combine the almond flour and sugar in the bowl of a food processor fitted with the metal blade. Process for about 1 minute, or until very fine. Set aside.

To make the meringue, place the egg whites in the bowl of the standing electric mixer fitted with the whip attachment. Beat on low to aerate. Add the sugar, raise the speed to high, and beat for about 3 minutes, or until soft peaks form. Take care not to overwhip or the meringue will be dry and it will be difficult to fold in the dry ingredients.

Remove the bowl from the mixer and, using a rubber spatula, fold the almond mixture into the meringue until well blended.

Transfer the batter to a pastry bag fitted with the #2 tip.

Carefully pipe fifty 2.5-centimeter (1-inch) rounds of the macaroon batter onto the parchment-lined baking sheet. Set them aside for about 1 hour, or until the macaroons form a skin on their surface. This is extremely important, as the skin helps the macaroons hold their shape during baking.

Bake the macaroons for about 10 minutes, or until firm and just beginning to brown around the edges. (The macaroons should not color much during baking.) Watch carefully, as the high sugar content can cause the cookies to burn quickly.

Immediately transfer the macaroons to wire racks to cool.

Using an offset spatula, lightly coat the flat bottom of 25 of the cooled macaroons with a thin layer of jam. Cover the jam with another macaroon, bottom side down, pressing gently to make a sandwich cookie.

Serve the macaroons immediately or store them, air-tight in layers, at room temperature for a day or two.

TIPS
Buttercream, *ganache*, or pistachio or praline paste may be used as a filling in place of the jam.

A drop or two of food coloring along with 3 milliliters (½ teaspoon) of any extract or 15 milliliters (1 tablespoon) of fruit brandy can be added to the meringue.

EVALUATING YOUR SUCCESS
The baked macaroons should be smooth and round with no cracks, crunchy on the exterior, and soft and chewy in the interior.

The baked macaroons should be consistent in size, shape, and color.

There should be just enough filling to hold the two pieces together as well as to add a bit of moisture.

Demonstration

Macarons d'Amandes (Macaroons with Almond Paste Base)

Makes 70 to 75 cookies
Estimated time to complete: 45 minutes

Ingredients	Equipment
150 grams (5⅓ ounces) almond paste	Baking sheet
150 grams (5⅓ ounces) sugar	Parchment paper
½ teaspoon pure vanilla extract	Standing electric mixer fitted with paddle attachment
¼ teaspoon almond extract	Rubber spatula
55 grams (2 ounces) egg whites, at room temperature	Pastry bag fitted with the #4 plain tip
	Wire racks

Prepare your *mise en place*.

Preheat the oven to 162°C (325°F).

Line a baking sheet with parchment paper. Set aside.

Combine the almond paste and sugar in the bowl of a standing electric mixer fitted with the paddle attachment. Beat on low to just combine and then raise the speed to medium and beat for about 3 minutes, or until creamy.

Add the vanilla and almond extracts and beat to blend. Add the egg whites, a bit at a time, beating well and scraping down the sides of the bowl with a rubber spatula after each addition. Continue beating until the batter is smooth, light, and airy.

Transfer the batter to a pastry bag fitted with the #4 plain tip.

Carefully pipe as many 2.5-centimeter (1-inch) rounds of the macaroon batter as you can onto the parchment paper-lined baking sheet (you should get up to 75).
Bake the macaroons for about 10 minutes, or until they are firm and an even, light brown color. Watch carefully, as the high sugar content can cause the cookies to burn quickly.

Immediately transfer the macaroons to wire racks to cool.

Serve immediately or store, airtight in layers, at room temperature for a day or two.

TIPS
Do not beat the almond paste without the addition of sugar or it might separate.

Spices or citrus zest may be added to the batter for additional flavor.

The macaroons may be sandwiched together with jam or *ganache*.

EVALUATING YOUR SUCCESS
The baked macaroons should have a strong almond flavor and be soft and moist inside.

The baked macaroons should be consistent in size and shape and be of an even, light brown color.

About *Tuiles*

Tuiles are very thin crisp, almost brittle cookies that, when hot, are formed into a curved shape over a *tuile* mold or rolling pin. Once formed, the curved cookie resembles the traditional red roof tile for which they are named.

The classic *tuile* cookie is made from finely chopped almonds, but they can also be made with almost any other nut or seed or flavored with citrus, extracts, chocolate, spices, or honey.

Although *tuiles* or other crisp, thin, moldable cookies of the same style are traditionally formed over a mold, rolling pin, or bottle, they can also be formed using a cut stencil. The batter is, in fact, sometimes called "stencil paste." In this case, instead of letting the batter spread out while baking into a slightly irregular circle, it is shaped by a stencil form: A baking sheet is lined with a silicone liner. A commercially made or a hand-cut stencil is placed on the silicone and, using an offset spatula, the batter is spread over the cut stencil in a smooth, even layer. The stencil is then lifted off, leaving the shaped cookie, which can be baked as directed.

Tuile batter can also be used to form "tulips" or cup-shaped molds for holding fruit, ice cream, *mousses*, or other desserts. To do this, the batter is baked in the usual way and, while still hot, is carefully molded around upside-down custard cups or other small, rounded molds. The cooled cookie will then form a crisp, cup-shaped tulip.

Demonstration

Tuiles d'Amandes (Almond Tuiles)

Makes 50 to 60 cookies
Estimated time to complete: 90 minutes

Ingredients	Equipment
180 grams (6⅓ ounces) sugar	Large mixing bowl
65 grams (2¼ ounces) finely chopped almonds	Wooden spoon
65 grams (2¼ ounces) all-purpose flour	Plastic film
90 milliliters (3 ounces) fresh orange juice, strained	2 silicone baking liners
2 baking sheets	Metal spoon
65 grams (2¼ ounces) warm, melted unsalted butter	Offset spatula
Zest of 1 orange	*Tuile* mold or rolling pin
	Wire racks

Prepare your *mise en place*.

Combine the sugar, almonds, and flour in a large mixing bowl, stirring to blend with a wooden spoon. Add the orange juice and melted butter along with the zest and stir until well combined.

Cover the batter with plastic film and refrigerate for about 1 hour, or until well chilled.

Preheat the oven to 162°C (325°F).

Line the baking sheets with the silicone liners. Set aside.

Using a metal spoon, drop the batter by the table-spoonful onto the silicone-lined baking sheets, leaving about 5 centimeters (2 inches) between each cookie to allow for spreading.

Bake the *tuiles* for 7 to 10 minutes, or until they are paper-thin and nicely browned.

Using an offset spatula, transfer the hot cookies to a *tuile* mold or rolling pin so that they drape over to form a rounded tile shape. As soon as a cookie sets, transfer it to a wire rack to cool completely. Handle carefully, as the baked *tuiles* are very fragile.

If the *tuiles* harden on the baking sheet before being shaped, return them to the oven for a minute or so to soften.

TIPS

The orange juice and zest may be replaced with any other citrus juice and zest.

The raw batter may be stored, tightly covered and refrigerated, for up to 1 week.

The baked, shaped *tuiles* must be stored absolutely airtight, as any moisture or humidity will cause them to collapse.

It is a good idea to bake only the quantity you will need at one time, as *tuiles* are fragile and vulnerable to moisture.

Sesame *Tuiles:* The following ingredients can be mixed, baked, and formed according to the directions in the recipe above: 150 grams (5⅓ ounces) sesame seeds; 135 grams (4¾ ounces) sugar; 30 grams (1 ounce) all-purpose flour; 75 grams (2⅔ ounces) egg whites, at room temperature; 30 grams (1 ounce) warm, melted unsalted butter.

EVALUATING YOUR SUCCESS

The baked *tuiles* should be an even brown color, almost paper-thin, crisp, and lacy, with many small holes.

There should be no chewiness.

The baked *tuiles* should have a caramelized orange flavor.

Demonstration

Tuiles au Chocolat (Chocolate *Tuiles*)

Makes 50 to 60 cookies
Estimated time to complete: 90 minutes

Ingredients	Equipment
85 grams (3 ounces) all-purpose flour	Sifter
1 teaspoon Dutch-process cocoa powder	Standing electric mixer fitted with paddle attachment
75 grams (2⅔ ounces) unsalted butter, at room temperature	Rubber spatula
110 grams (3¾ ounces) granulated sugar	Plastic film
40 grams (1⅓ ounces) light brown sugar	2 baking sheets
150 grams (5⅓ ounces) egg whites, at room temperature	2 silicone baking liners
	Metal spoon
	Offset spatula
	Tuile mold or rolling pin
	Wire racks

Prepare your *mise en place.*

Sift the flour and cocoa powder together. Set aside.

Combine the butter with the granulated and brown sugars in the bowl of a standing electric mixer fitted with the paddle attachment. Beat on low to just combine. Raise the speed to medium and beat for a minute to lighten. Then, add the egg whites, a bit at a time, beating well and scraping down the sides of the bowl with a rubber spatula after each addition. Add the sifted flour mixture and beat for a minute or two or until well-combined.

Remove the bowl from the mixer, cover it with plastic film, and refrigerate for about 1 hour or until well chilled.

Preheat the oven to 162°C (325°F).

Line the baking sheets with the silicone liners. Set aside.

Using a metal spoon, drop the batter by the tablespoonful onto the silicone-lined baking sheets, leaving about 5 centimeters (2 inches) between each cookie to allow for spreading.

Bake the *tuiles* for about 7 to 10 minutes, or until they are paper-thin and nicely browned.

Using an offset spatula, transfer the hot cookies to a *tuile* mold or rolling pin so that they drape over to form a rounded tile shape. As soon as a cookie sets, transfer it to a wire rack to cool completely. Handle carefully, as the baked *tuiles* are very fragile.

If the *tuiles* harden on the baking sheet before being shaped, return them to the oven for a minute or so to soften.

TIPS

The raw batter may be stored, tightly covered and refrigerated, for up to 1 week.

The baked, shaped *tuiles* must be stored absolutely airtight, as any moisture or humidity will cause them to collapse.

It is a good idea to bake only the quantity you will need at one time, as *tuiles* are fragile and vulnerable to moisture.

VARIATIONS

The following variations are mixed, baked, and formed according to the directions in the master recipe above. For each one, combine the butter and sugar, then add the liquid (such as egg or purée), and finally stir in the dry ingredients.

Fruit *Tuiles*: 40 grams (1⅓ ounces) unsalted butter, at room temperature; 100 grams (3½ ounces) confectioners' sugar, sifted; 50 grams (1¾ ounces) fruit purée such as raspberry, pear, or passion fruit; 30 grams (1 ounce) all-purpose flour, sifted.

Chocolate Chip Lace Cookies: 110 grams (3¾ ounces) unsalted butter, at room temperature; 80 grams (2¾ ounces) light brown sugar; 75 grams (2⅔ ounces) granulated sugar; ¾ teaspoon baking soda; 1 large egg, at room temperature; 1 teaspoon pure vanilla extract; 60 milliliters (2 ounces) water; 130 grams (4⅔ ounces) finely chopped nuts; 115 grams (4 ounces) semisweet or bittersweet chocolate, finely chopped.

Honey Crisps: 85 grams (3 ounces) unsalted butter, at room temperature; 100 grams (3½ ounces) confectioners' sugar, sifted; 125 grams (4½ ounces) honey; 85 grams (3 ounces) egg whites, at room temperature; 200 grams (7 ounces) all-purpose flour, sifted.

Hippen (a German wafer cookie similar to a French *tuile*): 50 grams (1¾ ounces) unsalted butter, at room temperature; 50 grams (1¾ ounces) sugar; 50 grams (1¾ ounces) egg whites, at room temperature; 50 grams (1¾ ounces) all-purpose flour, sifted.

EVALUATING YOUR SUCCESS

The baked *tuiles* should be an even color, almost paper-thin, crisp, and lacey with many small holes.

There should be no chewiness.

The baked *tuiles* should have a strong aroma and taste of the main flavor.

Demonstration

Brandy Snaps

Makes 50 to 60 cookies
Estimated time to complete: 90 minutes

Ingredients	Equipment
110 grams (3¾ ounces) unsalted butter, at room temperature	Medium heavy-bottomed saucepan
170 grams (6 ounces) dark corn syrup	Wooden spoon
110 grams (3¾ ounces) light brown sugar	Medium bowl
100 grams (3½ ounces) all-purpose flour, sifted	Plastic film
4 grams (1 tablespoon) ground ginger	2 baking sheets
10 milliliters (2 teaspoons) brandy	2 silicone baking liners
Pinch ground white pepper	Metal spoon
	Offset spatula
	Tuile mold or rolling pin
	Wire racks

Prepare your *mise en place*.

Combine the butter with the corn syrup and brown sugar in a medium heavy-bottomed saucepan over medium heat, stirring with a wooden spoon for about 3 minutes, or until the butter has melted and the sugar has begun to dissolve. Stir in the flour, ginger, brandy, and pepper and continue to heat until all the ingredients have blended into a batter. Remove from the heat.

Transfer the batter to a bowl, cover it with plastic film, and refrigerate for about 1 hour, or until well chilled.

Preheat the oven to 162°C (325°F).

Line the baking sheets with silicone liners. Set aside.

Using a metal spoon, drop the batter by the tablespoonful onto the silicone-lined baking sheets, leaving about 5 centimeters (2 inches) between each cookie to allow for spreading.

Bake the cookies for 7 to 10 minutes, or until they are paper-thin and nicely browned.

Using an offset spatula, transfer the hot cookies to a *tuile* mold or rolling pin so that they drape over to form a rounded tile shape. As soon as a cookie sets,

transfer it to a wire rack to cool completely. Handle carefully, as the baked *tuiles* are very fragile.

If the *tuiles* harden on the baking sheet before being shaped, return them to the oven for a minute or so to soften.

TIPS
The raw batter may be stored, tightly covered and refrigerated, for up to 1 week.

The baked, shaped *tuiles* must be stored absolutely airtight, as any moisture or humidity will cause them to collapse.

It is a good idea to bake only the quantity you will need at one time, as *tuiles* are fragile and vulnerable to moisture.

EVALUATING YOUR SUCCESS
The baked *tuiles* should be an even color, almost paper-thin, crisp, and lacy, with many small holes.

There should be no chewiness.

The baked *tuiles* should have a strong aroma and taste of the brandy and spice.

About *Financiers*

Financiers are one of the great classic French *petits fours*. Traditionally a flourless tea cake (usually made with crushed almonds or almond flour), with a texture somewhere between a sponge cake and a moist cookie, *financiers* have recently experienced a renaissance in the contemporary pastry kitchen. *Financiers* are also known as *friands*, or "small delicacies," and may be topped with fruit, berries, or *crème Chantilly*. They are often used as an accompaniment to ice creams or other frozen desserts or as a component in elegant, plated restaurant desserts.

Financiers were originally baked in ingot-shaped pans, from which their name derives. Nowadays, they are usually baked in small shaped molds, similar to cupcake molds. The base of a classic *financier* is brown butter (*beurre noisette*), ground nuts, confectioners' sugar, and egg whites. When made with the traditional ingredients, the baked cake should have a wonderful warm, buttery flavor and aroma. More modern variations might include chocolate, fresh fruit, spices, nuts other than almonds, and even seeds. Whatever the flavoring, the little cakes should be well flavored and slightly crisp on the exterior, with a soft, almost chewy interior.

Demonstration

Financier aux Noisettes (Hazelnut *Financiers*)

Makes 40 to 50 little cakes
Estimated time to complete: 2 hours

Ingredients	Equipment
For the *beurre noisette*	Small heavy-bottomed saucepan
190 grams (6¾ ounces) unsalted butter	Medium mixing bowl
	Wooden spoon
For the cakes	Rubber spatula
30 grams (1 ounce) cake flour	Plastic film
30 grams (1 ounce) bread flour	*Financier, barquette*, or mini cupcake molds
190 grams (6¾ ounces) sugar	Pastry bag fitted with #5 plain tip
135 grams (4¾ ounces) hazelnut paste (see page 337)	Wire racks
150 grams (5⅓ ounces) egg whites, at room temperature	
Butter and flour for molds	

Prepare your *mise en place*.

Place the butter in a small heavy-bottomed saucepan over low heat and cook for about 15 minutes, or until the milk solids have separated out in the bottom of the pan, and the butter has turned a light, golden brown and has a very nutty aroma. Set aside to cool.

Combine the cake and bread flours in a mixing bowl, stirring with a wooden spoon to blend. Add the sugar and hazelnut paste, stirring until very well blended.

Then, add the egg whites, a bit at a time, beating well and scraping down the sides of the bowl with a rubber spatula after each addition.

Stir in the cooled *beurre noisette*, beating until the batter is smooth.

Cover with plastic film and refrigerate the batter for 1 hour, or until well chilled.

Preheat the oven to 177°C (350°F).

Butter and flour the molds.

Transfer the batter to a pastry bag fitted with the #5 tip and pipe an equal portion of batter into each of the prepared molds, filling the mold about two-thirds full.

Bake the *financiers* for about 10 minutes, or until they are golden brown.

Unmold the cakes onto wire racks to cool slightly. Do not allow them to sit in the molds or they will sweat and get too moist to hold their shape.

Serve warm or within a few hours.

TIPS

Be sure that the *beurre noisette* has cooled before adding it to the other ingredients, or its heat will cook the egg white and render the batter unusable.

Chilling the batter ensures proper leavening and gives the baked cakes the ability to hold their shape.

A small piece of fruit may be placed in the top center

of each *financier* before baking. This will add a dimension of flavor, as well as extra moisture.

EVALUATING YOUR SUCCESS
The baked cakes should have a rich, buttery, nutty

aroma and taste and be consistent in size and shape.

The baked *financiers* should be moist and cakelike in texture.

Demonstration

Financiers au Chocolat (Chocolate *Financiers*)

Makes 40 to 50 little cakes
Estimated time to complete: 2 hours

Ingredients	Equipment
For the *beurre noisette*	Small heavy-bottomed saucepan
190 grams (6¾ ounces) unsalted butter	Medium stainless-steel bowl
	Medium heavy-bottomed saucepan
For the *ganache*	Wooden spoon
140 grams (5 ounces) semisweet or bittersweet chocolate, chopped into bits	Rubber spatula
160 milliliters (5⅓ ounces) heavy cream	Medium mixing bowl
	Plastic film
For the batter	Half-sheet pan
50 grams (1¾ ounces) confectioners' sugar	Parchment paper
40 grams (1⅓ ounces) almond flour	*Financier*, *barquette*, or mini cupcake molds
40 grams (1⅓ ounces) all-purpose flour, sifted	Pastry bag fitted with #5 plain tip
⅛ teaspoon baking powder	Wire racks
110 grams (3¾ ounces) egg whites, at room temperature	
Butter and flour for molds	

Prepare your *mise en place*.

Place the butter in a small heavy-bottomed saucepan over low heat and cook for about 15 minutes, or until the milk solids have separated out in the bottom of the pan and the butter has turned a light, golden brown and has a very nutty aroma. Set aside to cool. Place the chocolate in a medium stainless-steel bowl. Set aside.

Place the cream in a medium heavy-bottomed saucepan over medium-low heat. Bring to just barely a boil, watching carefully—bubbles should form around the edge of the pan, but the cream should not vigorously boil.

Remove the cream from the heat and pour it over the chocolate. Let stand for a minute or two to allow the hot cream to soften the chocolate.

Using a wooden spoon, stir the chocolate into the cream, beating until the mixture is completely smooth and homogeneous. Scrape down the sides of the bowl with a rubber spatula.

Set the *ganache* aside, stirring occasionally to ensure that the chocolate is completely melted, for about 1 hour to come to room temperature.

Combine the confectioners' sugar, almond and all-purpose flours, and baking powder in a medium mixing bowl, stirring with a wooden spoon to blend. Add the egg whites, a bit at a time, beating well and scraping down the sides of the bowl with a rubber spatula after each addition.

Stir in the cooled *beurre noisette*, beating until the batter is smooth. Add the cooled *ganache*, stirring until thoroughly combined.

Cover with plastic film and refrigerate for 1 hour, or until well chilled and firm.

Preheat the oven to 177°C (350°F).

Line the pan with parchment paper. Set aside.

Butter and flour the molds.

Transfer the batter to a pastry bag fitted with the #5 tip and pipe an equal portion of batter into each of the prepared molds, filling the mold about two-thirds full. Place the filled molds on the parchment-lined sheet pan.

Bake the *financiers* for about 10 minutes, or until they are golden brown.

Unmold them onto wire racks to cool slightly. Do not allow the cakes to sit in the molds or they will sweat and get too moist to hold their shape.

Serve warm or within a few hours.

TIPS

Be sure that the *beurre noisette* has cooled before adding it to the other ingredients, or its heat will cook the egg white and render the batter unusable.

Chilling the batter ensures proper leavening and gives the baked cakes the ability to hold their shape.

A small piece of fruit may be placed in the top center of each *financier* before baking. This will add a dimension of flavor, as well as extra moisture.

EVALUATING YOUR SUCCESS

The baked cakes should have a rich, chocolaty aroma and taste and be consistent in size and shape.

The baked *financiers* should be moist and cakelike in texture.

Demonstration

Meringues aux Bananes (Banana Meringues)

Makes 40 to 50 meringues
Estimated time to complete: 90 minutes or overnight

Ingredients	Equipment
225 grams (8 ounces) egg whites, at room temperature	2 half-sheet pans
225 grams (8 ounces) sugar	Parchment paper
375 grams (13¼ ounces) ripe bananas, puréed	Standing electric mixer fitted with whip attachment
	Rubber spatula
	Pastry bag fitted with desired tips
	Wire racks

Prepare your *mise en place*.

Preheat the oven to 93°C (200°F).

Line the pans with parchment paper.

Place the egg whites in the bowl of the standing electric mixer fitted with the whip attachment. Beat on low to aerate. Add the sugar, raise the speed to high, and beat for about 4 minutes, or until stiff peaks form.

Remove the bowl from the mixer and, using a rubber spatula, carefully fold the banana purée into the meringue. Work quickly and carefully, so that the meringue does not deflate.

Immediately transfer the meringue to a pastry bag fitted with the desired tip and quickly pipe small circles, rosettes, teardrops, or other shapes onto each of the parchment paper-lined pans. Do not allow the meringue to sit—it becomes watery very quickly.

Bake the meringues for about 30 minutes, or until they are completely dried out, with an even, light brown color.

Carefully transfer them to wire racks to cool.

Serve the meringues immediately or store them, absolutely airtight in layers, at room temperature for up to 1 month. If any moisture or humidity is absorbed, the meringues will become soggy and unusable.

TIPS

These meringues may be piped into any shape desired; however, the classic shapes are rosettes and teardrops.

Baked meringues may be half dipped in tempered chocolate or *pâte à glacer* (see page 381) for added flavor and an attractive presentation.

EVALUATING YOUR SUCCESS

The baked meringues should be light brown, dry and crispy, and consistent in shape and size.

The finished meringues should have a subtle taste of banana.

Demonstration

Madeleines (Shell-shaped Tea Cakes)

Makes 12 to 15 little cakes

Estimated time to complete: 2 hours

Ingredients	Equipment
125 grams (4½ ounces) sugar	Medium mixing bowl
110 grams (3¾ ounces) all-purpose flour, sifted	Wooden spoon
½ teaspoon baking powder	Plastic film
Pinch salt	*Madeleine* molds
Zest of 1 orange	Pastry bag fitted with #5 plain tip
2 large eggs, at room temperature	Wire racks
110 grams (3¾ ounces) unsalted butter, melted and cooled slightly	
Butter and flour for molds	

Prepare your *mise en place*.

Combine the sugar, flour, baking powder, and salt in a medium mixing bowl, stirring with a wooden spoon to blend. Add the zest. Stir in the eggs, mixing just to combine. You do not want to incorporate too much air into the batter. Finally, stir in the butter.

Cover the bowl with plastic film and refrigerate for 1 hour, or until well chilled. The chilling is important, as it makes the batter easier to pipe and ensures a higher rise during baking. At this point,

the batter may be stored, covered and refrigerated, for up to 4 days.

Butter and flour the *madeleine* molds.

Preheat the oven to 205°C (400°F).

Immediately transfer the batter to a pastry bag fitted with the #5 plain tip and pipe it into the prepared molds.

Bake the *madeleines* for about 7 minutes, or until the cakes spring back in the center when lightly touched.

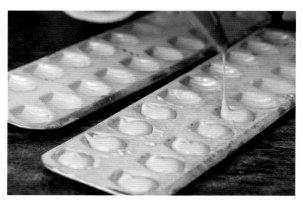

Immediately and unmold them onto wire racks to cool slightly.

Serve warm or within a few hours.

TIPS

Other flavorings, such as ground spices, nuts, or extracts, may be used in place of the orange zest.

Madeleines are best served warm, shortly after being baked. They do not keep well.

EVALUATING YOUR SUCCESS

The baked cakes should have a distinctive hump on the center top, be lightly browned around the edges, and have a strong orange flavor.

Madeleines should be only slightly sweet.

Madeleines are traditionally served rounded side up.

Demonstration

Langues de Chat (Cat's Tongues)

Makes 30 to 40 cookies
Estimated time to complete: 30 minutes

Ingredients	Equipment
115 grams (4 ounces) unsalted butter, at room temperature	2 half-sheet pans
225 grams (8 ounces) sugar	Parchment paper or silicone baking liners
Zest of 1 lemon or orange	Standing electric mixer fitted with paddle attachment
120 grams (4¼ ounces) egg whites, at room temperature	Rubber spatula
140 grams (5 ounces) cake flour, sifted	Pastry bag fitted with #3 plain tip
	Wire racks

Prepare your *mise en place*.

Preheat the oven to 177°C (350°F).

Line the pans with parchment paper or silicone liners.

Combine the butter with the sugar and zest in the bowl of a standing electric mixer fitted with the paddle attachment. Beat on low to just combine. Raise the speed to medium and beat, scraping down the sides of the bowl with a rubber spatula from time to time, for about 4 minutes, or until light and fluffy.

Add the egg whites, a little at a time, scraping down the sides of the bowl after each addition. Do not over-mix, or too much air will be incorporated into the batter and the cookies will rise quickly while baking and then collapse.

Add the flour and beat to just combine.

Transfer the batter to a pastry bag fitted with the #3 plain tip and pipe the chilled batter into batons 1.3 centimeters (½ inch) wide by 6 centimeters (2½ inches) long onto the prepared baking sheets. Bake the cookies for about 7 minutes, or until they are just lightly browned around the edges.

Immediately transfer them to wire racks to cool. Serve warm or store, airtight, at room temperature for up to 2 days, or frozen for up to 1 month.

TIPS

Langues de chat ("cat's tongues") refers to the shape of the baked cookies.

Although citrus zest is the classic flavoring for these cookies, other flavors and extracts can be used.

The baked cookies become stale quickly, so they must be stored airtight.

EVALUATING YOUR SUCCESS

The baked cookies should be lightly browned around the edges and consistent in size and shape.

The cookies should have a distinct citrus flavor.

Demonstration

Russian Tea Cakes

Makes 30 to 40 cookies

Estimated time to complete: 1 hour

Ingredients	Equipment
55 grams (2 ounces) walnuts, toasted and cooled	2 baking sheets
90 grams (3¼ ounces) sugar	Parchment paper or silicone
225 grams (8 ounces) unsalted butter, at room temperature	baking liners
½ teaspoon pure vanilla extract	Food processor fitted with metal blade

250 grams (8¾ ounces) all-purpose flour, sifted

¼ teaspoon salt

For the finish

250 grams (8¾ ounces) confectioners' sugar

Standing electric mixer fitted with paddle attachment

Rubber spatula

Large flat dish

Wire racks

Prepare your *mise en place.*

Preheat the oven to 149°C (300°F).

Line the baking sheets with parchment paper or silicone liners.

Combine the nuts with half the sugar in the bowl of a food processor fitted with the metal blade. Process, using quick on and off turns, until the mixture resembles coarse cornmeal. Do not overprocess or the mixture will turn to paste. Set aside.

Combine the butter with the remaining sugar in the bowl of a standing electric mixer fitted with the paddle attachment. Beat on low to just combine. Raise the speed to medium and beat, scraping down the sides of the bowl with a rubber spatula from time to time, for about 4 minutes, or until light and fluffy. Make sure that the mixture is well creamed or the cookie dough will be difficult to shape.

Beat in the vanilla, followed by the reserved ground nut mixture, flour, and salt, beating and scraping down the sides of the bowl from time to time until the mixture is well blended.

Roll the dough into 2.5-centimeter (1-inch) balls and place them on the prepared baking sheets, leaving about 2.5 centimeters (1 inch) between each one. At this point, the cookies may be well wrapped in plastic film and refrigerated for up to 4 days, or frozen for up to 1 month.

Bake the cookies for about 15 minutes, or until lightly browned around the edges.

Place the confectioners' sugar in a large, flat dish. Remove the cookies from the oven and let them cool for a few minutes. While they are still hot, roll each one in the confectioners' sugar to lightly coat. You may have to do this more than once, as the hot cookies may dissolve the first coating or two.

Place the cookies on wire racks to finish cooling.

Serve the Russian tea cakes or store them, airtight, at room temperature for up to 4 days, or freeze for up to 1 month.

TIPS

The nuts must be thoroughly cooled or the additional heat from the processing will turn them into paste instead of flour.

The walnuts may be replaced with pecans.

EVALUATING YOUR SUCCESS

The baked cookies should be hemispherical in shape and consistent in size.

The finished cookies should be completely coated in confectioners' sugar.

Snowshoe Tommy Bars

Makes 24 bars

Deer Valley Resort, where I work, is one of Utah's premier resorts, known far and wide for its cuisine and guest service. These chewy blond brownies are named for a miner who, long before chairlifts were built and modern skiers hit the slopes, traipsed around the valley carving his initials into the aspen trees.

14 grams (1 tablespoon) melted butter

Flour for pan

185 grams (1½ cups) all-purpose flour

7 grams (1½ teaspoons) baking powder

½ teaspoon salt

170 grams (6 ounces) unsalted butter, at room temperature

330 grams (11⅔ ounces) tightly packed light brown sugar

3 large eggs, at room temperature

10 milliliters (2 teaspoons) pure vanilla extract

170 grams (1 cup) semisweet chocolate chips

95 grams (1 cup) rolled oats

80 grams (1 cup) shredded coconut

80 grams (½ cup) chopped pitted dates

70 grams (½ cup) raisins

50 grams (1¾ ounces) chopped pecans

Preheat the oven to 162°C (325°F).

Using a pastry brush, lightly coat the interior of a 23-by-30.5-centimeter (9-by-12-inch) baking pan with the melted butter. Lightly dust the pan with flour.

Sift the flour, baking powder, and salt together. Set aside.

Combine the butter and sugar in the bowl of a standing electric mixer fitted with the paddle attachment. Beat on low to just blend. Raise the speed to medium and beat for about 4 minutes, or until light and fluffy.

Add the eggs one at a time, beating well after each addition and scraping down the sides of the bowl with a rubber spatula.

Add the vanilla and beat to blend.

With the mixer on low, gradually add the sifted dry ingredients, beating well to thoroughly blend and scraping down the sides of the bowl with the rubber spatula.

Remove the bowl from the mixer and, using a wooden spoon, stir in the chocolate chips, oats, coconut, dates, raisins, and pecans.

When incorporated completely, scrape the mixture into the prepared pan, spreading it into an even layer.

Place the pan in the preheated oven and bake for about 45 minutes, or until the batter is still moist but not raw in the center.

Remove from the oven and set on a wire rack to cool.

When cool, cut into twenty-four 5-centimeter (2-inch) bars, or into any size you desire.

Demonstration

Lemon Cookies

Makes 20 to 25 sandwich cookies
Estimated time to complete: 1 hour

Ingredients   **Equipment**

100 grams (3½ ounces) unsalted butter, at room temperature   2 baking sheets
100 grams (3½ ounces) confectioners' sugar   Parchment paper or silicone baking sheets
Zest of ½ lemon   Standing electric mixer fitted with paddle attachment
Pinch salt   Rubber spatula
5 large egg yolks, at room temperature   Pastry bag fitted with #4 plain tip
125 grams (4½ ounces) cake flour, sifted   Wire racks
                                                                  Small offset spatula
For the finish   Small stainless-steel bowl
100 grams (3½ ounces) raspberry jam   *Bain-marie*
250 grams (8¾ ounces) *Pâte à Glacer* (see page 381)

Prepare your *mise en place*.

Preheat the oven to 177°C (350°F).

Line the baking sheets with parchment paper or silicone liners.

Combine the butter and sugar in the bowl of a standing electric mixer fitted with the paddle attachment. Beat on low to just combine. Add the zest and salt, raise the speed to medium, and beat, scraping down the sides of the bowl with a rubber spatula from time to time, for about 4 minutes, or until light and fluffy.

Add the yolks one at a time, scraping down the sides of the bowl with a rubber spatula after each addition.

When the eggs have been completely incorporated, add the flour and beat to just combine.

Transfer the batter to a pastry bag fitted with the #4 plain tip and pipe it into rounds about 2.5 centimeters (1 inch) in diameter on the prepared baking sheets. Take care that the cookies are all the exact same size,

as they will be sandwiched together when baked.

Bake the cookies for about 7 minutes, or until lightly browned around the edges.

Transfer them to wire racks to cool.

Using a small offset spatula, lightly coat the bottom of one cookie with just enough raspberry jam to hold the sandwich together. Press the bottom of another cookie on top of the jam. The finished cookies may be wrapped, airtight, and frozen for up to 1 month.

Place a clean sheet of parchment or silicone on a cooled baking sheet.

Place the chocolate glaze in a small stainless-steel bowl and then into a *bain-marie* to just melt.

Dip each sandwich cookie halfway into the glaze. Do not use too much glaze or there will be a "foot" on the finished cookie where it pools. Place the dipped cookies on the prepared baking sheet to allow the glaze to harden.

Serve or store, airtight, at room temperature for up to 4 days.

TIPS
TIPS

This batter should be used as soon as it is mixed.

Do not use too much jam or the cookies will be too sweet.

EVALUATING YOUR SUCCESS

The baked cookies should have a distinct lemon flavor and be consistent in size and shape.

There should be just enough jam to add moisture and a bit of sweetness to the finished cookie.

The chocolate glaze should only cover the cookies halfway and should not have a "foot" left by pooling.

Demonstration

Palets aux Raisins Secs (Raisin Cookies)

Makes 40 to 60 cookies
Estimated time to complete: 8 hours for soaking raisins; 40 minutes to complete

Ingredients	Equipment
125 grams (4½ ounces) raisins	Small heat-proof bowl
250 grams (8¾ ounces) unsalted butter, at room temperature	Fine-mesh sieve
250 grams (8¾ ounces) confectioners' sugar	Cutting board
5 large eggs, at room temperature	Sharp knife
328 grams (11½ ounces) cake flour, sifted	2 baking sheets
	Parchment paper or silicone baking liners
For the finish	Standing electric mixer fitted with paddle attachment
100 grams (3½ ounces) confectioners' sugar	Rubber spatula
45 milliliters (3 tablespoons) rum	Pastry bag fitted with #3 plain tip
	Small bowl
	Wire whisk
	Pastry brush
	Wire racks

Place the raisins in a small heat-proof bowl with boiling water to cover. Set aside to soak for 8 hours or overnight.

Drain the soaked raisins through a fine-mesh sieve, discarding the soaking liquid. Transfer the softened raisins to a cutting board and, using a sharp knife, coarsely chop. Set aside.

Preheat the oven to 177°C (350°F).

Line the baking sheets with parchment paper or silicone liners.

Combine the butter and sugar in the bowl of a standing electric mixer fitted with the paddle attachment. Beat on low to just combine. Raise the speed to medium and beat, scraping down the sides of the bowl with a rubber spatula from time to time, for about 4 minutes, or until light and fluffy.

Add the eggs one at a time, scraping down the sides of the bowl with a rubber spatula after each addition. When the eggs have been completely incorporated, add the flour and beat to just combine.

Add the reserved raisins and mix to just incorporate.

Transfer the batter to a pastry bag fitted with a #3 plain tip and pipe it into rounds about 2.5 centimeters (1 inch) in diameter on the prepared baking sheets, leaving about 5 centimeters (2 inches) between each cookie to allow them to spread as they bake.

Bake the cookies for about 8 minutes, or until golden brown.

Meanwhile, make the glaze. Combine the confectioners' sugar and rum in a small bowl, whisking to blend. Set aside.

Remove the cookies from the oven and transfer them to wire racks.

Using a pastry brush, immediately coat each cookie with the rum glaze. Let cool.

Serve or store, airtight, at room temperature for up to 4 days.

TIPS
Chopping the raisins makes the batter easier to pipe.

Zante currants can be substituted for the raisins. They do not require soaking and chopping.

The glaze adds a touch of sweetness and a nice sheen.

EVALUATING YOUR SUCCESS
The baked cookies should be lightly browned around the edges, and the surface should be studded with raisins.

The cookies should be thin and slightly chewy.

The glaze should be transparent and shiny but not sticky.

Demonstration

Florentines

Makes 60 squares
Estimated time to complete: 90 minutes

Ingredients	Equipment
Flour for dusting	Half-sheet pan
Half recipe *Pâte Sucrée* (see page 94)	Parchment paper
180 grams (6⅓ ounces) sugar	Rolling pin
15 milliliters (1 tablespoon) light corn syrup	Pastry brush
100 grams (3½ ounces) unsalted butter, at room temperature	Docker or kitchen fork
80 grams (2¾ ounces) honey	Medium heavy-bottomed saucepan
105 milliliters (3½ ounces) heavy cream	Wooden spoon
Zest of 1 orange	Candy thermometer
250 grams (8¾ ounces) sliced almonds	Offset spatula
80 grams (2¾ ounces) diced candied orange peel or candied fruit	Wire rack
	Sharp knife

Prepare your *mise en place*.

Line the pan with parchment paper.

Lightly flour a clean, flat work surface. Place the dough in the center of the floured surface and, using a rolling pin, roll it out to a rectangle about 3 millimeters (⅛ inch) thick and large enough to fit the half-sheet pan. Using a pastry brush, lightly brush off the excess flour.

Lift the dough gently, fold it in half over the rolling pin, and slip it, still folded, into the prepared pan. Unfold the dough into the bottom of the pan and remove the rolling pin.

Slowly turning the pan, gently push the dough into the bottom and against the edges, taking care not to pull or stretch the dough. Use quick, light, pressing movements, making certain you do not make holes in the dough. The edges should be neat and pressed against the bottom edge of the pan, without coming up and covering the sides. Pinch any excess dough as necessary.

Using a docker or kitchen fork, dock the pastry. Transfer the pastry to the refrigerator for 30 minutes to chill.

Preheat the oven to 177°C (350°F).

Blind-bake the pastry as directed on page 90. Do not allow it to cook completely, as it will be baked again with the filling.

Remove the pastry from the oven and set aside. Do not turn off the oven.

While the pastry is baking, combine the sugar and corn syrup with 90 milliliters (6 tablespoons) water in a medium heavy-bottomed saucepan over medium heat. Cook, stirring occasionally with a wooden spoon, for about 4 minutes, or until the mixture begins to caramelize.

Stir in the butter and honey and bring to a boil.

Immediately add the cream and zest and again bring to a boil. Lower the heat and simmer for about 10 minutes, or until the mixture reach 124°C (255°F) on a candy thermometer.

Remove the pan from the heat and stir in the almonds and candied fruit.

Pour the hot mixture into the blind-baked pastry and, using an offset spatula, spread it out to an even layer.

Bake the Florentines for about 12 minutes, or until the candied mixture is bubbly.

Set the pan on a wire rack to cool, then, using a sharp knife, cut into 2.5-centimeter (1-inch) squares. Serve or store, airtight, at room temperature for up to 4 days.

TIPS

Take care not to overcook the filling or it will be too dark and have too strong a caramel taste.

Once the almonds have been added, don't stir vigorously, as you do not want to chop the nuts.

Spread the filling onto the pastry immediately after cooking, as it will begin to harden very rapidly.

EVALUATING YOUR SUCCESS

The caramel filling should be an even golden color.

The almond slices should remain whole, not shattered.

The candied fruit should be clearly visible on the surface of the baked confection.

The baked Florentines should have a sweet, honey flavor and be consistent in size and shape.

Demonstration

Sablés (Swirl Cookies Made from French *Sablé* Dough)

Makes 40 to 50 cookies
Estimated time to complete: 3 hours

Ingredients	Equipment
For the vanilla dough	Sifter
225 grams (8 ounces) unsalted butter, at room temperature	Standing electric mixer fitted with paddle attachment
100 grams (3½ ounces) sugar	Rubber spatula
Pinch salt	Bowl scraper
1 large egg yolk, at room temperature	Plastic film
1 teaspoon pure vanilla extract	Small bowl
270 grams (9½ ounces) all-purpose flour, sifted	Rolling pin
	2 pastry brushes
For the chocolate dough	2 baking sheets
270 grams (9½ ounces) all-purpose flour	Parchment paper or silicone baking liners
14 grams (1 tablespoon plus 1 teaspoon) Dutch-process cocoa powder	Sharp knife
½ teaspoon baking soda	Wire racks
140 grams (5 ounces) unsalted butter, at room temperature	
150 grams (5 ⅓ ounces) sugar	
Pinch salt	
1 large egg, at room temperature	
30 milliliters (1 ounce) whole milk	
For the finish	
Flour for dusting	
Egg wash (see page 62)	
200 grams (7 ounces) granulated sugar	

Prepare your *mise en place*.

For the vanilla dough, combine the butter, sugar, and salt in the bowl of a standing electric mixer fitted with the paddle attachment. Beat on low to just combine. Raise the speed to medium and beat, scraping down the sides of the bowl with a rubber spatula from time to time, for about 4 minutes, or until light and fluffy.

Add the egg and vanilla and beat, scraping down the sides of the bowl with a rubber spatula after each

addition, for about 1 minute, or until well blended.

Add the flour and beat just to combine.

Using a bowl scraper, scrape the dough from the mixer bowl, wrap it in plastic film, and refrigerate for about 1 hour, or until well chilled.

Wipe the bowl clean and return it to the mixer.

For the chocolate dough, sift the flour, cocoa powder, and baking soda together. Set aside.

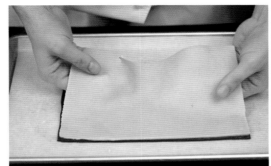

Combine the butter, sugar, and salt in the bowl of the standing electric mixer fitted with the paddle attachment. Beat on low just to combine. Raise the speed to medium and beat, scraping down the sides of the bowl with a rubber spatula from time to time, for about 4 minutes, or until light and fluffy.

Add the egg and milk and beat, scraping down the sides of the bowl with a rubber spatula after each addition, for a minute or two, or until well blended.

Add the sifted dry ingredients and beat just to combine.

Using a bowl scraper, scrape the dough from the mixer bowl, wrap it in plastic film, and refrigerate for about 1 hour, or until well chilled.

When both doughs are well chilled, lightly flour a clean, flat work surface.

Place the egg wash in a small bowl.

Set the chocolate dough in the center of the floured sur-

face. Using a rolling pin, roll it out to a rectangle approximately 28 by 41 centimeters (11 by 16 inches) and 3 millimeters (⅛ inch) thick. Use a knife to trim to size. Using a pastry brush, lightly brush off the excess flour.

Using a second pastry brush, very lightly coat the surface of the chocolate dough with a thin layer of egg wash.

Again, lightly flour a clean, flat work surface. Place the vanilla dough in the center. Using a rolling pin, roll the dough out to the same size rectangle as before and trim to size. Using the dry pastry brush, lightly brush off the excess flour. Carefully transfer the vanilla dough rectangle to the top of the chocolate dough rectangle.

Starting at a long side, gently roll the two layers of dough into a log shape. While rolling, take care that the layers stay firmly attached, with no space in the center, and that the log remains compact. If there is space between the layers, there will be holes in the cut cookies.

Wrap the dough log in plastic film and refrigerate it for at least 30 minutes, or up to 2 days. (At this point, the dough may also be frozen for up to 1 month. If frozen, it should be thawed before proceeding with the recipe.)

Preheat the oven to 177°C (350°F).

Line the baking sheets with parchment paper or silicone liners.

Generously sprinkle a clean, flat work surface with granulated sugar.

Remove the dough log from the refrigerator and unwrap it, leaving it sitting on the plastic film.

Using a pastry brush, coat the surface of the dough log with a thin layer of egg wash. Immediately roll it in the granulated sugar to generously coat the exterior.

Using a sharp knife, cut the dough crosswise into 6-millimeter-thick (¼-inch-thick) slices. Rotate the log slightly after each cut to help keep the cookies a perfectly round shape.

As they are cut, place the cookies on the prepared baking sheets.

Bake the cookies for about 7 minutes, or just until they begin to brown around the edges.

Transfer them to wire racks to cool.

Serve or store, airtight, at room temperature for up to 4 days.

TIPS

The doughs must be well chilled before rolling out or they won't hold an even shape.

If the doughs crack slightly when being rolled out, the cracks will not be noticeable in the baked cookies.

If desired, the vanilla dough can be rolled out slightly thinner than the chocolate, which facilitates rolling the log by starting with a thinner dough.

Use only a very thin layer of egg wash to hold the layer together; otherwise, the dough will get soggy.

The outer coating of sugar adds a nice crunchy texture to the baked cookies.

EVALUATING YOUR SUCCESS

The baked cookies should be just barely browned around the edges, round, and even in size and thickness.

The chocolate component should have a strong chocolate flavor.

The baked cookies should be dry but not hard or crumbly.

Demonstration

Nougat

Makes 30 to 45 squares
Estimated time to complete: 1 hour

Ingredients	Equipment
280 grams (9¾ ounces) almonds	Half-sheet pan
160 grams (5⅔ ounces) hazelnuts	Parchment paper
160 grams (5⅔ ounces) walnuts	Standing electric mixer fitted with whip and paddle attachments

40 grams (1⅓ ounces) pistachios

2 large egg whites, at room temperature

280 grams (9¾ ounces) honey

240 grams (8½ ounces) light corn syrup

600 grams (1 pound, 5 ounces) sugar

Cornstarch for dusting

Small heavy-bottomed saucepan

Medium heavy-bottomed saucepan

Candy thermometer

Silicone baking liners

Rolling pin

Sharp knife

Prepare your *mise en place.*

Preheat the oven to 93°C (200°F).

Line the pan with parchment paper.

Combine the almonds, hazelnuts, walnuts, and pistachios on the prepared sheet pan. Place in the preheated oven and toast, turning frequently, for about 15 minutes, or until nicely colored and aromatic.

While the nuts are roasting, prepare the base. If the nuts finish roasting before the batter is ready, they must be kept warm. Turn off the oven, but keep the door slightly ajar to prevent them from continuing to cook.

Place the egg whites in the bowl of a standing electric mixer fitted with the whip attachment.

Combine the honey with 40 grams (1⅓ ounces) of the corn syrup in a small, heavy-bottomed saucepan over low heat and bring to a boil.

Simultaneously combine the remaining corn syrup with the sugar and 75 milliliters (2½ ounces) cold

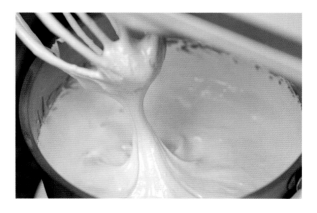

water in a medium heavy-bottomed saucepan over low heat and bring to a boil.

As soon as the honey mixture comes to a boil, begin whipping the egg whites. When the honey mixture has reached 130°C (266°F) on a candy thermometer, pour it over the whipping egg whites.

Continue whipping, and when the sugar mixture has reached 139°C (282°F) on a candy thermometer, pour it over the whipping egg whites.

When the meringue begins to stiffen, stop the mixer. Remove the whip attachment and replace it with the paddle attachment.

With the speed on low, add the nuts, mixing to just blend.

Place a silicone liner on a clean, flat work surface. Lightly dust it with cornstarch.

Pour the hot nougat out onto the cornstarch-coated liner. Dust the top of the nougat with cornstarch. Place a second silicone liner over the nougat and, using a rolling pin, roll the nougat out to 1.3 centimeters (½ inch) thick.

Allow to cool and then, using a sharp knife, cut the nougat into 2.5-centimeter (1-inch) squares.

Serve or store, airtight, at room temperature for up to 1 week.

TIPS

Nougat is often referred to as *Nougat Montelimar,* after the town in southern France where it is thought to have originated in the seventeenth century.

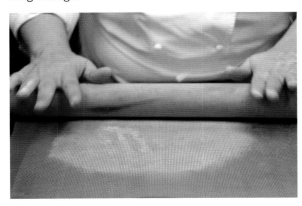

You must use the same total amount of nuts, but any combination of nuts can be used.

Diced candied or dried fruit can be substituted for a portion of the nut mixture.

Exotically flavored honeys can be used to add another dimension of flavor.

The nougat must still be warm when rolled or it will become too hard to work with.

If the nougat is too hard to roll after cooking, it is because the sugar mixture was cooked to too high a temperature.

If it is too soft, the sugar mixture was not cooked long enough.

The cut nougat can be dipped in tempered chocolate, if desired.

EVALUATING YOUR SUCCESS

The nougat should be slightly off-white, with no trace of blond or brown.

The finished nougat should be soft and chewy but firm enough to hold its shape when cut.

There should be nuts clearly visible in every bite, and each piece should be consistent in size and shape.

The nougat should have a strong honey aroma and taste.

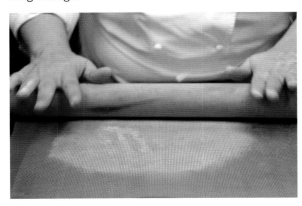

Demonstration

Pâte de Fruits (Fruit Jellies)

Makes 30 to 40 squares
Estimated time to complete: 90 minutes

Ingredients	Equipment
Nonstick vegetable spray	9-inch cake ring
750 grams (1 pound, 9⅓ ounces) sugar	Silicone baking liner
10 grams (2 teaspoons) pectin	Large heavy-bottomed saucepan
500 grams (1 pound, 1½ ounces) fruit purée of choice (see page 58)	Heat-proof spatula
75 grams (2½ ounces) light corn syrup	Candy thermometer
75 grams (2½ ounces) Trimoline (see page 499)	Small bowl
1 teaspoon citric acid (see Tips)	Large shallow bowl or plate
	Sharp knife

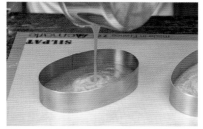

Prepare your *mise en place*.

Generously coat the interior of the cake ring with nonstick vegetable spray. Place the oiled ring on a silicone baking liner on a clean, flat work surface.

Combine 50 grams (1¾ ounces) of the sugar and the pectin in a large heavy-bottomed saucepan, stirring to combine. Add the fruit purée and place the pan over medium heat. Bring it to a boil, stirring occasionally with a heat-proof spatula.

As soon as the mixture comes to a boil, add 500 grams (1 pound, 1½ ounces) of the remaining sugar, along with the corn syrup and Trimoline. Cook, stirring frequently, for about 6 minutes, or until the mixture reaches 116°C (240°F/soft-ball stage) on a candy thermometer.

In a small bowl, combine the citric acid with 15 milliliters (1 tablespoon) cold water, or just enough to dissolve the crystals.

Once the mixture reaches the soft-ball stage, immedi-

ately remove it from the heat and stir in the citric acid. Stir to blend well.

Pour the mixture into the oiled cake ring and let it cool completely.

Place the remaining sugar in a large shallow bowl or on a plate.

When the jellies are cool, using a sharp knife, cut them into 2.5-centimeter (1-inch) squares (or any other small decorative shape you prefer) and dredge each piece in the sugar.

Serve or store, airtight, at room temperature for up to 1 week. Do not allow any humidity or moisture to touch the jellies or the sugar will melt and the finished candies will be quite unattractive.

TIPS

For strawberry, raspberry, or passion fruit purées, increase the pectin to 15 grams (½ ounce).

Citric acid is a commercially produced, water-soluble

product added to prevent crystallization and to heighten flavor. It is available from cake and bakery supply stores.

The traditional (and first) fruit jellies were made with quince, which is extremely high in pectin, so no additional pectin was required to set the candy.

EVALUATING YOUR SUCCESS
The finished jelly should be firm enough to hold its shape when cut but remain soft and slightly chewy.

The *pâte de fruits* should have a sweet, defined fruit flavor.

The granulated sugar coating should completely cover the candy.

Demonstration

Caramel Mou (Soft Caramel)

Makes 30 to 40 pieces
Estimated time to complete: 90 minutes

Ingredients	Equipment
Nonstick vegetable spray	9-inch cake ring
510 milliliters (17 ounces) heavy cream	Silicone baking liner
375 grams (13¼ ounces) sugar	Large heavy-bottomed saucepan
350 grams (12⅓ ounces) light corn syrup	Wooden spoon
50 grams (1¾ ounces) Trimoline (see page 499)	Candy thermometer
14 grams (1 tablespoon) unsalted butter,	Large shallow dish, optional
cut into cubes, at room temperature	Sharp knife
200 grams (7 ounces) semisweet or bittersweet	
chocolate, chopped into bits	
200 grams (7 ounces) unsweetened chocolate, chopped into bits	

For the optional finish
200 grams (7 ounces) confectioners' sugar
65 grams (2¼ ounces) Dutch-process cocoa powder

Prepare your *mise en place*.

Generously coat the interior of the cake ring with nonstick vegetable spray. Place the oiled ring on a silicone baking liner on a clean, flat work surface.

Combine the cream with the sugar, corn syrup, and Trimoline in a large heavy-bottomed saucepan over medium heat. Stirring constantly with a wooden spoon, bring the mixture to 118°C (245°F) on a candy thermometer.

Immediately remove the pan from the heat and stir in the butter and both of the chocolates. Stir just until the butter and chocolate have melted into the cream mixture (otherwise the caramel will begin to separate and be unusable).

Pour the caramel into the oiled cake ring and let it cool completely.

For the optional finish, combine the confectioners' sugar and cocoa powder in a large shallow dish.

Using a sharp knife, cut the cooled caramel into 2.5-centimeter (1-inch) squares (or any other small decorative shape you prefer) and, if desired, dredge each piece in the sugar-and-cocoa mixture.

Serve or store, airtight, in layers separated by parchment paper, at room temperature for up to 1 week. Do not allow any humidity or moisture to penetrate the caramels.

TIPS
If desired, you can first caramelize the sugar and then add the cream, corn syrup, and Trimoline, which will make the finished candy less sweet but produce deeper caramel flavor.

If the cooled caramel is too soft to hold its shape

when cut, it may be cooked further over low heat.

The cooked caramel should be homogeneous, with no lumps.

The cooling caramel should have a smooth, even surface.

The caramel should be soft and chewy but strong enough to hold its shape once cut.

The finished caramel should have a strong chocolate flavor and aroma.

The cut caramels should be consistent in size and shape.

References

Amendola, Joseph, and Donald Lundberg. *Understanding Baking*. New York: Van Nostrand Reinhold, 1992.

American Egg Board. *Eggcyclopedia*. Park Ridge, IL: The American Egg Board, 1999.

Arbuckle, W. S., *Ice Cream*, 4th edition. Westport, CT: AVI Publishing Co., 1986.

Beranbaum, Rose Levy. "Sugar Baking and Cooking." *The Research Report* (International Association of Cooking Professionals), October 1985.

Bilheux, Roland, and Alain Escoffier. *Professional French Pastry Series: Doughs, Batters, and Meringues*. New York: Van Nostrand Reinhold, 1988.

Bloom, Carole. *The International Dictionary of Desserts, Pastries, and Confections*. New York: Hearst Books, 1995.

Brunstein, Pascal: *Plaisirs de petits fours*. Paris: Passion Gourmande, Gourmande Passion, 1995.

Charley, Helen. *Food Science*, 2nd edition. New York: Macmillan Publishing Company, 1986.

Claiborne, Craig. *Craig Claiborne's The New York Times Food Encyclopedia*. New York: Wings Books, 1994.

Connell, Patricia. "All About Sugar." *Bon Appétit*, September 1988.

Corriher, Shirley O. *CookWise: The Hows and Whys of Successful Cooking*. William Morrow, 1997.

Culinary Institute of America. *The Professional Chef*. 7th edition. New York: Wiley, 2002.

Culinary Institute of America and Judith Choate. *The Fundamental Techniques of Classic Cuisine*. New York: Stewart, Tabori & Chang, 2007.

Dannenberg, Linda. *French Tarts: 50 Savory and Sweet Recipes*. New York: Artisan, 1997.

Davidson, Alan. *The Oxford Companion to Food*. New York: Oxford University Press, 1999.

Figoni, Paula. *How Baking Works: Exploring the Fundamentals of Baking Science*. Hoboken, NJ: John Wiley & Sons, 2004.

Friberg, Bo. *The Professional Pastry Chef*, 3rd edition. New York: John Wiley and Sons, 1996.

Gates, June C. *Basic Foods*, 2nd edition. New York: Holt, Reinhart, and Winston. 1981.

Gisslen, Wayne. *Professional Baking,* 5th edition. New York: John Wiley & Sons, 2008.

Godshall, M. A. "Use of Sucrose as a Sweetener in Foods." *Cereal Foods World*, April 1990.

Hamelman, Jeffrey. *Bread: A Baker's Book of Techniques and Recipes*. Hoboken, NJ: John Wiley & Sons, 2004.

Healy, Bruce, and Paul Bugat. *The Art of the Cake*. New York: William Morrow, 1999.

Herbst, Sharon Tyler. *The New Food Lover's Companion*. Hauppage, NY: Barron's, 1995.

Hillman, Howard. *Kitchen Science: A Compendium of Essential Information for Every Cook*. Boston: Houghton Mifflin Company, 1981.

Light, Joseph M. "Modified Food Starches: Why, What, Where, and How." *Cereal Foods World*, November 1990.

McGee, Harold. *On Food and Cooking: The Science and Lore of the Kitchen*. New York: Scribner, 2004.

Montagne, Prosper. *Larousse Gastromique*. New York: Clarkson Potter, 2001.

Pennington, Neil L. and Charles Baker, eds. *Sugar: A User's Guide to Sucrose*, New York: Van Nostrand Reinhold, 1990.

Potter, Norman N. *Food Science,* 4th edition. Westport, CT: AVI Publishing Co., 1986.

Schünemann, Claus and Günter Treu. *Baking: The Art and Science*. Calgary, Alberta, Canada: Baker Tech, Inc., 1988.

Shere, Lindsey Remolif. *Chez Panisse Desserts*. New York: Random House, 1985.

Sultan, William J. *The Pastry Chef*. Westport, CT: AVI Publishing Co., 1983.

Teubner, Christian, and Sybil Gräfin Schönfeldt. *The Great Dessert Book: Classic Light Desserts of the World*. New York: Hearst, 1983.

Time-Life Books. *The Good Cook, Techniques and Recipes: Preserving*. Alexandria, VA: Time-Life Books, 1981.

Wheaton, Barbara Ketcham. *Savoring the Past: The French Kitchen and Table from 1300 to 1789*. New York: Scribner, 1983.

Additional references:
Sugar material: Permission to reproduce entirely or in parts granted by The Sugar Association, Inc.

Glossary

Acetate: A flexible, clear plastic sheet, roll, or strip in varying degrees of thickness that is used as a smooth, nonstick surface in cake and chocolate work

Acetobacillus: Bacteria that create lactic and acetic acids by eating the sugars present in bread doughs and that impart a slightly sour taste to the baked bread.

Acidulated water: Water with an acidic ingredient, such as lemon juice or vinegar, that is used to prevent browning or other discoloration in cut fruits and vegetables.

Active dry yeast: Yeast that has been dehydrated and packed airtight to extend its viability.

Albumen: The white of an egg.

Allumette: French for "matchstick"; used to describe small, short strips of baked puff pastry, often topped with either sweet or savory items.

Almond flour: Finely ground blanched almonds.

Amylase: An enzyme in yeast-based baked products that breaks down starch into maltose and serves to soften the baked product and keep it from turning stale.

Appareil: A French word used to describe a mixture, filling, or ingredients for preparing food.

Apricot glaze: A shiny, translucent, apricot-jam-based coating used for desserts and pastries made from apricot jam and water that have been heated and strained. See also *nappage*.

Autolyse: In bread making, to allow a brief (usually 20-minute) resting period for a mixture of flour and water. During this time, the proteins hydrate and bond, which increases the volume of the dough and reduces oxidation.

Bain-marie: The French culinary term for a double-boiler or water bath. Also used to describe a metal container that is filled with hot water and used to keep food hot during service, or the process of placing pans filled with a product (such as custard) into a larger pan of water during baking to ensure even cooking and the retention of moisture.

Baker's percentage: A mathematical system used by bakers to determine bread formulas. Flour is considered 100 percent and all remaining ingredients are calculated as a percentage of the weight of the flour. This is a simple method for scaling a recipe up or down. Also called baker's math.

Barquette: A boat-shaped pastry shell with a savory or sweet filling.

Bavarois: See *crème bavaroise*.

Bench rest: A short, in-between proofing to allow the gluten in yeasted dough to rest.

Beurre: French word for "butter."

Beurre en pommade: Butter that has been softened so that it is malleable but remains very cool.

Beurre fondue: Melted butter.

Bevel: To cut off the edges of an un-iced cake to round them. Usually done before fondant is placed on the cake.

Beurrage: A square block of cold butter used in making puff pastry.

Biscuit: The French term for many types of sponge cake.

Biscuit à la cuillère: Ladyfinger.

Blanch: To quickly immerse a product, usually a fruit or vegetable, into boiling water to soften it slightly and then immerse it in very cold or ice water to stop the cooking process.

Blind-bake: To prebake a pastry shell before filling it. Often used for pies or tarts whose fillings either have

494

been precooked or do not require further baking.

Blister: Bumps that appear on doughs during baking that are caused by steam pockets.

Bombe glacée: Used loosely, a dessert and a frozen base mixture. More specifically, a frozen dessert traditionally made by filling a chilled, half-sphere mold with a firm mixture, such as ice cream or sorbet, sometimes in multiple layers.

Bonbon: A small confection or candy.

Brewer's yeast: Nonleavening yeast generally used for brewing beverages.

Cake board or cake circle: A thin cardboard upon which finished cakes are placed to provide support and stability. The boards may be rectangular (for sheet cakes) or round.

Cake comb: A flat, triangular metal tool with serrated edges all around that is used to make decorative designs on icings.

Cake marker: A tool used to mark exact wedges on the top of a cake to allow perfect slices to be cut.

Cake ring: A round metal (usually stainless-steel) ring mold without a bottom, used to create neat cake layers.

Caramel: Sugar cooked until it is either golden brown or a deep, rich brown, depending upon the degree and duration of heat applied.

Caramelization: Chemical reactions in sugars caused by the application of high heat. Any food containing sugars can be caramelized, which affects is coloring and flavor.

Chalazae: Twisted, ropelike strands of egg white attached to two sides of the yolk that serve to hold it in place at the center of the albumen.

Charlotte: A Bavarian cream served in a *génoise.*

Chemical leavener: A chemical agent, most often baking soda or baking powder, used to make a baked product rise.

Cheminées: Venting holes cut into pastry to allow steam to escape during baking.

Chiqueter: French term meaning to flute the edge of pastry dough for both décor and to help the steam pump up the pastry during baking.

Choux paste: See *pâte à choux.*

Cold water test: A simple method for testing the stage

of hardness of a candy or syrup by dropping a small amount of the product into extremely cold water. Not as reliable as using a thermometer.

Cookie cutter: A metal or plastic form used to cut out specific shapes in unbaked cookie dough. Also a professional sheet cutter that cuts out entire sheets of cookie dough at a time.

Cornet: A French term for "cone" that is used to describe a parchment-paper cone with a small hole cut at the end used to decorate or write on iced surfaces. Also used to describe cone-shaped baked products such as *pâte à cornet* decorations.

Coupe: A dessert of ice creams, sorbets, and fresh fruit served in a glass of the same name. It can also include chocolate sauce, chopped toasted nuts, and *crème anglaise.* In America, a *coupe* might be called a sundae.

Couche: A natural fiber cloth used when proofing bread proof dough.

Couverture: High-quality chocolate with at least 32 percent cocoa butter, to be used for tempering.

Creaming: The mixing together of fat and sugar until light and fluffy. This is often the first step in making a dough or batter and is followed by the addition of eggs.

Crème anglaise: A stirred custard used as a sauce or as a base for ice cream.

Crème au beurre: Buttercream icing.

Crème bavaroise: Bavarian cream, a classic molded dessert based on egg custard or fruit purée and served cold.

Crème brûlée: A baked custard with a crisped caramelized sugar crust or topping.

Crème caramel: A baked vanilla custard that, when inverted, has a loose caramel sauce.

Crème Chantilly: Sweetened whipped cream.

Crème Chiboust: A pastry cream lightened with Italian meringue and stabilized with gelatin.

Crème d'amandes: Almond cream—a mixture of sugar, butter, ground almonds, and eggs, sometimes flavored with rum.

Crème fraîche: A very heavy cream containing 46 to 48 percent butterfat.

Crème glacée: An eggless ice cream based on a mixture of milk, cream, sugar, and flavoring.

Crème légère: A pastry cream lightened with whipped cream.

Crème mousseline: A type of buttercream made by beating pastry cream into a large quantity of unsalted butter.

Crème pâtissière: "Pastry cream"—a cooked, custard-like cream used to fill many classic cakes and pastries.

Crimp: Pinching together a pastry (usually pie) crust rim to seal a top and bottom crust together. This may be done with the fingers or with a tool called a pastry crimper.

Croquembouche: Filled cream puffs dipped in caramel and arranged in a conical, tower shape.

Crumb: The interior texture of a baked pastry product.

Crystallization: The process whereby sugar molecules join together into granules. This occurs when liquid with sugar dissolved in it is heated, causing the water to evaporate.

Custard: A type of thickened pastry product made by the coagulation of egg protein in a liquid.

Dacquoise: A baked meringue disk or the cake made by layering these disks with whipped cream or buttercream.

Decorative cutter: A metal or plastic form used to cut decorative pieces from cookie dough, marzipan, or other firm doughs.

Demi-feuilletage: Puff pastry dough made with fewer turns than classic puff pastry.

Détrempe: A simple dough composed of flour, salt, water, and butter; a component of puff pastry.

Dust: To sprinkle a dry ingredient, usually flour or confectioners' sugar, on a work surface or over a product, either before or after baking.

Egg wash: A mixture of whole egg, egg yolk, or egg whites and liquid, usually milk, cream, or water, that is brushed onto pastries and other items before baking to add sheen, retain moisture, and aid in browning.

Elastic: Used to describe dough that can return to its original shape after stretching.

En croûte: Used to describe food that has been wrapped in a pastry covering and baked.

Enriched dough: A bread dough that contains dairy, eggs, fat, or sugar to make it richer and more tender than a simple dough.

Enrobe: To entirely cover a pastry or confection in chocolate, fondant, icing, or sugar.

Extract: A highly concentrated, alcohol-based, liquid flavoring, such as lemon, almond, or—most commonly—vanilla.

Fermentation: The process by which yeast converts sugars to alcohol and carbon dioxide. Also, the time allowed for dough to develop before it is shaped, proofed, and baked.

Feuilletage: See pâte feuilletée.

Feuilletage rapide: Quick puff pastry dough.

Feuilleté : A baked pastry puff.

FIFO: First in, first out. The rule of moving products from the kitchen before introducing new products.

Flamber: To pour alcohol over a product and ignite it.

Fold: To gently mix a light, airy ingredient, such as a meringue, into a heavier mixture, such as a batter, so that the airy ingredients don't deflate.

Fondant: Cooked, worked sugar that is flavored and used for icing. Also, the bitter chocolate high in cocoa butter used for making shiny chocolate coatings.

Fraisage: The process of crushing small clumps of dough and fat with the heel of the palm to incorporate thoroughly, usually used when making items such as pâte brisée.

Frangipane: An almond custard filling.

French meringue: The simplest type of meringue, made by beating egg whites with sugar.

Friand: The French term for a small, sweet pastry.

Friandise: A grouping of sweet confections and petits fours served after dessert. Also called mignardise.

Frost: To cover a cake with icing.

Fructose: A natural sugar that is a by-product of fruit and honey.

Ganache: A rich chocolate mixture made with heavy cream and chocolate.

Gâteau: The French word for "cake."

Gelatin: A thickening product that is odorless, tasteless, and colorless. Extracted from animal bones and connective tissues, it becomes a jelly when dissolved in liquid and allowed to set. It is used as a binder and thickener and to prepare jellied products.

Gelatinization: A reaction that occurs during the baking process whereby the starches in the mixture absorb moisture and swell, thickening the texture of the product.

Génoise: A foam cake made with whole eggs.

Glacer: To glaze by cooking food with sugar, butter, and water until a glossy coating is formed; iced, glazed, or crystallized.

Glaze: A thin coating on the surface of a product that is used make an attractive presentation as well as to prevent staling.

Gliadin: One of the two partial proteins that make up gluten.

Glucose: A liquid sweetener used in desserts that does not readily crystallize.

Gluten: The primary protein found in flour, and the elastic substance that gives a baked item its texture.

Glutenin: One of the two partial proteins that make up gluten.

Invert sugar: Sucrose that has been broken into fructose and glucose, a process that helps prevent crystallization.

Gum paste: An edible paste used in cake decorating. Homogenize: To create a mixture that comes together and does not separate.

Hydration: The amount of moisture in a bread dough, often expressed as the ratio of liquid ingredients to flour.

Icing: A sweet mixture used to coat and decorate cakes and other baked products; also called frosting.

Italian meringue: A meringue made with cooked sugar syrup that is poured into firmly whipped egg whites and then beaten into stiff peaks.

Knead: To work dough, either by hand or in an electric mixer fitted with the dough hook, into a smooth, malleable mass.

Lamination: Rolling and folding dough and butter in layers that will form flaky pastry when baked.

Lattice: The decorative design for the tops of pies or pastries created by interweaving strips of dough.

Leavener: An ingredient used in baked products to lighten the texture, increase the volume, and produce the desired crumb. Leavening agents might be egg whites, baking powder, baking soda, yeast, or cream of tartar.

Letter fold: A process for laminating doughs, whereby the dough is folded into thirds, as you would fold a letter to be placed in an envelope.

Liquefier: A liquid such as water, oil, or milk that is used to loosen a dough or batter.

Macerate: To soak an item in liquid to soften it and infuse it with flavor.

Maillard reaction: The browning that occurs in baked products because of a reaction between reducing sugars and proteins or amino acids. It is similar to caramelization, and the two reactions often occur simultaneously.

Marbleize: To work different-colored ingredients—usually chocolate, fondant, or cake batter—together to create the appearance of marble.

Marzipan: A thick, moldable sweet paste made from ground almonds, sugar, and egg whites used as a confection, cake covering, or decorative item.

Meringue: A stiffly beaten mixture primarily made of egg whites and sugar.

Mille-feuille: The French term meaning "thousand-layer" that refers to strips of baked puff pastry layered with pastry cream, jam, whipped cream, or other fillings.

Mise en place: A French term meaning "everything put in its place," used to describe a cook's systematic preparation and organization of all ingredients and tools necessary before beginning to execute a given recipe.

Mousse: A light and airy sweet or savory dish made by combining a flavored, puréed base with beaten egg whites or whipped cream.

Nappage: In pastry making, an apricot glaze used to coat tarts, pastries, or other desserts to seal in moisture and add sheen.

Nappant: For sauces, just thick enough to coat the back of a spoon.

Nougat: A sweet confection made from sugar, honey, nuts, and sometimes candied fruit.

Oxidation: The interaction between oxygen molecules and the variety of substances they contact.

Pain: The French word for "bread."

Parchment paper: A nonstick coated paper used to line pans and to make *cornets*.

Pâte: A pastry, dough, or batter.

Pâte à bombe: A dessert mixture made from egg yolks and sugar cooked to the soft-ball stage.

Pâte à choux: A twice-cooked dough used to make cream puffs and other airy pastries.

Pâte à glacer: Chocolate thinned with vegetable oil so that it will not set as hard and can be used to glaze cakes and other pastries.

Pâte brisée: A basic flaky tart dough made from flour, water, fat, and salt.

Pâte de fruit: Fruit jelly.

Pâte feuilletée: Puff pastry dough.

Pâte feuilletée inversée: A reverse puff pastry in which the butter encloses the dough.

Pâte sablée: A sweet pastry dough similar to short-bread that is sweeter, richer, and more crumbly than *pâte sucrée* and is sometimes leavened.

Pâte sucrée: A sweet, rich pastry dough softer than *pâte brisée*, generally used for small pastries or cookies.

Pâtisserie: An umbrella word used to refer to a pastry shop, pastry making, and the baked products produced in a bakery.

Pâtissier: The French word for "pastry chef."

Pâton: The package formed by folding the *détrempe* around the *beurrage*. The *pâton* is then folded, turned, rolled, and chilled many times, until a multilayered puff pastry dough has been created.

Pectin: A gelling agent available in liquid or powder form and used to thicken jams, jellies, glazes, and other products. It is also found naturally in some fruits.

Petits fours: Small, bite-sized confections or savory products.

Petits fours secs: French for "dry" *petits fours*; small, delicate cookies served with desserts.

Pipe: To push a semisoft ingredient, such as a dough, icing, or other pastelike substance, through a pastry bag or *cornet* to form a shape or decorate a surface.

Poured fondant: A pourable fondant used to coat *petits fours*, cakes, and other pastries, as well as to fill other products.

Praline paste: A thick paste made from ground caramelized almonds and hazelnuts and sugar.

Pre-fermentation: A method of taking a small portion of dough—just flour, water, yeast, and, occasionally salt —and letting it ferment for a period of time before adding it to a larger amount of dough to add superior flavor, increased volume, and moisture to the baked product.

Proofing: The fermentation time given to bread doughs to allow the leavening action of the yeast to fully develop before baking.

Proofing cabinet or box: An enclosed, temperature-and-humidity-controlled, rolling cabinet, usually metal, containing racks to hold sheet pans. It is used for fermenting yeast-based products.

Quatre-quarts: A classic French cake similar to an American pound cake, made from equal parts of butter, sugar, eggs, and flour.

Reverse puff pastry: Puff pastry made by enclosing the dough with the butter rather than the other way around.

Rolled fondant: A fondant icing that is malleable enough to be rolled like dough; used as a smooth covering for fancy cakes, such as wedding cakes.

Roulade: The French word for "roll," generally used to describe a thin sheet cake (or other similarly thin product) that is filled and rolled into a log shape.

Royal icing: A glossy white cake icing made from confectioners' sugar and raw egg whites with a touch of an acid (such as white vinegar or lemon juice).

Quick bread: Bread, often fruit- or vegetable-flavored, that gets its rise from fast-acting chemical leavening agents such as baking powder or soda.

Sabler: To cut butter into flour until a sandy texture is achieved.

Sanding sugar: Decorating sugar, also known as pearl sugar, whose crystals are substantially larger than those of granulated sugar.

Scald: To heat a liquid to just below the boiling point.

Scaling: The measuring and weighing of ingredients in a pastry kitchen.

Score: To make shallow cuts on the surface of an item to be baked, either for decoration or to allow steam to escape during baking.

Shelf life: The period of time that a product can be stored before it begins to go bad.

Short dough: A dough with a high percentage of fat to flour.

Sift: To shake a dry ingredient through a sifter to remove lumps, lighten it, or blend more than one ingredient together.

Silicone baking liner: A nonstick, heat-proof baking liner that can be used as an alternative to parchment paper.

Simple syrup: Known in French as *sirop simple*, a sugar-and-water solution used as a sweetener, moistener, glaze, poaching or preserving liquid, or as a base for candies, icings, frostings, and other desserts and drinks. Simple syrup is made by combining granulated sugar with water and heating just to the boiling point to dissolve the sugar. The ratio of sugar to water varies by application, but it is most often 1:1. Flavorings such as almond extract, fruit purées, and compound flavorings can be added to taste.

Slurry: A thick liquid made by whisking any of several starches into cold liquid until dissolved. It is then used to thicken sauces or gravies.

Smoothing: The process whereby fondant is rolled out without lines, bumps, or wrinkles so that it will lie smoothly over a cake.

Sponge: In bread making, the pre-ferment, slightly loose mix of flour, water, and yeast that is added to the main mixture after a short period of fermentation.

Staling: The process by which a pastry or bread loses moisture and becomes dry, with a change in the surface and the interior crumb.

Straight dough: A simple yeast dough, in which all ingredients are mixed together in order until a smooth, even dough is created.

Sucré: Sweetened or sugared.

Succès: A dry meringue used to make layer cakes and other pastries.

Sucrose: Regular granulated sugar.

Swiss meringue: A mixture similar to a French meringue, except that the egg whites and sugar are whisked constantly while heated over a *bain-marie* until they reach 54°C (130°F) and the sugar dissolves.

Tempering: The method of melting, cooling, and reheating solid chocolate to make it malleable.

Tourage: The process of folding, rolling, and turning pastry to create the hundreds of paper-thin layers characteristic of puff pastry.

Trimoline: A commercially prepared invert sugar paste that helps retain moisture and inhibits crystallization in cooked products.

Turn: The process used in laminated doughs whereby a folded dough is turned 90 degrees and then rolled out and folded again.

Viennoiserie: Baked goods other than breads.

Water bath: The culinary term for a double-boiler or *bain-marie*. Also used to describe the process of placing pans filled with a product (such as custard) into a larger pan of water during baking to ensure even cooking and the retention of moisture.

Yeast: A single-celled organism that when placed in the proper environment will grow and multiply, producing carbon dioxide to leaven baked goods. There are many types of yeast, including active dry, instant active dry, compressed fresh, cream, SAF, Brewer's, and wild yeast.

Zest: The thin, oily, and brightly colored outer layer of citrus skin.

Conversion Charts

Conversions of Common Pastry Items from Volume to Weight

Ingredient	Weight/Cup in Grams	Weight/Cup in Ounces
Crumbs (bread or cake)	100 grams	3.5 ounces
Currants	150 grams	5.3 grams
Dates (whole, pitted)	170 grams	6 ounces
Eggs (white, whole, or yolk)	225 grams	8 ounces
Figs	200 grams	7 ounces
Flour (A.P., unsifted)	135 grams	4.8 ounces
Flour (A.P., sifted)	115 grams	4 ounces
Flour (bread, unsifted)	140 grams	5 ounces
Flour (bread, sifted)	120 grams	4.3 ounces
Flour (cake, unsifted)	125 grams	4.4 ounces
Flour (cake, sifted)	95 grams	3.4 ounces
Flour (whole wheat, unsifted)	130 grams	4.5 ounces
Fructose	180 grams	6.3 ounces
Fruit juice	250 grams	8.8 ounces
Honey	340 grams	12 ounces
Lard	205 grams	7.3 ounces
Milk	245 grams	8.6 ounces
Milk (evaporated)	250 grams	8.6 ounces
Milk (powdered)	100 grams	3.5 ounces
Milk (sweetened condensed)	305 grams	10.8 ounces
Molasses	340 grams	12 ounces
Nuts (chopped)	130 grams	4.5 ounces
Oats (rolled)	85 grams	3 ounces
Oil	215 grams	7.5 ounces
Peaches (dried)	160 grams	5.6 ounces

Peels (candied)	115 grams	4 ounces
Pineapple (canned, crushed)	250 grams	8.8 ounces
Potato (grated, uncooked)	100 grams	3.5 ounces
Prunes (pitted)	175 grams	6.3 ounces
Raisins	150 grams	5.3 ounces
Rhubarb (cooked)	240 grams	8.5 ounces
Rice (uncooked)	190 grams	6.8 ounces
Shortening	190 grams	6.8 ounces
Sugar (granulated)	200 grams	7 ounces
Sugar (powdered)	100 grams	3.5 ounces
Vinegar	235 grams	8.3 ounces
Water	235 grams	8.3 ounces
Baking powder (double acting)	4.4 grams	0.17 ounce
Baking powder (single acting)	3.4 grams	0.13 ounce
Baking soda	5.3 grams	0.2 ounce
Caraway seed (ground)	3.3 grams	0.13 ounce
Cardamom seed (ground)	2 grams	0.07 ounce
Cinnamon (ground)	2.7 grams	0.1 ounce
Cloves (ground)	2.7 grams	0.1 ounce
Cream of tartar	3.4 grams	0.13 ounce
Extracts	5.4 grams	0.2 ounce
Ginger (ground)	1.9 grams	0.07 ounce
Jam, jelly, or marmalade	6 grams	0.2 ounce
Citrus zest	2.7 grams	0.1 ounce
Mace (ground)	2.3 grams	0.08 ounce
Nutmeg (ground)	2.3 grams	0.08 ounce
Poppy seed (whole)	3.3 grams	0.13 ounce
Salt	5 grams	0.18 ounce

American and Metric Measurements and Conversions

American Volume Measurements				
1 gallon	= 4 quarts	= 8 pints	= 16 cups	= 128 fluid ounces	
1 quart		= 2 pints	= 4 cups	= 32 fluid ounces	
1 pint			= 2 cups	= 16 fluid ounces	
1 cup				= 8 fluid ounces	
1 tablespoon				= 1/2 fluid ounce	= 3 teaspoons

Metric Volume Measurements

1 liter	= 10 deciliters	= 100 centiliters	= 1 mililiters

American Volume to Metric Volume

1 gallon	= 3.78 liters	
1 quart	= 0.946 liters	= 946 milliliters
1 pint	= 0.473 liters	= 473 milliliters
1 cup	= 236.6 milliliters	
1 fluid ounce	= 29.57 milliliters	

fluid ounces x 29.57 = # milliliters per # fluid ounces

Example: to determine the metric equivalent to 12 fluid ounces

12 x 29.57 = 354.8 milliliters in 12 fluid ounces

American Weight Measurements

1 pound	= 16 ounces

Metric Weight Measurements

1 kilogram	= 1000 grams

Metric Weight to American Weight

1 kilogram	= 2.2 pounds	= 35.2 ounces
1 ounce	= 28.37 grams	

grams / 28.37 = # ounces per # grams

Example: to determine the number of ounces equivalent to 750 grams

750 / 28.37 = 26.44 ounces = 1 pound 10.44 ounces

Temperature Conversions

0° Celsius	= 32° Fahrenheit
37° Celsius	= 98.6° Fahrenheit
100° Celsius	= 212° Fahrenheit

Degrees Fahrenheit to degrees Celsius [(F°-32) x 5] / 9 = C°

Example: 212°F converted to °Celsius

[(212°F –32) x 5] / 9 = [180 x 5] / 9 = 900 / 9 = 100° C

Degrees Celsius to degrees Fahrenheit [(C° x9) / 5] + 32 = F°

Example: 37°C converted to °Fahrenheit

[(37°C x 9) / 5] +32 = [333 / 5] +32 = 66.6 +32 = 98.6° F

Acknowledgments

It is with great appreciation that I thank the following people who made this book possible:

First and foremost our writer, Judie Choate, for her clarity and simplicity in making the professional pastry course so accessible. Matthew Septimus once again delivered inspiring photographs. Tina Casaceli, our head of pastry, shepherded the team through the breadth and complexities of the course. Without Kim Witherspoon, our agent, and Leslie Stoker, publisher of STC, there would be no book, so thank you for believing! Special thanks go to our editor, Luisa Weiss, and our designer, Debra Drodvillo.

And of course,

Jacques Torres
Gary Apito
Alain Sailhac
Nils Noren
Jürgen David
Christina Wang
Suzanne Sobel
Tara Hill
Melanie Miller
Wendy Knight
Robin Cohen

And the staff and students of the pastry department of The French Culinary Institute.

Thank you all!

Dorothy Cann Hamilton

Index